Register Your Book

at www.phptr.com/ibmregister/

Upon registration, we will send you electronic sample chapters from two of our popular IBM Press books. In addition, you will be automatically entered into a monthly drawing for a free IBM Press book.

Registration also entitles you to:

- Notices and reminders about author appearances, conferences, and online chats with special guests

- Access to supplemental material that may be available

- Advance notice of forthcoming editions

- Related book recommendations

- Information about special contests and promotions throughout the year

- Chapter excerpts and supplements of forthcoming books

Contact us

If you are interested in writing a book or reviewing manuscripts prior to publication, please write to us at:

Editorial Director, IBM Press
c/o Pearson Education
One Lake Street
Upper Saddle River, New Jersey 07458

e-mail: IBMPress@pearsoned.com

Visit us on the Web: www.phptr.com/ibmpress/

Praise for Search Engine Marketing, Inc.

"A very comprehensive, yet light-hearted guide for internet managers that demystifies search engine marketing and provides practical advice for success."

—Piers Dickinson
Global Internet Marketing Manager, BP

"Outlines every one of the major strategic steps to develop your search marketing initiatives. This book teaches Web marketers what to do from the beginning so they can implement a successful search marketing program—the strategic steps to define the scope and cost of your search marketing program, develop a team, create a proposal, get executive approval, manage, and measure your search marketing program. You have to read it to appreciate it!"

—Cynthia Donlevy
Web Marketing & Strategy, Cisco Systems, Inc.

"Getting your site indexed is the most fundamental, yet one of the most challenging, aspects to search engine marketing. *Search Engine Marketing Inc.: Driving Search Traffic to Your Company's Web Site* is a detailed and comprehensive guide through the pitfalls and opportunities of this complicated subject. I started reading Chapter 10, "Get Your Site Indexed," and haven't really put it down since. It is a wonderfully well-written and detailed reference that you will come back to again and again to get more out of your SEO efforts. From price engines to paid placement, Chapter 14, "Optimize Your Paid Search Program," covers everything you *need* to know about paid search. I have yet to come across a more useful book for SEM pros. From budgeting to bid strategy and optimization, Mike and Bill take you through the steps to create successful paid search campaigns. Whether you are just starting out in paid search or are already a power player, you will learn something new from this book."

—David Cook
Search Marketing Manager, Buy.com

"This book has no silver bullets or snake-oil potions that will magically propel your site to the top of every search engine. What it offers instead, is the most comprehensive, well-thought-out, and well-motivated treatment to date of all aspects of search engine marketing, from planning to execution to measuring. If you are involved in any way in the economic aspects of Web search technology, you need this book on your shelf."

—Dr. Andrei Broder
Yahoo! Research Fellow and Vice President of Emerging Search Technology

"Mike Moran and Bill Hunt have delivered a masterpiece on enterprise search marketing. Both engaging and results-focused, *Search Engine Marketing, Inc.* guides the marketer through the basics of why search is important and how search engines work to the more challenging organizational tasks of selling a search marketing proposal to executives and executing on a search marketing plan.

Unlike many previous search engine optimization books that have treated search marketing as a guerilla approach disjointed from other organizational needs, *Search Engine Marketing, Inc.* shows how to incorporate search into the overall marketing mix in order to increase both customer value and business return-on-investment.

Full of real examples from other enterprise search marketing organizations and thoughtful treatment of the business issues surrounding search, this book is the reference volume for bringing a successful search marketing program to fruition in the organization."

—Jeff Watts
Search & Community Manager, National Instruments

"Search Engine Marketing, Inc. is the ultimate source on how to implement a search marketing campaign. The book provides actionable instructions on topics from how to get the finances within your organization to how to make your pages rank well in search engines. Beyond that, the book explains conversion metrics and projecting your success. For anyone within a large organization, looking to make a difference with the corporate Web site; the book is a 'no-brainer.' For any professional SEO or SEM, the book is a must read. The manner in which Bill Hunt and Mike Moran organized the book is both unique and smart. Both Bill and Mike are also extremely professional public speakers on the topic of Search Marketing. I have been to dozens of search marketing conferences and I can honestly say, I am as impressed with this book as I am with their top presentations."

—Barry Schwartz
CEO, RustyBrick, Inc.

"Bill and Mike's book provides an excellent in-depth resource for companies examining their search marketing strategy. In addition to actionable SEO tips, this book outlines how to successfully develop a search strategy, determine what to outsource versus keep in house, and how to precisely outline the business case and 'sell' search to executive decision-makers. If your company is wondering how to enter the search space—or if you're revising your online strategy—read this book."

—Heather Lloyd-Martin
Author, *Successful Search Engine Copywriting*

"Required reading for anyone interested in how to apply leading-edge search marketing within large enterprises. With search marketing now of critical importance, the authors provide practical advice and approaches that are both sophisticated and invaluable."

—Rob Key
CEO, Converseon, Inc.

Search Engine Marketing, Inc.

ON DEMAND COMPUTING BOOKS

Business Intelligence for the Enterprise
Biere

On Demand Computing
Fellenstein

Grid Computing
Joseph and Fellenstein

Autonomic Computing
Murch

RATIONAL® SOFTWARE BOOKS

Software Configuration Management Strategies and IBM Rational® ClearCase®, Second Edition
Bellagio and Milligan

Implementing IBM® Rational® ClearQuest®
Buckley, Pulsipher, and Scott

Project Management with the IBM Rational Unified Process
Gibbs

IBM Rational® ClearCase®, Ant, and CruiseControl
Lee

Visual Modeling with Rational Software Architect and UML
Quatrani and Palistrant

WEBSPHERE® BOOKS

IBM® WebSphere®
Barcia, Hines, Alcott, and Botzum

IBM® WebSphere® Application Server for Distributed Platforms and z/OS®
Black, Everett, Draeger, Miller, Iyer, McGuinnes, Patel, Herescu, Gissel, Betancourt, Casile, Tang, and Beaubien

Enterprise Java™ Programming with IBM® WebSphere®, Second Edition
Brown, Craig, Hester, Pitt, Stinehour, Weitzel, Amsden, Jakab, and Berg

IBM® WebSphere® and Lotus
Lamb, Laskey, and Indurkhya

IBM® WebSphere® System Administration
Williamson, Chan, Cundiff, Lauzon, and Mitchell

Enterprise Messaging Using JMS and IBM® WebSphere®
Yusuf

MORE BOOKS FROM IBM PRESS

Irresistible! Markets, Models, and Meta-Value in Consumer Electronics
Bailey and Wenzek

Service-Oriented Architecture Compass
Bieberstein, Bose, Fiammante, Jones, and Shah

Lotus® Notes® Developer's Toolbox
Elliott

Developing Quality Technical Information, Second Edition
Hargis, Carey, Hernandez, Hughes, Longo, Rouiller, and Wilde

Performance Tuning for Linux® Servers
Johnson, Huizenga, and Pulavarty

RFID Sourcebook
Lahiri

Building Applications with the Linux Standard Base
Linux Standard Base Team

An Introduction to IMS™
Meltz, Long, Harrington, Hain, and Nicholls

Search Engine Marketing, Inc.
Moran and Hunt

Can Two Rights Make a Wrong? Insights from IBM's Tangible Culture Approach
Moulton Reger

Inescapable Data
Stakutis and Webster

DB2® BOOKS

DB2® Universal Database V8 for Linux, UNIX, and Windows Database Administration Certification Guide, Fifth Edition
Baklarz and Wong

Understanding DB2 9 Security
Bond, See, Wong, and Chan

Understanding DB2®
Chong, Liu, Qi, and Snow

High Availability Guide for DB2®
Eaton and Cialini

DB2® Universal Database V8 Handbook for Windows, UNIX, and Linux
Gunning

DB2® SQL PL, Second Edition
Janmohamed, Liu, Bradstock, Chong, Gao, McArthur, and Yip

DB2® for z/OS® Version 8 DBA Certification Guide
Lawson

DB2® Universal Database V8.1 Certification Exam 700 Study Guide
Sanders

DB2® Universal Database V8.1 Certification Exams 701 and 706 Study Guide
Sanders

DB2® Universal Database for OS/390
Sloan and Hernandez

The Official Introduction to DB2® for z/OS®, Second Edition
Sloan

Advanced DBA Certification Guide and Reference for DB2® Universal Database v8 for Linux, UNIX, and Windows
Snow and Phan

DB2® Express
Yip, Cheung, Gartner, Liu, and O'Connell

Apache Derby—Off to the Races
Zikopoulos, Baklarz, and Scott

DB2® Version 8
Zikopoulos, Baklarz, deRoos, and Melnyk

Search Engine Marketing, Inc.

Driving Search Traffic to Your Company's Web Site

Mike Moran and Bill Hunt

IBM Press
Pearson plc

Upper Saddle River, NJ • Boston• Indianapolis • San Francisco

New York • Toronto • Montreal • London • Munich • Paris • Madrid

Capetown • Sydney • Tokyo • Singapore • Mexico City
www.phptr.com/ibmpress

IBM Press Program Managers: Tara Woodman, Ellice Uffer
IBM Press Consulting Editor: David West

Cover design: IBM Corporation

Published by Pearson plc
Publishing as IBM Press

Library of Congress Number: 2005925506

IBM Press offers excellent discounts on this book when ordered in quantity for bulk purchases or special sales, which may include electronic versions and/or custom covers and content particular to your business, training goals, marketing focus, and branding interests. For more information, please contact:

U. S. Corporate and Government Sales
1-800-382-3419
corpsales@pearsontechgroup.com.

For sales outside the U. S., please contact:

International Sales
international@pearsoned.com.

ISBN 0131852922

Text printed in the United States on recyled paper at Courier Stoughton in Stoughton, Massachusetts.
7th Printing December 2006

Dedications

To my wife, Linda, and my children, David, Madeline, Marcella, and Dwight, with great appreciation for their support for me.

—Mike Moran

To my wonderful wife, Motoko, and my children, Mariko and William, for their tremendous patience, encouragement, and support.

—Bill Hunt

Contents

Foreword

Search engine marketing is one of the fastest growing segments of online advertising, with U.S. Bancorp Piper Jaffray's Safa Rashtchy forecasting online search becoming a $7 billion industry worldwide by 2007. Unfortunately, search marketers historically have had to rely heavily on tribal knowledge and trial and error to create successful campaigns. That is all about to change. Bill and Mike have parted the veil of secrecy and written an excellent book that teaches current and future search marketers how to successfully design, implement, and track a search engine marketing campaign.

When I started my first search marketing campaign at Intel, I would have given almost anything for a book like this that explained the process of creating a search marketing campaign. I went to the Search Engine Strategies conferences put on by Jupitermedia and talked to a number of agencies, but I had a hard time getting the information I needed to run an in-house campaign. There were quite a few agencies that would have loved to run my campaigns for me, but no one was willing (or able) to share the intricate details that are necessary to run an in-house campaign. I could easily get details about the generic benefits of search marketing, but how did they apply to Intel? How could I measure success for an awareness campaign when everyone else was talking about e-Commerce? Most importantly, how could I put a proposal together that would show to Intel decisionmakers the benefits of search marketing when all the other marketers at Intel and our agencies were focused on traditional media? If I had this book then, my life would have been a lot easier, and our initial forays into search marketing campaigns would have been a lot more successful than they were.

One of the chapters I am most excited about is the chapter on selling a search marketing proposal to the right people. You can pay an agency to build your keyword lists, write your creative, and even optimize your entire site, but without an approved proposal, you will not have the budget to even consider a pilot program. Bill and Mike walk you through the entire process from calculating the business value and assembling a search marketing proposal, through selling the proposal to stakeholders, and finally selling the proposal to your executives. The book demonstrates a thorough and well-documented process that will help you get the budget you need to test and see whether search marketing is the right vehicle to communicate with your customers.

This book deserves a place in the library of every search marketer, whether they are in an agency or are trying to run a search marketing campaign in-house. I will definitely be adding it to my library and will strongly recommend it to all I know who are involved with search marketing.

Martin Laetsch
Manager, Worldwide Search
Intel Corporation

The views expressed here are the views of the individual, and not the views of Intel Corporation.

Preface

Search marketing demands a curious mix of business, writing, and technical skills. No matter what skills you have, you probably have *some* of the skills needed to succeed, but not *all* of them. This book will fill the gaps.

If you possess marketing skills, or you have a sales or other business background, you will quickly see the ways that search marketing draws upon your previous experience, but you will also learn how it is different. Like any form of marketing, you will focus on the target markets you want to reach—in this case, searchers looking for certain words. You will segment those markets. You will realize that your Web pages are your marketing communications materials. You might see parallels to direct marketing as we relentlessly measure our success, or perhaps you will see the possibilities for search marketing to burnish your brand image. Regardless, like all marketing, you will learn to design your search marketing program to meet your company's larger goals. Unlike other forms of marketing, search marketing is not designed to interrupt people with an advertising message. Successful search marketing meets people at their point of need. When searchers want something, you must be ready to satisfy them with what they want, even if you would prefer to sell them something else.

As critical as marketers are to success, search marketing is, at its core, a writer's medium. Like direct marketing, a well-crafted message is critical to enticing a searcher to click your page. Once at your site, the words on your page also influence whether the prospective customer buys your product or abandons your site. But search marketing relies on skilled writing to an even greater extent, because the search engines choose the pages they show based on *words*. You will learn how to write the words that your customers *and* the search engines are looking for. If you are a writer, you will find search marketing a challenge like none you have ever seen, but one that can reward your company richly.

If you have technical skills, you are needed, too. Search marketing depends on your Web site's design and operation. Many commonly used Web technologies stop search marketing cold. You will find that search marketing is similar to other technical projects—you must understand the requirements so that you can develop the solution. You need to develop a business case to see the value so the work can be prioritized and funded for your busy IT team. You will need a project plan to execute on schedule. You will have standards and operational procedures that keep the system running smoothly. If you are a Webmaster, a Web developer, or any kind of technologist, your skills are vital to search marketing success.

If you are looking for a book about the secrets of search marketing, this book does have a few. However, they might be secrets of a surprising kind. Some people think of search marketing as an arcane pursuit where you need to know the "tricks" to get search engines to show your site. But those tricks are not the secrets of search marketing—you do not need tricks to succeed. What you really need is a firm understanding of how search marketing works, a methodology to plan your search marketing program, and the information required to execute it. The biggest secret of search marketing is that knowledge, hard work, and flawless execution are all you need. This book shows you how to get all three.

In Part 1, we cover the basics of search marketing. What is search marketing? Why is it so difficult? How do search engines and search marketing work? And what are searchers looking for anyway? Marketers and writers will learn more about search technology. Technologists will be exposed to the opportunity search marketing offers your company. You will all learn how to segment searchers based on their behavior, so you will know what they want from your site. Part 1 will teach you all the background you need to formulate a custom search marketing program for your company—which is what you will do in Part 2.

Part 2 takes you step by step through developing a proposal for your own search marketing program. You will learn how to identify the goals of your Web site and measure your current success in meeting them. You will learn how well you are doing at search marketing today and how much it is worth to do better. We show you how to estimate your costs, choose your strategy, and get your proposed program approved by your executives and by all the folks in your company who you need on your side. Because search marketing demands cooperation from so many people in your company, we show you proven ways to get each kind of person to work hard on your program.

Part 3 explores all the details you need to execute your program. Every Web site poses different challenges to a search marketing program. You will learn how to diagnose problems on your site and correct them. We teach you methodologies for every part of the search marketing process that you can apply to your own business. And we explain how to measure everything in your program so that you can improve the operation of your program every day.

 Throughout the book, you will see icons that signify special material on two important subjects. The first, shown at right, is the **spam alert** icon, which warns you about overly clever tricks that pose a real danger to your search marketing campaign. You are probably familiar with e-mail spam, when you get unwanted messages in your inbox, but search marketing has its own meaning for spam—any technique that is designed mainly to fool the search sites to gain an untoward advantage. That is an overly broad definition, but we explain exactly where the ethical lines are drawn every time you see this icon. Spam can be hazardous to the health of your search marketing program, because search sites have rules to control search marketing behavior—when you break the rules, you will suffer the consequences. Whenever you see this icon, you will know that there is a line that you cross at your own peril.

You will also see, shown at right, the **global tip** icon, which alerts you about techniques that are especially relevant to international search marketing campaigns. Most of the advice in this book is pitched to an audience of U.S. companies and companies using Google, Yahoo! Search, and other English-language worldwide search sites. You will learn, however, that searchers in many countries use search sites specific to that country, and that your non-English content sometimes has special issues that must be addressed. We highlight those areas in the book for you. Whether your Web site serves international visitors now, or you are considering doing so in the future, these tips are important for you.

No matter what your background, you are already partially prepared to become a **search marketer**. In this book, you will learn why it is so important to form a team of skills outside your own. Marketers, writers, technologists, and folks from other fields must collaborate to make search marketing work. You will find out why it is that the larger your Web site, the harder that collaboration can be—but you will also learn how to pull it off. Your business can coordinate these diverse skills to create a successful search marketing program. You just need to know how.

Whether you have been turned off in the past by experts selling quick-fix voodoo or you have just found search marketing too complicated or too intimidating, put that behind you. This book explains everything you need to know in simple terms that you can understand no matter what your experience. If you can use a Web browser, you can learn search marketing.

Every day, more and more business is done on the Web. And, increasingly, people looking to do business start with a search. Remember, if they can't find you, they can't buy from you. Discover how your company can be found.

Acknowledgments
from Mike

Leading my list of people to thank is Bill Hunt, my co-author. When I first met Bill, I was an expert in search technology, but knew almost nothing about search marketing on the Web. To me, if there was a problem with a search engine returning the wrong results, then we should dive in and tweak the ranking algorithm until it worked. Uh, right. Bill quickly showed me the rules of the search marketing road, and I started to learn search from the outside in—how to change our site to get what we want. In our work together at ibm.com, Bill has helped me through every difficult problem and has made it fun. Working on a book is never easy, but working with Bill made it as easy as possible.

I would like to thank my IBM management, including John Rosato and Lee Dierdorff, for their encouragement to complete this book. (I want to stress that the opinions expressed in this book are mine alone and do not necessarily reflect those of the IBM Corporation or IBM's management.) I also want to thank Doug Maine, David Bradley, and Jeanine Cotter, my former executive management at IBM, who were willing to take a chance on search marketing at IBM. This book is a compilation of what worked, but I want to thank them for riding out the things that did not work out as well.

I want to thank Jeff Schaffer from my IBM team, a good friend with a wonderful mind, who worked with me to develop many of the original ideas in the Web Conversion Cycle. Special thanks go to IBM teammate Alex Holt for reviewing every page of the book and offering helpful suggestions.

The team at IBM Press, especially our editor Bernard Goodwin, was very helpful, and Daria Goetsch reviewed several chapters and provided helpful comments. Many others provided assistance and encouragement along the way, including Andrei Broder, Kevin Chiu, Gideon Sasson, and others who I am probably forgetting.

Most of all, I want to thank my wife, Linda, and my children, David, Madeline, Marcella, and Dwight, who made so many sacrifices so "Daddy could write his book," being patient while I spent many hours writing on top of an already heavy workload from my day job at IBM. Without their love and support, I certainly could never have completed this book. I have read many acknowledgments of authors thanking their families for the heavy burdens they carried while the book was written, and I now understand what those other authors were saying. My family deserves every accolade for helping me complete this. I love them very much.

But my wife, Linda, requires a special acknowledgment for her work on this book, because it goes so far beyond anything an author would ever expect of a spouse. Before this book ever went to the publisher, Linda proofread it. And copyedited it. And the publisher was very pleased with how clean it was (crediting Bill and me far too much). But even those exhausting tasks do not scratch the surface of what Linda put into this book.

Linda is herself an accomplished magazine writer and book author, thus bringing a level of professionalism and experience to the craft of writing that she painstakingly taught me throughout the writing of this, my first book. But Linda brought even more to this book than her writing skills. Linda has worked as a programmer in a large company and is the Webmaster of three Web sites, so she is actually the perfect audience for this book. Her keen technical mind and corporate experience made her the ideal reader. We spent hours brainstorming ideas for the book, honing them until we agreed on the best way to explain them. As Bill and I "completed" each chapter, I would present it to Linda to see whether it made any sense to her, as someone who should understand it perfectly. And occasionally it did. But more frequently, Linda pointed out a critical flaw in terminology, a better organization for the same information, an improvement to a figure, or simply a technical error that we had overlooked. It sounds trite to say that this would not be the same book without Linda, but it is true. You would not believe how much harder to understand it would be. Linda did not just proofread or copyedit the words, she inspected the ideas. She judged the nomenclature, the style, the consistency, the flow—she worked over every thought and every word. Linda was truly our editor, in every sense of the word.

—Mike Moran

Acknowledgments
from Bill

I would like to thank Mike Moran, my co-author on this book, for his encouragement, vast knowledge, and willingness to partner with me to write this book while managing an already heavy workload. Without Mike's encouragement, gentle nudges, constant pacing, occasional kick in the backside, and, of course, his sense of humor, I could never have started this book, let alone finish it. I am indebted to Mike for his writing style that gave my rants a consistent voice that made them more than informative and actually interesting to the reader. Furthermore, Mike has been my mentor, teaching me how to effectively navigate the complex maze of a large corporate structure to actually demonstrate that search engine marketing is the ultimate marketing tool. It was under this tutelage that the methodologies included in this book were allowed to incubate and be tested on one of the greatest Web sites in the world.

A very special thank you and debt of gratitude goes out to Linda Moran for her unbelievable support for Mike and me on this book. Linda's assistance in reading and critical reviews of the book was helpful beyond belief. Mike and I wanted to write a book that was informative and helpful to the beginner and advanced optimizer alike. Linda's reviews and recommendations for changes were absolutely correct and, I believe, integral to us achieving that goal. In addition, thank you Linda for sacrificing your time with Mike to allow him to work with me on this demanding project.

I would like to thank the brilliant team of search marketing strategists from Global Strategies—Jeremy Sanchez, Andy Weatherwax, and David Turner—for their tremendous knowledge, support, ideas, research, content reviews, and undying encouragement of this effort. I need to thank them for picking up the slack with our clients while I was writing, which allowed us to keep them happy and pay the bills.

A thank-you goes out to the members of the IBM Search Effectiveness team, who have helped me to refine many of these techniques and be my sounding board. Thanks go to Marshall

Sponder for his honest reviews and assistance in refining the metrics for the enterprise, to Daniele Hayes for her insights into managing paid placement, and to Jessica Casamento for challenging me to develop intuitive audit tools to be used by the business units.

I also want to thank the IBM Corporate Webmaster team, especially Klaus Johannes Rusch for his technical insight and help to understand how to really motivate and work with Webmasters.

I want to thank my IBM management team, specifically John Rosato and Lee Dierdorff, for their support for Mike and me in working on the book and their support of search engine optimization efforts. I need to further thank John for his relentless desire to rank well and deliver almost impossible traffic increases to the site, both of which forced me to work harder to crack the code of delivering effective enterprise search engine marketing. Thank you to the IBM marketing team, including Lisa Baird, Eric Siebert, Richard Toranzo, David Manzo, and Claudio Zibenberg, for their support of search engine marketing and making it part of the marketing mix.

I want to give special thanks to my wife, Motoko, and my children, Mariko and William, for their tremendous support and encouragement during this project and for the many sacrifices they made so that I could take the time to write—even on vacation!

I need to offer a heartfelt thank you to Motoko for not only her support on this book but her dedication to my career, often at the sacrifice of her own, for the past 20 years. It is so true that behind every successful man is a strong woman, and Motoko is just that woman! Without her tremendous support, love, and understanding, this book and my overall success would not have been possible. I further need to thank her for allowing me to become the expert in Japanese SEO by keeping me current and providing many deep insights that I could have never realized alone. Thank you!

Additional thanks go to Andy Weatherwax who cleaned up my mess with the graphics and created many of the custom images. Thank you to Kevin Lee of Did-it for reviewing the paid search segments of the book and giving honest feedback and guidance that helped ensure accuracy and relevancy.

The team at IBM Press, especially our editor Bernard Goodwin, was very helpful and kept us from floundering during our first writing experience. Tara Woodman for helping us through the IBM Press process. Kristy Hart for the production support that turned our binder of paper into an actual book. Daria Goetsch for reviewing several chapters and providing insight to make some complex thoughts easier to understand.

Many others provided assistance, examples, and encouragement along the way, including Andrei Broder, Rob Key, Adam Glazer, Roger Balmer, Marshall Simmonds, Derrick Wheeler, Detlev Johnson, Joe Morin, Sherwood Stranieri, Danny Sullivan, Chris Sherman, Tor Crockatt, Neeraj Agrawal, Mike Grehan, and many others to whom I apologize for not listing here.

—**Bill Hunt**

About the Authors

About Mike Moran

Mike Moran is an IBM Distinguished Engineer with more than 20 years experience in search technology working at IBM Research, Lotus, and other IBM software units. He led the product team that developed the first commercial linguistic search engine in 1989, and has been granted four patents in search and retrieval technology. He led the original search marketing strategy for ibm.com, as well as the integration of ibm.com's site search technologies.

Mike has worked on IBM's Web site for the past seven years and is currently the Manager of ibm.com Site Architecture. In addition to his search work, Mike has spearheaded ibm.com projects in Content Management, Personalization, and Web Metrics.

In addition to Mike's broad technical background, he also holds an Advanced Certificate in Market Management Practice from the Royal UK Charter Institute of Marketing, helping bridge the gap between technology and marketing concepts. Mike can be reached through his Web site (www.mikemoran.com).

About Bill Hunt

Bill Hunt is the CEO and Founder of Global Strategies International (www.globalstrategies.com) and one of the pioneers of search engine marketing, getting his start in early 1994. Bill is an internationally recognized search marketing expert, conference speaker, and contributor to numerous marketing journals and books. Over the years, Bill has led numerous large search marketing projects for clients such as AT&T, IBM, Intel, The Hartford, and Zurich Financial. Bill can be reached through his blog (www.semincbook.com).

GSI specializes in helping Fortune 500 companies develop, implement and manage their global enterprise search marketing programs. With offices in the United States, Japan, the United Kingdom, and Switzerland, GSI has the experience to help companies execute their search marketing programs "from the inside out."

The Basics of Search Marketing

You are ready to go. You are motivated. You are just itching to dive into search marketing. But where do you start? The basics, that's where.

First, in Chapter 1, "Why Search Marketing Is Important . . . and Difficult," we examine what search marketing is all about. We look at the way search usage is exploding and why search marketing is so valuable to your organization—how it can drive visitors to your Web site. You will be convinced that your Web site cannot ignore Web searchers any longer. But before being overcome by irrational exuberance, we also take a cold look at why some companies find search marketing so hard to do—and why the larger your Web site, the tougher it is.

Building on that overview, Chapter 2, "How Search Engines Work," dives into how search engines work—what happens when someone is looking for a word, where the results on the screen come from, and how *your* Web site can show up right on that search results page. You will take a guided tour of the leading search engines and learn which ones to pay attention to.

That sets the stage for Chapter 3, "How Search Marketing Works," where we dig into search marketing methods. We teach you the three basic search marketing techniques, pointing out the benefits of each, so you can start thinking about which ones are most important to you. We also explain how each technique works and review which search companies you will work with for each one.

We wind up Part 1 with Chapter 4, "How Searchers Work," where we peek inside the mind of the searcher. Find out what these folks are *really* looking for when they type in one or two words. Learn to use your knowledge of searchers to your advantage.

Regardless of what job you have now, by the time you complete Part 1, you will have all the background needed to be a search engine marketer. You will know the terminology and the concepts. You will be ready to learn how to create your very own search marketing plan.

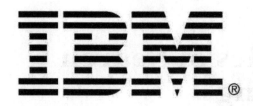

CHAPTER 1

Why Search Marketing Is Important . . . and Difficult

Search marketing. Perhaps you've heard this term kicked around, but you don't know what it means. Or, if you do know, you don't know where to start. As with anything new, if you take it step by step, you can learn it. A systematic approach can lead to search marketing success in any organization.

When a searcher types a word into Google, finds your home page, and clicks through to your site, you have attracted a visitor from a search site. If you do nothing at all, searchers will still find your site—sometimes. To maximize the number of searchers coming to your site, however, you must take specific actions to attract visitors to your site from search sites. That's **search marketing**. This book shows you how to become a **search marketer**. This chapter covers the following topics:

- *Web search basics*. What do we mean when we talk about "Web search"? You might think you know the basics already, but it is important that you *thoroughly* understand search fundamentals as you start your search marketing career. The advanced topics you need to learn will come more easily if you do not skip over the basics. In this chapter, we describe several different types of search, we introduce the leading search sites on the Web, and we talk about what makes them successful.

- *Search and your marketing mix*. You are probably not reading this book as an academic exercise—you want to know how to get more visitors to your Web site. You already spend your marketing budget on other ways to entice people to visit. How do you reallocate some of that budget to fit search into the mix? In this chapter, we demonstrate the huge opportunity of search marketing and show why you need to make room for it in your company's marketing mix.

- *The challenge of search marketing.* Attracting searchers to your site is appealing, but it's harder to do than you might think. And the larger your Web site is, the more difficult it can be. In this chapter, we explain why so many Web sites struggle to attract search visitors. But don't worry. The rest of this book shows you how to overcome these challenges.

Before examining the promise and the challenges of search marketing, we need to explore what we mean by Web search.

Web Search Basics

You know search is important. You want to attract search visitors to your site. You are reading this book because you expect to learn what you need to know so your site succeeds at search marketing. And the most fundamental fact behind what you already know is that more and more Web users are searching.

Congratulations on spotting the trend! Your intuition that search usage is growing is correct. Seventy-six percent of all Web users performed at least one search in January 2004, totalling 114 million Web visitors to search sites. Fully 64 percent of Web users employ search as their *primary* method of finding things and 59% of US users employ search *daily*. The top three search sites account for more than 5 percent of all Web site visits!

Beyond the numbers, search is becoming a cultural phenomenon. If you have never "Googled yourself" (searched for your own name in Google), I bet you are going to do so now. Even people who do not use the Web have heard of Google and Yahoo! The Web is growing in popularity every year, and search is growing right along with it. And younger market segments cannot be reached as easily through traditional advertising, because teens and young adults now spend more time online than watching television. When you add it all up, your Web site cannot ignore the increasing importance of search to your visitors.

But that does not make you an expert in how to *do* search marketing. You might not know the first thing about how to get your site into the top search results. Maybe you heard that your competitors are succeeding at search marketing—and one of your customers told you that your site cannot be found. You want to fix it, but how?

Despite how little you might know, you need to learn just two things to get started:

- *The kinds of search results.* When a search site responds to a searcher, different kinds of search results display. To begin your search education, we explain each type of display.
- *Where searchers go.* You might have a favorite search site, but not all searchers use what you do. Some search sites are even specific to a particular region or country. You need to understand which search engines are the most popular so that you can focus on them in your marketing efforts.

Let's begin with an overview of Web search results.

Kinds of Search Results

When we talk about search, we are actually referring to two distinct ways that search results land on the screen, as shown in Figure 1-1:

- *Organic results*. Also known as **natural** results, organic results are what made Google famous. Organic results are the "best" pages found for the words the searcher entered. When people refer to **search engine optimization** (SEO), they are talking about how you get your site's pages to be shown in organic search results. Organic search is what most people think of when they talk about Web search, and searchers click organic results 60 percent of the time. Searchers trust organic results, and therefore organic search must be part of your search marketing program. It can take time to succeed at organic search, but your time investment will pay off in the long run.

- *Paid results*. This term refers to a variety of revenue-generating activities by search sites, encompassing both paid inclusion and paid placement. **Paid inclusion** guarantees that a site's pages have been catalogued by the search site, so that they can be returned when they closely match an organic search. **Paid placement** allows a Web site to pay to have its page shown in response to a particular search word entered, regardless of how closely the page matches what the searcher entered. Paid search programs are the quick fix to attracting searchers to your Web site, and search marketers are responding. The paid search market hit $2.9 billion in 2004 and is expected to rise to $10 billion by 2009.

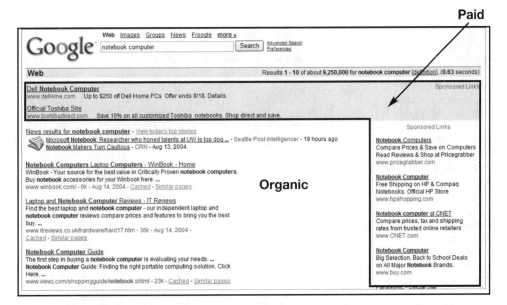

Figure 1-1 Types of search results. Google's results page has always separated paid from organic results, but other sites have at times combined them.

Another form of paid search is known as **paid listings** or **directories**, as shown in Figure 1-2. Directories are manually maintained classification systems that list Web sites according to each subject category that describes them. Directories are maintained by human editors who examine every Web site submitted to them by the site owner and decide under which subject a site should be listed. You can see in Figure 1-2 that an editor decided to list Tivo's company Web site under the Digital Video Recorder category. (Because the results are created manually, search geeks and other technologists do not consider directories to be a kind of search, but Web users do.)

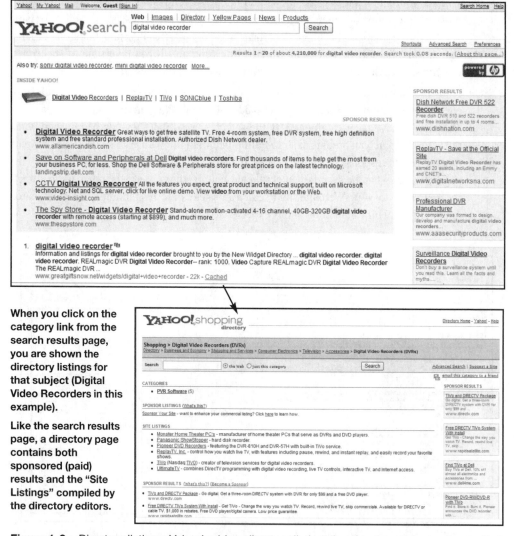

When you click on the category link from the search results page, you are shown the directory listings for that subject (Digital Video Recorders in this example).

Like the search results page, a directory page contains both sponsored (paid) results and the "Site Listings" compiled by the directory editors.

Figure 1-2   Directory listings. Yahoo! adds a directory listing showing the subject category that matches the result, giving the searcher one more choice.

Search engine marketing (SEM) is a broader term than SEO that encompasses any kind of search results. SEM is everything you do to raise your site's visibility in search engines to attract more visitors. Regardless of what term you use, search marketing is a critical way for your site to attract new visitors.

Now that you have learned about the types of search results, we can survey the most popular search sites around the world. In this book, we refer to search sites such as Google and Yahoo! as **search engines**.

Where Searchers Go

If you have a favorite search engine that you use all the time, you might not realize how many other search engines people use. Some search engines operate in just one country or one region, and others do nothing but help people comparison shop for products. Each search engine is competing vigorously for its share of this growing business, but searchers are beginning to show brand loyalty, as Figure 1-3 shows.

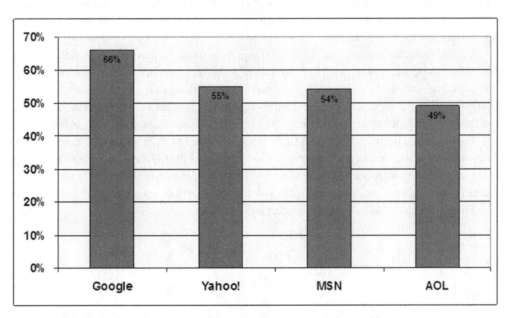

Figure 1-3 Searcher loyalty. Google leads in the percentage of searchers that do not switch to a different search site.

Sources: OneStat (May 2004) and iProspect (April 2004)

Among worldwide search engines, Google and Yahoo! are currently the two top competitors, but the landscape can change quickly. As late as 2004, Yahoo! and Google were partners! Let's look closely at the worldwide leaders in search and at leaders within particular countries and regions.

Google

A **googol** is a mathematical term for a 1 digit followed by one hundred 0s, and served as the inspiration for the Google search engine name, signifying the immense size of the search index it searches. Founded in 1998 by Stanford graduate students Larry Page and Sergey Brin, Google (www.google.com) has become so well known that "Googling" (searching for) someone's name has even been mentioned on popular TV shows.

Like many Web businesses of the 1990s, Google started small and grew as the Web exploded. Unlike many of the dotcom companies of that era, Google resisted going public until 2004, and eschewed advertising, preferring to grow through word of mouth. Google has been such a wonderful search engine that this strategy has worked. Google is used by more than 80 million searchers a month—40 percent of all Web users—tops of any search engine. Google is one of the five most-visited Web sites in the world, offering results in 35 languages— with half of its visitors from outside the United States.

Google started by offering the most relevant organic results that the Web had ever seen, which is still its most striking feature. The I'm Feeling Lucky button that takes you directly to the first search result testifies to the confidence Google has in its organic search capability. Google, like others, has a huge number of pages in its search index—more than four billion—but seems to find the right one for each search.

Unlike some competitors, Google initially kept its business focused on search, only recently straying into the territory of a portal, the way Yahoo! and others have offered news, weather, shopping, and other services. Google has always made its money through forms of paid search, allowing advertisers to purchase space on the results page based on what search words were entered. Over the years, Google has grown into one of the largest paid search companies in the world.

For the search marketer, Google is the 800-pound gorilla of the industry. You cannot ignore Google in your search strategy for organic or paid campaigns. But Google is not the only search engine in town. Although Google is the most popular search engine in the world, it receives less than half of all searches, as shown in Figure 1-4. You must include other search engines in your plan to maximize the benefits of search marketing.

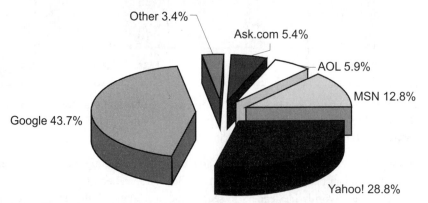

Figure 1-4   Share of searches. Google is the leader, but has less than half of the total share.

Source: comScore Media Metrix (October 2006)

Yahoo!

Yahoo! (www.yahoo.com) is one of the most-visited sites on the Internet, but its visitors do a lot more than search. Yahoo! is a leading portal, offering news, e-mail, shopping, and many other functions to visitors who register. The Yahoo! search engine is the #2 search engine in the world, with more than one fourth of all searches, but Figure 1-5 shows the difference in focus for Yahoo! and Google.

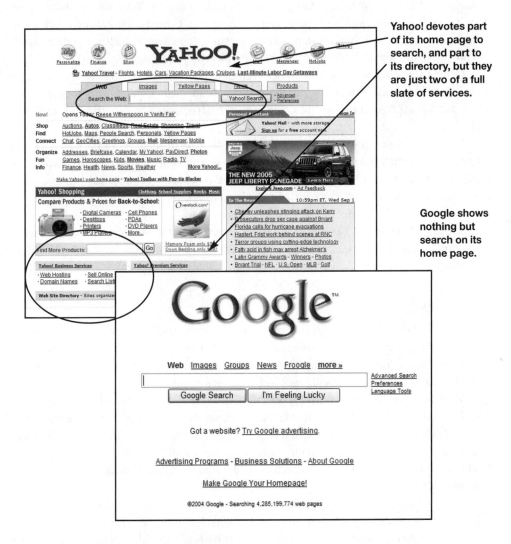

Yahoo! devotes part of its home page to search, and part to its directory, but they are just two of a full slate of services.

Google shows nothing but search on its home page.

Figure 1-5 Yahoo! and Google home page focus. Google is "all search, all the time," whereas Yahoo! is a "full-service portal."

Reproduced with permission of Yahoo! Inc. © 2005 by Yahoo! Inc. YAHOO! and the YAHOO! logo are trademarks of Yahoo! Inc.

Yahoo! is one of the oldest Web companies around, founded in 1994 by Stanford Ph.D. students David Filo and Jerry Yang. Yahoo! began as a Web directory—initially free to any company in its list—but later Yahoo! began charging a fee for each listing. Yahoo! quickly became a popular destination as its editors catalogued the growing Web, site by site, into its subject hierarchy. Yahoo! visitors believed they could find every Web site about any subject in just a few clicks.

When Yahoo! began offering organic search capability, it licensed the technology from other companies—at one time licensing Google's search technology. In 2003, Yahoo! shifted gears, acquiring several organic and paid search companies so that it could control its own technology. Yahoo! suffered no major drop-off in popularity, attesting to its search quality. If Yahoo! Search does not match the popular buzz of Google, it seems plenty good enough for its loyal users.

Google leads Yahoo! in total searches each month, especially outside the United States. Yahoo! Search has made strides in recent years to match Google in the number of languages supported, but Yahoo! frequently lags far behind Google in popularity in countries where they go head to head.

Yahoo! is a force within the United States, but its share of searches varies widely in other countries. U.S. search marketers must target Yahoo! as part of their plans, but marketers elsewhere should analyze the leading search engines in their country before finalizing their plans. Yahoo! should be targeted in countries where it handles a high percentage of total queries, but that needs to be decided on a country-by-country basis.

Although Google and Yahoo! get the lion's share of attention, other excellent worldwide search engines should also be targeted by search marketers in their plans. Although you will get less traffic from these engines than from Google and Yahoo!, it all adds up.

MSN Search

The Microsoft Network (MSN), Microsoft's answer to America Online's service, was launched in conjunction with the Windows 95 operating system, but has steadily trailed AOL in popularity despite Microsoft's dominance of the PC software business. Even at its height, MSN membership never cracked 10 million, while AOL once had 30 million members.

MSN Search (www.msn.com) is ranked third in the search race by most counts, with more than 10 percent of all searches worldwide, but Microsoft has long tried to increase its share of searches. Microsoft introduced new technology for MSN Search in early 2005, and is rumored to be developing a new search facility built in to a future version of the Windows operating system. Windows users would then be able to search their own computer, their company's servers, and the Internet within the same search.

Today's MSN Search, in contrast, looks a lot like the others, as Figure 1-6 shows. In late 2006, Microsoft overhauled the look and feel and added a "Live Search" logo, reinforcing its Windows Live strategy. As we write this, it's not clear whether the MSN Search brand is being de-emphasized or outright replaced by Live Search.

Paid placement advertising
from Microsoft adCenter

Organic results from MSN's
proprietary technology

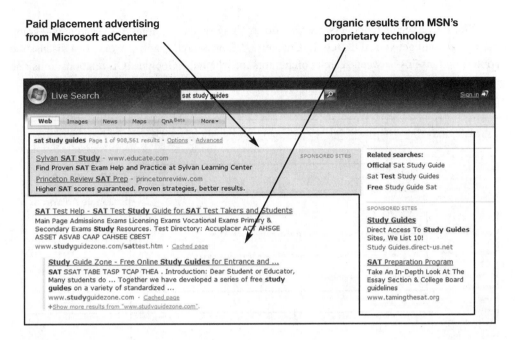

Figure 1-6   MSN Search results. Like most competitors, MSN returns both organic results as well as variations of paid listings.

Worldwide search marketers must focus on MSN Search because of the sizable number of visits you can attract to your site. MSN uses its own technology for organic search and is migrating to its own paid search facility as well. Microsoft adCenter handles the paid results in the US and a few other countries while MSN still syndicates Yahoo!'s Precision Match for other countries.

AOL Search

Now part of media giant Time Warner, America Online (founded as Quantum Systems in 1985) was an online company before most people knew what the Internet was. AOL was the original portal, gradually making its proprietary service more and more Web-oriented over the years. Still notable for its ease of use, AOL is the world's largest Internet service provider (connecting people to the Internet), at one time offering online access to more than 30 million people.

AOL Search (search.aol.com) is used mostly by AOL users, but that is still a lot of people—adding up to nearly 6 percent of total Web searches, good enough for fourth place worldwide. AOL has a partnership with Google, so search results on AOL Search are nearly the same as for Google (for both organic and paid search), as you can see in Figure 1-7.

Worldwide search marketers need not do anything special to target AOL searchers—going after Google will get you AOL, too. In Chapter 2, "How Search Engines Work," we discuss the various relationships between search competitors, of which the Google-AOL relationship is one of the most prominent.

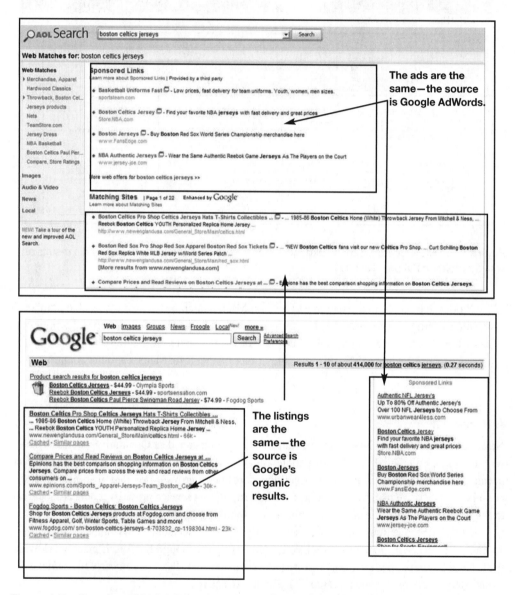

Figure 1-7   Google or AOL? AOL's results are nearly the same as Google's for the same search.

Ask.com

Founded as Ask Jeeves in 1996 as a 'natural language' search engine, Ask.com allows searchers to ask a question ("What is the population of India?") and get an answer, not just a list of documents containing the words. This approach yields good answers to popular questions; because it depends on human editors selecting the best answers, however, it does not work well for more esoteric subjects the editors did *not* handle. In recent years, Ask.com has acquired several organic search engine companies and built a search engine many believe is the closest rival to Google in quality. Figure 1-8 shows a sample results page from Ask.com that melds question answering with strong organic search results.

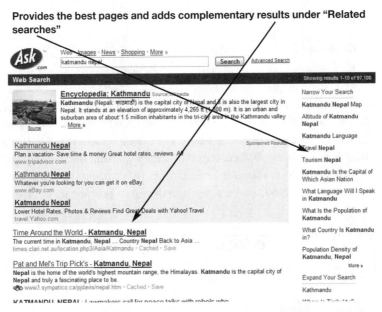

Figure 1-8   Ask.com search. Ask.com treats Katmandu as a location, returning links to related topics in addition to regular search results.

To gain market share, Ask.com also acquired Excite, one of the original Internet portals and still a popular search site. Today, Ask.com attracts more than 5 percent of all searches, when you add up the visits to all of its properties. Worldwide search marketers can reach Ask.com searchers through Google's paid search (which Ask.com uses), but need to pay attention to Ask.com organic search results, too. Ask.com has been growing in popularity; so although it has a relatively small share of searches today, it bears watching.

Metasearch Engines

Metasearch engines provide a way of searching multiple search engines, with the expectation that searching several different engines will provide better results than any one alone. Unfortunately, it does not, and relatively few searchers use metasearch engines.

Some metasearch engines, such as HotBot (www.hotbot.com), merely show a search input box and ask the searcher to choose which engine to search with. HotBot has its own search engine (using Yahoo! search technology), but also provides results from Google and Ask.com.

More complex metasearch engines actually search multiple search engines at the same time and mix the results together on the same results page. InfoSpace (www.infospace.com) searches Google, Yahoo!, Ask.com, and several other search engines. InfoSpace actually owns several metasearch engines that work this way, including WebCrawler (www.webcrawler.com) and Dogpile (www.dogpile.com), but none of these metasearch engines draw many searchers.

Search marketers do not need to concern themselves with metasearch engines—if you are listed in the worldwide search engines, the few searchers who use metasearch engines will find your site, too.

Local Search Engines

Until now, this discussion has focused on search engines that cover the whole world, but many popular search engines attract searchers from a local area—just one country or region. If your site attracts visitors from several countries, you might want to include **local search engines** in you plans. But before we look at a few local search engines, keep in mind that often a worldwide search engine is also the local search engine leader. For example, Google is the #1 search engine in the United Kingdom, Germany, France, Italy, Netherlands, Spain, Switzerland, and Australia. Figure l-9 show two typical local search engines, Onet.pl (www.onet.pl), Poland's leading Internet portal, and Seekport (seekport.co.uk), a new search engine popping up in several European countries.

Figure 1-9   Local search engines. Onet and Seekport are just two of the many local search engines that search marketers need to know.

Beyond search engines that operate in just one country or region, **local search** also refers to searches that operate within a geographic area—even inside a city. Yellow Pages sites, such as Verizon SuperPages, are the most common U.S. examples of local search engines. But worldwide search engines, including Yahoo! and Google, also use local search technology that detects the use of geographic terms in searches and finds results related to that area. So, a search for "Newark electrician" might find contractors in that city. But because not all searchers use geographic terms, and because those terms are frequently ambiguous (Newark, *New Jersey* or Newark, *Delaware*?), search engines are beginning to automatically detect the physical location of the searcher (using knowledge of the Internet's physical layout) and use that information in the searches.

Shopping Search Engines

One of the fastest-growing areas of search marketing is **shopping search**. Shopping search engines allow comparison of features and prices for a wide variety of products, and customers are flocking to them. Just 9 percent of all Internet users worldwide used a shopping search in 2002, but that grew to 15 percent in 2003 and continues to rise.

Consumers like comparison shopping search engines because they allow simultaneous comparison of similar products across many purchasing factors, such as price, reviews, and availability, as shown in Figure 1-10. Shopping search engines cover a wide range of consumer products, including electronics, office supplies, DVDs, toys, and many others. Internet users who visit shopping sites already have a good idea of what they are looking for, with price and availability often determining from whom they buy.

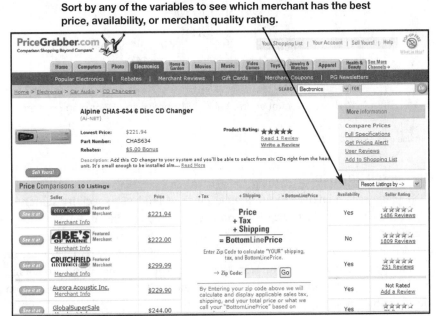

Figure 1-10 Shopping search engines. PriceGrabber, like any shopping search engine, has a product comparison page searchers can sort multiple ways.

To take advantage of shopping search engines, search marketers should ensure that no data is missing for products. For example, make sure you provide availability data (in stock, ship within two weeks, and so on) for your products. If you do not, when shoppers sort the product list by availability, your products will fall to the bottom of the list. Figure 1-11 shows the leading shopping search engines. If your site sells products available in shopping search engines, do not ignore this opportunity. We review specific strategies in more detail in Chapter 14, "Optimize Your Paid Search Program."

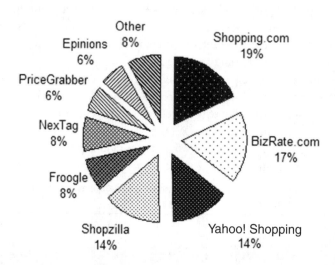

Figure 1-11   Shopping search market share. Yahoo! Shopping and Shopping.com are the leaders.

Source: Hitwise (November 2005)

Specialty Search Engines

Whereas shopping search engines locate a wide range of products, **specialty search engines** focus on just one or two product categories, or a certain type of content. Figure 1-12 shows a great example of a specialty search engine that focuses on information technology solutions. Because the content is limited to pages on a certain subject, the searcher retrieves more relevant results. Similarly, Technorati (www.technorati.com), which limits itself to blogs, and PODZINGER (www.podzinger.com), focusing on audio, may find more relevant information within those content types.

When IT managers search for "security" in Google, they get news stories and several top results that have nothing to do with what they are looking for.

It's not Google's fault—"security" has many meanings— but IT managers must scan down the page to find the first relevant result. Even searching for "IT security" doesn't help because "it" is such a common word.

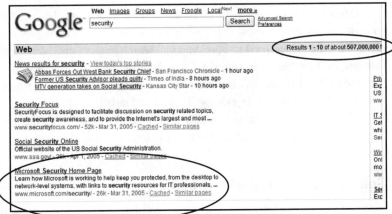

At IT.com, IT managers get a screen full of relevant results, because the content is limited to the subject of information technology.

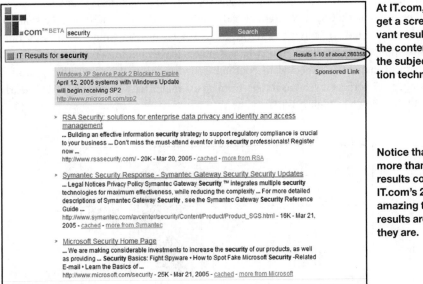

Notice that Google more than 500 million results compared to IT.com's 260,000. It's amazing that Google's results are as good as they are.

Figure 1-12   A specialty search engine. IT.com carefully limits its search results to IT solutions, providing more relevance to its niche market than Google can.

Most industries have at least one of these specialty engines, but consumer marketing has specialties, too. For example, the search facility at CNET (www.cnet.com), the computer and electronics site, shows products (as shopping search engines do), but also shows subject category matches and matching Web pages. So, searchers for "digital cameras" get a list of cameras along with their CNET reviews. This blend of product content, reviews, and comparison shopping is a near-perfect environment for electronics product marketers.

Search marketers should research the specialty search engines that cover their product lines, because specialty searchers are ready to buy.

Search and Your Marketing Mix

Now that you know a little bit about Web search, let's see why it should be part of your Web **marketing mix**—the advertising and other expenditures that your business allocates in its marketing budget. When *we* use the term *marketing mix*, we want you to think broadly—beyond what folks traditionally consider marketing. If your Web site is part of a for-profit business, then selling products is exactly what you do, but even nonprofit businesses have some kind of marketing mix—a budget that is allocated in various ways to attract visitors to the site to do something. If it is not to buy a product, it might be to donate money, or vote for your candidate. Whatever your Web site's purpose, search marketing should be part of the budget for attracting visitors to your site.

Your competitor's marketing mix might already include paid search; after all, the share of advertisers' budgets devoted to search marketing increases each year. Some businesses fund organic efforts from marketing budgets, too (whereas others use technology budgets for organic search). U.S. paid placement is expected to continue growing faster than any other sector of online advertising, at 17 percent a year, as it rises from an estimated $2.4 billion in 2004 to nearly $5 billion in 2009 (as shown in Figure 1-13).

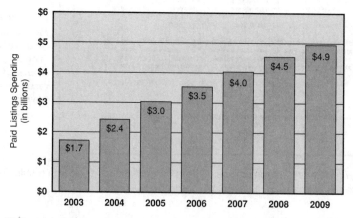

Figure 1-13   U.S. paid placement spending. Paid placement continues to grow, albeit more slowly than in years past.

Source: JupiterMedia (July 2004)

A BRIEF HISTORY OF WEB SEARCH

Search technology predates the Web by more than 20 years; after all, computers were first used to catalog documents and retrieve them in the 1960s. But although search technology grew to handle databases of thousands and later millions of documents within large organizations, nothing prepared the search industry for the size of the Word Wide Web. For the first time, billions of documents could be included in a single search, and search technology was not initially up to the task.

The first popular solution to this new Web search problem was not really a search engine at all. A small California company began to manually categorize every site on the Web in 1994, listing each site in a subject taxonomy that Web visitors could use to find what they were looking for. At first, it had no real search capability—visitors could merely find the desired subject and get to the home pages of sites about that subject—but it was a popular way to find things on this new World Wide Web. Thus began the first Web directory, called Yahoo!.

At the same time, true search solutions began to emerge. WebCrawler, Excite, Lycos, and others began examining each page of every Web site and allowing searchers to look for any word on any page. But no real leader emerged until late in 1995 when Digital Equipment launched the AltaVista search engine. AltaVista differed from the rest; it delivered strikingly more relevant results than its predecessors. For the first time, searchers could find what they were looking for in one or two searches, with the best results near the top of the list. Almost overnight, the Web world was abuzz with news of this magical new way to find Web sites.

For more than a year, Web users argued over the relative merits of Yahoo! Directory versus AltaVista search, but in 1997 two new choices emerged. Ask Jeeves developed a question-answering interface that provided access to answers to hundreds of thousands of commonly asked questions, such as "How many inches are in a meter?" that no directory or search technology could handle. Goto.com also made its debut in 1997, offering a unique system for advertisers to bid against each other for every search word, with the highest bidder receiving the #1 ranking for his page. Goto.com (later renamed Overture) launched the paid search industry.

But Web search changed forever in 1998 with the launch of Google. Google was able to find hundreds of millions (now billions) of pages on the Web while providing much better results than other search engines. Google eschewed the question answering of Ask Jeeves, instead improving on the search-oriented approach of AltaVista, and at first it had no directory or paid placement. But it worked—searchers were struck by how frequently Google seemed to find the exact right answer at the top of the list. Searchers soon abandoned AltaVista in droves for the new favorite.

Google has continued to innovate, by introducing the first search toolbar for browsers, by steadfastly separating paid search results from organic on its results page, and through new paid search techniques. Google introduced the AdSense paid search program, which combines both bidding and the popularity of an advertisement to decide which one is #1.

Yahoo!, which once used Google as the organic search that complemented its directory, has now made an about-face, acquiring several organic search companies to form a new organic Yahoo! Search (replacing Yahoo!'s use of Google) in 2004. Yahoo! acquired Overture (formerly Goto) for its paid search, rebranding it as Yahoo! Search Marketing Solutions in 2005. Google and Yahoo! are now the two largest competitors in the search market, but a little history shows how quickly that can change, as anyone associated with AltaVista can attest.

But the rise of search marketing is not just a U.S. phenomenon; it is a worldwide trend. European marketers already spend 13 percent of their online ad budget on paid search and expect it to increase to 15 percent by 2005. The picture in Asia is also striking; for example, China's paid placement spending is expected to increase fivefold by 2006 and Japan's by 560 percent by 2008. Around the world, search marketing expenditures have grown dramatically in recent years. Let's look at why.

Prospective Customers Use Search

One of the most basic reasons to spend your scarce marketing budget on search is that searchers buy products: 33 percent of all searchers are shopping, and 77 percent of those who research online before purchasing use search to do it. Lest you think that not enough people are online for search marketing to be worth your while, note that total Web users passed the 300 million mark worldwide in 2004. As simple as it sounds, your customers are on the Web, and they use search to buy. Your site must be found by these searchers who are ready to buy.

Think about the new way that people purchase products. They no longer call your company to have you mail them a brochure. They "Google" your offering ("verizon wireless"). Or maybe they look for your competitor's ("sprint"). Or they search for its generic name ("cell phone service").

If your company's Web site is not listed in the first few search results for these searches, you're out! You are out of the customer's **consideration set**—the group of companies that will be considered for the customer's purchase. If you are not in the customer's consideration set, you have no chance to make the sale to that customer.

Even if the goal of your Web site is not online purchase, your customers must find you to learn about your offerings, download information, or find the location of a retail store. Searchers are far more qualified visitors to your site than someone who clicks a banner ad, for example, so attracting search visitors is just good business.

The main reason to make search part of your marketing mix is that that's where your customers are, but there are other reasons.

Search Marketing Is Cost-Effective

Beyond your customers' use of search, the case for including search in your marketing mix is compelling for another reason: Search marketing expenditures are a good value.

European marketers report that they pay approximately €2 (euros) each time a searcher clicks their paid listings, and 55 percent regard that cost as "relatively cheap." Seventy-six percent of marketers believe paid search is better than banner ads for achieving their business goals, and 80 percent of businesses surveyed are satisfied with the return on investment for search marketing expenditures—35 percent are *very* satisfied. In fact, search marketing has the lowest cost per lead of *any* marketing method, as shown in Figure 1-14.

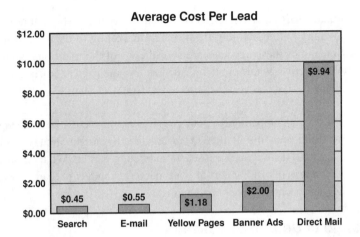

Figure 1-14 Comparing advertising value. Search is the leader in return on advertising investment.

Source: Piper, Jaffray & Co. (March 2003)

Why is this important? Because if you want to start spending money on search, you need to stop spending on something else. When you understand that search is the most effective way to spend your scarce marketing dollars, you should be able to easily make the tradeoffs required to reduce some existing budgets (direct mail, perhaps?) to find the money for your new search expenditures.

Search Marketing Is Big Business

You can tell a new marketing technique is taking off by noticing the number of consultants that hang out their shingles to help you do it! Several kinds of firms are involved in search marketing:

- *Search consultants.* A brand new kind of consultancy has sprung up in the past several years, variously known as SEO consultants or SEM consultants. These new firms, led by iProspect, Fathom Online, and Global Strategies International, handle search marketing and nothing else.

- *Traditional advertising agencies.* At the other end of the spectrum are the old-line advertising agencies that have been around for years. Just as firms such as Young & Rubicam and Ogilvy & Mather handle TV, radio, and print advertising, in recent years they have taken on Web advertising. Starting with banner ads, they have now moved into search marketing, too. Some ad agencies handle paid search only, whereas others offer SEO consulting for organic search, too.

- *Interactive advertising agencies.* In between the two extremes, interactive agencies handle anything online, ranging from search marketing to banner ads to e-mail campaigns. Sometimes these agencies are subsidiaries of the traditional ad agencies, such as OgilvyInteractive, whereas others, such as Avenue A | Razorfish, are smaller, independent firms.

All of these firms are competing for your growing interactive marketing budget—almost 3 percent of all advertising spending in 2003. Your organization might already work with one of these companies, or might be looking for a search marketing partner. What is most important at this point is your interest in allocating part of your marketing budget to search, because you will soon see that achieving success is rather challenging.

The Challenge of Search Success

Now that you know the basics of Web search, and you know how big a marketing opportunity it is, it must be time for a reality check: Search marketing is *not* easy to do.

And, unlike most marketing efforts, the bigger you are, the harder it is. We know that in marketing, size has inherent advantages. The bigger the budget, the more advertising you can buy, the more free media coverage you can coax, the better a public relations person you can hire, and on and on. But search marketing is different.

Companies with well-known brand names assume it is easy for their Web site to rank highly in search results, but John Tawadros (of search marketing firm iProspect) explains that "the field is more equal. Just because you're a big name doesn't mean much to the search engines." In fact, well-known brands have lots of competition for search rankings, both from their competitors and from their allies—many resellers rank highly for well-known brands. Amazon may rank well when a searcher searches for "sony dvd player"—possibly even higher than Sony's Web site.

It is actually easier in some ways for small Web sites to succeed in search marketing than large ones. For instance, fewer people need to know what to do, and the whole Web site is managed one way by one team. As soon as your site is large enough that you hear some telltale conversations about separating your team or even your site into multiple parts, then search marketing has just gotten tougher:

- *We need multiple teams of specialists.* "The copy writers and the HTML coders really should be in different departments. . . ."

- *We need multiple product sites.* "Each product line should really run its own separate Web site. . . ."

- *We need multiple audiences.* "We should really have different user experiences for consumers than for our business customers. . . ."

- *We need multiple countries.* "It is really easier for everyone if the Canada and the U.S. sites are separate. . . ."
- *We need multiple technologies.* "We decided to keep using the Apache server for the marketing information but we are putting all of the commerce functions into WebSphere. . . ."

Make no mistake—those preceding conversations are actually the sweet sound of success! Your Web site has grown too large to be run in the old simple way. Good for you that your site is growing and needs to be managed differently, but it makes search marketing much more difficult, for many reasons. Let's look at each of these situations and see what can go wrong for search marketing.

Multiple Specialist Teams

As soon as your Web team grows to more than about a dozen employees, people will start thinking about splitting the group into multiple teams and eventually several departments. No matter how you split things up, you will start to see communication problems that did not exist before.

If you divide the group by specialties, maybe the Webmasters, JavaScript programmers, and system administrators go into the Web technology group, and HTML coders, copy writers, and graphics artists form a Web creative group. That works well for most tasks, because, for example, each copy writer can work closely with the other copy writers to set standards and ensure that the writing is consistent across the site.

Unfortunately, search marketing gets more difficult precisely because it cannot be handled solely as a specialty. Your specialists must understand what they are personally required to do to make your search marketing a success. Your JavaScript programmers must place their code in files separate from the HTML files. Your copy writers must use the right words in their copy. Your Webmasters must choose the right naming convention for your pages' URLs (Uniform Resource Locators—the Web page addresses that start with www).

The key point you need to understand is that search marketing is a team effort and that medium-to-large Web sites have multiple teams that must work together for your search marketing to succeed. Oh, and one more thing: None of these specialists will be focused on search marketing—*that's* your biggest challenge.

Multiple Product Sites

Your organization might be so highly decentralized that your customers do not even think of your separate products as coming from the same company. How many of you know that Procter & Gamble makes Crest toothpaste, as well as the Cheer, Gain, and Tide laundry detergents? And how many even care? P&G's customers do not need to know what company makes these products— they know the brand names, and that is enough. And if they need to learn more about the new whitening ingredient in Crest, they are much more likely to go to www.crest.com than www.pg.com. So, Procter & Gamble created separate Web sites for each major brand, as shown in Figure 1-15.

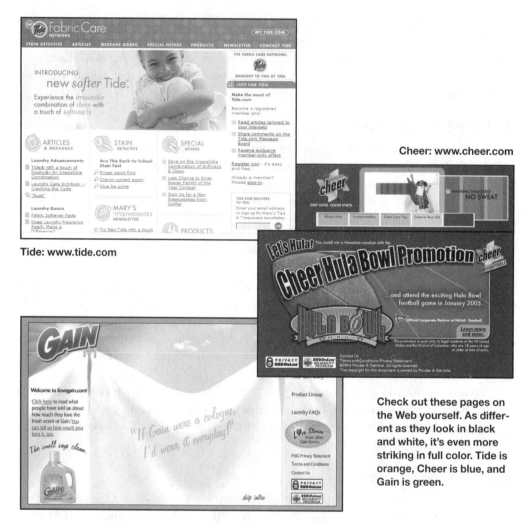

Cheer: www.cheer.com

Tide: www.tide.com

Gain: www.gainlaundry.com

Check out these pages on the Web yourself. As different as they look in black and white, it's even more striking in full color. Tide is orange, Cheer is blue, and Gain is green.

Figure 1-15   Multiple product sites. Three Procter & Gamble laundry detergent home pages look like they are from completely separate companies.

And each Web site might get its own team. There might be a Crest Webmaster, a Cheer Webmaster, a Gain Webmaster, and a Tide Webmaster, with the other specialists divided by product, too. Multiple product sites foster excellent communication among the specialists assigned to each product, but can create a situation in which there may be almost no communication *across* products.

For most Web tasks, this might not be problematic, but for search marketing, it can be. The Tide, Cheer, and Gain sites should each be found when searchers look for "laundry detergent"— but the respective teams might be fighting over those searchers rather than working together.

To lead search marketing across P&G, you must coax these disparate product groups to sometimes collaborate instead of always competing. Perhaps they should team up to create the ultimate "laundry detergent" page that showcases each of their products. This is harder to pull off than it sounds, because collaboration might violate the competitive corporate culture.

Alternatively, the three detergent marketers might pool their search knowledge so they *each* rank in the top ten. Moreover, this technique squeezes some competitors off the front page (because P&G has three listings out of ten). P&G marketers might warm to this approach because it is similar to how they stock supermarket shelves with multiple products to control the shelf space. None of these separate Web teams need to collaborate for other Web tasks; for search marketing, however, they do—that's *your* problem.

Multiple Audiences

Perhaps your company is highly customer-centric, conducting all sales and marketing based on audiences, or market segments. So, you have a Web site for large business customers, another for small-to-medium customers, and a third for consumers, even though they buy many of the same products. Of course, each of these sites can be run by separate teams that might not need to work together with the other sites' teams. (Are you starting to see a pattern here?)

Separate, audience-focused Web sites can be an effective way to communicate with your customers, because you can tune your marketing message to each audience's unique needs. Large businesses might want more customized service, whereas smaller firms might be willing to take a one-size-fits-all solution to their problem—these differing needs can be addressed with somewhat different offerings that are described differently on your Web site.

IBM sells the same computer software and servers to several different audiences, but large customers might have negotiated special pricing based on volume and special configurations, whereas small customers are more interested in ease of installation and service. So, the same underlying technology might be sold à la carte to large businesses but as a packaged "solution" to small businesses. To follow through on this strategy, IBM offers large customers discounted pricing in one part of its site, and markets solutions to smaller businesses elsewhere, as shown in Figure 1-16.

IBM's home page has separate links for medium businesses, large businesses, and other market segments. Clicking each link leads to a home page tailored for just that audience.

Figure 1-16   Multiple audience sites. IBM uses different marketing messages for different audiences, with a different area of its Web site for each.

And dividing this Web site based on customer size usually works well—until you consider search marketing. Unfortunately, when a prospective IBM customer searches for "Web commerce" in Google, there is no way to know whether the searcher has a small Web site that needs a turnkey solution or is from a large company wanting to purchase and run its own commerce software on its server. Neither the large company group nor the small company solution group is focused on search marketing, and so—say it with me now—"you will have to do that."

Multiple Countries

Another common way to divide up a Web site is by country, and like all the other ways discussed so far, it makes a lot of sense. (That's why companies do it!) Your company probably does not sell the same exact products in every country, so it makes sense that each country might have its own Web site for customers in that country to visit. Each country might have different languages, currency, cultural norms, laws—it is easy to understand why Web sites are so frequently divided this way.

But this clever organizational idea, once again, hurts search marketing efforts. Some searchers use country-specific search engines, but many use global search engines, such as

Google. What happens when a Canadian searcher enters "four-slice toaster" into the global search engine? Google might be able to determine the language of the query as English, but there may be excellent English-language pages on toasters in the United Kingdom, Australia, Canada, the United States, and many other countries. Your company might also have excellent matches for all of those countries—each toaster page is similar to those in the other countries, but is specific to the country. (It shows the toaster that conforms to UK electrical standards and is priced in British pounds, for instance.) Google might just show the UK pages, even though it is not the one the Canadian searcher wants, and suppress the rest as being "similar pages." If the wrong country page displays, your visitor cannot buy your product easily—he might be asked to pay in British pounds when he has Canadian dollars in his wallet.

You can see that if your corporate Web site is divided by country, you might find Web teams responsible for different countries battling to capture searchers with the same query—they want their pages to "win" so that your other country pages are the ones suppressed. Worse, you might have well-known brand names, such as Coke, that are used in many countries regardless of language. How do you know which country those searchers want? Figure 1-17 shows how Coca-Cola handles this problem on its home page, but your company could face this problem for hundreds of brand names that cannot all be listed on your home page.

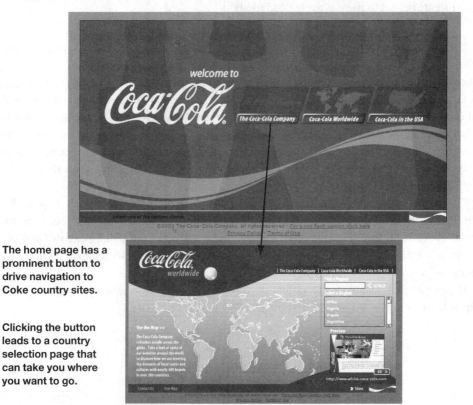

The home page has a prominent button to drive navigation to Coke country sites.

Clicking the button leads to a country selection page that can take you where you want to go.

Figure 1-17 Handling country sites. Coca-Cola highlights country selection on its home page to get searchers and other visitors to the right place.

Once again, there may be no incentive within your company for different country teams to collaborate on search marketing—they are not required to work together on most other things. All together now: "It's your job."

Multiple Technologies

Until now, this discussion has focused on the problems of multiple Web teams driven by the choices your company has made about how to organize. However, another problem grows as Web sites grow: the technology menagerie. A Web site can employ a dizzying array of technology:

- *Content management systems* help authors create and store the content for each page.
- *Web servers* display pages on the visitor's screen.
- *Application servers* run programs for the visitor to perform tasks on your site (such as viewing an appliance's service records).
- *Commerce servers* display your merchandise and enable visitors to purchase.
- *Portals* display content based on the visitors' interests (such as showing items for sale that are related to items already purchased).

Each of these components (and more) needs to be carefully configured to support your search marketing efforts. This configuration is complicated when your Web site has been pieced together across a large organization, however, because your site probably uses *different* components in each part of the site. So, your multiple product sites (or audience sites or country sites) might each have its own team using different technologies to run each site. In the initial rush to get every part of your company on the Web, a divide-and-conquer strategy might have ruled the day, with each division doing its own thing. Unfortunately, you are paying for that now, because every combination of technology that displays a Web page must be configured properly to make search marketing work.

The more technology combinations you have, the harder it is to get them all working for search. Frequently, you need to coordinate multiple changes to fix one problem because, for example, the content management system and the portal are both contributing causes. And (by now you are waiting for it), none of these technical specialists will think search marketing is part of *their* job—it is *your* job to get them to fix each problem.

If you find that your Web site suffers from the technology menagerie or any of the other problems listed here, don't despair. We show you how to solve each one.

Summary

Since the rise of the Web in the 1990s, more and more of your customers have turned to the Web, and more specifically to Web search, to find what they are looking for. Most searchers are clicking organic search results, although some are selecting paid search listings. Regardless, your Web site cannot ignore these searchers without losing them to your competitors. By focusing on searchers as part of your marketing plans, you *will* raise your sales (or raise whatever your Web site's goal is).

But paying attention to searchers takes more work than you might expect. To maximize your search marketing success, you cannot focus on just one or two search engines. Search engines come in many flavors and colors, ranging from worldwide sites to single-country engines to specialized shopping searches. Depending on your business, we discuss later how any or all of these might be key parts of your search marketing plan.

It is even more complicated for some organizations because the larger your Web site is, the more elusive search success can be. Large Web sites have multiple teams split by technical specialty, product line, country, and other organizational boundaries. Your company's organizational structure might be perfectly aligned for its overall goals, but can fracture search marketing.

Organizational splits hurt search marketing precisely because search marketing cannot be treated as a specialty performed by just one department. Rather, successful search marketing efforts pervade your entire Web organization, transforming jobs all along the way. Do not worry if you cannot imagine how you will persuade all these folks to change the way they do their jobs—we show you how.

Your multiple Web teams fail at search marketing because of their search ignorance— ignorance that can be overcome only through knowledge, knowledge that must start with you, the search marketer. The following chapter examines what a search engine actually does. As you learn how search engines work, you will be better prepared to train your far-flung Web teams to transform their jobs and to take advantage of the huge search marketing opportunity.

How Search Engines Work

You type a few words into Google, and you get a screen full of highly relevant results in seconds. But how did it happen? How does a search engine find the right pages? You have learned that search engines return both organic and paid results, and we repeat a figure shown in Chapter 1, "Why Search Marketing Is Important . . . and Difficult," as Figure 2-1.

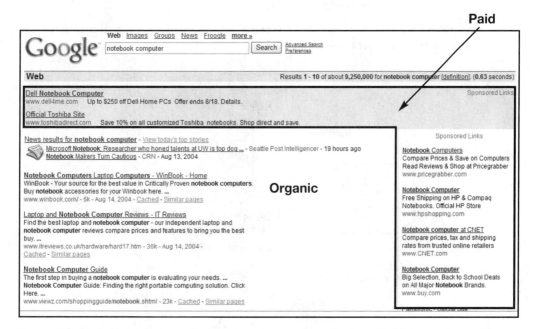

Figure 2-1 Types of search results. The Google search results page clearly separates paid from organic results; other search engines combine them.

In this chapter, we examine exactly how a search engine works, showing both what happens at the time a searcher enters words to be searched and what happened beforehand to prepare the search engine for that search. We spend most of our time on the more complicated organic search, but we explain how paid results are chosen, too.

Although it looks like Google is scanning each and every Web page the moment it displays your organic search results, it is not really that magical. It turns out a lot of preparation led up to that "magical" moment when the words are searched—search experts call that preparation **indexing**. Indexing is the process that creates a **search index**, a special database that holds a list of all the words on all the pages on the Web. Later in this chapter, we explain how the organic indexing process works. For now, just be aware that a lot of the magic of organic search engines occurs long before anyone enters anything to search.

Without yet knowing how the search index is created, you can still learn how the organic search engine *uses* that index when search words are entered. At the moment that words are typed into Google, the search engine does three major things, as shown in Figure 2-2:

- *Matches the search query.* The search engine must analyze the words the searcher typed in and pick the pages that match those words.

- *Ranks the matches.* Most search queries return many matches, so the search engine must sort the matches so that the best ones are at the top.

- *Displays the search results.* After the best matches are chosen, the search engine displays them on the screen for the searcher to see.

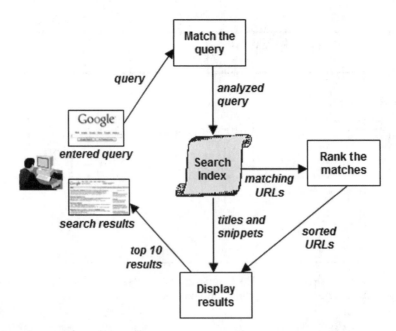

Figure 2-2   How organic search engines work. Every search engines matches search queries, ranks the matches, and displays them as search results.

Matching the Search Query

The **search query** is the technical name for what searchers type into a search engine to get search results. When someone enters "glaucoma treatments" into Google (or any other search engine), that is the search query. Experts usually describe each word in the search query as a **search term**. (In this example, "glaucoma" and "treatments" are search terms.) The search engine goes through several basic steps to find the pages that match, starting with **analyzing** the query.

Analyzing the Query

As soon as the searcher types his query and presses the Enter key, the search engine goes to work analyzing the query—examining each word (search term) in the query and deciding how to find the best Web pages in the search index that match. Search engines do not all analyze queries the same way, but most engines share some basic analysis techniques. That is what we look at in this section.

Finding Word Variants and Correcting Spelling

In English and other Western languages, the same word can be written in different cases ("Glaucoma Treatments" rather than "glaucoma treatments"). Most search engines pay no attention to case, which is usually what the searcher wants, because a word that starts a sentence (for example) is just as good a match as one that does not. Occasionally, searchers might want a query for "the White House" to match only occurrences in the proper case (and not match a sentence such as "He lives in *the white house* on Fourth Street"), but search engines generally find better matches by ignoring case.

In the same way, simply matching the exact words in the search query does not always locate what searchers are looking for. For Western languages, most words have multiple forms—singular and plural nouns, verb conjugations—that mean basically the same thing. Many of these words look similar to each other: *house* and *houses* mean essentially the same concept in a sentence, and they look basically alike. But others that are equally related, such as *mouse* and *mice*, look a bit different. Verbs such as *is* and *were* look completely different but mean about the same thing. Some search engines know that these **word variants** should be searched for whenever one is used in a query, so a search for "mouse" looks for "mice," too.

But that is not all that search engines do. We have all seen search engines correct our spelling for us, sometimes just going ahead and changing our entry into a correctly spelled word, but usually asking us "Did you mean . . .?" and prompting us with a more common word. Although a wonderful feature for searchers, search marketers should beware of clever product names that look like misspelled words—they might get corrected to real words, making it harder for searchers to find your product. And if customers cannot spell your product names correctly, the spelling-correction algorithms will not always help, so choosing names people can spell easily will work in your favor.

Detecting Phrases, Antiphrases, and Stop Words

A **phrase** means something slightly different in search parlance than in its normal use. You might know that most Web search engines allow searchers to enclose multiple words in double quotation marks when they should be searched together, as though they are a single word. These enclosed words are what search engines call a phrase. Phrase searches look for the words exactly as they are in the query, in the same order, and prove useful for finding specific information.

What you might not know is that modern search engines analyze queries to look for phrases even when the searcher does not use quotation marks. Search engines can identify words that occur frequently together and give preference to pages that use the words together.

Similarly, many searchers enter extraneous words that really are not what they are looking for, as in this query: "What is the treatment for glaucoma?" You can imagine that "What is the" does not help find the proper pages and might even throw the search engine off by finding pages that contain *what, is,* and *the*. These search terms are called **antiphrases** and are ignored (or at least treated as less important) in queries by smarter search engines.

This is important to search marketers because you might have a brand name (such as "Where's Waldo?") that looks more like a searcher's question rather than the actual query. Search engines use other techniques to recognize popular examples such as "Where's Waldo," but if your brand name is not well known, the search engines might not handle it well. If you can avoid cutesy names that will confuse search engines, you will be better off.

Finally, some words are just more important than others. Extremely common words (such as *a* or *the*) are usually called **stop words** because in the old days search engines would not ever look for them. Modern search engines know to pay attention to stop words at times, such as when you are searching for the rock group "The Who." As a search marketer, if you can avoid using stop words as critically important words in your brands and your trademarked names, that will make your names more easily searched.

If you work for clothing retailer The Limited, however, you probably do not have the luxury of changing the name! Unfortunately, you might find it is harder to get high search rankings because Google insists on looking simply for *limited* even when searchers enter "the limited." Now, The Limited is a well-known company, so when searchers enter "the limited," they will still probably find the right page. If your small business is called The Company, however, you might not be so lucky. And even a company as large as The Limited would find it hard to get high rankings for queries such as "the limited sale" or "the limited locations" when there are so many other pages that have those words on them.

Examining Word Order

Some search engines consider word order when they search, so the results differ depending on whether the search is for "Little Joe" versus "Joe Little." These engines try to find pages in which the words occur in the same order as they do in the query.

Again, this is a boon for searchers, but not always for search marketers. If your product has the catchy name of Enterprise Management Storage System, do not be surprised if some customers remember it as Enterprise Storage Management System or Storage Management Enterprise System. To the extent that your names are memorable in the correct order, that will aid searchability.

Processing Search Operators

A few savvy searchers know how to use the plus and minus operators in their queries, such as "big brother –tv" to find the Big Brother charitable organization rather than the TV show of the same name. Similarly, searchers can demand that a term be included in the results, as in "+the white house" to avoid sentences that talk about a white house (and ignore *the* as a stop word).

As search engines get smarter, it is less and less important for searchers to use these operators, but search marketers need to know them. If you have a choice, you want to avoid using brand and trademarked names that require these operators to produce good results.

Choosing Matches to the Query

After the query has been analyzed, the search engine must decide which results to present. With so many possibilities, how does the search engine find matches so quickly? Different approaches are taken for organic and paid results, and we look at the organic approach first.

Selecting Organic Search Matches

An organic search engine uses its search index to locate the matching pages. Basically, the query analysis determined which words to look up—not just the words that were typed as the query, but any word variants (*mouse* and *mice*)—and which to ignore (stop words and antiphrases). The engine goes to work looking up each word in the query to see which pages contain the word.

The search index can be thought of as an alphabetic list of every word that occurs on every page of the Web (as shown in Figure 2-3). The index contains a list of every Web page that contains each word. So, when you look up the word "glaucoma," you get a list of every page that contains that word.

That is the simplest case. It is more complicated when searchers enter more complex queries. If the searcher were looking for "glaucoma treatment," the engine would look up every page that contains each word, giving it a list of pages that contain the word *glaucoma* and a list of pages that contain the word *treatment*. Most search engines, faced with this decision, decide to show just the pages that contain both words. So they look through the two lists and find which Web pages are listed on both.

Some engines have more sophisticated rules about what they show for multiple-word queries. Consider a query such as "glaucoma eye treatment." Because the word *eye* is so much more common than the other words, some search engines might show some pages that contain the words *glaucoma* and *treatment* even if they do not happen to contain the word *eye*.

When you start adding word variants (*eye* and *eyes, treatment* and *treatments*), you can see that there might be many lists of pages that the search engine must look through quickly to determine the final list of pages to display.

For each word entered by a searcher, the search engine finds that word in the keyword table and looks up the documents that it is found within.

Keyword Table

Keyword	Document Numbers Containing Keyword
glaucodot	43278, 652389, 722227, 7234532, 8231234...
glaucoma	*1345*, 46891, 233343, 1827365, 9273524...
glaucomotous	2343, 261562, 2563516, 2635265, 4536524...

Document Table

Document Number	URL	Title	Description
1344	www.reliableauto.com/about	Reliable Auto – The one to trust for your next pre-owned car	For more than 50 years, Reliable Auto has been the leading car dealer in the central valley...
1345	www.glaucoma.org	Glaucoma Research Foundation	The Glaucoma Research Foundation is a national non-profit organization dedicated to conquering...
1346	www.cameras.com/us/sale.html	50% Off All 5 Mega Pixel Cameras	Our "Don't Settle For Less" sales event is your best reason yet to upgrade to five mega pixel quality...

Figure 2-3 How pages are retrieved from the index. Organic search engines check an index for the list of pages that contain each word in the search query.

Selecting Paid Placement Matches

Paid placement results are not retrieved from a search index, the way organic matches are, but the search engine does consult a database that stores all the listings that advertisers have submitted. Each advertiser selects the words and phrases that should match its listing, and submits a bid amount—that amount is charged to the advertiser each time the ad is clicked by a searcher.

EVALUATING ORGANIC SEARCH RESULTS: WHAT ARE PRECISION AND RECALL?

Search experts traditionally evaluate organic search engines according to measurements of precision and recall.

Precision measures the percentage of search results that are "correct" answers for a query. Precision attempts to show how well the search engine provides "good" results rather than "bad" results. So, looking at the list of ten results, the searcher can subjectively decide whether each one seems an appropriate answer to the search query. Time was that a person could actually examine every result for a particular query, but with hundreds of thousands of results being returned on the Web, no one can actually measure precision anymore (at least not precisely!).

In contrast, **recall** compares the number of correct search results returned for a particular query to the total possible correct results that *should* have been returned for that query. Recall tries to measure the fraction of correct results that were found, rather than missed, by the search engine. Historically, researchers could actually examine every document in a collection and decide subjectively which ones should have been returned for a particular query. With the advent of the Web, this is no longer possible, although sometimes it is still noticeable when a result that should have been present is missing.

The search engine uses the query analysis to decide which words should be searched for (just as with organic search) and looks up those words in the paid listing database. Each listing associated with the query terms is retrieved from the paid listing database.

Although the process sounds similar to organic search, in practice it is far simpler. The advertisers typically control exactly which words should match their ads, so far less analysis is required to find synonyms, for example. Moreover, rather than sifting through billions of pages, there are far fewer advertisements to pick from. In short, paid placement results are chosen much the same way that organic results are—the query is analyzed, and the results that match the words in the query are selected. For paid placement, however, there is typically a lot less work for the search engine to do.

Ranking the Matches

Merely displaying the list of all the pages that contain the words in the query is not much help when there are more than a dozen pages. And with Web search, that is almost always the case. So, one of the most important parts of a search engine is the **ranking algorithm**—the part of the search engine that decides which pages show up at the top of the results list.

Both organic results and paid results must be ranked, but the organic ranking algorithm is by far the most complicated, so we tackle that first.

Ranking Organic Search Matches

A search engine's organic ranking algorithm is one of the trickiest parts of designing a search engine, so let's start by examining the simplest kind of ranking algorithm.

Precision and recall work against each other. If a query returns only one page, and it is a correct answer, that is 100 percent precision (all answers are correct), but the recall measure is probably awful. (Likely, many other pages on the Web should also have been found.) Likewise, if a query returns all four billion pages on the Web, it has 100 percent recall (all the correct answers have been returned, and none missed), but precision is lousy because the vast majority of answers are wrong.

If no one can actually measure recall and precision on the Web, why are they important? Obviously, they are no longer important as measurements, but they remain important as concepts. Precision is important with searches that return many results. Lots of extraneous results frustrate searchers. Less frequently, searchers complain that they cannot find certain results they expect. Low recall of pages is the culprit, even if most searchers do not express the problem that way.

Although only experts (and now you) know these concepts, all searchers understand intuitively that they do not want to see wrong answers and do not want to miss correct answers. And the experts often drive search engine popularity, which is why *you* care about these concepts. "Buzz" among the digerati can drive usage of one search engine versus another. So if you think that "Google is slipping" or you hear experts talking about how "Yahoo! is improving its recall" or "Ask.com has more accurate results," it might be a sign of a popularity shift coming.

Ranking is just another word for **sorting**, the act of collating results into a certain order. Shopping search engines typically use simple ranking algorithms that the searcher can choose. When the searcher is looking for a product to buy, the shopping search engine might start by ordering the results by price (lowest to highest), but the searcher can decide to sort the list by other columns, such as availability (in stock, within one week, and so on), or any other features of the product.

But the kind of organic search that Yahoo! and Google use over billions of Web pages requires a much more sophisticated approach to ranking. For some kinds of information, such as news stories, ranking results by the date of the information (newest first) might make sense, but most organic search results are ranked by **relevance**, the degree to which the pages match the subject of the query.

More and more, organic search engines differentiate themselves on how their relevance ranking algorithms work, but every search engine uses certain standard techniques. We look at several factors that go into ranking algorithms, but one of the most interesting parts of designing a search engine is the interplay between those factors. Each factor is an ingredient in the ranking soup, and some engines use more of one ingredient than another—one reason why different search engines show different results for the same query. Some place more value on one ranking factor than others do.

Because your goal as a search marketer is to get your pages to the top of the list, it is crucial that you understand why search engines put some pages at the top and others far down the list, where few searchers will ever see them. As we discuss these ranking factors, we constantly talk about tendencies, such as, "All else being equal, pages with more of the terms will rank higher than pages with fewer of the terms." But ranking algorithms are deliciously complicated and all else rarely equal. Suffice it to say that if you pay attention to each of the factors as you design your site, you will have the best chance at high rankings.

We also try to use the parlance of search marketers and refer to a **keyword**. Unfortunately, *keyword* is a somewhat ambiguous term—at times it means an individual word in a query, but at other times it denotes the entire query. We use keyword or query to refer to the entire string of words a searcher types, but refer to a word or a search term when it is important to emphasize an individual search query word.

Keyword Density

Perhaps the simplest thing search engines look for is how many of the terms in the search query are actually found on the page. All other things being equal, pages that have more of the terms in the query (some search engines require *all* of the important terms) tend to rank higher.

However, it is more than mere term occurrence. It is more than just having all the terms of a particular query on your page. **Keyword density**, also known as **keyword weight**, is critical. In the old days of search, the more frequently the terms occurred on the page, the better. A page with a **term frequency** of ten occurrences for the word *glaucoma* was considered better than one with two, when that is what a searcher is looking for.

But the advent of Web search drove people to look for quick fixes in search rankings, and they started littering pages with words. (If 10 occurrences were good, why not 50?) So search engines have cracked down on keyword density. Now they look for a particular keyword density on a page and have decided that pages with around 7 percent of the words matching the query (a 7 percent keyword density) are "good" matches.

Most search queries, however, have more than one word. So search engines look at frequencies even more deeply. Ranking algorithms often decide between pages with a higher density in one term versus another. That is why a query for "glaucoma eye treatment" might look for pages with heavier densities of *glaucoma* and *treatment* rather than *eye*. Search engines can make these decisions based on the frequency of occurrence of a word throughout the entire Web. So, because the engine knows the word *eye* is much more common than *glaucoma*, the word *glaucoma* is a better differentiator for which pages best match that query. Similarly, pages that mention *glaucoma* frequently along with *treatment* are probably better than pages that mention *treatment* frequently along with one occurrence of the word *glaucoma*.

However, there is even more to it than that. If you think about it, the best possible pages might have the words *glaucoma* and *treatment* right next to each other. So pages that have higher **keyword proximity** (the terms are closer together) are often better than those that contain the terms separated by a few words, or worse, a few paragraphs. Web search engines work hard to find as many of the terms in the query as possible, with as many occurrences on the page as possible (up to that magical 7 percent threshold), as close to each other as possible. As you might imagine, it is critical for you, the search marketer, to write your pages using these keywords and phrases. We teach you how to do that in Chapter 12, "Optimize Your Content."

Keyword Prominence

Besides knowing that a page contains the words in a search query, isn't it important to know *where* they appear on the page? You better believe it. All other things being equal, pages where query terms appear in important places, such as the page title, tend to rank higher than pages where the terms are buried at the page bottom. Pages that feature query words in titles and initial paragraphs are said to have high **keyword prominence**, because the keywords appear in more prominent places than on other pages.

Why do search engines emphasize keyword prominence? Because search engines are, at heart, pattern-matching machines. They are tuned to recognize various patterns associated with pages that strongly match queries—pages with a pattern of keyword matches in prominent places are stronger matches than others.

So how does the search engine evaluate the prominence of terms it finds in various parts of the page? Here are the major categories, which are also depicted in Figure 2-4:

- *Title*. This is the most important part of the Web page to a search engine. The title is what displays in the search results page, and it is also shown in the window title for the browser. You can think of a Web page's title as similar to the title of a magazine article, which usually strongly indicates what the entire article is about.

- *Headings and emphasized text.* Most search engines give more weight to terms found in bold headings, and to italicized or colored text, assuming that these are more important occurrences of the terms. Headings are most similar to bold section headings inside a magazine article that break up the running text and indicate what the paragraphs below are about.

- *Body text.* Body text includes all the words that appear on the page, but body text that appears closer to the top of the page is considered more important than text found in the middle or at the bottom of the page. Pictures on the page also contain alternate text that search engines use to "learn" what each picture is about.

- *Description.* Web pages generally contain a summary that some search engines still show under the title in the search results. Most search engines, however, no longer show the description nor give it any more weight than body text.

You can find much more detail on how to craft your pages to be more attractive to search engines through clever term placement in Chapter 12.

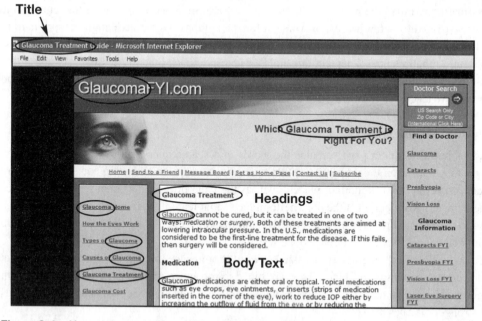

Figure 2-4   Keyword prominence within a page. Search engines treat matching words differently based on where those words are found on a page.

Link Popularity

It might seem to you that term frequency and term placement techniques would suffice for good relevance ranking, but, in practice, they do not. These techniques formed the state-of-the-art in ranking before the Web, but the sheer number of pages on the Web has overwhelmed their effectiveness. Luckily, the Web also made possible a new factor, called **link popularity** (sometimes called **link analysis**), that dramatically improves ranking when used in conjunction with these older techniques.

Link popularity is a fancy name for a simple concept—Web pages that other pages link to are better pages than Web pages that no one links to. It makes sense, doesn't it? The best pages on the Web are linked to by lots of other pages, and bad pages are not. Now there are certainly perfectly good pages that are new that no one has discovered yet, but the more links there are to a page, the more it *tends* to be a high-quality page with up-to-date and valuable information. If it weren't, people would stop linking.

For this reason, link popularity has emerged as a major factor in results ranking, sometimes outweighing the other two factors previously discussed. So, other things being equal, pages with more links to them tend to rank higher than other pages. It is easiest to see why this is a good idea by looking at an example.

Consider a search for the word "glaucoma"—a one-word search query. It seems simple enough, but just imagine how difficult a task this is for the search engine. A million pages contain the word *glaucoma*. Why should we expect that the pages that have the most *glaucoma* occurrences or that contain *glaucoma* in the title are the best ones? There must be tens of thousands of pages with *glaucoma* in the title anyway. How does any search engine pick the top ten from such a long list?

Link popularity is the answer. The best pages for *glaucoma* are the ones that are the most respected sources of information. And the best surrogate a search engine can find for respect is how well each site is linked to the rest of the Web. Now, this being a book about search engines, we can't leave it that simple, but that is the basic idea.

For a few reasons, the actual algorithms that search engines use are more complex than a simple count of the number of links. One reason is that all links are not equal. If you think about this, you will agree it is true. If you knew that one site about glaucoma was linked to by the American Medical Association's Web site, and another glaucoma site was linked to by someone's personal Web page, which one would you trust more? Undoubtedly, it would be the AMA link. But how can a search engine tell the difference between those links?

It's simple, really. Every Web site on the Internet is given a calculation of its **authority**, or its intrinsic value, based on the links that come to it. So, as you might expect, the AMA site has high authority, because it has thousands of links coming in, and many of those links are themselves from highly respected sites. And each high-authority site, such as the AMA, conveys some of that authority to each site it links to. So sites that are linked to by high-authority sites have a little bit of that authority rub off, which they can then pass along to the sites *they* link to. It is complex to calculate, but every search engine uses this type of calculation to help rank its search results.

Google's algorithm, known as **PageRank**, is the most well known. Google calculates the PageRank of every page on the Web as a number between one and ten. To continue with the previous example, if the AMA page that links to a glaucoma site has a PageRank of six, and the personal home page has a page rank of one, the AMA page confers great authority to its link, whereas the other conveys almost none. Now if that personal home page turns out to be that of a well-known glaucoma researcher and other sites begin to link to that page, its PageRank might rise to three and thus confer more status on pages to which it links.

But links alone are not specific enough to yield good search rankings. A site might receive many inbound links from well-respected sites, but those links might be on different subjects from what is being searched for. Suppose the AMA linked to the glaucoma site because an AMA board member is on the board of the glaucoma organization, and the link was to that board member's biography? What at first seemed like a credible endorsement of glaucoma information now seems like quite a bit less than that.

To be sure about the relevance of the link to the searcher's query, search engines use **anchor text**, the words that appear as the name of the link on the page. Therefore, a link from the AMA site to the glaucoma site that is actually named "glaucoma" is much more pertinent than one that contains the name of the AMA board member. That is why the search engine uses the names of the links as part of the link popularity analysis, giving much higher consideration to links that contain search terms in the link names.

Search engines are fiendishly complicated, so in truth these algorithms are even more intricate than described here, but this is enough for you to understand the basics. Chapter 13, "Attract Links to Your Site," explains strategies you can use to improve the link factor for your site.

Ranking Paid Placement Matches

Paid placement matches use much simpler ranking algorithms than organic search, but they still require a bit of explanation.

The oldest way of ranking paid matches is the simplest: The highest bidder wins. Overture, the paid placement company now owned by Yahoo!, invented the paid placement genre and introduced the **high bidder auction**. Each advertiser bids the amount of money it will pay when a searcher clicks its advertisement, and the search engine displays the highest bidder's ad first among the paid results. Bids can change minute to minute, but the search engine always shows the current high bidder at the top of the list. Many paid placement search engines still use high bidder auctions, but the top engines are moving away from it.

Google, never one to shy away from innovation, pioneered the **hybrid auction**. Advertisers participating in Google's AdWords program bid the amount they are willing to pay for a searcher's click, just as with the highest bidder approach, but the highest bidder does not always get the top spot at Google. Instead, Google weighs the combination of the bid and the clickthrough rate (the percentage of searchers that click on the result after it has been displayed), choosing the best combination of bid amount and clickthrough rate (and sometimes other factors) as #1.

In this way, Google's ranking method rewards more relevant results (those with higher clickthrough rates) because they will rank higher than less-relevant results that have higher bids. Although this ranking algorithm might provide benefits to the searcher by showing more relevant results, it is not motivated entirely by altruism—Google maximizes its overall paid placement revenue using this technique, whereas the high bidder auction maximizes only the bids. MSN Search has moved away from the high bidder approach to a hybrid auction for its ranking algorithm and Yahoo! has announced it will follow suit.

Displaying Search Results

After the search engine knows which pages match, and what rank order to show them in, it is time to display them on the search results page. Displaying the results is a lot simpler than some other parts of the process, but there are a few important things to pay attention to.

Each search engine has a different layout for its search results, but they are more similar than different, with each showing a mixture of organic and paid results. Most search engines distinguish organic and paid results through different visual treatments and different locations on the page, but some do not, integrating paid results with organic results in the list so as to make them indistinguishable. Figure 2-1, appearing earlier in this chapter, shows how Google displays its results.

Organic search results look similar no matter what search engine you use. They all use the title of the page followed by a **snippet**—a summary of the text from that page that contains the search terms. The search terms usually display in bold, drawing the searcher's eye to them. You should understand that everything displayed in the search results is drawn from what the search engine previously stored in its index. The search engine never examines the actual page while it is displaying search results, which is why the results page can sometimes contain outdated information, or even display pages that no longer exist (which are discovered when searchers click them). The information displayed on the results page was correct when the spider last crawled the page, but the page might have changed (or even been removed) since.

Paid results have also become more uniform in appearance over time, because ads that look like organic results (a title and a short text description with no picture) seem to get higher click-through than glitzier-looking graphics. The advertiser is in near-complete control of the ad that displays, although the search engines have editorial guidelines that stop overblown claims and remove results that are irrelevant to the searcher's query.

When the searcher clicks a particular search result (organic or paid), the chosen page is displayed, but not by the search engine. The search results screen merely links to the Web site page that was listed in the organic search index or the paid placement database, just like other hypertext links to that page from anywhere else. If everything has gone well, the information the searcher is looking for is on that clicked page. If not, the searcher can click the Web browser's Back button to see the results page again.

Now that you understand how both organic and paid results are found, ranked, and displayed, you need to learn how those organic search matches found their way into the index.

Finding Web Pages for the Organic Index

Sounds easy, right? Searchers enter queries, and then the search engine looks up the search terms in its organic index, it ranks the best matches first, and then displays the results. But how did all those pages get into the index in the first place? That is what Figure 2-5 shows, and the rest of this chapter explains. This information is critical to you, the search marketer, because if your pages are not in the index, no searcher can ever find them.

Spider

The search engine spider visits the HTML page and scoops up all of the text on the page, assigning the page a unique number.

Document #7222

Text Analyzer

The search engine removes the tags, keeping only the text.

```
</span>  <br /><img src="//www.ibm.com/i/c.gif" width="1" height="9" border="0" alt
="" class="display-img" />

<h1 class="smalltitle">Course description: Introduction to Programming XML and Related
Technologies</h1>

<img src="//www.ibm.com/i/c.gif" width="1" height="6" border="0" alt="" class="display-img" /
></td></tr></table>

              <!-- End Title -->
```

Introducing to programming xml . . .

Index

Finally, the search index is created with each keyword stored along with informa-tion about what pages it was found on (not shown).

Keyword	Document Numbers Containing Keyword
introduction	7222, 566539, 35245, 56324...
to	7222, 652389, 722227, 7234532...
programming	7222, 46891, 233343, 1827365...
xml	7222, 261562, 2563516, 2635265...

Figure 2-5   How organic search engines index pages. Every search engine finds Web pages, analyze their content, and builds a search index.

To build up the inventory of pages in the search index, search engines use a special kind of program known as a **spider** (sometimes called a **crawler**). Spiders start by examining Web pages in a **seed list**, because the spider needs to start somewhere. But after the spider gets started, it discovers sites on its own by following links.

Following Links

A spider uses the same links you click in your Web browser. When the spider examines the page, it sees the Hypertext Markup Language (HTML) code that indicates a link to another page (see Figure 2-6)—the same HTML code that your browser formats to show you the page.

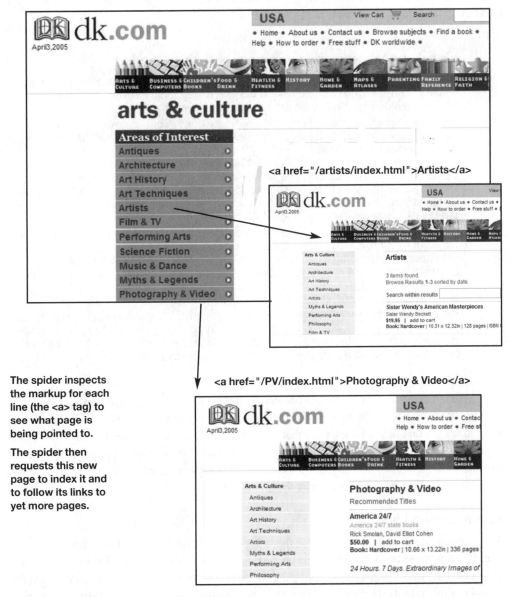

Figure 2-6 How spiders follow links. Every spider sees the same HTML code that your browser sees, and can follow links to other pages.

The spider scoops up the HTML for each page, noting links to other pages so it can come back to collect the HTML of those pages later. You can imagine that, given enough time, a spider can eventually find every page on the Web (or at least every page that is linked to another page). This process of getting a page, finding all the links on that page, and then getting those pages in turn, is called **crawling** the Web. Later in this chapter, we explain what the spider does with the HTML it collects from all of those pages that it crawls.

HOW MUCH OF THE WEB IS INDEXED BY SEARCH ENGINES?

It sounds easy. Spiders visit the pages and send them to the search index. Those little spiders keep crawling until they index the entire Web, right? Wrong. The truth is that the great majority of Web pages are *not* indexed in search engines.

Over the years, there have been many estimates of the gap between the number of indexed pages and all Web pages. In 1999, Lawrence and Giles found that the (now defunct) Northern Light search engine indexed just 16 percent of the estimated 800 million publicly available Web pages (*Searching the World Wide Web* by Steve Lawrence and C. Lee Giles, 1999). But the next year, Michael Dahn claimed the problem might be twice as bad as reported, because the "publicly available" Web may underestimate the total Web by half (*Counting Angels on a Pinhead: Critically Interpreting Web Size Estimates* by Michael Dahn, 2000).

Not to be outdone, in 2001 two studies estimated the total number of Web pages to be far larger than previously reported. Sherman and Price proclaimed the "Invisible Web is between 2 and 50 times larger than the visible Web" (*The Invisible Web* by Chris Sherman and Gary Price, p. 82, 2001). In *Deep Content: Surfacing Hidden Value* (BrightPlanet, 2001), Michael Bergman posited the Web contains 550 billion pages and search engines see only 0.03 percent of them.

Regardless of the wildly divergent numbers, the point is that an enormous number of pages are not indexed, and your Web site probably contains some of them. Each page on your site that is not indexed is completely invisible to searchers, which reduces traffic to your site, so your goal is to get as many indexed as possible.

Your organization's Web site is undoubtedly known to the search engine spiders, and you certainly have some pages listed in their search indexes. But you might not have as many of your pages listed as you think, and any page that is not in the index can *never* be found by the search engine. So, it is important to have as many pages in the index as possible. Chapter 10, "Get Your Site Indexed," shows you how to find out how many pages are indexed from your organization's site and some simple ways to get more of them indexed.

Remembering Links

Following links is important because it is the best way for a spider to comprehensively crawl the Web. But it is important for another reason, too. Spiders must carefully catalog every link they find—checking which pages link to your page and checking the words displayed that describe the link (the **anchor text**). Earlier in this chapter, we discussed how search engines rank search results; they do so with this information. Figure 2-7 shows how spiders collect the link information that is so important to ranking the results.

The anchor text for this link is "Destination Maps"

```
            <td class="secNavBoxContent" valign="top" width="50%">
    <a href="/travel/plan/destination_maps/index.jsp">Destination Maps</a></td>
            <td class="secNavBoxContent" valign="top" width="50%">

    <a href="http://delta-air.deltavacations.com" target="_blank">Delta vacations</a></td></tr><tr>
            <td class="secNavBoxContent" valign="top" width="50%">
    <a href="/travel/plan/aircraft_types/index.jsp">Aircraft Types & Layout</a></td>
```

Figure 2-7 How spiders collect link information. Spiders pay attention to which pages link to every other page and what words they use on each link.

Keeping Up with Changes

As you can imagine, Web crawling is not the most efficient way to keep up with changes to those billions of Web pages. New pages can be added, old pages removed, and existing pages changed at any time—the spider will not immediately know that anything has changed. It can be days or weeks before the spider returns to see what happened. That is why a searcher sometimes gets a "page not found" message when clicking a search result. The spider found that page during its last crawl, but it has since been removed or given a new address.

This can be an especially vexing situation for some business Web sites. Your site might have fast-changing content, such as product catalogs that list what you have available each day. If you have new products introduced frequently, or a volatile supply environment, your pages on your site might not be a close match to the pages the spider has put in the search index. Chapter 3, "How Search Marketing Works," covers a service some search engines offer called **an inclusion program** that can help address this problem.

Even without inclusion programs, however, the best spiders try to compensate to keep their indexes "fresh" by varying their rates of revisiting sites. Spiders return more frequently to sites that change more quickly. If a spider comes to two pages on the same day and then returns to both exactly a month later, if one of them has changed and one has not, the spider can decide to revisit the changed page in two weeks, but wait six weeks to return to the unchanged page. Over time, this technique can greatly vary the return rate for the spider, raising the freshness of the index by revisiting volatile pages most frequently.

Spiders also revisit more often to sites that have the highest-quality pages. Google, for example, tends to revisit pages with higher PageRank more frequently (perhaps once per week) than other pages. The Yahoo! spider, in general, does not return to sites as frequently as Google, but also pays more attention to well-linked pages.

Feeding the Index Without Crawling

By far, the most pages in organic search engines are gathered by the search engine's spider, but it is not the only way to get your data into the search engine.

Some search engines allow your site to send its data instead of waiting for the spider to crawl your site. Yahoo! Search, some shopping search engines, and some others allow your site to provide a **trusted feed**; that is, your site sends pages to the search engine, which are processed and stored in the index as soon as they are received.

Some engines charge for trusted feeds (Yahoo!), some (especially shopping engines) require them but do not charge, and others (Google) do not accept them at all. (Google's shopping engine, Froogle, does accept them.) In Chapter 10, we examine the use of trusted feeds as part of your search marketing program.

Analyzing the Content

Now that you see how spiders find pages on the Web, it's time to see what search engines do with all those pages. The first thing that you will find is that not every document in the search index is an HTML-coded Web page.

Converting Different Types of Documents

Up until now, we have assumed that all Web pages are made of HTML, but many are not. Modern search engines can analyze Adobe Acrobat (PDF) files and many other kinds of documents. Trusted feeds, in particular, tend to use their own formats.

When search engines come across a non-HTML document, they convert these documents to a standard format that they use to store all the other documents. For simplicity's sake, we examine the rest of the text analysis work as if all the documents are coded in HTML, but you know now that it is a bit more complicated than that.

Deciding Which Words Are Important

If you take a look at the average Web page, you will see a lot more than just the text that appears on the screen. If you view the HTML source, in fact, most of what you see is **markup**, or HTML **tags**. Because you do not want the names of these tags found when you search, you might imagine that search engines throw them away, but they do not. They use the markup to help them analyze the text.

When you look at a Web page on your screen using your browser, some words stand out more than others. Some words are in color or bold type; others are set in a larger size; some are set apart as headings. Also, because most Web pages are written in "newspaper style," the most important information tends to come near the top of the page.

As discussed previously in this chapter, search engines realize that emphasized words and words near the beginning of the page are more important than the rest of the words on that same page. This is the step of the index building process in which search engines decide which placements of words make them more important than others. In Chapter 12, we show you how to use this information to your advantage as you create and edit your own Web pages.

Spotting Words You Don't Normally See

Some of the most important tags are ones that you do not usually see. Because search engines see the actual HTML code, they can learn things about the page that you would never notice unless you viewed the HTML source yourself. These tags that contain information about the page are often called **metatags**.

The most important metatag is the **title** tag, but the title tag might not do what you expect. The words at the top of the Web page—the ones that your eye tells you make up the title—are probably generated by a heading tag or by an image. The actual HTML title tag shows up in the title bar of the browser window, as shown in Figure 2-8. (The words coded in the title tag also appear as the name of the page when you bookmark it or save it as a favorite.)

The title from the HTML source file...

...is displayed in search results ...

... and shown by the browser in the window tool bar.

Figure 2-8   How titles are used. You can see titles in several places if you look hard, but the search results page is where it matters the most.

Even though you often do not notice the title, search engines know that this tag provides a lot of information about your page. The theory is that the title contains the words that best describe the page. Search engines pay special attention to the words you use in your title tag, as mentioned in the ranking discussion earlier in this chapter. Moreover, search engines display the title when they show your page in the search results. Searchers use the title as a big factor in deciding whether to click through to your page.

Another important metatag stores the **description** of the page. As with the title, search engines expect that the words in your description summarize your page, and some search engines give words found in your description special importance. Unlike the title, searchers rarely see the description. In the past, many search engines displayed your page's description right under its title in the results list, but few do that today. Therefore, the description tag is less important than it once was. Chapter 12 covers metatags in detail.

Deducing Information from the Page

Search engines also analyze the page to figure out things that are not coded in the HTML. One thing that almost every search engine figures out is the language of the text. Search engines examine the beginning of the page and recognize that the words are from a certain spoken language, such as French or Korean. This recognition helps the search engine to limit its results to pages that are in the language the searcher understands.

Some search engines also deduce other things that are not explicitly coded on the page. Ask.com, for example, algorithmically analyzes the words and links on every page to determine each page's **communities**, recognizing that pages about a certain subject, such as woodworking or car repair, tend to use similar words and form a commonly linked community. Ask.com uses this information to hone in on pages considered experts within the community of each search query, believing this improves the search results.

More and more, the secret sauce of search engines is composed of special text analytics such as Ask.com communities, where the search engine deduces information about your pages that was not there when you coded them.

What Search Engines *Don't* See

But as smart as search engines sometimes seem to be, it is striking how much they miss. The most striking misses are the pictures. Search engines read and understand text of any kind, and as you have read, they even deduce information beyond what is encoded in the text.

But pictures have no meaning to search engines. Although a person can look at a picture and immediately recognize that it is a zebra, a search engine cannot make any sense of the pattern in that image file. Some search engines, such as Google, can find zebra images through tricky use of text, such as noticing that the image file is named zebra.gif or that some text associated with the image contains the word *zebra*, as shown in Figure 2-9.

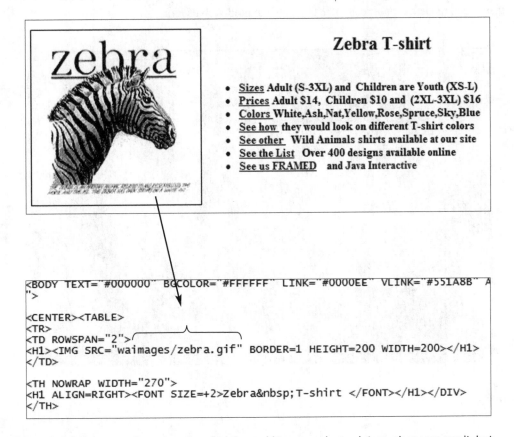

Figure 2-9 How search engines "see" pictures. You recognize a picture when you see it, but search engines see only the text associated with the image.

In fact, one way to think about search engines is that they use the Web the way sight-impaired people do. Blind Web users employ software called screen readers that literally read the text on the screen out loud to them, using the computer's speaker. Screen readers can speak any text, but they have nothing to say when confronted with a picture—any picture—even a "picture" of text.

Search engines suffer from a similar "blindness." This is an important reason not to use images for display text—the large titles that often occur at the top of the page. Even though sighted visitors to the page can easily read the words displayed from the image, search engines cannot, as shown in Figure 2-10. (Another important reason to avoid images containing text is that screen readers cannot read them to sight-impaired Web users.)

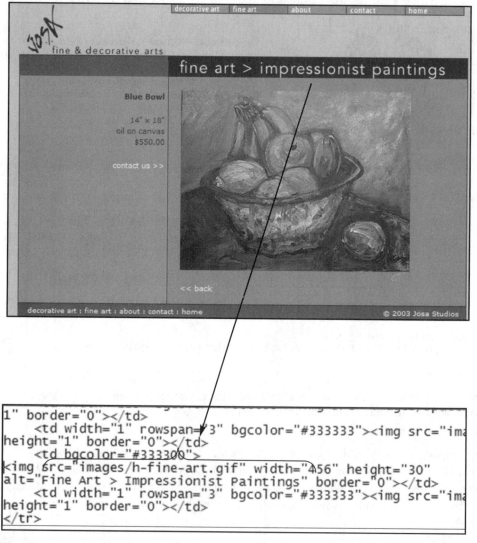

Figure 2-10   How search engines miss words. You can read the text as it is shown on the screen, but search engines only see the image tag's text.

These examples show how important it is for you to use alternate text that strongly describes all of your images so that search engines (and sight-impaired readers) understand them as well as possible.

Building the Organic Index

So far, the spider has crawled the pages, and the search engine has analyzed the markup and text on each one. The next step is creating the search index, which is a specially designed database that the search engine uses to quickly find the matching pages in response to any search query.

A search engine "remembers" which words are on which pages by storing them in its search index. In its simplest form, a search index contains a record for every word, followed by a list of the pages that contain that word. So, when searching for the word "glaucoma" in Google, the Google search engine looks in its index for the record for *glaucoma* and retrieves the list of pages.

When a search engine creates its search index, it examines the unique words on each page that the spider finds, and for each word it checks to see whether a record exists in the index. If so, it adds the Web page's address (Uniform Record Locator, or URL) to the end of the record. If no record for that word exists, a new record containing that URL is created. The actual URL would take up a lot of space in the index, so the search engine converts each URL to a unique number that it stores in the index. Figure 2-5 showed how a simple search index might look.

In addition, the search engine stores the metadata about each page for use in displaying the search results. So, it stores the URL, the title, and any information needed to display the snippets that highlight where the terms were found. That way, when it must display that page as a search result, it has all the information in the index to do so.

Search Relationships

Search engines compete with each other, but they also collaborate. Many search engines use technology from their competitors to present results. Understanding how each engine delivers its results helps you target the most effective search marketing efforts.

Search engines are deceptively simple in appearance. Visitors to search engines enter the words they are looking for and the search engine shows the results. But this outward simplicity masks a complex set of business relationships.

Ask.com uses Google's paid placement. Yahoo! used to use Google's organic search, but it bought a few organic search companies and does not use Google anymore. Figure 2-11 provides a glimpse of how complex it all can be—and it changes constantly. (By the time you read this book, it will certainly have changed again.)

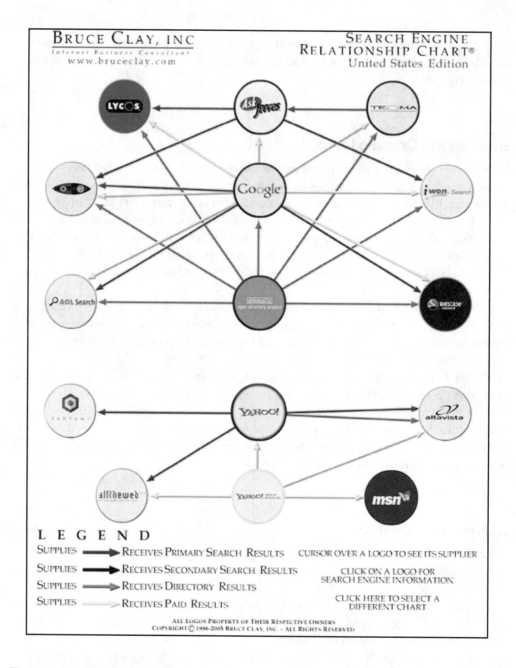

Figure 2-11   Search engine relationships. Many search engines utilize technology owned by their competitors.

Source: Bruce Clay Associates (October 2005)

Why is this important to you? Because what you do as a search marketer sometimes has broader ramifications than you might think—the paid placement you buy from one search engine might show up in others, for example.

Do not be concerned if you do not understand everything on the chart—honestly, you might *never* need to. What you *should* understand is that search engines are more complicated than they look, and you need to learn a little about how the important ones work so that your company can take advantage. In the next chapter, we break down organic search and paid placement (as well as other search marketing techniques) and sort out how these relationships affect you, the search marketer.

Summary

You need to know a lot more to be a successful search marketer, but you already know more than most people. You know what happens when a searcher enters a query into a search engine. You learned how engines match queries to the right pages in the search index. And you understand how pages get into those indexes in the first place.

So now you know how search engines work. Most of the rest of this book focuses on what to do when search engines do *not* work—when they do not show searchers the pages from your Web site. To cope with these problems, however, you needed to understand the basics of what search engines do when they are working. Armed with this base, you are ready to go into more detail.

This chapter focused on how search engines work. Chapter 3 focuses on how search *marketing* works—it introduces the tools in your search marketing toolbox.

How Search Marketing Works

Now that you know how search engines work, it's time to learn how to work *them*. How do you get your site prominently shown? What are your options? What does it all cost? How fast can it start working? In this chapter, we show you what is on the search menu and help you decide what to order. This chapter covers the following topics:

- *Organic search*. Search engines find the most relevant match for the searcher's query. You, the search marketer, optimize your pages, wait for the spiders to come (or pay to send your content), and see your pages in the organic listings. Google and Yahoo! are the best-known organic search engines, but many local and shopping search engines also provide results based on query relevance.

- *Directory listings*. A directory lists the Web sites it deems most closely related to a subject in its subject category list. You submit your site to human editors to be shown under the right subject category. Yahoo! Directory is the oldest and best-known directory, with Open Directory the main challenger.

- *Paid placement*. Search engines show listings from whoever paid them the most money (regardless of how relevant they are). You bid against others to place your listing or advertisement at the top of the results. Yahoo!'s Precision Match and Google AdWords are the two most popular programs. Most search engines shows paid placement listings as "Sponsor Listings."

No matter what your budget is or what kind of site you have, you can create an effective search marketing program using these techniques. Let's dig into organic search first.

Organic Search

Organic search refers to the way search engines find the most relevant match to a searcher's query. Organic search results are driven purely by the relevance of the matches to the query words that the searcher entered, and are *not* influenced by any payments made to the search engine by search marketers. Google and Yahoo! provide organic search results, but so do many other search engines that you might not think of, including shopping search engines (such as Shopping.com) and specialty engines (such as Orbitz, the travel site, at www.orbitz.com).

Search marketers use many techniques to improve their site's organic search results—these techniques are frequently referred to as **search engine optimization** (SEO). For some organizations, organic search is by far the least expensive of all search marketing techniques, but for others it can be frightfully expensive, demanding costly technology or content changes. Let's look at the basic steps for organic search:

1. *Get your pages in the search index.* Pages missing from the index cannot be found by searchers, so you need to get as many of your site's pages into the index as possible. To get your pages indexed, most search engines send spiders to your site, but most shopping search engines require that you send them your data in a trusted feed. If spiders are having trouble indexing your pages, you might need to make changes to your site so that they can succeed. No matter what it takes, you must get your content indexed.

2. *Choose the right keywords.* You must figure out what words searchers are typing in. Later in this book, we show you how you do that, but for now, you just need to understand that different searchers use different queries to try to find the same thing, and that they use different approaches in a shopping search engine than in Google. To discover the keywords that you should target, you can do the work yourself, hire a consultant to help you do it, or have the consultant do it for you.

3. *Optimize your content.* After you have deduced what people are looking for, you can tune your content to match. Again, we get into the details of how you do that later. Just remember that you have to update your content to match what searchers are looking for. To optimize your content, you can do it yourself, or you can hire a consultant to help you do it.

Sometimes these steps can be simple, but often there are so many approaches to improve organic search that decision-making can be difficult. Later in this book, we explore these approaches in depth so you can decide which ones are right for you. For now, let's just look at how different options have different price tags.

What It Costs

Organic search is an interesting search marketing technique, because utilizing the technique can cost nothing, or it can be expensive, depending on the situation you are in and what you decide to do about it.

It is possible that your site might already be well represented in search indexes and might already rank well in organic search for many queries. If so, it might be inexpensive to improve your results even more, by choosing more keywords to sprinkle into your content, for example. If your site has few pages indexed and is missing in action in the search results, however, optimizing your content for organic search can be a daunting prospect—it can be complicated and expensive to make the changes required.

With organic search, you do not need to optimize every page on your site (although that is great to do)—you need only optimize the pages that you want returned for the keywords you are targeting. One reason you might shy away from optimizing every page is that it can be expensive to do. Figure 3-1 shows you the range of prices you should expect to pay to optimize your pages.

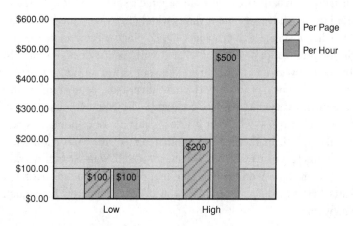

Figure 3-1 Organic search costs. Use these averages to estimate your costs to optimize some of your pages.

Source: Marketing Sherpa (October 2003)

The biggest costs for organic search come from hiring search marketing consultants, changing the content and technology of your site, and paying for inclusion of your pages in the search index.

Search Marketing Consultants

If you need expert advice on choosing keywords, optimizing your content, or getting your pages indexed, it does not come cheap. If you want to start small, you might find some search marketing firms that will help you optimize a few pages for important keywords for between $5,000 and $20,000. Conversely, if you need a consultant to thoroughly address problems in a large site, expect to pay hundreds of thousands per year.

If your budget allows it, however, you can benefit greatly from hiring an expert to jump-start your organic search marketing program. Your site's problems in search are lowering your revenue, and every day they are not fixed is more money down the drain. It can be cost-effective to accelerate your efforts by using an expert who gets more visitors coming to your site quickly.

Under normal circumstances, however, it is not absolutely necessary to use consultants. You and your team can learn enough to do it yourself. Just keep in mind that it will take you considerably longer to move up the learning curve on your own, which may not be cost-effective based on your available budget and the business opportunities that you are losing each day. It is a big decision to hire (or decide not to hire) a search marketing consultant. Chapter 8, "Define Your Search Marketing Strategy," walks you through the process.

Content and Technology Changes

What you spend for your organization's own resources to make content and technology changes to your site is usually your largest expense for organic search marketing. Figure 3-1 provides a rule of thumb for how much it costs, but it varies widely from Web site to Web site. Part 3 of this book is devoted to diagnosing search problems and helping you correct them.

Although you are unsure of exactly what it will cost, it does not have to be scary. You probably do not know how much it costs to update your site to introduce a new line of products, or to acquire another company, or to support a new advertising campaign, but these are business decisions that are made every day in every company. The Web team knows that it is part of its job to support these initiatives—whatever it takes is just a cost of doing business. Your biggest job will be to make search marketing just another part of the Web team's job—just another everyday cost of running your Web site. Chapter 9, "Sell Your Search Marketing Proposal," tackles how you convince the Web team to take that on. After you are successful, and the Web team makes search-related changes every day, you *still* will not know how much it costs, but at least it will be happening.

Organic search success usually requires fine-tuning to allow spiders to crawl your pages and to ensure your pages are found by the right search queries. If your site has a small number of HTML pages, updating the content is not pricey. If you have a huge dynamically generated site, however, it can be expensive to fix the technology so that spiders can see those dynamic pages. In addition to changes required by spiders, shopping search engines (and some others) depend on your data being sent to them, which forces you to write or buy a program that does that. On top of that, you always need to update your content to provide proper keyword prominence and density to get high rankings. All these content and technology changes cost money.

Content changes are typically less costly and easier to manage than technology changes. It is expected that content will be constantly updated, so if you can convince your Web team to write with search engines in mind, they will do that as a matter of course. It is not any more expensive to write a new page that includes mentions of the important search keywords for that page. Technology changes, however, are not so easy.

Many Web sites inadvertently make it difficult for spiders to index their pages. In Chapter 10, "Get Your Site Indexed," we work through the most common site design problems and the technology changes required to correct them. Usually, they require some kind of technology change, for example:

- We must change the commerce URLs so that they do not have so many dynamic parameters.

- We have to update the content management system so that writers can modify the titles and descriptions for every page.

- We have to modify the metadata template for all HTML pages so that we do not block the spider from crawling each page.

- We need to change the menus in the left navigation bar so that they do not require JavaScript.

- We must remove session identifiers from the URLs.

Don't worry if you don't understand the list. That's the point, actually. Every item in that list is something that your technology folks might need to do to fix your site so that spiders can crawl your pages. (And we cover many more, too.)

It is possible that your site suffers from few or even none of these technology problems. If so, organic search optimization will likely be inexpensive. If your site suffers from some of these problems, however, it can be expensive to get them fixed. Technology projects can be costly, hard to manage, and slow to complete. It is not unheard of for a large company to spend millions of dollars over several years to eradicate all of these organic search problems.

Inclusion Programs

Paid inclusion is the one organic search technique where you pay search engines. In contrast with paid placement, where you bid on keywords to be listed in the paid results, paid inclusion gets your pages into the index to be shown in the *organic* results. With paid inclusion, you pay a fee to the search engine for each page that you want included in its search index.

But why pay to be included in the index when spiders come to your site for free? As you will learn later in this book, organic search spiders cannot index all pages. Your site might have problems that prevent the spider from indexing your pages—paid inclusion can help you. Or you might need the spider to revisit your site more frequently because your content constantly changes—that is another good reason to pay for inclusion.

Although paid inclusion guarantees your page is listed in the index, it does not make it any more likely to be displayed #1 for any searches. The organic search engine works the same as always, but with paid inclusion, you have ensured your page is *in* the index, in case it is the right page for a query.

Yahoo! offers paid inclusion, but none of the other worldwide engines do, so it will not solve all of your spider problems. Google alone offers a free inclusion program, called Google Sitemaps. Shopping search engines usually require you to send your product database to them— that is a particular kind of paid inclusion called a **trusted feed**. We cover inclusion programs in detail in Chapter 10. For now, just realize that you may need to pay for inclusion or to use free inclusion programs to improve your organic search results.

The Benefits and Challenges

Despite the wide disparity in what an organic search marketing effort can cost, no search marketer can skip organic search. Organic search is critical to any search marketing program, even if you also use other search marketing techniques. But organic search offers a unique set of benefits and challenges.

Highly Qualified Visitors Will Come to Your Site

Organic searchers who click your pages are **highly qualified** visitors to your site. They are much more likely to make a purchase than some other kinds of visitors you receive.

To understand why, think about the motivation of visitors reaching your site from a successful banner ad. Those visitors set out to find some information (possibly on a subject wholly unrelated to your site), and while reading that article, spot your ad. Intrigued, they click through to your site. These visitors are far less qualified than searchers because they did not start out with interest in your products. You can build the interest and still make the sale, but that is a lot harder to do than to sell to someone already interested.

In contrast, searchers initiate their search on a subject related to your organization's site. That's why the search engine shows *your* page in the results. Those searchers want to learn about what your site can tell them. You are far more likely to sell to search visitors than to someone who clicks a banner ad, simply because searchers might intend to buy whereas banner visitors were doing something else when you caught their eye. People using shopping search engines, as you might expect, are *especially* likely to buy.

Visitors clicking directory listings to your site fall somewhere in between banner ad visitors and searchers as to how qualified they are. Some might be as motivated as searchers, but others are just surfing around when your listing gets their attention.

Searchers who click paid placements are qualified, too, but searchers trust organic results more, and are more likely to act on them. As discussed in Chapter 4, "How Searchers Work," many searchers focus on organic results to the exclusion of the paid listings on the page. Your site must appear in organic results to attract those searchers. But this benefit of appearing in the organic results leads to a challenge, because it is not easy to get your page ranked #1 in organic results.

With paid placement, for example, anyone with a big enough budget can buy the #1 paid result, and they will get visitors to click through to their site. Organic search, in contrast, can require a lot of effort in modifying content and technology on your site, and no one can guarantee when (or if) it will pay off in higher-qualified visitors. That's the basic organic search challenge.

You *Can* Do It on a Budget

Although scary problems exist that can make organic search a challenge for some Web sites, there are ways to succeed at organic search inexpensively. Your site probably has many pages in the search index already, and you can tune the content for these pages to rank higher and draw more traffic.

Moreover, the work that you do on organic search lasts. Paid placement success stops the minute you stop paying the search engines. After you optimize an organic page, however, you can continue to get high rankings with little work for a long time.

Despite organic search's low cost in some situations, we cannot emphasize enough that some situations can make organic search an expensive proposition. Chapter 7, "Measure Your Search Marketing Success," shows you how to assess the situation in which you find yourself.

What You Do Works Across Search Engines

Unlike paid placement, where an ad listed with Yahoo! does not appear in Google, most organic search techniques work across all search engines. Whatever you do to allow Google's spider to crawl your site will probably also help the Ask.com spider. Similarly, improving your keyword prominence and density helps your pages rank higher in all search engines. Just by its nature, organic search tends to require the same techniques for all search engines.

Beyond this natural tendency, currently only four organic search technologies are used by the major worldwide search engines, as shown in Table 3-1. That is a big change from a few years ago, when there were a dozen technologies around. With a dozen technologies, it was rarely worth pursuing any organic search technique that worked for only one technology. Now, with only four technologies in the game, it can be worthwhile to do things that affect only one technology, because numerous search engines use each technology. One example is paid inclusion— only Yahoo! offers it, but it affects all of the search engines syndicating the Yahoo! organic search technology, so it makes sense to consider.

Table 3-1 Organic Search Technology. Ask.com, Google, MSN, and Yahoo! are the suppliers of organic search technology to all major organic search engines.

Search Technology	Inclusion Program	Syndication
Ask.com	No	Ask.com
		Excite
		Iwon
		Teoma
Google	Free	AOL Search
		Google
MSN Search	No	MSN.com
		MSN Search
Yahoo! Search	Paid	Yahoo!
		AlltheWeb
		AltaVista

How to Get Started

Organic search is probably the easiest search marketing technique to get started with, because you are *already* started. It is highly likely that spiders already crawl your site, placing your pages in their indexes. If you search for your company's name, your home page might already be shown high in the list.

So what does it really mean to get started with organic search? It goes back to the basic steps laid out earlier:

1. *Get your pages in the search index.* Nothing else you do will matter if your pages are not in the search index. Chapter 10, "Get Your Site Indexed," teaches you how to get them there.

2. *Choose the right keywords.* To get serious about organic search, you need to focus on the queries searchers use that should find your site. There are many ways to do that, all detailed in Chapter 11, "Choose Your Target Keywords."

3. *Optimize your content.* To rank well for popular queries, you need to ensure that your pages contain the words in the queries, and have them in the right numbers, sprinkled in the right places. Chapter 12, "Optimize Your Content," shows you how.

Organic search is critical to any search marketing plan. Because it requires a great deal of expertise to succeed, most of the rest of this book shows you how. However, there are also other techniques for you to learn, starting with directory listings.

Directory Listings

Directory listings were the first of the paid vehicles within search and are commonly done at a site known as a **directory**—a site typically maintained by human editors who list Web sites by their subject. Figure 3-2 shows that someone looking for information can sometimes find things more easily by navigating directories than by searching. Searchers looking for "hospital white-board" might find nothing useful, but by following directory links find exactly what they are looking for.

Directory listings typically guarantee you a blurb about your Web site (or a part of your Web site), with no promise of where you will show up in the list (top? bottom? middle of the pack?) or how many people will click your link. The directory's editors decide what subject category to use for your site, although you can request a specific category. Most organizations get just one link from a single category to their site's home page, but medium-to-large companies that have Web pages on multiple subjects can get multiple directory listings.

Yahoo! was the original directory, and is still the most important. Although Yahoo! has expanded as a company into many other pursuits, ranging from organic search to e-mail to shopping, the Yahoo! Directory was how it all started. None of the other paid directories, such as LookSmart, are critical for search marketers to target nowadays because they have plummeted in popularity.

Searching for "hospital whiteboards" yields poor results . . .

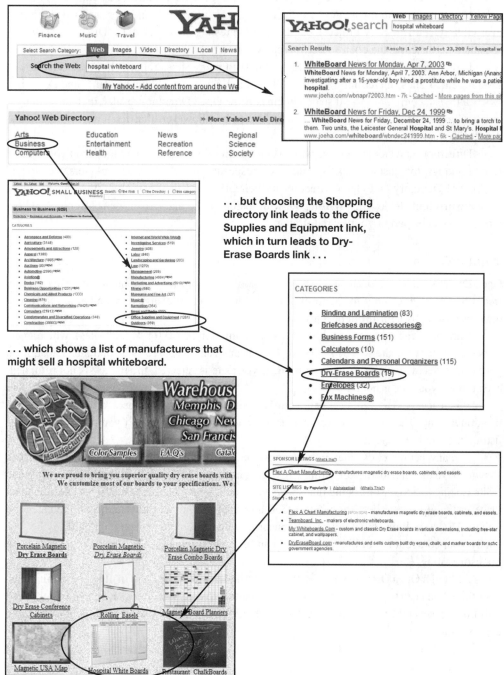

. . . but choosing the Shopping directory link leads to the Office Supplies and Equipment link, which in turn leads to Dry-Erase Boards link . . .

. . . which shows a list of manufacturers that might sell a hospital whiteboard.

Figure 3-2 Using directory listings. Sometimes people can find what they want using a directory when searching for the same thing would end in failure.

One free entrant, Open Directory (www.dmoz.org), uses volunteers as editors and is the only competitor to Yahoo! Directory worth spending any time on. Open Directory is also referred to as ODP (Open Directory Project), but its most interesting alias is DMOZ (Directory Mozilla), so named because it is the open source directory counterpart to the open source Mozilla browser.

Directories frequently syndicate their results to many sites. Yahoo! shows its directory at several search sites, including Yahoo! itself, AlltheWeb (www.alltheweb.com). and AltaVista (www.altavista.com). Almost all search engines show Open Directory results, including Google (as its Google Directory) and AOL Search. Remember, however, that far fewer searchers use directories than use search queries.

Directories are an inexpensive way to get attention for your site, and they help your search result rankings, too, just as links from any well-respected sites do. Search marketers need to target Yahoo! Directory and Open Directory in their plans—in fact, getting a directory listing is often the first thing to do when starting out with search marketing. Let's take a closer look at how directories can be part of your search strategy.

What It Costs

Open Directory is free. For the longest time, Yahoo! Directory was, too, but today Yahoo! offers free directory listings only for nonprofit organizations. Yahoo! charges an annual fee for every directory listing by a for-profit business.

Currently, Yahoo! charges $299 for a site submission ($600 for "adult" sites), which guarantees only that your site will be *reviewed*. That means Yahoo! charges you, and then it examines your site to decide whether it will be listed. If your site is rejected, the money is not refunded, even though your site is not listed.

When accepted as a Site Listing, your Web site is ranked in alphabetic order by your organization's name. The $299 fee covers the review and a one-year listing. If you fail to renew your listing in 12 months, it is deleted.

If many people click your link, it might be added to a special Most Popular list that is shown above the alphabetic site listings. If your site is not popular, you might be able to upgrade a Site Listing to a Sponsor Listing that shows your site *above* the alphabetic list (in addition to its place in the alphabetic list) for between $50 and $300 per month, depending on the category. Yahoo! Directory limits the number of Sponsor Listings it accepts, so you might already be shut out by your competitors. In Figure 3-3, you can see an example of a company that upgraded to a Sponsor Listing.

Although Open Directory is free, you might find that you pay for it in other ways—namely, your time. You need to be patient waiting for the editors to consider your site, and you might need to follow up several times to finally get their attention. For some, saving $300 is not worth the aggravation.

YAHOO! SMALL BUSINESS
directory

B2B > Tablet Computers and Webpads
Directory > Business and Economy > Business to Business > Computers > Har

Search [   ]   ⦿ the Web ◯ just this category

INSIDE YAHOO!

Finance: Business News and Quotes on Yahoo! Finance
Small Business: Business Resources on Yahoo! Small **Business**

SPONSOR LISTINGS (What's this?)

Motion Computing - offers a tablet PC and accessories.

SITE LISTINGS

- Airspeak - makers of the Flair.
- Agcess Technologies - makers of Qbe, a personal computing t
- Electrovaya - offers tablet PCs and powerpads featuring a high SuperPolymer technology.

Figure 3-3 High-visibility directory listings. You can upgrade to a Sponsor Listing in Yahoo! Directory to be displayed at the top of the heap.

Reproduced with permission of Yahoo! Inc. © 2005 by Yahoo! Inc. YAHOO! and the YAHOO! logo are trademarks of Yahoo! Inc.

The Benefits and Challenges

It is wise for a search marketer to pursue directory listings, both paid (Yahoo! Directory) and free (Open Directory) for several reasons, including the following:

- *Increased traffic.* Although Web users have gravitated more to full-text search the past few years, a sizable amount of traffic still pours in from directory listings. Web users still use directories in large numbers, and your site benefits from those extra visitors.

- *Improved search rankings.* As discussed in Chapter 2, "How Search Engines Work," one of the ways search engines decide which pages to show first is by analyzing links to each matching page. Links to your site from a reputable directory are influential because your site passed a human editor's quality test. Search engines weigh links from Yahoo! Directory and Open Directory heavily when ranking search results—we cover this topic in depth in Chapter 13, "Attract Links to Your Site." It is possible that Sponsor Listings and Most Popular links, because they add extra links to your page, might help search rankings above what the alphabetic Site Listing link brings.

- *Simplicity.* Unlike many search marketing techniques, directory listings are simple. You can submit exactly the wording that you want to appear in your blurb—you have no pesky content or technology changes to make to your site—and no technical expertise is required.

- *Low cost.* For most businesses, $300 is a small price to pay for the benefits that paid listings provide, and an Open Directory entry is free. Almost any other search marketing technique costs more, so this is often the best way to start your search marketing.

Although it is always a good idea for your Web site to get listed in directories, beware of a few pitfalls:

- *Lack of responsiveness.* Yahoo! Directory responds to paid submissions within seven days, but makes no promises for free (nonprofit) submissions. Likewise, Open Directory has no committed turnaround time for your submissions. To make matters worse, some companies have complained that when they have been listed under the wrong category, it took weeks to get Yahoo! to correct the error, and Open Directory is even slower.

- *Editorial changes.* Although you can submit under any subject category, and you can send in any words that you want used, sometimes directory editors wield their red pens. What shows up in the listing is what the editor put there, even though it might not be what you wanted (or might not even be accurate).

- *Limited exposure.* Whereas organic search can bring up any page on your site, directories link just to the home page of most businesses. Larger Web sites might be granted a dozen entries under different subject categories, and large, popular Web sites might have a hundred links, but that is about the limit. You cannot easily point someone deep within your site the way organic search can. Moreover, fewer visitors will come to your site from directories than from search engines.

Despite the challenges, paid directory listings are among the best investments you can make, and the steps to get them are simple.

CASE STUDY: GETTING MULTIPLE DIRECTORY LISTINGS

If one directory listing for your company is good, wouldn't 20 be better? Yes, but the directories do not usually hand out so many. They are directories of *Web sites*, and typically list only the home page of a site under its appropriate category.

WebMD, the popular health information site (www.webmd.com), believed it had a case for multiple directory entries because it has more than 100 disease and illness condition centers, each with hundreds of pages of information.

WebMD submitted 25 of its condition-center URLs to Yahoo! Directory (paying the fees) and were granted a directory listing for each one. But the Open Directory editors were tougher. Open Directory rarely provides a Web site with multiple listings. WebMD spent six months working with the editors in various categories in Open Directory, arguing that each condition center was equal in quality to the Web sites that were already listed in the categories.

Persistence paid off. Today, WebMD has about 50 Open Directory listings.

How to Get Started

There are three steps to get listed in a directory:

1. *You submit your site.* To submit to Open Directory or Yahoo! Directory, you navigate to the subject category that best describes your site, and then click the Suggest URL link (Open Directory) or Suggest a Site link (Yahoo! Directory), as shown in Figure 3-4.

2. *Editors review your site.* When the editors review your submission, they examine all of the information in your submission form and visit your live site.

3. *Editors list your site.* If your site checks out, it will be listed. The editors choose exactly which subject category your site is listed under, and they edit the words in your blurb.

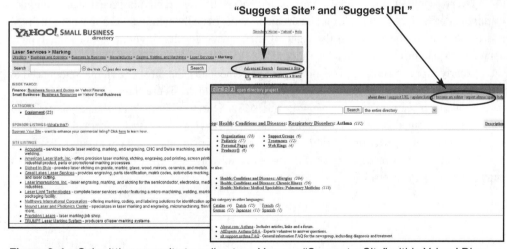

Figure 3-4 Submitting your site to a directory. You can "Suggest a Site" within Yahoo! Directory and "Suggest URL" within Open Directory to submit yours.

Reproduced with permission of Yahoo! Inc. © 2005 by Yahoo! Inc. YAHOO! and the YAHOO! logo are trademarks of Yahoo! Inc. Reproduced courtesy of the Open Directory Project. Please visit dmoz.org for more information.

Typically sites are accepted, but if your site does not clearly identify your company, or if it cannot be viewed by all Web browsers, or your site is under construction, or it is not available all the time, your site might be rejected for a listing. Yahoo! reserves the right to reject sites for other reasons, too, but it rarely does.

Whereas Yahoo! Directory promises turnaround to paid submissions within a week, Open Directory uses volunteer editors who review thousands of submissions each month. It usually takes months for an Open Directory submission to be accepted as a listing, but do not resubmit if you get impatient—that just moves you to the end of the line.

Paid Placement

By now, you have gotten a taste for the difficulty of revamping your site to garner organic search traffic. Although it pays off handsomely, organic search success takes skill, effort, and time. Paid search seems far easier. Select a keyword, plunk down your credit card, and overnight you have the #1 search position! It *can* work that way—*if* you know what you are doing. Let's explore paid placement, the fast (and sometimes easier) method of paying your way to the top.

Paid placement is where the action is, generating nearly $3 billion of ad revenue for search engines just in the United States. Google makes 95 percent of its revenue from paid advertising.

Paid placement has been described as a cross between day trading and direct marketing. Most paid placement requires bidding against other search marketers to win the top spot for your site. Bidding can be intense, changing every second as companies jockey for position. Every word in your listing matters—making the difference between an ad that gets clicked and one that does not.

Every search engine displays paid placement results differently, but most search engines distinguish paid placement ads from the organic results (usually calling them sponsored listings) and display them above and to the right of the organic results. Figure 3-5 shows a typical approach to paid placement taken by Yahoo! for a search for "ski equipment."

Nearly every search engine displays paid placement ads, but most search marketers need to place ads with just three of them—MSN, Yahoo!, and Google. These three companies carry 97 percent of paid placement ads. (As we write this, MSN Search still uses Yahoo! paid placement in some countries, but it has announced plans to move to its own Microsoft adCenter paid placement engine in all countries over time.) Table 3-2 shows a list of paid placement competitors. Each one has different fees and restrictions on the content it accepts, and each one has different search engines that display its results.

Paid ads from Yahoo!

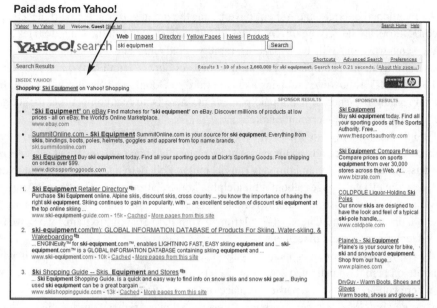

Figure 3-5   Paid placement results. Yahoo! Search presents paid placement results at the top and right of its results page.

Reproduced with permission of Yahoo! Inc. © 2005 by Yahoo! Inc. YAHOO! and the YAHOO! logo are trademarks of Yahoo! Inc.

Table 3-2   Paid Placement Programs. Google and Yahoo! are the leaders, but there are also other choices for paid placement.

Search Engine	Program	URL	Activation Fee	Content Restrictions	Syndication
Google	AdWords	adwords.google.com	$5	Adult and gambling	Google AOL Ask.com Netscape
Yahoo!	Precision Match	www.overture.com	$50	Adult and gambling	Yahoo! Alta Vista
MSN	Microsoft adCenter	advertising.msn.com	$5	Objectionable and illegal terms	MSN Search Windows Live Search
MIVA	MIVA Pay-Per-Click	www.miva.com	$50	Objectionable and illegal terms	WebCrawler Dogpile InfoSpace Lycos
Kanoodle	Keyword Target	www.kanoodle.com	$50	Objectionable and illegal terms	WebCrawler CNET Search

As mentioned, Google and Yahoo! have by far the greatest traffic for paid placement, but other competitors are not giving up. MSN has introduced adCenter in the United States and several other countries and will be expanding rapidly. FindWhat and Espotting merged to form MIVA (www.miva.com), combining Espotting's focus in Europe with FindWhat's strength in the United States. MIVA, however, remains a distant third to Google and Yahoo! in Europe. Except for the impending presence of MSN paid placement, there is no real competition to Google and Yahoo! in the Asian paid placement market.

Google and Yahoo! also offer a variant of paid placement known as **contextual advertising**, where you bid to place ads on the pages of Web sites that have articles about subjects related to your ads. For example, if your company runs a hotel in Philadelphia, you might want to display an ad on a travel site's pages about Philadelphia tourist attractions. Contextual advertising, although appropriate for some search marketers, is not the first place for you to start, so we reserve that discussion until Chapter 14, "Optimize Your Paid Search Program," when we review advanced techniques in paid placement.

By far, the most money is spent on paid placement based on bidding, which is what we concentrate on here. Sophisticated search marketers also use a technique known as **fixed placement**, where you negotiate for a particular place on a page for a given search query, usually paying for impressions (the number of times your ad is shown), rather than for clicks. Specialty search engines are more likely to offer fixed placement than worldwide search engines. Fixed placement is *not* the way a rookie search marketer should break in—you need to know what you are doing before you negotiate a long-term, hard-to-change commitment. As you grow in your search marketing experience, however, you might find that some fixed-placement opportunities make sense as part of your overall search marketing plan.

What It Costs

One of the best things about paid placement is that you can control the costs. You can buy as many or as few keywords as you want, and you decide how much you are willing to pay for each click. And you can adjust anything at a moment's notice, so you can control your budget.

As you embark on a paid placement program, here are the kinds of costs to keep your eye on:

- *Creative costs*. Whether you do it in-house or you hire a consultant or ad agency to do it for you, it costs money to create the titles and descriptions that display onscreen. Remember, the number of searchers who click through to your site depends completely on the killer title and description you write, so this is no place to skimp on the budget. Agencies can usually do three or four new ads an hour, charging anywhere from $50 to $200 an hour to do so.

- *Management costs*. Tracking and adjusting your bids can be a lot of work, but it is the key to maximizing the return on your paid placement investment—these campaigns do not run well on autopilot. You also need to keep track of your creative changes and deadlines, reconcile your bills, and verify your clickthroughs. You can hire an ad agency or search consultant to manage your paid placement campaign for you. Conversely, if you manage it in-house, budget at least one full-time person to manage a large campaign consisting of more than a thousand keywords. In addition, you should invest in bid management software or services to automate a lot of manual work.

- *Per-impression fee*. Usually referred to as CPM (cost per thousand—M is the Roman numeral for 1,000), you pay each time your ad displays onscreen, whether a searcher clicks or not. Typically, CPM pricing is used only for fixed-placement advertising, not bid-based advertising, and it varies from $10 to $30 per thousand impressions (or about 1¢ to 3¢ per single impression).

- *Per-click fee*. Often called CPC (cost per click), it just means that each time a searcher clicks your advertisement, the search engine charges you a fee. Typically, you open an account for a set amount and start bidding for placement. Whenever a searcher clicks your ad, the current bid (per-click) fee is deducted from your account, with your ad disappearing if your account reaches zero. CPC prices range from about 10¢ (usually the lowest bid allowed) to $30 or sometimes more, with the average around $1.

- *Per-action fee*. Also known as CPA (cost per action), you pay only when the searcher takes "action"—typically a purchase of your product. In practice, CPA pricing is used mainly for fixed placement or shopping searches, not bid-based advertising, and runs anywhere from $5 to $50. Some paid placement engines, however, are beginning to experiment with CPA pricing, so you may someday have a choice between CPC and CPA pricing for your keywords. In addition, a new kind of action, a phone call, is also becoming a popular pricing model—it's called pay-per-call pricing.

CPM, CPC, and CPA fees are usually mutually exclusive—you pay only one of them on any particular deal. Table 3-3 shows what a paid search campaign might cost when priced according to each method. Some advertisers prefer one method over another, but there is no surefire way to pay less on a consistent basis—it all depends on how many searches, clickthroughs, and purchases there are.

Table 3-3 Comparing Pricing Formulas (What you pay depends on the activity multiplied by the rate, but no magical method will always save money.)

Method	Searches	Clicks	Actions	Rate	Total Cost
CPM	1,000,000			1¢ per impression	$10,000
CPC		50,000		20¢ per click	$10,000
CPA			1,000	$10 per action	$10,000

Every pricing method has advantages and disadvantages. Chapter 14 reviews paid search strategies in more detail, and provides examples to help you choose the best option for your objectives.

MANAGING YOUR BIDS WITHOUT GOING CRAZY

As easy as it can seem to get started with paid placement, you will find that it takes some work to manage the bids in multiple search engines for hundreds (sometimes thousands) of keywords. If you do not carefully monitor your campaign, you will find that you are being outbid (and losing traffic) or that you are paying more than you need to. Unfortunately, monitoring your bids can be labor-intensive, especially in hyperactive markets where others are constantly monitoring and adjusting *their* bids.

In a high bidder auction, if you are willing to pay 45¢ per click, but you see that the high bidder is paying just 20¢ each, you can bid 21¢ and snag the top spot. Now you have the top spot, *and* you are paying well under your budgeted maximum. It is critically important that you continue to monitor, however, because your competitor (or someone else) could bid 22¢ and you will lose the top spot. If you are monitoring, you can keep raising your bid to stay #1 until you hit your limit of 45¢.

You might be able to remain at #1 without monitoring for quite a while if you just bid 45¢ right off the bat. But if the next bid is 20¢, you are wasting 24¢ on each click, because you would get the same #1 position for 21¢. That 24¢ is known as a **bid gap**. You want to eliminate bid gaps as soon as they appear.

Even paid placement engines that use hybrid auctions (clickthrough rate and bid), such as Google, require monitoring. While there are no bid gaps to close, you'll still find competitors raising their bids or increasing their clickthrough rates (by improving their ad copy, perhaps). When they do, their ads may pass yours in the ranking, so you might then want to make changes of your own.

You need to spend a lot of time monitoring your bids frequently to make sure that you maintain your position, do not exceed your limit, and eliminate bid gaps as soon as they appear. Or, you could use bid management software.

Every paid placement program provides a way to automate your bidding. You can set "caps" for your bids (45¢ in our example), set intervals for how frequently your position is assessed, choose the rules for how bids are modified—all without having to personally check constantly. If you use only one paid placement program, you can use the free bid management tool that is part of the program. (Figure 3-6 shows Yahoo!'s.) If you use multiple programs, you might be better off paying for a bid management tool that can manage your campaigns across all of your paid placement programs. We examine some of the more popular bid management tools in Chapter 14.

The Benefits and Challenges

Paid placement offers a proven way to attract visitors to your Web site, but put that credit card away for a minute. For all of the benefits of paid placement, you can quickly burn through your budget, getting few sales, if you are not careful. Managed well, paid placement is an indispensable part of a search marketing plan for lots of reasons—if you know what you are doing.

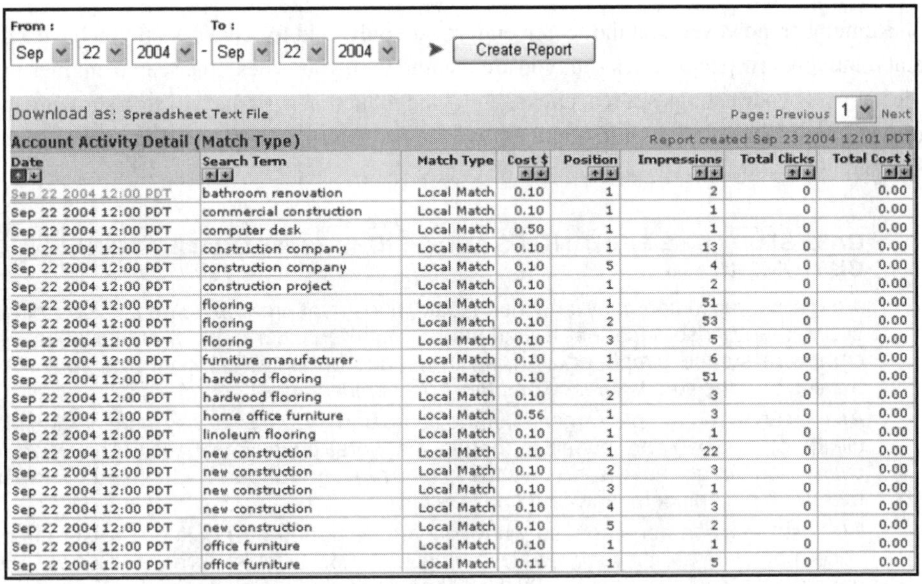

Figure 3-6 Sample bid management tool. Yahoo!'s bid management tool offers many options for managing your paid placement bids

Reproduced with permission of Yahoo! Inc. © 2005 by Yahoo! Inc. YAHOO! and the YAHOO! logo are trademarks of Yahoo! Inc.

Highly Qualified Visitors Will Come to Your Site

Just as with organic search, paid placement attracts visitors who are already interested in what your site does. If they weren't, they would not have been searching in the first place. So it makes sense that searchers who click paid placement listings are more likely to buy than visitors arriving at your site from clicking a banner ad or directory listing, for example. But paid placement listings get lower clickthrough than organic search, and searchers say that they trust them less, so organic search might still have the edge in converting searchers into buyers.

Paid placement provides near-total control over what your listing says, allowing you to further qualify searchers so that only the "right" ones click through. In organic search, although you can pick your page's title, the snippet that appears below the title is chosen by the search engine from the words that appear on your page. Paid placement allows you to choose the exact words that appear—you can tune them again and again until you maximize clickthrough and sales.

Remember, however, that the search engines are only paid for clicks, so if you have a great ad that relatively few people click (but you are pleased with your sales), the search engines might not be happy. If your listings get few clicks, high bidder auction systems will stop showing them, whereas Google (and other hybrid auctions) will lower your rankings. At that point, you must make changes to your ad to try to increase the clicks.

> **CASE STUDY: THE RIGHT TITLES AND DESCRIPTIONS QUALIFY YOUR CUSTOMERS**
>
> A large insurance company launched a paid placement program to boost sales for discounted auto insurance that it marketed through a senior citizens organization. The campaign started simply enough, as they bought the typical keywords you would expect, such as *auto insurance* and *low-cost car insurance*.
>
> As they analyzed the performance of the campaign, they found they were getting high clickthrough (yea!) and low sales (boo!)—the worst possible situation. They paid for every click but got next-to-no revenue in return. They wondered whether their experiment with paid placement would end in failure.
>
> But just then, someone noticed what everyone else had overlooked. The auto insurance they were selling required customers to be 55 or older to apply. Quickly, they changed their ad copy to say, "Over 55? Looking for auto insurance? Apply now!"
>
> The turnaround was immediate. The clickthrough rate dropped dramatically, but that was okay because nearly all of those clicking now were older than 55 and thus eligible to apply. And apply they did. Now that the right people were clicking, they were far more likely to apply.
>
> The campaign that was almost cancelled went on to score a huge success, all because the changed ad copy drew clicks from only the most qualified customers.

You See Immediate Results

The biggest difference between paid placement advertising and organic search is that paid placements offer near instantaneous traffic to your site. You can launch a campaign immediately by paying your money, writing your ads, and bidding your way to the top of the paid results—all without changing a line of code on your Web site. And you can constantly fine-tune your ad copy and keyword purchases to further improve your clickthrough rate and sales. Organic search, in contrast, takes much longer to kick in, and much longer to fine-tune, because spiders take a while to revisit your site each time you make a change.

It Is Inexpensive to Get Started

Getting started in paid placement usually costs less than most other forms of search marketing. You do not have to make expensive changes to your site nor do you have to negotiate long-term deals with search engines. For as little as $50 and a credit card, you can open a paid placement account.

But you need to get near the top of paid placement listings for popular queries to get heavy traffic. Only the top few ads are syndicated to the other partners—so top paid results in Google are shown in Ask.com, too, but lower-ranking ads are not. Typically, the top four ads are shown on the first results page, followed by the next set of four on each subsequent page until all the ads have been displayed. So every searcher sees the top ads, but only the few searchers that page forward see the others.

And, as you will see in Chapter 11, popular queries have a lot of competition. Although some keywords generate high traffic with low per-click fees, most high-traffic keywords require high-priced bids. You can easily burn through your budget if you are not careful. Blindly raising your bids to stay #1 can end up costing you more than the traffic is worth.

KEYWORD BATTLES: HOW TO BLOW YOUR BUDGET IN ONE EASY LESSON

Because paid placement has increased in popularity among search marketers, it is rare to find a popular keyword phrase without any bidders. It is also increasingly likely that bidders are using bid management software to control constant changes to their bids to maintain their place as #1, for example.

When two or more sites decide to be #1 for a particular keyword, a **keyword battle** ensues. Each time one site raises its bid, another increases *its* bid to leapfrog the original site. Unless one side eventually reaches their bid limit, the bidding can escalate dramatically. That's good for the search engines, but not for search marketers.

Sometimes these battles are fought intentionally, with each side consciously raising its bids, but all too often the battle is a mistake. The typical keyword battle arises between two sites with bid management software instructed to always be #1 for that keyword. As you might expect, neither site's software can succeed at being #1 for long—just the length of time in between bids. In this situation, the dueling software keeps bidding higher until one side exhausts its budget, usually within a couple of days.

It does not have to be that way. When you set up your bid management software, you can still request that it be #1, but also set a limit of the highest bid you are willing to pay. That way, your bid management system stops escalating its bid when it reaches the limit you set, defusing the battle, and saving your budget for opportunities with higher return on your investment.

You Pay Only for Visits to Your Site

Many advertisers prefer paid placement's fee structure—you pay only when searchers click your ad, not when they view your ad. With banner ads and other types of paid advertising, you are charged for impressions—you pay every time your ad is shown.

But you must be on the alert for **click fraud**—someone clicking your link expressly to charge your account, but having no intention to buy. Although search engines have sophisticated tools to detect click fraud, unscrupulous competitors of yours could engage in this unethical activity.

Pay attention to any suspicious click patterns, such as clicks increasing dramatically for just a couple of queries, with no commensurate increase in sales. Monitor discussion boards to see whether competitors are encouraging readers to click your listing without any real interest. If you suspect click fraud on your account, contact the search engine immediately—they will provide free clicks to you to make up for it.

You Can Target Your Audience

Because paid placement offers tight control over the keywords you buy and the exact wording of your listing, you can create highly targeted ads that cannot be duplicated in organic search campaigns. In organic search, the same page might be found for many different queries and might not be optimized for each kind of searcher—with paid placement, each ad can be chosen especially for searchers entering an exact query.

Paid placement also helps you reach large audiences, because ads are syndicated across many different search engines. However, sometimes this can be a problem. You might be happy with the policies of Yahoo! and Google, but you might be embarrassed over what content is on the same page as your listing on one of their syndication partner sites—they might have much looser policies on controversial content. You cannot control which partner sites might show your ads, except to opt out of syndication to *all* partners, which can cut your traffic substantially. (Many image-conscious companies *do* opt out, despite the loss of traffic.)

The newest way to target more granular audiences is through a technique called **local search**—displaying your ad to visitors from a particular city or region. Prior to the advent of local search, businesses with natural geographic boundaries had no way to effectively use paid placement. Small businesses, such as plumbers, would be throwing money away to buy a keyword such as *stopped drain* because anyone in the world could be searching. But medium-to-large businesses suffered, too. A retail chain that dominates several states had no way of using paid search because it was not cost-efficient to pay for searchers throughout the United States.

Local search has changed all that. Slowly growing at about 15 percent a year, local search appeals to the same kinds of advertisers that currently buy printed Yellow Pages ads: doctors, lawyers, retailers, travel agents, contractors, and many others.

The major search engines (Google, Yahoo! Search, and Ask.com) and some traditional Yellow Pages publishers (Verizon and SBC) offer local search. Each local search engine has different capabilities, with most based on Zip codes, cities, or other geographic information in queries. Yahoo! integrates its Yellow Pages and White Pages content into its mapping data to offer local results, and Ask.com partners with CitySearch (www.citysearch.com) for similar function. Some paid placement engines even analyze the location of a searcher's computer on the Internet (its **IP address**) to guess where the searcher is physically located, to provide **geographic targeting** when searchers do not even tell the search engine their physical location.

Yahoo! (local.yahoo.com and yp.yahoo.com) and Verizon's SuperPages (www.superpages.com) are the current leaders in local search, with Verizon drawing 16 million visitors per month and Yahoo! attracting several times that. Verizon claims that more than 80 percent of its searchers contact an advertiser, and half say they are likely to make a purchase. We take a closer look at local search engines in Chapter 14.

How to Get Started

There's nothing tough about getting started in paid placement. Table 3-2 listed the URLs for you to visit to fill out your sign-up form—all you need is a credit card and an Excel file with your target keywords, your listings, and the URLs searchers should go to when they click your ad. Following a review by the search engine (lasting one to five days), your ads are approved and you can start bidding.

Occasionally, a listing is rejected after review. Each search engine sets its own policies, but most shy away from controversial content, which varies based on local laws and customs. (In Germany, for example, it is illegal to advertise any religious Web sites.)

Search engines are becoming more careful about the copy they allow in advertising. Although one of the great things about paid placement is the control you have over the wording of your listing, search engines must ensure that their searchers are not misled by exciting offers leading to less-than-scintillating Web pages. Reviewers are becoming sticklers for your offer matching what is on your Web page, so make sure that your ad is consistent with the URL on your site to which it leads. If you do not, your campaign might be delayed during your wrangling with the paid placement editors.

Summary

You are on your way as a search marketer! You have learned the three basic techniques in search marketing: organic search, directory listings, and paid placement. Each technique proves advantageous under the right circumstances, but each one must be handled with care to avoid the pitfalls. Table 3-4 summarizes the strengths and weaknesses of each technique.

Table 3-4 Search Marketing Techniques Comparison (Organic is hard to do but yields high reward, whereas paid happens quickly but requires higher investment.)

Search Marketing Technique	How Much Expertise Is Required?	How Much Traffic Can It Drive?	How Qualified Are the Visitors?	How Soon Do You See Results?
Organic search	High	High	High	Slow
Directory listings	Low	Low	Low	Moderate
Paid Placement	Moderate	High	High	Fast

Perhaps the best news of all is how complementary these techniques can be. Directory listings improve your organic search rankings. When your site is shown in *both* organic and paid results for a search, searchers click one of your listings more than 90 percent of the time.

Why do searchers behave this way? That is what is examined in the next chapter. Understanding why searchers do what they do is critical for you as a search marketer. If you do not understand searchers, you cannot predict which keywords they will use or what content will strike their fancy. Let's examine the research into searcher behavior in Chapter 4.

How Searchers Work

Management Would Be Easy . . . If It Weren't for the People is the whimsical title of Patricia J. Addesso's excellent book (American Management Association, 1996). Similarly, search marketing would be a lot easier if we did not have to worry about those pesky searchers.

You know the best search query to use to find your hit product, but searchers might not. Searchers might not know your product's name, or might not be able to spell it. Or they might not know that you call them "notebook computers" because they think of them as "laptops." If you optimize your pages for "notebook computers," you sure are going to miss a lot of those "laptop" searchers.

Searchers are not experts. They are not experts in what is on your Web site. They are not even experts on how to search. If you are expecting them to be, then they will continue to use search to find their answers—they just will not find them from you! One of the hardest things about any kind of marketing (and search marketing is no different) is to put yourself in your customer's shoes. *You* might know how to find the information on your site, but searchers do not. Your searchers are probably not like you, because you know a lot more than they do about searching and you especially know more about your Web site.

The preceding two chapters examined how search engines work and how search marketing works, but this chapter examines how *searchers* work—how they think, what they do, and what you can do about it. Not surprisingly, any effective search marketing program requires a solid understanding of the Web searcher. This chapter covers the following topics:

- *Visitor behavior.* Before we look at the particulars of how searchers behave, we need to take a look at some general findings on the behavior of visitors to Web sites.

- *The searcher's intent.* When formulating the query, every searcher has some objective in mind. Understanding the searcher's intent helps you provide the right information for the search engine to return—we can categorize search queries into several distinct types.

- *The searcher's click.* What links on the search results page do searchers click? We review the latest research into why searchers click where they do.

- *The searcher's follow-through.* Getting the searcher to visit your site is only half the battle. You need to develop your model of what visitors do on your site after they search to be sure that they will follow through—to buy your product, or sign up for your newsletter, or vote for your candidate.

Anyone who spends time studying people realizes that they interact with the world in unexpected and complex ways, and searchers are no exception. Let's start by examining the basic principles of how Web site visitors behave.

Visitor Behavior

No matter what your Web site's goals are, your visitors have goals of their own. They might be figuring out why their geraniums keep dying, or choosing which cell phone service to buy, or checking their doctor's advice about their high cholesterol. You must start with an understanding of what visitors to your Web site are trying to accomplish before you can help them reach their goals.

For some of you, thinking about visitor behavior is second nature—you might be a product marketer, or maybe you are responsible for voter research in a political campaign. If you are in a more technical role, however, such as a Webmaster or a Java programmer, you might not have thought much about this subject at all. Before we examine how to track visitor behavior, you need to understand some of the basic principles.

Fortunately, all the complex factors that affect visitor behavior have been studied for many years, because before they were "Web visitors" they were just plain folks—and research scientists have studied people's behavior for decades. If you are selling something, there is a wealth of information on **buyer behavior**. Political scientists regularly research **voter behavior**. No matter who your visitors are, there is probably a lot of information you can learn about their motivations, their beliefs, and their thinking—all of which help predict their likely behavior.

Because many of you are using search marketing to sell something, this chapter focuses mainly on sales examples, but we also examine the behavior of visitors with other goals (such as attracting votes for a candidate) so that you discover the underlying principles.

Buyer Behavior

Each of us buys things frequently, but somehow we forget our own experiences when we start selling things to other people. If your site's goal is to sell something, you need to be attuned to what your prospective buyers are looking for. There is no shortage of terms used to describe buyer behavior, but one important way to differentiate buyers is by the type of information they are seeking.

Some buyers are in the early stages of consideration of a purchase. Some marketing gurus call this **primary demand**, using the economic term *demand* to indicate when a buyer feels a need for something. Buyers experiencing primary demand have a problem, but they might not know whether there is any solution for it. Or they do not know which of several types of solution to choose. Contrast this with **selective demand**, where the buyer wants a particular brand of product or even a specific model.

If this is all you ever understand about buyer behavior, you will still be miles ahead of some of your competitors. You can imagine how a primary demand buyer might need a lot of education about various solutions to his problem before he is ready to hear about different products, whereas a selective demand buyer would be bored by such information and just wants to get detailed product information.

Consider someone who needs the snow shoveled from her driveway, which you can now identify as a primary demand situation. This buyer does not know whether she wants to hire a snow removal service or buy a snow blower, an electric snow shovel, or just a new shovel. How would you pitch what you are selling to such a person? If you happen to sell snow blowers, telling this buyer that your snow blower is the highest rated in the industry and it is on sale this weekend is pointless. She does not even know if she *wants* a snow blower. An article that shows the pros and cons of the various ways to remove snow, on the other hand, is exactly what the buyer wants to read. Here is where your powers of persuasion come in handy. Does your article point out the benefits of snow blowers as opposed to other methods? Because buyers are distrustful, your article should be sure to point out the legitimate situations in which other solutions are worthwhile, but you can certainly favor snow blowers as the solution of choice in most situations.

Your goal is to *inform* the primary demand buyer, allowing her to *become* a selective demand buyer. Notice that only when the buyer is convinced that she needs a snow blower does it make sense for you to extol the virtues of your snow blower over your competitor's. At that point, all the information deemed inappropriate earlier (its high rating and its sale price) might become important to that same buyer.

Human beings are complex creatures, and many different factors go in to decision making. The more that you know about what drives your visitors' buying behavior, the more easily you can tailor your Web site to address their needs.

Voter Behavior

Maybe your Web visitors are not buyers at all. Perhaps yours is a persuasion site trying to elect the next governor. You need to consider everything you know about voter behavior when designing your site. You need to understand how voters decide whom to vote for and you must decide what motivates voters to go to the polls rather than sitting the election out at home. (It is no use to persuade those who do not actually cast their vote.)

As discussed with buyer behavior, human behavior is complex. Different voters might view the same situation and make different decisions. Some political scientists believe that it is important in close elections to appear to be the front-runner, because "bandwagon behavior" causes undecided voters to go with the apparent winner. Other experts note that the leader often struggles to get supporters to the polls, because of the perception that the candidate is going to win anyway. Do voters look at your candidate differently because he is the challenger and not the incumbent? Regardless of what your pollster is telling you about your voters, you want voters exposed to certain themes and specific messages, and your understanding of voter behavior is a key part of deciding what your Web site says.

The same principles apply to visitors to other kinds of persuasion Web sites. In the medical field, it is increasingly recognized that **patient behavior** is important to any successful outcome, especially when it comes to so-called high-risk behaviors such as smoking, drug taking, or sexual promiscuity. Understanding the behavior of your site's target audience helps you design the messages that will persuade them to your point of view.

The Searcher's Intent

Now that you understand the basics of Web visitor behavior, let's talk specifically about search. Web searchers have behaviors all their own that start with the query itself.

Throughout history, human beings have sought to bring order to information by sorting and grouping documents to find them when they need them. But the advent of computer **information retrieval** (that is, search) made possible a massive increase in the number of documents available to find the needed information. And mostly, that's good. The problem arises when we expect those poor human beings to know how to find information in a whole new way. Folks who are comfortable using library card catalogs, book indexes, and other paper techniques find that none of those skills translate into using Web search.

So, although searchers are growing more sophisticated each year, the task of actually choosing the words for the query is one of the most difficult parts of searching. A few years ago, searchers mostly entered one- or two-word queries, and although queries are getting longer each year, it is still hard for search engines to know exactly what the searcher intends by a query.

It's actually a simple question: What does the searcher really want when he enters a query? But the answer is hardly as simple. When a searcher enters "home improvement," is he remodeling his bathroom or interested in Tim Allen's TV show? Researchers from top search engines say one of their biggest frustrations is making sense of the searcher's query. Despite this, it is not a hopeless cause. You *can* dramatically improve your search marketing by thinking about the "need behind the query." This knowledge helps you deliver the best possible content to your visitors when they search.

Andrei Broder, Yahoo! Research Fellow and Vice President of Emerging Search Technology, segments searchers into three categories:

- *Navigational searchers* want to find a specific Web site (perhaps because they do not know the exact URL), and use queries such as "irs web site" or "valley hospital."

- *Informational searchers* want information to answer their questions or to learn about a new subject, and use queries such as "what is scuba" or "hard water treatments."

- *Transactional searchers* want to do something (buy something, sign up, enter a contest, and so forth), and use queries such as "sydney weather" or "treo 600 activation."

We need to examine each kind of searcher so that you can reach them with content from your Web site. Understand that real people shift roles all the time—the same searcher might enter informational queries to learn about a new product and suddenly decide to use a transactional query to buy it. A clear understanding of the types of searchers and their respective intent will help you reach more searchers with less effort.

Navigational Searchers

Navigational searchers are looking for a specific Web site, perhaps because they have visited it in the past, or someone has told them about it, or because they have heard of a company and they just assume the site exists. Unlike other types of searchers, navigational searchers have just one right answer in mind. Table 4-1 shows some examples of navigational searches.

Table 4-1 Examples of Navigational Queries (Searchers expect a single correct result from any navigational query, the home page of the site they are looking for.)

Search Query	Probable Destination
greyhound bus	www.greyhound.com
internal revenue service	www.irs.gov
jetblue airlines	www.jetblue.com
toys are us	www.toysrus.com
barnes and noble	www.bn.com

Even when they use the same query, navigational searchers might not have the same destination in mind, as Table 4-2 shows.

Table 4-2 Confusion with Navigational Queries (Searchers expect a single correct result from any navigational query, but exactly what result is not always clear.)

Search Query	Probable Destinations	Organization
delta	www.delta.com	Delta Airlines
	www.deltafaucet.com	Delta Faucets
usc	www.usc.edu	University of Southern California
	www.sc.edu	University of South Carolina
cardinals	www.stlcardinals.com	St. Louis Cardinals baseball team
	www.azcardinals.com	Arizona Cardinals football team
hoover	www.hoovers.com	Hoover's Online
	www.hoover.com	Hoover Vacuums

Although it might be ambiguous as to what the navigational searchers want, it is clear what they do *not* want. They do not want deep information from a Web site—they want the home page. They know what site they want, and only that site will do. And, in most cases, they want just the home page for that site—no other pages.

AFFILIATE "SPAM" FRUSTRATES NAVIGATIONAL SEARCHERS

At a standing-room-only session on Internet travel deals at a popular New York City tourism conference, one woman stood up after a panel discussion and launched into a complaint about a particular hotel chain. She was furious that this hotel had hundreds of Web sites, each offering different prices and conflicting information. Not one of them showed the phone number so that she could actually call the hotel and book a reservation directly. This rant elicited cheers of support and sympathy.

The session moderator calmly tried to retake control of the session by explaining that those sites were affiliate sites and they did not actually belong to the hotel chain. Each site was a legitimate affiliate marketing partner of the hotel chain that gets a small commission for every reservation it books on behalf of the hotel. Unfortunately, some of these sites use unethical techniques (spam) to get top search rankings, frustrating navigational searchers who find these affiliate sites rather than the official site for the actual hotel.

This explanation did not make the attendees any happier, but at least they now understood what they were seeing. Another woman in the audience made the suggestion that searchers add the word "official" to their search query. For example, the query "official hilton hotel" actually returns the "official" Hilton Web site high in the results list in the major search engines, avoiding the spam (at least until spammers catch on and start adding that word to their own sites).

Frequently, novice search marketers find navigational searchers the hardest to fathom—this type of search does not make any sense to them. "Why would someone go to a search engine to search for my company when the URL is our name?" they ask. But Table 4-3 reflects the popularity of navigational searches within the top 20 most frequently searched terms. As you look at the table, you will see that the top searches revolve around popular current events (Paris Hilton's TV show, the *Spider-Man* movie, the Tour de France, and so on), but just below you find a set of navigational queries, some of which are the same week after week.

Table 4-3 The Popularity of Navigational Searches (Although these searches might seem pointless, many searchers use navigational searches to find Web sites.)

Rank	Search Phrase	Type of Search
1	paris hilton	Informational
2	tour de france	Informational
3	britney spears	Informational
4	spider-man 2	Informational
5	cameron diaz	Informational
6	jessica simpson	Informational
7	beyonce knowles	Informational

Rank	Search Phrase	Type of Search
8	google	Navigational
9	yahoo	Navigational
10	wwe	Navigational
11	ebay	Navigational
12	jeopardy	Navigational
13	mapquest	Navigational
14	nascar	Navigational
15	maria shapapova	Informational
16	yahoo.com	Navigational
17	ashlee simpson	Informational
18	jetblue	Navigational
19	anime	Informational
20	hotmail	Navigational

Source: www.wordtracker.com *(July 2004)*

If, by now, you are becoming convinced of the importance of navigational searchers to your search marketing efforts, you might be wondering what you can do to make sure those searchers find your site. Usually, you do not need to do much. Most navigational queries don't have a lot of competition—when someone enters the name of your company into Yahoo! Search, your Web site should show up. As Table 4-2 shows, if your company's name is shared by other companies, there might be some competition, but there is much less competition than for other kinds of queries. Most corporations should be in the top few results of most search engines for searches on their company name or their popular brand names.

Take steps now to make sure your Web site ranks well for navigational queries:

- Ensure your site is in the major search engine's indexes. Most organizations are already indexed, but see Chapter 10, "Get Your Site Indexed," if yours is not.

- Make sure the search engines show a good description for your home page for searches on your company name. If you do not like what you see, add a strong sentence with your company name to your page—the search engines will take that information and show it in the results. Figure 4-1 shows what can happen if you do not have a strong description.

- Remember that "negative" sites (yoursite-sucks.com) often rank close to (or occasionally higher than) your Web site, as shown in Figure 4-2. See Chapter 9, "Sell Your Search Marketing Proposal," for ideas about increasing the search exposure of your site and limiting the visibility of your detractors.

Google finds the best possible
site for this navigational query
as its #1 result . . .

. . . but the displayed snippet looks
more like a legal contract than a
page a searcher would click on.

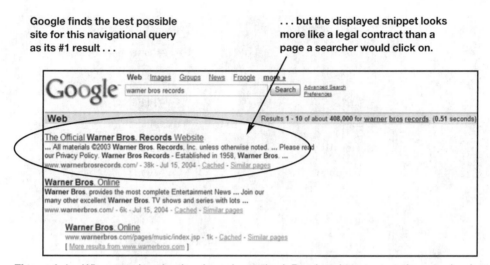

Figure 4-1   When good navigational queries go bad. Poorly written text on the page leads to a
result that few searchers would click.

Your company might battle "negative" sites, such as this one that dogs Amway.

Figure 4-2   "Negative" Web sites. Navigational queries can turn up sites that you would rather
not have your customers see.

Because people often use navigational queries to locate a company when they cannot figure out how to type the URL directly, you might also consider registering domains for common
misspellings of your company name. That way, people might find your company without resort-
ing to navigational searches at all.

Informational Searchers

Informational searchers want to find deep information about a specific subject. Informational searchers believe this deep information exists, but they don't know where it's located. Unlike navigational queries, informational queries do not have a single right answer—the best search results are several pages from multiple sites that all shed some light on the subject.

Almost every Web user is an informational searcher at one time or another. Most searchers start with a simple query, refining it until they locate good answers (or give up). The intent of informational searchers proves the most difficult to deduce because their queries can mean so many things. Many informational searchers enter only a single phrase, such as "new york." Whether that searcher meant New York City or the State of New York, and whether she wants to visit New York or learn about its history, discerning her intent is next to impossible.

CASE STUDY: IS THE SEARCHER'S INTENT INFORMATIONAL OR TRANSACTIONAL?

At the peak of the dotcom boom, a leading art and print site was spending millions of dollars on paid search placements for art-related search queries. The marketing manager knew that "monet" was one of its most heavily trafficked queries, but recently the visits from Yahoo! for "monet" had decreased significantly. What had changed?

Examining the Yahoo! search results for "monet" revealed a new site in the organic listings offering the complete history of Monet. Apparently many searchers were looking for information on Monet and were probably heading to that new site, instead of the art and print site.

In response, the marketing manager placed more historical information about Monet on his site and soon found his Monet page ranked highly in the Yahoo! organic listings. As expected, he began to see the traffic to this new Monet page increase significantly from the organic listing. The surprise was in the *paid* search clicks—they dropped even further. Worse, there were no more buyers of Monet prints even though overall traffic had doubled when you added up both paid and organic referrals. Why?

The marketing manager decided to perform a test. He added a survey to the new Monet page offering a drawing for a free print for anyone who would reveal their purpose in coming to the site. Of the survey respondents, 95 percent indicated they were students simply looking for biographical information on Monet and information about his paintings. These were informational searchers that had no desire to ever buy a Monet print.

Armed with this information, the marketing manager switched his paid placement buys from an informational query ("monet") to specific transactional queries (the names of Monet paintings such as "water lilies"). This strategy not only increased traffic but also increased sales, by capturing people who were *not* entering "monet" as their search query, but were truly ready to buy a specific print.

As you can see, careful study of the searcher's intent pays off in more visitors who are focused on your site's goal. It can be just as important to avoid the wrong traffic as to get the right traffic, because every art student who clicked the paid placement page cost the art and print site a few cents in pay-per-click fees that were completely wasted. By focusing on queries that real purchasers use, the art and print site reduced the art students and attracted more art buyers at the same time, thus selling more while paying less for paid placement.

The informational searcher is the mainstay of any search marketing program. Informational searchers have not yet chosen the product they want to buy (for example), so they are still "up for grabs." Informational searchers allow you to present your products before they have chosen a specific product.

The key to satisfying informational searchers is to provide clear "learn about" content related to your products or services. If you are selling riding lawnmowers, explain why riding lawnmowers are superior to the hand-push kind. If you offer a smoking-cessation program, why does yours work while others fail? No matter what your Web site sells, why is yours better? Whatever your Web site does, why do you do it better?

By researching the informational queries that searchers use (explained in detail in Chapter 11, "Choose Your Target Keywords"), and by optimizing your pages to meet those information needs (covered in Chapter 12, "Optimize Your Content"), you can attract informational searchers to your site.

Transactional Searchers

Transactional searchers make things happen. They are not looking for information—they want to *do* something. Transactional queries cluster around specific tasks, such as buying products, accessing databases, and downloading various types of files (images, software, or songs). When searchers enter the name of a book, or the model number of a digital camera, they are intending to make a transaction, namely to buy the item. But there are many other kinds of transactional queries. Anyone trying to download a fix for a computer, or signing up for a newsletter, or donating to a charity is a transactional searcher.

Transactional queries are the hardest of all queries to incorporate into an optimization program. Transactional queries are often related to specific products, and should return product catalog pages, which unfortunately have little content on them and do not rank well in search engines. The text-rich informational searcher pages that solved shoppers' problems with your products are gone, replaced by barren catalog pages with model numbers, specifications, and a picture. It is hard work to dress up these catalog pages for search engines.

The most important goal for improving these catalog pages is to make the search result's snippet relevant to the query. You improve your chances of both being found by the search engine and being clicked by the searcher by incorporating the query's words into the title and other parts of the page. In addition, you should feature any special pricing or other offer prominently on the page to catch the attention of the searcher. If your page can reassure searchers that it is a good choice, even better.

Figure 4-3 demonstrates why paid placement advertisements are not always clicked by searchers. Clearly the searcher is looking for a specific model of camera, yet all but the fifth result fail to incorporate the camera model into the offer. The other paid results might cause searchers to have to start from scratch and enter the model number all over again once they get to the Web site, a sure way to turn off searchers.

A query for "canon s60 digital
camera" signifies someone
ready to buy . . .

. . . but the top four sponsored links don't
contain the model number. The searcher
probably clicks #5.

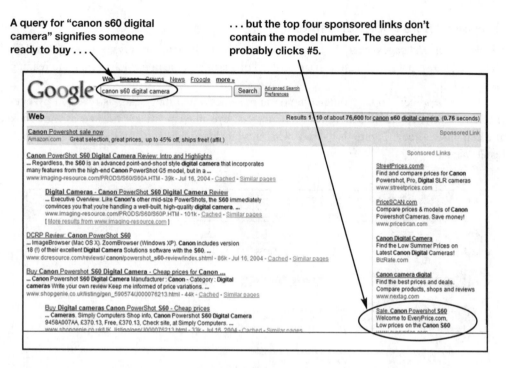

Figure 4-3   Enticing transactional searchers to click. Transactional searchers expect to see
what they typed in your offer, or they might not click.

The Searcher's Click

Now that we understand why searchers enter the queries they do, we need to learn what they do
with the search results. We already learned that searchers have *different* needs motivating their
search queries, but now we will see that searchers *share* certain behaviors when dealing with
search results.

Just because your site ranks at the top of the results does not mean that searchers will view
your page. You need to give them a reason to click.

Searchers see only a few things about your page on the search results page: the title, the
snippet, and the URL. Your copy writer selects the title, and your Webmaster chooses the URL,
but the *search engine* picks the snippet from your page based on the searcher's query. Take
another look at Figure 4-1. Someone searching for "warner bros. records" is told in the title that it
is the "official site," but the legal disclaimers might scare people away.

Let's take a deeper look at how searchers look at search results, why they click where they
do, and what is happening when searchers do *not* click a result at all.

How Searchers Look at Results

People do not read pages when they use the Web—they *scan* them. So it is no surprise that Web searchers also scan a search results page, instead of starting in the upper-left corner and reading each word.

Searchers seem to use some common approaches when they scan, as revealed by **eye-tracking analytics** studies, in which test subjects' eye movements are tracked as they look at a computer screen. Figure 4-4 shows what a typical searcher actually looks at on a search results page.

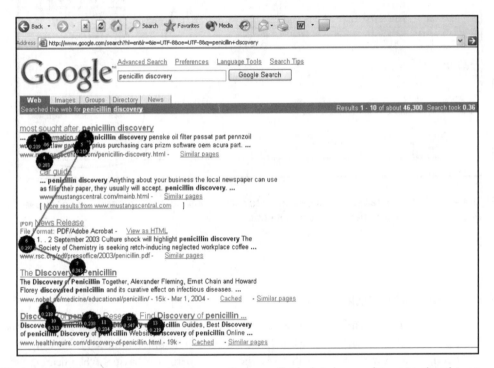

Figure 4-4   What searchers see on the results page. Each dot shows where searchers' eyes track.

Source: Human-Computer Interaction Group at Cornell University

Eye movement studies (and other studies) disclose what searchers scan for:

- Searchers "mentally divide" the page into sections and focus on the organic results area the most. Four out of five searchers ignore the sponsored links (paid listings).

- Nearly all users look at the first two or three organic search results.

- Searchers spend less time looking at organic results ranked below #3, and *far* less time scanning results that rank seventh or lower, possibly because these results require scrolling down on the page. Eighty-eight percent report scrolling down only when there is no relevant result in the top three.

- Within each result, searchers spend 43 percent of the time viewing the snippet, followed by 30 percent reviewing the title.

If you did not realize it already, you can see that high rankings for search queries are the key to getting noticed. The first hurdle to being clicked by searchers is to get their attention—rank highly on the results page and have an eye-catching title and snippet. But after you get their attention, what makes them click your page?

Why Searchers Click Where They Do

Searchers click pages because they expect those pages will satisfy a need. So navigational searchers expect to land at the right site, information searchers expect to find their answer, and transactional searchers to take action—or at least get one step closer.

No matter what they do, one thing to keep in mind is that they do it fast. Most searchers choose the first promising link they see, and they do it in less than five seconds. They look at only the top two or three links, and they are most likely to click the first link. Searchers also seem to favor organic results over paid, clicking them 60 percent of the time.

But why does a searcher click one result rather than another? No matter what type of query—navigational, informational, or transactional—studies show that searchers tend to click a result that contains the exact query words in its title and snippet. In addition, for informational and transactional queries, seeing trusted information sources and brand names (and reviews and comparison information) correlates with searcher clicks. For transactional searchers, showing a low price (along with promises of discounts or other offers) enhances clickthrough, especially when the searcher can buy online.

After you begin getting good search rankings for your pages, you will want to continue to learn about what motivates searchers to click on *your* page in the search results, but you also need to understand what stops them.

When Searchers *Don't* Click Results

Although search engines can often seem magical in the way they find the right page for a query, the truth is that about half of all searchers do not click a result on the first page of search results. What are they doing?

Are they usually moving to page two of the search results? No. About seven in ten searchers enter a new query when the top ten results are unappealing. In fact, many searchers plan to start with a broad query, making it more specific as they go. In addition, about one fourth of searchers go to a different search engine and use the same query.

ENHANCING YOUR PAGE'S "CURB APPEAL"

Realtors have long provided tips to home sellers on enhancing "curb appeal"—that certain something that makes a house enticing to a potential buyer. If you consistently enhance your titles and snippets, your pages will have the curb appeal you need to drive heavy clickthrough rates.

The most examined part of a search results page is the snippet, the two- to three-line page excerpt that search engines use to show where the query words were found on that page. Searchers spend 43 percent of their time looking at the snippet before deciding to click that link.

Typically, the search engines take the first full sentence of page text that contains the query words. It moves down the page pulling in additional clauses containing the query words until it reaches the maximum character limit. If a page does not contain the query words within a sentence (or at all), the search engine takes the content found in the HTML description tag. If you understand how this snippet is created, you can adjust your content so that the search engine will use the snippet you want, rather than something cobbled together as in Figure 4-1.

Above the snippet is the title, the underlined (usually blue) text taken from the HTML title tag from the page. The title normally garners 30 percent of the searcher's scanning time, or higher if the title contains the query words. Figure 4-4 shows that the searcher's eyes stopped on every bold occurrence of the query words. Figure 4-5 shows the overall percentages of how searchers spend their time.

Smart search marketers spruce up their pages to increase their appeal to searchers, so that their high rankings for search result in a high clickthrough rate, too. Chapter 12 shows you more tips on increasing curb appeal.

Title: 30% ———————▶
Snippet: 43% ———————▶
URL: 21% ———————▶
Other: 5% (Includes, cached, similar pages)

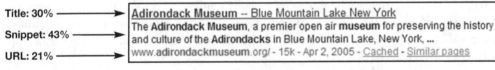

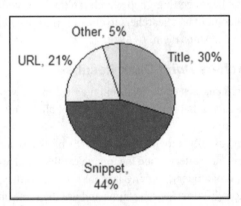

Figure 4-5   Seeing each search result. Searchers mainly focus on the title and the description snippet.

Source: Human-Computer Interaction Group at Cornell University

The Searcher's Follow-Through

Just getting people to click your link on the search results page is not enough. Your Web site has a purpose, whether it is persuading a customer to purchase more of your product, coaxing a prospect to provide his e-mail address, or convincing someone to exercise. No matter what you do in search marketing, the job is not done unless the searcher not only finds your site, but also follows through.

Visitors landing on your site from search engines exhibit specific behavior when they arrive—searchers typically decide within ten seconds whether to click further. Searchers tend to click further when your page contains the following:

- The searcher's exact query words in the page heading or another prominent location
- Pictures of your product
- Wide selection (for informational searchers)
- Price, features, and value (for transactional searchers)

But what stops them from completing their task? Like it or not, people are far less patient with Web sites that do not work their way than they are with offline businesses.

Consider what you would do if you drove to the store, spent a few minutes putting items in your cart, and went to the register and saw a rather long line—maybe you will be waiting for five or ten minutes to check out. Most of us would grin and bear it. We might be annoyed, but we would wait semi-patiently and check out. If it happened frequently enough, however, we might start avoiding that store.

Now think about an equivalent experience on the Web. You spend a few minutes placing several items in your cart, and then you get to the checkout and it is slow. Each time you click it takes 10 to 15 seconds to respond. Then it takes 30 seconds on the next screen. What would you do?

Many of you would abandon that site and go somewhere else, even though it means starting all over (and though you would wait 10 minutes in a brick-and-mortar store to do the same thing). Why? Because it is so quick to go to another Web store, that is why. You know that you will only spend a few minutes doing it, and you will recover all your lost time, whereas it might take considerably longer to retrace your steps in a physical store.

Successful Web sites construct the optimal path for their visitor to follow to complete any task, and the only way to do that is to understand your visitor's behavior. Throughout this chapter, we have discussed how searchers get to your site, but now we need to consider how they follow through after they have arrived. To understand your Web visitor's behavior, you need to develop a **behavior model**. We show you one technique for developing behavior models called the Web Conversion Cycle.

The Web Conversion Cycle

You work with behavior models every day, but perhaps you do not think of them in those terms. If you own a retail store, it is understood that customers enter the store, look around at the merchandise, pick a few things out, and take them to the register to pay. That is a behavior model. Your Web visitors use a model, too, and you need to take that into account when you try to measure the success of your search campaign.

Just like the retail store, your Web site is designed to drive to a **conversion**, such as purchasing a product. But both the retail site and your Web site have secondary goals, such as allowing returns or repairs of products, which you can also count as successful Web conversions.

We should account for the main user goals in our behavior model, which we call the **Web Conversion Cycle**. In Chapter 5, "Identify Your Web Site's Goals," we help you define your own Web Conversion Cycle to model visitor behavior on your Web site. But for now, let's look at just one example, as shown in Figure 4-6.

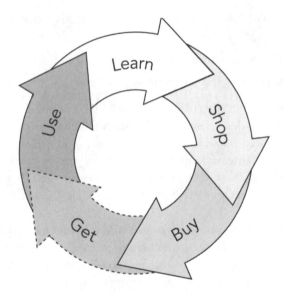

Figure 4-6   A behavior model for personal computer sales. Visitors satisfy their information needs before buying, "get" the computer offline, and return for technical support.

As we look at our example of the Web Conversion Cycle, we can see that visitors might start out with a problem (primary demand) and must Learn about what kinds of solutions exist. When informed, they can choose a type of solution and Shop for a particular product (selective demand). If they are persuaded that they have found the right product and the right deal, they can Buy the product, and then wait to Get it before they Use it. Let's look at each step in more detail.

Your visitor starts by **learning** how to solve her problem, and is said to be in the Learn step. The information on your site was carefully written to discuss her problem and gradually lead her to explore your products, which can solve her problem.

At the moment she begins examining pricing or comparing features of your product, she is **shopping**. Visitors in the Shop step need different information than those in the Learn activity—learners are trying to figure out what kind of product can help them, whereas shoppers are gathering information leading to the purchase of a specific product.

After your shopper chooses a specific product, she is **buying**. In the Buy step, she lands on a particular product page, examining the information carefully to decide whether to place the item in her cart. The Buy activity includes all the steps of placing an item in her cart, checking out, and actually completing the purchase.

After buying the product, the visitor waits to **get** the purchase, which typically takes several days. During the Get step, she might check online order status to see when the item is shipped and might use tracking numbers from overnight shipping vendors to ascertain the delivery date of her order.

After she has received her purchase, she begins to **use** it. Depending on the product, there might be many specific steps in the Use activity, ranging from assembly, to installation, to asking "how to" questions, to solving a problem. If the customer is happy with the product, she might decide to return to your site to purchase something else from you.

How Visitor Behavior Affects Search Marketing

There are lots of ways to use the Web Conversion Cycle in your business, but we can start by examining how these visitor behaviors affect the search queries they enter and how you can design your pages to capture those searchers for your site. Let's look at four of the most important steps in the Web Conversion Cycle and see where search fits in.

The Learn Stage

Many visitors start out needing to Learn more about what you sell before they consider a purchase, and they frequently use informational search queries to do so. To ensure visitors find your site when they enter the informational queries, write articles with objective information comparing multiple solutions to the problem. The articles should lead visitors to conclude that your product is the best solution in most cases. Make sure that you help them understand the product category and show them a few choices (retailer) or show them why yours is best (manufacturer).

The Shop Stage

Not all visitors start at the Learn step. Some know what kind of product they want to buy, but need to Shop for the particular brand or model. They are still entering informational queries, but they are more specific now than in the Learn step. Learners search for "computer," whereas shoppers look for "laptop computer."

As you design your site, you must ensure that you have product category pages, not just model pages. For example, create a page that lists of all of your DVD players with an explanation of how they work. That way, you capture search traffic for shoppers entering the "dvd players" query, not just buyers using queries that name particular brands or models. Use the three-second rule from direct marketing: Can the customer tell what you are selling in three seconds? If not, simplify your copy.

The Buy Stage

The most valuable searchers to capture for your site are the ones who are ready to Buy. Even if they did not visit your site to Learn or Shop, if you can capture them here, you can make the sale.

When searchers want to buy your product, they enter specific transactional queries, such as "sony dvd player" or "dell inspiron 1150." Your pages are probably already using the right words for these pages to ensure being found, but you must also add content that answers any lingering questions to encourage the visitor to put the product in a cart and check out.

The Use Stage

For some products, especially technology products, the majority of Web site visitors need help while trying to Use the product. A few years ago, customers needing help were more likely to come directly to *your* site to solve their problem, but more and more they now head to Yahoo! or Google to search for their answer.

You want these searchers to find your site for several reasons, including the following:

- If you can solve their problems, they will value your company more highly, which might lead to future business. It might seem illogical, but studies show that customers report higher satisfaction with companies that promptly correct problems than they report for companies that do not cause any problems in the first place!

- People who solve their own problems on your Web site will not contact you by phone. You save the phone costs and the costs of your personnel interacting with your customers.

- If you can get customers to come to *your* Web site for their problems, rather than going somewhere else, you might generate revenue from a service call, or from upgrading a warranty, or by selling an add-on product, or by convincing them to scrap what they have and buy a new one that works better.

CASE STUDY: USING THE WEB CONVERSION CYCLE IN YOUR SEARCH STRATEGY

You might look at the Web Conversion Cycle and say to yourself, "If only things really went this smoothly!" and you are correct—all visitors do not sail through the steps as easily as it appears in the diagram. Real life is rarely as neat and clean as shown here, but a simple model helps you analyze what is really going on. Let's look at a realistic example of how the Web Conversion Cycle might work with your search marketing strategy.

Suppose that you are the marketing manager for TurboTax for Intuit Inc. (the successful maker of Quicken). Some prospective customers are clearly looking for a solution to the problem of filing their income taxes and might enter the query "income tax return." These searchers are in the Learn activity. Now you can imagine the search engine providing several different types of answers to that query:

- *How-to information*. Advice from the government or other well-respected sources on how to fill out tax forms yourself, usually in layman's terms.
- *Tax services*. Descriptions of accounting firms and tax-preparation firms, such as H&R Block, that will fill out your tax return for a fee.
- *Tax software*. Explanations of computer programs that you can buy to complete your tax return using your personal computer.
- *Comparisons*. Articles that contrast doing it yourself, using accounting and tax-preparation firms, and using tax software to determine the best way to complete your tax returns.

As the TurboTax marketing manager, you have undoubtedly placed pages on your site that explain the workings of computer tax software. Even better, you could place pages on your site that compare the advantages of tax preparation software versus having it prepared by professionals (or doing it by hand). Both types of content will help you get high rankings in search engines for the query "income tax return."

But some searchers will be further along in the buying process. They might be searching for "computer tax software" because they have already decided how to solve their problem and are shopping for exactly the right solution. This particular kind of informational query is looking for the product category, and is typical of those in the Shop activity. The pages you created on tax software to satisfy informational searchers will also serve you well here. In addition, pages devoted to features of TurboTax might also rank well.

Other searchers know exactly what they are looking for. They are in the Buy activity— in this case they want to buy a copy of TurboTax. For these queries, you, the marketing manager, must create pages that clearly show how to buy the product and perhaps display some special offers that might help people decide now. Because the customer has already decided on your product, your search marketing here is focused on selling directly from your site rather than having a retailer or other distributor make the sale.

Other searchers need help with your product. They are in the Use activity, which is a common reason to visit a software manufacturer's Web site. Technical support issues trigger queries such as "turbotax printing error." And do not forget Intuit's favorite Use query: "turbo tax upgrade" (which for tax software comes along every March). That is the kind of query that can close the loop in the Web Conversion Cycle and return the customer to the Learn activity.

Summary

Understanding the "need behind the query" can provide a significant advantage to search marketers. You use this knowledge to deliver the best possible content to searchers at the very time they need it.

This chapter covered the various types of searchers and how they approach their queries. You learned how they view search engine results and how they decide which result to click, all of which is summarized in Table 4-4. You also learned how Web visitors follow a behavior model that describes what they do on your site—and whether they complete that action.

Table 4-4   Understanding Searchers (Different types of searchers use different queries to do the same thing—in this case, each searcher wants a book on weight loss.)

Searcher Type	Search Query	What Searchers Want	Why Pages Rank Highly	Why Searchers Click
Navigational	amazon	Amazon home page	Query words in title and URL	Query words in title and snippet
Informational	low carb diet	Deep information from several sites	Text-rich pages with query words	As above, with trusted sources and brands
Transactional	south beach diet	Buy page from bookseller	Query words in title and text	As above, with a great offer

In Part 1 of this book, you have learned the basics of Web search—what it is, how it works, and what you can do about it. You have also learned that the searcher drives everything you do as a search marketer. In Part 2 of this book, the focus changes to examine your site's goals and how to measure success. No matter what your organization does, your Web site has a specialized purpose, and search marketing must support that purpose. The next chapter shows how to isolate the exact mission of your site before you embark on any search marketing effort.

PART 2

Develop Your Search Marketing Program

Search marketing is unlike other marketing programs, because it requires the support of many people within your organization. To gain their support, you need to develop a very clear program whose value can be explained to anyone. Part 2 is where you learn to do that.

First, in Chapter 5, "Identify Your Web Site's Goals," we identify your Web site's underlying goals. Is it an e-Commerce site? A site to build brand awareness for higher offline sales? A way to get volunteers for your nonprofit organization? Regardless, your Web site has a purpose, and your search marketing program must help your organization fulfill that purpose.

With your goals identified, Chapter 6, "Measure Your Web Site's Success," explores how your Web site measures its success in reaching those goals. You learn to track Web events that mark successful visits to your site. This chapter also looks at other Web metrics, such as visitor traffic and sales revenue.

With that as a backdrop, you are ready to measure your search success in Chapter 7, "Measure Your Search Marketing Success." You will choose the focus area for your first search marketing campaign, assess your current search marketing situation, and calculate the business opportunity of a successful campaign.

Chapter 8, "Define Your Search Marketing Strategy," broadens the scope to your entire search marketing program, introducing you to the strategic decisions required for organization-wide success. You will choose your program's scope, decide which groups will perform various search marketing tasks, and decide whether you will work with a search marketing vendor or run a completely in-house program. Finally, you will project the cost of your own search marketing program.

Part 2 concludes with Chapter 9, "Sell Your Search Marketing Proposal," in which you learn how to assemble your proposal for a search marketing program in your organization. To gain support for that proposal throughout your company, you must persuade numerous technical and business specialists, as well as a host of executives. This chapter shows you how to get that crucial organizational buy-in.

CHAPTER 5

Identify Your Web Site's Goals

So why are you trying to attract search traffic anyway? Every reader of this book will have a slightly different answer to that question, because each Web site has an intrinsic purpose, one that your search marketing efforts must support. In Chapter 4, "How Searchers Work," we examined the motivation of searchers, but in this chapter we are examining *your* motivations as a search marketer. Every Web site needs to drive traffic, but there are many different reasons for doing so. Your site might be selling online, or gathering contact information for offline follow-up, or maybe just generating market awareness. Your organization's site could also be focused on something else entirely.

No matter your goals, attracting traffic from search engines requires an understanding of search from the inside. Most of this book contains tips that do not vary much based on your specific goals for your site. However, your precise goals can sometimes be important, because your goals determine how you *measure* your search marketing success. In Chapter 6, "Measure Your Web Site's Success," we show how to measure success based on your goals, and in the rest of the book we ensure you know which search marketing strategies help achieve those goals. So, let's dig in and identify your goals for your site.

For some of you, this will be a simple exercise, because you think about the goals of your Web site every day. But maybe you are like the trout, who when asked, "How's the water?" replied, "What water?" Maybe sometimes you get so mired in the day-to-day details that you have trouble remembering what your overall goals are.

Regardless of who you are, your Web site probably has one or more of the following goals:

- *Web sales*. Ring the digital cash register! Your customer buys your product on the Web.

- *Offline sales*. Ring that *other* cash register! Your customer uses the Web to research your product, but buys it in a brick-and-mortar store or over the phone.

- *Leads*. Find a new customer! Your customer uses the Web to research a problem and leaves contact information.

- *Market awareness*. Tell your story! Your customer learns about what you do or engages in an activity (sponsored by your brand).

- *Information and entertainment*. Inform people! Your visitor wants to learn something or have fun killing time.

- *Persuasion*. Change someone's mind! Your organization might be trying to help people with a problem or medical condition, or you might be trying to influence public opinion.

No matter how many of these goals are your Web site's goals, you want to draw traffic from search engines. Understanding each goal will help you better focus your search efforts.

Web Sales

Ringing the digital cash register is an easy goal to understand, and it is easy to measure success. If your site has a shopping cart and sells directly to visitors, Web sales is one of its goals. Amazon.com is probably the best-known example of a pure Web sales site, but many corporate Web sites sell something directly to visitors.

Saying that your goal is "Web sales," however, is a broad goal. It helps to be more specific about exactly what kind of business you have, because different kinds of businesses need different search marketing strategies.

Online Commerce Versus Pure Online

An **online commerce** site offers items that can be purchased right on the site, but it delivers the items offline. In contrast, a **pure online** site not only sells on the Web, but delivers electronically, too—there is no physical package sent to the buyer. Your business might be squarely in one of these camps, or it might be a hybrid, where some of your products are delivered online and some are delivered offline. So, although we contrast online commerce businesses from pure online businesses, keep in mind that in real life businesses fall on different points of a continuum, not always at the extremes.

Many successful Web businesses are pure online businesses. Charles Schwab sells investments—the buyer makes the purchase online and might receive a mail confirmation, but the asset is owned immediately. Downloaded software and music are other examples of pure online businesses. In contrast, online commerce businesses include everything else actually sold on the Web—books, packaged software, CDs, and so many other things now. Every day, something new is available for sale on the Web, to be shipped to the buyer's address. In many ways, Federal Express and the rest of the package delivery industry is the biggest winner in the e-Commerce revolution.

But why is this distinction between online and offline delivery important? Because the faster the buyer gets the product, the more impulse purchases are made. And impulse purchases differ from a well-researched purchase in important ways. Those differences go to the heart of your search marketing strategy.

When we examine pure online businesses, we see that they inspire the most impulsive purchases possible. Think about how online trading has rocked the securities industry in the past ten years. Time was, buying or selling stock was a big decision, one not made often. Advice was frequently sought from a stockbroker, a financial advisor, or even friends and family. Buying or selling an investment usually received careful consideration.

What happened when investments could be bought and sold online? Everything changed. First, there was huge competition over the lowest fees charged for each sale, the simplest customer experience, and the trustworthiness of the electronic broker. But that was only the beginning. Completely new needs began to emerge. Brokers began to compete on the information available—real-time quotes, investment analysis, and portfolio management tools. And then day traders emerged. Day traders are the ultimate impulse purchasers in the electronic brokerage business. And they are highly sought-after customers because the churn in their accounts brings in large fees. They are the high rollers of the brokerage business.

This kind of change is underway in music today, as brick-and-mortar retailers that first came under attack from Web retailers such as CDNow now also fear Apple iTunes, the music download store. Digital commerce and digital delivery inexorably result in more impulse purchases at lower prices. Whereas we formerly thought a bit before trooping to the store to buy a $15 CD, now we think nothing of downloading a single song for 99¢. You can see the same shift underway for books and can imagine it affecting many other industries as the years go by.

THE SEISMIC SHIFT TO IMPULSE PURCHASES

The shift to more impulsive purchases is not limited to pure online businesses. A 2000 Angus Reid study showed nearly 25 percent of all Web purchases were made on impulse, but by 2003, a User Interface Engineering study showed it had grown to almost 40 percent. Analysts describe various factors that can increase impulse purchases for your site.

- *Offer a deal*. Two 2000 surveys by Yankee Group and Ernst and Young each found price to be the #1 reason consumers cited for making unplanned purchases.

- *Make it easy*. The Web impulse purchase champion, Amazon, has shown that a well-designed site with one-click purchasing and personalized offers results in higher sales. Many book lovers acknowledge that they buy more books from Amazon then they did when they had to schlep to the bookstore. And making physical delivery more convenient continues to drive a shift to impulse purchases. Best Buy lets customers buy online and pick up the product at a local brick-and-mortar store. Amazon guarantees delivery on a particular date for some products. Most online commerce sites offer some form of "Buy Today, Ship Today." Many companies use text chat windows for people to ask questions while looking at pages on the Web site. Basically, every roadblock you remove brings higher impulse sales.

- *Perfect your site navigation*. User Interface Engineering found that 87 percent of impulse purchases were made by visitors who navigated a site's product categories, instead of using the site's search engine. It appears that although customers might find your site using Google and other search engines, you will increase your impulse sales if you provide clear navigation after they get there. Apparently customers who navigate your product categories are exposed to more product pages and more merchandise ads than those who use your site's search facility, and higher impulse sales result.

What does this shift to more impulsive purchases mean for search marketing? First off, it means more of your business comes to you from search engines than ever before, but it means more than that. Impulse purchasers search for different things. A day trader is not looking for the same brokerage features as a conservative investor, and the same is true for other industries. People buying CDs are more likely to use the name of the artist and the name of the album in their search query, whereas folks downloading tunes for their iPods might use the name of the song. As you saw in Chapter 4, there is a difference between informational and transactional searches—impulse purchases tend to be far more transactional than informational.

As your business moves from *offline* to *online commerce* to *pure online*, you might see similar shifts in searcher behavior that need to drive your search marketing strategy.

Retailers Versus Manufacturers

In offline businesses, manufacturers and retailers usually do not compete with each other. Distribution networks connect manufacturers to retailers directly or through wholesalers, and are so efficient that most manufacturers do not even sell their products directly to end customers. The Web has changed that manufacturer-retailer relationship in many industries.

On the Web, any manufacturer with a commerce system and a UPS label can deal directly with the end customer, completely bypassing the wholesalers and retailers. At first, people talked about **disintermediation**, a fancy term that basically means the manufacturers cut out the middlemen. But what happened, as usual, is more complex and nuanced than disintermediation, and has varied by industry.

Many consumer manufacturers have added the ability to sell direct to customers or have expanded the volume sold directly. Book publishers that rarely sold books except through intermediaries now sell more direct than ever before. Manufacturers of little-known products that had trouble getting wide distribution have huge advantages in selling direct on the Web. But Amazon and other online retailers show that, for many businesses, immense value still remains in aggregating the wares of many manufacturers in one place. Many manufacturers well-schooled in drop-shipping large volumes of their products to a warehouse found they are not necessarily proficient at shipping one item to someone's home and dealing with the customer service issues that go along with it. Book publishers, for example, cannot offer the low prices and fast shipment to customers that Amazon does, because the publisher's low direct sales volumes prevent investment in the most efficient distribution systems.

Dr. Michael Hammer, the originator of the reengineering concept, gave the example that a central air-conditioning manufacturer *can* sell direct on the Web, but there are so many questions before purchase and so many thorny installation problems (as well as post-installation maintenance needs) that it might not make any sense to do so. That manufacturer's Web site might be better devoted to offline sales through its traditional dealer network. So, manufacturers must think carefully about the value of direct sales to their end customers before pursuing a disintermediation strategy. Many manufacturers are better off pursuing offline sales as their Web site's primary goal, as we discuss later in this chapter.

Just as manufacturers and retailers have different business strengths, so do their Web sites, as shown in Table 5-1.

Table 5-1   Strengths of Manufacturer and Retailer Web Sites (The strong points of manufacturer sites differ from those of retailer Web sites.)

	Manufacturer (e.g., Sony)	Retailer (e.g., Buy.com)
Breadth of products offered	One manufacturer	Many manufacturers
Depth of product information	Deep and detailed	Surface only
Objectivity of product information	Biased to own product	More objective
Frequency of return visits	Moderate	High

Figure 5-1 shows two Web pages, one from Sony, a manufacturer of DVD players, and one from retailer Buy.com. At sony.com, you obviously see only Sony DVD players, whereas buy.com shows DVD players from many manufacturers. Sony's site is likely to have much more detailed information about its products and underlying technology (including how it works and what the benefits are) than any retailer does, but the content is also slanted in favor of Sony, rather than being objective. Whereas many retail sites just show warmed-over manufacturer information, smart retailers show third-party reviews and solicit customer reviews, providing more balanced choices, because there is no allegiance to any particular manufacturer.

The manufacturer emphasizes the brand messaging . . .

. . . and builds navigation around all products . . .

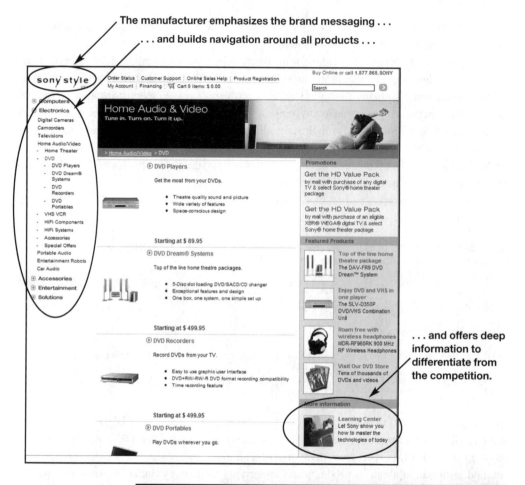

. . . and offers deep information to differentiate from the competition.

The retailer stresses navigation within the product category . . .

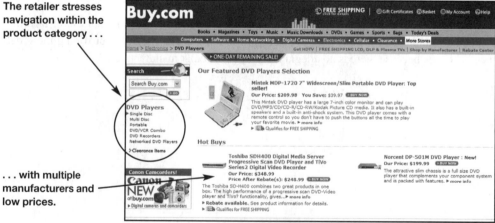

. . . with multiple manufacturers and low prices.

Figure 5-1   Comparing manufacturers and retailers. Both sell DVD players, but each has a different emphasis in making the sale.

Beyond their relative strengths and weaknesses, the very goals of manufacturers and retailers differ, too. Buy.com does not care which DVD player customers buy as long as they buy from them. Likewise, Sony does not care who customers buy from as long as they buy a Sony DVD player. These differing goals lead to different Web approaches, with Sony emphasizing deep product expertise and branding that leads to a Sony product purchase. Buy.com emphasizes customer experience, one-stop shopping, competitive prices, and quick shipping.

Obviously, both manufacturers and retailers also care about customers considering their companies for future purchases. Even here there are differences, however. A manufacturer's brand image for product value and quality is a different proposition than a retailer's reputation for low prices and strong service, and their Web sites are designed accordingly. Manufacturers sometimes differ from retailers in **frequency** of return visits, too. Some retailers get more frequent return visits than manufacturers, so features that depend on return visits, such as personalization, might be more useful to retailers.

These important differences between retailers and manufacturers also lead to somewhat different search strategies. Both retailers and manufacturers emphasize informational and transactional queries, but it is usually easier for manufacturers to get high search rankings for queries that contain their brand names and model numbers. Thus, a query for "sony playstation" is much easier for Sony to rank #1 for than it is for Buy.com. Buy.com and other retailers might do better than Sony, however, for the query "video games."

Even if your business is not purely a manufacturer or a retailer, some of these principles might still apply. Dealers that act as manufacturer's representatives often sell just one manufacturer's products, so they are basically extensions of the manufacturers, and their Web sites usually have the same strengths and weaknesses as those of manufacturers. Dealers that sell competing products from multiple manufacturers might resemble retailers more than manufacturers on the Web.

Retailers and manufacturers also differ in terms of the importance of navigational queries. In general, manufacturers are more recognizable than retailers, although that is not always the case. No matter how well known (or unknown) your company is, you want to take steps for your company's Web site to be found when its name is entered. But it is more important for some businesses than others. It is more likely that customers will aim for a manufacturer of a product rather than its retailer. Many more searchers look for "sony dvd player" than "buy.com dvd player" (or even "amazon dvd player"). A well-known retailer such as Buy.com does need to pay attention to being found for navigational queries, but informational queries are more important.

Manufacturers and retailers that sell online have many characteristics in common, but they also have different strengths that bring value to their customers in the buying process. These varying strengths influence both the design of their Web sites and their search marketing strategies.

Offline Sales

Ringing that *other* cash register can be trickier to measure than ringing the digital cash register. You might be trying to get people to come into your store or buy over the phone. Perhaps you sell direct on the Web, too, but you find that people often ask questions before buying. Or maybe you have no e-Commerce capability at all. You might be a forklift manufacturer, a car dealer, or you might sell many other big-ticket items. Your site encourages research and comparison because most of your sales close through more traditional channels. Your company might be a product manufacturer or a manufacturer's representative. If this sounds like your business, your primary goal is offline sales. As discussed before, however, your goals might not be so black and white. You might have a mix of products, some of which are conducive to online sales and some that are better served with an offline approach.

For products where you do emphasize offline sales, you need to work hard at your **call to action**, which is sales-speak for the thing you are trying to get someone to do. Where the call to action for Web sales might be as simple as a shopping cart icon next to a sales pitch, your offline sales site must move the customer to the sales channel where you will eventually close the deal. Depending on your business, that channel can take different forms, as depicted in Figure 5-2:

- A toll-free telephone number
- Directions to your store
- A list of locations of stores that carry your product
- A link to a retailing Web site that sells your product online

Some companies have even more elaborate ways of shifting people to the channel to close the sale. Some auto manufacturer Web sites let customers fill out forms to request price quotes from local dealers. IBM offers a button on selected Web pages called Call Me Now; visitors can enter their phone number and have an IBM product expert call them back in a couple of minutes to answer questions (and maybe close the sale).

Studies confirm that customers frequently have questions they want answered before buying. After a study on customer behavior, Laura Evans of the consulting firm Ten/Resource (as quoted in *Internet Retailer*) noted, "I was surprised that, when armed with information from the Web that they took into the store, they still wanted to talk to a salesperson to confirm what they learned."

Regardless of the methods your company uses to move people from the Web site to the offline sales channel, the search strategy for offline sales is similar to that for Web sales, optimizing your site for a mix of informational and transactional queries. Likewise, companies with well-known names also need to focus on their ranking for navigational queries.

Web sales sites and offline sales sites differ most sharply in how they measure success. For Web sales, measurement is simple: Your Web traffic measurement system tells you how many people came, and your e-Commerce system tells you how many people bought. But offline sales are much tougher to measure. In Chapter 6, we help you close the loop on your offline sales measurements.

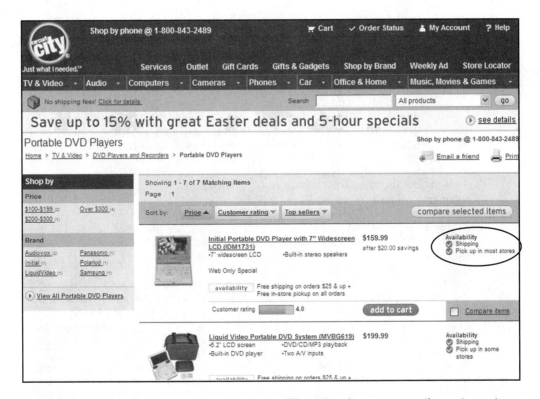

Figure 5-2   Calls to action for offline sales. Your offline sales site must move the customer to the channel that will eventually close the deal.

Leads

Finding a new customer is the goal of many Web sites. Similar to offline sales, Web sites looking for leads attract visitors that eventually buy elsewhere, but those visitors tend to switch channels far earlier in the sales process. When someone walks into your home improvement store with a printout of the Web page with the snow blower's model number and price, you are making an offline sale. Someone who downloads your article on the difference between snow blowers and electric snow shovels is a lead. Many corporate sites exist entirely to generate leads, such as consulting firms, construction contractors, or other companies that normally bid a custom service for each customer.

"LEADS R US:" ARE YOU AN AFFILIATE MARKETER?

Often leads are handled within the same company, but they can be passed to other companies, too. A special kind of business, called an **affiliate marketer**, exists solely to create leads for other businesses. Affiliates are usually paid based on sales (typically online sales), but their goal is the same as other lead-passing Web sites: to get a customer interested in a product and close the sale elsewhere.

Although some offline businesses work in similar ways to affiliates, affiliate marketing has really grown up on the Web. Pioneered by Amazon, affiliate marketing provides a way for a retailer or manufacturer to attract traffic from other Web sites (the affiliates) by setting up financial compensation for affiliates to send prospective customers their way. Amazon has since renamed its affiliates **associates**, but the name *affiliate* has stuck to describe this unique form of Web marketing.

An **affiliate program** is created by the **affiliate program sponsor** (the retailer or manufacturer) to enroll companies such as yours as affiliates, providing you with links to place on your Web site. When your visitor clicks your affiliate link, the visitor is taken to the program sponsor's Web site, where they might purchase one of the sponsor's products.

Depending on the terms of the affiliate program, that visitor's click might cause you, the affiliate, to get paid for directing the visitor through the affiliate link. Most affiliate programs, however, require more. Most programs pay commissions on online sales made to any visitor that you sent. A few pay for leads, such as when the visitor you supplied provides contact information (name, phone number, e-mail address, and so on).

To succeed at affiliate marketing, you typically must build a strong information site, attracting visitors on specialized subjects with your interesting content. The best affiliate marketing sites draw a crowd with their information and sell products related to those same subjects. StarTrek.com is a successful Amazon affiliate that has newsletters, interviews, movie capsules, and lots of other interesting information for "Trekkers." While looking at a movie capsule, however, readers also see discreet Buy It Now buttons for videos and DVDs that link directly to the Amazon product pages. StarTrek.com clearly has unique information that attracts a core audience who sometimes purchase products. If your site presents merely warmed-over product information cribbed from the program sponsor, you might have trouble attracting search traffic, because search engines go to great lengths to lower your rankings for transactional queries.

If you think about it from the searcher's perspective, it makes sense for Yahoo! and other search engines to lower affiliate rankings for those queries. If a searcher is seeking a specific product, the product's manufacturer and well-known retailers for that product are the best matches. An affiliate link to one of those retailers is not a great match, because the searcher has to click through the affiliate link to get to the retail site that could have been directly shown in the search results. In other words, why show the affiliate site when Yahoo! can show the program sponsor's site directly?

So, if you are an affiliate marketer, don't try to compete with your program's sponsor on transactional search traffic. Instead, opt for the kind of content that your sponsor does not provide, such as impartial product reviews, usage tips, or some other angle that is hard to find. Then target informational queries with your search marketing strategy. When you get the visitors to your site, enough of them will click through your affiliate links if the products appeal strongly to your audience.

Regardless of how the sale is closed, the main distinction between a lead and an offline sale is when in the sales process the customer switches to the offline channel. Customers who do online research and immediately switch offline are leads, whereas customers who know the model number and the sale price walking into the store are offline sales.

You need a different search marketing strategy to handle customers who switch earlier in the process. Using the terminology developed in Chapter 4, businesses seeking leads should optimize their sites for informational rather than transactional queries, because leads-oriented Web sites are optimized for the early online research part of the sales cycle. If you are selling above-ground swimming pools, your prospective customers do not know the name or number of the exact model they want. This might be the only time they ever buy one in their lives. They *cannot* enter a transactional search query until after they have entered an informational query and done a lot of research. You want to snag those customers early in the process and sell them when they are doing their initial research. So, articles favorably comparing above-ground pools to in-ground pools (they are less expensive, they can be disassembled and moved to a new home, they require less maintenance, and so on) will attract customers who are still deciding what kind of pool they want—those informational searchers.

If one of your site's goals is identifying leads, you want to concentrate on techniques for attracting informational searchers, although well-known companies also need to pay attention to navigational queries. As with offline sales sites, measuring sales can be tricky for sites generating leads. In Chapter 6, we show several techniques for judging your lead-passing Web site's success.

Market Awareness

Telling your story is at least a secondary goal for every organization's Web site, but lots of Web sites exist almost solely to enhance brand image. If your company sells children's cereal, the games you put on your site do not have any direct impact on sales, but they might create loyal little consumers tagging along with their parents in the grocery aisle. Many low-priced consumer goods companies have Web sites to raise awareness. Entertainment sites for current movies have a like purpose.

If you have a site designed mainly for market awareness, you might emphasize contests, quizzes, games, or other ways of generating interaction with your visitors. But some market awareness sites are changing in subtle ways. Movie sites, for example, frequently do some Web sales (for the soundtrack, for instance) or they link to Moviefone or Fandango to directly sell tickets at the proverbial theater near you. Cereal sites are starting to sell DVDs, action figures, and other toys on top of the free interactive games.

If your site exists mainly for awareness, do not overlook opportunities for Web sales of other products, but make sure that your site fulfills the awareness need first. Cereal sites that spend too much time amusing children with games might upset a mom who wants to learn more about the cereal's nutritional content.

Regardless of what your awareness site is trying to do, your search strategy focuses mostly on navigational searches. Cap'n Crunch cereal mostly gets searches (from kids or moms) for "capncrunch" or even "captain crunch," but not for the specific games or action figures on the site (unless they have an ad campaign for them). Searchers will be typing in the name of the cereal, the name of the movie, or other brand names.

Market awareness sites are also more likely to be "trendy" than sites with other purposes, because they are great places to start "buzz" about a product (movies are again a good example).

Because it can take a while to get organic search engine results (you must design and optimize your pages and wait for search spiders to find them), market awareness sites often benefit from paid placement techniques, as discussed in Chapter 3, "How Search Marketing Works."

Information and Entertainment

Informing people is a basic goal of any Web site, but some sites exist for that sole purpose. During the Web's "Content is King" phase in the late 1990s, many sites arose offering visitors just another form of media, much like TV or magazines. Some of these sites are adjuncts to offline media, such as CNN's Web site or *Sports Illustrated*'s. These sites exist in part to increase market awareness of the mother ship, as discussed earlier. However, an information and entertainment site can also be an end in itself, existing only to provide information on a particular subject.

Your information and entertainment business might be based on a combination of ad revenue and premium subscriptions, for content that is not available to the general public. CBS MarketWatch is a good example of such a site, with business news available to everyone, but "premium products" that offer more exclusive analysis or investment management tools to subscribers. Many interactive game sites offer some free games, but offer multiplayer games by subscription only.

The few well-known information and entertainment sites, such as ESPN, should focus on navigational queries, but informational queries are the lifeblood of all information and entertainment sites. MarketWatch might capture new visitors with its breaking business news, but makes a profit on premium services. Similarly, game sites might capture traffic for a "multiplayer games" query, but they make money only through subscriptions.

Because the queries for information and entertainment sites are so varied and so topical, paid search often does not pay off. Organic search optimization techniques can be built in to the process of creating each news story and the search engines learn that these sites change quickly and the spider visits frequently.

One specific paid search service is of interest to information and content sites. As discussed in Chapter 3, Google AdSense and similar services can place contextual advertisements on your site's pages that relate to the content of each page. Whereas other kinds of sites *buy* contextual ads as part of their search marketing mix, information and entertainment sites *sell* them, with search engines acting as a broker between the buyers and sellers.

Persuasion

Changing someone's mind about an issue or a behavior is the primary goal of an ever-increasing number of Web sites. These information-oriented sites exist not to make money, but rather to persuade people to do something: give to charity, vote for someone, stop smoking, donate blood, or volunteer to be a Big Brother. All of these causes have Web sites that try to persuade people to particular point of view. Increasingly, Web sites are an integral part of any public relations or political campaign, and are also critical to charitable organizations. If your Web site falls into this category, you are probably trying to influence public opinion or to help people with a particular problem.

Influencing Public Opinion

The Web is fast becoming the tool of choice in influencing opinions. Shallow TV ads are losing credibility with citizens and are increasingly being used to direct people to Web sites for more information, as shown in Figure 5-3. These Web sites are written to persuade people to a point of view, with calls to action that differ somewhat from those of businesses. Obviously navigational queries are important to campaigns with TV and other media ad campaigns, but all of these sites emphasize informational queries, focusing on the best search words ("springfield school budget" or "iraq war") to attract visitors.

Figure 5-3   Competing persuasion sites. Burning public issues more and more are argued by competing pro and con sites on the Web.

These influencer sites are not selling a product, but they can function the same way that lead-passing Web sites do, by moving the visitor to deeper involvement. If you are running a political campaign Web site, you can offer e-mail newsletters, forms to volunteer as a campaign worker, or the ability to donate money.

Usually, nonprofit organizations try to influence public opinion, but sometimes for-profit businesses do it, too. Verizon might want to dampen public support for workers on strike. Wal-Mart wants public support for building stores in new areas.

However, most opinion influencers are indeed nonprofit organizations. Many are political campaigns, both candidates for public office and other ballot initiatives. Bond issues, school budgets, and other ballot questions are more and more being argued by dueling pro and con sites on the Web. Other sites mobilize public opinion against government actions, ranging from anti-war sites to those opposed to building that expensive new sports stadium.

No matter what the cause, influencing opinion is a different kind of goal than driving sales. Online sales are a snap to measure, but with public opinion it is quite hard to know how successful you have been. How can you tell that a voter cast a ballot for your candidate? And how can you tell it is because of your Web site? Usually, you cannot tell, but you *can* use surrogates that help you measure effectiveness, much the way offline sales and leads can be tied to Web activities. Your Web site can use calls to action (sign our petition, join Citizens for Kerry, volunteer to stuff envelopes, sign up for our e-mail newsletter, and so forth) that can be counted to plot your progress.

Public relations campaigns are also different in their duration. Selling a product is usually a long-term effort—you can build your brand over the years. But PR campaigns sometimes last only a few weeks; you must ramp up quickly and might abruptly stop (on election day, for example). Traditional organic search optimization might start up too slowly to get the quick traffic boost you need. In contrast, paid search marketing (as discussed in Chapter 3) can be started at a moment's notice and can be turned off the instant it is no longer needed (such as when your candidate withdraws from the race). The immediacy of paid search (at start and finish) makes it an appealing technique for influencing public opinion when time is of the essence.

Helping People

Charitable organizations have goals that are the hardest to measure of all. How can you tell whether people stop smoking, much less whether they did so because of your Web site? Just as with the influencer sites previously discussed, calls to action can serve as surrogates for your real goal and help you track something measurable. Evan Balzer, the Director of Market Research and Internet Operations for Guideposts (the publisher of the inspirational magazine of the same name), says that "helping those in need" is a primary goal of their Web site (www.guideposts.org), but that they are also beginning to attract volunteers and donors to their organization.

Obviously, raising money and becoming a volunteer are major calls to action, but there are many others. Organizations frequently measure themselves on the basis of information distributed, so the success metrics might be the number of pages viewed, papers downloaded, or free subscriptions ordered. Balzer notes that Guideposts tracks the number of downloads of their inspirational material as a key measure of their success in helping people who come to their site.

Like other persuasion-oriented sites, charities must emphasize informational queries, because that is what people at their point of need will use. You can see how "stop smoking" and "lung cancer" would be important targets for the American Cancer Society. But such a well-known organization must also consider its ranking for navigational queries such as "cancer society."

Unlike quick PR campaigns that benefit from paid search techniques, helping organizations typically have long-term missions wherein slow and steady work in organic search optimization of informational queries yield great results. Organic approaches are usually less expensive, too, so it fits more easily into constrained charity budgets.

HOW DO I JUGGLE SEVERAL GOALS FOR MY SITE?

Your Web site might have multiple goals—many do. IBM has some products (server accessories and software upgrades) that it sells online to customers, many other products (mainframe servers and business consulting) it sells offline, and some (servers with industry software) that it sells by passing leads to resellers. Like most companies, IBM also wants to create market awareness for its "e-business" and "on-demand" campaigns. How does IBM juggle all of these goals?

IBM, like most large businesses, has lots of goals, but each individual area usually has only one or two. Typically goals do not conflict—if you provide comparison and benefit information for informational queries (that you might close offline or by passing a lead), you can still provide transactional information, too. Different queries are chosen by searchers to satisfy different goals, and they can satisfy different goals for you, too. As Figure 5-4 shows, you can provide overlapping information and use linking to make different kinds of information available. You can help information seekers to either buy online or to switch channels to make transactions.

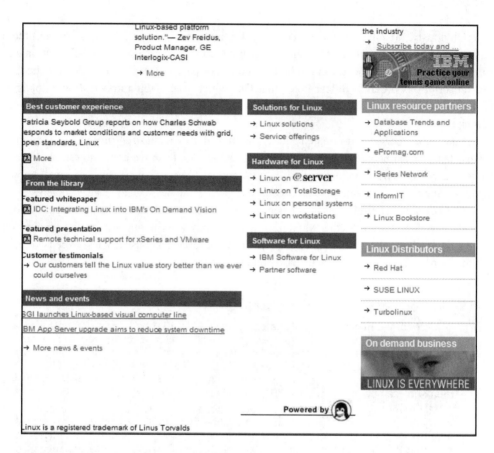

Figure 5-4   Juggling multiple goals. You can provide overlapping information and use linking to make different kinds of information available.

Summary

Every Web site is created for a purpose, most for more than one. As time passes, however, we sometimes lose sight of why the Web site exists. It is critical that you, the search marketer, keep in mind the overarching goals of your Web site so that you choose the appropriate search marketing strategy. Remember also that no Web site stands still—goals can and do change as the years go by. You must regularly examine your goals and choose a search marketing strategy to match.

This chapter examined many different site goals, ranging from all varieties of sales and marketing to information and entertainment. You learned how to identify your site's goals and what kinds of searches will be used to find your site, as summarized in Table 5-2.

Table 5-2 Site Goals and Search Strategies (Your Web site's goals drive the types of queries and search approaches you must emphasize.)

Web Site Goal	Search Query Type			Search Marketing Approaches
	Navigational	Informational	Transactional	
Web sales	Medium	Medium	High	Organic and paid
Offline sales	Medium	Medium	High	Organic and paid
Leads	Medium	High	Low	Organic and paid
Market awareness	High	Low	Low	Emphasis on paid
Information and entertainment	Low	High	Low	Emphasis on organic
Persuasion	Medium	High	Low	Organic and paid

Chapter 6 examines how to use your site's goals to measure success, setting the stage for measuring your success specifically in search marketing.

Measure Your Web Site's Success

Search marketing is not an end in itself. The purpose of search marketing is to drive traffic to your site so your site can reach its goals. Before you can concentrate on search marketing, however, you need to know how to measure your Web site's success. Only by measuring your site's success can you prove the business case for search marketing.

Beyond the business case, metrics are important to *any* activity that you intend to continuously improve. Management guru Peter Drucker's famous quote, "If you can't measure it, you can't manage it," could easily have been coined for the Web, where seemingly *everything* is measurable. Metrics are the lifeblood of any ongoing marketing campaign, including search marketing. In the preceding chapter, we looked at your Web site's goals. Now we show how you measure success at achieving those goals. This chapter covers the following topics:

- *Counting conversions*. Every time a visitor achieves your Web site's goal (buying something, entering contact information, donating to your campaign, and so on), you have converted that person from a mere visitor to someone having a new relationship with your organization (a customer, a lead, a donor, and so forth). The first step in measurement is to identify what the right conversions are for your business and to accurately count them.

- *Counting visitors*. Just knowing the number of conversions does not tell you enough. What you really want to know is what percentage of visitors you convert. You can figure that out only by carefully counting visitors, too.

- *Counting dollars*. The most persuasive thing to count is dollars—the extra revenue you earn due to search engine marketing. You can learn to translate into dollars the impact of every visitor who converts, using those dollars as justification for your search marketing efforts.

Even if you are not really a "numbers person," you can learn to quantify what visitors do into extra revenue for you. Let's start with most critical site metric by counting conversions of your visitors.

Count Your Conversions

It all goes back to the goals you laid out in Chapter 5, "Identify Your Web Site's Goals." Depending on what your goal is, you measure success in different ways. You might hear sales sites discussing how to **monetize** search—to convert your search results into its business impact in dollars. We look at each of the goals discussed in Chapter 5 and determine what visitor outcome you should measure for your business. We call these successful visitor outcomes **conversions**. After we take a close look at what conversions are, we explore which conversions make sense for each kind of business.

Conversion is a sales term that refers to converting prospects into customers, and you might often hear about a business raising its **conversion rate**, the ratio of "lookers" to "buyers." For a Web sales business, you can think of the conversion rate as the number of visitors divided by the number of orders. Raising the sales conversion rate means that you book more sales with the same number of folks coming into the "store" (your Web site). Table 6-1 shows how to calculate your Web site's conversion rate.

Table 6-1   Calculating the Sales Conversion Rate. Dividing the number of orders (buyers) by the number of visits (lookers) yields the conversion rate.

	September
Number of orders	4,000
Divided by: Number of Web visits	100,000
Conversion rate	4%

We can use the concept of conversion more broadly than just for sales. There is no reason you cannot apply the same kind of conversion rate calculation to *any* goal for your Web site. Instead of discussing only sales conversions, you can track **Web conversions**, any Web activity that can be counted as reaching your site's goal.

In Chapter 5, we showed that every Web site has a goal for its visitors to achieve, which we are now calling a Web conversion. In this chapter, we measure the effectiveness of each site by **counting** its Web conversions. For example, your Web site's goal might be creating as many leads to an offline channel as possible. Perhaps you have placed a form on your Web site that enables visitors to provide their contact information, which gets routed to your offline sales force. You can treat each completed contact form as a Web conversion, and you can calculate your Web conversion rate as shown in Table 6-2.

Table 6-2 Calculating the Web Conversion Rate. Dividing the number of leads (completed forms) by the number of visits yields the conversion rate.

	December
Number of leads	7,500
Divided by: Number of Web visits	100,000
Conversion rate	7.5%

Now that you understand the concept of Web conversions, we can examine the same list of Web site goals that we covered in Chapter 5 and see how you can measure Web conversions for each one.

Web Sales

If the goal you chose for your site in Chapter 5 is Web sales, the conversion metric you should count is the number of Web orders taken by your site. To analyze what a visitor is doing on his way to becoming one of your "conversions," we again turn to the Web Conversion Cycle methodology introduced in Chapter 4, "How Searchers Work."

We first looked at a visitor behavior model for a Web sales site in Chapter 4, and we show it again here as Figure 6-1. The Web Conversion Cycle models how visitors use your site, as each activity leads to the next one. Visitors might set out to Learn more about a need or problem they have and what solutions there are. Once informed, they can narrow their choices to a particular kind of solution to Shop for a specific product, comparing prices and features, perhaps. After they identify the best product, they are ready to Buy the product, and then wait to Get it before they can Use it.

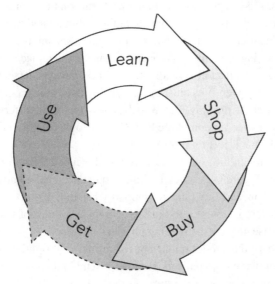

Figure 6-1 A behavior model for personal computer sales. Visitors satisfy their information needs before buying, and then return for technical support.

There is nothing terribly hard to understand about any of these steps, and it might exactly fit the kinds of products you sell. For example, a personal computer fits this model quite well. Customers start out not really knowing what to buy—there are laptops and desktops, and there are even different kinds of desktops that actually sit on your desk or "towers" that go under your desk. Most people need to Learn more about what is out there before they even know what category of computer is right for them, and they can do that right on your Web site, if you have this kind of information available for them.

After the customer has chosen a particular category, such as a laptop, she needs to decide which one. She must analyze Dell versus ThinkPad versus Apple, and she must also make decisions about operating systems, weight, battery life, screen resolution, memory, disk space, and lots of other features. These are all the tasks that shoppers go through while they Shop for a computer, and they are increasingly done on the Web. If you are a retailer, you can provide objective information for all the brands you carry, and manufacturers can differentiate their wares against their competitor's.

After she has narrowed down her choices to just a few, she begins thinking about whether to Buy. She starts to think about where she can get the lowest price and the fastest shipping for one of the models that she wants. The Web is also a great place to do this, if you have designed your site to make it easy to compare prices (including shipping) for different models and if you explain shipping options and any special offers that are available.

After purchasing, she wants an e-mail confirmation. While waiting to Get her computer, she can check the status of the order at any time right on the Web site. If she has chosen express delivery, you can help her track the package through UPS or any other shipper, also right on the Web. Because most of the Get interaction occurs off-Web, we show that step using dotted lines in Figure 6-1.

The moment she receives her computer, she can begin to Use it. She can install it and get right to work. As she does, she can get answers to her problems on the manufacturer's Web site. She might sometimes have trouble throughout the life of the computer and come back to get technical support. If the manufacturer has done a good job in support, she might at some point want to upgrade her computer by adding more memory, or she might want to replace her computer with a new model, in which case she begins to Learn all over again as she considers a new purchase.

This example shows why Web sites must be designed with customers in mind—customers might use the Web every step of the way. But *your* business might be different than PCs. You might need different steps in *your* version of the Web Conversion Cycle. Read on to design your own Web Conversion Cycle that is just right for your business.

What if you have a pure online business, where you download the software that you sell? Your model might look like Figure 6-2, which is similar to the personal computer model, where customers need to Learn, Shop, and Buy (and get support when they Use it), but there is no truly distinct Get step—the software is downloaded to their computer as part of the Buy step. So, no order status is needed because no package is being physically shipped.

It is also possible that your model might not require any substantial post-sales support, such as an e-book store. In that case, your model might resemble the one in Figure 6-3, where (after the Buy step) your customers do not return to your Web site until they need to consider their next purchase.

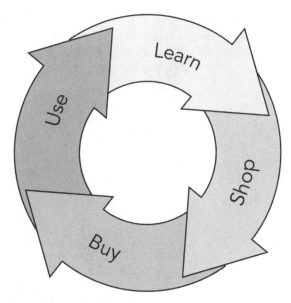

Figure 6-2 A behavior model for a software download store. For pure online businesses, there really is no distinct Get step.

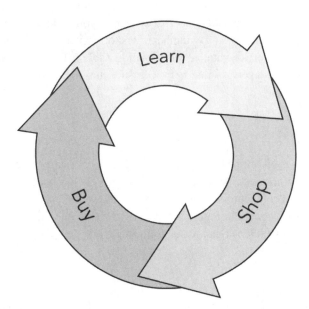

Figure 6-3 A behavior model for an e-book store. Products that require no post-sales support might not require an explicit Use step.

In Figure 6-4, we show how a Web bookstore might operate, where you physically ship your product (requiring a Get step) but usually have no post-purchase customer interactions until the next buying opportunity.

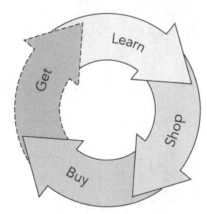

Figure 6-4   A behavior model for a book store. A Get step is required, but no Use step because no post-sales support is required.

Regardless of which version of the Web Conversion Cycle is right for your Web sales business, it is simple for you to calculate your success. The same e-Commerce system that takes your customer's order can count the number of sales that you make from your site, and your Web traffic metrics system can count the number of visitors to your site. You use these two numbers to calculate your conversion rate, as was shown in Table 6-1 earlier. Later in this chapter, we show you how your conversion rate helps measure the impact of your search marketing campaign in dollars.

Offline Sales

If your business focuses on offline sales, you need to take special care in deciding what to count as Web conversions. Offline sales businesses have visitor behavior models that closely resemble those of their Web sales competitors, except that some steps occurs offline—often through face-to-face interaction or by phone. In Figure 6-5, we use the example of an automobile manufacturer, and we depict offline interactions with the customer with dotted lines.

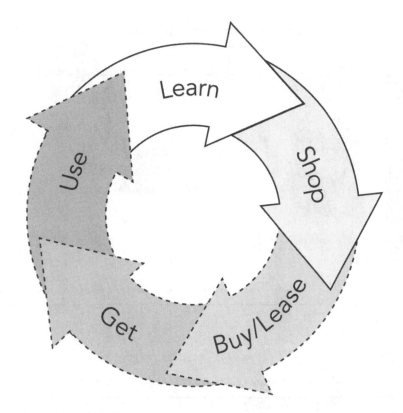

Figure 6-5 A behavior model for an automobile manufacturer. In some models, visitors move offline after the early research stages.

For offline sales, just as for Web sales, the customer needs to Learn about what kinds of cars are available, because so many choices exist (and they increase each year). People do not buy cars every year, and they typically do a lot of research on the Web before making a decision.

Increasingly, people are starting to Shop for a new car on the Web. If your customers typically walk into a dealer showroom with a Web printout of exactly what they want, they have actually completed the Shop step on the Web. Figure 6-6 shows how Cadillac does it, but most auto manufacturers have similar facilities. If your Web site does not offer this capability, *your* Web Conversion Cycle would show the Shop step with dotted lines because your goal is to shift your customers to offline channels following the Learn step.

Simple steps that lead to an offline purchase.

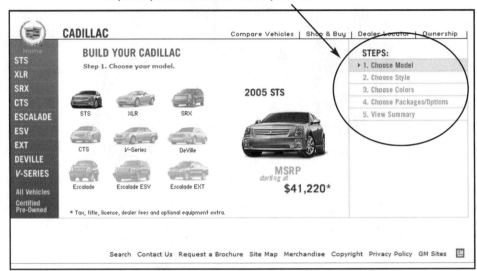

After the choices are made, shift the Buy/Lease steps to an offline dealer.

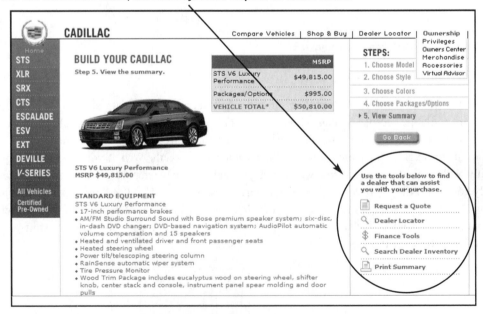

Figure 6-6   Shop for a Cadillac on the Web. Cadillac's site lets you "build" your Cadillac and present the result to a dealer for purchase.

Relatively few cars are actually purchased on the Web, so the model in Figure 6-5 shows the Buy/Lease step in dotted lines, emphasizing that it happens offline. It is possible that this step might shift to the Web at some point in the future, with customers dropping by the dealer to Get their new car, but most customers still haggle and purchase in person today.

Customers still Get their cars at the dealer and return to the dealer (or elsewhere) for maintenance while they Use their cars, with relatively little interaction with your Web site, so these steps are shown as offline, too.

Although Web sales and offline sales share significant similarities, one crucial difference exists: It is easy to know how many visitors to your Web site also bought your product on your Web site, but it is a lot harder to accurately measure offline sales driven by the Web. No matter what you do, you will never have perfect measurements, but there are some basic ways to tie offline sales to the Web:

- *Provide a special phone number.* If your goal is to shift Web visitors to your call center to take the order by phone, you can use some simple tricks to tie the call to your Web site, such as displaying a phone number that appears only on your Web site and is not used in TV or print ads or any other materials. That way, anyone who uses that number must have come from your site. A variant on this is to call your regular number but advise them to "Ask for Operator 123" or "Ask for Alice." (Not all of your visitors will do this, however, so you might have them "Ask for Alice to receive a free mouse pad with your computer.")

- *Call them.* You can provide a form on your Web site that lets Web visitors complete their contact information so you can call them. IBM has had success with a Call Me Now button. When the button is clicked, the customer is prompted to supply a phone number, and an IBM telephone salesperson calls the customer within a few minutes.

- *Bring this printout.* As you saw in Figure 6-6, Cadillac encourages customers to select the color and options for their car before coming to the dealer. The dealer can note any customer who brought in that printout for tracking purposes. If your product does not require extensive customization, you could provide an online coupon for a freebie or a discounted price the customer can print and bring to the store.

- *Request for quote.* Cadillac's Web site also demonstrates an RFQ capability, where the car the customer "built" can be shown to a local dealer who prices it. The customer needs to fill out contact information to receive the quote, so any sales made to this customer can then be accurately tracked as assisted by the Web site.

If, as you read this list, you are thinking that these techniques are excellent goals for your Web conversion rate, you are catching on! Your Web traffic metrics system can count the number of visitors who come to the site, and you can also count how many visitors reach each of these goals. Your Web traffic metrics system can count how many folks click a Call Me Now button, or print out a form, or request a quote, but you need to take steps in your call center procedures to ensure that your Web callers are accurately logged. No matter what the right technique is for your business, you can calculate your Web conversion rate as shown in Table 6-3.

Table 6-3   Web Conversion for Offline Sales Sites (You can track different Web conversion rates for each goal you have for your site.)

December Out of 100,000 Visitors, How Many . . .	Number of Web Visitors Converted	Web Conversion Rate
Called a special phone number?	10,000	10%
Brought discount coupon to a dealer?	3,000	3%
Requested an online quote?	1,000	1%

However, your Web conversion rate still needs to be expressed in terms of dollars. That's why it is critical to choose Web conversions that can be linked to offline sales, as we have in these examples. Your offline procedures must ensure that call center operators log each call accurately or that dealers report the printouts brought in, for example. By doing so, you ensure accurate sales reporting, because if you track these events in your sales reporting system, you will learn how much of your sales derive from the Web, as shown in Table 6-4.

Table 6-4   Web Conversions for Offline Sales (You can track different Web conversion rates for each goal you have for your site.)

December Web Average Order: $2,000	Conversion Conversions	Sales Offline Rate	Sales Orders	Revenue
Special phone number	10,000	1%	100	$200,000
Discount coupon	3,000	10%	300	$600,000
Online quote	1,000	10%	100	$200,000
Totals	14,000	3.6%	500	$1,000,000

If you examine Table 6-3 and 6-4 together, you can begin to see how to measure the impact of your Web site in terms of sales, even though your site makes no direct sales. By creating a way to tie the offline sales back to the Web site, you can see that your site was the catalyst for $1 million in sales in December. You can also calculate your *sales* conversion rate (not your Web conversion rate) for your Web visitors as shown in Table 6-5.

Table 6-5   Sales Conversion Rate for Offline Sales (You can track your offline sales conversion by dividing offline orders by total Web visitors.)

	December
Number of offline orders	500
Divided by: Number of Web visits	100,000
Sales conversion rate	0.5%

When you can measure the conversions of your Web site, you can do a little math to express your goals in purely monetary terms. Table 6-6 shows how to monetize each Web conversion so that you know the value to your business.

Table 6-6   Web Conversions in Terms of Revenue (You can calculate, on average, how much each and every Web conversion is worth.)

December Average Order: $2,000	Web Conversions	Sales Revenue	Sales Revenue per Conversion
Special phone number	10,000	$200,000	$20
Discount coupon	3,000	$600,000	$200
Online quote	1,000	$200,000	$200

This table tells you that every time your Web site persuades someone to call on the phone, it is worth about $20 in revenue, whereas printing discount coupons or requesting quotes are worth about $200 each. When you understand this, you can see how improving your Web site so that more visitors take these actions can directly affect your sales.

These examples show how, even for an offline sales site, you can tie your Web conversions to your true sales. Later in this chapter, we show how to build on these calculations to measure the dollar impact of your search marketing efforts.

WHAT IF I CAN'T TRACK MY OFFLINE SALES BACK TO MY WEB SITE?

Don't worry. If you have no systems in place that enable you to track your offline sales back to your Web site, all is not lost. After all, it is not that hard to set up special phone numbers or print discount coupons. But maybe you cannot get your organization to take even those minimal steps. If you truly cannot track actual sales instigated by the Web, the next-best thing is to estimate them. How to go about that estimating depends on your business (as always), but there are a few possibilities.

- *Ask customers when they buy.* If you close most of your sales on the phone, add a question to the call center script to ask customers whether they used your Web site before calling.
- *Update your warranty cards.* If your product already requires the return of a warranty card, change your questions to ask about use of your Web site.
- *Add a question to a survey.* Your business might regularly survey your customers. Add one question to the survey to see whether customers used the Web site before their last purchase.

None of these methods are as scientific as tracking actual sales, but they are better than nothing. After you choose your estimation method, the number that you calculate can be used in the rest of our formulas to estimate sales conversion rates and any other statistic. You can also use estimates to perform trend analysis, checking the ups and downs month to month. If possible, however, you should try to eventually implement systems that accurately track sales.

Leads

Web sites designed to generate leads can measure their conversions in much the same way as sites that generate offline sales. Let's first examine a typical behavior model for a leads site, in this case a swimming pool dealer, in Figure 6-7.

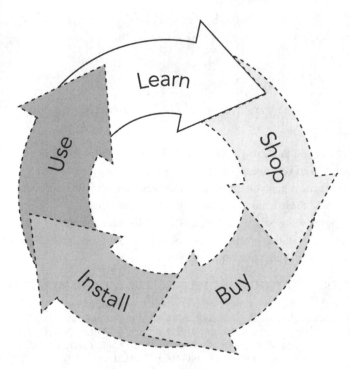

Figure 6-7   A behavior model for a swimming pool dealer. Some models shift offline quickly in the sales process.

The first thing that you notice is all those dotted lines! For the typical lead-oriented site, visitors Learn on the Web site, but tend to do everything else offline. For customers looking for a swimming pool, they want to get information about whether to choose above-ground or in-ground pools on the Web. When a customer begins to Shop for a specific pool, however, he needs a dealer to come to his house and tell him what it costs to be installed in his backyard. Similarly, the Buy, Install, and Use steps all occur offline, for the most part, although some dealers might have some helpful do-it-yourself pool-maintenance tips on the Web.

If your business is not based on product sales, you might need a different model. Consider how a consulting firm might model visitor activities, as shown in Figure 6-8. This model is different from product-oriented businesses. In product-oriented businesses, the products are largely offered as is (or can be somewhat customized), whereas a customer requiring consulting services is focused on explaining the problem to suppliers so they can solve it.

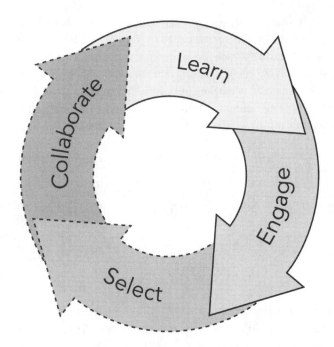

Figure 6-8 A behavior model for a consulting firm. Highly customized services require a model focused on agreeing on the service being provided.

Consulting customers need to Learn about their problem so they can understand what kinds of solutions can be provided, but they quickly move to Engage with a few possible consultants. The Engage step typically includes a Request for Proposal (RFP), in which customers describe their specific situations. The Engage step is more frequently being executed online, as customers describe their problems and provide contact information in Web forms. The Select step, in which the customer receives written responses to the RFP and selects a consultant to work with, is almost always done offline, as is the engagement itself, during which the consultant and the customer Collaborate to solve the problem. Successful consulting firms make it a point to use engagements to teach their customers about other problems they can solve, starting the Learn step all over again.

After you develop the right version of the Web Conversion Cycle for your lead-oriented Web site, you are faced with the question of how to measure its success. Although methods can vary from business to business, it is usually easier to measure leads than offline sales. **Lead management** systems help your business store contact information for each visitor who fills in his contact information, and they help track the progress of that lead all the way through to a sale. So, the easiest way to measure your site is to ensure that your Web contact form (the one that all leads fill out) is connected to your lead management system. When it is, your lead management system will track the number of leads submitted from the Web, and will show you exactly which sales resulted. You can use this information to calculate the value of each lead, as shown in Table 6-7.

Table 6-7   The Value of Leads (You can calculate the average worth of each lead as well as the Web conversion and sales conversion rates.)

December Average Order: $2,000	Total	Conversion Rate	Sales Revenue per Event
Web visitors	100,000	100%	$20
Web leads	2,000	2%	$1,000
Orders from Web leads	1,000	1%	$2,000

You can divide total sales (in this case, $2 million) by the number of orders to determine that the average order size is $2,000. Using the same logic, you can divide sales by the number of leads to learn that each lead is worth an average of $1,000. This calculation shows you the value of improving your Web site to drive more and more leads. Similarly, if you take the same calculation back one more step, you can divide total sales by the number of Web visitors to see that each visitor to your Web site is worth about $20. Later in the chapter, we show how to use these calculations to put together your business case for search engine marketing.

Market Awareness

Because their goal of "raising awareness" for a product is so nebulous, it is critical that market awareness sites carefully choose exactly what to count as their Web conversion metric. If you take care in designing your Web site to drive to specific Web conversions, you *can* calculate measurements that can show the value of your market awareness Web site.

Figure 6-9 shows a specific example of a market awareness site for a children's cereal. The Web site is promoted on the cereal box itself and in TV ads for the cereal, leading kids to Discover the Web site. Once there, they Engage by reading stories and playing games that reinforce the brand as fun for kids. The goal of the site is to get kids to Enroll in a club by providing their mailing address. Club members are mailed a monthly newsletter with fun games for the kids, action figures to buy, and cereal discount coupons for their parents. Because most cereal companies sell multiple cereals, the Enroll step might also trigger mail solicitations for other kids' cereal clubs, starting the cycle again.

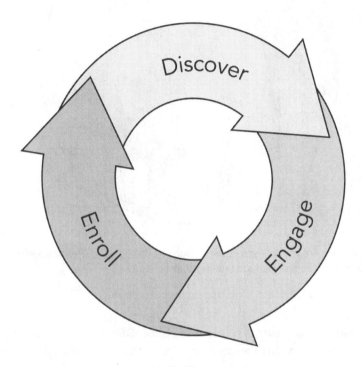

Figure 6-9   A behavior model for a children's cereal. The Web site is used to form deeper relationships with children who influence parents to buy.

You are probably getting the idea by now. You can track club enrollments as your Web conversion and coupon redemption as your sales conversion. After tracking for a while, you might find that club members buy two more boxes of cereal a month than nonmembers, demonstrating the value of the Web site.

Information and Entertainment

Information and entertainment sites frequently derive most of their revenue from advertising, but they often sell premium services, too. For premium service sales, the number of orders is the proper Web conversion metric. You can use the Web Conversion Cycle methodology to model premium services sales, as shown in Figure 6-10.

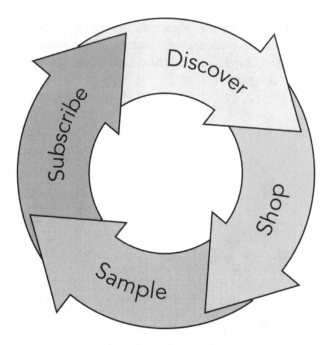

Figure 6-10   A behavior model for a subscription information site. Premium services are constantly marketed with free trial periods leading to purchase.

The first step for these sites is taken when visitors Discover the site, often from a search query, and continues as each visitor returns to the site for free content and discovers that premium services are available. On espn.com, for example, "Insiders" can view exclusive content not available to others. These premium stories are shown alongside the free stories and a sales pitch for Insiders is shown each time a nonmember clicks on them, as shown in Figure 6-11.

Scores are free, but RealTime scores carry the "in" symbol for Insiders only.

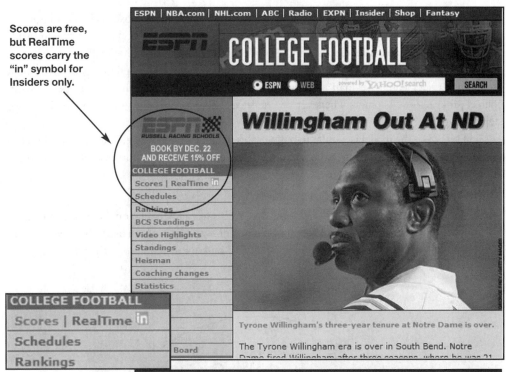

When a nonmember clicks an Insider link, the premium service is described and a chance for a free trial offer displays.

Figure 6-11   Premium services on an information site. ESPN shows Insider premium content alongside free content.

The enticement for ESPN Insider places the visitor in the Shop phase, as he is continually exposed to the value of premium membership each time he sees a link that is exclusive to Insiders. The next step is to entice the visitor to Sample the premium service, typically with a 30-day free trial; visitors Subscribe at the end of that period if they have not explicitly cancelled. Most premium services capture e-mail addresses for the trial period, which they use to periodically contact prospective customers whenever new services become available, beginning the Discover step over again.

In this case, the model is similar to online sales in that the Web conversion and the sales conversion is exactly the same event, so calculating the revenue value of visitors is relatively simple.

Persuasion

So far we have looked only at businesses, but any Web site can benefit from behavior modeling. Figure 6-12 shows a possible model for a political campaign that you can use to both choose and measure your Web conversions. Just as with buyers making a purchase, each voter might go through several steps in response to the candidate.

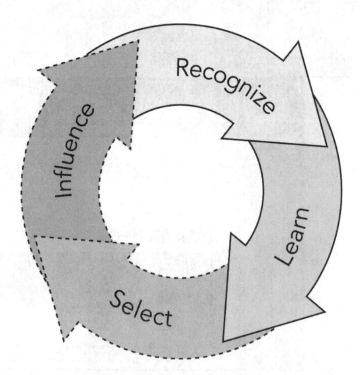

Figure 6-12   A behavior model for a political campaign. Each voter's activity can be modeled throughout the campaign right up until election day.

The first step is for a voter to Recognize the candidate's name, which might happen online (searching for a candidate's name) or offline (seeing the name of the candidate's Web site in a TV ad). At some point, the voter decides to Learn more about the candidate's background and positions on the issues, and comes to the Web site. Voters eventually Select the candidate they will vote for, but this is an offline conversion that cannot be accurately measured before election day. The trick for the Web site is to set up a Web conversion that *can* be measured. That is why the Influence step is so important.

If your Web site can attract people who are willing to influence other people, you can be fairly certain you have their votes locked up. What's more, they might start attracting more supporters. So the best Web conversions for your site might be influencer goals:

- *E-mail a friend.* Provide a function that sends a position paper to someone else with a personal note from your visitor. This goal has the added value of placing the friend's e-mail address in your solicitation database.

- *Volunteer to work for the campaign.* There is never any shortage of work to do, and free labor conserves funding for TV ads and other expenses.

- *Donate to the campaign.* The Web is becoming a powerful force in raising political contributions in the United States, as Howard Dean's 2004 campaign for the Democratic U.S. presidential nomination showed. Dean raised $40 million in just a few months, much of it by accepting contributions right on the Web site.

Other Web conversions besides influencing others might also correlate to racking up votes at the polls, such as subscribing to e-mail newsletters or downloading position papers. Use of the Internet in politics is in its infancy, however, so you might find that you need to experiment. But whether your site is persuading a voter or someone else, you must decide what your Web conversions are so that you can measure your information and entertainment site's effectiveness.

Count Your Traffic

We've spent a lot of time discussing how to measure your Web site's effectiveness at achieving conversions, and each time we do, we talk about visitors to the site. As you have seen, you cannot determine your conversion rate unless you know how many visitors are coming. But how do you count visitors? *That* is what this section explores.

Web metrics experts refer to visitors coming to your Web sites as **traffic**, and the way Web traffic is measured has changed a lot over the years. You need to understand the fundamentals of traffic measurement because it is a critical part of tracking your success.

Page Views

The most fundamental metric in Web measurements is the **page view**, which is just what it sounds like—a count of how many Web pages have been shown to your site's visitors. Web metrics reports always summarize page views for a particular time period, so you can see how many page views occurred in a day, a week, or a month.

By analyzing the trends of page views, you can see whether your views have gone up this month from last month, or from the same month last year. (For a toy retailer, comparing January's page views to those of last January is usually more instructive than comparing to the Christmas-inflated December numbers.)

More importantly, the page views of individual pages can be analyzed, so that you can see which particular pages on your site have been viewed the most, and you can analyze the trends for each page over time.

HOW PAGE VIEWS ARE MEASURED

No search marketing campaign can be measured without counting page views. But despite how simple it is for you to count the page views by your Web browser, it has taken years of evolution for Web metrics systems to accurately count them.

In the early days of the Web, most Web sites were measuring **hits**, the number of computer files that your Web server displayed to your visitors. At the time, this made some sense because most Web pages consisted of text from a single file. If every page consisted of one file, the number of hits was the same as the number of page views. It was easy to count hits, because your Web server writes a record into a **log file** every time it serves a file. Web measurement programs, such as WebTrends, emerged to analyze log files and produce reports summarizing the number of page views. So far, so good.

Unfortunately, by the end of the 1990s, hits had no meaning at all: Almost all pages were complex combinations of multiple text and numerous image files. The hits metric could tell you how many files were shown to visitors, but could not reveal how many actual pages were viewed. Existing Web metrics facilities tried to compensate for this situation with tortured algorithms that estimated "true" page views, sometimes by examining how close together in time the hits were retrieved and which user they were served to. So, if the Web log file showed that eight files (hits) were shown to the same network address in a split second, the metrics facility assumed this was one page view.

But lots of situations caused these algorithms to fail. Large companies with complex server environments served single page views from multiple servers: The company logo image file came from one server and the text from another. Now the metrics programs had to gather up all the log files from *every* company server to see that there were many hits to the same network address at the same time. And even then, the algorithms ran into problems because the servers had their internal clocks set slightly differently, so you could not tell how close together the hits actually were!

In addition, all America Online customers (more than 25 percent of many Web sites' visitors) appeared to be coming from a small range of network addresses from somewhere in Virginia—the addresses of AOL's servers. So, the metrics programs could not tell which hits were for one visitor versus another—several at a time shared the same network address because they were routed to your site from the AOL server's network address.

So, the algorithms were failing both because they could not gather together all the hits from multiple Web servers with valid times, and because they could not tell which hits went to which visitors. It was clear that a new approach was needed. Variously known as "single-pixel tracking" or "Web beacons," this technique depends on you adding a one-pixel image file to each Web page on your site. When each page is served to a visitor, the hit for this unnoticed image is stored in your Web log file and can be counted as a surrogate for a page view.

Most Web metrics programs can use this technique today, and that ensures the accuracy of your page view metrics. If your metrics package still does page view estimates based on hit algorithms, you might want to invest in a better package.

Visits and Visitors

More interesting than analyzing page views is examining just who is viewing those pages. Most Web metrics programs can identify a series of pages that have been viewed by the same visitor, by using **cookies**. The Web metrics program "drops" a cookie file on each visitor's computer when she enters the site. This file contains a unique identifier not shared by any other computer's cookie. The Web metrics program reads the identifier from the cookie file each time a page is viewed and remembers which computer viewed that page.

Identifying visitors allows metrics programs to provide you with better information. Now, instead of merely counting page views, you can count the number of **visits** to your site. Visits, called **sessions** by some metrics facilities, let you see how many people are coming, not just how many pages were viewed by all people. For example, 2 Web sites might each show 100 page views, but 1 site has 4 visits with 25 page views each, whereas another might have 10 visits that average 10 views each. If you count just page views, all you know is that 100 pages were viewed. If you count visits, you know that 1 site got 4 visits, but they stayed and looked around for a while, whereas the other site got 10 visits from people who looked at fewer pages in each visit. This information is critical because you cannot get more conversions from more page views— you get more conversions from more visits.

In addition to identifying visits, you can also track the number of **visitors** (sometimes called **unique visitors**), because you can track whether the *same* visitor has returned to your site multiple times. So, the metrics report could show 100 page views in 10 visits by 8 different visitors, because a couple of those 8 visitors had more than 1 visit. This is important, too, because for many Web sites, people tend to visit multiple times before they convert; therefore, knowing the number of *new* versus *returning* visitors can tell you even more than tracking visits alone.

It is true that Web metrics programs accurately count all of these measurements, but it is critical that you use a *single* metrics facility across your entire site. Although small sites would undoubtedly do so, large Web sites with hundreds of thousands of pages might implement different metrics facilities for different parts of the site. If you are in this situation, collecting accurate measurements across your entire site is impossible.

To see why it is impossible, suppose that you have two metrics systems, one used in the sales part of your site and the other in the support area. In this situation, you cannot just add up the number of visitors in each system to get your total, because each system drops a visitor cookie when it sees a new visitor. Any visitor whose visit crosses both sales and support pages will be double counted. It will seem like two separate visits when it was, in fact, one. If you have even more than two systems, the problem is even worse. Double-counting your visits lowers your reported conversion rate and makes your efforts appear less effective than they are, because sales are reported accurately but the number of visitors that created the sales is artificially high.

If you must live with a situation where multiple metrics facilities are used for the same Web site, just keep in mind that the visit and visitor numbers will not be accurate when added up for the total site. It is *still* better to use those inaccurate numbers than to ignore them, because you can perform **trend analysis** on even inaccurate numbers because the inaccuracies are relatively constant. For example, if you add up visitor totals across three separate metrics systems, they will not be right, because some of those "visitors" are actually the *same* folks who headed into different parts of your site. Regardless, if you see that you added up 30 percent more visitors this month than you added up last month, you can probably conclude that *something* good is happening, even though you really cannot be sure that the improvement is actually 30 percent as opposed to 22 percent or 45 percent. It is definitely worth the effort to get to a single metrics system so that your numbers *are* accurate, but do use whatever data you have, no matter how imperfect. It's better than nothing.

Count Your Money

Earlier in this chapter, we spent a lot of time analyzing the behavior model for visitors to your Web site and determining the business value of what they do. You can use that analysis to make the case for investing in search engine marketing. If you are running a political campaign, this section does not apply to you because you cannot justify your spending based on higher revenue. For everyone else, however, this is the section that will get your search marketing campaign funded. Businesses invest money because they can count the revenue that comes in after that investment.

The simplest business case for search engine marketing for any business is this: If they can't find it, they can't buy it. But that will not convince too many green-eyeshade types like your Chief Financial Officer. And, like anything else, a search marketing program requires investment.

So, how do you convince accountants to open the checkbook? Start with the Web Conversion Cycle. Go back to the model you developed earlier in this chapter—the one that best fits your business. No matter what the model, you have chosen what to count as your Web conversions. Maybe yours are simple, because you sell direct on the Web and you just need to count Web orders. Or maybe they are more complicated to track, such as leads or offline sales. But no matter what your conversions are, you can use the formulas presented earlier to place a dollar value on each Web conversion. Check out Table 6-8 for a summary.

Table 6-8   Calculating the Value of Web Conversions (You can calculate the average worth of each Web conversion for any Web site goal.)

Web Site Goal	Formula
Web sales	Total sales ÷ Total orders
Offline sales	Total sales from Web ÷ Total Web conversions
Leads	Total sales from Web ÷ Total leads

Table 6-8 can be simplified even further, because the formula listed for offline sales actually works for any goal. No matter what your goal, if you can count the total sales that came from the Web and you can divide that dollar figure by the total number of Web conversions, you will find the value of each conversion.

Although that is interesting, and useful for showing the value of your Web site, it does not yet justify spending money on search marketing. To make that case, we need to take the model one step further. We need to identify the value of each visitor to the site.

The formula for the value of each visitor is also simple: Divide the total sales from the Web by the total number of visitors. Table 6-7 provides an example of this calculation, where 100,000 visitors come to the site and each visitor was worth about $20. This calculation is the basis of your search engine marketing business case, because the purpose of search engine marketing is to increase the number of visitors to your site. Table 6-9 shows a simple example of how the calculation could work for the site modeled in Table 6-7—the 10 percent rise in traffic yields 10,000 new visitors worth $20 each for a $200,000 increase in revenue, for example.

Table 6-9   Calculating the Value of Increased Traffic (You can calculate the sales impact of additional traffic to your site.)

If Traffic Increases By	Revenue Increases By
5%	$100,000
10%	$200,000
15%	$300,000

If the flinty-eyed accounting types at your business do not need any more than what is shown in Table 6-9, consider yourself lucky and go get the money to start your search marketing campaign. Most businesses, however, need more than this. They need to know exactly how much you are projecting to increase site traffic, and they want to know what it will cost. These are reasonable questions, but we are not yet able to answer them. We will save them for Chapter 7, "Measure Your Search Marketing Success."

Summary

As you saw in Chapter 5, every Web site has a goal—a purpose it was designed to fulfill. Most sites are designed to sell, to inform, to persuade, or some combination of all of them. In this chapter, we explored the various behavior models that apply to Web site visitors, and we showed how to measure what visitors do on your site.

 We looked at several different versions of the Web Conversion Cycle model, each customized for a different Web site. We hope that you developed the appropriate model for your Web site, too. Throughout the rest of this book, we return to the Web Conversion Cycle concept at various points, identifying those passages with the icon shown here.

In this chapter, you also learned how to choose the right events to count (we call them Web conversions), and you now know how to translate those events into revenue dollars. More importantly, you know how to calculate the revenue value of each visitor who comes to your site, forming the basis of the business case of your search marketing campaign.

We are just getting started, however. In Chapter 7, we go beyond existing Web site measurements to a set of new metrics that help you move your organization where it needs to go. We start by assessing where your site stands today and show you the opportunity that you are missing. We build on the calculations we introduced in this chapter to show what search engine marketing is worth to your own Web site.

You probably know that "you get what you measure." In the next chapter, we show you how to track the measurements that prompt the behavior you want. So, say goodbye to generalities. No more theory. Let's put your site under the microscope.

CHAPTER 7

Measure Your Search Marketing Success

It might seem backward to talk about how to measure the impact of your search marketing at this point. After all, don't you do that after the campaign? Well, yes and no. Certainly, you cannot measure what happened until after it has happened, but you must focus on measurements up front to justify the initial investment in search marketing. Unless you can project the value, you will never get that investment funded in the first place.

Defining your search metrics from the beginning helps you justify the investment, and it also focuses your activities. Too often, search marketing is treated as an art rather than a science— a set of arcane incantations that when repeated with fervor (and mixed with eye of newt and toe of frog) will somehow magically lead to success. Nothing could be further from the truth.

Although intuition is a normal part of anything you do, it should be the exception rather than the rule. Without measurable results, you cannot tell a skilled practitioner from a quack, or a successful campaign from a flop. When you painstakingly measure everything you do, you can do more of what works and less of what does not. You make these adjustments every day and gradually improve your results. Intuition can still be important, but even then, informed intuition is the best kind.

Enough philosophy! It's time to roll up your sleeves and get to work. Instead of just listing the search metrics and explaining them to you, we walk you through an example. At the same time, we encourage you to choose your own example—your first search marketing campaign— and work through the measurements in your own business.

In this chapter, we take several steps to understand search metrics:

- *Target your first campaign.* You can always change your mind later, but you will find that choosing the first target for search marketing now will make it easier to study search metrics. Most people find that learning with their first campaign in mind is highly motivating.

- *Assess your current situation*. The first use for search metrics is figuring out what shape you are in right now. Your assessment provides objective evidence of the importance of your search marketing plan—both the overall plan and each piece of the plan. Every task in your plan will be driven by what you find in your assessment. You will finalize your choice for your first search marketing campaign and you will take action based on your own situation.

- *Calculate your opportunity*. Another use for search metrics is "what if" analysis that shows you how well you will be doing after you execute your plan. Although no one can promise exactly what your results will be, you can estimate your outcome to show the potential impact on your organization.

There are many more search metrics than we cover in this chapter, so we return to the subject of metrics in Chapter 15, "Make Search Marketing Operational." In this chapter, however, we focus on the basic metrics required for you to show the business case for search marketing. Your first search marketing campaign is the place to start.

Target Your First Search Marketing Campaign

Before you dive into search metrics, you need to first choose a project to measure. To do so, you must decide the area of your site that you want to drive search traffic to. Which product sale? Which marketing program? A sign-up form? You have to pick something.

You might be saying to yourself, "How should I know where to start search marketing in my business?" Don't worry. It's not as hard as it sounds. And, you can always change your mind. As you read through this chapter, you might realize that you should have started search marketing somewhere else in your organization. If so, just retrace your steps and figure out the new campaign.

To choose your first campaign, go back to the goals of your Web site from Chapter 5, "Identify Your Web Site's Goals." If your site sells online, pick a top-selling product and try to raise sales. If you generate leads for offline sales, choose a hot new product and work on increasing leads. No matter what your site's goals are, you can choose some area of your Web site and declare, "This is the best place to start." After you choose the target area, you will then discover what search queries to target in your campaign.

Choose the Target Area of Your Site

What makes a particular area of your Web site the best place? After all, your first campaign is important. You want it to succeed and to persuade others that it succeeded. To choose your "best place," follow these rules when you make your selection:

- *Pick something high profile*. If you want to get attention with your first campaign, don't pick some sleepy product that no one cares about. If you do, you might execute a great search marketing campaign and still ring up few sales.

- *Make sure the business impact can be measured*. Using the methods outlined in previous chapters, you can measure almost any outcome and place a value on it. But make sure that your organization already has those measurements in place, or that you can put them in place. If your first campaign delivers 50 percent more leads to the sales force, that is great; but it is not so great if no one knows how much a lead is worth. You have obviously succeeded, but it is hard to decide how much to continue to invest. That is a bad thing.

- *Keep it simple.* Your first campaign should not tackle difficult problems that we cover in this book. It is also easier if you avoid areas of your site that already have some paid search activity, because it makes your impact harder to measure. Leave the advanced topics for later and take on something manageable now. When you conduct your assessment, you will get a clue as to how hard your problem might be.

- *Make it practical.* If your top-selling product has a team that is always hopelessly busy with their own plans, maybe you should choose your #2 seller. If your #2 product team is located two time zones away, maybe the #3 team that sits in your building would be your best choice. Think about who maintains the content for your targeted area and pick a group that you can work with easily.

So take some time and think it over. Which part of your Web site offers the best tradeoff between business impact and degree of difficulty? Answer that question and keep that answer in mind as we explore search metrics. As you look deeper into your current situation, you might find that you have chosen a project too difficult for your first one. If so, you will realize it while you read this chapter, and you can always change your mind and circle back.

While you are thinking through your target project, we walk you through a fictional case study of our own. Imagine what you would do for Snap Electronics, a large consumer electronics manufacturer with a well-known brand name and an equally large Web site (www.snapelectronics.com) that does brisk online sales. (Snap is a completely imaginary company not patterned after any existing corporation.)

Snap Electronics has a long history of innovative consumer electronics designs ranging from TVs to DVD players to home theater systems. Snap is well known for its breakthroughs in ease of use—its tag line is, "Our products are a snap." As you look at our rules for choosing the right product area to target, Snap's evaluation is shown in Table 7-1.

Table 7-1 Snap Electronics Product Suitability (You assess the suitability of a product area for your first search marketing campaign according to a few simple rules.)

Product Area	High Profile?	Measurable?	Simple?	Practical?
Televisions	Yes	No	Unknown	Yes
DVD players	Yes	Yes	Unknown	No
Home theater	Yes	No	Unknown	No
VCRs	No	Yes	Unknown	Yes
Digital cameras	Yes	Yes	Unknown	Yes

As we consider the contenders, we realize that most of Snap's TVs and home theater systems are sold offline, so it is harder to measure the impact of your search marketing campaign for those products. We also remember that the group that handles DVD players is redesigning its entire site for a launch in two months, so they are probably not in the mood to hear from us now. We dismiss VCRs because the technology is fading, so it is not as high profile as the others. But digital cameras might be promising.

Snap was late to the digital camera party, but introduced several innovative models under a new SnapShot brand that (as usual) were markedly easier to use than competing models. Snap blanketed TV and magazines with advertising touting SnapShot's easy design, raising brand awareness. But after the successful launch, marketing costs need to come down this year. Snap cannot continue to spend so much on advertising year after year. Each of these factors make SnapShot digital cameras a strong candidate for Snap's first search marketing campaign.

As we sum up the factors we considered in Table 7-1, we see that the digital camera product area is high profile, we can measure its online sales, and the product team seems practical to work with, but Snap's one concern is simplicity. No complicating paid search campaigns are underway for digital cameras, which is good. But it is still hard to judge the difficulty of changing the digital camera content to rank well in search, because we have not yet investigated the site deeply enough. We will have to wait for the assessment to find out how simple this campaign might be.

Focus on the Keywords Searchers Use

Perhaps you are not sure what searchers might enter into search engines when they want to buy a digital camera. Fortunately, there are lots of ways to find out, which we cover in Chapter 11, "Choose Your Target Keywords." But you do not need that much sophistication yet.

Which keywords do you think are the most popular for finding a digital camera? Kind of obvious that "digital camera" might be one of the phrases, huh? After you have settled on one or more phrases, it's time to find variations. Again, you will learn much more about this process in Chapter 11, but for now we will use a simple approach that employs the Yahoo! suggestion tool. (As we write this, Yahoo! is changing its Overture brand name to Yahoo! Search Marketing Solutions, but they did not have the newly branded URLs available in time for publication.)

Yahoo! offers a free **Keyword Selector Tool** (inventory.overture.com/d/searchinventory/ suggestion) for you to research keyword variations. Figure 7-1 shows how it works for the phrase "digital camera." If you type that phrase into the suggestion tool, Yahoo! displays the most popular search queries containing those words in the past month. The tool also shows the **count** for each keyword—the number of searches made in the last month for each query on Yahoo! and its partner sites.

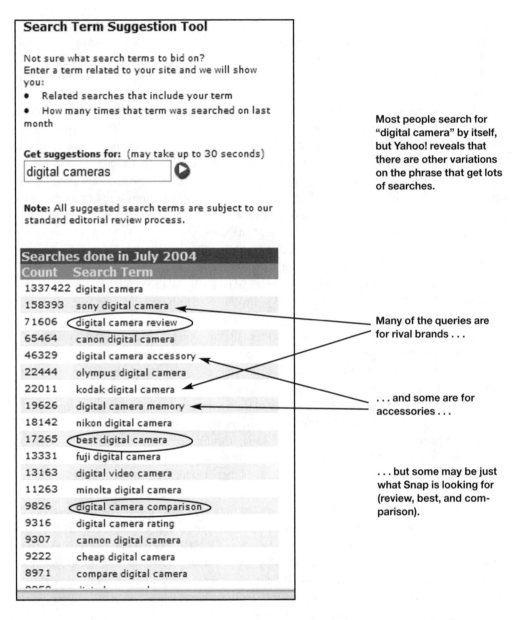

Figure 7-1 Choosing your keywords. See the variants searchers use when looking for a phrase such as "digital camera"—and how often they use them.

Reproduced with permission of Yahoo! Inc. © 2005 by Yahoo! Inc. YAHOO! and the YAHOO! logo are trademarks of Yahoo! Inc.

It was easy for Snap to think of "digital camera" as the phrase searchers are likely to enter, but your site might be a bit harder than that. You might need to do some brainstorming. Ask other people, look at your Web pages, and check out your competitors' pages. Think about what words you use to describe your products to your family. What do industry pundits call this kind of product?

It is tempting to settle for the names your company uses for its products—sometimes those *are* the most popular names. (Searchers do use some brand names a lot, such as iPod or Windows.) But most companies are not blessed with a product whose brand name overshadows its generic name. Try to think of the generic (not proper name) phrases people use to find you—do not use the name of your company or your product. Brand names are also good keywords to target, but your goal with this tool is to identify variations on the most common search query, so try to think of the most popular way to refer to your product. In Snap's case, the most popular query is "digital camera" rather than their brand name, "SnapShot."

So, after you have amassed your generic keywords and variations, what do you do with this list? Well, it is clear from looking at the "count" column from the suggestion tool (in Figure 7-1) that lots of folks are searching for "digital camera" all by itself. All of Snap's competitors are trying to rank #1 for the query "digital camera"—anyone in their business would want that—but maybe they are overlooking these other keyword combinations.

You might be dreaming about ranking #1 for "digital camera" (and someone does rank #1, so it *is* possible). But it takes quite a bit of work to get that top ranking because so many others want that ranking, too. Although we will not drop the idea of getting a high ranking for an extremely popular keyword such as "digital camera," we need to look at less-popular queries, too. These less-popular queries generate plenty of traffic, but fewer companies target them, making it easier to get a high ranking for them. You will see that these medium-popularity keywords are often the perfect targets, generating just enough traffic to be noticeable but without the intense competition for high rankings that comes with the top keywords. Some of the queries on this list might be perfect for Snap, whereas others might not, which we will determine by analyzing each one.

So, let's look at the list of Yahoo! suggestions shown in Figure 7-1. The first disappointment is that Snap's competitors are being searched for by name—Sony, Canon, Kodak, and even the "Cannon" misspelling—but Snap is not. Searches for Snap's brand names (such as "*snap* digital camera" and "*snapshot* digital camera") are apparently lower on the list. Regardless, brand name phrases are important for Snap, and one that its competitors *cannot* rank well for. That means that even though fewer people search for those brand names, Snap has a good chance at a top ranking, so it can drive substantial traffic.

Next, we see that some of these queries are for accessories: "digital camera accessory" or "digital camera memory" or "digital camera battery." Those searchers might buy accessories, but that is a different campaign from cameras. Because there are so many competing cameras in the marketplace, most of these searchers are looking for accessories to cameras Snap does not manufacture anyway. Cross those queries out, too.

We also see that one of the queries, for "digital video camera" is not for the right product. That is a query for a different product—a different search campaign. Delete that one, too.

What's left? After wiping out the competing brands, accessories, and incorrect products, there are only a few left, but these are the most important keywords to look at:

- Discount digital camera
- Digital camera review
- Best digital camera
- Digital camera comparison
- Compare digital camera
- Cheap digital camera

For some companies, all of these might be good targets for search marketing. They all bring heavy traffic and they all seem like queries that informational and transactional searchers use—those are the ones most qualified to sell to.

But for Snap, two of them do not belong—"discount digital camera" and "cheap digital camera"—because Snap is a premium brand that offers innovative easy-to-use designs, but at a price. The SnapShot models are *not* cheap, and it is futile to try to sell them that way. So cross those two off, too, leaving us with the list of targeted keywords shown in Table 7-2.

Table 7-2 Snap Electronics Keyword Targets (You create your short list of keywords to target—these are the initial keywords for Snap's first campaign.)

Keyword Phrase	Monthly Queries	Query Type
digital camera	1,337,422	product category
snapshot digital camera	4,879	brand + product category
snap digital camera	6,243	company + product category
digital camera review	71,606	product category variation
compare digital camera	10,326	product category variation
best digital camera	17,865	product category variation
digital camera comparison	11,863	product category variation

Don't read too much into the wide variation in the numbers. Although the query for "digital camera" receives far more traffic than the others, we're fooling ourselves if we think Snap can swoop right in and get the top ranking for that keyword. Remember that the competition for these "mega-keywords" is fierce, so a top ten ranking is hard to achieve without a lot of work. Moreover, you recall that many of those searchers are seeking information about how to *use* digital cameras, rather than buy them, so those searchers are not as highly qualified as someone searching for "digital camera review," for example. Each of these keywords gets enough traffic for Snap to target, and it is easier to get good rankings for less-popular keywords that have fewer other companies targeting them.

Take a deep breath. That wasn't too hard, was it? You can do the same thing with the area of your own site that you picked. Brainstorm the right words and come up with seven to ten phrases that will generate more traffic to your site. You will likely find that your top keywords fall into the same types: your brand name and a generic category name, along with a few variations. This is true regardless of whether you are driving traffic to a site for a product or not. The Police Athletic League will want to capture queries for "police athletic league," of course, but also wants to generate traffic for "boys' clubs" and "children's sports," too. Most of the time, your organization has a "brand" name (what you call it) and a generic name (what most people call it). You will rank higher for your brand name, but fewer people will search for it, so you need to target both brand names and generic names to maximize your success. Remember, prospective customers who are not searching for your brand name can find your site *only* if you target the generic name. Otherwise they will find your competitors.

Perhaps you are already so familiar with your Web site that you know your first campaign is simple to conduct, but many people cannot tell. They need to assess the simplicity of the campaign to be sure. Armed with our target keywords, now we're ready to assess our site on how well it draws search traffic for each of those queries.

Assess Your Current Situation

No two search marketing situations are the same, which is why you need to assess your situation on its own merits. No matter how little search marketing you have done up to this point, you are probably drawing some amount of organic search traffic. But regardless of how much or how little traffic you are drawing, you cannot tell how well you are doing unless you take a more systematic approach. The first step in your new system is to decide exactly which pages on your site you want the search engines to show when searchers enter a query.

Identify Your Search Landing Pages

It's not enough to choose the keywords that relate to your campaign. You need to identify pages on your site that you want those queries to lead to. When a searcher enters one of those keywords, which page from your site do you want shown in the search results?

COMING IN FOR A LANDING

At first, banner advertisers did not understand the importance of landing pages, but they do now. Let's look at an example to illustrate why.

If a digital photography site's banner ad offers "30% Off a SnapShot X5," that ad could simply be linked to the existing page on Snap's site for that model. When the ad is clicked, visitors would go to the regular SnapShot X5 product details page with "Snap-Shot X5" at the top of the page. They would see the detailed list of features and a picture of the X5. At the bottom of the page, they would see a small notice that says "Now 30% Off" next to the Add to Cart button. As we said, Snap *could* link its banner ad to this page, but if it does, that will not maximize sales.

Why? Because the product details page does not reinforce the offer in the banner ad. A better approach is to use a landing page that repeats the offer for this specific

To answer that question, it is useful to understand the concept of a **landing page**. Originating in banner advertising, the landing page is the place on your Web site visitors will go when they click a particular banner ad. **Search landing pages** are similar to banner landing pages—they are designed to reinforce the searcher's intent. Search landing pages emphasize the keywords the searchers entered to get there, so that visitors to your site from search engines will know they are in the right place and begin to make their way through your site. One difference between search landing pages and banner landing pages is their longevity. Because banner ads are often tied to time-sensitive promotions and discounts, marketers frequently design a new landing page for each banner ad, because no appropriate page already exists. Marketers throw away these special landing pages at the end of the campaign. Searchers, on the other hand, use much the same queries month after month, so it is less important to design new search landing pages—many sites have perfectly appropriate existing pages that reinforce the searcher's intent.

You must identify good search landing pages for each keyword that you picked—pages that reinforce the keywords they are searching for. Let's go back to our example and see how to identify search landing pages for Snap Electronics.

As we look over our list of keywords, we see that several of them might share the same search landing pages. The queries "digital camera," "snap digital camera," and "snapshot digital camera" might all lead to the same place, perhaps the product category page that lists every model of digital camera that Snap sells. You can see this product category page in Figure 7-2.

Just as we saw that several queries above can share the same product category page as their search landing page, the keywords "digital camera comparison" and "compare digital camera" should also share a common landing page (because both are seeking the same information). But Snap's site does not have any page that compares cameras against each other. We could try to use the same product category page used above, but that seems unwise because it contains mostly fuzzy marketing speak—these information seekers want detailed specifications and features. Snap must create a new search landing page to handle these comparison searches.

Our attention turns to "digital camera review." Snap has a page titled "News and Awards" that lists several links to digital photography sites with positive reviews and awards for SnapShot cameras. That looks like a good choice for that keyword.

banner ad. When visitors click through from the ad, the banner landing page amplifies the offer—it says "30% Off SnapShot X5" in big letters at the top of the page, and it shows a picture of the X5 with its key features. At the bottom of the landing page, it provides buttons that let visitors go to the existing X5 product details page for more information or to add the X5 to their carts.

You will sell more when you employ landing pages, because you have reinforced what the visitors are trying to do. They clicked the ad because it said "30% Off SnapShot X5," so when the landing page emphasizes that they are "in the right place" after they click, they are much more likely to continue reading about the offer. If the ad sends them to the product details page instead, they might be disconcerted as to whether they are in the right place and might not be sure they are getting the discount. If it takes time to figure out they are in the right place, many visitors will not take that time and will not take that offer.

Snap
Electronics
                                             "Our products are a snap!"

TELEVISION   AUDIO/VIDEO   HOME THEATRE   CAMERAS

SnapShot Digital Cameras

SnapShot sets the standard in ease-of-use. Get one before they
are gone!

- clickpick.com *review (February 9, 2005)*

SnapShot Point and Shoot

You'll point, you'll shoot, and you'll fall in love
with our affordable introductory model.

SnapShot Pro

You can depend on this all-weather workhorse
for outstanding image quality and reliability.

SnapShot SLR

Redesigned from the ground up, our most
powerful model uses interchangeable SLR
lenses.

Figure 7-2   SnapShot product category page. Informational searchers looking for "digital camera" want to land on an overview page.

That leaves the query for "best digital camera." It is hard to know exactly what these searchers are looking for, because what makes something the "best" is subjective. After a little thinking, we decide to target the most expensive SnapShot model in the product line, the Snap-Shot SLR X900.

Summing up our analysis, we chose existing pages to serve as our search landing pages for most of the queries, but the two "comparison" keywords require a single new landing page to be created for them. Table 7-3 shows the complete list.

Table 7-3 Snap Electronics Landing Pages (You must choose an appropriate search landing page for each targeted keyword in your list—Snap's are shown here.)

Keyword Phrase	Landing Page URL
digital camera	www.snapelectronics.com/stores/Cat?cat=6&lang=1&cntry=840
snap digital camera	www.snapelectronics.com/stores/Cat?cat=6&lang=1&cntry=840
snapshot digital camera	www.snapelectronics.com/stores/Cat?cat=6&lang=1&cntry=840
digital camera review	www.snapelectronics.com/cameras/news
best digital camera	www.snapelectronics.com/stores/Prd?prd=9&lang=1&cntry=840
digital camera comparison	New search landing page needed
compare digital camera	New search landing page needed

See If Your Existing Landing Pages Are Indexed

Now that you have identified the best pages on your site for searchers to find for each of your targeted keywords, it is time to check whether those pages are indexed by the search engines. Certainly, if they are not indexed, they cannot be returned by the search engines for those or any other queries.

We decided earlier that the "comparison" keywords required that Snap create a new search landing page for them, so inevitably that page is not already indexed. Snap will have to ensure this page gets indexed when it is created. But let's check out Snap's existing pages to see where they stand.

Every search engine has a special inclusion operator you can use to see whether a URL is included in its index. For Google, you search for "allinurl:" in front of the URL (such as "allinurl:www.snapelectronics.com/cameras/news") and Google will return the page in its result list if it is indexed, or no results if it is not. Table 7-4 shows the special search query to use for each of the major search engines to see whether your page is indexed—some are fussy about whether you enter the http:// prefix to the URL or not, so follow the syntax shown in the table. (Sometimes the syntax changes, so check the Help page for each search engine if you have any trouble.)

Table 7-4 Special Operators to Check Inclusion (You use special search queries for each search engine to check to see whether your page is included in its index.)

Search Engine	Special Inclusion Operator
AOL Search	allinurl:www.snapelectronics.com/cameras/news
Ask Jeeves	url:http://www.snapelectronics.com/cameras/news
Google	allinurl:www.snapelectronics.com/cameras/news
MSN Search	url:http://www.snapelectronics.com/cameras/news
Yahoo!	url:http://www.snapelectronics.com/cameras/news

It takes some time, but you can check each of your URLs in each search engine. Table 7-5 shows the results for Snap. For space reasons, we have eliminated the leading "www.snapelectronics.com" from the URLs in the table.

Table 7-5   Snap Electronics Inclusion Check (Each search engine indexes some of the pages from your site [indicated by "Yes"], but not others.)

Target URL www.snapelectronics.com . . .	AOL Search	Ask.com	Google	MSN Search	Yahoo!
/Cat?cat=6&lang=1&cntry=840	Yes	No	Yes	No	No
/cameras/news	Yes	Yes	Yes	Yes	Yes
/Prd?prd=9&lang=1&cntry=840	No	No	No	No	No
New page needed	—	—	—	—	—

The inclusion check for Snap yields some disconcerting results. We already knew that Snap needed to create one new page and get it included, but now we see that two of Snap's other pages are also problems—only the "News and Awards" page is indexed by every search engine. We do not have any insight into *why* these pages are not indexed—we will have to wait until Chapter 10, "Get Your Site Indexed," for that—but at least we know that there is some work to do. That is a critical part of our assessment. Some sites have difficult (and expensive) technical problems that prevent spiders from indexing their pages. Because there are only four pages that we have identified, the worst-case scenario is that we need to create a few new pages on the site that search spiders can find to replace the existing pages that they are not indexing. In later chapters, we will see that you *never* create special pages for your site for the sole purpose of ranking well in search (that is an unethical spamming technique), but you should replace pages that cannot be crawled with those that can.

Harkening back to the question of whether the digital camera area of Snap's Web site is a simple enough choice for our first campaign, it appears to be. Some of the critical pages are indexed already, and we have identified other pages that we might get indexed. If we fail to get them indexed, we could create a few new pages to compensate. Overall, it seems to be a simple proposition, so finalize the choice for Snap's first marketing campaign—it is the SnapShot digital camera.

Check the Search Rankings for Your Landing Pages

Now that you know which pages are in and out of which search indexes, it is time to see whether those that are included are ranking in the top ten, and if not, where they are.

There are two ways to check search rankings. You probably thought of the first way: entering the queries by hand and scrolling through the search results until you see your page. You can do it that way, but checking multiple queries in several search engines can get old fast. So, you might want to try the other way of checking rankings—using an automated tool.

Usually tools cost money, however, and you might not have any money to spend. In Chapter 15, we take a look at several fee-based rank checkers, but here we introduce the best free tool, shown in Figure 7-3, Keyword Tracker from Digital Point Solutions (www.digitalpoint.com/tools/keywords). Keyword Tracker checks rankings only in Google, Yahoo! Search, and MSN Search, whereas fee-based checkers handle many different search engines, but it can still save you some time.

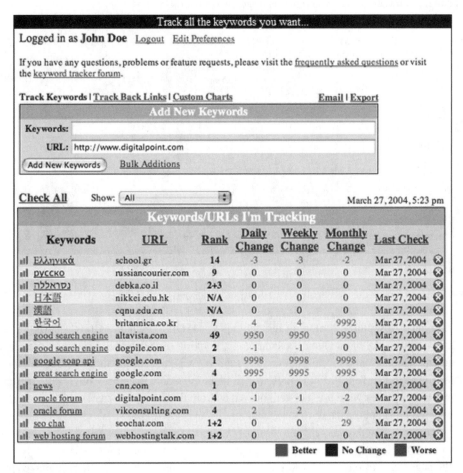

Figure 7-3 Search ranking checker. Keyword Tracker shows where your site's pages rank in Google for your targeted keywords.

Whether you do it by hand or use a rank-checking tool, the basics are the same. You record the organic search rank (paid does not count) of your site's page for the targeted search query. You start counting from the #1 organic result on the first page—that is the top result on page one (which may be underneath paid results in some search engines). For search engines that show ten results on a page, the last result on page one is obviously #10, with the first one on the second page #11, and so on from there.

Of course, the higher the rank, the better, but you might not realize just how critical it is to rank in the top ten. Consider, however, that only 5 to 40 percent of all searchers view results past the first page. Not many searchers are getting to result #11. Of those searchers who do click the first page, 60 percent of them are clicking organic results, so appearing in the top ten of organic results is clearly the place to be. Of course, searchers do not split their clicks evenly among the top ten, so the higher up in the list you are, the more visitors you will get. Table 7-6 shows the results that Snap Electronics found for its targeted keywords.

Table 7-6   Snap Electronics Ranking Check (Some queries return your pages at the same rank in different search engines, but others do not.)

Keyword Phrase	AOL Search	Ask.com	Google	MSN Search	Yahoo!
digital camera	45	—	45	—	—
snap digital camera	3*	2*	3*	4*	2*
snapshot digital camera	3*	1*	3*	1*	1*
digital camera review	—	44	—	34	31
best digital camera	—	17*	—	47*	22*
digital camera comparison	—	—	—	—	—
compare digital camera	—	—	—	—	—

* Page found from snapelectronics.com site, but not the targeted landing page.

One interesting thing to note in this table is that AOL Search and Google have the same rankings, because AOL uses Google's technology. Looking further into the rankings, we see that although the landing page for "digital camera review" was indexed in all the search engines, it was not found in the Top 100 in Google (or in its clone, AOL Search). Conversely, the target pages for other queries were *not* indexed, but pages from the Snap Electronics site *were* returned for the query—just not the pages that were targeted.

For "snap digital camera" and "snapshot digital camera," the Snap home page was returned. It is not the page that was targeted, but it is better than being missing completely. Similarly, the page that was returned by Ask.com, MSN Search, and Yahoo! for "best digital camera" is a interesting one. Titled "The SnapShot Difference," it explains why SnapShot cameras are better than all others—what technology is included and why SnapShots are so easy to use. This page seems better to target than the most-expensive camera's product detail page.

The bad news, however, is the dismal rankings of most of these pages. Unless searchers explicitly specify Snap's company's name or product's name, they are not going to find snapelectronics.com with these keywords. We do not yet know *why* Snap's pages are ranking so poorly, but we explore those reasons in later chapters of this book.

Check Your Competitors' Search Rankings

If Snap is not getting the top spot, who is? It's easy to take a look and see. Figure 7-4 shows the results for "digital cameras" in Google. You can see that the first page lists retailers and review sites rather than camera manufacturers such as Snap.

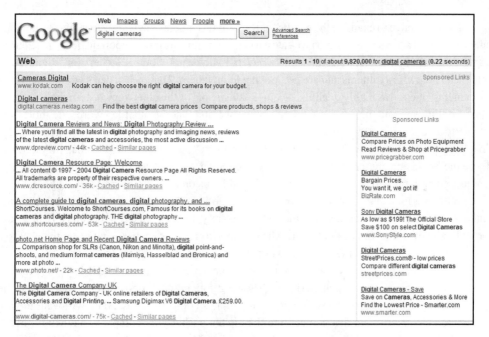

Figure 7-4 Google results for the "digital cameras" keyword. A broad keyword such as "digital cameras" returns many sites besides the camera manufacturers.

One look at the Google results for "digital cameras" tells you that this will be a difficult keyword to get high rankings for—none of Snap's competitors are on the first page, either. But where *are* Snap's competitors? Studying the Google results for a few of the targeted queries can result in a competitor-ranking matrix, as shown in Table 7-7. You can see where each competitor's Web site ranks for each query. For example, the first page from snapelectronics.com returned by Google for the "digital camera" keyword is result #45, whereas Kodak has a page from its site ranked #12.

Table 7-7   Snap Electronics Competitor-Rankings Matrix (Major digital camera manufacturers have wide variation in Google rankings for the primary keywords.)

Keyword Phrase	Snap	Kodak	Canon	Sony	Olympus	Nikon
digital camera	45	12	15	21	42	46
snapshot digital camera	3	—	—	—	—	—
snap digital camera	3	—	—	—	—	—
digital camera reviews	—	—	10	6	22	19
best digital cameras	—	—	—	—	—	—
digital camera comparison	—	—	8	9	58	24

It is instructive to examine the results for the "digital camera" keyword. None of the manufacturers have even a top ten ranking, as we saw earlier. But is this the most important query for Snap to target if they want to attract potential camera buyers? Maybe not. Some searchers for "digital cameras" need help *using* cameras and are not looking to buy them. That means that searchers for "digital cameras" are not as highly qualified as those using some of the other keywords in the list.

Looking beyond the "digital camera" query, we find that the other keywords are more hospitable to manufacturers and suggest more qualified buyers. Focusing first on the searchers for Snap's own SnapShot brand ("snapshot digital camera"), we can conclude that they already desire the brand and are far more likely to buy from Snap. We also see that Snap already has a #3 ranking, so perhaps part of Snap's campaign should focus on moving up to #1.

When we look at the remaining keywords, we notice that, although only Sony has a top ten ranking, the rankings for the manufacturers look healthy. Despite this, Snap is missing in action for all but its own SnapShot brand name. Clearly, this competitor matrix is pointing the way to a search strategy of emphasizing those keywords favored by more qualified searchers.

The matrix has another value, too. When it is time to persuade other people in your organization to invest in or work on search marketing, showing your competitors' rankings usually gets the competitive juices flowing. When you appeal to people's competitiveness, they will want to win. Remember, too, every page that you get into the top ten pushes your competition down further—you are helping yourself while denying them exposure at the same time.

See What Traffic You Are Getting

All the rankings in the world don't mean much if searchers don't click through to your site. So although we know there is a strong correlation between high search rankings and high search traffic, we need to track that traffic to accurately measure the business impact of search marketing—tracking rankings is not enough.

So the next step is to check the traffic that Snap is getting for each keyword. As you saw in Chapter 6, "Measure Your Web Site's Success," Web metrics software can track page views, visits, and visitors, but they can also count which of those visitors came to your site from search engines. Metrics facilities determine where each visitor comes from by examining the **referrer** for each page view. The referrer is the actual URL of the Web page that the visitor viewed before coming to your page.

Clearly, referrers can be used to see which visitors followed links to your page from other pages within your site or from pages on other sites. But metrics facilities provide special support for **search referrals**—referrals that come from a URL known to be a search engine (such as www.yahoo.com). Your metrics software comes with a list of the popular search engine URLs, and you can add any that are missing. This list is used to generate a report showing how many page views were referred from search engines.

But search referrals have even more information buried inside those URLs that you will come to rely on. Each search referral tells you more than what search engine it is from (www.*yahoo*.com). Metrics facilities also dissect these URLs to actually show you the search query that the visitor used to find you! Table 7-8 shows a few examples from Google, Ask.com, and Yahoo!, respectively.

Table 7-8 Search Queries Hidden in Search Referrals (You can see the actual search query used by any search visitor who comes to your Web site.)

http://www.**google**.com/search?sourceid=navclient&ie=UTF-8&oe=UTF-8&q=**digital+camera**

http://web.**ask**.com/web?q=**digital+camera**&o=0&qsrc=0

http://search.**yahoo**.com/search?p=**digital+camera**&ei=UTF-8&fr=fp-tab-web-t&cop=mss

Metrics facilities carefully accumulate these search referrals so that they can show how many visits your site received, or a page on your site (or even a set of pages) received from a particular search engine. They can also show how many visitors used specific search queries. Or how many used a specific query from a specific engine.

For example, Snap might want to know how many visitors they get to the Snap home page from Google, Ask.com, and Yahoo! (which the metrics facility adds up from the referrals shown in Table 7-9). But Snap can also find out how many people reached that page using the "digital camera" query, regardless of which search engine they used, by analyzing the same referrals.

Table 7-9 Snap Electronics Visitors from Search Engines (Your metrics facility can add up your search referrals across all search engines for each targeted query.)

Keyword Phrase	Search Referrals
digital camera	1,412
snapshot digital camera	5,278
snap digital camera	4,044
digital camera reviews	0
compare digital cameras	0
best digital cameras	0
digital camera comparison	0
Total Search Referrals	10,734

Snap Electronics does not have any paid search campaigns underway for digital cameras, but as you tabulate current search referrals for your own site, be aware of any paid activity. If you are using paid search, you need to assess that, too, because it affects your referral numbers, but we do not cover that until Chapter 14, "Optimize Your Paid Search Program."

Assessing your site is a critical step, but knowing where you stand is just the beginning. Let's see where you can go from here.

Calculate Your First Campaign's Opportunity

It's interesting to find out how many searchers are being referred to your site with the keywords you have targeted, but you also need to know how many searchers do *not* come to your site. Those are the people that you want referred your way—they are your search marketing opportunity.

Obviously, although search marketing can drive new visitors to your site, you might need to make other changes to your site to increase conversion. Although marketing opportunities certainly exist, they are not particular to *search* marketing because your changes affect every visitor to your site, regardless of how they landed there. To go beyond search marketing visit Jim Sterne's excellent Web site (www.targeting.com), which is loaded with ways to measure your Web site's success and to make improvements.

Now you have learned enough to estimate the traffic increase a well-designed search marketing campaign can produce, and we do so through the next few pages.

Check Your Keyword Demand

The number of searches for any particular query is referred to as **keyword demand**. So, although search referrals tell you how many of those searchers clicked through to your site, keyword demand tells you how many searchers used that keyword in total. Keyword demand counts the people that chose a result from your site as well as all of those searchers for that keyword who chose to click someone else's site.

We explain keyword demand in detail in Chapter 11, exploring several sources of keyword demand information, but we can give it a "once over" here. Table 7-10 shows the results for our targeted keyword phrases from the Yahoo! Keyword Selector Tool that we used earlier to choose our targets. In that table, you'll see that we multiply the number of searches in the Yahoo! tool by 2.2 to approximate the number of searches for that keyword in all search engines, because at the time Snap did the analysis, Yahoo! was serving about 45% of the paid placement ads worldwide. As we write this, Yahoo! is serving just 28% of the ads, because MSN has stopped using Yahoo! ads and because Yahoo!'s own search facility has a lower market share than it once did. So when you do your analysis today, you might want to multiply the Yahoo! keyword demand by 3.5 to approximate the worldwide demand across all search engines. In Chapter 11, we introduce other keyword tools that you can use instead of the Yahoo! Keyword Selector. (Keyword Discovery, for example, shows worldwide demand without you needing to perform any calculation.)

Table 7-10 Snap Electronics Keyword Demand Matrix (You can find out how many searches are being performed for each of the keywords on your target list.)

Keyword Phrase	Yahoo! Searches	× 2.2 =	Keyword Demand
digital camera	1,337,422		2,942,328
snapshot digital camera	4,879		10,734
snap digital camera	6,243		13,735
digital camera reviews	71,606		157,533
compare digital cameras	10,326		22,717
best digital cameras	17,865		39,303
digital camera comparison	11,863		26,099
Totals	1,460,204		3,212,449

Discover Your Missed Opportunities

Although it is helpful to see how many searches are performed on your targeted keywords, you must remember that you are already getting some search traffic to your site. How many searchers are you missing? To answer that question, we must develop a **missed-opportunity matrix™**.

Because every searcher that uses your targeted keyword is an opportunity to bring a visitor to your site, merely subtracting your search referrals from the total number of searches yields the number of searches where no one came to your site. You can also calculate your share of the search traffic by dividing the number of your referrals by the keyword demand. Table 7-11 shows how simple it is to calculate missed opportunities for Snap Electronics.

Table 7-11 Snap Missed Opportunity Matrix (Juxtaposing the actual search referrals with the keyword demand shows how many searchers were missed.)

Keyword Phrase	Keyword Demand	Actual Search Referrals	Share of Search Traffic	Missed Opportunities
digital camera	2,942,328	1,412	0.05%	2,940,916
snapshot digital camera	10,734	4,044	38%	6,690
snap digital camera	13,735	5,278	38%	8,457
digital camera reviews	157,533	—	0%	157,533
compare digital cameras	22,717	—	0%	22,717
best digital cameras	39,303	—	0%	39,303
digital camera comparison	26,099	—	0%	26,099
Totals	3,212,449	10,734	0.33%	3,201,715

Project Your Future Traffic

Now it is time to calculate what you really want to know: How many more search referrals can you reasonably obtain if you execute a strong first search marketing campaign? Although those searchers that failed to come to Snap's site are literally missed opportunities, it is not realistic to expect that any one site could collect all the clicks for any query. The question then becomes how to estimate the *reasonable* number of clicks that can be achieved after a successful first search marketing campaign.

Before we begin our analysis of future traffic, you should know that it is impossible to accurately calculate something as nebulous as a "reasonable number of clicks." Anyone who tells you that he can pinpoint the answer is oversimplifying the complexity of searcher behavior. But we can make **estimates** to help make a business decision on how to invest in search marketing. Although it will not be terribly precise, it will help you make a better decision than using the seat of your pants.

Studies show that 62 percent of searchers click a result on the first page of results and that 60 percent of those clicks are on organic results rather than paid. Multiplying those numbers together tells us that 37 percent of all searchers click an organic result on the first page. At the time that Snap projected its first campaign's results, however, the research showed that 48 percent, not 62 percent, clicked on that first page, so Snap did its research based on 29 percent (48 percent multiplied by 60 percent) clicking on an organic result on the first page. As you do your projections, use the resources in Chapter 16, "What's Next?" to stay up to date with the latest research on the percentage of searchers that click on the first page of results. Snap used the then-current 29 percent figure for the rest of its calculations, but you should use the latest numbers.

Although helpful, that statistic does not tell us nearly enough for us to calculate our real opportunity, because searchers frequently click more than one result from the same search—first clicking on #1, then #3, and finally #4 before going off to do something else. So, although 29 percent of searchers click an organic result on the first page, there are more pages clicked than 29 percent. What we need to know is how many clicks there are *per search*. And honestly, no one knows, except the folks running the search engines themselves, and they consider the information to be proprietary. Anecdotal evidence indicates that between 1.8 and 2.8 results are clicked for each search—if we take the more conservative 1.8 number and multiply it by 29 searchers, we get 52 clicks for every 100 searches.

So we have estimated 52 clicks per 100 searches as the average, but not all searches are average. Some produce more than 52 clicks and others produce less. But even that isn't all, because those 52 clicks per 100 searches are not spread around evenly. Far more of them are clustered at the top of results page, where the highest-ranked pages are shown. The exact results that searchers click vary greatly from query to query. Table 7-12 shows four different distributions that all average 52 clicks, and there is no way to be sure what distribution any particular query yields.

Table 7-12 Distribution of Clicks by Search Ranking (Although 52 clicks are the average number per 100 searches, they can be distributed widely for each query.)

Search Ranking	Number of Clicks			
	Weak Informa-tional Results	Strong Informa-tional Results	Brand Informa-tional Results	Navigational Results
#1	8	15	20	50
#2	5	12	9	5
#3	5	10	6	5
#4	4	5	6	4
#5	4	3	4	3
#6	3	2	3	2
#7	1.5	2	2	1
#8	0.5	1.5	1	1
#9	0.5	1	0.5	0.5
#10	0.5	0.5	0.5	0.5
Totals	32	52	52	72

Although you cannot be sure of the number of clicks you can get, you can make some reasonable assumptions. The first two distributions shown in Table 7-12 are for informational queries, where the "weak" results list has no clearly superior result and the "strong" list has markedly better results at the top of the list. Contrast these two distributions with the last two, where a brand query ("snapshot camera") might return the manufacturer (Snap Electronics) or a leading retailer (in the #2 through #5 slots, perhaps), leading to stronger clickthrough (especially at the top of the list). When searchers enter a navigational query ("snap electronics") where there is truly a "right" answer for most searchers, we might see a distribution like the one in the last column where the #1 result gets the lion's share of the clicks.

So, by looking at the table, we can take some educated guesses as to how search ranking can affect the number of clicks to your site. If you rank in the top three, you might get clicks for 8 percent to 30 percent of the queries for a particular keyword. If your page ranks four through ten, perhaps you will get a click for 0.5 percent to 7 percent of searches. If your page shows up on the next two result pages (ranked #11 through #30), you will pick up a few clicks—maybe clicks totaling 0.25 percent of all searches. One quarter of 1 percent might not sound like much, but it is better than nothing, which is your likely fate beyond position #30. At the other end of the spectrum, some search marketers report getting clickthrough rates of more than 50 percent, especially when their listing is in the top three of both the organic and the paid placements for the same query. If we carefully examine the tail end of the table (the last few results), using the graph in Figure 7-5, we can see that seemingly small differences might be significant for popular queries.

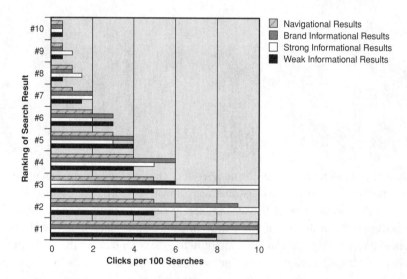

Figure 7-5   Little differences add up. The tail distribution shown in Table 7-12 varies a lot from query to query even though the numbers seem small.

If you are considering mounting both an organic and paid campaign, your clickthrough rate could be considerably higher than what is shown here. Recall that 40 percent of the 87 clicks (35 clicks) are for paid results. It is typical to get 5 percent clickthrough or more for a top three paid placement. If your plan includes a top paid placement bid for each keyword, you should add 5 percent of the paid clicks to the organic clicks you anticipate. Table 7-13 shows how the range of clickthrough rates dramatically affect the number of searchers that come to snapelectronics.com each month.

Table 7-13   Snap Electronics Traffic Potential Model (You can use the estimated monthly keyword demand to estimate search referrals at various clickthrough rates.)

Keyword Phrase	Monthly Keyword Demand	Estimated Monthly Search Referrals				
		0.25%	1%	5%	10%	25%
digital camera	2,942,328	7,356	29,423	147,116	294,233	735,582
snapshot digital camera	10,734	27	107	537	1,073	2,683
snap digital camera	13,735	34	137	687	1,373	3,434
digital camera reviews	157,533	394	1,575	7,877	15,753	39,383
compare digital cameras	22,717	57	227	1,136	2,272	5,679
best digital cameras	39,303	98	393	1,965	3,930	9,826
digital camera comparison	26,099	65	261	1,305	2,610	6,525
Totals	3,212,449	8,031	32,124	160,622	321,245	803,112

The next step requires a cold look at what your potential improvement in rank can be for each keyword. Let's haul out yet another table to show the potential improvements from a successful search marketing campaign. Table 7-14 shows a **projected-rankings matrix**, with the current rank for each of Snap's targeted keywords along with a guess at what the new improved rank might be.

Table 7-14   Snap Electronics Projected Rankings Matrix (where Snap and its competitors rank in Google today gives clues for where Snap could rank in the future.)

Keyword Phrase	Current Rankings			Projected Rankings Snap
	Kodak	Canon	Snap	
digital camera	12	15	45	10
snap digital camera	—	—	3	1
snapshot digital camera	—	—	3	1
digital camera reviews	—	10	—	15
best digital cameras	—	—	—	30
compare digital cameras	12	15	—	8
digital camera comparison	8	17	—	10

When you develop your projected-rankings matrix, you are realistically assessing where your pages *can* rank—in this case for Google. (A more complete approach, avoided here for brevity, would be to analyze each of the major search engines and all major camera competitors.) Taking the phrase "digital camera," we can see that it might not be realistic for Snap to get a top ranking—the current top results include no camera manufacturers, showing high-quality camera review sites instead. But it is entirely reasonable for Snap to move from "off the charts" to a respectable #10.

Similarly, when we look at the keyword "best digital cameras," we see that all the camera manufacturers are missing in action. But there might be some hope here. We note that none of the other manufacturers use that phrase on their pages, possibly because large corporations do not want to appear boastful. Snap does not like to toot its own horn either, but many third-party digital camera reviews actually call the SnapShot the "best digital camera"—Snap can quote these reviews on its site without appearing boastful, and the search engines will find the words on Snap's pages. Armed with this information, it might be reasonable to project that Snap can break through at least to the top 30 for this query where the other manufacturers did not.

When you develop your own projected-rankings matrix, you must make similar decisions, keyword by keyword, and you need to be as realistic as possible. You might find that your projections are conservative at times, but that is better than overpromising and underdelivering.

After you have decided what rankings you can achieve, you need to assign your clickthrough rate for each keyword, as discussed in Table 7-12. For each keyword, you need to decide what the right click distribution is across every organic search result, and then assign the appropriate percentage to your result based on the position you expect to achieve. Table 7-15 shows Snap's decisions. Projected "top 30" rankings are valued at a 0.25 percent clickthrough rate, whereas a #1 ranking for a quasi-navigational query such as "snap digital camera" might get 20 percent clickthrough. Multiplying that rate by the estimated monthly searches produces the projected visits resulting from the search marketing campaign.

Table 7-15   Snap's Organic Traffic Model (For each keyword, Snap can project the percentage of clickthrough per organic search and project added referrals.)

Keyword Phrase	Monthly Keyword Demand	Current Monthly Visits		Current Rank	Projected Rank	Projected Monthly Search Referrals		Added Search Referrals
digital camera	2,942,328	1,412	0.05%	45	10	0.50%	14,711	13,299
snapshot digital camera	10,734	4,044	38%	3	1	50%	5,367	1,323
snap digital camera	13,735	5,278	38%	3	1	50%	6,867	1,589
digital camera reviews	157,533	—	0.00%	—	15	0.25%	394	394
best digital cameras	22,717	—	0.00%	—	30	0.10%	23	23

Keyword Phrase	Monthly Keyword Demand	Current Monthly Visits		Current Rank	Projected Rank	Projected Monthly Search Referrals		Added Search Referrals
compare digital cameras	39,303	—	0.00%	—	8	1.50%	590	590
digital camera comparison	26,099	—	0.00%	—	10	0.50%	130	130
Total	3,212,449	10,734	0.33%			0.87%	28,082	17,348

If Snap Electronics planned to place a top paid placement bid in Google, Yahoo!, and MSN for every keyword, they could add as much as 5 percent to their clickthrough rates to generate a larger number of added referrals. But Snap wanted to take a more conservative approach. Rather than buying each of these keywords across three search engines, Snap decided to buy just *one* keyword in Yahoo! as an experiment. They chose the most popular keyword, "digital cameras." This approach allowed them to gain experience with paid placement without having to make a big commitment of money and management time. Based on the results of the experiment, they will decide how to approach paid placement in the future.

Snap's approach required them to project the added search referrals for paid placement for the "digital cameras" keyword, which was fairly easy. Snap took the number of Yahoo! searches for "digital cameras" from Table 7-10 (1,337,422) and multiplied by a 1 percent clickthrough rate. Many paid placements yield 5 percent clickthrough rates or more, but Snap decided to make a conservative projection for their first paid campaign. Multiplying the Yahoo! searches by that 1 percent clickthrough rate produced an additional 13,374 monthly search referrals from paid placement.

If we add the 17,348 organic search referrals from Table 7-15 to the new paid search referrals, it results in 30,722 new search referrals each month. That kind of number will draw the attention needed to get your search marketing program off the ground. It is hard for anyone running a Web site to turn down additional traffic, but you can make your case for search marketing even more enticing by projecting not just traffic, but conversions.

Project Your Future Conversions

Regardless of what your Web site's goals are, you saw in Chapter 5 that you can choose certain visitor events as your conversions. Obviously, if you are selling your product online, it is easy for you to translate your conversions into revenue, but you saw in Chapter 6 that that you can translate most conversions into some kind of business value.

Continuing our fictitious scenario for Snap Electronics, we can project our digital camera search marketing campaign's conversions and its incremental revenue. Snap needs to know a few numbers to do so:

- *Projected added search referrals*. As we calculated earlier, the estimate for the extra traffic to Snap's site due to successful search marketing consists of referrals from both organic and paid search. Snap's total comes to 30,722 more visits.

- *Conversion rate*. What percentage of visits results in sales? If Snap knows the conversion rate for digital cameras (the percentage of visitors to the digital camera pages that buy digital cameras), that would be the best conversion rate to use. But many companies, especially large companies, have trouble isolating individual product metrics. In Snap's case, isolating digital camera conversion rate is not possible, but they do know that their overall conversion rate is 2 percent. They can use that 2 percent conversion rate as a conservative estimate, because they expect that the digital camera conversion rate is higher than average.

- *Average transaction price*. What is the typical price paid for a digital camera? Snap should be able to monitor all digital camera sales and divide the total sales by the number of transactions to find out the average transaction price. In some cases, you need to use the average transaction price across all products, rather than the product you are targeting, but Snap happens to know that its average digital camera price is $348.

After you have compiled the necessary numbers, you can put them together to project the incremental revenue from search marketing for digital cameras, as shown in Figure 7-6.

	Added Monthly Search Referrals	30,722
Multiply by:	Conversion rate	0.02
	Added monthly sales	614
Multiply by:	Average transaction price	$348
	Added monthly revenue	$213,672
Multiply by:	12 months	12
	Added yearly revenue	$2,564,064

Figure 7-6   Projecting Snap's search campaign's revenue. A simple formula converts projected incremental search referrals into projected revenue.

As you calculate the opportunity for your own first campaign, you might be wondering how big the opportunity can be if you go all out with a site-wide search marketing program, consisting of many individual campaigns. In Chapter 8, "Define Your Search Marketing Strategy," you decide how broad your overall search marketing program should be, and in Chapter 9, "Sell Your Search Marketing Proposal," you will see how large the profit could be.

Summary

Search marketing is, after all, *marketing*, so you need to be armed with the business impact of your search marketing plans. No matter what your site's goals, you can use search marketing to drive traffic to your site to achieve those goals. In this chapter, you learned how to project the traffic your campaign will generate and how to translate that traffic into its business impact. Figure 7-7 summarizes the steps we took to get there.

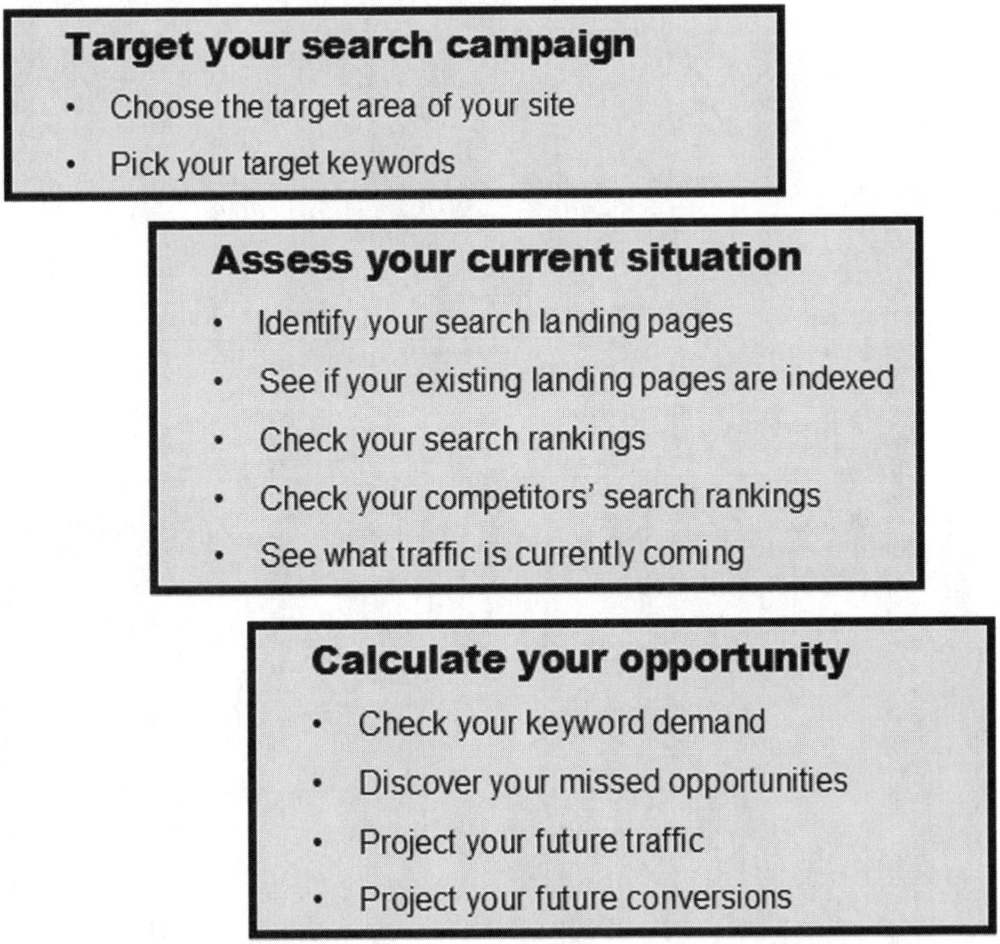

Target your search campaign
- Choose the target area of your site
- Pick your target keywords

Assess your current situation
- Identify your search landing pages
- See if your existing landing pages are indexed
- Check your search rankings
- Check your competitors' search rankings
- See what traffic is currently coming

Calculate your opportunity
- Check your keyword demand
- Discover your missed opportunities
- Project your future traffic
- Project your future conversions

Figure 7-7 Measuring search success steps. For each campaign, you can define your measurements up front to show the expected value.

In the next chapter, we look past your first campaign and dive into your search marketing strategy. What are the tasks required? Who should perform each task? How large should your overall search marketing program be? What will your program cost? Read on and see how your opportunity can be realized.

CHAPTER 8

Define Your Search Marketing Strategy

Strategy. Do you get a bit suspicious just hearing the word? "Strategy" discussions sometimes seem disconnected from reality—the kind of "where the rubber meets the sky" conversations that are funny in a Dilbert cartoon. But when you hear some consultant show a bunch of pretty charts with no semblance of understanding your business, or the risks being run, or the effort required, it's not funny anymore—it's scary.

When done properly, strategy is critically important before you undertake any task. We try to avoid the pixie dust and give you a set of practical tasks to shape your search marketing program and carry it out. The major strategic steps to develop your search marketing program are covered in this chapter, as follows:

- *Choose the scope of your search marketing program.* The most important part of your strategy—the part you must decide first—is: How big are you going to do this? You must choose the breadth of your program across your organization. (A product line? Division? Country? The whole company?) In the preceding chapter, you chose your first search marketing campaign. Now you will decide how large your entire search marketing program will be—a program consisting of many campaigns.

- *Divide the work.* Some duties need to be centralized in a new search team, whereas the existing Web teams should perform others. As you set the strategy for your search marketing program, it is important to understand what these duties are and who the best people are to take them on.

- *Choose your approach.* How are you going to execute your search marketing program? Will you use an internal team alone or will you engage an external firm to assist you? You must understand the reasons to choose one approach or the other.

- *Project your costs.* The final part of your strategy must total up the investment required. In Chapter 7, "Measure Your Search Marketing Success," we identified the opportunity. In this chapter, we assess the cost of reaching the opportunity. We actually total up two different costs—one is the investment you need right away to run your first campaign. The other is the cost of your full search marketing program, projected over several years.

At the end of this chapter, you will know exactly what your search marketing program will set out to do, you will know how you intend to accomplish it, and you will know approximately what it will cost. (You will also calculate what your first campaign will cost.) Let's begin by deciding the breadth of the program.

Choose the Scope of Your Search Marketing Program

Any strategy starts with a firm definition of what the project will do. When you set out to succeed in search marketing for your Web site, your most critical question might be the scope of your program. On what scale are you working? A single business unit? Corporate branding across the enterprise?

Before answering that question, you need to remind yourself of the distinction between your first search marketing campaign and your overall search marketing program. Figure 8-1 shows how Snap's overall program consists of many campaigns, starting with the digital cameras campaign we have discussed. Although we show just four in the figure, Snap's program will eventually consist of dozens of campaigns as it gradually covers each product in its product line.

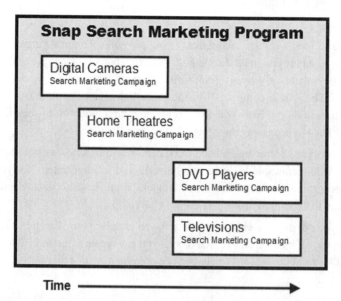

Figure 8-1   Search marketing campaigns within the program. Snap's digital cameras campaign is just the first in its overall search marketing program.

You need clear objectives for your search marketing program before you start. Are you looking for a long-term solution or just a quick fix to get a few keywords ranking well? Are you expecting to do just a few campaigns or do you have dozens (or hundreds) of product lines? Without asking yourself these questions up front, you are likely to take the wrong actions.

Occasionally, these questions are moot. If you are reading this book because a particular executive has ordered you to "fix search" (as sometimes happens), you will *know* your program's organizational scope—it covers the executive's organization. In short, if the Snap executive for home entertainment had charged us with improving search traffic, we probably would not have chosen digital cameras as our first campaign! We would choose home entertainment as our program scope, and we would pick one of those products (such as home theater systems) as our first campaign.

Much of the time, however, *you* will be the one making the recommendation, so you need to take a close look at your situation. To make a smart decision on your search marketing program's scope, you must consider both the size and structure of your organization. We tackle size considerations first.

Size Matters

Although every company differs, large and small companies typically face different challenges in search engine marketing. (If your organization is medium sized, you might have some problems of each.) Because these are generalizations, your company might have some differences from its stereotype, but understanding what can go wrong can help you analyze your own situation.

Normally, large organizations have the advantage in marketing, but small companies frequently have the upper hand in *search* marketing. Big companies still have some advantages, but it is a far more level playing field than with other areas of marketing. Let's investigate the success factors for search marketing and see how they relate to company size.

Flexibility

Smaller companies are generally "light on their feet"—more flexible than their larger counterparts. This flexibility provides small companies with fundamental advantages in search marketing, starting with a basic willingness to pursue search marketing in the first place.

Large companies are often "stuck in their ways"—they execute the same kind of marketing programs year after year—and it can take them a long time to even try search marketing. Some corporate types are risk averse, not wanting to go out on a limb for the new thing. Small companies are often more willing to take a chance on an unproven approach and are more likely to raise investment in search marketing quickly when they see it is working.

Large companies are often slower than small ones, which hurts search marketing in several ways. First, search marketing inevitably requires changes to your Web site. The faster you can make those changes, the faster your search success can begin. Moreover, continuing success depends on frequent fine-tuning. Smaller sites tend to be able to make changes with more speed and less bureaucratic wrangling.

Name Recognition

Small companies often have the advantage in search marketing, but not here. Large companies have a big edge in publicity. Searchers know their names and the names of their products. Searchers are more likely to include those names in searches, a big edge for the large companies that own those names.

But it does not end there. The bigger and more well known the Web site, the more other Web sites will link to it. Whereas little companies must beg and plead for every link, big sites get them without even asking. Because everything that big companies do seems newsworthy, they attract news coverage for every tiny product announcement (which means links from news organizations and other well-respected sources). Customers, suppliers, and resellers link to large companies to bask in their reflected glory. Large corporations frequently have multiple sites that are interlinked, adding to their advantage. The link popularity that large sites enjoy helps their rankings immeasurably.

But small companies can attract links as well, as we explain in Chapter 13, "Attract Links to Your Site." Every day, some large companies find themselves ranked lower than smaller companies for searches for the own products. These small companies are often resellers for the large company, and they rank higher just because they have done a better job at search marketing.

Resources

Larger organizations typically have a huge edge in marketing resources, but they are often slow to devote them to something new, such as search marketing. So, although larger budgets can be an advantage in paid search (and can be helpful for organic campaigns as well), sometimes small companies spend more than big companies do.

In addition, the largesse of big companies sometimes gets in their own way. Small companies are much quicker to seek outside expertise, and might get better advice from consultants than corporations get from their less-experienced internal personnel who are not search marketing experts.

When it comes to money, more is better than less. But most big companies squander this advantage with the overly complex design of their Web sites. Search spiders greatly prefer simple sites without JavaScript navigation or dynamic pages or other expensive technical gimmickry that small companies typically cannot afford. There are good reasons to use these techniques, but when they are overused or used incorrectly, they quash search marketing. Small companies tend to have simple, clean designs that spiders love. In Chapter 10, "Get Your Site Indexed," we look at how overdesigned pages can be adapted to be more search-friendly.

Analyze Your Organizational Structure

When deciding your search marketing program's scope, think about how your Web teams are organized. Figure 8-2 shows four kinds of organizations—yours might be different yet. Regardless, you need to consider how *your* organization works when choosing the scope of your search marketing program. Your organization certainly has some elements of these four if it is not a direct match.

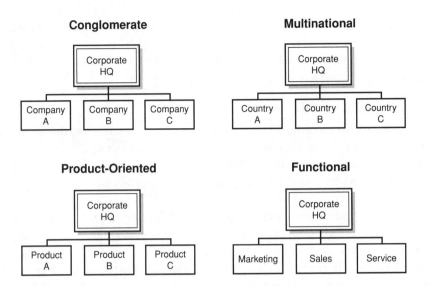

Figure 8-2 Analyzing your organization. Most organizations have some underlying principle that they are organized around, so figure out yours.

There is no "right" way to organize and you might firmly believe that your organization ought to be reorganized. (Take heart, it probably will be soon.) What is important for your success as a search marketer is to understand your *current* organizational style.

Functional organizations

Functional organizations tend to have a small number of products that are similar to each other and are sold to the same customers—many small-to-medium companies are organized functionally. Your teams have been divided into specialties based on what people do (such as marketing versus sales)—their *functions*.

If your organization has one Webmaster group, a single team of programmers, and one marketing department (for example), your Web organization is structured more by function than one with groups for every country (or every product, or every audience, and so on). The more your Web organization is organized functionally, the easier it is to adopt a site-wide scope for your search marketing program. You can use existing functional groups within your organization to carry out many search marketing tasks.

One of the challenges of search marketing in a functional organization is to persuade the functions themselves to collaborate. In the good old days, the marketing department was in charge of delivering brand messages to groups of customers (market segments) and the sales department was in charge of selling the product to each individual customer, and they did not have to work together all that closely. With the advent of the Web, you might find these long-standing functional relationships in flux, because no one can agree where Web marketing leaves off and Web sales begin, for example. They need to collaborate now, whereas they did not need to work together as closely in the past.

Despite these challenges, implementing search marketing in a functional organization is less challenging than in some of the others we touch on later, simply because you do not need to coordinate across many different groups of specialists. All the marketing folks are in one group, for example, so you can train them all in search marketing at one time.

Product-Oriented Organizations

Product-oriented organizations might have centralized a lot of business functions into corporate headquarters, but they leave manufacturing and sales to product groups. Does each product have its own Web site? Do the Web sites share the same technology and content infrastructure or different ones? The more they work the same, the more easily you can engage in a site-wide search marketing program.

Do the products have a common set of customers? Do some of the search queries overlap between your products? The closer they are to each other, the more likely a company-wide search marketing program can succeed.

On the other hand, if your products appeal to completely different market segments, or each product area has a separately managed Web site, you might need to treat each product area as its own scoped search marketing program.

Product-oriented organizations (in which each product has its own Web site and Web team) require significant coordination for site-wide search marketing programs to succeed. You might need to bring together a dozen Web programming teams to explain how search marketing changes their jobs. You might require agreement from several groups for new standards and procedures.

Apple Computer is a good example of a product-oriented company (whose products share common customers), but because its Web site uses a single approach, its search marketing might be centralized, too. The more different ways that your Web team operates your Web site, the more coordination you must do.

Alternatively, if your products are sold to different customers who use different search queries, and your product sites are organizationally separate, you might pull back from centralizing a lot of tasks, and use the same approach discussed below for conglomerates—setting up separate search marketing programs for each product. General Electric does not sell aircraft engines and light bulbs to the same customers, nor use the same Web site for each, so perhaps its search marketing programs should differ for each product line, too.

There's no one right answer. What you decide depends largely on how your company is organized today.

Multinational Organizations

Multinational organizations tend to have strong global brands that are managed centrally, but each country has substantial control over how it is done.

As before, you need to look at the details of how things are done in your organization. Look for parallels to search engine marketing. Are technology investments managed centrally? Advertising? Marketing? Find one or two examples of central management of something similar to search marketing and use them as prototypes for setting the scope of your search marketing program.

IBM is an example of a company that is organized by country. It has centralized a lot of its marketing and advertising, however, so centralizing search marketing is accepted by the corporate culture. Other companies might provide the country organizations with more autonomy, so they might need to do more of the search work locally, with separate search marketing programs in each country.

Conglomerates

Conglomerates are *highly* decentralized. Your corporate Web site (www.conglomerate.com) might be a small undertaking that exists mainly for investors because all the action happens in the individual companies that make up the conglomerate. Each company makes its own decisions about what to do and how to spend its money with little direction from corporate. Each company has its own Web site (www.company.com) that many customers do not even realize is part of the conglomerate, because the brand identity mainly resides with each company.

In some conglomerates, such as Berkshire Hathaway, a centralized search marketing effort makes no sense because their corporate culture is not centralized. You are far better off setting up separate search projects in each individual company, possibly sharing ideas and consulting across the companies.

Finalize Your Search Marketing Program's Scope

Now that you have analyzed the type of organization you work in, you are ready to make some decisions about your search marketing program's scope. How broad should the program be in your organization? Should it cover your entire enterprise, just your business unit, only your country, or something else? Choosing your program's scope affects which executive(s) and which Web team(s) you need to persuade, a topic we address in Chapter 9, "Sell Your Search Marketing Proposal."

If you work in a small organization, this decision will not take terribly long; in a medium-to-large company, however, it might take some thought. Consider the points we covered as you analyzed your organizational structure. Do you work in a highly decentralized conglomerate or a highly centralized functional organization? In a conglomerate, you might decide to limit your program's scope to one of the semi-independent companies, whereas you might decide to tackle the entire enterprise in a functional organization.

You should also consider your *role* in your organization. If you are the Webmaster for the North American Web site, maybe that is the easiest scope to tackle first. If you are a product manager, maybe the best scope to start with covers just your product. If there is an executive you know you can convince to invest, perhaps his organizational scope is the right one for you. Remember, you can think big for your search marketing program's scope, but still start small with a single campaign. It is common, in medium-to-large companies, for the initial search marketing campaign to be limited to a single product. Think about what is practical for you.

Company size also plays into your program scope decision. The larger the company, the more difficult it is to take on the whole organization at once. Larger Web sites suffer from many technical and organizational complexities that make the effort more difficult as you make the scope larger. Similarly, the larger the scope you choose for your program, the longer it takes to get approval. You might decide to start small to show some success before requesting an enterprise-wide commitment.

The lesson is for you to think critically about your own situation. No matter what generalizations we write here, your company is not a generality—it is your own specific reality. You might work in a culture that likes to try new things, so maybe you can give paid search a shot. Perhaps your conglomerate has a tradition of working together on marketing, even though everything else is separate, so you can undertake an enterprise-wide search marketing program. If your product-oriented organization centralized its technology group, maybe you can tackle organic search across your whole site. Think carefully about your situation and choose the best program scope for your organization.

The folks at Snap Electronics carefully considered what the best scope would be for their search marketing program. Because Snap is a large company with significant name recognition, it has already attracted many links to its Web site, giving it a big leg up on organic search. Unfortunately, as you saw in Chapter 7, some of Snap's most important pages are not in the search indexes, and it is not clear how easy that will be to fix. Snap's management is generally open to new ideas, but is a bit suspicious of paid placement because it sounds too much like the dreaded banner ads (which Snap got burned on a couple of years ago). Snap is a highly product-oriented organization, but its marketing is aligned by country.

After taking all of this information into account, Snap chose to focus on the United States, its largest market, across its entire product line. So, Snap's overall scope for its search marketing program covers its U.S. products and its first campaign will be for digital cameras. Snap decided to concentrate on organic search, targeting the five major worldwide search engines: Google, Yahoo!, Ask Jeeves, MSN Search, and AOL Search. Although concentrating on organic search, Snap chose to experiment with paid search, too, deferring a final scope decision on paid search until the experiment is complete. These basic scope decisions will drive the rest of Snap's strategy.

Divide the Search Marketing Work

Successful search engine marketing requires highly specialized work. If you thumb through the remaining chapters in this book, you will see all sorts of arcane techniques important to your success. You can't rely on everyone learning search marketing on their own, however. You cannot rely on specialists being motivated to do search marketing. (Although it is true that *some* specialists will embrace search marketing without a larger program in place, most will not.) And no amount of evangelism on your part will prove sufficient by itself—you cannot execute an enterprise program based on the sheer force of your personality.

You need to organize. And when you organize, you will split into two groups:

- *The central search team.* When you start your search marketing efforts, the central team is *you*. In a medium-to-large organization, that is not enough. (In Chapter 15, "Make Search Marketing Operational," you will learn which skills you need and how to staff your central team.) Although we use the word *central* throughout, central is relative—

relative to the program scope that you have chosen. So, if you have chosen a scope of a single country within your multinational company, the central team manages search marketing throughout the country, not throughout the enterprise.

- *The extended search team.* Your organization already has an existing team (maybe lots of teams) to manage your Web site today. These specialists decide your Web site's strategy, write the content, create the pages, design applications, and do many other things. You must take advantage of these existing resources as your extended search team, because search marketing cannot succeed unless *they* do the right things. You need to understand these specialists and speak their language, because you must convince them to add search marketing tasks to their day-to-day jobs.

You need to carefully plan what work will be done centrally and what will be done by your extended search team. You must make search marketing part of the normal processes that every Web specialist performs each day. If you do not, you are fighting a losing battle with a new search crisis every day:

- Last month, they finally fixed the title tag so customers can find our top-selling product page in search engines, but yesterday they updated the page again and the title is now wrong, as before.
- They just released a new version of the e-Commerce application, and no spiders can see the pages anymore. Now we have to wait until the *next* release to get them back in the search index so customers can find them.
- They just changed the left navigation bar across the entire site, but now search spiders cannot follow the links, so interior pages are not being crawled for storage in the index. Now we have to get them to change it all over again, which could take months.

What do all these problems have in common? The amorphous "they" in each scenario are the folks on *your* extended search team. But they don't know they are. Or they don't know what they need to do. See, they are probably good at what they do. They probably work hard, and they want to do the right thing. You just need to make "doing the right thing" possible for them.

Exactly how you do that depends on how your organization works today. Methods that work in some organizations might be rejected in others. But here are some ideas on how to prevent these three crises:

- Last month, they finally fixed the title tag so search engines can find our top-selling product page. Last week, the page needed to be updated for an unrelated reason, and the title was inadvertently messed up. The central search team checked the page as part of the normal review process and spotted the problem before it was promoted to production.
- The release plan for the next version of the e-Commerce application included a new technique for displaying pages, but in the customary design review it was found that it did not adhere to the searchability standard. The technique was modified to comply before the coding began.

- The team assigned to redesign our Web site's linking structure came up with three alternative ways to implement their new navigation idea. Because that redesign team included someone from the central search team, they realized that one of their approaches would stop spiders from crawling the site, so they chose one of the other ways.

Sound like a dream? It's not. But it does take planning and hard work to get your organization to function this way. It will not happen by itself. Defining the search marketing tasks, and then dividing them between the central and extended teams, is where you start turning that dream into reality.

Search Marketing Tasks

Before you can divide the work, you need to make a list of exactly which tasks are involved in search engine marketing. Some search marketing tasks apply to organic search, others to paid search. Many are used for both. This list is not intended to be exhaustive—we've got the rest of the book for that—but we want to show the broad categories of tasks that search engine marketing requires:

- *Choosing the search marketing strategy.* Someone needs to set the search marketing strategy. Do we hire a search marketing agency? Do we do everything in-house? A little of each? Are we focusing on organic or paid? Where does the budget come from? How can we prove return on investment? All of these questions must be answered by someone.

- *Targeting search engines.* Which search engines are you trying to get traffic from? Are they the same worldwide or do you need to target different engines in different countries? Someone must decide.

- *Planning keywords.* This is a fancy search marketing name for deducing which query words your visitors will be searching for. To optimize your content so that your pages have the right words on them, someone needs to decide what those words are. Who does that?

- *Managing bids.* If you are using paid search services, you must bid against your competitors to get a sponsored listing on the search results page. Each time your competitors change their bids, you might want to change yours. Every paid search campaign needs someone to manage it.

- *Optimizing content.* If you are pursuing organic search, a lot of the work revolves around changing the content on the pages—titles, descriptions, and any other words you see— and making sure that the HTML is coded and maintained properly. Each page has someone (if not lots of "someones") assigned to maintain its content.

- *Developing technology.* Web sites are based on technology, even if your site uses only a simple Apache Web server to display HTML files. As they grow, many Web sites start using more technology to display their pages and provide other functions, from e-Commerce servers to registration systems to personalization techniques. Each of these technologies can make or break your organic search marketing efforts by making it easy, hard, or even impossible for spiders to crawl your site. Someone needs to make sure that the technology is developed to be search engine–friendly. Whose job is that?

- *Defining standards.* Every Web site has standards for how HTML tags should be used, or what URL patterns are acceptable, or what kinds of software technology might be used. Many existing standards need to be amended and some new ones need to be created to make organic search marketing work. Someone is in charge of each one.

- *Selecting search marketing tools.* Search engine marketing, like anything else, requires specialized tools to manage your bids, check your page rankings, analyze your pages, identify which sites are linking to yours, and many other functions. Someone must be in charge of identifying the need for a tool, justifying the expenditure, selecting the best one, and making sure it is installed and operating properly (and that those who need to use it know how). Who is that someone?

- *Reporting metrics.* How many visitors came to your site from search engines this month? What is the trend from last month? Which queries seem to be the most popular? Which popular queries do not find our pages in the search engines? Someone must be assigned to track and report these measurements. Who?

Don't worry if you do not deeply understand all of these tasks yet. You don't need to. By the time you finish this book, you *will* understand them (and more). It is also normal for the list to seem overwhelming—we help you tackle them one task at a time. Right now you know enough to decide which tasks ought to be performed by your central search team and which ones you need the extended team to do. Later in this book we help you get each one done properly.

Decide Which Search Marketing Tasks to Centralize

There is no one-size-fits-all organization. You might have to experiment to see what works. You might find that some of the tasks above might need to be modified, divided up differently, or even shared between groups. That's okay. Every organization and process is a work in progress anyway. In this section, we give you some rules of thumb that work in many organizations. In the next section, we help you analyze your organization to see whether you want to break any of these rules.

As we look at each task, and decide whether to centralize them or give them to the extended team, keep in mind that *centralize* is a relative term—relative to the scope of your search marketing program, that is. If you have chosen your program scope to cover a division of your company, your central search team operates across the entire division; if your program's scope is your whole company, the central search team works company-wide.

When deciding which tasks to centralize, the most important guideline is to decide whether the task is new for your organization, or whether you already have a team that performs that task (or *should* perform that task). Many search marketing tasks require changing the way someone's existing job is done (such as a copywriter adding keywords to page titles)—those tasks usually belong with your extended search team. Other tasks require deep search marketing expertise or heavy additional workload and are not being done in your company today (such as setting the search marketing strategy)—likely tasks for the central search team. Let's look at each of the major tasks and think through how they might be divided in your organization:

- *Choosing the search marketing strategy.* If this task could be performed well by the extended team, you probably would not need this book. This task requires enough search marketing expertise and enough time that it needs to be centralized in almost all cases.

- *Targeting search engines.* Your central search team is probably best equipped to select the worldwide engines to focus on (such as Google and Yahoo!), but picking the right *local* search engines in each individual country around the world might be best done by the people on your extended team that maintain your Web site in each country. If you work for a small company with few international sales, just focus on Google, Yahoo! Search, MSN Search, Ask.com, and perhaps a few others. However, a large multinational company, with sales in dozens of countries, must explicitly target local search engines in each country, in addition to the big worldwide players. Let your extended team members in each country do that.

- *Planning keywords.* Some organizations can allow the extended team to handle all keyword planning, if the keywords for one business unit do not overlap with the ones desirable to other business units. For many businesses, however, it is essential for the central search team to arbitrate keyword contention between the business units. It would not be good for General Motors to discover its Buick division trying to outbid its Cadillac group for the paid search keyword "luxury sedan." Both business units would be paying more than necessary. Better for the GM central search team to create a great landing page for "luxury sedan" that shows off both Buicks and Cadillacs, allowing visitors to click either one to learn more. That way, Buick and Cadillac can pool their paid search budgets for that keyword and drive traffic to both of their sites. So, even if you distribute bid management to the extended team, be sure that the central team monitors any overlapping bids across the organization. In addition, some keywords truly apply to the entire organization, and therefore must be handled centrally.

- *Managing bids.* Where this task lands depends mostly on who pays for it. If you are running your paid search campaigns centrally, the central team holds the budget and manages the bids. But if each business unit is managing its own paid search budget, they will undoubtedly want to manage their own bids. In a large organization, it is easier to let each business unit handle its own paid search budget rather than manage it centrally, just because of the amount of work involved in juggling thousands of bids simultaneously.

- *Optimizing content.* This task is rarely one the central search team can do well. The central team will educate and help the existing content teams to do their job with search in mind, but they cannot make the actual changes themselves. Your organization might have a single content team that maintains the entire site, in which case the central search team can work closely with it—maybe even be part of the content team. If, like most businesses, the folks that maintain content are scattered hither and yon across the various parts of your organization, however, the central search team must evangelize each team, helping them to understand what processes they must change to optimize their pages on a daily basis.

- *Developing technology.* If you have a central information technology group, it is already purchasing and developing all of your Web site's technology. You just need to get them to understand how their decisions affect search marketing. Let them tell *you* how to make it work—whether they need your help when they do their designs, or they need to update code review procedures, or add some automated tests that prove their new technology works with search engines. If your IT group is *not* centralized, you might need to hire a technical architect for the central search team who can work with each IT group so that they each make the needed process changes. No matter what, your central team cannot take over the technology role, so you need to figure out the best way to persuade this crucial part of your extended team to meet search marketing requirements.

- *Defining standards.* Wherever possible, have the extended team modify your *existing* standards. For example, you probably already have content tagging standards—make sure those standards include what makes a good title for search marketing purposes. Modifying an existing standard allows you to police compliance using whatever procedure already exists; if your central team creates a new standard, however, you need to set up your own compliance process. For every task you need to persuade the extended team to do, try to find an existing standard and persuade the standard owner to modify it. The central team should define new standards only when they are clearly needed and have no obvious extended team owner.

- *Selecting tools.* It is usually best for the central team to choose the tools and pay for them out of a central budget and distribute them to the extended team. You need specialized search marketing expertise to make good selections, and your life will be easier if everyone is using the same tools. You will get a volume discount, and you will have only one set of tools requiring training and support.

- *Reporting metrics.* Your Web site certainly has a group already responsible for traffic metrics, so you can ask them to add a few reports on referrals from search engines (if they do not have them already). But most Web metrics groups will balk at providing reports that are not traffic based, such as summaries of search rankings for important keywords, or a list of all the pages that do not have titles. You will probably have to devote part of your central team for these new reports that fall out of your metrics team's comfort zone, but it cannot hurt to ask.

Regardless of the advice given here, use your own good judgment when deciding what to centralize and what to leave with the extended team. Consider the existing groups in your Web organization to be your extended search team and try to get them to do everything appropriate, because search marketing must permeate so many jobs in your organization to be successful. You will find that your existing organization provides the best clues as to which search tasks should be centralized and which ones the extended team must be persuaded and trained to do.

Different Organizations Centralize Different Tasks

There's no recipe for who does what. As you formulate your plans, you need to carefully consider which tasks should be centralized and which tasks should be distributed to the extended team. Some tasks might need to be shared across the two. Table 8-1 lists a subset of these search marketing tasks and summarizes some possibilities of how centralization decisions might differ based on your organization type. Even when each organization has chosen the same scope (in this case, their entire Web site), the table shows that they might make different decisions about how each search marketing task is executed.

Table 8-1   Centralizing Search Marketing Tasks (Different types of organizations centralize different tasks even with the same site-wide search marketing scope.)

Task	Functional	Product-Oriented	Multinational	Conglomerate
Targeting search engines	Central	Central	Extended	Central
Planning keywords	Central	Extended	Extended	Central
Reporting metrics	Central	Central	Central	Extended
Defining standards	Central	Central	Central	Extended

Our friends at Snap Electronics faced the same decisions on dividing tasks between central and extended teams. Snap decided to pursue both organic and paid search, so every task on our list requires a decision. Snap adopted the approach suggested above for a product-oriented organization. As its search marketing program's scope eventually expands to encompass countries outside the United States, however, it might adopt the multinational approach, allowing each country team to choose the local search engines to target.

You can see that there are many ways to divide up the search marketing work between a central and an extended search team. There are no sure-fire answers, but if you carefully consider the type of organization you work in, you can choose a mix of responsibilities that offers the best chance of cultural acceptance, and therefore success.

Choose Your Search Marketing Approach

Now that you have analyzed the search marketing tasks to perform and made some preliminary decisions about who in your organization will perform them, it's time to decide exactly how to get started. Do you have the expertise on your team to do this? Or do you need to hire some outside help?

You might hear people talk about the choice between outsourcing search marketing and "doing it in-house," but that is a false choice. Certain search marketing tasks, such as changing the content or doing proper redirects, are almost never done by outsiders—your extended team does them. You will *always* do some of the work in-house.

The real question is whether you hire an external vendor to help you. Do you conduct your search marketing program with completely internal resources, or do you also hire an outside firm to augment your own personnel? To answer that question, you need to consider several factors:

- *Corporate culture*. If your executive never "throws money away on consultants," you are unlikely to persuade him on this one. So, one reason to avoid an external vendor is that it does not fit your corporate culture. Most companies, however, benefit from the specialized expertise that search marketing vendors bring. Search marketing is exactly the kind of focused specialty where a consultant can be extremely valuable.

- *Budget*. It is sad but true that some organizations do not have the money to hire an external firm, or at least they believe they do not. This can be extremely shortsighted. Some "starter packages" from search marketing firms cost just $5,000 to $10,000 for a quick analysis with a recommendation for a single product line, for example. You might spend that much to do it yourself, and you would be unlikely to do it as well as the outside firm. Your time is not really free, and you might spend a lot more time doing it than an expert would, especially when you consider the specialized tools and experience a professional brings to the task.

- *Expertise*. Do you have the necessary skills to staff a central search team internally? If not, could you afford to hire someone who has those skills? Would you know how to locate such a person? If you have sufficient expertise available in-house, you do not need any external firm to help. Be aware, however, that a good search marketing firm has a breadth of expertise that you could never find in one or two people. You might need help on arcane technical topics—topics such as rewriting URLs to help dynamic pages get indexed. To solve that problem requires deep expertise in search marketing as well as skills in the particular brand of Web server software you purchased to run your Web site.

- *Time*. In Chapter 7, you probably found that search marketing is an extremely valuable opportunity for your business. It follows that every minute you fail to cash in on that opportunity is costing you money. So, one factor to consider is how quickly a vendor can get your program in gear as opposed to you going it alone—and how much that is worth. If you can see results two months faster, would that more than pay for the professional fee?

- *Quality*. Do you believe that you can get the same (or better) results from your completely in-house search marketing program as if you hired an outside vendor to advise you? It is not easy to assess this factor, but it is worth pondering. A search marketing firm has worked with lots of clients and has undoubtedly seen something before that is similar to your situation. That experience might result in more traffic from your search campaigns.

After assessing these factors in your situation, you might still not be able to decide what to do. If you are undecided, you can interview several search marketing firms to see whether they convince you to hire their firm. They can develop proposals for you to help estimate what your search marketing costs might be—many will do that for a modest fee (or perhaps no fee if you are a large company that could make them a lot of money). Next, we look at how to engage a search marketing firm and select one if you are interested.

Select an External Search Marketing Vendor

As discussed briefly in Chapter 1, "Why Search Marketing Is Important . . . and Difficult," the search business is becoming big business. There are many companies clamoring to become your search marketing vendor, and more firms enter the industry each year. How do you decide which one is right for you?

Any time you select a vendor to provide services to your company, it makes sense to follow a methodical step-by-step process. Your procurement department can help you with some of these steps, but there are specific tips you need to know. We provide those tips as we walk through each step.

Decide Your Vendor Requirements

"Common sense is not so common," goes the old saying. And so it is with selecting vendors. You would think that every company would make a list of what is needed before buying, but many do not. Because we know how sensible you are (hey, you were so smart you bought this book), we are confident that your first step is thinking through your requirements for a search marketing vendor.

You have already made a decision in Chapter 7 on which search techniques you would like to use, so you should ensure that your vendor has expertise in organic, paid, or both, depending on what you picked. Some vendors do much more of one kind of search marketing. Know what you need.

Decide which search marketing tasks you would like the vendor to perform. Help you with the strategy? Keyword planning? Make your list so that you can check the firm's expertise for each task that you want help with. Your list will drive the questions you ask when you talk to each firm.

Do you have any other requirements? Do you want the firm to be available for in-person meetings (so maybe they should have an office located near you) or is it okay that they do the work remotely? Do they need international experience?

Make a list of every requirement and decide how you will grade each one. For example, if you require that your vendor meet your team frequently in person, you might use specific criteria to grade each company:

- *Strong.* Every member of the vendor team on your account is available in a local office.
- *Moderate.* The key members of your vendor account team are local, but some members are not.
- *Weak.* Few or none of your vendor account team members are nearby.

Think carefully about every requirement you have. Decide up front what you are looking for from a vendor to meet that requirement. Then prioritize your requirements. Which ones are critical—no vendor can be selected unless they qualify—as opposed to those that are of medium importance or just nice to have? After you have chosen your requirements, your scoring criteria, and your priorities, you can look for the search marketing vendors that meet them.

Create Your List of Vendor Candidates

Before you can start listing individual firms, you should first decide whether a particular type of search marketing vendor meets your needs better than others. You can consider three major types of firms:

- *Search consultants.* Called search engine optimization (SEO) or search engine marketing (SEM) consultants, these new firms specialize in search marketing. Some of the leading firms include iProspect, Efficient Frontier, and Global Strategies International, but many smaller firms can do a great job for your business, too. Typically, search consultants are smaller firms whose resources could be overwhelmed by a large account, and they have commensurately higher risks of failure. Like most small companies, they are usually far more flexible in the way they work with your company, which can be critical if you work for a large organization used to doing things its own way. Some search consultants are stronger at organic search than paid search, but most handle both well. A great place to find search consultants is the Search Engine Marketing Professional Organization (www.sempo.org).

- *Traditional advertising agencies.* Branching out from their traditional advertising business in TV, radio, and print media, well-known agencies such as Young & Rubicam and Ogilvy & Mather have moved to the Web. Agencies tend to be more proficient at banner ads and paid placement than organic search, but they are steadily making strides there, too. These companies have enormous strategy experience and huge resources to throw at almost any problem, but might not always provide the most personal attention to your account. Your company might already have a relationship with one or more of these companies.

- *Interactive advertising agencies.* Consisting of mostly small firms (although usually larger than search consultants), these firms handle all Internet marketing needs, including e-mail and banner ads, but have begun to focus more on search marketing. Traditional ad agencies have created interactive agencies as well (such as OgilvyInteractive). Some interactive agencies are better at paid search than organic search, but others have strong SEO expertise. Small firms suffer all the expected small company vendor risks, but also provide more personal attention than their larger agency counterparts. You can find a list of agencies by visiting the Interactive Advertising Bureau Web site. (Visit iab.com/about/general_members.asp for a list of "general" members; see iab.com/about/assoc_member_list.asp for "associate" members.)

Perhaps one type of company fits your situation better than the others, or maybe you want to interview a couple of firms in each category, so that you can evaluate the full gamut of vendors available. Regardless, you must put together a list of firms to consider.

Recommendations from others, Web searches, and trade association lists (such as Search Engine Marketing Professionals Organization) can all help you compile your list. You can visit each firm's Web site and read comparisons of each firm to come up with your "short list" of vendors to consider. In Chapter 16, "What's Next?," we list several industry conferences where you will find vendors selling their wares—it never hurts to meet them and hear a five-minute sales pitch before going further. Depending on your organization's location, you can also consult *Buyer's Guide to Search Engine Optimization Firms: US, UK & Canada* by Marketing Sherpa (www.marketingsherpa.com), which contains ratings of more than 100 organic search vendors.

After you have your short list of vendors, you can use your requirements list to put together a matrix to assess each vendor against the others. Snap Electronics put together such a matrix, as shown in Table 8-2. (The vendors shown, like Snap itself, are fictitious operations that are not intended to bear any resemblance to real firms.)

Table 8-2   Snap Electronics Vendor Scorecard (Set up a matrix to assess your vendors against each requirement according to the criteria you have decided.)

Vendor Requirements	Priority	Stolid Advertising Agency	Mega Internet Marketing, Inc.	Boutique SEO
Organic search experience	High			
Paid search experience	Medium			
Search strategy	Medium			
Keyword planning	High			
Technical expertise	High			
Business reliability	Medium			
Local presence	Low			

In the interest of space, we are showing a short list of both requirements and vendors for Snap. Yours would likely be considerably longer for both. Right now, there are no ratings for each vendor in that table, but we will fill them in as we meet each one.

Meet the Vendors

Now that you have a scorecard, it's time to start the game. Depending on the size of your company, and the size of the deal the vendor anticipates from you, you might be able to get a free proposal for your search marketing plan. If you have a small organization, you can at least get them to conduct a teleconference with you during which they "strut their stuff" and answer your questions. So what questions should you ask? That's what we will show you here.

The first set of questions should cover the vendor's methodology. After reading this book, you should be able to ask specific questions about each technique that your vendor proposes to use. You need to ensure that your vendor does not use unethical spamming techniques and that your consultant's approach is right for your situation. You should expect a document or presentation that lays out the strategy the firm intends to use.

HOW DO YOU SPOT A SPAMMER?

No smoking gun proves a search marketing vendor practices unethical techniques, but you can use this list to raise enough red flags to eliminate suspicious candidates:

- *Do they guarantee top rankings*? No reputable firms will promise you top results—too many variables are out of their control. Firms that promise top results will usually do *anything* to get them. Spam techniques might have temporary results, but they will be caught in the long run and your site will be banned.
- *Do they promise that top rankings require only minimal changes to your site*? You might be dealing with a **link farm** operator. Another way to spot a link farmer is that they want you to include special HTML on your pages. They hide links to their other clients on your pages (and hide links to you on other clients' pages).
- *Do they talk about special code that gives them an edge*? If you hear them discuss "cloaking," or "IP delivery," or using different versions of pages for the spider than are used for the visitor, be wary.

If you get a "yes" answer to any of these questions, you might be dealing with a spammer. One way to flush out a spammer is to check the references provided. Another way to spot a spammer is to act as though that is exactly what you are looking for. Talk up how you have heard that you need to do some really secret stuff to get high rankings and that you need an expert who knows how to do it. A spammer will likely take that bait, but an ethical search marketer will talk you out of it and explain the right way to do it.

Each firm should be able to itemize the steps they will take to diagnose any problems on your site and work with you to correct them. How specific they can be depends on whether they have done only a quick site audit or a full-blown proposal for you.

You need to be realistic in your expectations. If you are a small company looking for a $10,000 contract, you cannot expect any vendor to provide you a 30-page proposal before you have signed a deal with them. On the other hand, a large corporation that wants a long-term relationship should expect a free detailed proposal before signing a six-figure agreement.

Some vendors will perform a site audit that clues you in to search marketing challenges before you sign up with them. Even if they do not, you should be able to review a step-by-step pro forma project plan—maybe your plan will be a bit different, but each vendor should be able to show what they typically do. Unless a vendor has done a site audit, you cannot expect a specific plan for your site, but they should be able to tell you what they do in certain hypothetical situations.

One last methodology question might be important to you. You might care deeply how wedded your vendor is to their own methodology. If you work in a large, inflexible organization, you might require supreme flexibility in your search marketing vendor's methodology. If your vendor insists on only one right way to do its work, you might not be able to carry out the plan.

Beyond methodology questions, there are the normal business questions you would ask of any prospective vendor. Your procurement experts can help you analyze the pricing, contract terms, and the firm's financial viability. Remember that in the fast-moving Internet world, a company's financial health can change rapidly, so be sure to check out a firm's records, not its past reputation. Your procurement specialist should also weigh in on whether liability insurance is required.

Perhaps the most important set of questions center on the account team that will be assigned to your company by the vendor. A high-priced dream team might call on you before you sign the deal, but are they going to be your actual account team after you sign? Insist on meeting *your* account team beforehand. Those folks will be working with you every day and their opinions and experience will prove far more important than the rainmakers who close the deal. There's nothing wrong with a junior staff member doing preliminary keyword research or running reports or other preparation work—that saves you a lot of money—but the real brain work must be done by experienced senior search marketers.

Ask the members of your account team how long they have been employed by the firm, and whether they are permanent employees (who get W-2 statements) or are contractors (receiving 1099s). Team members that are longstanding permanent employees provide reassurance that your account team might remain stable, without members jumping to new jobs and leaving you with a rookie to break in. All team members should be covered by nondisclosure agreements for confidential information. If possible, ensure that team members do not also work on search marketing for your competitors.

Question account team members about their specific expertise and search marketing experience. They should be able to name their other accounts and supply references you can contact. Those references should testify to the team's results in previous search campaigns. Insist on talking to former clients, not just current ones. Firms routinely recite long lists of impressive clients, but you should only be impressed by the clients that you verify are satisfied.

As you ask these questions, fill in your scorecard. Table 8-3 shows Snap's scorecard.

Table 8-3 Final Snap Electronics Vendor Scorecard (Using the criteria that you set at the beginning of the process, each vendor can be graded against the others.)

Vendor Requirements	Priority	Stolid Advertising Agency	Mega Internet Marketing, Inc.	Boutique SEO
Organic search experience	High	Weak	Moderate	Strong
Paid search experience	Medium	Strong	Strong	Moderate
Search strategy	Medium	Strong	Strong	Moderate
Keyword planning	High	Moderate	Moderate	Strong
Technical expertise	High	Weak	Moderate	Strong
Business reliability	Medium	Strong	Moderate	Weak
Local presence	Low	Moderate	Weak	Strong

Snap used its interviews with each vendor to decide its rating on the requirements. Not all of the assessments were clear-cut, and no real leader emerged. The final decision came next.

DO YOU NEED A GLOBAL SEARCH MARKETING VENDOR?

Maybe your business has been a global marketer for many years. Or perhaps the Web has put global markets within your reach that were impossible before. Regardless, more and more businesses are marketing globally on the Web. If you are hiring a search marketing vendor for a program with global scope, you need to ask more questions to find the right match.

Unfortunately, there are no easy answers to some of these questions. You will quickly find that each vendor you interview has a different story about how they execute global programs, so it quickly comes down to what you need. You must ruthlessly prioritize which countries and languages you *need* coverage for, because a vendor strong in one area might be weak in another. Know which countries and languages are your top priorities—that cannot be compromised—and be willing to accept a little less for other markets.

After you have your target market list, check out the vendor's expertise, country by country:

- *Local presence*. Does the vendor have native speakers residing in the country? Many do not. Does that person work for the vendor? Many have subcontracted relationships with local search marketers—sometimes two or three levels of relationships, which can make things sticky if you run into disagreements.
- *Integration*. How do they enforce the strategy of the overall program in each country? How do they report results across the whole program? Many do not have any way of performing these critical operational tasks.
- *Search engine relationships*. Do they have verifiable relationships with the local search engines and directories? Many local search engines work only with certain firms, so make sure you are working with those firms, too.
- *Local references*. Insist on speaking to customer references in each country. Search marketing vendors can have wildly different capabilities from country to country, so make sure you check them out in every top-priority locale on your list.

After you have spoken to each vendor, think carefully about the right tradeoffs. If 80 percent of your revenue is from the United States, is it worth compromising global markets to get the best vendor for the United States? Could you hire multiple vendors to get stronger coverage across your target markets, or would the coordination headaches be too great? You might not have an easy decision; if you ask the right questions, however, at least you will have fewer nasty surprises.

Make Your Decision

If you have done a good job recruiting strong candidates to become your search marketing vendor, your final decision will not be easy. You need to return to your original priorities. Which requirements are the most important and how does each vendor stack up on those?

Snap faced a difficult decision among the three vendors on its short list. To simplify the choice, Snap focused on its highest priorities: organic search experience, keyword planning, and technical expertise. Boutique SEO was rated "strong" on all three counts. Boutique's only weakness was business reliability, due to its small size and short experience. Snap decided to take that risk, negotiating a low-priced deal to compensate for the risk. Boutique, as a hungry small firm, was eager to land the high-profile Snap account as a great reference customer (that will help persuade new customers to sign with them).

Your decision might be just as difficult as Snap's. Before you decide, however, also consider whether you should run your program completely in-house, with no search marketing vendor on your payroll.

Run a Completely In-House Search Marketing Program

It is not easy to go it alone—without hiring an outside vendor—but it can work, if you know what you are doing.

The biggest benefit to doing it in-house is that your program will take an "inside-out" approach rather than an outsider's approach. Your in-house team understands your organization. Your depth of knowledge will allow you to set your priorities based on which campaigns are the easiest to do—that can be good. Sometimes external vendors know a lot about search marketing but not much about your company—they can possibly lead you astray. Of course, if you manage the vendor properly, you will not run this risk.

The hard part of going it alone is in finding the needed expertise in-house. It is rare that you can find search marketing experts inside an organization that, up until now, has not been doing any search marketing. It is possible you can find such skills if your search marketing program is run on a small scale (one division, perhaps) and you want to expand to an enterprise-wide program.

Failing to find the needed expertise, you can develop your search experts from within. You can send folks to classes and conferences, and buy them books (they each need three copies of this one), teaching them what they need to know. This approach can work, but it is slow—usually taking months of startup time before you really get rolling.

Typically, you will be in a hurry, forcing you to hire experts from the outside. The best of both worlds can be to hire an "embedded strategist" who acts as a facilitator to the organization—you try to hire the same kind of person who a search marketing vendor hires.

If you can locate, develop, or hire the search marketing experts that you need, you will likely find that you still do not have the same experience that hiring an outside vendor brings. Vendors work with many different companies and see myriad situations. You are unlikely to replicate that experience in a one- or two-person search team. You will, however, save a lot of money. Internal search experts are typically cheaper than buying the same expertise from outside. With a few key hires and an investment in training, you can staff a strong internal team and create additional loyalty from employees gaining new skills.

And that loyalty might prove vital, because a 100 percent in-house approach has a key danger of employee attrition. Search marketing skills are hot and getting hotter in today's job market. External search marketing vendors can usually pay more for your employees than you do (because those companies charge more to cover the costs). If you lose your key team members to competitors or vendors, your search marketing efforts can be severely damaged, at least in the short term. Although members of a vendor account team also might depart, the vendor is more easily able to withstand those changes and replace people with others of high skill. Replacing defectors from *your* in-house team with equally talented people might be considerably more challenging.

In short, it is possible for you to run a successful search marketing program with no outside vendor, but it has its own set of challenges and risks. If you can find, train, or hire the experts you need—and retain them—your search marketing efforts will bear strong results while also costing less than using an external firm. You might find, however, that the slow "ramp up" time to start your program, coupled with the risks of hiring less-skilled resources and unexpected employee defections, might not make the cost savings worth the pain.

Project Your Search Marketing Costs

Deciding your search marketing strategy is critical to formulating your program, especially when it comes to assessing your costs. You cannot win approval for a program when you have no idea how much you need to spend to carry it off.

To paint your cost picture, you need to go back to your strategy decisions. You need to keep your scope in mind—how broad is your program? A search marketing program that handles only a few areas of your site is not nearly as big as one that covers the whole site. Your program scope directly impacts your costs.

You must also know what your approach is to budgeting. Will you budget to build or will you build to budget? That's the shorthand way of asking whether you will add up all your possible costs and ask for that budget (budget to build) or you are being told a budget and can build a program that includes any tactics you can afford under the budget.

The budget to build approach is the most accurate, and we use it here. If, on the other hand, you are handed a budget, you use the same calculations to determine your costs, but you prioritize your most important costs and you choose your program's scope based on what you can afford.

Organic Optimization Costs

If your search marketing strategy includes organic search, you must project how much money to budget to carry out your organic optimization efforts. If you remember assessing your organic search situation in Chapter 7, you will recall that you identified which of your site's pages should match your targeted keywords, and whether those pages are stored in search indexes. As you learned, it can be quite difficult to get some pages included in the search index—in Chapter 10, we explore all of the reasons that spiders can be blocked from your site. Because it is hard to estimate the cost of eliminating these spider problems, we simplify our cost projections by assuming that we will create new pages that are designed to be crawled by the spider to replace the hard-to-crawl pages if we have to.

Even if your pages are already in the search index, you still need to work on them. You need to update the titles and content on your pages to include mentions of your targeted keywords, as discussed in Chapter 12, "Optimize Your Content." You need to make these changes not only so that your pages achieve high rankings in the search results, but also so that your title and snippet invite the searchers to click through to your site.

After you read Chapters 10 and 12, you might be able to project your costs much more closely, but you can use techniques right now to come up with a ballpark estimate. As you saw back in Chapter 3, "How Search Marketing Works," it usually costs between $100 and $200 to optimize each page for organic search. If your content costs are typically low and you are mostly editing existing pages, your costs might be closer to the $100 mark, whereas large organizations creating new pages might pay $200 or more. These costs are just averages; so if you know exactly how much it costs to create new pages or edit pages on your site, use that figure for higher accuracy. If you do not know your own costs, take into account how difficult it is to make changes to your site. If you have a simple process that requires only a few people to touch the page, you will spend much less than a large organization with intricate workflows where pages are checked by people ranging from the copy editor to the brand manager to the corporate counsel.

After you know your per-page cost, you then need to estimate the number of pages you must change—we will do that based on the area of your Web site that you targeted in Chapter 7. If the targeted area required that you optimize 10 pages for organic search, and optimization costs you $123 a page on average, you will spend $1,230 for each area of your site. If you have 100 products, that adds up to $123,000 to optimize your whole site.

Returning to our case study for Snap Electronics, you recall that Snap identified five pages it had to optimize for its digital camera campaign. To be conservative, they estimated higher costs, assuming they would have to change at least 25 pages. Because Snap had kept no records on its content-update costs, it decided to use the high-end $200 figure, yielding a $5,000 cost per product line. Because Snap has 78 product lines in the United States (its total scope of its search marketing program), Snap estimates it will cost $390,000 to optimize its content for organic search. You can see how seemingly small costs can add up quickly in a large company.

Paid Placement Costs

If you decided to pursue paid search as part of your strategy, Yahoo!'s current high bidder auction makes it simple. Unfortunately, Yahoo! has already announced that they will be moving to a Google-like paid search ranking technique that combines clickthrough rate and bid, which may complicate matters. Yahoo! has promised that they will provide an estimated number of ad impressions based on the bid you are contemplating, so it may remain simple to project your costs. We won't know for sure, however, until we see how Yahoo!'s new approach works. In the meantime, here's how Yahoo!'s current system can help you estimate your costs.

Point your Web browser to http://searchmarketing.yahoo.com/rc/srch/ and click on the View Bids Tool link, then enter one of your targeted keywords. As shown in Figure 8-3, you will be shown the top bidders for that keyword in Yahoo! along with each one's **bid limit**—the highest amount that each bidder will pay.

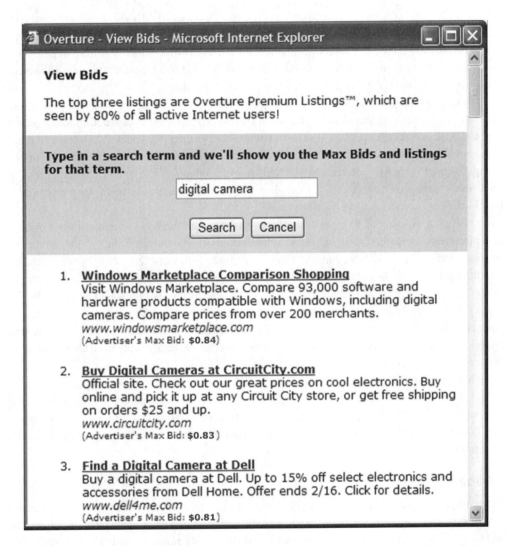

Figure 8-3 Snap's Yahoo! bid limits. Yahoo! shows the highest bid your competitors will pay per click on a result for the keyword "digital camera."

Reproduced with permission of Yahoo! Inc. © 2005 by Yahoo! Inc. YAHOO! and the YAHOO! logo are trademarks of Yahoo! Inc.

Depending on what the other bidders are doing, the bid limit might or might not be what the bidder is currently paying for each click—but it is the amount that bidder is *willing* to pay. So if you want to estimate what it would cost you to take the #1 spot (for example), you would need to budget at least 1¢ more than the bid limit of the current top bidder.

Now you might not be aiming at the top spot. Perhaps you are happy with the third position, for example. (You should understand that the top three positions are syndicated to many search engines, but lower results are shown far less.) Choose the position that you want, and add 1¢ more to the current bid limit for that position. To be conservative, you might want to add more than a penny. Eyeing Figure 8-3, you can see that Snap might need to pay 85¢ or more to garner the top spot, because the first three bids are more than 80¢ each. If you outbid them, they might raise their bids.

Using an estimate of 85¢ per click, Snap can calculate the budget required for a Yahoo! paid placement campaign for digital cameras by multiplying the bid rate (85¢) by the number of monthly queries (1,337,422 as counted by Yahoo! in Table 7-10 from Chapter 7) by the estimated clickthrough rate (Snap conservatively projected 1 percent) to yield the estimated monthly Yahoo! cost of $11,368. Multiplying that cost by Snap's 78 product lines yields a cost for the overall search marketing program of $886,704 per month for paid placement. Clearly, that is more than anyone at Snap wants to risk for such an unproven idea, so they decide that they will project a much smaller cost more befitting with the experimental status they have chosen for paid placement.

Multiplying $11,368 by 12 produces the yearly paid search budget for the first campaign of $136,416, which Snap rounds up to $150,000 for its proposal. Anticipating that the experiment will be at least somewhat successful, Snap decides to double that budget for the overall program to $300,000 a year, but the outcome of the experiment will ultimately tell them whether that is the right figure.

Personnel Costs

Depending on your particular strategy, you might find that personnel costs are the largest expense in your program. Perhaps you will have just a small central search team (maybe it is just you), but whatever personnel time is expended on search will cost something. You might know exactly how much your organization allots for each person assigned to a project—if you do, use that. Most organizations budget between $75,000 and $150,000 each year for each "head count," so your company probably lands somewhere in that range.

If you can get away with it, it is best to avoid calculating the costs of the extra work your extended search team must do to support search marketing. In some organizations, you might be required to take a shot at this number, but it varies widely based on your situation. You are better off making the case that this is part of their job, and always should have been part of their job. The marketing department does not have to justify why the Web team should change copy when they develop a new slogan—it is part of their job. Point out that this is part of developing a good Web site that meets your business needs, and should be absorbed as part of their current workload. You can show real return for the work you are requesting, which is more than can be said for a lot of the work they do that no one ever questions.

If you have decided to hire an external vendor, you should have received an estimate on what will be charged. You can do small one-time audits for as little as $5,000, but a full-blown program in a large enterprise can easily run hundreds of thousands of dollars. Whatever you decided, you need to include that cost in your proposal for your program.

Snap Electronics decided to staff a three-person central search team. The team leader is an experienced Snap Web marketer (who already knows the U.S. product managers) whose mission is to sell the program internally and to manage the central search team. Snap will hire an organic search expert and a paid search expert from outside the company, because they cannot seem to find those skills internally. Snap's finance department insists that all proposals use a flat rate of $130,000 per person for planning purposes, so the three-person team is budgeted at $390,000 each year.

Boutique SEO, the vendor that Snap chose, initially provided an estimate of $140,000 annually to provide strategy and keyword planning services, but Snap felt that was more than it wanted to pay. Snap wanted to keep the total personnel costs at half a million dollars or less, because investments more than $500,000 required higher-level executives to approve. Snap negotiated with Boutique to train its central search team to perform keyword planning internally, instead of doing the keyword planning at Boutique. This change reduced the annual costs to $110,000. When that $110,000 is added to the $390,000 cost for the central search team, it totals a more palatable $500,000 combined annual investment. Making this change will slow down the rate of rollout of the search marketing program because it will take longer to do the keyword planning across the entire product line, but it was believed that the tradeoff was worth it to get the program approved more easily.

Summary

We have covered a lot of ground in this chapter. You chose the scope of your search marketing program, decided what strategy to adopt, and estimated the costs involved. All of these points are critical to your next step: convincing the rest of your organization to approve your program.

In Chapter 7, you chose your first search marketing campaign—one that you believed would be high impact and relatively easy to do. Your first campaign lets you start small, show success, and build from there. Recall that your alter egos at Snap chose digital cameras. We can itemize the costs of Snap's first campaign in Table 8-5. To keep things simple, we assess the costs for the entire central search team and the SEO vendor to our first campaign, but you might want a more complex calculation to spread those costs over multiple campaigns.

Table 8-5   Snap's First Campaign Costs (Startup costs incurred in Year 1 for organic search drop off in Years 2 through 5.)

	Organic Search	Paid Search	Personnel	Total
Year 1	$5,000	$150,000	$500,000	$655,000
Year 2	0	$150,000	$500,000	$650,000
Year 3	0	$150,000	$500,000	$650,000
Year 4	0	$150,000	$500,000	$650,000
Year 5	0	$150,000	$500,000	$650,000
Total	$5,000	$750,000	$2,500,000	$3,255,000

Snap Electronics made its search marketing program scope decision right along with you, choosing an ambitious U.S. program across all of its products that emphasizes organic search and experiments with paid search. Table 8-6 summarizes Snap's estimated costs for the first five years of its program. The organic search costs are one-time only, but the remaining costs apply each year.

Table 8-6   Projected Costs for Snap's Search Marketing Program (Each expense must be totaled to develop your overall business case to be persuasive.)

	Organic Search	Paid Search	Personnel	Total
Year 1	$390,000	$300,000	$500,000	$1,190,000
Year 2	0	$300,000	$500,000	$800,000
Year 3	0	$300,000	$500,000	$800,000
Year 4	0	$300,000	$500,000	$800,000
Year 5	0	$300,000	$500,000	$800,000
Total	$390,000	$1,500,000	$2,500,000	$4,390,000

These costs look large, but the benefits look larger, as you will see in the next chapter. We take the work we did in Chapter 7 to analyze the opportunity across the scope of the program that we chose in this chapter. For Snap Electronics, we calculate the revenue opportunity for all U.S. products.

We're just getting started, however. In Chapter 9, we go beyond the numbers to close the deal. How do you convince all the members of your existing Web team (your extended search team) to change their jobs to include search marketing? And how do you persuade the toughest audience of all—your executives—to part with the cash you need to get started? In the next chapter, we show you how to convince your organization to take a chance on a search marketing program.

Sell Your Search Marketing Proposal

It's time to close the deal. Time to get the approvals for your proposal to start a search marketing program. Next to actually managing a search marketing program, the most complicated activity is getting "buy-in" from your extended search team and your executives. How hard that is to do depends on the scope of the search marketing program that you selected in Chapter 8, "Define Your Search Marketing Strategy." The larger your scope, the tougher your approval process will be.

In this chapter, you learn how to do the following:

- *Assemble your proposal.* You calculated the revenue opportunity for a single campaign in Chapter 7, "Measure Your Search Marketing Success," and the costs for both your first campaign and overall program in Chapter 8, "Define Your Search Marketing Strategy." In this chapter, we put them together and craft a proposal that you can use to persuade others in your company. Your proposal will contain business cases that justify the investment in both your first campaign and the program as a whole. Your proposal will also include a step-by-step plan with a time line to implement your first search marketing campaign.

- *Sell your proposal to the extended search team.* Your organization already has an existing team (maybe lots of teams) to manage your Web site today. These specialists decide the strategy, write the content, create the pages, design applications, and do many other things. You must take advantage of these existing resources as your extended search team, because search marketing cannot succeed unless *they* do the right things. You need to understand these specialists and speak their language, because you must convince them to add search marketing tasks to their day-to-day jobs.

- *Sell your proposal to your executives.* In most places, no money gets released without executive approval. You will learn what executives are looking for in a proposal, so that yours will be approved.

In some organizations, you can sell your proposal to the executives, who then order the extended team to execute, but in most companies that will not work. Many corporate cultures do not allow executives to bless a proposal until there is consensus among all affected. You can assess how your organization works to decide whether to talk to the extended team first, the executives first, or to work them in parallel. Regardless of which you approach first, you need to assemble your proposal so you have something to talk about, so let's do that now.

Assemble Your Search Marketing Proposal

In the preceding chapters, you've laid the groundwork for your proposal, but you need to put it all together. Your proposal contains two business cases—one for your overall search marketing program and one specifically for your first search marketing campaign. This way, you explain why search marketing is important strategically, for many campaigns, but also focus on a tangible, practical first effort. Your proposal must also include a detailed plan of tasks on a time line to execute the first campaign, but we start with the business cases.

The Business Case for Your Search Marketing Program

A business case serves two primary purposes. First, it is an unbiased and objective analysis of projected costs required to achieve expected benefits. The second objective is to convince your decision makers to accept your recommendations. In short, your business case ought to persuade *you* before you use it to persuade others. Too often, business cases get a bad name because they are cobbled together as a pretext for doing something that does not actually have much value. Search marketing has a great deal of value—you do not need a sham business case. You can build a case to convince even the most tight-fisted bean counter.

In Chapter 7, we discussed the revenue opportunity for your first search marketing campaign, and in Chapter 8 we calculated the cost, both for your first campaign and your overall search program. Here, we put them together to show the payback of search marketing—the payback of pursuing search marketing across the full scope of the search marketing program that you chose in Chapter 8. We look at the bigger picture, going beyond your first campaign. How can you project the revenue opportunity of your search marketing program across your program's entire scope? We first return to your calculations from Chapter 7 for the revenue opportunity and expand it to the entire program. Then we revisit your costs based on the work you did in Chapter 8.

Your Search Marketing Program's Revenue Opportunity

If you followed the logic to determine the revenue opportunity for mounting a search marketing campaign, you might be wondering how we can estimate the revenue opportunity for your entire search marketing program. What if you embarked on a search marketing program across all your products? How much incremental revenue could you drive? There is no precise way to answer these questions. No matter what we do, we will be making some assumptions. But we can come up with ballpark figures that give you a glimpse into your search marketing potential.

Returning to our fictitious firm, Snap Electronics, we recall that they chose as their search marketing program scope their entire U.S. product line. To estimate the total search marketing potential for Snap's site, we can extrapolate from our first campaign.

Table 7-15 from Chapter 7 projected the number of additional organic search referrals Snap could achieve with a well-executed search marketing campaign for digital cameras. Because Snap's scope emphasizes organic marketing over its 78 product lines within the United States, we can examine our projections for Snap's first campaign and then apply them across the entire scope. Table 7-15 shows that the referrals to the digital camera area of Snap's site total just 10,734 each month, but are projected to rise to 28,082 referrals, a 162 percent increase. We can apply this same percentage increase to Snap's overall U.S. search referrals—the referrals associated with any keyword, not just those related to digital cameras—to estimate the traffic increase possible for Snap's entire search marketing program. In Snap's case, its Web metrics facility showed 52,634 organic search referrals for its U.S. site last month. Multiplying by 162 percent yields an opportunity for 137,901 organic search referrals—an increase of 85,267 each month across Snap's whole U.S. site.

But we need to estimate our paid referrals, too. Because paid placement is an experiment, Snap decided to limit its spending to $300,000, just twice the cost of the first campaign for digital cameras. It stands to reason that we should double the added referrals for that first paid placement campaign as our best estimate for the overall impact of paid placement. If $150,000 brings 13,374 added referrals for digital cameras, spending $300,000 might bring twice as many: 26,748.

To estimate the overall added referrals for our search marketing program, we can total the organic search projection (85,267) and the paid search one (26,748) to produce 112,015 added referrals per month.

As we did with digital cameras, we can calculate the revenue impact of the entire Snap search marketing program for all U.S. products, as shown in Figure 9-1. We had used the site-wide conversion rate of 2 percent in Chapter 7, so that remains the same, but we now use the average transaction price of all U.S. sales on the site, which rises to $493. It is $13 million in incremental revenue a year!

	Added monthly traffic	112,015
Multiply by:	Conversion rate	0.02
	Added monthly sales	2,240
Multiply by:	Average transaction price	$493
	Added monthly revenue	$1,104,320
Multiply by:	12 months	12
	Added yearly revenue	$13,251,840

Figure 9-1 Projecting revenue for Snap's search marketing program. We use a familiar formula to project incremental search revenue program-wide.

Although no one can predict the exact numbers with pinpoint accuracy, clearly Snap has a lot to gain from a search marketing program across the U.S. product line. As you work through your organization's opportunity, you might find a similarly exciting prospect in your own backyard.

Your Search Marketing Program's Costs

You saw in Chapter 8 that, as tough as it is to project revenue opportunity, it might be even harder to figure out what it all will cost. Nonetheless, we can use the estimates we calculated in the preceding chapter to project our costs over the next several years.

In your situation, you might make different (and more complex) assumptions, but in our Snap case study, we keep it very simple. The organic search costs we estimated ($390,000) can be assumed to be incurred in the first year. That is probably an unrealistic expectation, because most companies would make their investment over a period of years, but spending money earlier is the most pessimistic business case, so we do it that way.

The organic search costs are a one-time cost—after the technology and the pages are cleaned up, your central search team and your improved standards and processes will keep them clean. But the other costs are annual, and need to be reflected in each year's cost projection. You can review Tables 8-5 and 8-6 in Chapter 8 to refresh your memory for the cost calculations both for the first campaign and the overall search marketing program.

Your Search Marketing Program's Business Case

We can construct a business case for the Snap Electronics search marketing program based on the revenue we calculated in Figure 9-1. To keep things simple, we round off the revenue number and assume it to be constant over all five years. Obviously that is also unrealistic, because you would likely see a gradual rise in revenue from a slow start, but it makes the example simpler to understand. Table 9-1 consolidates our work from these previous two chapters to show the estimated profit over five years from Snap's search marketing program.

Table 9-1   Snap's Search Marketing Program Business Case (In a large company, the payback from search marketing can be sizable across the enterprise.)

	Revenue	Cost	Profit
Year 1	$13,250,000	$1,190,000	$12,060,000
Year 2	$13,250,000	$800,000	$12,450,000
Year 3	$13,250,000	$800,000	$12,450,000
Year 4	$13,250,000	$800,000	$12,450,000
Year 5	$13,250,000	$800,000	$12,450,000
Total	$66,250,000	$4,390,000	$61,860,000

Even in a company as large as Snap Electronics, $61 million over five years is a big deal. So big a deal, in fact, that they reduced their numbers drastically before they showed this business case to their executives. They reasoned that search marketing was a great idea even if they were wildly off in their calculations, so they wanted to be careful not to overpromise the benefits and risk early disappointment.

This book is not devoted to developing business cases, so there are certainly many more sophisticated methods to use. Check with your finance folks to see whether they have a methodology that they like. Whatever method you use, the payback for your search marketing program is likely to be *very* positive. And that is the point of this exercise. Estimate what search marketing can do for your organization, and then make the decision to get started.

Your First Search Marketing Campaign's Business Case

The business case for your overall search marketing program shows why search marketing should be strategic to your organization, but you need to have a more tactical proposal. Few businesses would lay out sizable cash in the first year for a totally unproven idea. Therefore, your proposal also needs to make a strong case for your first search marketing campaign.

In Chapter 7, we calculated Snap's revenue opportunity for its digital camera campaign in Figure 7-6, and we carry those revenue projections into our business case in Table 9-2 (along with the costs we estimated in Table 8-5 in Chapter 8).

Table 9-2   Snap's First Campaign Business Case (The digital camera product line does look like a promising initial target for search marketing at Snap.)

	Revenue	Cost	Profit
Year 1	$2,550,000	$655,000	$1,895,000
Year 2	$2,550,000	$650,000	$1,900,000
Year 3	$2,550,000	$650,000	$1,900,000
Year 4	$2,550,000	$650,000	$1,900,000
Year 5	$2,550,000	$650,000	$1,900,000
Total	$12,750,000	$3,255,000	$9,495,000

As with the overall program business case, we round off the overly precise revenue projection we calculated in Chapter 7. The reason you round off is that you want the precision of the estimate to show the precision of the model—our model is not precise enough to estimate anything down to the dollar, so why show a number that makes the model look more precise than it is? How much would you trust a man who sticks his hand into a cold stream and announces "49.2 degrees"? Being overly precise takes away attention from the real message to your executives: "Search marketing is a big opportunity—even though our numbers are estimates and might be very far off, you can *still* see the right decision to make."

That wraps up the business case sections, but you need to create a more complete proposal for your search marketing program. As we continue assembling our proposal, we need to explain exactly what we will do to deliver on the business case for the first campaign.

The Plan for Your First Search Marketing Campaign

What tasks will you undertake? When will they happen? You will not have a persuasive proposal without a plan. You need to show, task by task, who will take the actions required to deliver the value promised in your business case. You also need to show the time line for each action. Every search marketing campaign needs a plan with several phases:

- *Organization phase.* You have completed much of the organizing for your first campaign already, but it can be one of the longer phases of some projects. The primary organizational tasks include choosing the team, deciding the approach (organic, paid, or both), setting the scope of the campaign, and performing preliminary keyword analysis to help set the budget and opportunity. We have worked through each of these steps in Chapters 7 and 8 for your first campaign, but you will take these steps for every campaign.

- *Auditing phase.* For organic search, you need to audit your technology and content to determine what problems afflict your site. The diagnoses for these problems drive the later phases.

- *Learning phase.* Early in your organization's efforts, it is typical for gaps to exist in search marketing knowledge. As your company grows in experience, more of the problems found in each campaign's audit can be handled without requiring additional learning.

- *Implementation phase.* Finally the wrenches start to turn and the search marketing machine comes to life. Both organic and paid campaigns are tuning content (Web pages or ads) and monitoring traffic and conversions. For paid campaigns, bid management is a major task; organic campaigns are constantly seeking links from other sites and ensuring spiders can index content.

Snap Electronics put together the plan shown in Figure 9-2 to explain the campaign for its digital camera product line. You can see that each phase of the project takes a month or two to execute—*your* project plan might be shorter or longer, depending on what you want to do, the pace of your organization, and how thoroughly you persuade your extended team and your executives (which we cover later). Each phase in the plan lists the major tasks that must be accomplished, the group that leads each one, and the others that must assist that task's completion. The central search team leads many tasks, but your extended search team must lead some, too (especially in the implementation phase). You might want to produce a more exhaustive chart that shows all the tasks in each phase, but for brevity we showed just the major ones to give you the idea.

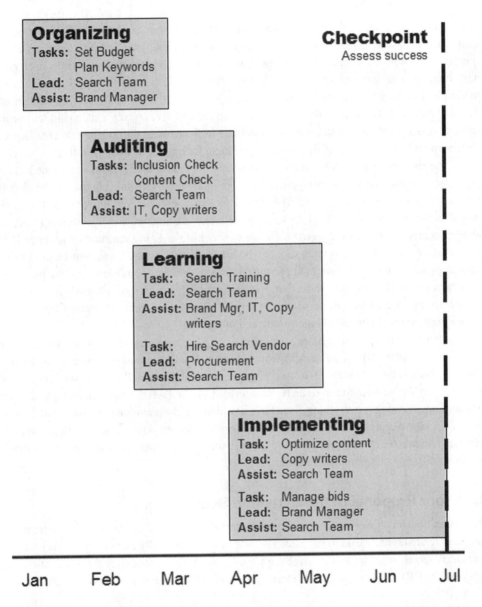

Figure 9-2 Snap's first campaign time line. A simple visual that shows what needs to be done can explain the campaign in one glance.

This chart is very important in explaining your plan. Your executives and your extended team will each want to know exactly what you plan to do. They will want to know what your timeframe is and who will perform each task. When you speak to the extended team, each group will scan this chart looking for its name. The copywriters will see that they are leading a task in the implementation phase, which will make them nervous. It is important that you explain how you will help and why they ultimately need to own the task. When they understand why search marketing is important and that you are deferring to their ownership of the content, they will understand why they must lead the optimizing content for organic search marketing.

The checkpoint line on Figure 9-2 is also very important. Your plan must include a checkpoint for evaluating success—give yourself enough room in the schedule not just to complete the actions, but for them to show results. You should not expect to have everything "done"—you will find it is *never* done. There is always one more tweak to improve the clickthrough rate, and another competitor that leapfrogged you to the #1 spot last week. Implementation never ends, but you must periodically assess your success, both to fuel continuous improvement in your first campaign, and to justify investment in future campaigns in your overall program. So, pick a date on which you will show the results that you promised in your campaign's business case (or at least a strong step toward those results). Chapter 15, "Make Search Marketing Operational," shows many ways of continually measuring and improving.

After you have pulled together your campaign's plan, recognize that this is really just a first draft for your plan. To get agreement from others, you will undoubtedly need to make some changes. Now is the time for you to start "shopping your plan around" to the rest of your organization to get the go-ahead to execute it. Remember Dwight Eisenhower's famous quote, "Plans are nothing; planning is everything." You have now done all the planning that you can do by yourself. Your *real* planning starts when you explain your plan to others and hear their suggested changes. As much as you might persuade them to follow your plan, you also need to be flexible about modifying your plan to suit them.

Sell Your Proposal to the Extended Search Team

No matter how much work your central search team does, every search marketing program relies on the extended search team to succeed. The extended team actually manages your Web site. The extended search team writes the page copy, codes the HTML, programs the applications, and chooses the URLs. The central search team knows what to do, but the extended search team must do it.

Who makes up the extended team? Business people (such as sales reps and marketers), writers who develop copy for your Web pages and for your advertisements, technologists (such as Webmasters and Web developers), and operations personnel who keep your Web site humming.

In a small company, the extended team is also small, but in a large company the team can be thousands of people. For medium-to-large Web sites, you will work with a daunting array of specialists. You need some of these specialists for organic search marketing, some for paid, and some for both. Not every organization has each of these specialists, and sometimes the roles go by different names, but every specialty has its own language and its own search marketing blind spots.

So read the descriptions as *roles* rather than *jobs*. Someone in your organization is doing these tasks, regardless of what you call that person. Your job (er, role) is to find them and get them to do what you need.

Now that you have your proposal in hand, you need to evangelize the extended team to persuade them to approve it. If they don't believe in your proposal, it will not work well, no matter how many executives order them to execute it. Remember that your proposal has several parts—business cases for both your strategic search marketing program and your first campaign, plus a plan of the tasks to execute for your first campaign. Each part of your proposal is there for a reason, either to persuade people as to the value of search marketing, or to show that it is possible. Use your proposal to fuel your sales pitch to your extended search team.

Start by explaining your ideas using whatever methods seem to work in your organization. If people need you to show up in person with a PowerPoint pitch in tow, do that. If your company expects regular conference calls to answer questions and check progress to your goals, do that. If you find that you need to create an intranet Web site that lists all of the tips for search improvement, go for it. They might like an e-mail newsletter? Try it. There is nothing different about selling this idea from selling any other new concept in your organization. You work there and you probably know how to do it.

> ### CASE STUDY: PERSUADING THE EXTENDED SEARCH TEAM IN A LARGE COMPANY
>
> The Web's largest auction site, eBay, is no different from your company when it comes to search marketing. Corey Cleek, the head of eBay's International Marketing Team, knew that he needed to mobilize the extended search team to turn around eBay's search marketing.
>
> Cleek outlined how eBay got it started: "We first brought all of our Internet marketing partners together and focused on the ones that were 'search-specific.'" Cleek then embarked on an "internal road show," delivering a PowerPoint presentation month after month, to any department that would listen. The road show yielded valuable feedback from people within eBay who had experience in search marketing campaigns for other companies. "We gathered enthusiastic interest from every business unit that wanted to get [search marketing] working for them," Cleek says.
>
> "When it comes to natural optimization of the eBay site, we have a long ways to go," Cleek admitted, but eBay shows that a focus on paid search can pay off when you first persuade the extended team.

But first, a warning: Do not expect the extended team to listen. That might be the toughest lesson to learn for the central search team. You read this book, you are fired up, and you expect everyone else to be as excited about this as you are. Well, they're not.

Search marketing is *your* job. It's not theirs. At least they don't think it is. *That* is what you need to change. You must start by explaining why search engine marketing is important. Show them how your competition is doing this better than you. Explain the technical challenges to the "techies" and the business value to the marketers. Challenge them.

But when you do, remember that someone walks in every day with another new task they should add to their already jam-packed days. They are busy, just as you are. Figure out how to make it fun. Figure out how to make it easy. You *can* persuade them, but you must understand who they are so that you can speak to them in *their* language.

We show you how to do that right now. We look at several kinds of specialists on your extended team and help you reach them. Each one has a special perspective on the world, and you can learn what motivates them. After you win them over, and not before, you will be on your way to search marketing success.

Business People

Money talks. Use the search marketing opportunity information you put together in Chapter 7 to persuade the business people of the importance of search marketing. Whatever drives sales will drive the investment you need to jump-start search marketing.

Who are the "business people"? Most are sales and marketing personnel, all trying to sell your products to customers. We also discuss how to work with your legal department, whose job is to protect the business from unnecessary risk.

The business people are very important to convince, because they will make your case to the rest of your organization. Remember, marketing and sales people excel at persuading people. Get them to help you persuade your organization.

If you work at a nonprofit organization, the principle is the same, even if the particulars are different. Your "business people" might not be marketers or sales reps, but they are responsible in some way for the growth of your organization. Your Web site has some overarching goal that we identified in Chapter 5, "Identify Your Web Site's Goals," and anything that supports that goal will justify the investment that you seek. For a business, it is usually sales, but those of you working in nonprofits can use organizational goals to convince people in similar ways. We use business-oriented roles here, but you can translate "brand manager" to "campaign manager" if your Web site supports a political campaign.

Now it's time for you to learn how to talk to brand managers, sales people, public relations folks, and lawyers to persuade them to participate on your extended search marketing team.

Brand Managers

Brand managers focus on promoting a particular set of products within your company. They have detailed knowledge of their products and are well skilled in marketing techniques, such as market segmentation, advertising, and message management. Brand managers are responsible for targeting the right people to buy your products and then reaching them with the message that causes them to take action.

In a small company, you might have only one brand (often the name of the company), and you might call this role the **marketing manager**. In a company the size of Honda, for example, you have a brand manager for the Civic and another for the Accord. In fact, Honda might need one brand manager for each *model* of Civic and Accord.

Brand managers typically review and approve all marketing activities associated with their product set, and are accustomed to dealing with their traditional marketing channels (face-to-face sales, telemarketing, retail, and others, depending on your business). They are *not* typically well schooled in Web marketing, although that is beginning to change. Even those that do understand Web marketing are unlikely to understand *search* marketing.

Your first task with a brand manager is usually one of education. You must convincingly show why search marketing is a good way to spend scarce marketing budgets. Because neither paid nor organic search marketing is ever completely free, it is critical that the brand manager be your biggest supporter. In addition, you will need his help whenever one of the other specialists does not fall into line. When the brand manager says that search marketing is a priority, everyone else will listen.

So, how do you get the brand manager behind the search marketing program? If your brand managers are Web savvy, they are already using search personally, and you merely need to show them a few queries for their products so they can see how little traffic they must be getting. If you are dealing with brand managers who do not use the Web, you must show them how many people *are* using the Web and cite some of the other statistics discussed in Chapter 1, "Why Search Marketing Is Important . . . and Difficult."

Regardless of how Web savvy they are, show them the missed opportunity reports described in Chapter 7 (Table 7-11). Brand managers tend to be swashbuckling risk takers, always on the lookout for the next opportunity to sell more, so they are usually easy to convince.

Sometimes, brand managers will object to search marketing because they do not have any budget to spend on it. In that case, show them that the cost of searchers converting to customers is lower than for other forms of marketing, such as direct mail. That usually persuades them to shift some of the budget from their other marketing activities to search. If there really is no money to spend, start with free organic search techniques and ask the brand manager to help you spread the word to the other teams that must be convinced to change how they do their jobs. Although brand managers will not get into the technical details, they will apply pressure in the right places if you convince them to.

After you have persuaded a brand manager to give search marketing a try, your first campaign is critical. It must show strong results to lead to a second campaign. Brand managers should be heavily involved in choosing the keywords to target for the campaign, but they might need your help. They often have blind spots when it comes to a customer's perception of your product—brand managers tend to expect that customers will enter only brand names ("honda accord") rather than generic ones ("family sedan"). You need to convince them to work on both kinds of queries.

Brand managers also must review and approve all paid placement advertising. As they do, educate them so they are thinking about qualifying customers as well as selling to them. They typically do not think about the cost per click—they usually want to get everyone to click because that is their experience from offline and other online media. You need to show them how to optimize the tradeoff between clickthrough rate and sales. Teach them what every good sales rep knows—that it is just as important to dissuade the wrong searchers from clicking (and draining your budget) as it is to persuade the right ones to click. Top sales reps do not waste their time on prospects who will not buy; you should not waste your search marketing budget on them either.

And keep selling the brand managers on search marketing even after you have campaigns in high gear. Take care to regularly report success to the brand managers as search marketing takes off, so that they are not tempted to move to another new and exciting initiative a few months down the road. If they were easy for *you* to convince, the next person coming along with a bright idea might persuade them to dump your project in favor of a new high flyer.

Sales People

In larger companies, there might be specialists who use particular channels to pump up sales directly, or to assist in sales being made by others. Although none of these roles are as critical as the brand manager, there are ways you can get help from them:

- *Direct marketing*. Those responsible for the direct sales from your Web site can be critically important to search marketing. They are interested in anything that drives higher sales, and they are often the perfect folks to operate paid placement campaigns, with their knowledge of why people click and buy from an ad. They are experts at calls to action and rotating advertisements. In addition, direct marketing folks are frequently the best people to track search success (organic or paid) because they have affiliate programs or other Web sales tracking mechanisms in place that can also track search-related sales.

- *Lead generation*. If your business is based on offline sales, your Web site's major goal might be passing leads. The folks responsible for lead generation from the Web site will be most interested in promoting search marketing when they see how it yields more leads. You can ask them to capture the search referrers in their lead-generation forms to track those leads back to search. They can also report which keywords seem to bring the highest number of visitors.

- *Partner relations*. If your company sells through distributors, resellers, or other partners, the partner relations team regularly interacts with these other companies. You can teach them how to request links to your Web site from each partner site. Partner links that go straight to the product pages on your site are the best (rather than a generic link to your home page).

No matter what kind of business you have, there are folks who sell things using the Web. Sales people are usually excited about any new idea that can drive sales. Find them and get them to sell search marketing throughout the organization.

Public Relations

Public relations people are also instrumental in obtaining links from other Web sites, which we cover in detail in Chapter 13, "Attract Links to Your Site." But the PR department can help search marketing in several other ways, too.

PR people are responsible for the press releases that are hugely important for organic search marketing. When people get wind of the news, they tend to search for the rest of the story. If your press releases are optimized to be found by search engines, and they contain links to deeper information in your site, you can turn information searchers into conversions. If your press releases are truly newsworthy, your PR folks can directly feed your stories to press release wires or online press release sites, causing search engines to highlight your stories as news. (This works especially well with product launches and other announcements.)

The PR people are also responsible for your organization's image, so Web "negative" or "hate" sites targeted at your organization (www.yourdomainsucks.com) are their problem. You can explain strategies to your PR department that minimize the impact of these hate sites when searchers are looking for your company:

- *Check search results regularly.* Your PR team should be on the lookout for the emergence of these sites and should regularly execute queries using your leading brand names, your company name, and the names of high-profile executives. Hate sites depend on search results to get attention, so spotting them quickly helps you take action sooner.

- *Take legal action when warranted.* If the hate site is misusing your trademarks, or has lifted copyrighted material from your Web site without permission (such as product images), you can pursue legal remedies.

- *Crowd them out of the search rankings.* Search results never contain more than two listings from any one domain, but you might be able to get a little help from your friends. First, make sure your pages are optimized so that you get your legitimate two listings (#1 and #2 is what you are shooting for). Next, if your company has multiple domains (for subsidiaries, international affiliates, and so on), you can ethically optimize those sites for your company's target keywords. Your vendors, business partners, and other friendly companies might also have pages on their sites that legitimately speak of their relationship with your company—you can assist them to optimize those pages. Never do anything unethical to divert searchers to places that are not relevant, but you should cultivate the help of friendly sites. If your friends provide more relevant results than your enemies, the hate sites will be pushed down in the list so they do not draw as much attention.

PR teams are typically very open to search marketing opportunities when you explain to them what they need to do. They are just as interested in getting positive publicity as you are, so if you show them how search can provide that, they will be on board.

Lawyers

Lawyers are not marketers, but we talk about them among the business people because they frequently pass judgment on marketing material—the content on each page so critical for organic search as well as paid placement advertisements. In many corporations, the legal department checks every word before it goes live on the Web site, so that errors are avoided (those "expose us to a lawsuit" kinds of errors).

In some industries, including pharmaceuticals and financial services, protracted legal reviews can significantly affect a search marketing campaign's flexibility. Lawyers are sometimes derisively known as the "business prevention people" for their "go-slow" approach that mitigates all risk, but your organization has made a policy decision about what risks they want to run, and loss of speed is a tradeoff that they are making. Rather than whining about it, it is smarter to factor legal reviews into your time lines under these circumstances. Your competitors might be laboring under similar constraints, anyway.

It is important to educate your legal team on search marketing for several reasons. First, if they understand the importance of quickly changing copy on pages, they might try to accelerate their review cycles. Another reason to train the legal team is to give your paid search program some oversight, particularly as you make decisions about other companies' trademarks. Finally, your legal team is perfectly positioned to negotiate links to your products and services from outside suppliers as part of any deal, improving your search rankings for your site.

When you work with your legal team, you will find them picky about using the best word for search optimization. For example, searchers might be looking for "hair restorer" but your lawyer knows your company cannot legally make that claim about their product. How do you work something out? Sometimes you can try some clever copy, such as in Figure 9-3, which uses your search keywords but does not run afoul of legal restrictions.

> **LOOKING FOR A HAIR RESTORER?**
>
> In truth, there is no universal hair restorer. Baldness, a common male problem, can be caused by myriad different conditions, and no two men respond to treatment the same way.
>
> But there is hope. Clinical studies show that FollicFill, a new scalp treatment specially designed for male pattern baldness, delivers remarkable results.

Figure 9-3   Evading the law(yer). Not every legal team will go for this, but if your lawyers understand the importance of search marketing, they might.

When your legal team sees the value of search marketing, they might occasionally take a risk to support it, rather then never taking the risk, as they do now.

Writers

Search marketing depends on having the right words—that is what writers do. We examine three different kinds of writers: copywriters (who develop "sales-y" descriptions of products), content writers (who create objective information about a subject), and translators (who convert content to other languages).

If you do not win over the writers, you will never excel at organic search marketing, because those keywords must be littered across your pages. In addition, you need well-written paid placement ads for maximum clickthrough. No one but the writers can perform these tasks, so pay attention to how to persuade them.

Copywriters

Web **copywriters** create marketing copy for a company's products and services. As you might expect, they write action-oriented prose that is sometimes more flowery than you would see in an encyclopedia, for example. That is what they have been taught to do, but search marketing usually requires a different style than a sales brochure.

Searchers are looking for both your product's brand name and its generic name ("tivo" *and* "digital video recorder"), and organic search engines want to see those words prominently and frequently on your page. Copywriters are typically unaware of what search engines need, so your first job is to teach them. Similarly, copywriters sometimes overlook the fact that customers search for generic names, not just brand names, and that they are unfamiliar with acronyms and other insider terms. You need to explain to them what search engines and customers need from their writing so that your business converts searchers to customers.

Sometimes copywriters object to changing their style of writing. They have succeeded in their careers writing as they do, and they might be reluctant to change. Some might complain that sprinkling keyword phrases throughout their copy is repetitive and poor writing, but you need to overcome their objections. Without search-friendly copy, you will be hard-pressed to attain high rankings in organic search.

Copywriters know that their job is to generate sales, so you can usually persuade them to alter their styles when they see that their pages are not found by search engines—especially if your competitors' pages are. Show them the kinds of queries their customers enter and show them which pages show up. Let them see that their precious words are not being read.

Do not listen to their complaints about the "repetitive" style. Challenge them to integrate search requirements as just one more constraint they deal with. Tell them that you know that they are talented writers and that you are confident they can write search-friendly pages that are well written, too. Show them how they need only make a few tweaks to what they already do—that will be enough.

Content Writers

We distinguish **content writers** from copywriters, not because they have a different role to play in search marketing, but because they view themselves differently and you need to speak to them differently. Content writers create the prose for Web pages just as copywriters do, but rather than selling products, their pages convey information.

Web sites that present news, health, travel, and other information employ content writers. Content writers often have an academic or news reporting background and are skilled at taking a subject and making it simple and interesting. What they do not have is any understanding of what search engines need. *That* is where you come in.

Just as with copywriters, it is imperative that content writers produce pages with the keyword prominence and density needed to match the queries required. Like copywriters, they will object to your changing their style—often decrying censorship or lack of editorial integrity. Unlike copywriters, content writers are not trying to sell anything, so you need to talk to them differently.

Luckily, content writers are just as interested in having their words read as any other writer. When you show them that their prospective readers are not finding their treatise on the best restaurants in Des Moines—they are reading that information from a competitive site—*that* will get their attention. You can appeal to their pride as writers and tell them they can make it interesting while taking search marketing into account, just as you did with copywriters.

But you have one other advantage that makes all the difference in the world. Content writers are relentless researchers, because they must constantly check their facts before they write. That means that they are searchers themselves. If anyone can put themselves in the shoes of searchers, it is content writers. When you show content writers how hard it is for searchers to find their pages, they will usually come around quickly.

CASE STUDY: PERSUADING WRITERS TO WRITE WITH SEARCH IN MIND

A large content Web site, with dozens of staff writers, realized that it was receiving far fewer visitors from search engines than it could be, and embarked on a search marketing initiative. Almost before starting, the writing staff went into full revolt, irate at the idea of "compromising their editorial integrity." What to do?

The first rule in these sensitive situations is to move gingerly. Rather than coming in full of advice, we approached them cautiously, full of questions. In this case, the best way to start was asking the writers how they came up with their story ideas. This led to a freewheeling discussion detailing a number of sources for ideas, including news stories, their personal interests, and the popularity of similar stories. We looked at a current article as an example.

Together, we examined the writer's most important keywords for that article and used Overture's query tracking tool to show other variants of those words that were missing—missing from the article but not missing from searchers' minds. The writers' eyes started to open to the idea that many potential readers were searching for their articles but never finding them.

That was just the start. Next, we began searching for the keywords missing from the story and looking at the search results. The writer of the article gasped, commenting that the search results showed the next five variations of his article that he should write. The mood of the meeting completely changed, as writer after writer tried this technique to get ideas for future stories.

In a single meeting, the writers had become convinced that their readers were just like them. The same way that they searched to find story ideas, their readers were searching to find the information *they* desired. At that point, we showed them how they could pepper their writing with keywords and ensure they have given them the proper prominence and density.

Training in keyword prominence and density was exactly what the writers needed all along, but only by approaching them with respect and interest in their job were the writers open to learning the lesson.

Translators

You might not think of translators as writers, but they are. And how they translate your content to other languages can make or break your search performance. If you have thoroughly optimized your English content for organic search, but the translators do not use the right French keywords (with the proper prominence and density), your French query rankings will be literally lost in the translation.

You must show the translators how their work is critical to good search rankings. Just like other writers, they will object to you cramping their style; if you demonstrate how their current practices are preventing their readers from finding their pages, however, they will come around.

Technologists

Technologists might be the most unapproachable specialists, because their knowledge seems so deep in areas other people do not understand. Sometimes technologists are so specialized that they intimidate each other. But that cannot stop you. Unless you train the technologists in search marketing, your organic search efforts will fall short.

It probably sounds by now that no matter what specialist we discuss, we tell you how important it is to get them on your side. Unfortunately, one of the biggest challenges of search engine marketing is that *everything* is important. Unless you convince each member of your extended team to do the job right, search marketing will not work. Webmasters, Web developers, information architects, and style guide developers are next up on your dance card.

Webmasters

The most important technology role for organic search marketing belongs to the Webmaster. On small sites, this role might belong to a single person, but it is not unusual to have dozens of Webmasters on large corporate sites. Webmasters make sure your site does not go down and that it responds quickly when visitors arrive, but they do a lot more, too. They set the domain names and URL names. They decide which servers display each Web page. They handle load balancing—and a lot more.

Some Webmaster tasks are critical for organic search marketing, so we concentrate on those:

- *Site availability.* When spiders come visiting, your site must be up and respond quickly (typically in less than 10 seconds) for your pages to be indexed. If spiders continually find slow or unavailable pages on your site, they will visit infrequently or not at all. Spiders can visit at any time of the day or night, so there is no safe time for your site to be down.

- *URL names.* Webmasters name the domains and subdomains (such as www. subdomain.domain.com) and they frequently decide how directories (folders) are named as well (www.domain.com/directory). Some search specialists believe that ensuring that your URLs are named after keywords helps your search rankings, but even if they do not, you need the Webmaster to help you with URL naming. Here's why: After a page is named with a certain URL, you do not want it changed—if it is, the links to that page from other sites will not work, and your search rankings will be affected.

- *URL redirects.* One way that Webmasters change the URLs on pages is to code something called a **redirect**, which tells a browser (or a spider) that the page has changed to a new URL. There are several kinds of redirects, all of which work for browsers, but there is only one type that works for spiders. Obviously, you want your Webmaster to use that one, which we explain in detail in Chapter 10, "Get Your Site Indexed."

- *Directions for the spiders.* The Webmasters control a special file, named **robots.txt**, which contains instructions to spiders on how to crawl your site. This file can tell spiders to go away completely, to crawl everything, or something in between. You must ensure that your Webmasters allow the spiders to crawl all of the pages that need to be indexed in search engines. We cover robots files in Chapter 10.

With so many critical search marketing tasks, you can see how important it is for Webmasters to understand the right way to perform each one. But, as you have probably guessed, many Webmasters do not understand even the basics of search marketing. Some Webmasters completely block spiders from their sites, mistakenly believing they are improving site performance by keeping those pesky spiders from wasting the time of our precious Web servers!

Because Webmasters are very technically proficient (and you might not be), it can be very intimidating to approach them, but you must do so. If you pay proper deference to their technical abilities, you will probably find that they truly have the best interests of your site in mind. They really do care that your visitors see your pages load quickly and get what they are looking for. When you explain how important search marketing is for your visitors, they will listen. Webmasters usually use search themselves, so showing them how hard it is to find your site will be convincing.

Occasionally, the Webmaster team is concerned about how many more visitors will show up at the site if your search marketing is successful. You might need to help them justify more servers to handle the additional load that you expect as you succeed.

After you have them on your side, the Webmasters can be your best ally in spreading the word to other technologists. The Webmasters work with many people in the course of their job, and they often enforce standards and evangelize best practices to others.

Web Developers

Web programmers develop the HTML and JavaScript code that displays the pages in your visitor's Web browser. They are typically at the receiving end of lots of changes from different sources—brand managers who changed the logo for a product, designers who decided that the navigation bar should be royal blue, copywriters who have updated the kind of information they want on the product details pages, and many more. When you approach your Web developers with yet more changes, they will roll their overworked eyeballs, thinking, "Here we go again."

But don't be too concerned. If you have done your work convincing the brand managers and sales people of how important search marketing is, the Web developers should be easy to persuade. They are very knowledgeable about Web pages and will immediately understand why you need the changes you do. They are usually avid searchers themselves and will probably find your project interesting.

You need to ensure that they are trained to code HTML and JavaScript the way you need them to, which we cover in Chapter 12, "Optimize Your Content." Also in Chapter 12, you will learn how to audit your pages to find specific search problems—the Web developers will get the results of these audits to correct those problems.

Training and persuading this group will pay off, because if they design pages to be search-friendly from the start, they do not have to correct problems later.

Information Architects

Information architects do not really consider themselves technologists, but the average person does. They decide the navigational structure of the site—how information is divided into separate pages, which pages link where, what nomenclature is used on a link to ensure people know what it is, and many other tasks. Although not as critical to search marketing as some other technologists, they can help you simplify your site's navigation so that spiders are not blocked.

Information architects think deeply about what your visitors need and what they will understand, always striving to satisfy their needs in the simplest way. Unfortunately, what is simple for visitors is not always simple for spiders. Many compelling user experiences are based on using JavaScript pull-down navigation—it looks pretty, it is easy to use, but spiders cannot follow it at all, so every page behind that JavaScript code is missed by the spider.

As with every other specialist, your first job is one of education. You need to explain (using the information provided in Chapter 10) how spiders are stymied by JavaScript, and how that affects our site's visitors terribly. That will get an information architect's attention. You need to explain what the alternatives are and persuade the architects to choose something more search-friendly.

Information architects also control the primary navigation pages on your site, such as the site map or your "Products A–Z" page. Because these pages are so important to getting spiders to crawl more of your site, there are specific techniques we discuss in Chapter 10 that you will want your information architects to know.

Once in a while, you will get objections that the search-friendly way is ugly, or harder to use. Remind them that there are visitors without JavaScript enabled that will be tripped up by their design, too. If you cannot convince them to junk the JavaScript, at least get them to implement alternative paths to the same pages, possibly through site maps that spiders can navigate.

Like the other specialists, information architects have their job to do. They see the world a certain way and they do their job within that perspective. When you widen their perspective, most adjust and cooperate with you, because down deep they want the best for their site just like you do.

Style Guide Developers

Style guide developers create and maintain the rules governing the look and feel of the Web site, including page layouts, color schemes, information architecture, and many other areas. All Web sites of any size have a style guide. For small sites, this is a part-time job for one or two people, but larger sites have a full-time person or even a team that maintains the style guide. Each standard in the guide is enforced, often by reviewing projects while they are still under development—only after they pass the standards are they launched on your Web site.

Style guide developers require Web site design and information architecture skills, and often know HTML, too. These skills help style developers to understand and suggest changes to the standards, as well as to explain them to the people designing the pages on the site. As you might expect, however, style guide developers usually do not possess search marketing skills. Because the standards in the guide are used throughout the site, rules that inhibit search marketing can have broad implications.

Your job as a search marketer is to make sure the style guide is analyzed with organic search in mind, and to identify the rules that need to be changed. After those changes are made to the style guide, they will be enforced along with the rest of the guide, providing you with an important tool to make your entire site more search-friendly. Don't underestimate the power of the style guide to mold behavior across your organization. Make sure that your style guide motivates the behavior you want.

Unfortunately, it is not always easy to get developers to make the changes to the style guide that search marketing requires. People attracted to a job based in enforcing stringent rules are not always the most flexible people on Earth. And your story about why the standards should be changed to accommodate search might not sound any different to them than all other changes that have been requested. There are ways to reach theses folks, however.

The most important mission for style guide developers is to maintain the brand image and the overall consistency of the site. So, your challenge is to explain to them how your site's poor search results negatively affect the brand image. Show them how your competitors' brands are being shown in response to important informational queries, whereas your site is notably absent. When explained as a poor branding experience, style guide developers tend to be persuaded. If you cannot persuade them to do anything, enlist the brand managers, Webmasters, and other specialists to lobby for your changes, because the style guide developers are accustomed to listening to them. If you do not convince them to make *all* of the needed changes, take what you can get and come back for more another time.

Site Operations

If you thought that after you get your search marketing program going that you are home free, think again. Search marketing is not a one-time thing, and you will fail unless you engage the operational management of your site to put ongoing focus on search. (We know that you are getting sick of hearing about how many different groups you need to work with, but rest assured that we will show you how.)

For search marketing, the two most critical groups within site operations are Web metrics and Web site governance. The metrics team helps track and publicize your success, and the governance folks enforce the standards so painstakingly written into your company's style guide.

Metrics Specialists

Metrics specialists are the keepers of the statistics—how many visitors come to the site, customer satisfaction survey results, the number of sales, and many more. You learned in Chapter 7 that we want to track new metrics on the success of search marketing—both organic and paid.

In some Web organizations, there is no central metrics role. The Webmaster might report traffic metrics. The marketing team might report survey results. The finance department might report sales. Regardless, you need to spread the search marketing word to your organization's metrics specialists, because you need them to help you report search marketing metrics.

Metrics specialists are already experts at collecting some of the critical search marketing metrics, but no one might have ever asked before. They know how to tease search referral statistics out of your log files using your company's traffic metrics tool. They know how to correlate sales with those referrals. They have the quantitative analysis skills to track trends and to tell you when changes are statistically significant.

It's a real coup if you can convince metrics specialists to devote some of their time to search metrics, and even better if you can incorporate a few search metrics into their regular reporting. These weekly or monthly reports tend to be reviewed by many different people working in your Web organization, including your executives. That will help you draw attention to the importance of search and to your growing success. Perhaps you could get them to include the compliance reports described in Chapter 15 that show how well each part of your Web site is adhering to best practices in search marketing.

At times, metrics specialists will object to taking on the extra work associated with search metrics, but if you can show them how important search marketing is to your overall site objectives, they will usually come around. Metrics specialists want to demonstrate their value to your organization. Any time they can trot out a new statistic and open some eyes, it makes them look good. If you can show metrics specialists that the brand managers are looking for these numbers, they will quickly figure out how to absorb the extra workload to report search metrics.

Web Site Governance Specialists

A **Web site governance specialist** is a clunky name for someone who enforces your site's standards. What process on your site puts teeth in your style guide? It is not enough for your style guide to be rewritten with organic search in mind—you need to police everyone to comply with those rules. Perhaps there is a single group devoted to compliance with your standards; regardless of how your site does it, however, you need to get your organization to enforce search standards.

As usual with all of these specialists, it is unlikely that governance specialists have more than a middling familiarity with search. They do not typically have every standard committed to memory, so how do they enforce compliance? Typically, they enforce the standards that they know. So your job is to help them understand why search is important and which specific standards are critical for success. If you get these specialists familiar with search marketing, they can help enforce the standards critical to your success.

Sometimes your discussion will not be welcomed, because governance specialists have too much to do as it is. This position is typically underfunded because it is hard to show the business value of the standards police, so when you come around adding more rules to enforce, it can be hard to hear. Your best approach is to make the compliance work as simple as possible— automating everything you can. Chapter 15 shows how your checklists can simplify the governance specialist's job, even explaining how software tools can automatically check compliance with some standards.

Much like the Webmasters, your governance team is ideally positioned to spread the word across the organization. They work with every group that puts up a Web page, and they typically have the power to order compliance to the rules. The governance team can block a project manager trying to launch a change to the Web site—that is the ultimate "teachable moment." That project manager will make sure the next project is designed to be search-friendly from the start.

The governance specialists are the people who make the difference between paying lip service to search standards and really "walking the talk." If you persuade the governance folks of search marketing's importance, they will help transform your site one project at a time.

Sell Your Proposal to Executives

To sell your executives on your search marketing proposal, you must think like an executive. To understand what executives are looking for, we explore the questions on their mind, and then show you how to close the deal at the end of your presentation.

Ten Questions Your Executive Might Ask

In a sense, there is nothing different about search marketing from any other proposal you would sell to an executive. With any proposal, your executive wants to understand what it's about and why we should do it. We have found that almost all executives are interested in the same information to make their decisions. Not every executive asks all of these questions, but you should be prepared to answer them, or, better yet, answer them in your presentation without waiting for them to be asked.

What Is Search Marketing and Why Do I Care?

Typically, your executive will not understand the basics of search marketing. Although you should gloss over the details, a couple of charts that explain Google and provide some of the "gee whiz" numbers we showed in Chapter 1 should convince any executive to hear you out the rest of the way.

Demonstrate that search is a growing area of marketing and that it complements current marketing activities. If you have done surveys of your customers, or you have industry surveys showing that your own customers are using search, that's even better.

How Does This Help Me Achieve My Corporate Goals?

Remember spending all of Chapter 5 figuring out what your Web site's goals are? This is why.

The more closely the benefits of a search marketing program align to the executive's existing goals, the higher the probability that you will get your program approved. With every executive, showing that your organization's goals are being met by your proposal makes the sale easier. However, different executives have somewhat different goals and concerns. Make sure you know who is on the receiving end of your pitch:

- *Chief Executive Officer or any sales executive*. This can sometimes be your easiest sell. They typically will be convinced by your business case and do not care about the details of the work to be done. A credible business justification coupled with a realistic plan will persuade them to take a chance on your proposal.
- *Technology executive*. This might be your toughest sell. You must show that same compelling business case, but you must also convince this executive that the IT team will not be saddled with an impossible job. It is critical that you demonstrate a grasp of the details, especially its feasibility within your proposed budget. Walk through the plan step by step, explaining exactly what needs to be done. Show how you can make the IT exec a hero by taking on this low-risk project that will raise revenue.
- *Marketing executive*. How warm a reception you get from this executive might vary depending on whether the marketing group is responsible for the content on the site or not. In many organizations, the marketing group manages the copywriters, and this exec will be concerned about what is expected from his team. As with the technology executive, your confidence about what the copywriters need to do will carry the day. When an executive knows his team can do what is required, there is no danger to his reputation, so the benefits of the project carry the day. Marketing executives with no content responsibilities should be very excited about search marketing, but some might be concerned that other favorite marketing programs will be cut to fund search marketing.
- *Chief Financial Officer*. Numbers, numbers, and more numbers. Show your business case and show how search marketing is cost-effective compared to other marketing programs. CFOs are sometimes risk-averse, so showing that other companies are succeeding at search marketing can be very important.

You probably get the idea. Think carefully about the executives you need approval from, and make sure you appeal to their needs and concerns.

Where Do We Stand Today?

Most executives are born problem solvers. As these fix-it types size up your proposal, they will ask themselves, "Exactly how bad is this, compared to all the other pressing problems I know about?" The best way to answer that question is to show them. Show your executives that when your customers search for your products, they don't find your company. Show them over and over. Query after query. That usually gets their attention.

For some executives, just performing the searches in front of them is compelling, but others want to see more data. You can dig out the ranking check that you did back in Chapter 7 (in Table 7-6). Seeing how poorly your site ranks for a slew of keywords across all the search engines will win over even the most skeptical data wonk.

If your executives use the Web, remind them of the way *they* search. Are they checking out result #45? No? Neither are your customers.

What Are Our Competitors Doing?

Executives are, by nature, notoriously competitive. They are supremely motivated to beat the competition, and they do not like to lose. Go back to Chapter 7 and break out your site's competitor-ranking matrix (Table 7-7). If you can show executives they are losing and convince them they can win, you will get strong consideration for your proposal.

You can use your competitors in other ways, if you know how to pitch to your executives. Risk-averse executives will be comforted if one or two of your competitors are actively pursuing search marketing. Alternatively, if none of your competitors are engaged in search marketing yet, you can play that up with a visionary executive as the new way to get an edge.

What Are You Proposing to Do?

This question requires a very crisp answer—you need a high-level version of your plan, such as the one shown in Figure 9-2. Executives get proposals every day. They have a sniff test for which ones are practical enough to implement and which ones are pipe dreams. It is not enough for you to show a business case.

Executives check a proposal's practicality in several ways:

- *Consensus.* If you have agreement from key members (preferably leaders) of your extended search team that they will do the work, it can go a long way.
- *Speed.* The faster you can deliver, the less time the executive needs to wonder whether it will work.
- *Specificity.* The more detailed your plan is—granular tasks, with people assigned to each one, on a defined schedule—the more credence an executive will place in that plan.
- *Measurability.* Executives tend to trust plans with objective measurements that can be checked after the fact. Snap Electronics presented a detailed grid of all projections so that results could be measured each month. In Chapter 15, we show the kinds of operational metrics that can be tracked to show the business impact of search marketing.

If you are presenting to an executive who wants to see the details, make sure you explain the cause and effect of each action with its beneficial result. If you are recommending to the IT executive that all dynamic URLs be rewritten into a spider-friendly format, be ready with the explanation of why that is important. Do not assume that you can show a laundry list of actions without justifying each one. Eliminate any actions that are not absolutely necessary, at least from your first plan. Propose the Volkswagen, not the Mercedes.

What Business Value Do You Expect to Achieve?

This is a broader question than it might seem. Yes, you should present the missed-opportunity matrix you developed in Chapter 7 (Table 7-11). And we do want you to show your business opportunity—the case for your entire scope and the one for your first campaign. But you need to think more broadly than that. Remember the work that you did in Chapters 5 and 6, "Identify

Your Web Site's Goals" and "Measure Your Web Site's Success," respectively? Explain how the search marketing program directly leads to higher sales or more leads or whatever conversion your executive is interested in. Don't just show the numbers; demonstrate your logic, too.

Keep in mind that anyone can show big numbers, but the executives are judging whether your plan will *deliver* on those numbers. If you have a track record of solid proposals, or you can demonstrate that others have followed this plan to success, or your executives have all read this book (okay, that is unlikely), they will believe that executing your plan will actually produce the promised results.

How Much Does It Cost?

You will, of course, be ready for this question. You have the costs estimated and totaled for a full search marketing program across your entire scope, but you also have today's request—funding for the first campaign.

You need to be prepared for a lot more questions on cost than just the raw numbers. Executives know that estimates are just that—estimates. They want to know why you believe these estimates are correct. They want to assess the risk that the actual costs could be higher.

There are several ways to buttress your estimates. If you are using an external search vendor, you can present the cost estimates from each vendor to show what the range can be. Another approach is to show the details behind the estimates, if your executive can judge that level of detail. You can also appeal to the expertise of your extended search team, who can validate your cost projections for the tasks they must perform.

How Long Will It Take?

This is a difficult question to answer. Make sure that you understand this question. Because you are down in the details, you might think the question refers to when the actions in your plan will be executed. It does not. Your executives want to know when they will see the results.

You need to be careful when you provide your answer, because some factors are hard to predict:

- *Will resources be available*? You cannot assume a "green lights all the way" schedule. Make sure that your extended search team is committed on the schedule that you are planning. Ensure you have contingency built in for unforeseen problems.

- *How frequently do spiders visit your site*? Some sites have spiders visiting every day, but does yours? If you have a small site, or you have lots of spider problems, they might not visit more than once a month, so plan accordingly. If it takes you three tries to get the perfect density of keywords on your pages, will that take three months or three days? You must take the frequency of spider visits into account in your planning or you will have the wrong time line.

• *How much iteration will it take*? Whether you are managing an organic or a paid campaign, you usually do not get everything perfect the first time around. Paid placement ads are not written perfectly, so they get lower clickthrough. The technology project delivered the wrong fix for a spider problem. The brand manager released a set of new models that changed which keywords are the best choices. These examples demonstrate that search marketing depends on taking a shot, checking how close you are to the target, and taking another shot. Do not make promises based on hitting the bull's-eye the first time.

Everyone wants to promise quick results, but it is more important that you show credible results. Coming back to an executive to ask for more time will not position you well for your second search campaign.

When executives ask you how long it will take, they might actually be asking a different question: "When will I see payback?" This question tells the executive how fast the costs of the program are recouped, and is usually expressed in units of time. Fortunately, most search marketing campaigns pay back in a matter of months. In Chapter 7, we analyzed the monthly revenue expected (in Figure 7-6). You can plot your revenue and expenses month by month to be ready for this question.

Why Should I Fund This Project over Current Projects?

Be prepared for this question. There is no "new money" for a search marketing program. Whatever money you want is money that cannot be spent on something else. You must demonstrate that your search marketing program will generate better results than whatever it replaces, which is not that easy.

You can fall back on studies, such as the one mentioned in Chapter 1 (Figure 1-17), but you will have a far stronger case after you have executed your first campaign, when you will have hard numbers from your own business. Perhaps the studies will persuade executives to approve your first campaign as a test. Then you can make a direct comparison of the traffic and conversion numbers for search marketing versus other marketing techniques.

What Are the Risks?

All projects have risks and a search marketing campaign is no exception. You can line up all the usual suspects—cost overruns, schedule delays, and overbooked resources—but search marketing has its own special risks.

The biggest risk concerns organic search. No matter what anyone tells you, high organic search rankings cannot be guaranteed, no matter what you do. Consider that there is only a single #1 spot for each query. If ten companies perform that perfect search marketing campaign, only one of them can be #1. If your keywords are highly competitive, it might be very difficult for you to get the rankings (and therefore the traffic) that you want.

Similarly, ultra-competitive bidding in paid placement is also a risk. When you investigate your chosen paid keywords, you might assume that paying a few cents more than the current bid maximum will land you #1, but others might raise their bids in response. You could find yourself in a bidding war that is unaffordable for you. You might have the Hobson's choice of losing traffic or blowing your budget.

Despite these possible risks, search marketing is rarely a high-risk proposition.

Close the Deal

If you are armed to answer the executive's questions, you need to be prepared to do something else as well: get your proposal accepted. You must enter every executive meeting knowing exactly what requests you want to make of that executive that day. Do not explain your whole proposal "as an FYI." Know what you want and ask for it.

Here are the typical things you should request:

- *Approve this project.* We figured you remembered this one. But be very specific. Make sure you have the money and you are authorized to spend it. Sometimes (in large companies especially), "approvals" take weeks before you can actually spend any money.

- *Order the extended search team to cooperate.* You want your "letter from the king" to use with any recalcitrant extended search team members. Although most people will listen to your search evangelism and go along with the plan, a few can be painful to persuade— maybe impossible. At that point, you want your executive to stand behind your plan and use his power to get the objectors into line.

- *Review the metrics with us every month.* At first, there will not be much to see, but as your program reaches its full scope, and you introduce the operational metrics explained in Chapter 15, you will have a wealth of data to analyze. You will want executives to review the metrics so that they can take action to correct problems. You will find that situations will arise, such as ill-considered technology changes or poor content coding, where executives can focus resources and attention to get them corrected.

Your thorough proposal, prepared while reading the previous few chapters, will convince almost any executive. Make sure that you are prepared for success—that you know precisely what you need from that executive to maximize your success.

Summary

Nothing is easy about executing a search marketing program in any organization. Your organization has dozens, maybe even thousands, of folks who all need to do things the right way, but they are ignorant (and possibly apathetic) about what to do, and they are so busy that even asking them to listen to you might take some persuasion.

But, in this chapter, you learned how it is done. You assembled your proposal, because that is the basic selling point for any audience. You are familiar with the critical daily tasks. You now know how to decide which tasks should be performed by a central team, and which must be done by the rest of your Web team, your extended search team. You have met each kind of specialist on that extended team and you are armed with approaches to persuade them to do their part in improving search marketing for your site.

We also helped you to persuade the toughest audience of all—your executives. You know what questions they will ask, and you know what requests you have for them.

We are just getting started, however. In Part 3, we go beyond the planning to the execution—what specific tasks must you undertake to make your search marketing plan a reality? In the next chapter, you will determine how many of your pages are indexed by organic search engines and you will find out how to get virtually all of them included.

Execute Your Search Marketing Program

Search marketing is at the convergence of business and technology. To successfully execute a search marketing program, you need to tame the technology while sticking with sound business procedures across your team. That is what Part 3 is all about.

We begin in Chapter 10, "Get Your Site Indexed," by getting your Web site indexed for organic search. Your technologists must ensure your site is *designed* to be indexed; otherwise, the search engines will not find you.

Chapter 11, "Choose Your Target Keywords," focuses on your target market: searchers. What words are they using to find what they want? Which ones should you be targeting in your search marketing campaigns? Your marketers must understand how to identify what searchers are looking for.

After you know your target keywords, it is time to optimize your content in Chapter 12, "Optimize Your Content." Your writers and your technology team must work together so that each page is designed and written to please a searcher. That way, your pages will rank highly in organic search and drive Web conversions for both organic and paid search.

Chapter 13, "Attract Links to Your Site," addresses the challenge of drawing links to your site. Learn why links are important to organic search engines and what you can do to build your site's link popularity.

Paid search takes center stage in Chapter 14, "Optimize Your Paid Search Program." Although many search marketing techniques apply equally to organic and paid search, many tasks are specific to paid placement. Find out how to set your budget, manage your campaigns, and make adjustments along the way.

Chapter 15, "Make Search Marketing Operational," helps you design your operating procedures to manage your search marketing performance each day. We explain the best practices for developing your central search team, measuring your success, and diagnosing the inevitable problems that pop up.

We wind up with Chapter 16, "What's Next?" in which we explore exciting new developments in search marketing and show you how to further your education as a search marketer.

By the end of Part 3, you will know how to turn your search marketing program into a well-oiled marketing machine—a successful mix of business and technology. Your program will not always work flawlessly, but you will be able to identify your challenges and take action to correct each one. Day by day, you will make the right decisions to improve your search marketing effectiveness.

CHAPTER 10

Get Your Site Indexed

"You've got to be in it to win it," the lottery commercials blare, but they do have a point. Winners did have to buy a ticket, or they would never have won. To win the organic search lottery, your site needs to buy its tickets, too—you need the pages of your site indexed. The more pages you have indexed, the more chances you have to win the search lottery. And take heart, because you have much better odds at winning the search lottery than the Powerball lottery.

To win, however, you need to know the rules of the game—and to play by them. In the search lottery, you must learn the rules that **spiders** play by, so that your site plays by them, too. After you understand what spiders cannot or will not do, you can make sure that your site does not run afoul of the rules. Because when you break these spider rules, your page will not be indexed. And if your page is not in the index, it cannot be found by searchers.

It might sound simple, but getting Web pages indexed by search engines can be challenging for corporate Web sites. Corporate Web sites are often designed without spider rules in mind, so their pages are frequently left out of search indexes. As you start your organic search marketing efforts, getting your pages indexed is the first step to take, because it can take some time for your team to correct the design problems you find on your site. You need to discover whether your pages are indexed, to diagnose indexing problems when they are not, and to correct them.

This chapter answers three basic questions:

- *What if your site is not indexed?* Most corporate Web sites have at least some of their pages indexed, but a few sites have no pages indexed at all. We show you how you can check on yours and what to do in the rare event that all of your pages are missing from the search index.

- *How many pages on your site are indexed?* In Chapter 7, "Measure Your Search Marketing Success," we did a quick assessment of whether the landing pages for your first search marketing campaign were indexed. In this section, we look across your entire site to see where you stand.

- *How do you get more pages indexed?* That's the most important question to answer. What problems are preventing your site from having all of its pages indexed and what can be done to correct them?

Remember, for organic search, pages that are missing from the index can never be found by searchers. This chapter helps you include as many of your pages as possible in each search index. Let's start by addressing an unusual but critical situation—what if your site has *no* pages in the search indexes?

What If Your Site Is Not Indexed?

If your business has been around for a while and has a Web site, your site is overwhelmingly likely to be indexed by all the leading search engines. It is rare for corporate sites to be completely missing from search indexes, although it is quite common for individual pages from the site to be missing. (We show you how to figure *that* out later in this chapter.)

One way to tell whether your site is indexed is to search for it and see whether it is found. (Yeah, we figured you thought of that one.) If your company has a common name (AAA Plumbing), you might want to search for more than just the name ("aaa plumbing syracuse"). It's common for site owners to panic when their sites are not shown by the search engine for these navigational queries for company names. It's easy to jump to the conclusion that the entire site is not indexed, but that is rarely the case.

You can also use a search toolbar in your browser to check to see whether your pages are indexed. If you use the Google toolbar (or one for another search engine), you can navigate to your home page and take a look at the toolbar—most toolbars indicate that the page is indexed in some way. Figure 10-1 shows how Google's toolbar does it. You can see whether your site is indexed by that toolbar's search engine, although it does not help you figure out whether your page is indexed by other search engines. (We show you how to do that later in the chapter.)

Nearly all corporate sites have their home pages (and at least a few other pages) in the leading search indexes, but if somehow you do not, read on. It is unlikely but possible that your site is missing in action—it *has* happened, even to relatively large companies. Or perhaps your search marketing program's scope does not cover your whole company, but *all* the pages within your scope are missing from search engines. In that case, you need to ask a few questions:

- *Is your site banned by the search engines?* Search engines have very specific rules for being included in their index. Sites that violate these rules might find all of their pages removed from the search index.

- *Is the spider visiting your site?* Your pages cannot be indexed if the spider never comes. Check to make sure.

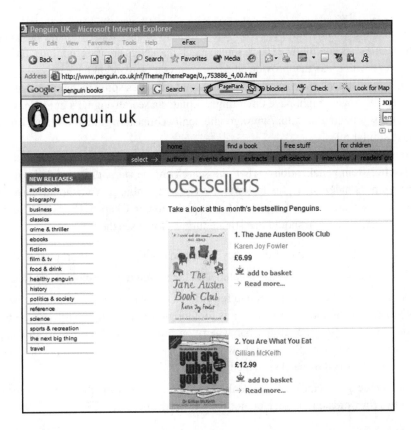

Figure 10-1 Toolbars show indexed pages. Google's toolbar indicates the current page in the browser is indexed with the green PageRank bar.

- *Are other sites linking to yours?* Spiders find your site by following links from other sites, so you must verify that your site is linked into the larger Web.

If you can find at least a few pages of your site when you perform searches in the major search engines, you can skip ahead to the next section to determine how *many* pages you have indexed. If your site is not found at all, however, you can explore these questions to solve the mystery of the missing site.

Verify Your Site Is Not Banned or Penalized

The most difficult situation occurs when one or more search engines have **banned** or **penalized** your site. If your site is well represented in some search engines, but completely missing in others, your site might be banned. Sites are banned when search engines detect that those sites are trying to "fool" the search engine to rank that site's pages more highly than they deserve.

Search engines do not ban sites on a whim—they do so only when your site has persistently violated their rules. As you might expect, some search marketers are unscrupulous, trying to take unfair advantage with tricks that provide an edge. Your company might have unwittingly become involved with an unethical search marketing consultant who uses **spam** techniques that try to fool the search engine, or you might have unwittingly violated a search engine's guidelines. (You can look at Google's guidelines at http://www.google.com/webmasters/guidelines.html; other search engines have similar rules.)

If your violation of the rules is not severe enough for a search engine to ban your site, you still might suffer from penalization—when the search engine starts dropping large numbers of your pages from its index or begins to lower your search rankings. You should make sure that signs of penalization are checked regularly (we explain how in Chapter 15, "Make Search Marketing Operational"), and you should investigate further if you see the following:

- Your site's search engine referrals have dropped drastically in a short period of time.
- The number of your site's pages included in the search index rapidly decreases.
- The search engine shows fewer and fewer links to your site each month, maybe decreasing to zero. A simple way to check this for Google's index is to use the Google toolbar—you will see a gray PageRank bar when you browse your Web pages. In Chapter 13, "Attract Links to Your Site," we show you easy ways to check the number of links to your site that are stored by each search engine.
- Your home page can be found only by a direct search on the URL—informational queries for words on the page do not seem to work anymore.

If you suspect a problem, you first need to diagnose the cause. In the next section, we discuss a spam technique called **cloaking**. We cover **doorway pages** and other stupid content tricks in Chapter 12, "Optimize Your Content," and **link farms** in Chapter 13, "Attract Links to Your Site." These are the most common spam techniques. If your site has been banned or penalized for using these techniques, you can clean up your site and request reinstatement, which is usually granted (although reinstatement sometimes requires an extended period of explanation and begging).

Make Sure the Spider Is Visiting

If the spiders are not coming to your site, your pages cannot be indexed and your site will not be found by organic searchers. Your Webmaster can help you check your Web servers' **log files** to see which search spiders have been visiting your site. (Most Web servers are configured to log search spider visits, but some servers might need to be adjusted by your Webmaster to capture this important information.) Figure 10-2 shows an extract of a log file showing that a spider has visited. The log file indicates the name of the **user agent** that accessed the page noted, which indicates the software that was used to see the page.

```
66.249.69.3 - - [29/Nov/2004:13:24:03 -0500] "GET /robots.txt HTTP/1.0" 200 4524 "-" "Googlebot/2.1
(+http://www.googlebot.com/bot.html)"
66.249.69.3 - - [29/Nov/2004:13:24:03 -0500] "GET / HTTP/1.0" 200 11119 "-" "Googlebot/2.1
(+http://www.googlebot.com/bot.html)"
66.196.90.83 - - [29/Nov/2004:18:03:31 -0500] "GET /robots.txt HTTP/1.0" 200 4524 "-" "Mozilla/5.0
(compatible; Yahoo! Slurp; http://help.yahoo.com/help/us/ysearch/slurp)"
66.196.90.110 - - [29/Nov/2004:18:04:11 -0500] "GET /promotion HTTP/1.0" 302 222 "-" "Mozilla/5.0
(compatible; Yahoo! Slurp; http://help.yahoo.com/help/us/ysearch/slurp)"
66.196.90.110 - - [29/Nov/2004:18:05:49 -0500] "GET /enterprise.html HTTP/1.0" 200 6758 "-" "Mozilla/5.0
(compatible; Yahoo! Slurp; http://help.yahoo.com/help/us/ysearch/slurp)"
207.46.98.51 - - [29/Nov/2004:19:24:55 -0500] "GET /robots.txt HTTP/1.0" 200 4524 "-" "msnbot/0.3
(+http://search.msn.com/msnbot.htm)"
207.46.98.51 - - [29/Nov/2004:19:28:37 -0500] "GET /style.css HTTP/1.0" 200 5145
"http://www.globalstrategies.com/" "Mozilla/4.0 (compatible; MSIE 6.0; Windows NT 5.1; SV1; .NET CLR
1.1.4322)"
207.46.98.51 - - [29/Nov/2004:19:28:48 -0500] "GET /images/logo.gif HTTP/1.0" 200 2030
"http://www.globalstrategies.com/" "Mozilla/4.0 (compatible; MSIE 6.0; Windows NT 5.1; SV1; .NET CLR
1.1.4322)"
207.46.98.51 - - [29/Nov/2004:19:28:48 -0500] "GET / enterprise.html HTTP/1.0" 200 2030
"http://www.globalstrategies.com/" "Mozilla/4.0 (compatible; MSIE 6.0; Windows NT 5.1; SV1; .NET CLR
1.1.4322)"
```

Figure 10-2 Spotting spider activity. Carefully examining your log files can prove that spiders are visiting your site.

Most of the visits to your site generate a log listing of something like "Mozilla/4.0 (compatible; MSIE 5.5; Windows NT 5.0)," which indicates that the Internet Explorer Web browser (version 5.5) was used to access your site. As you might expect, the vast majority of the user agents listed in your log file are from Web browsers. But a small number of log entries might show you that the spiders are crawling. Googlebot, as you might surmise, is Google's user agent. Yahoo! aptly named its spider Slurp. Table 10-1 shows some the names of some of the leading spider's agents, but there are many more, and they change their names frequently.

Table 10-1 Spider User Agent Names (Each search engine sends a spider to your site that you can spot by its agent name in your Web server logs.)

Search Engine	Spider Agent Name
AOL	Googlebot
Ask.com	teoma_agent1
Google	Googlebot
MSN	msnbot
Yahoo!	Slurp

By examining your log, you can tell which spiders are crawling your site, and how frequently they do so. Spammers use these user agent names for more nefarious purposes, however. Variously known as **cloaking** or **IP delivery**, they use a high-tech version of the old "bait-and-switch" scam. Here's how it works. The spammer sets up a URL served by a program dynamically and waits for someone to request it. When the request is received, the user agent name and its IP address are checked. If a browser is making the request (with Mozilla in the name, for example), the program returns the page that human visitors should see. If it is a search engine's spider, however, the program sends back a page full of keywords designed to attain a high search ranking. Later in this chapter, we discuss situations where you can legitimately use IP delivery techniques, but using this technique to fool a search engine about what visitors see on the page is clearly spam and the search engines will deal with it harshly. Unless you know that what you are doing is acceptable, cloaking is a very dangerous game that can get your site banned. Cloaking can bring quick rankings, but when competitors see what you are doing, they will complain to the search engines and shut you down.

Each search engine spider has its own frequency for returning to your Web site. Spiders return to a typical Web site at least once a month, but popular corporate Web sites might be revisited weekly, or even daily. By analyzing how frequently spiders crawl your pages, and which pages they check the most, you will know how quickly content changes on your site will be reflected in search indexes.

Although it is rare to find a site that the spiders do not visit at all, it can happen for a few reasons:

- *Your site is not linked.* If you have a brand new site that is not linked to by any other site in the spider's path, you will not get any spider visits. If the search engine spider does not know your site exists, it obviously cannot visit.

- *Links to your site are not effective.* Some links cannot be followed by spiders, for many reasons that we get into later in this chapter. Or the links to your site are from sites that themselves are not crawled by spiders, perhaps because they are also new, or possibly because they are banned for using unethical techniques. You can use the Google toolbar to check the PageRank of sites that link to yours—that shows you how valuable a link you are getting. If your linker has a zero PageRank, it is not doing you any good in Google because that site is not indexed.

- *The spider has given up.* Perhaps the spider was visiting your site at one time, but your site was blocked so that the spider could not index any pages in the search index. After a few months of fruitless visits, spiders sometimes permanently stop visiting.

If your site truly is not being visited by spiders, the remedy depends on which of the above reasons is the cause. If your site is not linked or links to your site are not effective, the best way to get the spider to visit is to make sure other well-respected sites link to yours (explained in more detail later). If the spider has given up, first remove the spider trap (also explained later), and then you should manually submit your site to the search engines.

Search engines vastly prefer to find new sites by following links because analyzing link patterns is one of the ways engines judge relevance; if your site is linked and spiders are not visiting, however, you should manually submit your home page's URL. (If you create a new site but are too impatient to wait until someone links to you, you can also submit, but waiting to be found from a link will help your pages rank higher.)

Every major search engine, except Ask.com, has a way to submit your site, but not all of them are free. Search engines that offer free submission often refer to their "Add URL" page as the place you should go—at Google it's at www.google.com/addurl (with others listed in Table 10-2). Remember, if your site is missing from multiple search indexes, you need to submit to *each* search engine. Typically, pages submitted are included in the search index within a few weeks—you can check your log files to see whether the spider is visiting.

Table 10-2   Submitting URLs (Each search engine allows you to request inclusion of your site—some charge nothing, whereas others have paid inclusion programs.)

Search Engine	Free or Fee?	URL
AOL	Free	www.google.com/addurl
Google	Free	www.google.com/addurl
MSN	Free	http://search.msn.com/docs/siteowner.aspx?t=search_webmaster_ref_gettingsiteindexed.htm
Yahoo!	Fee	http://docs.yahoo.com/info/suggest/

Submitting to local or country-specific search engines is no different from worldwide search engines. The spiders can detect the language of the site and will add it into the appropriate-language version of the index, which we cover in detail in Chapter 12.

WHAT NOT TO DO IF YOUR SITE IS MISSING FROM INDEXES

Before you get excited about submitting all your Web pages to the search engines, a word of caution is in order. Many "experts" will advise you to submit your site early and often, and to submit many pages from your site. *Don't.* It is more complicated than that.

Submitting your site should be a last resort because you have tried everything else without success—you cannot get anyone to link to your site, or your site has been blocked so long that the spider has given up. If you are forced to submit, submit only your home page. Your site map should help the spider find everything else, so make sure your map is comprehensive. Often, people submit their sites over and over without ever checking to see whether the spider is blocked from their site. Before submitting, follow the advice in this chapter first. If you do, you will probably see that you do not need to submit after all.

Even worse than manually submitting your site is automatic submission. You might have received unsolicited e-mails offering to submit your site to thousands of search engines for $19.95. The e-mail might include some compelling statistics about millions of visitors this service will generate. Avoid "automated submissions" entirely. If you are lucky, these services just set you back $20 and do no harm. But some search engines consider these automated submissions to be spam and many actually have measures in place to block such submissions. At best, these submissions are ignored, but at worst your site could be penalized or banned for excessive submissions.

A surefire way to get your pages included is to pay a search engine to put them in the index. As discussed in Chapter 3, "How Search Marketing Works," paid inclusion not only guarantees to keep your pages in the index, it also promises that they will be revisited by the spider regularly. Only Yahoo! (of the major worldwide engines) is offering paid inclusion, but several search engines offered it a few years ago, so the trend might change yet again. Fees are typically charged for each page included and for every time a searcher clicks your page. Remember that paid inclusion does not guarantee your page will be shown by the search engine—only that it is in the index to be found. Later in this chapter, we look at paid inclusion in detail.

Get Sites to Link to You

As we have emphasized, the best way to get indexed is through a link from another site (one that is already indexed itself). If you have a well-established site, you have probably already attracted many links, but a new site obviously does not have any.

The best kind of link is one from a high-profile site, such as a directory, but almost any link has some value. By creating high-quality content on a subject, you will eventually attract links from other sites, but you can also execute a **campaign** to attract links. Chapter 13 is devoted to attracting more links to your site, an important subject whether it is new or well known.

How Many Pages on Your Site Are Indexed?

The number of your site's pages that you want indexed is *all* of them—all of the **public** pages, anyway. Many of your pages might be **private**—unavailable to the general public because they are secured behind passwords—but that's fine, because you do not want private pages indexed for the whole world to see anyway. No, the real problem is when public pages that you want to be searched are missing from the index.

Later in this chapter, we look at *why* some of your public pages are missing from search indexes, but first, we simply check how many pages you already have indexed. We calculate your site's **inclusion ratio**—the number of pages indexed divided by the number of pages you have on your site.

Determine How Many Pages You Have

Although this might sound exceedingly odd to those of you with smaller sites, it is not always easy to know how many pages are in a Web site. Especially for large decentralized sites, it might require a lot of thought to even estimate the total number of pages in your Web site. If you can easily estimate the number of pages on your site, feel free to skip ahead to the next section to check how many pages you have indexed.

As you begin the task of counting your Web pages, keep in mind that you should be counting "publicly available" pages only. That means no private (secured) pages—pages locked behind passwords—ought to be part of your calculation, because you do not *want* those pages on public display in a search engine. So, if you have special pages that show your customers their invoices or their order status, it makes sense that you have them password-protected so each customer sees only his own information. Don't count these pages in your site total, because you do not want them in the search indexes anyway.

For the purposes of calculating your inclusion ratio, it is wonderful if you know *precisely* the total number of pages on your site, but it is not required to be so accurate. If you do not know the exact number, there are several ways to make a reasonable estimate:

- *Ask your Webmaster.* Your Webmaster might not know either, but he has probably been asked this question before and at least he has thought about the answer. Question your Webmaster's logic in guessing the total so you can evaluate its credibility.
- *Check your corporate search engine.* If you have a search engine that allows visitors to search only your site, check to see how many of your Web site's pages are in your corporate search index. (Be aware that if your corporate search engine's index is updated through crawling, your corporate search index will be missing many of the same pages that Google and other Internet search engines are missing.)
- *Add up the counts from your content sources.* Most Web pages are really document pages—they have a document somewhere in your content management system or your e-Commerce catalog. Granted, you might not be able to count all of your pages accurately using this method, but it helps you make a more accurate estimate than taking a stab in the dark.
- *Use a special spider.* You can unleash your own spider on your site. Special spiders, such as the free Xenu (http://home.snafu.de/tilman/xenulink.html) and the $98 OptiSpider (www.optitext.com/optispider), are designed to find pages on your site that you might have overlooked, and they can count what they get. Unfortunately, as with a corporate search engine, many of the same barriers that block Internet search spiders will block these special spiders, too. The good news is that special spiders can show you where they were blocked, so that you can take the corrective actions we show later in this chapter.
- *Check each search engine.* This might seem odd, but each search engine has stored a different number of pages from your site. This is probably the worst method to use for estimation, but it is better than a complete guess. In the next section, we show how to coax the search engines to tell you how many of your pages they have included in their indexes.

After you have estimated how many pages are on your site, you are ready to check how many pages you have indexed in the major search engines.

Check How Many Pages Are Indexed

Search engines understand that you want to know how many pages of your site are indexed, and they have made it easy to do. Every search engine has a special search operator designed to show you how many pages it has stored in its index for a particular site.

To check how many pages you currently have included in Google, enter the query "site:yourdomain.com" to find the number of pages on the *yourdomain* Web site. For example, the query "site:coach.com" shows how many pages are indexed from the handbag manufacturer's site, as shown in Figure 10-3.

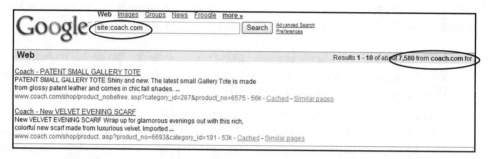

Figure 10-3   Checking how many pages are indexed. Coach.com has thousands of pages included in the Google search index.

Google is not alone—AOL, MSN, and Yahoo! all provide that special "site:" operator for you to see how many of your pages are indexed. Yahoo! goes so far as to offer a beta tool called Site Explorer (http://siteexplorer.search.yahoo.com). But Ask.com forces you to use its Advanced Search interface to search for a word on all your pages (such as your company name) with yourdomain.com in the Domain or Site field.

Instead of entering these special operators by hand, you can use one of several tools to take the drudgery out of the reporting. MarketLeap (www.marketleap.com), a search marketing consultancy, offers their Search Engine Saturation Reporting Tool, as shown in Figure 10-4.

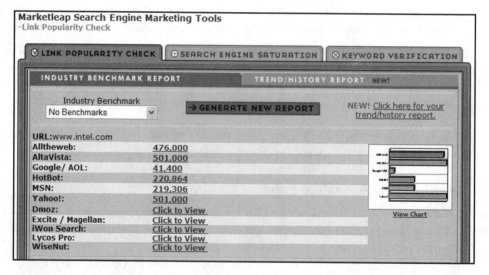

Figure 10-4   Tool for checking indexed pages. MarketLeap's Search Engine Saturation Report shows how many pages are currently indexed by engine.

You can see from this report that at least 181,000 pages from Intel's public Web site are indexed in Google. (Some of these pages might be duplicates, but most are unique.) Intel is also well represented in Yahoo! with nearly 72,000 pages indexed. Although both Yahoo! and Google index much of Intel's site, you can see there is a 100,000 page difference between the two engines. Different spiders crawl Intel's site differently, resulting in different pages being indexed.

Calculate Your Inclusion Ratio

You probably already guessed how to calculate your inclusion ratio (the percentage of your site's pages residing in a search index). Just take the number of pages found in a search index (Ask.com, for example) and divide that by the total number of pages you have estimated to be on your site. For example, if Ask.com reports that you have 10,000 pages indexed, and your content management system has 15,000 documents in it, your Ask.com inclusion ratio is $10,000 \div 15,000 = 0.67$ or 67 percent.

So what is the right metric to shoot for? It is minimally acceptable for you to have about 50 percent of your publicly available pages in the search indexes. Fifty percent is the minimum, but you *can* get nearly 100 percent included, if you work at it.

On rare occasions, you might find a Web site whose inclusion ratio exceeds 100 percent. No, the search engine is not handing out special bonus pages. Instead, you may have a serious problem on your site. The search index might contain duplicate pages, possibly because you have many dynamic URLs (which are explained later in the chapter). Even more serious, your site's private content (information that should be protected from public view) might be in the search index through a security error. Or, you might have underestimated the total pages on your site, which would be the happiest cause of a runaway inclusion ratio.

If you have nearly 100 percent of your site's pages indexed in all search engines, rejoice, and then skip the rest of this chapter. Most companies don't. Most Web sites have far less than 100 percent indexed—some have less than 5 percent. Next, you will learn how to increase your inclusion ratio, perhaps to 100 percent.

How Can More Pages from Your Site Be Indexed?

After you have determined that your site is indexed, and you have calculated how many pages you have indexed, you are certain to be greedy for more. The number of pages you can have indexed is limited only by the number of pages on your site. Many sites have millions of pages included, whereas some prominent Web sites have only their home page indexed.

You can take several steps to raise the inclusion ratio of your site, including the following:

- *Eliminate spider traps.* Your Web site might actually prevent the spiders from indexing your pages. You will learn what the traps are and how you can spring the spider from each one.

- *Reduce ignored content.* Spiders have certain rules they live by, and if your content breaks the rules, you lose. Find out what those rules are and how to reduce the amount of content spiders ignore on your site.

- *Create spider paths*. You can coax spiders to index more of your site by creating site maps and other navigation that simplifies the link structure for all of your site's pages.

- *Use inclusion programs*. One way to ensure inclusion is to pay your way in, for those search engines that allow it. Google offers a free inclusion program.

Many complain about the inability of spiders to index certain content. Although we are the first to agree that spiders can improve their crawling techniques, there are good reasons why spiders stay away from some of this content. You have a choice as to whether you wring your hands and complain about the spiders or set to work pleasing them so your pages are indexed. You can guess which path will be more successful.

If your site is suffering from a low inclusion ratio, you can take several steps, but eliminating spider traps is the most promising place to start.

Eliminate Spider Traps

As we have said before, spiders cannot index all pages. But we have yet to say what causes problems with the spiders. That's where we're going now.

Spiders are actually rather delicate creatures, and they can be thrown off by a wide variety of problems that we call **spider traps**. Spider traps are barriers that prevent spiders from crawling a site, usually stemming from technical approaches to displaying Web pages that work fine for browsers, but do not work for spiders. By eliminating these techniques from your site, you allow spiders to index more of your pages.

Unfortunately, many spider traps are the product of highly advanced technical approaches and highly creative user-experience designs—which were frightfully expensive to develop. No one wants to hear, after all the money was spent, that your site has been shut out of search. Yet that is the bad news that you might need to convey.

Luckily, spiders become more sophisticated every year. Designs that trapped spiders a few years ago are now okay. But you need to keep up with spider advances to employ some cutting-edge techniques.

So here they come! Here is how you eliminate the most popular spider traps.

Carefully Set Robots Directives

Pretend that you are the Webmaster of your site, and you just learned that there is a software probe that has entered your Web site and appears to be examining every page on the site. And it seems to come back over and over again. Sounds like a security problem, doesn't it? Even if you could assure yourself that nothing nefarious is afoot, it is wasting the time of your servers.

Too often, that is how Webmasters view search spiders: a menace that needs to be controlled. And the robots.txt file is the way to control spiders.

It is a remarkably innocuous-looking file, a simple text file that is placed in the root directory of a Web server. Your robots.txt file tells the spider what files it is allowed to look at on that server. No technical reasons prevent spiders from looking at the disallowed files, but there is a gentleman's agreement that spiders will be polite and abide by the instructions.

A robots.txt file contains only two operative statements:

- *user-agent*. The user agent statement defines which spiders the next disallow statement applies to. If you code an asterisk for the user agent, you are referring to all spiders, but you can also specify the name of just a particular spider using the list provided in Table 10-1.

- *disallow*. The disallow statement specifies which files the spider is not permitted to crawl. You can specify a precise filename or any part of a name or directory name—the spider will treat that as a matching expression and disallow any file that matches that part of the name. So, specifying *e* eliminates all files starting with *e* from the crawl, as well as all files in any directory that begins with *e*. Specifying / disallows *all* files.

Figure 10-5 shows a robots.txt file with explanations of what each line means.

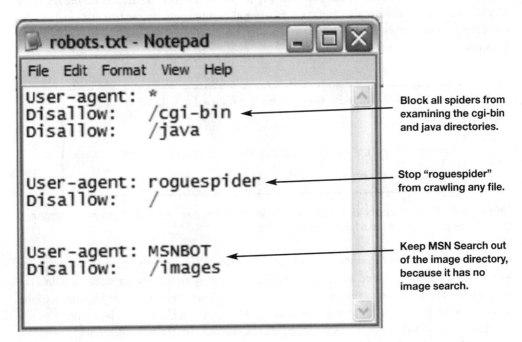

Figure 10-5 Coding robots.txt files. Robots.txt files direct the spider on how to crawl your Web site, or direct them to avoid your site completely.

Webmasters have a legitimate reason to keep spiders out of certain directories on their servers—server performance. Most Web servers have programs stored in the cgi-bin directory, so it is a good idea to have your robots.txt file say "disallow: /cgi-bin/" to save the server from having to send the spider all those program files the spider does not want to see anyway. The trouble comes when an unsuspecting Webmaster does not understand the implications of disallowing other files, or all files.

Although many Webmasters use the robots.txt file to deliberately exclude spiders, acciden-tal exclusion is all too common. Imagine a case where this file was used on a beta site to hide it from spiders before the site was launched. Unfortunately, the exclusionary robots.txt file might be left in place after launch, causing the entire Web site to disappear from all search indexes.

In addition to the robots.txt that controls spiders across your entire site, there is a way to instruct spiders on every page—the **robots metatag**. In the <head> section of the HTML of your page, a series of metatags are typically found in the form <meta name="type"> (where the "type" is the kind of metatag). One such metatag type is the robots tag (<meta name="robots">), which can control whether the page should be indexed and whether links from the page should be followed.

If the robots.txt file disallows a particular page, it does not matter what the robots metatag on that page says because the spider will not look at the page at all. If the page is allowed by the robts.txt instructions, however, the robots metatag is consulted by the spider as it looks at the page.

Figure 10-6 shows the variations available in the robots metatag for restricting indexing (placing the content in the index) and "link following" (using pages linked from this page as the next page to crawl). If the robots metatag is missing, the page is treated as if "index, follow" was specified.

Instructs spiders to index the page, but not follow any links on the page:

```
<meta name="robots" content="index,nofollow">
```

Instructs spiders not to index the page, but to follow all links to other pages:

```
<meta name="robots" content="noindex,follow">
```

Figure 10-6   Coding robots tags. Robots tags on your Web page direct the spider on whether to index the page, follow links from it, or do neither.

Although you would normally want your pages to be coded without robots metatags (or with robots metatags specified as "index,follow"), there are legitimate reasons to use a robots tag to suppress spiders. Some pages on your site should be viewed only from the beginning of the sequence, such as a visual tour or a presentation. Although there is no problem with allowing searchers to land in the middle of such sequences, some site owners might not want them to, so they could code a robots tag on the first page of the presentation that says "index,nofollow" and specify "noindex,nofollow" on all the other pages.

Another reason to use a "noindex" robots tag is to prevent an error for the visitor. Your com-merce facility might require a certain route through pages to work properly—you cannot land on the site at the shopping cart page, for example. Because there is no reason to have the shopping cart page indexed, you can code "noindex,nofollow" on that page to prevent searchers from falling into your cart.

But most of your pages should be available to be indexed. When many pages from your site are indexed, but a few are not, this tag is frequently the culprit. Unfortunately, it is common for this tag to be defined incorrectly in templates used to create many pages on your site. Or misguided Web developers employ the tags incorrectly. This was the case at Snap Electronics.

If you recall from Chapter 7, Snap's search landing page for the keyword phrase "best digital camera" was not in any of the indexes. Examining the pages showed that a number of Snap pages had restrictive robots tags. The product directory page was using the <meta name="robots" content="index,nofollow"> version of the tag. This caused the spider not to follow any of the directory page's links to the actual product pages. Moreover, even if this problem had not existed, each of the actual product pages had the <meta name="robots" content=" noindex,nofollow"> version of the tag. The Web developers indicated it was done so that the commerce system would not be overloaded by search engine spiders. After educating the developers about search marketing, the tags were removed and the pages were indexed.

Eliminate Pop-Up Windows

Most Web users dislike pop-up windows, those annoying little ads that get in your face when you are trying to do something else. Pop-up ads are so universally reviled that pop-up blockers are in wide use. Many sites still use pop-ups, however, believing that drawing attention to the window is more important than what Web users want.

Many Web sites use pop-up windows for more than ads. So, if user hatred is not enough to cure you of pop-up windows, maybe this is: Spiders cannot see them. If your site uses pop-ups to display related content, that content will not get indexed. Even worse, if your site uses pop-ups to show menus of links to other pages, the spider cannot follow those links, and those pages cannot be reached by the spider.

If your site uses pop-ups to display complementary content, the only way to get that content indexed is to stop using pop-up windows. You must add that content to the pages that it complements, or you must create a standard Web page with a normal link to it. If you are having trouble convincing your extended search team to dump pop-ups, remind them that the rise of pop-up blockers means that many of your visitors are not seeing this content either.

If you are using pop-up windows for navigation menus, you can correct this spider trap in the same way, by adding the links to each page that requires them and removing the pop-up, but you have another choice, too. You can decide to leave your existing pop-up navigation in place, but provide alternative paths to your pages that the spiders *can* follow. We cover these so-called spider paths later in the chapter.

Don't Rely on Pull-Down Navigation

As with navigation displayed through pop-up windows, spiders are trapped by pull-down navigation shown with JavaScript coding, as you see in Figure 10-7. And spiders are stymied by pull-downs for the same reason as with pop-ups: They cannot simulate clicking the links. As you might expect, the same solutions prescribed for pop-up navigation will work here as well—you can redo the links in normal HTML or you can provide alternative paths that allow the spider to reach those pages.

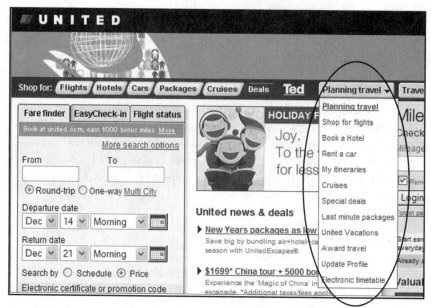

Figure 10-7   Pull-down navigation prevents crawling. Pull-down windows block spiders from indexing any pages linked from them.

In addition to those solutions, there is one more way to remove the JavaScript spider trap, through the use of the <noscript> tag. People familiar with HTML know that some older browsers do not support JavaScript, and that some Web users disable JavaScript on their browsers. These browsers that are not running JavaScript cannot execute the JavaScript code found on Web pages, which can cause big problems. If your pull-down navigation requires JavaScript, non-JavaScript browsers cannot display any navigation to their users.

Enter the <noscript> tag. Page designers can add this tag to provide alternative code for any browser that does not support JavaScript. Spiders will not execute JavaScript, so they process the <noscript> code instead. If you must use JavaScript navigation, you can place standard HTML link code in your <noscript> section. However, for search spiders to follow the links, they must contain the full path names (starting with http) for each linked page. To further ensure the spiders can find these pages, list these pages in your site map.

Simplify Dynamic URLs

So-called **dynamic** pages are those whose HTML code is not stored permanently in files on your Web server. Instead, for a dynamic page, a program creates the HTML "on-the-fly"—whenever a visitor requests to view that page—and the browser displays that HTML just as if it had been stored in a file.

In the earliest days of the Web, every Web page was created by someone opening a file and entering his HTML code into the file. The name of the file and the directory it was saved within became its URL. So, if you created a file called sale.html and placed it in a top-level directory called offers on your Web server, your URL would be www.yourdomain.com/offers/sale.html

(and that URL remained the same until you changed the file's name or moved it to a new directory). These kinds of pages are now referred to as **static** Web pages, to distinguish them from the dynamic pages possible today.

It did not take long to bump into the limitations of static pages—they contained the exact same information every time they were viewed. Soon the first technique for dynamic pages was defined, called the Common Gateway Interface (CGI), which allowed a Web server to run a program to dynamically create the page's HTML and return it to the visitor's Web browser. That way, there never needs to be a file containing the HTML—the program can generate the HTML the moment the page is requested for viewing.

You have probably noticed that some URLs look "different"—they contain special characters that would not occur in the name of a directory or file. Figure 10-8 dissects a dynamic URL and shows what each part of it means.

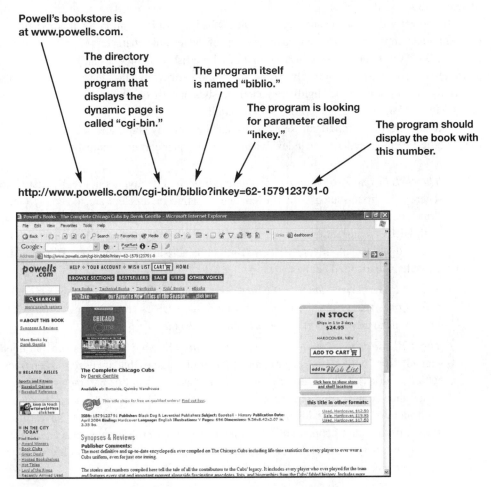

Figure 10-8 Decoding a dynamic URL. Each part of a dynamic URL has a specific meaning that governs what content appears on the dynamic page.

The **parameters** in each dynamic URL (the words that start with the ampersand character [&]) is what causes complications for spiders. Because just about any **value** (the words that follow the equals sign character [=]) can be passed to the variable, search spiders have no way of knowing how many different variations of the same page can be shown. Sometimes different values passed to each parameter indicate a legitimate difference in the pages, such as in Figure 10-8—each book has a different number. But other times, the values do not have anything to do with what content is displayed, such as so-called "track codes," in which the Web site is designed to log visitors coming from certain places for measurement purposes. A spider could look at the exact same page thousands of times because the tracking parameter in the URL is different each time. Not only does this waste the spider's time (when it could be looking at truly new pages from other sites), but sometimes it causes these pages to be stored in the index, resulting in massive duplication of content. Clearly spiders must be wary of how they crawl dynamic sites.

In the early days of dynamic pages, spiders had a simple solution for this dynamic site problem—they refused to crawl any page with one of the tell-tale characters (? or & or others) in its URL. But CGI programs were just the first of a long list of techniques allowing programs to generate Web pages dynamically. Over time, more and more Web pages have become dynamic, especially on corporate sites. Highly personalized sites consist of almost 100 percent dynamic pages. Most e-Commerce catalogs consist of dynamic pages.

Because so much important Web content has become dynamic, the search engines have tried to adjust. Search spiders now index dynamic pages under certain circumstances:

- *The URL has no more than two dynamic parameters.* Okay, it's not really that simple. There *are* circumstances where even two dynamic parameters are too many (see the "rule" on session identifiers below), and there are *other* circumstances in which pages with URLs having more than three parameters are still indexed. If you must use more than two parameters in your URL, you might be able to use a technique known as **URL rewrite**, as explained below.

- *The URL has fewer than 1,000 characters.* Ridiculously long URLs are ignored, but shorter ones seem okay. There is no reason to have URLs anywhere near 1,000 characters, so make them as short and as readable as possible.

- *The URL does not contain a session identifier.* Session identifiers are parameters named "ID=" or "Session=" (or some other similar name) that are used to keep track of which visitor is looking at the page. Spiders hate this kind of parameter because the exact same content uses a different URL every time it is displayed—a spider could put thousands of copies of identical pages in its index because they all have different URLs. If your pages contain this parameter, have your programmers use an alternative approach, as we describe below—spiders will not (and should not) index all of these duplicate pages.

- *Every valid URL is linked from category lists or site maps.* Because some dynamic pages can use almost any value for its parameters, there is no way for the search spider to know every valid product number for your product catalog. You must ensure that there are spider paths to every valid dynamic page on your site. This technique reduces risks for the spiders in crawling the pages, so it encourages many to index your pages.

If your site relies on passing more than two parameters in the URL, you might benefit from the URL rewrite technique, which allows your dynamic URL to resemble a static URL. For example, the URL in Figure 10-8 might be rewritten as http://www.powells.com/book/62-1579123791-0 so the page appears static. This is a completely ethical technique that search spiders appreciate, with the benefit of showing more readable URLs for your human visitors.

Each server platform and content management system has its own method of rewriting URLs. The most widely used Web server, Apache, uses "mod_rewrite," which is very powerful. (Just so you know, when technical people call a tool "powerful," it means that you can do anything you want with it, if you could only figure out how.) Using mod_rewrite to change URLs is not dissimilar from performing woodcarving with a chain saw. You can do it, but you can also hurt yourself along the way. The mod_rewrite module allows an unlimited number of rules to be defined, requiring great attention to detail to ensure proper results, as explained at Apache's Web site (http://httpd.apache.org/docs-2.0/mod/mod_rewrite.html).

Snap Electronics used IBM's WebSphere Commerce Server, which has a similar capability it calls "URL Mapping." Snap used Websphere's URL Mapping technique to convert its dynamic URLs for its e-Commerce catalog to appear to be static URLs. This allowed many of its product pages to be crawled that were missing from search indexes previously.

As noted above, pages with session identifiers cause problems for spiders—your pages will not be indexed unless you remove them from your URL parameters. You might be wondering, "Why did my Web developers use session identifiers in the first place?" It's not that complicated. As visitors move from page to page on your site, each program that displays a new page wants to "remember" what your visitor did on prior pages. So, for example, the order confirmation page wants to remember that your visitor signed in and provided credit card information on the checkout page. Simple enough, but where does the session identifier come in?

Your developer decided (correctly) that the best way to share information between these separate programs that display different pages was to store the information in a database that each program can read and change. So, the program that displays the checkout page can store the credit card and sign-in data in the database—then the program that displays the order confirmation page can read that data from the database. But how does the order confirmation page know which record in the database has the information for each person that views the page? That is where the session identifier comes in.

When the visitor reaches the checkout page, the checkout page program creates a session identifier—a unique number that no other visitor gets—that it will associate with that visitor for the rest of the session (that visit to the Web site). When it stores information in the database, that program stores it with a "key" of the session identifier and any of the other programs can read that information if they know the key. Which brings us back to the original problem—the developer is passing the key to each program in the URL session identifier parameter.

Your developers can provide this function without using session identifier parameter, however. If your programmers are using a sophisticated Web application environment, a "session layer" usually provides a mechanism for programs to pass information to one another—that is the best solution for the session identifier problem. If your Web infrastructure is not so sophisticated, you can use a cookie to hold the session information. If you go the cookie route, be careful not to trap the spider by forcing all visitors to have cookies enabled. We discuss why that is a problem in our next section.

Eliminate Dependencies to Display Pages

Web sites are marvels of technology, but sometimes they are a bit too marvelous. Your Web developers might create such exciting pages that they require visitors' Web browsers to support the latest and greatest technology. Or have their privacy settings set a bit low. Or to reveal information. In short, your Web site might require visitors to take certain actions or to enable certain browser capabilities in order to operate. And although that is merely annoying for your visitors, it can be deadly for search spiders, because they might not be up to the task of viewing your Web site.

If you are as old as we are, you might remember the Pac-Man video game, in which a hungry yellow dot roamed the screen eating other dots, but changed course every time it hit a wall or another impediment. Search spiders are very similar. They will hungrily eat your spider food pages until they hit an impediment—then they will turn tail and go in a different direction. Let's look at some of the most popular technical dependencies:

- *Requiring cookies.* "Cookies" are information stored on the visitor's computer that Web pages can use to remember things about the visitor. For example, if your site says "Welcome Jane" at the top of the page every time she returns to your site, the name *Jane* is probably stored in a cookie on Jane's computer. When Jane views your page, her browser reads the cookie and displays her name in the right spot. Normally this works just fine, but what if your Web page requires that Jane's browser use cookies for this function, or else it displays an error page? First, some of your site visitors turn off cookies (for privacy reasons) and would not be able to view your site. But search spiders cannot accept cookies either, so they are also blocked from your pages. The bottom line is that your site can use cookies all it wants, but it should not *require* them to view a page. If your site's design absolutely depends on all visitors accepting cookies (such as to pass a required session identifier), this is a legitimate reason to use the IP delivery technique we discussed earlier in this chapter. By detecting a spider's user agent name and IP address, your program could allow spiders to look at the page without accepting the cookie, while still forcing cookies on all Web browsers. Make sure that your developers are careful to deliver the same page content to the spider as to the visitor, so you are not accused of spamming.

- *Requiring software downloads.* If your site requires certain technology to view it, such as Macromedia Flash, Java, or something else, your visitors must download the software before entering your site. In addition to being somewhat inconvenient for your visitors, it completely blocks spiders. Spiders are not Web browsers, so they cannot interact with your site to download the required software. In addition, spiders can only read document formats, such as HTML and PDF files—files that contain lots of text to index for search—so when they run into software download requirements, they go elsewhere. Your entire site might be blocked from indexing if you have this spider trap on your home page.

- *Requiring information.* Frequently, sites are designed to be personalized in some way, which can be very good for visitors, but sometimes the designers go too far. Sites that require visitors to answer questions before viewing your pages are annoying to your visitors, and (you are getting the idea now) unusable by spiders, because all the spiders see is the HTML form that requests the input, and they cannot enter any words to get your site to show the actual pages. If visitors must enter their e-mail address before they download a case study or their country and language before seeing your product catalog, you are asking for something that spiders cannot do. So the spiders cannot enter the required information to see the case study or the product catalog, and they will mosey on down to your competitor's site. Similarly, if your pages require an ID and password to "sign in" before you show them, the spider is unable to. The simplest way to think about this issue is that if your site prompts the visitor to do anything more than click a standard hypertext link, the spider will be at a loss and move on.

- *Requiring JavaScript.* By far the most common dependency for Web pages is on JavaScript. JavaScript is a very useful programming language that allows your Web pages to be more interactive, responding to the visitor's cursor, for example, and JavaScript also allow your Web pages to use cookies, as discussed earlier. Used properly, JavaScript causes no problems for spiders, but frequently it is misused. In the next section, we discuss the pitfalls of JavaScript usage, but for now, just understand that your page should not *require* JavaScript in order to be displayed. Spiders cannot execute JavaScript, and some Web visitors also turn it off for security reasons. If your page tests for JavaScript before it allows itself to be displayed, it will not display itself to spiders, and none of its links to other pages can be followed.

To see these problems for yourself, turn off graphics, cookies, and JavaScript in your browser or use the text-only Lynx browser (lynx.browser.org)—if you do not want to download Lynx, you can use the Lynx Viewer (http://www.delorie.com/web/lynxview.html). You will see which pages force the use of certain technologies, and you will get a good look at what a spider actually sees. Any time you need to do anything more complicated than clicking a link to continue, the spider is probably blocked.

Use Redirects Properly

The inventor of the Web, Tim Berners-Lee once observed that "URLs do not change, people change them." The best advice to search marketers is never to change your URLs, but at some point you will probably find it necessary to change the URL for one of your pages. Perhaps your Webmaster might want to host that page on a different server, which requires the URL to change. At other times the content of a page changes so that the old URL does not make sense anymore, such as when you change the brand name of your product and the old name is still in the URL.

Whenever a URL is changed, you will want your Webmaster to put in place something called a **redirect**—an instruction to Web browsers to display a different URL from the one the browser requested. Redirects allow old URLs to be "redirected" to the current URL, so that your visitors do not get a "page not found" message (known as an HTTP 404 error) when they use the old URL.

A visitor might be using an old URL for any number of reasons, but here are the most common ones:

- *Bookmarks*. If a visitor bookmarked your old URL, that bookmark will yield a 404 error the first time the visitor tries to use it after your change that URL.

- *Links*. Other pages on the Web (on your site and other sites) link to that old URL. All of those links will become broken if you change the URL with no redirect in place.

- *Search results*. As you can imagine, search spiders found your page using the old URL and indexed the page using that URL. When searchers find your page, they are clicking the old URL that is stored in the search index, so they will get a 404 if no redirect is in place.

Now that you understand that URLs will often change for your pages, and that redirects are required so that visitors can continue to find those pages, you need to know a little bit about spiders and redirects.

Spiders, as you have learned, are finicky little creatures, and they are quite particular about how your Webmaster performs page redirects. When a page has been permanently moved from one URL to another, the only kind of redirect to use is called a **server-side redirect**—you might hear it called a "301" redirect, from the HTTP status code returned to the spider. A 301 status code tells the spider that the page has permanently changed to a new URL, which causes the spider to do two vitally important things:

- *Crawl the page at the new URL*. The spider will use the new URL provided in the 301 redirect instruction to go to that new location and crawl the page just as you want it to. It will index all the content on the page, and it will index it using the new URL, so all searches that bring up that page will lead searchers to the new URL, not the old one.

- *Transfer the value of all links to the old page*. You have learned how important it is to have links to your page—the search engine ranks your page much higher when other pages (especially other important pages) link to your page. When the spider sees a 301 redirect, it updates all the linking information in its index; your page retains under its new URL all the link value that it had under its old URL.

Unfortunately, not all Webmasters use server-side redirects. There are several methods of redirecting pages, two of which are especially damaging to your search marketing efforts:

- *JavaScript redirects.* One way of executing a redirect embeds the new URL in JavaScript code. So, your Web developer moves the page's real HTML to the new URL and codes a very simple page for the old URL that includes JavaScript code sending the browser to the new URL (such as <script language="JavaScript" type="text/javascript"> window.location="http://www.yourdomain.com/newURL"</script>).

- *Meta refresh redirects.* A meta tag in the <head> section of your HTML can also redirect a page—it is commonly called a "meta refresh" redirect (such as <meta http-equiv="Refresh" content="5; URL= http://www.yourdomain.com/newURL" />). This tag flashes a screen (in this case for five seconds) before displaying the new URL.

Search spiders normally cannot follow JavaScript, and in any case, both of these techniques are commonly used by search spammers so they can get the search spider to index the content on the old URL page while taking visitors to the new URL page (which might have entirely different content). These kinds of redirects will not take the spider to your new URL and they will not get your new URL indexed, which is what you want. Make sure that your Webmaster uses 301 redirects for all page redirection, and make sure that your Web developers are not using JavaScript and "meta refresh" redirects.

How your Webmaster implements a 301 redirect depends on what kind of Web server displays the URL. For the most common Web server, Apache, the Webmaster might add a line to the .htaccess file, like so:

```
Redirect 301 /OldDirectory/OldName.html
http://www.YourDomain.com/NewDirectory/NewName.html
```

You would obviously substitute your real directory and filenames. Understand, however, that some Apache servers are configured to ignore .htaccess files, and other kinds of Web servers have different means of setting up permanent redirects, so what your Webmaster does might vary. The point is that your Webmaster probably knows how to implement server-side redirects, and search spiders know how to follow them.

Server-side redirects are also used for temporary URL changes using an HTTP 302 status code. A 302 temporary redirect can be followed by the spider just as easily as a 301. Webmasters have various reasons for implementing 302s, but one that is important to search marketers, so-called vanity URLs. Sometimes it is nice to have a URL that is easy to remember, such as www.yourdomain.com/product that shows the home page for one of your products. You tell everyone linking to your product page to use that vanity URL. But behind the scenes, your Webmaster can move that page to a different server whenever needed for load balancing and other reasons. By using a 302 redirect, the spider uses your vanity URL in the search index but indexes the content on the page it redirects to.

Before implementing any 301 or 302 redirect, your Webmaster should take care not to add "hops" to the URL—in other words, not adding a redirect on top of a previous redirect. For example, if the vanity URL has been temporarily directed (302) to the current URL and now needs to be directed to a new URL, the existing 302 redirect should generally be changed to the new URL. If, instead, the Webmaster implements a permanent (301) redirect from the current URL to the new URL, you now have two "hops" from your vanity URL to the real page. Not only does this slow performance for your visitors, but spiders are known to abandon pages with too many hops (possibly as few as four). Use a free tool at www.searchengineworld.com/cgi-bin/servercheck.cgi to check how your URLs redirect.

Make sure that your Webmaster is intimately familiar with search-safe methods of redirection, and confirm that the proper procedures are explained in your site standards so that all redirects are performed with care. Make sure that redirects are regularly reviewed and purged when no longer needed so that the path to your page is as direct as possible.

Ensure Your Web Servers Respond

If it sounds basic, well, it is; however, it is a problem on all too many Web sites. When the spider comes to call, your Web server must be *up*. If your server is down, the spider receives no response from your Web site. At best, the spider moves along to a new server and leaves your pages in its search index (without seeing any page changes you have made, of course). At worst, the spider might conclude (after a few such incidents over several crawls) that your site no longer exists, and then deletes all of the missing pages from the search index.

Don't let this happen to you. Your Webmaster obviously wants to keep your Web site available to serve your visitors anyway, but sometimes hardware problems and other crises cause long and frequent outages for a period of time, possibly causing your pages to be deleted from one or more search indexes.

A less-severe but related problem is slow page loading. Although your site is technically up, the pages might be displayed so slowly that the spider soon abandons the site. Few spiders will wait 10 seconds for a page. Spiders are in a hurry, so if good performance for your visitors is not enough of a motivation, speed up your site for the spider's sake.

Reduce Ignored Content

After you have eliminated your spider traps and the spiders can crawl your pages, the next issue you might encounter is that they ignore some of your content. Spiders have refined tastes, and if your content is not the kind of food they like, they will move on to the next page or the next site. Let's see what you should do to make your spider food as tasty as possible.

Slim Down Your Pages

Like most of us, spiders do not want to do any unnecessary work. If your HTML pages routinely consist of thousands and thousands of lines, spiders are less likely to index them all, or will index them less frequently. For the same time they spend crawling your bloated site, they could crawl two others.

In fact, every spider will stop crawling a page when it gets to a certain size. The Google and Yahoo! spiders seem to stop at about 100,000 characters, but every spider has a limit programmed into it. If you have very large pages, they might not be getting crawled or not crawled completely.

Once in a while, someone decides to put all 264 pages of the SnapShot DLR200 User's Guide on one Web page. Obviously, the 264-page manual belongs on dozens of separate Web pages with navigation from the table of contents. Breaking up a large page also helps improve keyword density by making the primary keywords stand our more in the sea of words. Not only is this better for search engines, your visitors will be happier, too.

The most frequent cause of fat pages, however, is embedded JavaScript code. No matter what the cause, there is no technical reason to have pages this large, and you should insist they be fixed. It is even easier to fix JavaScript bloat than large text pages—all you need to do is to move the JavaScript from your Web page to an external file. The code works just as well, but the spider does not have to crawl through it.

We recently reviewed the home page of a large consulting company and found their home page source code equal to 21 printed pages of text. Ninety percent of that content was JavaScript, much of which could be placed in external files and called when the page is loaded. Doing so leaves the remaining 10 percent of real content, which becomes tasty spider food. If your Web pages suffer from this kind of bloating, cutting them down to size will improve the number of pages indexed (and often their search ranking).

Validate Your HTML

When you surf your Web site with your browser, you rarely see an error message. The Web pages load properly and they look okay to you. It is understandable for you to think that the HTML that presents each page on your site has no errors. But you would be wrong.

Here is why. Web browsers, especially Internet Explorer, are designed to make visitors' lives easier by overlooking HTML problems on your pages. Browsers are very tolerant of flaws in the HTML code, striving to always present the page as best as possible, even though there might be many coding errors. Unfortunately, spiders are not so tolerant. Spiders are sticklers for correct HTML code.

And most Web sites are rife with coding errors. Web developers are under pressure to make changes quickly, and the moment it looks correct in the browser, they declare victory and move on to the next task. Very few developers take the time to test that the code is valid.

You must get your developers to validate their HTML code. They must understand that coding errors provide the wrong information to the search spider. Consider something as seemingly minor as misspelling the <title> tag as <tilte> in your HTML. Browsers will not display your title in the title bar at the top of the window, but because the rest of the page looks fine, your developers and your visitors probably will not notice the error. The title tag, however, is an extremely important tag for the search engine—a missing title makes it much harder (sometimes impossible) for that page to be found by searchers. Validating the code catches this kind of error before it hurts your search marketing.

Sometimes the errors are more subtle than a broken <title> tag. Comments in your HTML code might not be ended properly, causing the spider to ignore real page text that you meant to be indexed because it takes that text as part of the malformed comment. In addition, browsers will sometimes correctly display pages with slight markup errors, such as missing tags to end tables, but sometimes search spiders might lose some of your text. So, the page might look okay, but not all of your words got indexed, so searchers cannot find your page when they use those words. Occasionally, HTML links—especially those using relative addresses where the full URL of the link is not spelled out—work fine in a browser but trip up the spider.

It is easy for your developers to validate their code. Just send them to http:// validator.w3.org/ and they can enter the URL of any page they want to test. There are several flavors of valid HTML, from the strictest compliance with the standards to looser compliance that uses some older tags. As long as your page states what flavor it adheres to in the <doctype> tag, it will be validated correctly, and search spiders can read any flavor of valid HTML code. Make sure that your everyday development process requires that each page's HTML be validated before promotion to your production Web site.

Reserve Flash for Content You Do *Not* Want Indexed

Macromedia is a very successful company that has brought a far richer user experience to the Web than drab old HTML, allowing animation and other interactive features that spice up visual tours and demonstrations. This technology, called Flash, is supported on 98 percent of all browsers and can make your Web site far more appealing. (There are other graphical user environments similar to Flash, but Flash content is the vast majority, so we will just refer to everything as Flash, which is not far off.)

But (and you knew there was a *but* coming) spiders cannot index Flash content. Because Flash content is a lot closer to a video than a document, it is not clear how to index that content even if the spider could read it. Clearly, there is a lot less printed information in Flash content than on the average HTML page. So does that mean that you should not use Flash on your site? No. But it does mean you should use it wisely.

Reserve your use of Flash for content that you are happy not to be indexed—that 3D interactive view of your product or the walking tour of your museum's latest exhibit. You can also use Flash for application development, such as your online ordering system—something that you would not want indexed anyway. Do not use Flash to jazz up your annual report, unless you accept that no one can search for any words in the report to find it. And do *not* make your home page a Flash experience, unless you are exceedingly careful to ensure that spiders have another way into your site besides walking through the Flash door—give the spiders a plain old HTML link to boring old HTML pages. (Remember, you cannot pop up a question asking whether visitors want Flash or non-Flash because spiders cannot answer that question either.)

When you do use Flash, make sure you always have an HTML landing page to kick off any Flash experience. That way you can have a short page that describes the great walking tour of your museum and allows visitors to click the Flash content. By using this technique, you will give the search engines a page to index that might be found by searchers looking for your walking tour—they will find the dowdy HTML page that leads to the exciting Flash tour.

If you have a Web site built entirely in Flash content and you absolutely cannot change it to HTML, you can legitimately use the IP delivery technique discussed earlier to get your content into the search index. Here's how. Your Webmaster must implement an IP detection program that runs whenever a page requiring Flash is to be displayed. That program uses the user agent name and IP address to recognize the difference between when a spider is calling and when a Web browser is calling. The Flash content is served up as usual for Web browsers (for your visitors), but spiders get a different meal—they are served an HTML page that has the same text on it as the Flash content. This use of IP delivery is entirely legitimate because you are serving the same text content to visitors and spiders. Be extremely careful, however, never to serve *different* text to visitors and spiders, because that would (rightly) be considered spamming. Ensure that your publishing process forces your Flash and your HTML content to be synchronized after every update so that you do not inadvertently violate spam guidelines.

So remember, use Flash for things that are truly interactive and visual—not documents. Or if you *must* use Flash for documents, make sure there is an HTML version of the document as well for spiders.

Avoid Frames

If your site's design has not been updated in a while, you might still have pages that use **frames**. Frames are an old technique of HTML coding that can display multiple sources of content in separate scrollable windows in the same HTML page. Frames have many usability problems for visitors, and have been replaced with better ways of integrating content on the same page—using content management systems and dynamic pages. But some sites still have pages coded with frames.

If you are among the unlucky to have frame-based pages on your site, the best thing to do is to replace them. Your visitors will have a better experience, and you will improve search marketing, too, because spiders have a devil of a time interpreting frame-based pages. Typically spiders ignore everything in the "frameset" and look for an HTML tag called <noframes> that was designed for (ancient) browsers that do not support frames.

There are techniques that people use to try to load the pertinent content for search into the <noframes> tag, but it is a lot of work to create and maintain. Our advice is to ditch frames completely. Creating a new frame-free page will end up being a lot less work in the long run and will improve the usability of your site, too.

Create Spider Paths

Now that you have learned all about removing spider traps, let's look at the opposite approach, too. Sometimes it is very difficult, costly, or expensive to remove a spider trap. In those cases, your only option is to provide an alternative way for the spider to traverse your site, so it can go around your trap. That's where **spider paths** come in.

Spider paths are just easy-to-follow routes through your site, such as site maps, category maps, country maps, or even text links at the bottom of the key pages. Quite simply, spider paths are any means that allow the spider to get to all the pages on your site. The ultimate spider path is a well thought-out and easy to navigate Web site—if your Web site has no spider traps, you might already have a wonderful set of spider paths. With today's ever-more-complex sites full of Flash, dynamic pages, and other spider-blocking technology, however, you need to make accommodations for spiders trapped by your regular navigation.

Site Maps

Site maps are very important, especially for larger sites. Human visitors like them because they enable them to see the breadth of information available to them, and spiders love them for the same reason.

Not only do site maps make it easier for spiders to get access to your site's pages, they also serve as very powerful clues to the search engine as to the thematic content of the site. The words you use as the anchor text for links from your site map can sometimes carry a lot of weight. Site maps often use the generic name for a product, whereas the product page itself uses the brand name—searchers for the generic name might be brought to your product page because the site map linked to it using that generic name. Work closely with your information architects to develop your site map, and you will reap large search dividends.

For a small site, your site map can have direct links to every page on your site. You can categorize each page under a certain subject, similar to the way Yahoo! categorizes Web sites in its directory, so that your site map lists a dozen or so topics with links to a few pages under each one. Your site map does not need to follow your folder structure—sometimes the site map can offer an alternative way of navigating the site that helps some visitors. This simple approach probably works until you have about 100 pages.

When your site reaches several hundred pages, you cannot fit that many links on one site map page. You should modify your site map to link to category hub pages (maybe corresponding to the same topics that you used for your original site map). Because you might have just 10 to 15 links on your page (1 for each category), you might want to add a descriptive paragraph for each category to augment the link. From each category hub page your visitor can link deeper into the site to see all other pages. This approach can work even for sites with 10,000 pages or more.

Very large Web sites (100,000 pages or more) frequently have multiple top-level hub pages that, taken together, form an overall site map, because they cannot fit all of their topics on one site map page. IBM's Web site (www.ibm.com) uses this approach, with its top three hub pages for "Products," "Services & Solutions," and "Support & Downloads," as you can see in Figure 10-9. These three pages are shown in a navigation bar at the top of every page on the site, including the home page, making it very easy for spiders. Each page lists a number of categories relevant to the page—the "Products" page lists all of IBM's product categories, with a similar list on the "Services & Solutions" page, and the "Support & Downloads" page provides links to the support centers for IBM products. Taken together, these pages form an extensive site map that spiders feast on, returning at least weekly to see whether any important links have been added to IBM's site. In addition, search engines consider these pages to be highly authoritative, with Google assigning them a PageRank of 9 or 10 at times.

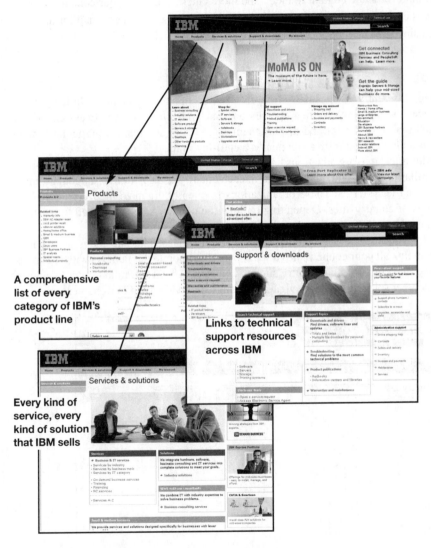

Products, Services & Solutions, and Support & Downloads are shown at the top of each page, including the ibm.com home page.

A comprehensive list of every category of IBM's product line

Links to technical support resources across IBM

Every kind of service, every kind of solution that IBM sells

Figure 10-9 A system of site map pages for a large Web site. IBM has three hub pages that are visited regularly by the search engines.

Your site map might not do as well as that of a popular site such as ibm.com, but it shows the importance of a site map page as the key page on your site for spiders. If you have new content that you want the spiders to find quickly, add a link to it from your site map page. Remember, too, that because some search engine spiders limit the number of links that they index on a page, links within the site map should be ordered by level of importance. You should also try to include text on your site map page, rather than just a list of bare links. Adding text to this page provides the spiders with more valuable content to index and more clues as to what your content is about. Some Web servers can automate the process–Snap Electronics generated a site map for its entire product catalog using IBM's WebSphere Commerce Server.

Country Maps

As you have seen, different Web sites have different versions of site maps that might list product categories, services, or anything else that appears on your Web site. You can always categorize your pages in an organized manner and display them as a kind of site map. A particular kind of spider path that is a bit different from a site map is a **country map**.

Many medium-to-large organizations have operations in multiple countries, often requiring them to show similar products and other content in each country using different languages, monetary currencies, and legal terms. These organizations frequently organize their corporate Web domain as a series of country sites. Depending on how the country sites are linked to the main domain, spiders might easily find them all or might be completely stopped.

That is why you need to use country maps. Country maps, like site maps, are search-friendly pages that link all your country sites to your overall corporate domain. As with site maps, your country map must link to each country site using a standard HTML link—not a JavaScript pull-down or any other spider-trapping navigation discussed previously in this chapter.

Figure 10-10   Effective country map techniques. Castrol's worldwide home page provides multiple paths for spiders to reach country sites.

Figure 10-10 shows the country map used by Castrol. It is easy to follow for a spider, making it effective for search marketing.

Regardless of what kind of Web site you have, spider paths are an invaluable way to get more pages from your site indexed. Whether you use country maps, site maps, or a related technique, you will provide the spiders with easy access to every page on your site, leaving en escape hatch to avoid those pesky spider traps. Next up, we look at one last way of getting more of your pages in the organic search index—telling the spiders what pages to index.

Use Inclusion Programs

As we discussed in Chapter 3, an inclusion program is a way for you to get your pages added to the search index, and to get the index updated rapidly every time the content on your pages change. Some inclusion programs are free, while others are referred to as "paid inclusion."

Let's look at free inclusion first. Some shopping search engines, such as Froogle, include your pages for free, but most require payment. But the most important free inclusion program is not from a shopping search engine, but from Google. Google Webmaster Central (www.google.com/webmasters) provides Webmaster tools for search marketers to give more control over getting their pages indexed in Google.

Paid inclusion programs usually guarantee your pages will be indexed and they guarantee how quickly it will happen. Google's Webmaster tools Sitemap protocol (commonly called "Sitemaps") makes no promise that your pages will be included or how often they will be refreshed. Regardless, many search marketers are rushing to take advantage of Sitemaps, just on the possibility that they could add pages to Google's index that have been missing for so long. Some sites have succeeded in adding hundreds of thousands of pages to Google's index using Sitemaps. The Sitemap protocol also allows you to tell the Google spider when pages were modified and which pages change most frequently, so that the spider may come back to check those pages more often.

Google offers several different ways of creating Sitemaps, which we will cover later in this chapter, but for now the most important thing to understand is that Sitemaps are low risk. Using Sitemaps doesn't replace Google's regular crawl of your site, so you really can't lose. Sitemaps may help you get more pages included in Google's index, and it may get them refrehsed faster, but it won't take away any pages that you already have indexed. Oh, and did we mention that it's free?

Paid inclusion, on the other hand, has been around much longer than free inclusion programs, but it has the same purpose—to get your pages in the index. Not many years ago, almost every major search engine (except Google) had paid inclusion programs, but today only Yahoo! has one (among worldwide search engines). Paid inclusion has come under criticsm from Consumer Reports and other industry watchdogs demanding more disclosure on which search results have been included for a fee. Possibly in response, MSN Search has most recently withdrew its paid inclusion program in 2004. Despite that trend, some experts believe that paid inclusion will grow. JupiterResearch, for example, projects the current $110 million market will surpass $500 million by 2008.

There are two related types of paid inclusion programs:

- *Single URL submission*. It is fast and simple. You enter your URL into a form, and the search spider comes every two days and indexes the page. The spider will not follow any links on the page—if you want more pages to be crawled every two days, you must pay for them individually and submit them URL by URL. Because a spider is visiting your page, you might have work to do. Although paid inclusion can overcome some technical problems with free crawling, it is not a panacea. (Why is it that nothing is *ever* a panacea? Not sure why we even need the word in the dictionary.) Although you do not need to fix spider traps that affect links (such as pop-up windows and JavaScript navigation), you do need to make sure that your page has valid HTML and is optimized for search (as discussed in Chapter 12).

- *Trusted feeds*. To handle large volumes, trusted feeds make more sense. Rather than asking the spider to crawl each URL, you can send your pages directly to the search engine. Although very efficient for large Web sites, you have some technical tasks to perform to make it all work, which we explain later. Some specialty search and almost all shopping search engines require the use of trusted feeds to load your data into their search indexes. Trusted feeds can also be sent whenever the data changes (so you do not have to wait for the spider to come back), and they can prove a godsend for a site riddled with spider traps.

Yahoo! offers both kinds of paid inclusion programs, called Site Match and Site Match Xchange. Site Match is a single URL submission program, designed for submitting fewer than 1,000 URLs. Site Match Xchange handles more, allowing you to provide either a trusted feed or a single URL from which the spider can crawl all of your pages. (Remember, if you opt to provide a single URL, such as a site map, to be crawled by the spider, you must be sure that your site is free of the spider traps listed earlier in the chapter, whereas trusted feeds avoid these spider problems.)

Both single URL submission and trusted feed programs have similar cost structures, although the actual prices might differ. You should expect the following costs for both kinds of programs:

- *Annual fee*. For each URL you submit, there is a yearly charge, usually discounted by volume.

- *Per-click fee*. Each time that a searcher clicks a page you paid to be included, the search engine charges a fee. (Many shopping search engines and Yahoo! charge per-click fees.)

- *Per-action fee*. Each time that a searcher purchases a product you included, the search engine charges a fee. (Only some shopping search engines charge this fee.) Search engines charge either a per-click or a per-action fee, never both for the same campaign.

As an example, the Yahoo! Site Match (single URL submission) program charges an annual fee based on the number of URLs submitted, ranging from $49 for one URL to $10 each for more than 10. Site Match subscribers also pay a fixed cost per click for each searcher choosing their page (with no cost per action). Most content categories are charged at 15¢ per click, although selected categories are priced at 30¢ each.

Turning to trusted feed programs, we see that Site Match Xchange is open to search marketers submitting more than 1,000 URLs or spending more than $5,000 per month. The per-click fee is the same as for Site Match, and there is no annual fee.

You can use Web feeds in addition to an inclusion program. You may have heard of Really Simple Syndication (RSS) feeds (and Atom feeds) that send blog entries to their subscribers. Used mainly to distribute blogs, RSS feeds support any data, even product catalogs. So, each time your catalog is updated, you can have your feed "ping" individual search engines to index the updated products—or even easier, ping Ping-O-Matic (www.pingomatic.com) which, in turn, pings *all* search engines. As long as at least one user subscribes to your feed from that search provider, your feed will be indexed—one My Yahoo! subscriber will cause the Yahoo! search engine to index a feed, for example.

Inclusion Programs Can Make Your Life Easier

Inclusion programs can improve your organic search marketing in several ways, including the following:

- *They index more of your site.* If you have some intractable spider traps making it impossible to get your site crawled, and it costs too much to fix them, inclusion programs can help. Google's program is free, and if you have the budget to pay for Yahoo! you can get most pages indexed that spiders cannot process. But your content must also be optimized—and it is time-consuming to create compelling titles and descriptions for your pages. In addition, you can use trusted feeds to get your products included in shopping search engines, but remember that you must automate the transmission of your data to the shopping engines. It *will* cost you some time and money up front to write the software to send your data to the engines every day.

- *They are cheaper than paid placement.* Per-click charges for paid inclusion are usually substantially lower than for paid placement, but you must be careful that you are not paying for clicks that you could get for free. If you can get your pages crawled by Yahoo! without paying for inclusion, that is obviously better. With shopping search engines, you typically *must* pay for inclusion to be in their index—there is no free lunch here.

- *They respond quickly to changes.* If your site is highly volatile—content changes rapidly as inventory and prices change—then paid inclusion allows you to add new pages to the index and delete old ones much more rapidly than you can waiting for the spider. You can control what products appear in the search index, even rotating your offers if desired, and you can do that for both Yahoo! and for shopping search engines. Also, because paid inclusion metrics are up-to-the-minute, you can respond to drops in your search ranking or lower clickthroughs as they occur. You can also find new keywords that your pages should be optimized for. Remember that Google's program, however, provides no turnaround commitments.

- *They let you test changes to your site quickly*. Paid inclusion's 48-hour turnaround lets you make frequent changes to your site to see how Yahoo! changes your ranking. Test many different combinations of content and check your corresponding rankings and traffic. Rather than waiting for weeks to see how several changes worked, you can test three different combinations in one week. When you find the best version of the page for Yahoo! you will likely find it was the best one for Google and other organic search results, too.

How to Get Started with Inclusion Programs

Signing up with Yahoo! for Site Match (the single URL submission program) is very simple, but implementing trusted feeds for Yahoo! and for shopping search engines takes quite a bit more work. Taking advantage of Google Sitemaps requires efforts somewhere in the middle.

Site Match submission requires just one step—filling out the submission form. Just enter the URLs for each page that you want included, along with the subject category of your site—the category chosen determines whether you are charged 15¢ or 30¢ per click.

Google Sitemaps are free, but they require more technical acumen to set up than Site Match. The work consists of three steps: setting up a Google account, creating and submitting the Sitemap, and updating it when needed. You don't have to be a genius to set up your account or to update your sitemap (you just press an update button from your account screen) but creating your first Sitemap can be a little tricky.

First off, you have several choices about *how* to create your Google Sitemap, some of which require more technical expertise than others. The simplest version of a Sitemap is just a text file that contins a list of URLs, one per line, but you can get a lot fancier than that. Google offers a Sitemap protocol that tells the spider when pages have been updated and which pages are the most important to crawl frequently. You can hand encode a file that uses that protocol, but most sites will find it smarter to automate the process, either by writing a custom program or by using the Sitemap generator provided by Google. Google also accepts syndication feeds (your Webmaster will know what these are), such as Really Simple Syndication (RSS) and Atomz. Most Web developers know how to generate at least one of these formats to feed Google's spider, and if you automate the creation of your Sitemap, you will ensure that it changes whenever your Web pages do.

When you have finished creating your Sitemap, you place the Sitemap file on your Web server in the root directory (or the top directory you want crawled) and submit the Sitemap from your Google account. That's it. Then you wait for the spider and hope for the best. Remember that Sitemaps won't remove all spider traps. If your pages require the use of JavaScript or are excluded by a robots.txt file, your Google Sitemap won't override these problems. But if you struggle with long dynamic URLs or pages hidden behind registration forms or many other problems, a Google Sitemap can be the only way to get your page indexed. And although they do require someone with technical skills to set them up, once they are running they require little technical exerptise.

Trusted feeds take a bit more work, as you might expect. Your programmers must create a file containing the content you want included and send that to the search engine. Different search engines accept different formats, ranging from CSV (comma-separated variable) files to Microsoft Excel spreadsheets to custom XML. (As mentioned earlier, some search engines will also crawl your site, but then you need to do all the work of removing spider traps and creating spider paths as described earlier in this chapter.) Just about every search engine accepts XML format, which is the cheapest to maintain in the long run. (XML is a markup language similar to HTML that allows tags to be defined to describe any kind of data you have, making it very popular as a format for data feeds.)

What data you must put in your feed depends on the search engine you are sending it to, because each engine has different data requirements. For example, Yahoo! requires the title, description, URL, and other text from the page. Shopping search engines typically expect the price, availability, and features of your products, in addition to the product's name and description. Most data feeds include some or all of these items:

- *Page URL.* The actual URL for the Web page for this search result. It can be a static or a dynamic URL, but it must be working—no "page not found" messages—or the search engine will delete the page from its index.

- *Tracking URL.* The URL that the searcher should go to when clicking this result. It can be the same as the page URL, but sometimes your Web metrics software needs a different URL to help measure clicks from search to your page.

- *Product name.* All variants of your product's name, including acronyms and its full name. Pay special attention to what searchers might type in to find your product name and include them here.

- *Product description.* A lengthy description of your product that should include multiple occurrences of the keywords you expect searchers to enter. (See Chapter 12 for more information on how to optimize your content for search.) Every search engine is different, but most allow 250 words for your product description.

- *Model number.* The number you expect most searchers to enter to find this product. If a retailer and a manufacturer have different numbers for the same product, you can sometimes include both, depending on the search engine you are submitting the feed to.

- *Manufacturer.* The complete name of the manufacturer of the product, with any short names or acronyms that searchers might use.

- *Product category.* The type of product, according to a valid list of products maintained by the search engine. Each search engine has somewhat different product lines that they support, with different names. You need to use the exact name for your product's category that each search engine uses.

- *Price*. A critical piece of information for shopping search engine feeds, which typically require tax and shipping costs, too. Be sure that your prices are accurate each time you submit your feed, because price is one of the main ways that shopping searchers find your product.

Inktomi, now owned by Yahoo!, pioneered the concept of feeding large amounts of data from commerce Web sites directly into its search index. Inktomi defined a custom XML format for supplying documents named IDIF (Inktomi Document Interchange Format), which is still used by Yahoo! today and is depicted in Figure 10-11.

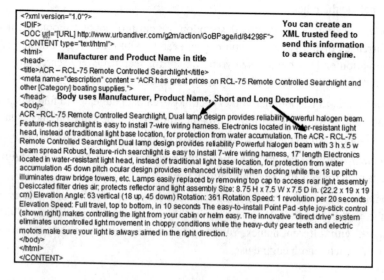

Figure 10-13   Sample trusted feed. To use the Yahoo! trusted feed program, you must regularly send them an XML file containing your data.

Making the Most of Paid Inclusion

It's not all that complicated to get started with paid inclusion, especially if you start with a single URL submission program, but most medium-to-large sites probably need to use trusted feed programs. You also need to use trusted feeds to send your data to shopping search engines, because they cannot be fed any other way. And anyone feeding shopping search engines needs trusted feed programs. They are a bit more complex to set up, as you have seen, so you want to make sure you get the most out of them and that you avoid any pitfalls along the way. Here are some tips to make your paid inclusion program a success:

- *Avoid off-limits subjects.* Most search engines have off-limits subjects that they refuse to be associated with. Because of local laws in various countries, some search engines reject "adult" (pornographic) content, sites with controversial themes, gambling sites, and pharmacy and drug information. All content submitted undergoes initial and ongoing quality reviews. If pages are rejected, some search engines, including Yahoo!, do not refund your fees.

- *Take advantage of "on-the-fly" optimization.* The better your source data and the better your feed-creation program, the better your feed can be. One advantage of trusted feeds over crawling is on-the-fly optimization—having your feed-creation program add additional relevant words to the feed that were not in your original source, such as keywords to your titles and descriptions. For example, Snap Electronics discovered that all of its product pages contain the words *Snap* and *SnapShot*, and the model number, and a picture, but they actually do not all contain the words *digital camera*. Snap made sure that the program that produces its trusted feed optimized its data on-the-fly, by adding the generic product keywords *digital camera* to the titles and descriptions of the trusted feed. That way the search engine has that information even though Snap forgot to optimize the original page to contain *digital camera*.

- *Do not add keywords unrelated to your content.* Although optimizing on-the-fly can be a real advantage for you, it can be very dangerous for the search engines, because it leaves them wide open to anyone unethically adding keywords that do not really describe the data, just so they can get high search rankings for those keywords. Regardless of whether you use a simple URL submission program or the more complex trusted feed, search engines are very strict about what content they accept. Many unethical search marketing techniques (known as spam) try to fool the search engines to find your pages when they really should not match, and every search engine takes measures to avoid being fooled. Shopping search engines are sensitive to errors in your trusted feed (such as sending "in stock" in the feed when the product is temporarily unavailable). If your pages use some of these tricks, expect search engines to begin rejecting your submissions.

- *Make your feed-creation program flexible.* Even if you start using trusted feeds for just a single search engine, be prepared to expand to work with others in the future. Each engine uses a slightly different format, so make sure your programmer is prepared to change the program to create feeds for other search engines when they are needed.

- *Seek out feed specialists if needed.* If your programmers cannot do the job, several vendors will be happy to step in and do it for you, including Position Tech (www.position-tech.com), MarketLeap (www.marketleap.com), Global Strategies International (www.globalstrategies.com), and Business Research (www.bizresearch.com). Each of these companies is "certified" by Yahoo! and some shopping search engines to produce trusted feeds. Companies that are not certified typically have to partner with a certified company, so you are better of working with a certified company directly.

- *Stay on top of daily operations.* In addition to the work of creating the program, you must ensure that your operations personnel run the program to send the data whenever it changes, or else the search engine will not have the most up-to-date information for your site. Don't do all the expensive upfront work and then fall down by not operating reliably.

Paid inclusion, especially trusted feeds, can require some work upfront, but they can pay off handsomely when executed properly. If your site would benefit from sales from shopping search engines, or you need to boost your pages indexed in Yahoo!, paid inclusion could be the extra organic lottery ticket it makes sense to buy. And Google Sitemaps are even better—they are free lottery tickets.

Summary

This chapter covered a great deal. If you started out having no idea whether your Web site was well indexed, and even less of a clue as to how to fix that, you cannot say that any more.

You learned how to check to be sure your Web site is indexed, and what to do in the unfortunate situation that it's not. You now know exactly how many pages you have in each index and approximately what percentage is indexed (your inclusion ratio). But you also know how to get all of your public pages indexed.

You learned how to recognize spider traps and eliminate them. You know what content spiders ignore. You can create spider paths through your site so that spiders can find every public page. And you got the lowdown on inclusion programs—why you use them, how they work, and how to take advantage of them.

In short, you've learned how to "kick-start" your organic search efforts, because it all starts with getting your pages included in the organic search index. However, you still have more to learn. In the next chapter, we explain how you know which keywords searchers use and how you should pick the best targets for your search campaigns. After you know that, you need to learn how to change your pages so that they are found for those keywords. So, get ready. It's time for you to discover which keywords your targeted searchers are using.

Choose Your Target Keywords

Get out your crystal ball! That's one way to guess the words that searchers use. If your crystal ball is as cloudy as ours, however, you might want to use a few other methods, too. That's what you will learn in this chapter.

In the preceding chapter, you learned how to get your site indexed for organic search, but getting indexed is not enough. You need to get your pages to be highly ranked in the organic search results to generate traffic to your site. Or you need to invest in paid search techniques for your site's pages to show up on that search results page. No matter whether you are focusing on organic or paid search or both, you need to know which keywords searchers are using. If you do not know which words searchers are entering, you cannot purchase the right keywords (for paid placement), nor can you make sure those words are prominently featured on your pages (for organic search). Each time you embark on a new search marketing campaign, you will choose your target list of keywords.

In this chapter, we show you that choosing the right keywords for your search marketing campaign does not have to be guesswork. We explain the basics of **keyword planning**—the method by which you choose your keywords. This chapter covers the following topics:

- *The value of keyword planning.* You will see how keyword planning improves brand awareness for your organization and how it helps you improve Web conversions—the ones you chose back in Chapter 5, "Identify Your Web Site's Goals," for your Web site.

- *Your keyword planning philosophy.* Most failures of keyword planning stem from misunderstanding the proper thinking behind keyword decisions. You will learn the philosophy of selecting "just right" keywords that are neither too broad nor too narrow.

- *Step-by-step keyword planning.* We dive into the planning process itself, showing you three proven steps to select the right keywords for any campaign.

At the end of this chapter, you will be able to choose the best keyword targets for every search marketing campaign you undertake. Let's start by getting an appreciation for why keyword planning is so important.

The Value of Keyword Planning

You might be tempted to skip the whole process of keyword planning. Maybe you think you already know what searchers are looking for. If you do, that's great. Unless you have done a comprehensive keyword analysis in the past, however, you don't really know what words searchers enter. Oh sure, you know *some* of them. But what about the ones you do not know? Every valuable keyword you miss is an opportunity for your competitors.

And what about the keywords that you are *sure* lots of searchers are using? Time and again, we have seen smart people focus scarce resources to target a keyword and find very little traffic as a result. Often, the words that *you* search with are not the same as what your customers use. You are an expert, and they are not.

So, the basic value of keyword planning is to make sure that your search marketing resources are focused on all the valuable keywords (so that you haven't missed any) and not targeting words of low value (which costs you unnecessary money and time).

But the value of keyword planning goes deeper than that. As you saw in Chapter 4, "How Searchers Work," searchers exhibit very specific behavior when they look for information. Keyword planning enables you to present searchers with the right content at the right time—your content, that is. As with all of search marketing, keyword planning derives its value from the basic goals of your site that you developed in Chapter 5. There are two basic reasons to engage in search marketing: building brand awareness and increasing Web conversions. Let's look at each one before we take on the keyword planning process itself.

Building Brand Awareness

Whether you like it or not, many people have never heard of your company. These people might be customers, if only they knew they should be buying from you. It is well accepted in other forms of marketing that raising awareness is the first step in landing a new customer, and many forms of advertising are devoted to nothing but brand awareness.

When someone sees your TV commercial about that new car, you hope that viewer might be in the market for a car at that moment and head down to the dealer to buy, but relatively few people are in that situation at any one time. The vast majority of people watching that ad have no interest in buying a car. But someday they will. Advertisers know that the messages in their constant commercials—the name of their company, the model of their car, and how exciting/practical/sexy/inexpensive/luxurious the car is—will stick in viewers' minds, who might remember the message later when they *are* in the market for a car. Marketers call this **brand awareness**.

Raising awareness of your brand identity is a basic part of any marketing effort, but it is just starting to be recognized as a legitimate goal for search marketing. You might or might not have a goal of building brand identity through your own search marketing efforts. If you do, keyword planning is essential to that goal. At the end of this chapter, when we prioritize the most important keyword candidates for your organization to target, you will take into account any brand awareness goals as you do so.

Remember, searchers might not know you offer a particular product or service. Unless they see it listed in the results, they will not think of you. Searchers researching a product or service for the first time might not be aware of *any* specific brand or company. They are just gathering information. They might not even have any intention to buy anything yet, because they are just looking into a problem and do not know they need anything to solve it. However, according to research from search marketing consultancy iProspect, more than 55 percent of Internet users expect to find big brand Web sites listed at the top of search results. That same study also found that over 66 percent of searchers believe that sites with the highest search listings are the top companies in their field.

Think about how this affects brand awareness. If you are not listed in the search results, you are not a "big brand" in the searcher's mind. If you are listed there, you must be. Such is the branding power of search.

These searchers (who are in the Learn phase of the Web Conversion Cycle discussed in Chapter 5) might or might not ever become your customers, but your product has a far better chance of being considered if they do decide to move to the Shop phase and eventually make a purchase. Marketers call the group of companies that shoppers might purchase from their **consideration set**. To be in the consideration set, you need to have high brand awareness.

So how does search improve brand awareness? The simplest way is to ensure that you are targeting broad keywords that capture prospective customers while they are still learning— before they have made any brand decisions. But there are other ways, too.

In your paid placement ad copy, always use a well-known brand name, if you have one. And if you don't, you might find that constantly using your brand names will begin to build some level of awareness. Searchers are much more likely to click results with brand names they know. So, paid placements for Snap Electronics should always have *Snap* in the ad, or *SnapShot* for its digital camera ads. Because that name is well known, searchers will choose it over a generic ad for *digital cameras*. When you purchase unbranded keywords, such as *digital cameras*, and you put your brand name in the ad, you are building brand awareness.

Another way to build brand awareness through search is with tie-ins to traditional advertising campaigns. As mentioned previously, most traditional advertising has some brand awareness goals, such as the TV commercial for cars. But where do people go after they see the commercial? Where do they go when they see your print ad in the airline magazine? They probably do not troop down to the dealership for a brochure. More and more, their next step is to go to the Web.

Perhaps you think that they remember the name of your company and they type in the URL of your Web site. Or they remember the URL you printed at the bottom of the ad? Well, maybe they do. However, it is more likely that they perform a search, for several reasons:

- They remember your company name, but they do not know what your Web site address is.

- They do not actually remember the name of your company; they just remember the name of the car.

- They did not catch anything from the ad except your slogan, but they were interested in that car.

If you do a good job generating attention with your print and on-air advertising, you prompt people to seek out your Web site, which they will often do by searching. If you are introducing a new product or a new concept about your product, you might find people wanting more information when no one was interested before. So, if you are raising interest offline, you must follow through online.

Frequently, search marketers are caught unprepared when a new offline (print or on-air) campaign begins. A keyword that was not important in the past is suddenly hot, but you have no search campaign in place to capture the traffic. Perhaps your company is introducing a new catch phrase. Maybe your product designers are adding a hot new feature to a product. Any of these events can draw attention and prompt searchers to start using new words—the words you use in your offline campaign. Stay in touch with your offline counterparts so that you are ready for sudden success from unexpected places.

Similarly, do not fret about being too early to target a keyword. Sometimes you should stick with an unpopular keyword when you know your organization is committed to building awareness. Searchers might simply not have been exposed to the term yet. Daniele Hayes, a manager of paid search programs at IBM, refers to this phenomenon as "keyword timing," noting that each keyword has its own life cycle, where it rises from out of nowhere, might become very popular (quickly or slowly) and eventually fades into oblivion.

Hewlett-Packard and IBM have dueling marketing campaigns that demonstrate keyword timing. IBM's is called "On Demand," with HP touting "Adaptive Computing." Keyword planning performed when these campaigns were launched revealed almost no searches for either term. As both companies ratcheted up their offline media campaigns, searches for these words took off.

It's not just big companies that can do this. Whenever you send out a press release or hold a gala event, it's news. Make sure your search marketing program has a campaign cooking to catch the happy result of your publicity. If brand awareness is one of your goals for search, keep that in mind as you go through your keyword planning process.

Increasing Web Conversions

As you saw in Chapter 6, "Measure Your Web Site's Success," the simplest justification for search marketing for most businesses is "If they can't find you, they can't buy from you." And, as you also saw, online purchases are only one kind of Web conversion—you decided what the important conversions are for your Web site and you will use search marketing to drive more of them.

How does keyword planning help you do that? The first benefit of keyword planning is driving qualified traffic to your site. Note the word *qualified*. You can drive traffic to your Web site in dozens of ways, if you have the budget, but the value of search marketing is that the searcher has initiated the interaction.

One of the largest advantages of search marketing is that it is a "pull" medium rather than the traditional "push" media (such as print ads, or radio and TV advertising). Searchers have taken the initiative to tell you what they are interested in, rather than you interrupting what they were doing to push your message in. The better you can interpret searchers' interests and present them with highly relevant content, the greater your conversion rates will be. That is where keyword planning comes in. Keyword planning helps you interpret what searchers actually want, so that you can target just those searchers that you can convert.

 So, although keyword planning can help you drive more traffic to your site, even better is that it shows you how to drive more *qualified* traffic to your site. Later, when we assign priorities to different keywords, we look at how to use your Web Conversion Cycle to decide your searchers' place in the buying cycle, thus increasing your Web conversions by selecting the proper keywords.

But before we dive into the keyword selection process, you need to learn how to think about keyword planning. Without the proper thought process, you will not make the decisions that will maximize your success.

Your Keyword Planning Philosophy

Goldilocks has a lot to teach us about keyword planning. When she tasted the porridge, she avoided the bowl that was too hot, and the one that was too cold, and settled on the one that was "just right." So it is with keyword planning.

You will hear a lot of theories about keyword planning, so you will need to make up your own mind. You will often hear variations on one of these two approaches:

- *The "hot" keyword approach.* You have to target very popular search terms if you want to drive substantial traffic to your site.

- *The "cold" keyword approach.* You need to target less-popular keywords that have little competition if you want to get a high ranking.

But the world just is not that simple. Either one of these approaches can be right in your situation, or they might both be wrong. The key is understanding your situation and developing a philosophy that matches your Web site's content. The keyword you select cannot be too hot or too cold for your Web site—it needs to be "just right." So let's look at the Goldilocks approach to keyword planning.

Don't Pick Keywords That Are "Too Hot"

Popular keywords are very seductive. We cannot help but have visions of instant success, with searchers streaming onto our Web site overnight. But, as is usually the case in life, it is not as easy as it seems. Let's look at why some words can be too hot for you.

Overheated Subjects

Be honest. Is your organization a household name? Do people naturally associate your products with its generic name? For example, anyone interested in a copier would naturally think of Xerox. They might also think of Canon or Ricoh, but most people would think of Xerox. Is that the kind of Web site you have? Your company is very identified with a product?

If so, you can think *big*. You *should* target the word *copier*, if you work for Xerox. You make every kind of copier there is. Color copiers, collating copiers, copiers that staple, punch holes, and do the fandango. You make every flavor of copier known to man, so why not go after that big broad word?

But what if you don't work for Xerox? What if you work for a small copier manufacturer? Yes, you have many good, loyal customers. And lots of folks think your copiers are even better than Xerox copiers. And they are cheaper, to boot. It is tempting to target that word *copier* too, isn't it? No need to check how popular that word is—you *know* it has a zillion searches every day. If you only get some of those searchers, that's okay. You want to fish where the fish are, right?

Well, no. That word *copier* is too hot for you, and you *will* get burned. You see, you do not make *every* kind of copier. You only make *color* copiers. Uh, *personal* color copiers, as a matter of fact. You *are* the leader in the emerging personal color copier market. But of all the people searching for the word "copier," only a few are looking for personal color copiers. *Those* are your potential customers—no one else. Now that does not mean that the only keyword that you should buy is "personal color copiers." It probably makes sense to buy "personal copiers" and "color copiers" and many more, too. But if you purchase paid placement for "copier," you probably are looking at a bad outcome:

- *You get very few clicks.* This is what will happen if your paid placement ad for the word *copier* is titled, "Personal Color Copiers at Low Prices." Most people searching with the query "copier" are not looking for a personal color copier, so they will not click. If your clickthrough rate is low enough, eventually the paid placement service will drop your ad completely. So, you will rack up next to no sales on your paid placement campaign.

- *You get many clicks, but low conversion.* This is your probable outcome if your "copier" ad says, "Low-priced copiers with free delivery." Now, you might have low-priced copiers and you might offer free delivery, but you only sell personal color copiers, so many of the folks will click your ad, see you do not have what they want, and abandon your site. After you are charged for the click, of course. Charged handsomely, in fact, because that word *copier* is very expensive (*because* it gets a zillion searches a day). So, you will rapidly run through your paid placement budget, racking up next to no sales.

But, you might ask, "Suppose I do not use paid placement? I can go after organic search." Think again. There are millions of pages with the word *copier* on them, so why should Yahoo! show yours on page one? There are many other companies that sell a wider range of copiers and are more well known (and have more links to their sites). On the other hand, you might have a great chance at getting a high ranking for *personal copier* or *color copier* or especially *personal color copier*.

And think about it. If you do optimize your page for those more attainable phrases, the word *copier* will be all over the page anyway. So if by some chance you do have a shot at ranking well for *copier*, you will. But it is more realistic to pick terms that are just right for your Web site, rather than too hot, because it will cost you just as much to perform organic optimization for the wrong keyword as for the right one. You just will not drive any qualified traffic with the wrong one. Just as with paid placement, most people searching for "copier" are not looking for you, anyway. So what is the point of ranking well for *copier* when it will not get you many conversions?

Before you go overboard in the other direction, however, there are times when a very broad keyword *is* "just right" for you. Consider whether Apple Computer should target the word *computer*. At first blush, you might reject *computer* as being too broad a term. After all, most people looking for a computer want a computer that runs the Windows operating system and many want servers, which Apple is not well known for. But do people that have specific ideas about what they want (such as a Windows server) actually search for the word "computer"? Probably not. It might be that the novices who know they want to buy "a computer" are exactly the kind of people who might buy an Apple.

The most important thing to learn is not to be seduced by the high volumes for the most popular keywords. Go after the keywords that are the closest match for your site, even if they are not the most popular ones. If it turns out that those popular keywords *are* "just right" for your site, by all means target them. But don't overreach. Don't go after words that are too hot for you, because you will not get the conversions you want anyway.

Overheated Meanings

There is no best-selling book titled *Lincoln: The Man, the Car, the Tunnel*, because even though a Lincoln Continental and the Hudson River crossing share the name of America's sixteenth president, they do not have much else in common. All of which is a roundabout way of saying that words with multiple meanings are another cause of "too hot" keywords. In addition, slightly different words sometimes have very different meanings.

Overheated meanings occur in a number of common situations:

- *Multiple audiences.* The keyword *security* means one thing to an antivirus software maker and something else to a home burglar alarm installer. As with the *copier* example, sometimes you can add qualifying words (*computer security* and *home security*) to bring down the temperature and make a keyword "just right." At other times, you might decide to just avoid that keyword entirely.

- *Related meanings.* If you sell auto insurance, the difference in your conversion rate between searchers for "car" and "car insurance" is substantial. Stay away from a broad term when a more specific one will do. Yes, some people buying cars are in the market for car insurance, too, but you are panning an awful lot of water for a few gold nuggets.

- *Multiple intents.* Although it is true that the word *hotel* and the word *lodging* mean the same thing, a hotel operator will find much higher conversion rates for the word *hotel* itself. Searchers for "lodging" are often looking for alternatives to hotels, such as bed-and-breakfast inns, which is why they used the less-common word. Job seekers look for the word "job," whereas employers search for help with "recruitment"—both might search for "recruiters" (which might be too hot a word).

- *Singular/plural meaning changes.* Search engines typically look for both the singular and plural forms of a word, but that can sometimes cause overheating. The word *sale* has a different meaning than *sales*—"appliance sale" might be searched for by a consumer, whereas a job-seeking salesman might want "appliance sales"—and that difference can overheat the keyword. *Cosmetic* and *cosmetics* are two more words that seem seductively similar in meaning, but in fact are not. Think carefully about every keyword you target to see whether changing from singular to plural changes the meaning.

- *Acronyms.* It is quite common for the same acronym to mean several things, causing the keyword to be overheated. Does *CD* mean a disc or a certificate of deposit? Does *SCM* stand for supply chain management or software configuration management or source control management? Actually, it stands for all three, which is why it is hard to get qualified traffic when your site matches just one meaning of the word.

Most search marketers follow "the more, the merrier" theory. If *women's fashion boots* is a good keyword for your Web site, *boots* will be even better! There are so many more people searching for "boots" that it is sure to drive a lot more traffic. The problem is that if you sell only women's fashion boots, that extra traffic will not produce many more conversions. Instead of looking for hotter and hotter keywords, look for "just right" keywords.

Don't Pick Keywords That Are "Too Cold"

Often, after being burned by a flaming keyword or two, people go in the opposite direction, afraid to go after any keyword that has too much competition. Even some search marketing consultants would rather go after "cold" keywords so they can show you how quickly they get high rankings in search. Goldilocks will tell you that this is not the right way either.

Sometimes cold keywords—ones with few or no searchers looking for them—are chosen by accident. An Italian tour operator targets "milano," but misses all the American tourists who use the anglicized spelling "milan." Or the shortest word forms of keywords are chosen, such as *manage your finances* instead of *personal financial management*—search engines usually find the shorter forms when you target the longer forms (but not always vice versa).

One particularly troublesome cause of accidental cold keywords is translating campaigns into other languages. If you take a search marketing campaign you have run in your native language (say, English) and merely translate those keywords to French, for example, you are likely to have chosen numerous cold keywords. Just as searcher intent differs in English for many terms with similar meanings, you might have chosen an accurate, but unpopular, French translation for your English keyword. Paid placement vendors can help you redo your keyword planning in global markets so that you pick "just right" keywords for your site in every local market.

Another accidental chill can occur when you assume that different audiences for the same product search the same way. Tor Crockatt, Global Editorial Director for MIVA (the paid placement vendor), loves to show examples of how searchers performing similar tasks do different things. Tor describes a major electronics manufacturer whose Scandinavian customers did research online but whose German customers did little research online (although they did buy the product online). If the manufacturer had assumed that buying habits were the same in Germany as in Scandinavia, many cold keywords would have been targeted around the Learn stage of the Web Conversion Cycle. Similarly, IBM has found that consumers tend to *shop*, whereas business people tend to *procure* or *purchase*, even when they are buying the same product. If you expect that every market segment will approach searching for your site the same way, you are likely to land in some cold spots.

Some choices of cold keywords are actually done on purpose, however, by intelligent people who really should know better. Wordtracker (www.wordtracker.com), the keyword research tool, features Keyword Effectiveness Index (KEI) analysis. KEI analysis (and similar techniques that go by other names) is a mathematical representation of the popularity of a keyword (the number of searches containing it) compared to its popularity in usage (the number of Web pages it is found on). As a tool, there is nothing wrong with KEI analysis—in fact, it can be quite useful in helping you avoid "too hot" keywords that are not right for your site. But it can be abused.

Some might use KEI analysis to dissuade you from going after any keyword with even a modicum of competition. That's misguided. Although it is true that the more pages a word appears on, the more difficult it is to get a top ten search result, the simple fact is that someone's site *is* ranking #1 for that word. How did they do it? Whatever they did is what you have to do just a bit better if you want to rank #1.

Just as it was silly for our personal color copier manufacturer to want to rank #1 for the hot *copier* keyword, it is equally silly to shy away from the keyword *personal color copier* just because many pages contain those words. If you have found a set of keywords that perfectly describe your site, it's time to fight for that ranking, not slink away to some backwater set of keywords that no one is looking for (just so you can say you have a #1 ranking). Remember, it costs just as much to optimize an organic page for a cold keyword as for a "just right" one, so spend your efforts on the ones that will pay off.

Before we move on to "just right" keywords, you should know that paid placement differs from organic search when it comes to cold keywords. In the case of paid placement programs, there might be little downside to targeting cold keywords. Even if very few searchers enter the keywords each month, if you are getting conversions at low per-click rates, there is no reason to stop (unless it is costing you too much time to manage). In general, however, stick to the "just right" words; they will have the best payoff.

Pick Keywords That Are "Just Right"

So why do "just right" keywords work? It is not that hard to understand, really. Search engines actually do a very good job of finding the right pages for each query, and people do a good job of clicking the right pages from what they see. What that means is that if you target keywords that are truly relevant to your site, and you follow through on the techniques in the rest of this book, you will likely improve your search traffic with highly qualified visitors. In short, sticking to keywords that truly reflect your site will make it easier for you to attract search rankings and will pay off in more conversions than if you do anything else.

Conversely, if you find that you are seeing the symptoms of targeting "too hot" keywords (low paid clickthrough, dropping organic search referrals, or low conversion rates), you have a choice. You can move back to "just right" queries, or you can change your Web site. If you want to compete for the "copier" query, what content can you put up to attract all copier buyers? Affiliate links for products you do not sell? Comparison information that shows why every copier buyer should buy yours? It is not easy, but there are times when you can expand your site so that it really is a good match for a broad query.

For those of you who are less ambitious (and more realistic), however, there is good news. The days of searchers entering single-word queries in large numbers are coming to an end. Although there are still cases where a single search word is very descriptive of what the searcher wants ("ipod"), there are far more situations in which only multiple words will truly pinpoint the information desired, and searchers are growing in sophistication.

Jeremy Sanchez, Senior Search Strategist for search consultancy Global Strategies International, says that "75 percent of all search queries in our trusted feed data are three terms or longer with very few search queries alike. For every 50 clicks a URL receives, 45 of the search queries are different." In a similar vein, a recent study showed that 70 percent of searches contain two or more words, with 25 percent using three words or more.

What this means is that more and more searchers are entering long keyword phrases that far more accurately pinpoint the pages they want. More searchers are using "just right" queries, so you can feel comfortable targeting them.

Our friends at Snap Electronics heeded this advice. They stayed away from the hot keyword *cameras* because they make only digital cameras, not film cameras. The word *cameras* might be okay for Kodak, but it was wrong for Snap. Snap recognized that *digital cameras* itself was still a very hot word, and that it would not be easy to get a high ranking there, but they also knew that it perfectly described their product line—they made a range of cameras and they needed to be seen there to reinforce their brand image as the best and easiest to use digital camera.

Enough philosophy! Now that you understand the value of keyword planning and you have a sound approach to make your decisions, let's get started.

Step-by-Step Keyword Planning

When you know the steps to take, you can usually get where you are going. Keyword planning is no different from any other specialized task, so let's take a quick peek at the steps for choosing a target list of keywords for any search marketing campaign:

- *Gather your keyword candidate list.* You start by compiling as long a list as possible of the words searchers might use to find your site. You will learn to brainstorm with your team to start the list, and then consult your Web site's many data sources to complete the list.

- *Research each keyword candidate.* It is not enough to have a long list of words—you need to learn which ones are attracting enough searches to be worthwhile, and whether related keywords should also be considered.
- *Prioritize your keyword candidate list.* Decision time. You will not be able to target every promising keyword you find. You will prioritize the keywords that are "just right" for your site.

If that seems like a lot of work, well, it is. But it is work you need to do. Proper keyword planning will actually save you enormous amounts of work later—all the wasted time of managing paid placement campaigns and optimizing your content for all the wrong keywords. We also introduce you to some tools and techniques that reduce the work as much as possible.

Gather Your Keyword Candidate List

Let's start making a list and checking it twice. Every Web site has a wealth of information to consult for keyword planning, even though you might not be aware of it.

We go through each source of data you can check, but the very first place to start is inside your own head, and inside the heads of your teammates. Bring together the folks most familiar with the subject of the search marketing campaign at hand—experts in the content of the product, service, or whatever the campaign is centered on. You will start your keyword planning with a brainstorming session.

Brainstorm with Your Team

You have probably participated in brainstorming sessions before—this one is no different. Approach it in the standard way. Get together the people who are knowledgeable about your search marketing campaign's focus, be it a product, service, or something else. Make sure all participants get to add their two cents and do not censor any ideas—you will remove erroneous choices and prioritize the most important keywords later. Let each one add words to your master list of keyword candidates. We prompt you along the way with techniques that lend structure to your brainstorming session, to make it easier for you to develop a more comprehensive list.

The easiest way to start your brainstorming is for everyone to make a list of all of the names you can use for the product, service, or other subject of this campaign. Focus first on *nouns*. Let's see what one Snap Electronics team member listed for its digital camera campaign: camera, digital camera, SnapShot, Snap digital camera, X5, X6, X7, SLR X800, and SLR X900. Each team put together a slightly different list that had more than 30 unique names on it by the end of the exercise.

The next step is to organize your nouns into categories, as shown in Table 11-1. Sometimes putting each name in its proper column helps to identify ones that are missing. If your names use acronyms, you might need to also include the full name of the product or service, if that is the phrase most people will use to search.

Table 11-1   Keyword Noun Brainstorming (Organizing each noun by its type can reveal omissions in your list.)

Category	Segment	Brand Group	Products
camera	digital camera	Snap SnapShot	X5, X6, X7, SLR X800, SLR X900
PC	notebook	ThinkPad	R40, R51, T41, T42
car	luxury sedan	Lexus	LS
chair	desk chair	Herman Miller Aeron chair	Graphite Frame, Titanium Frame

After you have a fairly complete set of nouns, break out the *adjectives*. Think in terms of qualifying words that hone in on more details, such as qualities, characteristics, or attributes. Some of the noun phrases identified in Table 11-1 can be viewed this way—*digital* camera or *luxury* sedan, but now it's time to list a lot more adjectives. Table 11-2 shows how Snap Electronics carried out this exercise. Listing several different categories of adjectives can help you flesh out the adjectives you need. Don't be concerned about which category your adjectives fall in, or whether you list one more than once—when you are done, it will not matter how they are categorized. The point of the exercise is to identify as many of those multiword phrases that describe your subject as possible. The categories just help you think of more adjectives.

Table 11-2   Keyword Adjective Brainstorming (Develop several categories of adjectives that describe your product, and have everyone fill in the blanks.)

Comparison	Qualifier	Function	Attributes	Action
best digital camera	cheap digital camera	fastest digital camera	8 megapixel digital camera	buy digital camera
easy digital camera	discount digital camera	lightest digital camera	slr digital camera	download digital camera software
	smallest digital camera			
	fastest digital camera			
	lightweight digital camera			

Complete this matrix with *your* product in mind, not by listing any plausible adjective for your industry. Snap makes high-end digital cameras, so they ultimately decided to shy away from the adjective *cheap*, even though someone wrote it down during brainstorming. It is common in offline advertising to use "opposite" terms to "convert" buyers of cheap product to high-end products, but that rarely works in search marketing.

By this time, you should have a solid list of keyword nouns and a longer list of phrases with adjectives to qualify those nouns. Before getting too self-satisfied, however, you should know that most folks have missed a number of very important keywords at this point in the process. It's time to think about the road not traveled.

It is natural for you to think narrowly about your product or service because you are an expert on that subject. Your list of candidate keywords contains all the words that you and your team would use to search, but it is probably missing a bunch of keywords your customers use. Broaden your list further by asking yourselves some questions:

- What do your customers need? What problems are they trying to solve? What words do they use to describe their needs and problems?

- What content do we have on our site that would satisfy someone's search? What words would you search for to find that content?

- How would you describe your product to a novice?

- What words do industry magazines and industry analysts use to describe your products? Is there a product category name that they use?

You might call your computer a notebook, but do others call it a laptop? Do novices search for "digital photos" or "computer pictures" or "computer camera"? If you do not know, write it down anyway. If your team is having trouble with this part of the exercise, bring in some folks from your target market and ask them the same questions. What words would they use?

If you take the time, you will get many of the right target keywords from brainstorming. You will never get all of them, but you have many other data sources to consult to complete your list of keyword candidates. Next up, you mine your Web log files for keyword gold.

Check Your Current Search Referrals

Some of your best keywords are right under your nose—they are keywords customers are already using to find your site. Chapter 7, "Measure Your Search Marketing Success," introduced the concept of search referrals, showing how your Web metrics facility can examine your Web log files to tell you the search queries that visitors use to find your site.

Search referrals are a gold mine for developing your candidate list for keywords, because they are phrases that searchers are using, *and* they relate to your products. Don't look only at the keywords that get lots of traffic—you are already succeeding with those. Notice keywords that you get little traffic for, too. Those low-volume keywords might actually be popular searches, but your site just does not rank very high in the results, so it attracts little traffic for those words.

Use your list of referrals to add more keywords to your master list. Do not *remove* a keyword already on the list because you do not see many (or any) referrals with that word. One of your goals is to find those keywords that your site is drawing little or no traffic for today. We have plenty of time to winnow the list later.

Consult Your Site Search Facility

If your site has its own search engine—one that returns the pages of your site for searchers—you can study the list of keywords those searchers enter to see what words you are missing. Check out the more popular terms most closely—no need to look at every keyword that was searched for just once in the last month.

As you study this data source, remember that the *context* for the searcher is different when the results are limited to your site than when searching in MSN or Ask.com. When Snap Electronics examined their log, they found that there were almost no searches for "snap digital camera" because the searchers knew they did not have to include the word "snap" in their query—they are already at Snap's site.

Depending on your business, you might find that there are many queries from visitors in the Use phase of the Web Conversion Cycle who are seeking technical support, for example. Snap found queries for downloading some digital camera utilities they offer, but realized that only existing customers were interested, so they are not great choices to target for their search marketing campaign.

Study Paid Inclusion Reports

If you use paid inclusion, you can pore over the metrics reports from your paid inclusion vendor to identify the keywords used to find specific pages on your site. This technique helps you identify keywords that you already have content for—showing you which pages might be good landing pages for each.

Check Out Your Competition

Take the time to look at the Web pages for your top competitors for the subject of your campaign. If your campaign revolves around one of your products, examine Web pages for competing products.

Look at what words *they* use. Obviously competitors have their own brand names and model numbers, but look deeper than that. What words do they use to describe their products? What words are found in their titles? Their keyword metatags? Crack open their HTML and look. Check out their site maps and their "Products A–Z" pages—what words do they use to describe the product's category? Add promising new keywords to your list.

Keep in mind, however, that just because your competitor uses a term that does not automatically mean that many searchers use that term. Your competitor might not have performed any keyword analysis to see whether it is a popular keyword.

If you have a page that legitimately mentions a competitor—such as a feature comparison page—that is perfectly okay. However, steer clear of any tricks using your competitors' brand names or other trademarks, such as dumping your competitor's trademarks into a description tag on your page. Searchers entering your competitor's names are not looking for your products. If you try to hijack those brand-loyal searchers with tricky pages that mention your competitors' brand names, you will annoy those searchers and risk a lawsuit for trademark infringement or unfair competition.

Research Each Keyword Candidate

You've brainstormed, you've checked multiple data sources, and you've compiled quite a list. By now, you should have many possible keyword targets, but you do not know how frequently searchers enter any of them. Bring on the keyword research tools!

Keyword research tools reveal which keywords on your list are heavily used by searchers and which ones are rarely used. Research tools can also expand your list by showing variations of your keywords that are also garnering traffic.

Keep in mind, however, that keyword tools are just that—tools. They are not magical, and they do not substitute for the step you just completed to gather your own keyword list based on your in-depth knowledge of your product. It is so easy to use these tools that you will be tempted to skip the gathering step, but over-reliance on keyword tools is one of the ways that search marketers miss some very valuable keywords and target keywords that do not match their product very well. In addition, it is seductive to fall in love with one tool and use it exclusively. *Don't.* Each one has different strengths and weaknesses, so researching with multiple tools results in better information for your decisions.

Wordtracker

Wordtracker (www.wordtracker.com) is the leading fee-based online keyword research tool, with a database of more than 350 million actual searches performed by the MetaCrawler and Dogpile search engines. Wordtracker uses this data to estimate the number of searches that are performed for each keyword across all search engines. This statistic is often referred to as **keyword demand**—Wordtracker calls it "count," as you can see in Figure 11-1.

Keyword ❷ explain	Count	Predict	Dig
digital cameras	11090	10005	✐
digital camera	6869	6197	✐
digital camera reviews	5872	5298	✐
digital camera review	1695	1529	✐
sony dsc-f717 cyber-shot digital camera $589.99	1642	1481	✐
canon digital cameras	1569	1416	✐
sony digital cameras	1442	1301	✐
kodak digital cameras	1169	1055	✐
compare digital cameras	1143	1031	✐
olympus digital cameras	1142	1030	✐
digital camera comparison	1131	1020	✐
nikon digital cameras	1041	939	✐

Figure 11-1 Wordtracker's Keyword Research Tool. Wordtracker shows the keyword demand ("count") for variations on the keyword entered.

Many search marketing consultants swear by Wordtracker's keyword demand numbers, for a reason that you might not think of. The number of searches performed for popular keywords on Yahoo! Search, Google, and other popular search engines is tainted by the fact that some of those searches (no one really knows how many) are not being performed by true searchers. Those tainted searches are being performed for the sole purpose of "rank checking"—a search marketer checking where a site ranks for a particular query. You have already become one of these "rank checking" searchers, and there are many others like you. Conversely, searchers at less-popular search engines, such as MetaCrawler and Dogpile, are almost 100 percent real searchers—not too many folks are bothering to check their rankings there.

There is one possible drawback to this supposed accuracy in keyword demand. Because there are relatively few MetaCrawler and Dogpile searchers, it is possible that they differ in fundamental ways from Google and Yahoo! searchers. Perhaps they are more sophisticated about search than the mainstream searcher. Maybe they are more technically astute. Search marketers should keep this in mind while they use Wordtracker.

Besides keyword demand, Wordtracker helps with several tasks in keyword planning:

- *Discover keyword variations.* You can take any word on your list and see which other words are searched for in combination with that word. This technique can help you find those three- and four-word "just right" phrases that describe your content perfectly. For global marketers, however, Wordtracker is a bit of a disappointment, because it works only for English keywords.

- *Take control over word variants.* Sometimes your best defense against an overheated keyword is to restrict your target to a particular word variant (*appliance sale* versus *appliance sales*, for example). Wordtracker enables you to see the precise number of searches for exact phrases—even for singular and plural forms. This feature helps you decide the particular phrases to optimize your organic content for, as well as whether to use "broad" or a more restricted form of matching for paid search (which we explain in depth in Chapter 14, "Optimize Your Paid Search Program").

- *Analyze keyword effectiveness.* We cautioned against reading too much into KEI analysis earlier, but it can be helpful in some situations as long as you remember that the keyword's applicability to your content is more important than the number of competing pages for that keyword.

- *Maintain your keyword lists.* Wordtracker enables you to create and manage multiple keyword lists for your many campaigns.

- *Export and e-mail your results.* You can export your keyword lists to Excel or just e-mail a list of results to yourself or another person.

Wordtracker has a number of subscription options, including daily, weekly, monthly, or annual pricing. Use the generous 30-day free trial to get a feel for how the system works to decide whether it's for you. It costs around $250 for a yearly subscription, so it is easily affordable within most search marketing budgets.

Yahoo! Keyword Selector Tool

You might remember trying out a tool from Yahoo!'s former Overture brand back in Chapter 7 when we did our preliminary research for our first search marketing campaign. You might recall that one of the major benefits of the Keyword Selector Tool (at http://inventory.overture.com/d/ searchinventory/suggestion) is the price. It costs nothing to use, in unlimited volume, and it is accessible to anyone.

It is a much simpler version of Wordtracker, showing the demand for various keywords, but has some important differences:

- *Data sources*. Yahoo!'s tool draws its keyword demand numbers strictly from the search engines that use Yahoo! paid placement, which are mostly Yahoo! properties, such as Yahoo! Search, alltheweb.com, and AltaVista. As with our caveat for Wordtracker, it could be that there is some bias in this sample, so do not expect perfect precision from these numbers.

- *Global reach*. Unlike Wordtracker's English-only approach, Yahoo! provides information for 15 countries and 20 languages, greatly aiding search marketing in global markets.

- *Granularity*. Keywords that differ from each other in small ways (singular/plural, word order, punctuation) are grouped for reporting purposes, so you cannot get individual keyword demand totals for "appliance sale" versus "appliance sales" searches. For paid placement research, this is rarely a problem, but it hinders organic optimization. Organic search engines do not always return pages with singular occurrences when the plural form is entered for a search query, so it is helpful to know which form is more prevalent.

- *Accuracy*. As discussed above, the demand shown for popular keywords might be inflated due to rampant rank checking on Yahoo! and its partner paid placement sites.

As with Wordtracker, the Yahoo! tool enables you to enter words to see their keyword demand totals, along with variations on that word that were also searched for, as shown in Figure 7-1. As noted in Chapter 7, you can multiply Yahoo!'s keyword demand numbers by 3.5 to estimate demand across all search engines. Because Yahoo!'s market share percentage changes each time it adds or loses a syndication partner, you need to use the resources in Chapter 16, "What's Next?" to recalculate your multiple from Yahoo!'s current market share. Snap Electronics used Yahoo!'s tool when Yahoo! had a 45 percent share, so Snap multiplied the counts by 2.2 to derive total keyword demand, but they would use 3.5 if they were doing that same calculation using the tool today.

Yahoo! does not match Wordtracker in its other features; if you are planning a Yahoo! paid placement campaign, however, there is no better source of information. To see a combination of Yahoo! and Wordtracker results in a single tool, you can use Digital Point's free Keyword Suggestion Tool (www.digitalpoint.com/tools/suggestion).

Trellian's Keyword Discovery

Trellian, the maker of SEO Toolkit and other search tools, now offers Keyword Discovery (www.keyworddiscovery.com), which has quickly become the biggest competitor to Wordtracker.

Keyword Discovery takes a different approach from Wordtracker, which uses metasearch engines for its data. Keyword Discovery uses historical data from 32 billion searches from 180 search engines from around the world, sometimes employing search logs provided directly by the engines, but often "sampling" the referral logs of sites receiving traffic from search engines. It's not known exactly what sites are being sampled, so some bias in the sample is possible here. Still, none of the other vendors claim to include Google and Yahoo! in their analysis–Trellian does.

Like Wordtracker, Keyword Discovery offers a list of keywords related to the one you've entered, including counts and KEI analysis of each keyword. Unlike other tools, Keyword Discovery provides suggestions for misspelled keywords related to yours, and offers 12 months of data that allows you to see seasonal trends. It's hard to judge the value of the data when it's unknown where it comes from, but Keyword Discovery does offer new features you can't get anywhere else.

Trellian offers two versions of Keyword Discovery, a standard edition (limited to 1,000 results per keyword) and an enterprise edition (offering up to 10,000 keyword results). Both editions are offered with monthly or yearly pricing as low as $600 annually.

Hitwise Keyboard Intelligence

Web market intelligence vendor Hitwise (www.hitwise.com) uses its Web visitor data to power its Keyword Intelligence tool (www.keywordintelligence.com), even providing country-specific information.

Alone among these tools, the Hitwise data collection technique ensures that the keywords shown were successful searches–that they resulted in a searcher actually visiting a Web site. Searches with no results or no clicks (including rank checking searches) are thus excluded from the data. Like each of these tools, it's hard to judge whether Hitwise's data sample is better than others'—it may skew to more popular queries.

Hitwise offers a basic version ($900 yearly) limited to 100 variations per keyword, while the 1,000-variation version weighs in at $1900 each year. Both prices are for just one geographic market, but at least Hitwise does offer country specific data, unlike most of its competitors.

Google AdWords Keyword Tool

 As shown in Figure 11–2, Google offers its own free tool (adwords.google.com/selectKeyword ToolExternal), similar to Yahoo!'s. Google's AdWords Keyword Tool supports over 40 languages and more than 200 countries. Google's tool, however, does not show keyword demand—it merely displays an estimate of the number of clicks you will receive with an average bid.

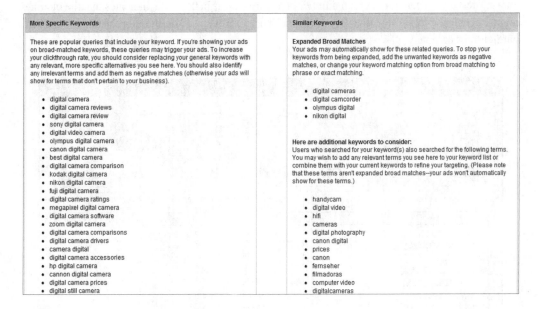

Figure 11-2   Google AdWords Keyword Tool.   Unlike most keyword tools, Google's does not show the keyword demand for your keyword.

Microsoft adCenter

Microsoft adCenter (advertising.msn.com/microsoft-adcenter) offers an eclectic collection of free tools as part of microsoft adCenter Labs (adlab.msn.com), but like Google, does not offer a way to estimate keyword demand. The adCenter Lab tools do provide interesting ways to expand your keyword list and are worth checking out.

Xybercode Ad Word Analyzer

For paid placement campaigns, it is helpful to know how many other advertisers you are competing against. Because only a few ads are shown on each results screen, you can quickly see whether you are bidding against only a few other advertisers or whether you are dueling with dozens. This information is important because the more advertisers you are battling with, the higher the price can go.

If you have enough time, you can manually enter all of your keyword variations into Google and Yahoo! and count the number of ads that you see (as you scroll through the results pages). But for just $67, you can purchase the Xybercode Ad Word Analyzer (www.adwordanalyzer.com/), which can do the work for you.

Ad Word Analyzer shows you several interesting statistics for a keyword, most notably the number of paid advertisements currently running on Google and Yahoo!. You can see in Figure 11-3 that there are currently 44 Google advertisers and 42 Overture (now Yahoo!) advertisers for the phrase "best digital camera." A high number of advertisers, as in this case, indicates that the bidding might be high and might stay that way over time. There are even ads running for the brand names of our fictitious company!

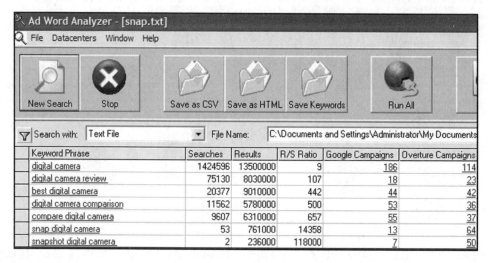

Figure 11-3   Xybercode'sAd Word Analyzer. See at a glance how many advertisers you are up against at Overture (Yahoo!) and Google.

Prioritize Your Keyword Candidate List

The keyword research tools helped round out your list by unearthing variations that you might have not thought of. They also brought you important information you will use now to prioritize your list—the popularity of the keywords (keyword demand).

Remember, you do not want to blindly target the keywords that are the most popular. You want keywords that are "just right" for your site. You use the popularity numbers for keywords to ensure that you are not choosing keywords that are too cold. Other than that, try to identify the keywords that are the closest matches for your site's content.

As you comb through the list, set a priority for each keyword:

- *Top priority.* The keyword is a close match to your site's content and is very popular or moderately popular or has high conversion rates.

- *Medium priority*. The keyword is a close match to your site and is somewhat popular with acceptable conversion rates.

- *Low priority*. The keyword is a close match to your site and has enough searches to be worth a paid placement bid, but not worthy of organic search optimization efforts.

With apologies for all the repetition, you should *not* be targeting any keywords that are not close matches to your site. You just waste your time as well as the searcher's time. Focus on only those keywords that you believe your site is truly a good response for—keywords for which the search engine honestly *should* return your site. Those are the only ones that will get you strong clickthrough rates and high conversion rates.

Your "top-priority" and "medium-priority" keywords are candidates for both organic search and paid search campaigns. Your lowest keyword tier is *not* useful for organic search, because there is a natural limit to the number of keywords that you can target organically. As you will see in the next chapter, when you optimize pages for organic search, you can only target three to four keywords per page. So, you will find that you eventually run out of pages that you can plausibly link together for the search engines to index for organic search.

For paid placement, this is not an issue, so you can freely target your low-priority words for paid search (as long as you believe it is worth the time to manage the extra words in your campaign). You can develop a separate search landing page for every paid placement keyword, and those landing pages do not need to be cohesively linked into your site. Each page can have just one or two links *from* the landing page to other parts of your site—no other pages on your site need link *to* each landing page—and searchers using other queries will not be bothered by the presence of the landing pages they do not land on. With organic, your landing pages *must* be linked together cohesively to coax the spider to index them, so there is a natural limit as to the number of keywords you can target organically before your site begins to look maddeningly repetitive, with multiple pages that say the same thing with slightly different words.

TEST HOW SEARCH ENGINES HANDLE ARABIC AND ASIATIC KEYWORDS

Global search marketers need to perform some tests before making final decisions on keyword priorities because search engines do not always do the best job of finding all keywords. Search engines sometimes process text incorrectly when there are no blanks in between words, as is the case for many Arabic and Asiatic languages. Search engines sometimes split the text in the wrong places, changing the meaning of the words. Search engines have an especially hard time segmenting Japanese words. Japanese uses four different ways to write its words, and can even combine these formats.

Western languages, except for German, do not suffer from these errors because each word is separated by a space. German employs many compound words, so sometimes search engines fail to find matching words if they do not "decompound" correctly.

Search marketers must test every keyword in these languages to ensure that it is correctly processed and the right pages are found. Perform searches in every major search engine in each country in question. Make sure good results are being returned. Sometimes you will find that the word that you wanted to use is not handled as well as another one. In that case, you might want to target a different keyword and optimize your organic content around that term.

To make your priority decisions for each keyword, you need to take into account popularity, of course, but you also need to remember your goals for your campaign. If your search marketing campaign is designed to build brand awareness, you need to decide which keywords are "must win" because your company must be shown for those words. You might even decide to target a few "too hot" keywords if you believe that the branding awareness you will build compensates for the lower conversion rates. Basically, your branding awareness keywords are marketing decisions—which keywords require you to be seen?

If your search marketing campaign is designed to increase Web conversions, as most are, your decisions are a bit more complicated. You need to prioritize based on which keywords bring the highest conversion. For organic search, it costs the same amount to optimize a page for any query, so your priorities are based purely on which keywords will drive the most conversions. For paid, your decision making is more complex, because the per-click cost of each keyword must be taken into account, too. The problem with prioritizing by conversion potential, however, is that you have no idea which keywords will have the highest conversions before the campaign starts.

As you will see in Chapter 15, "Make Search Marketing Operational," you will be able to track conversion metrics over time so that you can gradually place more emphasis on keywords that convert and de-emphasize those that do not. It is seductive to look at high conversion rates, but it is more profitable to go after a higher number of gross conversions. (Would you rather convert 10 out of 100 or 2 out of 4?) Regardless of what you will do after the campaign is underway, your problem now is to figure out which keywords to target to begin your campaign.

 First, using a technique pioneered by search consultancy Global Strategies International, you need to break out your Web Conversion Cycle. We use Snap Electronics as an example, dusting off their Learn/Shop/Buy/Receive/Use model for digital cameras. We can take every keyword on Snap's list and assign it to a particular phase of the Web Conversion Cycle. As we do, we quickly realize that any queries that Snap put into the mix for the Receive or Use stages are unlikely to bring any conversions. (Some Use queries might help you sell accessories or supplies, but that is another campaign.)

So Snap is left with the keywords associated with the Learn, Shop, and Buy phases, which are shown in abridged form in Table 11-3. (You should categorize *every* keyword according to your Web Conversion Cycle, but we are shortening the example.) To accurately categorize each query, you need to think about what each stage in the Web Conversion Cycle means. So, a searcher who knows nothing about digital cameras is in the Learn phase, and is likely to use search keywords such as "digital cameras" or "buy digital camera." A searcher who knows more would enter queries based on features of digital cameras (Shop phase), such as "8 megapixel digital camera," whereas searchers who know precisely what they want to buy (Buy phase) might enter the exact model number to shop for the lowest price.

Table 11-3   Snap Keywords and the Web Conversion Cycle (Snap categorized each of its prioritized keywords according to its customers' buying cycle.)

Learn	Shop	Buy
digital cameras	8 mega pixel camera	snapshot x5
digital camera reviews	lightweight camera	snapshot x6
best digital camera	easy digital camera	snapshot x7
buy digital camera	snap digital camera	snapshot slr x800
compare digital cameras	snapshot camera	snapshot slr x900

Snap already culled the list to remove any search keywords, such as "cheap digital camera," that are not close matches for their site's content. But how do we prioritize the rest? The answer is to think carefully about what Snap is trying to achieve in their campaign.

Keywords from the Buy Stage

Because you have no idea what kinds of conversion rates are associated with each keyword, you cannot accurately prioritize based on that, but you can take guesses. You can guess, for example, that Snap will achieve higher conversion rates for the keywords that mention its own brand and model names—those from the Buy stage. And because Snap already has product pages for each individual camera model, it will not be hard to optimize each page for its keyword. Those product pages already contain the "features and benefits" information that buyers need to confirm their decision and complete the purchase. All of this adds up to keywords that closely match Snap's site, and (we believe) will have high conversion rates. These keywords should be categorized as top priority.

But what about the Learn and Shop keywords? Well, you quickly see that some of the Shop keywords contain the brand names "snap" or "snapshot" in the search keyword, too. Once again, they should carry very high conversion rates for Snap. And they also seem like "must have" queries from a branding standpoint because Snap is aiming for brand awareness as well as conversions. Make those top priority, too.

Keywords from the Shop Stage

So far, you have picked out the keywords that seem to have high conversion rates, but you have not looked at the rest of the list. It's time to focus again on how close a match these keywords are to Snap's site. For the Shop list, the search "easy digital camera" is a direct hit for Snap's product line, but "8 megapixel camera" and "lightweight camera" (although accurate) are not quite as distinctive—other camera manufacturers can validly make those claims. When we examine keyword demand data from our keyword research tools, we see that "8 megapixel camera" is a somewhat popular query, whereas "lightweight camera" is less so. On that basis, we will make *easy digital camera* a top-priority keyword, assign *8 megapixel camera* a medium priority, and make *lightweight camera* a low-priority keyword to consider only for paid placement.

In real life, your list would be far longer than this, but this is the kind of decision process that you will go through. You will target very close matches almost regardless of popularity, because they will have high conversion rates. In fact, if they are less popular, it is easier to rank well for each keyword (although you must make sure you do not focus organic search optimization efforts on "too cold" keywords). For keywords that are related to your site, but not direct hits, you will make judgments based on popularity and anticipated conversion rate.

Keywords from the Learn Stage

When you examine the Learn search keywords, one jumps out as a great target: "digital camera reviews." You know that Snap has gotten wonderful reviews, so putting up a few pages that boast about those reviews (with links to the magazine sites that contain the actual review articles) is excellent spider food for that query. Snap's competitors do not always get the same rave reviews that Snap does, so this keyword is a direct hit for Snap's digital cameras. Make that one a top priority. Because some of the reviews literally say that Snap makes the "best digital camera," that keyword should be at least a medium priority, too.

But what about the others? Broad search keywords such as "digital cameras" and "buy digital camera" do not seem to promise a very high conversion rate, but they are in high demand. Because you do not know what the conversion rate might be, it is worthwhile to try out a few keywords that are very popular to see how much traffic you can draw and test what the conversion rate is. You do not want to spend precious resources on a large number of them at first, but you cannot completely ignore them, either. You might decide to make *digital camera* a top priority because it is extremely popular—Snap does make a broad range of cameras—but reserve *buy digital camera* for paid placement for now.

The keyword *compare digital cameras* might be a medium priority because Snap has enough different models that it can put together a few pages that compare them against each other. In addition, Snap might be able to use the pages that target *digital camera reviews* to subtly compare Snap to its competition.

 You can probably tell from this process that keyword prioritization is as much an art as a science. Your initial prioritization at the start of your campaign will almost never turn out to be the best one. It is important to mix in some words that you are not sure about to gather information, rather than to play it safe and choose only words you expect will drive high conversion rates. Conversely, you should not go all out with many dubious choices because this will expend more resources that could be put to better use elsewhere. Target the words that seem to promise high conversion, but also go after some keywords in every stage of the Web Conversion Cycle to learn which ones convert for you better than others. In Chapter 15, we show you how to adjust your campaign as you go.

Summary

Choosing your target keywords is the real beginning of any organic or paid search marketing campaign. After you have chosen the product or other focus of your campaign, you must carefully decide which keywords to target before you can start the work of organic search optimization and paid placement.

In this chapter, you learned the value of careful keyword planning, along with a philosophy that helps you make decisions every step of the way. Rather than blindly reaching for the most popular keywords, or gravitating to unpopular keywords because they are "easy" to get high rankings for, you saw how "just right" keywords closely target your site, almost regardless of popularity.

We walked through the entire keyword planning process step by step, discovering how to gather a list of keyword candidates, how to research each candidate to uncover hidden variations and determine its popularity with searchers, and how to prioritize the keyword list so that the most valuable ones get the most attention in the campaign.

In the next chapter, we focus again on organic search, offering guidance on optimizing your content for the organic keywords that you targeted—allowing that content to achieve the highest organic search rankings possible for those keywords. Now that you know which keywords you are going after, let's go to work to drive the right pages to the top of the organic search results.

Optimize Your Content

Two-time American presidential candidate Adlai Stevenson once said, "Words calculated to catch everyone may catch no one." Such is the dilemma of optimizing your content. You know that organic search engines are looking for specific word patterns on your page to decide whether it should be shown at the top of the results list, but you also know that your page must appeal to the searchers themselves. How do you avoid "catching no one"? We show you the way.

And, although optimizing content is mainly a task for search marketers pursuing organic search rankings, paid placement marketers should pay attention, too. Increasingly, paid placement landing pages are subjected to editorial review to ensure that the page is relevant to the keyword purchased. We note where our tips are for just organic, or for paid, too.

In this chapter, you learn how to optimize your content. This chapter covers the following topics:

- *What search engines look for.* Search engines are meticulously designed to return the best matches for a searcher's query, weighing dozens of factors to decide which pages rank first. We explain what search engines want to see.

- *The philosophy of writing for search.* After you know what search engines are looking for, it's oh so tempting to write your page copy with only search engines in mind. And it's wrong. We show you how to think about your *real* goal.

- *Step-by-step optimization of your search landing pages.* You will be introduced to each task in the content-optimization process, and learn how to perform each one.

When you have completed this chapter, you will be ready to take on your own Web site and make the content changes needed for successful search marketing. We begin by exploring what is important to search engines when they choose the results they return.

What Search Engines Look For

As you learned in Chapter 10, "Get Your Site Indexed," it can be a challenge just getting your page into the search index. When you do, you face your next challenge—what the search engine thinks of your page. An organic search engine categorizes your page according to dozens of criteria, some driven by explicit tagging, but others based on judgments the search engine makes from an analysis of your page. We investigate the most important criteria search engines look for, which they use to make two different kinds of decisions:

- *Filtering*. For each query, search engines decide which pages are in the search results list and which are not. If your page meets the filtering criteria, it will be in the list somewhere.

- *Ranking*. For each query, search engines sort the search results by relevance to decide which pages are shown at the top of the list. The better your page, and the closer it matches your query, the higher it will rank in the results.

What you put on your page is your best chance to influence the search engine's decisions as it filters and ranks the search results for each query. We check out filtering now.

Search Filters

Searchers use **search filters** to set their search's scope. Pages that are not included by the filters for a query do not appear in the results. For example, a searcher using the Yahoo! Australia and New Zealand site can choose to search the entire Web, or just Web pages from Australia or those from New Zealand. If the searcher's query for "digital cameras" limits results to pages from Australia, no pages from outside Australia will be shown, regardless of how closely they relate to the "digital cameras" search, because they are excluded by the Australian country filter.

The two most important search filters are for language and country, but we look at others, too.

Language Filters

 Big news! People like search results in the languages they know! Okay, that might not be the lead story on the nightly news, but it is very important for search marketers. When a searcher enters a query as shown in Figure 12-1, only pages written in Japanese will be shown in the search results.

Figure 12-1   Language filtering in Google. Searchers can choose to limit results to their local language.

In some countries, such as Japan and China, the vast majority of searchers want their results limited to their native languages; in other places, however, such as Sweden, searches can be conducted in Swedish or English. Searchers in different countries have different preferences.

For the search marketer, what is important is that the search engines *know* the language of your page. If your page is not correctly identified, it will be missing from searches that should include it, lowering your referrals.

So how do search engines decide the language of your page? There are several different methods:

- *Language metatag*. Many Web pages contain an HTML tag declaring the language of the page (such as <meta http-equiv="content-language" content="ja"> for Japanese). It sounds simple—the spider reads the tag and the search engine knows the language, right? Not so fast. A very high percentage of the language metatags are flat-out wrong. The tags are missing, they are syntactically incorrect, or they have the wrong language encoded. Search engines do look at this tag, but they never decide the language of the page based on this tag alone.

- *Character encoding*. Computer files (including HTML pages) require a key to correctly interpret the characters (letters, numbers, and so on) in the file. That key is called the character encoding, and is declared on Web pages in a metatag (such as <meta http-equiv="content-type" content="text/html; charset=shift-jis">). Web browsers and spiders assume the page is encoded for Western languages, so pages written in those languages do not require this tag. Asiatic, Arabic, and Cyrillic text *does* require the tag for proper display by browsers; so when the search engines see the tag for these languages, it provides high confidence as to the correct language of the page.

- *Content analysis*. Search engines make their final determination of the page's language by studying the character patterns in the content. The correct language can be detected with very high accuracy for pages with as few as two dozen words, with metatags being used only for pages where the language is unclear after analysis.

For the most part, search engines will correctly detect the language of your pages without any action on your part. For pages with very few words, it is important that the language and character set metatags on your page be encoded correctly to ensure that your pages are identified in the proper language.

Country and Region Filters

Often, searchers do not want to limit results to a language—they want all results within a particular *country*. This is particularly true of transactional searchers in the Buy stage of the Web Conversion Cycle. They want to buy from a vendor in *their* country that uses *their* currency and will not charge a king's ransom to ship the item.

Limiting by language does not do that. German pages exist in Germany, Austria, and Switzerland, French content in France and Canada, Spanish pages in Latin America as well as Spain—you get the idea—and English content all over the place. So, most search engines apply filters by country or by region. Searchers can always use the Advanced Search interface to specify these fil-ters, but relatively few do. Instead, most local searches have a default filter, or allow selection between two or three filters on the search page, specifying a particular country, region, or language.

So how do search engines know which country your Web pages are from? They look at where the page is hosted and they examine the URL itself. Every Web page has a URL, and the domain (www.company.com) is resolved to an IP address—a unique number that points to a server some-where on the Internet. Search engines can use that IP address to determine the country in which that server resides. Web pages hosted on servers within each country are part of that country's filter.

 But pages hosted outside a country can be included in a filter, too, if they are named appro-priately. Any URL that ends with the domain for a country is included in that country's filter. A British company might have a URL of www.britishcompany.co.uk (for example). The co in the name indicates it is a company, and the uk that it is a British company. So, a search within the UK brings back Web pages that end in uk—what technical types refer to as the "top-level domain." Some countries just use their country code (such as de for Germany) with no co to indicate com-panies (such as www.deutschefirma.de). It sounds logical, and it works—for Web sites that do business in a single country.

For the global search marketer in a multinational company, however, country (and region) filters can prove problematic. You want the country content on your site to be included by search engines when they filter by country, but it is not always easy to do, because of the way that the search engines' country filters work. Your multinational site is probably hosted centrally and uses com as its top-level domain, no matter what country the content is for.

Let's look at an example. Microsoft, like most multinational companies, maintains country "sites" that are part of its com top-level domain. Entering the URL www.microsoft.de redirects you to www.microsoft.com/germany—which does not qualify as a page from Germany. You see, according to the search engine's country filter rules, all pages considered to be from Germany must be hosted locally or have a top-level domain of de—Microsoft's page is hosted centrally and has no content under its de name, so the search engine indexes the content from its com domain (the www.microsoft.com/germany page). Later, when searchers limit results to pages from Ger-many, this page will not be found (because it is a com and not a de and is not hosted in Germany); when they limit to German language pages, however, it *will* be found (because it is rightly ana-lyzed to be written in German).

What is the global search marketer to do? First, don't panic. Many searchers understand this problem and regularly toggle between language and country filters to get what they want. If your target customers are not terribly sophisticated Web searchers, however, you might want to approach your Webmaster about changing the way your site is organized so that your country pages do use the top-level domains for each country. Or you can ask that your country pages be hosted at IP addresses within each country. Your Webmaster is unlikely to relish these suggestions, because they make your Web site harder to manage, but in the short term you might have no alternative.

In the long run, you should expect the search engines to address this issue. They are painfully aware of this problem and are taking some steps to ameliorate its impact. Some of the larger search engines already use your site's IP address to see whether your pages are hosted within the correct country, so that can help some of you. If you cannot adapt your site to use the proper top-level domains, we suggest ensuring that your URLs and content strongly reflect the country of the page. Microsoft's approach of adding germany (or de) to the URL while also placing the words *Microsoft Deutscheland* at the top of the page (itself written in German) might someday be enough clues for search engines to accurately discern the page's proper country. If you cannot satisfy what the search engines are currently looking for with their country filters, at least prepare your content to be as ready as possible for what they might be looking for someday. In addition, the better your content, the more likely it will draw links from sites that *are* included in the country filter—for some search engines, enough high-quality links from country pages can get *your* pages recognized as country pages, too.

Other Filters

Search engines offer searchers other filters that might sometimes be important to search marketers, but each search engine provides a different set.

Most search engines enable searchers to filter by type of content. Most have some kind of "picture" or "image" search, some can filter news stories, and most have an Advanced Search interface that filters by document type (such as Adobe PDF files or HTML files).

You might think it is valuable to be the #1 PDF file in Advanced Search, but it really is not, because so few searchers will take the extra time to use Advanced Search. In general, the more clicks required to execute a search, the fewer searchers will do so.

So before you get excited about these specialized searches, think like a searcher. If you work for a news organization, searchers for your site might make that extra click on the News tab in Google, so having high rankings for news stories could help you meet your search marketing goals. Image searches might be important to a seller of fine art prints. For the most part, however, none of these specialized searches are of much interest to the search marketer. (Some search engines offer a tab for shopping search, which might be important to you—we cover that in Chapter 14, "Optimize Your Paid Search Program.")

Most search engines enable searchers to set **preferences** that control how all of their searches work. Most preferences are unimportant to search marketers, such as the number of results on a page or whether search results open a new browser window, but one can be very important, because this preference is a filter.

The so-called Adult Content filter suppresses pornographic or otherwise sensitive material from the results. The issue for search marketers, as you might expect, is how accurate the filter is. In the past, news reports have trumpeted breast cancer sites (for example) suppressed by such filters, but modern search engines generally do a good job on these filters because of their strong text-analysis capabilities. Most search engines, by default, filter out just the most egregious scatological and sexual content, while leaving in explicit scientific and informational content. A strict setting can be chosen by searchers as their preference; if so, setting the preference just once then employs the strict filter forever. Search marketers whose site might contain sensitive material might want to monitor their page rankings so that they are not unfairly filtered, and might want to police word usage on their sites to avoid being filtered. Pay special attention to message boards on your site frequented by your visitors—if your visitors use inappropriate language in their posts, your site might be snagged by this filter.

You have finished your grand tour of search filters. Depending on the nature of your site, search filters might be critically important to your efforts, or you might not have to think about them much anymore. But now it's time to pay attention, as you learn what is behind a search engine's ranking algorithm.

Search Ranking Factors

A **ranking algorithm** is the mathematical formula a search engine uses to score pages against the query to see which pages are the closest matches. But what goes into that formula? How can your pages get consistently high scores for your targeted keywords?

It's time to answer those questions. Chapter 2, "How Search Engines Work," explored the basic concepts behind search ranking, but in this chapter we go deeper, explaining more of what search engines are looking for and, later in this chapter, showing you practical ways to help your pages score high. As you read this, keep in mind that the highest rankings mean nothing if your pages are excluded by the filters listed above—strike out on a filter and your page is out of the results list no matter how closely it matches the query.

If your page is *included* by the filters for a particular query, the ranking algorithm takes over, looking at every page containing those words and deciding how your page stacks up against the others for that query. There are no right or wrong answers from the search engine—the engine tries finds the highest-quality pages matching the query. The ranking algorithm contains many **factors**, components that are scored for each page. If your page scores the most points, according to the ranking algorithm's factors, it will get the #1 slot in the results.

In Chapter 2, we discussed how complicated a search engine's ranking algorithm is. Because a ranking algorithm is such a closely guarded secret, no one can publicly state how many different factors a ranking algorithm weighs, but some say there are more than 100. Clearly, not all 100 factors are equally important, so we concentrate on the more important factors here.

Ranking factors come in two main varieties:

- *Page factors.* Web search ranking algorithms rely heavily on components that have nothing to do with the query entered, such as the strength of links to the page, the number of visits to the page, and many more. These factors boost a page in the rankings for searches on any word that occurs on that page.

- *Query factors.* As you might expect, the particular query the searcher enters weighs heavily. The number of occurrences of the words in the query, where they are found on the page (title, body, and so on), and many other elements are weighed by the search engines when ranking results.

You can optimize your content for both page factors and query factors—neglecting either one will derail your search marketing program. We investigate page factors now.

Page Ranking Factors

The moniker "page factors" is a bit of a misnomer—Andrei Broder, a VP and Research Fellow at Yahoo! prefers to call them **query-independent factors**—because they are not so much *about* the page as *not about* the query. So-called page factors can take into account anything the search engine knows about the page itself, the pages that link to that page, the site that contains the page, and many other components. What this means is that any particular page's page factor score is exactly the same for *every* query—a page with strong page factors starts out with a high score for every word that is on that page.

Every Web search engine uses page factors as a critical component in its ranking algorithm—Google's PageRank is the most famous example. As explained in Chapter 2, when a searcher enters a broad query, such as the word "camera," the search engine needs a way to decide which few pages, among the millions that contain the word *camera*, are the ones to rank at the top of the list. The pages with the most occurrences of *camera* are probably not what searchers want; they want the most definitive pages. Only page factors can make that determination. Let's look at the most important page factors in a search ranking algorithm:

- *Link popularity.* As discussed in Chapter 2, Web search engines put great stock in your page if other Web sites link to your page for the subject of the search. For example, the Snap Electronics digital camera product category page (the hub page that we first saw in Figure 7-2 in Chapter 7, "Measure Your Search Marketing Success") has many links to it that all have the anchor text (the clickable words in the link) *digital cameras* or *SnapShot digital cameras*. That causes the page to rank highly for the queries for "digital cameras" and "snapshot digital cameras." Although link popularity is a critical page ranking factor, it does not have much to do with how you optimize your content (because anchor text in the links is on someone else's site, not yours), so we hold off on the in-depth treatment of links until Chapter 13, "Attract Links to Your Site."

- *Popularity data.* Now that many searchers use search toolbars—the Google and Yahoo! toolbars are the most popular, but many other search engines have them, too—they can gather information about which pages are visited the most. Unbeknownst to many toolbar users (although openly spelled out in their terms of use), the search engines keep track of which pages searchers are visiting, even when they are not searching. Ask.com, for one, confirms using popularity data to give more popular pages a "boost" in the rankings when searchers look for words that appear on those pages. Other search engines might be doing the same.

- *URL length and depth.* You learned in Chapter 10 that dynamic URLs with more than two parameters might cause spiders to avoid the page, but you should know that longer URLs, in general, reduce your page's ranking in a small way. Search engines are more likely to "boost" pages that are closer to the root directory of your site, so the same page located deep in your site (perhaps at www.yourdomain.com/news/announce/today/top.html) might rank a bit lower than if placed nearer to your home page (say, at www.yourdomain/news/top.html).

- *Freshness.* If your page has not changed in a long time, its rank might be reduced because search engines suspect its information is out-of-date.

- *Page style*. Pages that are grammatically correct allow the search engine to better score relevance. Pages that are organized like a newspaper article (important words at the top, somewhat repeated throughout, and reinforced at the end) are sometimes said to have an advantage. In many cases, folks who use unethical spam techniques are flagged by these factors because their content is written in a stilted way to repeat keywords *ad nauseum*.

- *Site organization*. One of the best ways to strengthen your page factors is good Web design. Work with information architects to make the site simple to navigate with a well thought-out linking structure. Use meaningful words in your URLs, but do not take the spam route by stuffing in three or four keywords between hyphens. Use as simple a page layout and design as possible.

- *Spam-free*. Every page on your site contains text that can inform a visitor and attract a search engine. When you try to mislead a search engine with spam techniques, your page will be penalized in ranking, possibly leading to your site being banned.

As mentioned previously, although it is easy for us to think about these factors as relevant to just one page, search engines are more sophisticated than that. They look at links to your whole site, not just one page. They check for profanity on your whole site, even if most pages are "clean." If most of your pages are updated frequently, do not obsess about changing your "History of the Company" page every two months.

STUPID CONTENT TRICKS: HOW TO GET YOUR SITE BANNED IN FIVE EASY STEPS

Tricking the search engines to rank your pages higher than they ought to is called **spamdexing**, or simply **spam**. Throughout this book, we have warned you about a host of spam techniques, because spamming can get your site banned from search engines—a nasty wrench thrown into your search marketing plans.

There are many different ways of tricking search engines, people being the clever creatures they are, but we cover only the *content* spamming techniques here. Our goal is not to teach you how to perform these techniques. Rather, you should know enough to spot them to prevent your site from running afoul of the rules and suffering the consequences. Or enough to discover them on a competitor's site so that you can justifiably turn them in.

- *Doorway pages*. Any page that is designed solely to achieve high search rankings, but otherwise has no value to visitors to your site, is a doorway page. Search landing pages are *not* doorway pages, and we talk about the difference later in this chapter.

- *Keyword stuffing*. Also known as **keyword loading**, this technique is really just an overuse of sound content-optimization practices. It's good to use your target keywords on your search landing pages, and use them often, but when you start throwing them in just to attract the search engines your pages can be flagged. Dumping out-of-context keywords into the alternate text for images, or into <noscript> or <noframes> tags, is a variation of this same unethical technique.

As you read the list, you might notice that you do not have a lot of control over some of these factors, and it is true, in general, that page factors are harder to influence than query factors. But you are not helpless. Although you cannot directly affect your site's popularity, for example, you can indirectly affect it in many ways—through search engine marketing, by attracting more links (as explained in Chapter 13), and many other ways of getting attention.

Query Ranking Factors

For you control freaks out there, start salivating. The query-dependent ranking factors, which we call **query factors** for short, are what you will spend most of your time on, as you lovingly craft each search landing page to best appeal to search engines, and (do not forget) the searchers themselves.

Page factors are constant across every query. A page with high-scoring page factors takes that score with it for every query. And although page factors are important, there must be something going on that is query related, or else the same pages would be at the top of the search results for every query. There *is* something going on— the query factors.

But before talking about query factors for ranking, there is one filter that we did not address back in the filtering section, because it makes more sense to discuss it now. A very powerful filter is used on every query—at least one (and typically all) of the words in the query are expected to be found on your page. If none of the words are on your page, that page is filtered out of the results list, no matter how wonderful its page factors are.

- *Hidden text*. HTML offers many opportunities to place text in front of the spider that the visitor will never see. Displaying text in incredibly small sizes, or with the same font color as the background color are hoary spam techniques. Newer approaches include using style sheets to write keywords on the page that are then overlaid by graphics or other page elements. In short, any time you can see text in the HTML source of a page that does not show up when you view the page in your browser, it is probably spam—the only exception is valid HTML comments, which the browsers and spiders both ignore.
- *Duplicate tags*. Using duplicate title tags or other metatags have been rumored to boost rankings in times past. The same style sheet approach that can hide text can also overlay text on top of itself, so it is shown once on the screen but listed multiple times in the HTML file.
- *Duplicate sites*. Why stop at duplicate tags when you can clone your whole site? You duplicate the content in slightly different form under several different domain names and then have each of your sites link to each other (to increase their page ranking factors). Maybe your sites can grab six slots in the top ten results.

And the really bad news about all of these techniques is that sometimes they do work. Search engines do get fooled—usually by people more industrious and harder working than us. Most of the time, however, spam techniques are like stock tips. When you hear the tip, it is probably too late. The stock price has already gone up and the search engines are already implementing countermeasures.

Now that sounds simple and obvious, doesn't it? Except that it is not precisely true. One exception applies to that filtering rule: if enough pages link to your page—if they link using the query words in the anchor text of their links.

Let's look at an example. Figure 12-2 shows the search results for the word "laptop" in Google. Apple has the #3 result, but the word *laptop* does not appear anywhere on the page. It must be that there are so many other pages linking to this one (containing the word *laptop* in the link) that Google is convinced (correctly) that this is a good result for that query, even without any occurrences of the word on the page itself. If Apple placed *laptop* on this page, maybe it would rank #1.

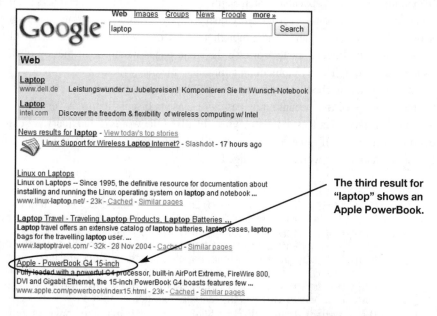

The third result for "laptop" shows an Apple PowerBook.

But the Apple PowerBook page does not contain the word *laptop.*

There must be a huge number of links to this page using the word *laptop.*

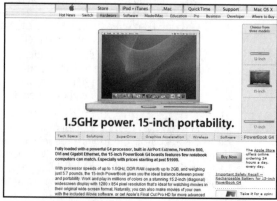

Figure 12-2   The power of page factors. Once in a while, the links to a page drown out the ranking factors from the content on the page itself.

That does not happen very often, however. The vast majority of the time, your page must contain the keyword to rank highly for that query. When your page gets past that filter (and the other filters we discussed earlier), it is *in* the results list and ranking takes over. Each page in that list comes with its predetermined page score, such as Google's PageRank, the score associated with that page based on its cumulative page factors. Pages with high page factors get a head start in the scoring. But then the query factors take over to decide the winner.

Some query factors can apply to any query, whereas others kick in for multiple-word queries only. Here are the universal query factors:

- *Keyword prominence*. All words do not have equal importance on a page. Words in a title or in a heading are more important than words in a body paragraph—these locations of keywords are their **placement**. Keywords also show their value by their **position**—how close to the beginning of a page element that they are. For example, words at the beginning of the body (or the start of the body) are usually more important than those that show up later in that same element. So, when we combine the concepts of placement and position, the most **prominent** keyword location is the first word of the page's title. Search engines look for a keyword in prominent places (and in prominent positions within those places) because it is one of the best clues to what the page is actually *about*. Pages with a keyword in prominent locations tend to be good matches.

- *Keyword density*. What percentage of the totals words on the page are the occurrences of the keyword? That is **keyword density** (sometimes called **keyword weight**). In Chapter 2, we mentioned that search engines look for around 7 percent keyword density, but that is just a guess. Your page will not be sent to the spammer's graveyard if you have 14 percent density, but it might not help you rank higher either. Density helps ensure that a page with 7 occurrences in 100 words is not outranked by a PDF with 12 occurrences in 5,000 words.

- *Keyword frequency*. As discussed in Chapter 2, search engines at one time placed much more stock in **keyword frequency**—the number of times the keyword actually occurred on the page. Given spammers' predilection for keyword stuffing, ranking algorithms began to favor keyword density. But frequency still matters. You cannot stick a page out there with the single word *camera* in the title and the body and expect high rankings for the query "camera." Yes, it has wonderful prominence and 100 percent density, but only two occurrences of the keyword. To get a top ranking for a keyword with strong demand, frequency is still important.

- *Query intent*. As search engines apply more and more analytical firepower to your pages, they are working to match the searcher's intent (such as navigational, informational, and transactional) to pages that satisfy that intent. Although no two search engines treat searcher intent in identical fashion, search engines generally respond to navigational queries with site home pages, whereas informational queries yield pages with several hundred words on them. Certain queries contain clues about the type of documents to return—a search for "maytag jetclean dishwasher manual" might return the PDF product manual or a page with a list of links to the PDFs, for example. Search engines are always looking at new ways to improve recognition and satisfaction of searcher intent, so the more accurately your content reflects its purpose, the better your edge.

- *Contextual relevancy.* The newest frontier for search engine relevancy is the searcher's **context**. Context includes components that are permanent or semi-permanent, such as gender, job role, and marital status. Context can also include more ephemeral factors, such as current geographic location, the subjects of pages viewed recently, and recent search keywords. Currently the major search engines try to guess a searcher's physical location so that queries for "hardware store" will see ones near them. Other contextual factors might become important in the future. Those search toolbars that collect page popularity information can associate recent page views and searches with the searcher, although none have claimed to put it to use for ranking as of yet. Similarly, Yahoo! offers many services that require registration, so it can collect more permanent information about the searcher. All of this information could be put to use at some point to improve relevance, if searchers do not object due to privacy concerns. Such "personalized" searches have the potential to complicate rank checking for search marketers by changing the whole idea of "ranking #1" to "ranking #1 for a certain percentage of people," but search engines are taking mere baby steps in this direction so far.

You can see that every query undergoes complex analysis, and your pages do as well. But queries containing more than one word are evaluated in an even more complicated way, because of the interplay between the words. Take a look at the factors that apply only to multiple-word queries:

- *Term rarity.* When queries contain more than one term (words are called "terms" in search parlance), the search engine wants to know which words are the most important across the Web, because that helps the search engine find the best pages. Consider the query "hotels in london" from the search engine's point of view. A search engine knows the frequency of every term's occurrence across the Web. The term *in* occurs on most English pages and is therefore not a "good discriminator"—it does not help the search engine pick the best pages for the query because pages containing the word *in* are just about as likely to be good answers as pages that do not. Rarer is the term *hotels*, but it is not as rare as *London*. For each term, the engine calculates its **inverse document frequency**—a logarithmic formula that produces very high values for rare words and very low values for common words. The search engine then takes each of the three terms and executes a formula for each page in the search results known as TF*IDF—normalized term frequency (what we have called keyword density) multiplied by inverse document frequency. This complicated math tells the search engines which pages have the highest keyword densities for the rarest terms in the query.

- *Term proximity.* As discussed in Chapter 2, the best pages contain all the terms in the query right next to each other in the same order they were listed in the query. So, pages containing *hotels in London* might be the best. But the search engines apply more judgment than that. Because the term *in* is so common, for this query pages containing "london hotels" might be just as good as those with "hotels in london." Other queries that contain no common words might emphasize word order more. In all cases, having all the words close to each other is a good thing—certainly better than a page that has numerous occurrences of *London* and *hotel* separated by several words or sentences.

Remember that search experts spend their whole careers crafting and polishing these formulas, so no short explanation will give you a complete understanding—and you do not need one. You do need to understand the basics of what search engines are looking for, however, and now you do.

Although we have dealt with page factors and query factors separately, to make them simpler to explain, on every query the search engine mixes them together to derive the best ranking for the results list—and different queries emphasize one set over the other. For example, imagine a query such as "digital camera." There are millions of occurrences of those words, and keyword density does not help much in determining the best pages. So page factors become critically important in deciding the top ten. But for the query "maytag jetclean dishwasher manual," relatively few pages contain all of those words, especially in proximity to each other, so query factors probably drive the top results more than page factors. Obviously any page that excels in both, for a particular query, could be the #1 result. But every search engine differs, and they handle different types of queries in different ways—that's one reason they have different results for the same query.

As you continue your education in search marketing, you will discover many articles that answer the basic question, "Just what are search engines looking for?" Each article has slightly different answers. Sometimes the articles contradict each other. Do not be concerned about that.

Search engines are fiercely complex, and they change all the time. In addition, "what search engines are looking for" strikes to the heart of a search engine's trade secrets—its ranking algorithm. So, maybe the article's writer observed a few situations and concluded something that wasn't quite true—the search engines will never publicly divulge the truth. Or maybe what one writer wrote might have been true when it was written, but is not true anymore. Perhaps two writers performed tests with two different search engines, and what is true for one is not true for the other.

Unfortunately, divining how search works through observation is hopelessly subjective. You will read conflicting and erroneous information about what search engines are looking for, so you need to take everything you read with a grain of salt—including what you read here. We do not have any inside information. We have lots of experience, just like most of those other writers, but what we write might not be any more accurate than anyone else's story. And by the time you read this, the search engines might have added a new wrinkle. If you believe you must keep up with the ever-changing algorithms, consult the resources in Chapter 16, "What's Next?"

But maybe you can take a different approach. What is more important than the *details* of how any particular search engine works is your *philosophy* for feeding them tasty spider food. How you *think* about what search engines want is more important than what they actually want at any particular moment in time. If your philosophy is to outsmart them at every turn, constantly tuning your pages to fit the latest ranking algorithm, that's one philosophy—one we do not recommend. Wouldn't you rather use an approach that does not need to be changed every week, one that people without any special training can learn and stick to? We advise a philosophy of writing for your visitor first—you will learn what that means next.

The Philosophy of Writing for Search

You have read hundreds of pages about how your site can appeal to search engines, and why it is so important, but now we turn the tables on you. The best philosophy for writing for search is: Write for people first, not for search engines.

We know, we know—that's what you were doing before you picked up this book. In fact, you were writing for people first, last, and only. We are not telling you to go back to that extreme. But neither should you take a pendulum swing in the other direction. Do not write for search engines and forget about people.

We are warning you about this because a far-too-common response of newbie search marketers is to optimize *everything* for search engines. To go overboard learning about every tiny part of search ranking algorithms and to overanalyze and overtune their sites to appeal to search engines every way they can think of. To "chase the algorithm," by constantly re-optimizing to keep up every time the search engines change. This is a huge mistake.

To see why, go back to the basics. What is the purpose of your Web site? To get high search rankings? No. Getting high search rankings is merely a means to an end. In Chapter 5, "Identify Your Web Site's Goals," you decided *your* Web site's goal. You have developed your search marketing program to support that goal. As you reconsider your Web site's goal, think again about your Web conversions. Selling a product. Downloading that white paper. Passing a lead to a manufacturer's rep. Getting a donation for your cause. Don't forget what your goal is: getting conversions.

If you get high rankings in search because you "chase the algorithm," but you have not written with people in mind, you might not get anyone to click through and eventually convert. Let's look at an example. To optimize a page for its "digital cameras" search marketing campaign, Snap Electronics could have produced the prose in Figure 12-3.

EASY DIGITAL CAMERAS, THE BEST DIGITAL CAMERAS, SNAPSHOT DIGITAL CAMERAS FROM SNAP ELECTRONICS

Digital cameras are hot and Snap's SnapShot digital cameras are the hottest. SnapShot digital cameras are not just the best digital cameras, but they are easy digital cameras, too. If you want digital cameras that are not just the best digital cameras, but are also easy digital cameras, you need to choose one of Snap's SnapShot digital cameras.

Figure 12-3   Overoptimizing your content. When you try to stuff keywords into every phrase, you produce stilted, unreadable copy that converts no one.

It makes your brain hurt just reading it, doesn't it? And the worst thing about the mind-numbing repetition of the "broken-record" approach is that it sometimes works. Sometimes search engines *will* give that kind of page a high ranking. But how many Web conversions do you think that kind of writing will draw? Most people reading that drivel would run screaming into the night.

Chasing the algorithm with tortured and torpid prose might win the battle (rankings) but lose the war (conversions). What is the alternative? Writing for people first. *First*, write strong, interesting, action-oriented copy. Your words must help your visitor complete their task—that's how you get conversions. Take a look at Figure 12-4.

SNAPSHOT DIGITAL CAMERAS—THE BEST DIGITAL CAMERA IS THE EASIEST ONE TO USE

Snap's award-winning SnapShot digital cameras have been named "2005's Best Digital Camera" by *Camera Views* magazine. Find out why, like all Snap products, SnapShot digital cameras are easy to use and best in class with the features you need:

- 8 megapixel (8MP) resolution
- Snap's patented OneTouch focus—the easiest to use in the industry according to clickpick.com

Figure 12-4 Writing for people first. You can write for your reader while still taking care to repeat the phrases needed for high search rankings.

Wasn't that better? Granted, we did not squeeze as many keywords into the same 60-word body (or 13-word title) as in the original, but you can read it without your brain imploding, which means that *some* people might convert (as opposed to *none*). And you just might find that you get the same search ranking for the well-written version as for the overoptimized one, because you have attracted far more links to the information-rich, visitor-friendly page.

Besides, chasing the algorithm will drive you nuts. Page ranking factors used by search engines can be extremely volatile—some believe that search engines regularly tweak their ranking algorithms as one way to doom search marketers who do chase their algorithms. And how do you know what is *in* that algorithm anyway? Well-respected search experts say that the optimal page size for search is between 250 and 550 words. Others say it is 350 to 600. Some say that you should change your pages frequently so that your content is fresh. Others say that you should stick with what is working. Who's right? Who cares? The only people who really know how the algorithms work are the search engine designers themselves—and they aren't telling.

Don't chase after any of these search factoids. You will miss the mark on actual conversions. And you will go insane tweaking your content. Get off the algorithm roller coaster and connect with your visitors instead. What do your visitors need to know? How can you help them get what they want? *That* is what will drive your conversions.

Yes, you should write with keywords in mind. You should use them early and often, in titles, and throughout the body. Yes. Do all of that. But not to the point of insanity. Not until your words seem like a computer tried to translate them from another language. Or that you were paid by the keyword.

And there are more reasons to avoid prose so laden with keywords. Search engines are wise to "keyword stuffing" and consider it a form of spam, actually causing your page to be penalized in the rankings. And if search engines do not flag all of those pages today, someday they will. They get smarter every year. Beyond search engine smarts, overoptimized pages also leave you vulnerable to being reported by your competitors to the search engines for spamming—causing a human editor to check the page and possibly ban your site. If the search engines do not catch you, your competitors probably will. So don't take the chance. In truth, only a few very smart operators with loads of time on their hands are able to consistently stay ahead of the search police and truly fool the search engines. It is a lot easier to have a different philosophy.

So, pick your own reason for writing for visitors first:

- *It's the right thing to do.* Ethically, you feel better about yourself because you know that when your pages come up, the searchers really do want to see them and you are providing a valuable service to them, rather than wasting their time.

- *You don't have time to chase the algorithm.* If you are one of those people waiting for a book called *The Four Habits of Highly Overworked People*, you know that you are not going to make time for a new full-time job of out-guessing the search engines. Even when you guess right, you need to make time to guess again next month. As the years go by, ranking algorithms increasingly reward rich content written in an engaging way, so the higher the quality of your content, the better your site will do as search engines continue to improve. Excellent content is the best way to invest your precious time.

- *You cannot afford the bad publicity from spamming.* If your executives are squeamish about any hint of negative reporting about your company, a story about unethical search practices is not a risk you are likely to take.

- *You are focused on conversions, not rankings.* You know that the illusory gains you make from overoptimizing do not bring you customer conversions anyway, so why not work for conversions first?

In the end, it is your decision, but we strongly advise you to play it straight. Be factual. Avoid the overheated hype. Unlike other forms of marketing and advertising, a straightforward approach is often the most convincing on the Web—even a "soft sell" can sometimes be best. Now let's look at some specific techniques for writing copy that puts the visitor first but will still appeal to search engines.

Step-by-Step Optimization for Search Landing Pages

If your head is spinning because you are trying to remember exactly what search engines are looking for at the same time you are trying to write for your visitors first, take a deep breath. You *can* do this, and do it well, if you are willing to take it one step at a time. Each step in the content-optimization process builds from the previous ones, as shown in Figure 12-5.

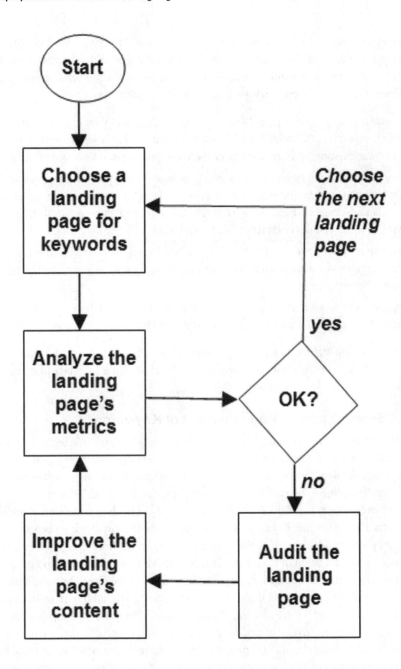

Figure 12-5 The Process for Optimizing Content. Search landing pages can be continuously improved to get high search rankings and Web conversions.

You can see from the process that some of the steps are iterative—for example, you continue to change content and check rankings until you get the search results you need. That way, you can take as many tries at them as necessary. Sometimes you get what you need right away, but other times it takes months. Let's look at an overview of each step:

- *Choose a search landing page for a set of keywords.* Start by looking at your keyword list from Chapter 11, "Choose Your Target Keywords." Pick a strong search landing page from your existing Web site for one or more of your targeted keywords from your list.

- *Analyze the landing page's metrics.* See how your page is performing. For each keyword that you are targeting for your landing page, find out how far down the search results list your landing page is. Find out how many search referrals you get to that page and how many of those visitors complete a Web conversion.

- *Audit your landing page.* If your page is not performing the way you would like (a strong possibility as you start search marketing), you can analyze your landing page to find areas of improvement.

- *Improve your landing page's content.* Your page audit shows how to optimize your content to get top search rankings, more referrals, and higher conversions.

Faithfully following each step will get you where you want to go. So don't feel overwhelmed at all there is to do—just take the first step by choosing a search landing page to start working on.

Choose a Search Landing Page for a Set of Keywords

The place to start optimizing your content is exactly where we left off in Chapter 11—with your list of targeted keywords. For each campaign, you follow the steps in Chapter 11 to develop a target list of keywords. Then, for each keyword, you need to identify the page on your site that is the best **search landing page**—the perfect place on your site for a searcher's query.

It is not necessary for every keyword to have a *unique* landing page; some landing pages can be used for more than one keyword. It *is* important for the keywords to be closely related, however, if they share a landing page. Harkening back to our fictitious company, Snap Electronics, you can imagine that some of their keywords for the "digital camera" campaign might share landing pages. The product category hub page for SnapShot Digital Cameras—the home page for Snap's entire digital camera product line—might be a good search landing page for queries such as "digital cameras," "snap digital camera," "snap camera," "snapshot," "snapshot camera," and "snapshot digital camera." Even though they are each somewhat different queries, a searcher wants to see the main "digital cameras" page on Snap's site in response to any of these queries.

We will repeat part of that sentence again, because it is *so* important: A *searcher* wants to see the main page on Snap's site for any of these queries. A searcher. You choose your landing page based on what the *searcher* wants to see, not necessarily what *you* want the searcher to see. It is very tempting for folks who have grown up in other forms of marketing to think "message first," as in, "What message do I want to deliver to this person?" Search marketing does not work this way. You *must* consider what information the searcher wants to receive as the primary point of the page. Only when you satisfy the searcher's need can you think about how to "spin" your message around that need.

How *Not* to Choose a Search Landing Page

Too often, dyed-in-the-wool marketing folks approach landing page selection the same way they do target marketing for print ads. They believe they should be able to select any message they want for the target audience. So you will ask, "What landing page should come up when searchers look for 'digital cameras'?" And the marketers reply, "Our 30-day holiday offer for a SnapShot SLR X900 and a free copy of Adobe Photo Elements!" This is probably a bad idea, for a few reasons:

- *Getting that page to rank highly in organic search for that query is hard.* The pages that rank well for the query "digital cameras" are ones that contain basic information about them. Remember, a broad query such as "digital cameras" might find a million Web pages that contain those words, so the ones that rank highest have many links to them using the words *digital cameras*—a 30-day offer page is unlikely to garner that kind of attention. The SnapShot digital cameras hub page might, over a period of months and years.

- *We are skipping several steps in the Web Conversion Cycle.* You need to match the type of query with the type of information on the landing page. An informational *query* (such as "digital cameras") needs to produce an informational *page*, not a transactional page that is screaming at searchers to "Buy Today!" Your landing page must be the *perfect* page for the searcher's query, or searchers will not click through (or will abandon your site immediately if they do click through). Visitors will be perturbed by your reaching for their wallets when they were just trying to figure out whether they even want a digital camera. So, in the unlikely event you could get a high ranking for your 30-day offer page, you will not get many conversions from people searching for "digital cameras."

- *That page will soon disappear.* Search marketing is not like other forms of marketing. Search marketing campaigns live a long time because they are based on searchers' queries. Searcher behavior sometimes changes quickly (usually in response to seasonal changes or current events), but more frequently it changes very slowly. Searchers for "digital cameras" are going to be around during the holiday season, but they will be there in January, too. Will this page? No. So if by some chance Snap *did* get high rankings, and people *did* convert, all the hard search marketing work is worthless the minute the offer expires. As soon as the 30 days are up, the offer page disappears from the site, and the search engines soon find other pages to put in its place—probably pages from other sites.

For all of these reasons, you need to take a more permanent approach to search landing pages. The closer you design your landing page to the searchers' intent, the easier it will be to put the words they are looking for in context on the page. (It would be odd to mention *digital cameras* six or seven times on the 30-day offer page, but it is quite reasonable on the SnapShot hub page.) Further, the closer your landing page is to the searchers' intent, the more likely it will draw those all-important links from other Web sites for that subject. And if it matches the searchers' intent, searchers are much more likely to click through to your page. It makes sense to choose permanent pages on your site for keywords that are permanently being searched for.

Does such slavish attention to searcher intent mean that Snap cannot show them the 30-day offer? Not at all. Snap can add a link to the 30-day offer page from the search landing page for "digital cameras" by placing a merchandising spot on the right side of the page (and lots of other pages, too). After searchers have satisfied their original intent, a merchandising spot with a nice picture of the SLR X900 and an Adobe logo might generate interest in the offer.

Landing Pages for Multiple Keywords

You can choose the same search landing page for multiple keywords, but it is important that they be closely related. You saw above that several related keywords might all target Snap's digital camera hub page.

Often, it is necessary for your keywords to share terms to make a single landing page effective. The search keywords "digital camera comparison" and "compare digital cameras" can easily share the same page because they are merely variants of the same words. One way to examine how closely your keywords are related is to assess the number of concepts they share—Tor Crockatt, Global Editorial Director for MIVA, refers to **meaning elements**. Table 12-1 shows some examples. There are no hard-and-fast rules on how to separate your keywords into meaning elements—the idea is to think about how closely keywords do relate to each other before choosing the same landing page for them.

Table 12-1   Keyword Meaning Elements (You can analyze your keywords to compare how many different concepts are embedded in each one.)

Phrase	Meaning Elements
digital cameras	1 (digital cameras)
discount digital cameras	2 (discount) + (digital cameras)
digital camera reviews	2 (digital camera) + (review)
snap digital camera	2 (snap) + (digital camera)
snap digital camera accessories	3 (snap) + (digital camera) + (camera accessories)

If you think that dozens of keywords should all land on the same page, however, you are fooling yourself. Different keywords imply different intents on the part of the searcher—they require different search landing pages. If you try to optimize your page for unrelated keywords, you will find that your words calculated to catch everyone will catch no one. Optimizing two unrelated keywords will dilute the density of each one, lowering the page's ranking for each keyword. Better to bite the bullet and choose a different landing page for each one.

In short, if you truly believe that two keywords are so closely related that searchers will want to see the same page, optimize your page for both. Otherwise, go with multiple landing pages.

When You Can't Find the Right Landing Page

What if you can't think of a good landing page for one of your keyword targets? When Snap Electronics looked at its targeted keywords in Chapter 7, the related search keywords "digital camera comparison" and "compare digital cameras" had no strong landing page already on Snap's site. You might be in a similar predicament, or perhaps you know of so many pages on your site that you cannot decide on the best landing page.

Either way, you can get help from search to try to find the best search landing pages. If your site's pages are all indexed by your site search engine, you can search for your keyword and check each page that comes up. Similarly, if you have followed the advice in Chapter 10 to get your pages indexed, you can get help from Yahoo! and other Internet search engines. Use the "site:" operator in your query the way you did in Chapter 10 when you were checking how many pages you have indexed. Just add your keyword to the "site:" operator, as Figure 12-6 demonstrates with the search keyword "liability insurance" for the Hartford Insurance company. The query "liability insurance site:www.thehartford.com" finds all pages containing "liability insurance" within the primary domain of The Hartford Insurance company (revealing 198 matches in Google). You can look at each result to select the best landing page for your keyword.

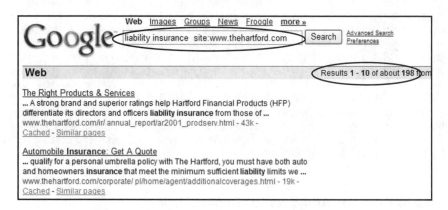

Figure 12-6 Finding possible search landing pages. Using the "site:" operator reveals the pages on your site that contain your targeted keyword.

If you have several possible pages that all seem plausible to you as landing pages, it is fine for you to optimize each one for the same keywords. It is more work than focusing on one page, but it pays off in the long run because a site with multiple pages linked together that are all optimized for the same keyword will receive higher rankings for its pages. Search engines do not look at just one page—they look at your whole site. In this chapter, we focus on choosing one page to keep things simple, but the more pages you optimize, the better your search rankings will be.

If you have exhausted these methods and still cannot find an acceptable page, it might be time to create a new page. (You will not draw any organic search referrals for that keyword if you have no content on your site that matches.) It is also common to create new landing pages for paid placement for special events or short-lived promotional campaigns.

> **SEARCH LANDING PAGES VS. DOORWAY PAGES: WHAT'S THE DIFFERENCE?**
>
> **Search landing pages** are pages you have designed for searchers to enter your site from a search engine. And so are **doorway pages**. But that is where the similarity ends.
>
> A doorway page is a spam technique designed to fool the search engine into providing a high ranking for a page that has no other purpose except search rankings. A doorway page is heavily optimized (usually by using other spam methods) to capture searchers and is usually kept hidden from other visitors to the site. Frequently, doorway pages get high rankings from a combination of content optimization and large numbers of links (using a spam technique called a **link farm**, which we expose in Chapter 13). A doorway page is a search landing page gone wrong—it serves no purpose on the site except search rankings and is not linked to by the other pages of the site—it has links *from* the doorway page *into* the site. So, it is a door that only opens in. Doorway pages go by other names, such as gateway pages or entry pages, but the name is not important. If the page is designed merely for the consumption of search engines, it is spam.
>
> Search landing pages are different. They are legitimate pages on the site that are linked from many other pages on the site. Although optimized for search rankings, they are designed for visitors first and search engines second.
>
> Some search landing pages—specifically those pages used only for paid search—are actually designed to be closer to doorway pages. You recall from Chapter 11 that some of our low-priority keywords were used for paid search only—this is the reason. You can create paid placement landing pages that are not part of the mainline site navigation and have links merely leading into the site. The difference between these pages and doorway pages is they are *not* being used for organic search at all. (You should use a robots tag or robots.txt file to block them from organic search.) Because you are not fooling the organic engines with these pages, they are *not* spam.
>
> So, be sure to heavily link organic search landing pages into your site's main navigation paths. You can create somewhat more hidden pages for use as paid placement landing pages, but be sure that they are never crawled by spiders—you don't want to be inadvertently guilty of spamming.

Analyze the Metrics for Your Search Landing Page

Now that you have chosen a search landing page for a small set of keywords, your next move is to check the performance of your page, according to all the measurements you can amass. Depending on your site's sophistication in search metrics, which will grow over time, you might have a sizable amount of page performance data available for your analysis:

- *Organic search rankings.* Check the organic search ranking of your search landing page for each keyword that you are targeting. Ideally, you will perform that checking in multiple search engines. In Chapter 7, we showed how to project your rankings—are you achieving the ranking that you expected? If not, you need to make some changes.

- *Search referrals.* If the rankings are good, you should see a high number of visits to the page referred by search engines for your targeted keyword. In Chapter 7, you projected the expected referrals based on good search rankings—are you achieving what you projected? If not, changes are required.

- *Web conversions.* Remember, the point of search marketing is not top rankings or even high referrals, but increased Web conversions. If your page is getting high rankings and referrals, but visitors do not convert, your landing page and other pages on your site need to be changed.

If you were only to track one metric for all of your pages, Web conversions would be the one because it correlates to your overall goal for search marketing. Until conversions increase, you have not succeeded. But it's helpful to track the others, too, because they can help you figure out what to do.

If you think about it, if search rankings are low, referrals and conversions will be, too. Similarly, if rankings are okay, but referrals remain low, conversions will continue to be low, too. However, you will take different actions in these two situations, because the ways to improve search rankings are not always the same as the ways to improve low referrals when you have high rankings. Moreover, the actions designed to raise low conversions differ from what you do to raise disappointing referrals. So all three measurements help you diagnose what is wrong with your pages.

And if these three measurements do not sound like numbers you calculate once and then forget about, well, you're right. You will be tracking these metrics for all of your landing pages *forever*; because page performance can change at any time, you need to constantly maintain your page to continue to succeed.

If you do not know how to gather these measurements, don't worry about that yet. We cover them each in depth in Chapter 15, "Make Search Marketing Operational," when we explain the various measurements you will want to stay on top of. For now, just understand that each time you optimize a page you will check several different measurements before declaring success. Later in this chapter, we explain how to change your page to improve these metrics, because you will be making changes to your pages until they meet your metrics projections.

Check Organic Search Rankings

Let's take a quick look at organic search rankings. We continue with the insurance example. Although there are 198 pages from The Hartford in the Google index containing the keyword *liability insurance*, Google will show no more than 1 or 2 of them (if any) in the top 10, and only a few others throughout the rest of the results. Google (and other search engines) limit the results for any one site because searchers want to see a variety of sites in response to their search.

Does that mean that The Hartford should not try to optimize all 198 pages? Not at all. The more pages are optimized, the more it helps all of their rankings. And many of those 198 pages might be perfect landing pages for other keywords related to liability insurance, such as *product liability insurance* or *professional liability insurance*. When pages are optimized for these deeper keywords, they enhance rankings for *liability insurance*, too, because the words *liability insur-ance* are contained within each of the deeper keywords.

In Chapter 15, we list several tools that automatically perform rank checking, but for this exercise it's fine to do the checking manually, by entering the keyword and working your way through the results list looking for your company's pages. You could also use the Keyword Tracker tool from Digital Point Solutions (www.digitalpoint.com/tools/keywords) that we used in Chapter 7 to check Google rankings. In Figure 12-7, you can see a Keyword Tracker report for "liability insurance" for The Hartford. Even though there were 198 pages indexed in Google with that keyword, only three of them rank in the top 1,000, with the highest at #51.

liability insurance			
Rk	Pg	Pos	URL
Google			
51	6	1	http://sb.thehartford.com/learn_insurance/property.asp
798	80	8	http://mb.thehartford.com/insurance_info/pdfs/520-602.pdf
843	85	3	http://mb.thehartford.com/reduce_risk/risk_tips_liability.asp

Figure 12-7   Checking search rankings for landing pages. The Hartford's top page for "liability insurance" ranks just 51st in Google.

Check your rankings for every keyword you are targeting for your search landing page, and it's best to check in multiple search engines. It is probable that your first ranking check for your search landing page will not show high rankings any more than The Hartford's check did. After you make changes to your page (we explain what kinds of changes later in the chapter), you wait for the search spider to come around again (which can take days, weeks, or sometimes months), and then you recheck your rankings. You continue this "lather, rinse, and repeat" cycle until you attain the rankings you need to meet the search marketing projections you made in Chapter 7.

Measure Organic Search Referrals

After you have optimized your page for high rankings, you need to check your organic search referrals. In Chapter 7, we showed how different types of queries yield different rates of referrals (in Table 7-12) and how you can use keyword demand to estimate the number of referrals (in Table 7-15). As soon as the search spider has crawled your updated page and it attains a new search ranking, you should see referrals change. Your Web metrics facility can show you referrals for your search landing page broken down by keyword, so you can do a before-and-after comparison to determine whether you are getting the projected clickthroughs on your page.

If your page has the high rankings you hoped for, but your referrals are not what you expected, you need to look at how to make your page more appealing for searchers to click. Later in this chapter, we show you ways to do that. As before, after you make changes to your page, you wait for the spiders to return and then check your referrals again. Sometimes you will find that changes you made to improve clickthrough damaged your search rankings, so you will need to try again.

Calculate Search Conversions

Eventually, you will achieve the rankings and referrals that you are shooting for, but you are not done until you start getting the conversions that you projected. In Chapter 15, we explain several ways to track your conversions from search, but let's focus on just the process now. In Chapter 7, you projected the number of conversions you expected to result from your search marketing campaign (in Figure 7-6). Now is the time to see whether you are achieving those goals.

If not, you need to use your Web traffic metrics facility to investigate where most of your visitors abandon your site—it's somewhere between the search landing page and the conversion page. To correct the problem and boost conversions, you might need to make changes to the search landing page itself or you might have work to do on other pages on your site. You will carefully make changes to your landing page so as not to disturb your rankings and referrals. The good news is that you need not wait for the spiders to see the effects of conversion changes—as soon as you change the pages, you can measure whether the changes improved your Web conversions.

Next, you see what to do about low conversions (and low rankings and referrals, too). If your landing page does not deliver the metrics you projected, what can you do to improve the situation? You start by **auditing** your search landing page.

Audit Your Search Landing Page

Your first check of your search landing page's metrics will typically be depressing. It is rare for a page that has not been optimized to rank well, and rarer still for referrals and conversions to be what you want—after all, that's why you embarked on search marketing in the first place. It's time to *audit* your page to diagnose problems and see what might be improved. Landing pages used only for paid placement are audited only for conversion problems, while you aim to improve rankings, referrals, *and* conversion for organic landing pages.

You will eventually develop your own eye for auditing pages, but in the beginning you can benefit from using **content analyzers**. As you do, just keep in mind that content analyzer tools are just that: *tools*. They are designed to *inform* your judgment, not *replace* it. Content analyzers typically offer advice only for search ranking problems, not referral or conversion problems, so you need to consider the advice carefully—it is no victory to improve your rankings while decreasing referrals or conversions. So don't blindly follow what any tool has to say—it is no search marketing oracle. Use your judgment about whether the advice fits your style and whether it will help you improve conversions as well as rankings. These tools can prove very helpful, but none provide *perfect* advice for all search engines in all situations—that's impossible—so don't check your brain at the door.

In addition to helping you perform audits properly, content analyzers can help you persuade recalcitrant members of your extended search team to make the required changes to aid search rankings. For some reason, many people are more easily persuaded when they see a report from a program than if you tell them the same thing. You should do whatever it takes to get writers to change their words (to optimize the content for higher search rankings). If it means running a content analyzer and walking them through the results, go for it. Figure 12-8 shows a sample report from Site Content Analyzer (www.sitecontentanalyzer.com).

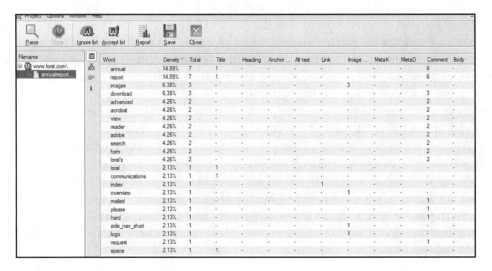

Figure 12-8 A content analyzer's report. Site Content Analyzer scores a search landing page's individual ranking factors for each keyword targeted.

Site Content Analyzer is not the only game in town. Many content analyzers are available to help you audit your search landing pages. Table 12-2 lists a few of the better-known ones.

Table 12-2 Content Analyzer Tools (Several programs can help you analyze your search landing pages to find areas to improve your content's search optimization.)

Product Name	URL	Price
Ranks Keyword Density and Prominence tool	http://ranks.nl/tools/spider.html	Free
Site Content Analyzer	www.sitecontentanalyzer.com	Personal Edition $80 Business Edition $120
WebCEO	www.webceo.com	WebCEO Free Free WebCEO Startup $19 WebCEO SmallBiz $179 WebCEO Professional $279
WebPosition Gold	www.webposition.com	Standard Edition $149 Professional Edition $349

Each tool has different features and might use different names for the content analysis techniques employed. The most full-featured versions allow analysis of your entire site, as discussed in Chapter 15. Another useful feature of high-end tools is a side-by-side analysis of your page against pages from your competitors. To show you how to use a content analyzer, we walk through a case study of such an analysis now.

Snap Electronics chose their "digital cameras" hub page as the right landing page for the "digital camera" search keyword, so they decided to perform a content analysis on their page (which ranked #45 in Google) against the three top-ranked pages in the Google results. If you think about it, examining what the top-ranked pages have going for them is a simple way to see where you are coming up short.

None of Snap's competitors, such as Canon or Kodak, are listed on the first page of results for "digital camera," so it might be an uphill battle for any camera manufacturer to crack the top ten. Regardless, Snap can probably learn a lot by seeing what kinds of pages *are* at the top of the list. The top three Google results for the search *digital camera* show the popular *Camera Views* magazine at the top, with the well-respected camera review site clickpick.com second, and Black Hat Cameras, a little-known camera retailer, in third place. (Like Snap, all three of these companies are fictitious.)

Scrutinize Your Title

After running the report against the four pages, Snap examined the title tag, as shown in Table 12-3. Snap's title was "Snap Electronics digital cameras for you." resulting in one occurrence of the keyword *digital cameras* in the middle of the six words, for 50 percent prominence and two words out of six for a 33 percent keyword density. In contrast, the competitors' pages led with the keywords, such as *Camera Views* title "Digital camera reviews from *Camera Views* magazine." The #2 and #3 pages had longer titles with two occurrences of the keyword, but they had the same density as Snap.

Table 12-3   Digital Camera Landing Pages Title Analysis (Each of the high ranking pages had a more prominent title than Snap's page did.)

<title> text	Snap #45	Camera Views #1	clickpick.com #2	Black Hat #3
Total words	6	7	12	12
Keyword frequency	1	1	2	2
Keyword density	33%	28%	33%	33%
Keyword prominence	50%	100%	100%	100%

Keep in mind that your goal is not to optimize your content by mindlessly repeating your keywords just to get a high score in the analyzer. But the analyzer can be helpful as a quick way to get a read on where your optimization places you among the top search results.

Snap's referrals and conversions for this page are very low, because it is ranked #45. But it's worth considering whether there are any changes needed to optimize referrals now. The title tag is crucial in driving referrals because it is the first thing searchers see about your page on the search results screen. As you learned in Chapter 4, "How Searchers Work," of the time searchers spend reviewing the search results page, 30 percent of that time is spent looking at titles. In contrast, the title has no impact on conversion because visitors do not look at the title after they land on your page.

"Snap Electronics digital cameras for you" is not a terribly compelling title. Perhaps the Snap Electronics brand name would cause some searchers to click, but the SnapShot brand is completely missing. And for those unfamiliar with the brand, there is absolutely no reason to click. We have some ideas later in this chapter to improve this title to boost both rankings and referrals.

Although Snap's page did not look as well optimized as the others, it seems easy to catch up. After all, how hard is it to rewrite a title?

Analyze Your Snippet

Snippets, the short blurb of text underneath the page title on the search results page, are excerpts of text from your page that aid a searcher to decide whether to click through or not. If your snippets provide searchers with an appealing synopsis of your page, you will raise your referrals for that page. Recall from Chapter 4 that searchers spend more time looking at snippets (43 percent) than any other part of the search results page.

Later we provide some tips for influencing the search engines to show snippets that bring you higher clickthrough rates, but for now, let's just think about what we want shown. The Google and Yahoo! snippets for the "digital cameras" query were almost identical, as shown in Figure 12-9.

**Yahoo! drew its snippet from the middle of Snap's page,
the only appearance of the keyword digital cameras.**

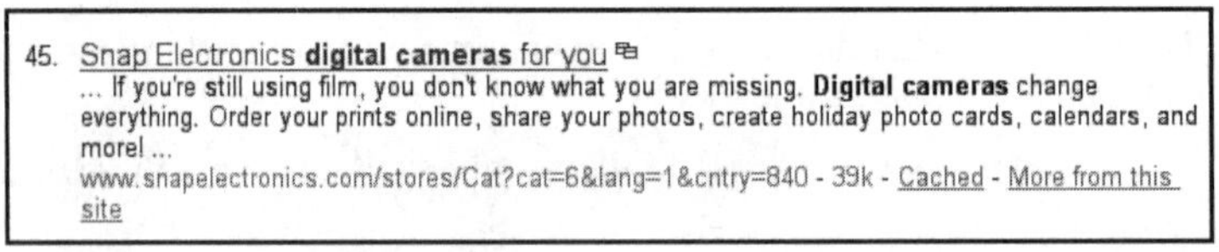

45. Snap Electronics **digital cameras** for you
       ... If you're still using film, you don't know what you are missing. **Digital cameras** change
       everything. Order your prints online, share your photos, create holiday photo cards, calendars, and
       more! ...
       www.snapelectronics.com/stores/Cat?cat=6&lang=1&cntry=840 - 39k - Cached - More from this
       site

**Google snippets tend to be shorter than Yahoo! snippets,
but this one is not remarkably different.**

Snap Electronics **digital cameras** for you
... **Digital cameras** change everything. Order your prints online, share your photos, create
holiday photo cards, calendars, and more! ...
www.snapelectronics.com/stores/Cat?cat=6&lang=1&cntry=840 - 39k
- Cached - Similar pages

Figure 12-9   Digital camera landing pages snippets. Google and Yahoo! snippets were rather similar in this case, although Google's is shorter.

This snippet has no strong call to action and no mention of the Snap or SnapShot brand names, making it less likely that a searcher would click through to this page. Snap decided it would try to optimize its snippets later in the process.

Evaluate Your Body Text

The body of the HTML page is the viewable text on the screen. We just analyzed how the body text is excerpted to form the snippet that drives referrals, but the body text is also important for high rankings and conversion.

Snap's metrics system reveals the conversions for the site as a whole, but it does not allow Snap to check search conversions for a single landing page. (In Chapter 15, we offer some ideas on how to do that.) Snap has been pleased with the overall conversion rate for digital cameras on the site, so this body analysis will concentrate on improving those low search rankings (#45 in Google and AOL and missing from the top 100 in the other major engines).

For a keyword as popular as *digital cameras*, with so many pages vying to be #1, it stands to reason that the body of each of high-ranking pages is heavily optimized, not just the title. Table 12-4 reveals the truth, which is not so clear-cut.

Table 12-4   Digital Camera Landing Pages Body Analysis (Of the four analyzed landing pages, Black Hat Cameras had by far the best optimized body content.)

<body> text	Snap #45	Camera Views #1	clickpick.com #2	Black Hat #3
Total words	637	0	85	1,240
Bold keywords	0	0	0	5
Heading keywords	0	0	0	1
Keyword frequency	1	0	2	42
Keyword density	0.3%	0%	4.7%	6.8%
Keyword prominence	64%	0%	100%	100%

Clearly Snap's page has a long way to go, with just one occurrence of the keyword *digital camera* in the middle of the body. But only Black Hat's site seems heavily optimized. Surprisingly, *Camera Views* is the #1 result with no mentions of the keyword at all!

When viewed with a browser, Snap's page shows the words *digital cameras* in a heading at the top of the page. That title helps visitors orient themselves, reassuring them they are in the right place—and that helps increase conversions. But examining the page's HTML revealed this text is generated by an image and that there is no alternate text specified. To the spider, that title is invisible. The image file needs to be changed to a heading tag, thereby adding a prominent occurrence of a keyword. (It is prominent because it is at the top of the page.) Similarly, the word *cameras* at the top of the screen is generated by an image map—the spider cannot see that one either. As hard as it is to believe, there really is only one occurrence of *digital cameras* on the page, so the page needs to be rewritten to achieve proper keyword density. Again, don't just load up on keywords to please the analyzer, but clearly you should be using your important keywords more than once.

Exploring the HTML for the competitors' pages does not reveal anything out of the ordinary, but it's clear that the folks at Black Hat know how to optimize a page. Although the page seems very long, it is richly peppered with keywords throughout, including occurrences in headings and in bold. The density is right around the magical 7 percent mark, and the prose is not stilted at all—it is quite well written.

This content analyzer calculates keyword prominence based on the first occurrence, so placing a keyword as the first words in the body merits a 100 percent score. If we use our judgment, however, we might decide that search engines might be more discriminating than that—they might use a weighted average of all occurrences. You might want to cluster a couple of occurrences in the first 25 words in the document, with the rest sprinkled throughout. As with the title, adding one prominent occurrence of a keyword is fairly easy, but it seems like working hard on density will pay off, as Black Hat's page shows. Beyond metrics, Black Hat's page has well-written content full of useful information for their visitors.

But what about that #1 result? *Camera Views* magazine must have quite a page factor score, which is what we look at next.

Examine Your Link Popularity

Snap's content analyzer provides a report on links to each page, which affects the search engines' page factors. (Link popularity has no effect on referrals or conversion, just ranking.) As you will see in Chapter 13, the quality of links is more important than the quantity of links. With that in mind, you can see how Table 12-5 explains how *Camera Views* magazine got the #1 result.

Table 12-5 Digital Camera Landing Pages Page Factor Analysis. The top three pages had significantly more and better links than Snap's page.

Page Factors	Snap #45	Camera Views #1	clickpick.com #2	Black Hat #3
Google PageRank	4	8	6	6
Number of links	34	7,960	192	9,250
PageRank 7+ links	0	6	4	0
PageRank 5-6 links	0	151	6	0
PageRank <5 links	34	7,803	182	9,250

Camera Views has almost 8,000 links to its page—many of them high-quality ones (from other sites with PageRank 5 and higher). The popular clickpick.com site also has a number of high-quality links, but not enough to move it up to #1.

But check out our friends at Black Hat Cameras. Black Hat has more links than the other pages combined. But they are not a well-known retailer, so how could that be? We do not have any proof, but it is possible that Black Hat is actually spamming the search engine using bogus links from a link farm. We talk about that more in Chapter 13. The lesson here is that whenever you analyze a competitor, you must be careful not to copy spam techniques. In this case, it appears that the optimization techniques used on the page itself are ethical, but you must be careful.

Because Snap wanted to use that same page as its landing page for other search keywords as well (such as "snap digital camera" and "snapshot digital camera"), the same content analyzer was used to check the page for the other keywords. The results were similar, showing that scant attention has been paid to any keywords on this hub page.

As Snap looked at other pages in the "digital cameras" area of the site, it was clear that they all needed the same kind of makeover as the hub page. None of them had strong titles, nor was their body copy optimized. In Chapter 13, we explore how Snap can beef up links to the page, but now let's look at how to optimize page content to boost search rankings, referrals, and conversions.

Improve Your Search Landing Page's Content

Here's what you have been waiting for—advice on improving your search landing page to meet your search marketing goals.

Before tackling each element on your page, let's keep in mind the process we are following. Each time we change the page, we wait for it to be recrawled by the spider and we check the performance metrics again. Is it ranking highly now? Producing sufficient referrals? Conversions? We continue to iterate change after change to the page until we drive the page performance we projected in Chapter 7 when we first conceived the campaign. Smart search marketers go so far as to log every change to their key pages so that they can see which update made an impact on the performance metrics.

Let's look at what changes you should consider for your search landing pages, starting with the most critical part of any page—its title.

Perfect Your Title

Your title tag is your best means of improving both search rankings and search referrals. Unfortunately, you typically need to trade one off against the other. If you load up your title with keywords to produce high rankings, its unreadable nature will hinder clickthrough.

This very tension between rankings and referrals causes search engines to give the title such weight for search rankings. Other metadata, such as the keywords metatag, are now largely or completely ignored by search engines, precisely because they were used *only* to achieve rankings—they do not appear on the page. Those tags could be optimized for search rankings, but there was no counterbalance to keep the content accurate—a wide-open invitation for spam. Because titles are shown to searchers, that helps police their accuracy. Remember that your Web feeds, such as RSS and Atom, also contain title tags for your posts that search engines look at.

Figure 12-6 shows some of the possibilities for the SnapShot hub page we have been ana-lyzing. Part of the tension between ranking effectiveness and referral effectiveness concerns the length of the title. There is no limit on the amount of text that can be used with a title tag, but search engines do not use all of it. It is not known how many characters in a title the search engines use for ranking purposes, but they clearly truncate the title displayed on the search results page at around 65 characters. Some experts advise creating a title somewhat longer than the trun-cation point to squeeze in an additional keyword, while tuning the title to be readable and com-pelling when truncated. Others believe that shorter titles of around 40 characters compel the highest referrals and that truncated titles turn off visitors.

Table 12-6   Digital Camera Landing Page Title Alternatives (There are many bad choices for titles, but many good ones, too.)

Title	Ranking Effectiveness	Referral Effectiveness
SnapShot home page	Just one keyword	No call to action
Snap digital cameras for you	Better, but not enough	Still no call to action
Save on Snap digital cameras	Still weak	Good call to action
Snap Electronics—SnapShot Digital Cameras	Keywords improved	No call to action
Snap Electronics—SnapShot Digital Cameras—Save on digital cameras	Strong on keywords	Good call to action
SnapShot Digital Cameras from Snap Electronics—Save on digital cameras	Strong keywords with improved prominence	Good call to action
SnapShot Digital Cameras—Save on the best digital camera from . . . Snap Electronics	Very strong keywords (including singular and plural forms) with strong prominence	Good call to action that reinforces brand image, but company name trun-cated onscreen
SnapShot Digital Cameras from Snap Electronics—Save on the best . . . digital camera	Very strong keywords with very strong prominence	Good call to action with brand image reinforce-ment, with repeated key-word truncated onscreen
Snap Digital Cameras—Save on a SnapShot digital camera	Very strong keywords with very strong prominence and density	Good call to action with no truncation

Ellipsis (. . .) indicates estimated truncation point onscreen.

When you craft titles for your pages, do not just copy what Snap did. Snap knows that it has a well-known brand name and that many of its highest-converting keywords contain its company name (Snap) and its brand name (SnapShot). Your business might not have that kind of name recognition, so you might be better advised to lead with the generic product name (digital cameras). Tailor your titles to what searchers are looking for and you *will* improve your rankings.

So what creates high-ranking effectiveness? You already know the answer. Keywords. High keyword density and prominence. If you want to optimize for multiple keywords (especially several multiple-word keywords), however, you run out of space very quickly.

What to leave out of a title soon becomes just as important as what you put in. Obviously, words that are neither keywords nor strong calls to action must go. Delete *home page*—in fact, *page* by itself is also useless. Wipe out *welcome*, *online*, *menu*—you get the idea. These flabby words do not drive rankings or clickthrough. Every "waste" word you remove leaves more room for words that matter and improves your keyword density.

Combine keywords wherever possible. When Snap writes "SnapShot Digital Cameras," a double dip takes effect: The page is optimized for the query *snapshot digital cameras* but for the *digital cameras* query, too. Repeat keywords if you can get away with it. It hurts readability if overdone, but if you can do it naturally, go for it. Try to use one singular and one plural form to ensure the page is found no matter which form the searcher uses.

To improve referral effectiveness, cram as many trigger words into the title as you can, making sure it is readable. Happily, for many situations, the keywords and the trigger words are the same—*Snap Electronics* and *SnapShot* are the kinds of well-known brand names that spur clicks. Other trigger words include local place names, low prices, prized features, and time-sensitive offers. But do *not* get the searcher off track—you need to reinforce the searcher's query first and foremost. If you can reinforce the searcher's query and still have room to add brand image terms or a strong call to action, do so.

Sometimes the title is not enough to cause a searcher to click. Fortunately, the searcher will see your snippet, too—you need to influence what text shows up there.

Influence Your Snippet

You've seen the "pitch" on the outside of an envelope of a direct marketing piece—a strong pitch causes more people to open the envelope and read the content inside. A snippet is the pitch on the outside of your search marketing "envelope." Your snippet is shown below your page's title on the search results page and can make the difference between a searcher clicking your page or passing you by.

Snippets are excerpts from your page's text that contain the searcher's keyword. Because you cannot predict every possible variation of search query that searchers will use to find your page, there is no way to control what displays in every case. However, you might find it to your advantage to massage your writing to influence snippets for the targeted keywords. To do that, you need to understand a little bit about how search engines choose their snippets.

Each search engine uses different rules for composing its snippets. Google, for example, rarely uses the description tag for its snippets, whereas Yahoo! frequently does. Search engines frequently take excerpts from text in the body of the page, normally choosing a section of text where all or most of the keyword terms are found together, or in close proximity. The first occurrence of the terms in proximity is frequently the excerpt chosen.

Just as with ranking algorithms, the rules search engines use to compose snippets change over time, so it is not usually worth the effort to chase the snippet algorithm. But you can benefit from a few tips as you write your page.

To influence the Yahoo! snippet, place your important keywords together at the start of the description. For example, Snap changed its description to begin "SnapShot digital cameras from Snap Electronics have been named 'Best Digital Camera 2005' by *Camera Views* magazine." A similar approach within your body text can influence Google.

For any search engine, ensuring that the first occurrences of your major keywords come together is a good thing. So, Snap should not allow the first occurrence of *digital cameras* to appear without its brand name. Make sure that your brand name (such as *SnapShot digital cameras*) is the first occurrence, so that searchers for *digital cameras* will see your brand name in the title *and* in the snippet.

Yahoo! appears to favor 150- to 200-character snippets, but sometimes shows longer ones. Google's snippets are generally shorter, around 100 to 150 characters. If you decide to craft a few snippet-worthy excerpts for a few high-priority keywords, remember the snippet length restrictions as you write.

This is a completely legitimate technique, because you are providing an accurate synopsis of what is on the page. The search engines are happy for you to take the care to consider what the snippet will say for popular queries, although they might change their snippet algorithms at any time. Remember, there is no reason to induce clickthrough for searchers who will not ultimately convert, so you want your snippets to be a factual representation of your page.

Snap Electronics rewrote their landing page to influence their snippets for *digital cameras*. The original copy was loaded with model names and features but did not mention digital cameras prominently. The first line of text in the body was changed to say, "SnapShot Digital Cameras feature a wide range of models ranging from the award-winning X5 to the top-of-the-line SLR X900 . . . ." This opening was considered a good compromise between what the marketing department wanted and what was required for strong search rankings.

The marketing department asked for its copy to be used for the description, but it was changed a bit to ensure it delivered a strong snippet. The new description begins "SnapShot Digital Cameras, named 'Best Digital Camera' by *Camera Views* magazine, features world-famous ease of use based on the OneTouch . . . ."

By tweaking its body text and description, Snap raised its odds of placing action-oriented text into its snippet that reinforced the brand image Snap wants to convey. For your high-priority keywords, similar attention might raise your search referrals.

Tune Your Description

Time was, description metatags were extremely important in search marketing, but they grow less important each year. In the old days of Web search, the search results page showed the description text under the page title for each result, but the emergence of snippets changed all that.

Because descriptions do not display as part of your viewable page in the browser, they have no impact on persuading a customer to convert. What little impact your description has is limited to rankings and referrals.

For some search engines, such as Google, descriptions have *no* impact on search rankings. Google typically ignores the description when deciding both whether your page appears in the search results and how high it ranks. Yahoo! seems to give text found in descriptions some weight, but far less than for text found in the body.

As discussed previously, snippets are *very* important in driving referrals to your page. Yahoo! frequently excerpts description occurrences of keywords for its snippets. Google has used descriptions in its snippets at times in the past, but seems to do so infrequently at the moment. Snippet algorithms change regularly, so you might want to check sources found in Chapter 16 for the most current information.

So what's a search marketer to do? Our advice is to spend a *little* time ensuring that your search landing pages have good descriptions. It does not take very long, and you never know when it might help. Use the tips presented in this chapter to optimize your description text in case it is selected as a snippet. There is no restriction to how long a description can be, but search engine snippets are about 100 to 200 characters, so there is no point making descriptions too long. You can knock yourself out crafting multiple sentences to influence your snippet for several keywords, but that is probably worth your time only for your most critical landing pages and keywords.

Fix Your Body Text

Before you became a search marketing expert, you might not have realized that there was any more to a Web page besides what you saw in your browser. All of the text and the images the browser displays on the screen are contained in the *body* of the Web page, signified by the <body> tag in your Web page's HTML.

Except for whatever is excerpted for your snippet, the body has no effect on search referrals, but it is very important for organic search rankings and the most important part of your landing page for Web conversions (for paid and organic search). In addition, paid placement vendors are increasingly inspecting paid search landing pages to make sure that the page is relevant to the keywords purchased for that page, so paying attention to your keyword prominence and density still makes sense.

As you saw, the most prominent placement for your targeted keyword is in the title, but to get strong rankings, you need keywords present in the body, too. Search engines look at the body as a single area when determining keyword density and prominence, but not all words in the body are treated equally for ranking purposes:

- *Headings.* Within the body, keywords found within headings are given higher weight than elsewhere. Because visitors treat headings as more important than other text, the search engines do, too. Although all headings carry more clout than surrounding text, an <h1> tag is more powerful than lesser headings. Keywords found in heading tags are among the most prominent placements on the page. Web feeds, such as RSS and Atom, use title tags for the headings of posts.

- *Opening text.* Keywords that occur at the top of the page have more impact than text that occurs later. Because most pages summarize their central concepts in the first few words, search engines give these words more authority when determining relevance. The most prominent body placement of a keyword is inside a heading tag within the opening text.

- *Emphasized text.* Bold and italicized keywords stand out to a visitor, so search engines give them somewhat more consideration, too.

- *Links.* This is the oddball of this group, because although the anchor text in a link tag is very important, its importance is credited to the page being linked to, not the page the link appears on. As discussed in Chapter 13, some of the most important text for your page is the text that *other* pages use when they link to your page. Links from other *sites* are considered far more credible than links within your own site, but it can be helpful for you to carefully choose your anchor text to reflect keywords even for intra-site links, because they do carry some weight.

- *Everything else.* Keywords found anywhere on the page have some value, but not as much as if they were in placements listed above. This content includes paragraph tags and many others, but none are treated as more important than the others.

Although different body elements count more than others, good writing is not assembled piecemeal—dropping a bold word here and a heading there. If you write naturally, you are likely to use the right number of keywords without making it sound like a keyword-stuffed mess. Some writers like to read their copy out loud so that they can listen to it as well as see it. They say that if it sounds stupid, it is.

Poorly optimized body copy can sometimes lean to the other extreme. Sometimes the targeted keyword is not mentioned even once in the body copy. (We saw that Snap had a meager one occurrence.) Here are some tips for crafting your body text for top rankings and high conversions:

- *Keep it short.* Search engines will index as many as 100,000 characters on your page, but it is virtually impossible to maintain strong keyword density over a very long page—the best pages are usually less than 1,000 words. Short pages aid conversion, too. Web visitors do not *read* your pages the way they read a book. They *scan* for what they are looking for—long pages are much harder to scan.

- *Write with variety.* Using variations of your keywords in your copy helps both rankings and conversions. Because searchers do not use the exact same keywords each time they search, peppering your text with both singular and plural forms, varying verb tenses, and using different word orders help your page be found no matter what searchers type. Moreover, writing with variety overcomes tendencies toward the stultifying, repetitive prose that marks amateurish search optimization. Because your writing is easier to read, you will attract more links to your site and higher conversions.

- *Think location.* Search engines are increasingly taking searchers' locations into account. If you are a local business, make sure that all the variations of your place names are woven into your content so that search engines know where you are located. Search engines increasingly attempt to match local searchers with local organizations.

- *Think local.* For global marketers, translating pages to local languages can endanger your search marketing. Don't settle for a correct translation—you must do your keyword research over again for each country and language and get the "just right" keywords. The difference between a correct word and the best keyword could cost you a lot of conversions. And insist on translators paying attention to the same prominence, density, and other writing techniques listed here.

- *Think like a newspaper reporter.* Start out with the most important information up front. Continue to emphasize important concepts throughout, and wind up with a strong conclusion.

- *Think like a direct marketer.* How do direct marketers get you to open the envelope? To read the copy? To respond? You must think about your title and your snippet and your body text as your direct marketing copy. Study how direct marketers use language to hook you and offer strong calls to action with a sense of urgency. Don't settle for "click here" links. And don't forget to analyze all the pages between your landing page and your conversion page—visitors can abandon your site as easily as they dump a direct-mail piece that misses the mark. Raise your conversions with compelling and action-oriented direct marketing copy throughout your site.

- *Avoid tricks.* Do *not* go overboard as a direct marketer. Avoid the dark side full of tricks and hype—they work even less well on the Web than they do in direct marketing. Stay accurate and factual. Eschew overblown hype-laden prose and, of course, stay away from stupid content tricks that spam the search engines.

The challenge of writing good copy with these tips in mind underscores how difficult it is to optimize for multiple keywords. You will find that aiming for good keyword prominence and density limits the number of keywords you target—they cannot all be the first words on the page. Even worse, the more subjects you write about, the harder it is to achieve proper density for any of them. Recalling our work on Table 12-1 on meaning elements, you can pepper partial keyword phrases into your writing to aid readability. Rather than constantly referring to "SnapShot digital cameras," you might use "SnapShot" and "digital cameras" separately sometimes. Examining your meaning elements will guide the best separations. As we learned in Chapter 2, search engines look for multiple-word keyword elements in proximity to each other, so it is not necessary for you to use the entire set of words together every time.

In addition to well-written copy, you want your page to be well designed. Technical folks like to speak about "clean" code—HTML that is so well structured and organized that it is easy to understand and maintain. That clean code is good for your extended team as they maintain the page, but it's a pleasure for spiders, too. And the easiest way to maintain clean code is with a Cascading Style Sheet (CSS for short).

Pages that use CSS files can be remarkably smaller than other pages because all the formatting instructions are in the CSS file, not on the page. It is common for half of a traditional HTML file to be formatting instructions, with the other half the text to display. The less formatting instructions, the easier it is for the spider, and the more of your pages can be crawled in less time.

CSS files also enable you to use more modern page-layout techniques rather than tables or (please, no!) frames. Tables are fine for information laid out in rows and columns, but too many Web pages are designed as one big table with the left navigation as a long column, for example. Although this produces the desired result onscreen, the tortured markup is very difficult to correctly maintain and for spiders to interpret. Sites coded without tables sometimes rank higher. CSS files enable you to use <div> tags and other techniques to place your text anywhere on the page, so you can put your most important content nearer the top of the page where the spider wants to see it.

As with all tools, you must be careful how you use style sheets. It is possible for you to define your own set of tags with names of your choosing, but make sure you keep the basic ones intact. Heading (<h1> through <h6>) tags, especially, should be used with their traditional names so that spiders know to treat that text with increased importance. You can define any appearance for these tags that you want, so being limited in the use of the name will not crimp your style.

Clearly, the body element of your Web page drives both your search rankings and Web conversions. We have seen many tips to improve the writing and the coding of your body text—it might seem a bit complicated to you. Don't worry. It gets easier from here as we look at some simple rules for managing the parts of your page that are *not* text.

Handle Nontext Elements Properly

As you know, spiders cannot understand images. They do not interpret JavaScript. So these parts of the page don't matter, right? Wrong. Carefully craft your nontext page elements to avoid these common problems:

- *Embedded scripts and style sheets.* Throughout this book, we have cautioned you on misuse of JavaScript, and to a lesser extent, style sheets. Used wisely, however, both JavaScript and style sheets improve your site's appearance and usability. But don't embed large scripts or style sheets within your Web pages. It is okay for a few lines to be embedded here or there, but anything longer should be "offloaded" (as the techies say) to an external file that is called by the page. You saw in Chapter 10 how bloated pages impede crawling. It is also true that these elements can push the real content further down into the file, harming keyword prominence.

- *Overemphasis on images.* There is no harm in having many images on your landing page, so long as they are not crowding out your text. If your page becomes so image-laden that there is precious little text left, you *can* cause a few problems. First, if you have fewer than two dozen words, the search engine might not correctly identify the language of your page, putting it at risk of being erroneously excluded from queries using language filters. That same lack of text can make it quite challenging to provide enough keyword occurrences to attain high rankings, and you might also hurt your page's conversion rate if the images are not as persuasive as some well-written text would be.

- *Text hidden in images.* Frequently, page headings are bold and big—and invisible to the spider. All because they are coded as images rather than as heading (<h1> through <h6>) tags. Heading tags are prominent placements of your keywords—don't hide the keywords from the spider.

- *Poor alt text.* Too often, descriptive text for images is either hurriedly constructed or missing completely. The HTML <img> tag is designed to help visually impaired visitors (and those who use text-only browsers) determine what the images contain, by allowing you to specify some alternative (alt) text. This text is shown (or spoken if you are visually impaired) when visitors mouse over an image. In addition, spiders will index this text, so make sure it is an accurate description of the picture. Use keywords in the alt text if appropriate, but don't "stuff" keywords unrelated to the picture—that's spam.

Painstaking attention to nontext page elements can improve your search rankings. If ignored or handled sloppily, nontext elements can undermine your best efforts on your text. So make proper coding of nontext elements one of your priorities.

Optimize Dynamic Content

We've served up a bevy of tips on optimizing your content—everything from working over your titles to coding alternate text for your images. All of those tips are important, and they apply to every Web page. If you are working on a static landing page—one that is stored in an HTML file on your server—you can skip this section. However, you have a few more things to learn if you need to optimize a dynamic page.

You recall that dynamic pages are generated on-the-fly by a software program whenever a visitor (or a spider) requests the URL. You know that dynamic sites can pose a number of problems for spiders, as discussed in Chapter 10. Now let's look at how dynamic sites generate their pages and how you can ensure they are optimized for search marketing.

Dynamic pages are created by software programs that use two different kinds of information:

- *Templates.* For each type of dynamic page, the software program fills in a shell with dynamic content (content that can be different every time the program displays the page). Figure 12-10 shows a dynamic page with the content in the template overlaid in gray.

The content in the template is the same on every page that uses that template. In this case, all books sold by Prentice Hall have a page driven by a template, and the template causes them to have a common look and feel.

- *Database information.* The dynamic content that makes each page different is drawn from some kind of database. It could be a content management system or an e-Commerce catalog or any kind of database at all. Prentice Hall maintains a database that has a record for each book that it publishes and the software that generates the page fills in the title, the author, the ISBN number, the price, the excerpt, and other information on the page.

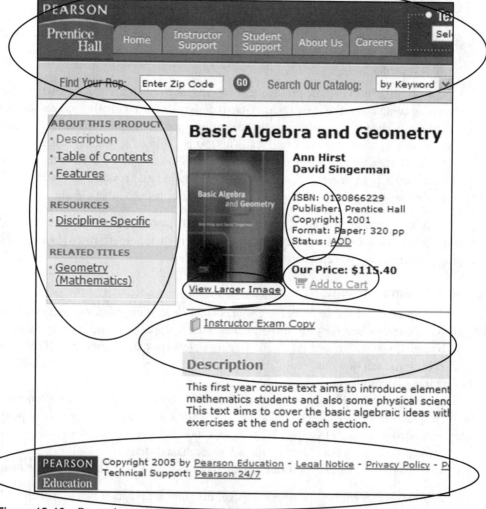

Figure 12-10   Dynamic pages use templates. The circled areas contain text generated by a template, with the rest of the text coming from a database.

The figure can show you how the template looks on the screen, but more is going on behind the scenes than that. The template actually contains all the HTML coding that formats the page—the database contains only the information to be filled into the template.

By now, you might be thinking, "That's all very interesting, but what does it mean to me?" Search marketers need to understand this split between template and content to optimize dynamic pages, because the template is controlled by different people than the content is.

Your Web developers usually control the template. In some cases, it is a separate file that is easily updated—most content management systems work that way. At other times, the HTML is stored inside the software program itself, which means that the programmers must modify the software to change the HTML.

The content, on the other hand, is managed by the operations people who maintain the database. Sometimes these folks are writers, because the content contains long prose fields that require the same care in writing as static HTML pages. For some kinds of pages, however, the content is a long list of features and specifications reminiscent of a printed catalog—if the content requires no writing ability, it might be maintained by data entry operators who key in the data and make sure it is correct.

So, every piece of text on the screen comes from either the template or the database. And every HTML tag comes from the template. That's important to understand when you want changes made to the dynamic page.

All the tips in this chapter apply to dynamic pages. Dynamic pages have titles, and you want them to drive rankings and referrals. Dynamic pages have descriptions. They have body text. To the spider, the HTML of a dynamic page looks the same as for a static page. Both kinds of pages are ranked against each other in the same ways.

If there is no static HTML file, however, how do you optimize a dynamic page? There is no single answer to that question—every situation differs slightly. Here are a few scenarios that will give you the idea of what you will be up against:

- *There are no title tags on my pages*. That's obviously not a good thing for search marketing. Without titles, your pages are unlikely to be highly ranked in the search results and will get low clickthrough. It turns out that the developer left the title tag out of the template for the product catalog. One template change later, your catalog pages have titles.

- *Yeah, but all the titles are the same*. Okay, that's still not great. It turns out that the developer just plugged some boilerplate text into the template, when it should have been taken from the database. Now the developer has changed the program so that the titles are being generated from the product name field in the database.

- *Um, but the titles are wrong*. Yeah, about that—the data entry folks said that the product name field has never been checked all that carefully because it was never used for anything before. Now that they know how important it is, they can fix the data in the next couple of weeks so the names are right.

- *Okay, but I noticed the descriptions have the same text on every page.* Well, that *is* a problem. We do not have a field in the database for description text for every product. We can add the field, but it will take a couple of months to change the database design and the template, and then wait for the operations team to write descriptions for every product in the catalog.

All right, it is not always as frustrating as that, but changing a dynamic page usually takes more persuasive powers and more time than getting a static page changed. That's the bad news. The good news is that when you persuade your extended team to change one dynamic page, they usually change them all. With static pages, when you have changed one, you have changed, uh, one. So it is harder to change one dynamic page than one static page, but it is easier to change them all.

Dynamic content has other benefits, too. It is perfect for trusted feed programs. If you want to participate in shopping search engines or any other paid inclusion program, having your content stored in databases makes it far simpler to do.

Another advantage of dynamic content is quality control. Static pages are usually created with HTML editing tools that cannot check the content of the page, except to validate the HTML. Because dynamic page content is drawn from databases, you can ensure that the database update process checks the content itself. For example, if your company's model numbers always start with two letters followed by five numbers, your update process can check for that when data is entered.

Let's explore a scenario for optimizing dynamic content. The page that Snap Electronics wants to optimize for its *digital cameras* keyword *is* a dynamic page. That means that no one can change its title directly, because no static page contains that title tag. That title tag is generated, along with the rest of the page, by a program that uses a template in conjunction with content stored in a database—in this case, Snap's e-Commerce catalog database.

An inspection of the template shows how the current "Snap Electronics digital cameras for you" title is generated. The template record that generates the title (text: "<title>Snap Electronics" field: PRODCAT text: "for you</title>") produces the title tag followed by the company name, grabs the product category field from the catalog database ("digital cameras" for this page), and finally adds the "for you" text and the title end tag.

The marketing team at Snap prefers the new title to be "Snap Digital Cameras —Save on a SnapShot digital camera," but it might take some thinking to pull it off. The Web developers proposed a new template record (text: "<title>Snap" field: PRODCAT text: "—Save on" field: PRODCAT text: "</title>"), which would produce a title of "Snap digital cameras—Save on digital cameras"—not exactly what the marketing folks had in mind.

The marketing folks asked the developers why they could not add the word *SnapShot* to the template, to come closer to the original idea, but the developers explained that the template is used for all product catalog hub pages, and they cannot use the SnapShot brands name on pages for VCRs and TVs. (They have their own brand names.) As it was, every product catalog hub page would now have the "Save on" call to action in its title, but the marketing folks thought that was okay. The impasse was averted when the developers agreed to change the product category name to "SnapShot digital cameras" in the database. By adding the word "Electronics" to the template record, the title now reads 'Snap Electronics SnapShot digital cameras—Save on Snap-Shot digital cameras"—not exactly what marketing wanted, but acceptable for now. The developers agreed that they could eventually add a title field to the database allowing the data entry folks to enter any title they wanted for each product in the catalog, but that will take a couple of months to pull off.

Dynamic content is the most efficient way to power large sites with many similar pages. With the right attention to detail, you can optimize your dynamic site for search as easily as a static site.

Summary

Content is king, at least in the land of search engines. The quality and relevance of your content is the biggest factor in succeeding in search marketing—*that* is why optimizing your content is so important.

In this chapter, you learned what search engines are looking for and how you approach writing for them. This chapter covered the steps in a content-optimization process that stresses iteration—working the process over and over until you succeed. No one will optimize a page properly the first try. Failure is normal. What matters is how many times you will take another crack at it until your pages finally deliver the search marketing value you expected.

We deferred the discussion of one of the major ways search engines discern the quality of pages—link analysis. In the next chapter, we investigate the importance of links to your pages. We show you how to increase the high-quality links to your site that attract more visitors and impress the search engines, too.

CHAPTER 13

Attract Links to Your Site

Suppose that you open an e-mail that has a link in it to a news story on the Web. You click it, and read the headline of the story: "Senator Possibly Implicated in Voter Fraud." You read the story, assessing its credibility. Would the story be credible if it were from the Web site of NBC News? The *Washington Post*? The Drudge Report? The *National Enquirer*? Some blogger you have never heard of? You are unlikely to give the same credence to that report regardless of the source, because not all sources have the same reputation in your mind. Now understand, some people might have a higher opinion of some sources of information than you do, and regardless of anyone's opinion, even the source held in the lowest regard can be correct on a particular story while the most-respected can be wrong.

Despite occasional surprises, reputation *is* an effective shortcut for evaluating the quality of information presented to us. Organic search engines use a similar shortcut. Search engines judge the reputation of every Web site so that they can present the highest-quality content—the content with the best reputation. Search engines have a few ways of judging the quality of content, discussed as **page ranking factors** in Chapter 12, "Optimize Your Content." By far the biggest element of a search engine's view of your page's reputation is driven by links.

If your Web site is well known, you might already have attracted many links. Perhaps you think that you have no need to improve the links coming to your site. But even some large companies, such as WebMD (www.webmd.com), the well-known medical information site, attract fewer links than they could. WebMD had more than 12,000 links at one time, but virtually all of them to its home page, with few links to the disease information pages that drive referrals from informational queries. WebMD ranked #1 for queries for "webmd," but not for "allergies." A campaign to attract links to WebMD's interior pages changed all that, and it can help your site, too.

Although links are used by search engines just for organic results, search marketers planning only paid campaigns might want to read on as well, because links help your site regardless of their impact on search. Links drive visitors to your site—visitors who follow those links—and those added visitors mean more Web conversions. But links also improve your organic search results, and in this chapter you learn all about the relationship between links and organic search:

- *Why search engines value links.* Every link to your page is a "vote" for its quality. Organic search engines tally the votes when they decide which pages possess the highest quality for their search results.

- *Your link-building philosophy.* Many search marketers pull their hair out trying to out-guess the search engines' ranking algorithms, but there is a better way.

- *Step-by-step link building for your site.* Link building is not easy, but when you know what to do, you can pull it off. Your site will benefit both from improved search rankings and from more visitors following the links.

Before starting your own link-building campaign, let's examine why links are so important to search engines.

Why Search Engines Value Links

"Content is king"—or at least it reigned during the Internet boom years of the late 1990s. But content is not the real change ushered in by the Web. The Web content itself is not remarkably different from what you can read in books, magazines, or newspapers. What *does* differ is the ease with which surfers can move from one piece of content to the next—that's the power of links. Links changed the way people consume content; they can now navigate easily across different sources that once required meandering amid library stacks—after schlepping to the library in the first place.

Just as links transformed readers' content consumption, links changed the game for search engines, too. With the advent of Google in 1998, search engines began to use links to judge the quality of every page on the Web. Although Google was the first to apply this insight to Web searches, precursors to hypertext links have historically been employed to judge the value of information.

Scientific papers have long relied on **citations**—references to previous papers that attest to the correctness of a basic concept. Scientists vie for the honor of having the most citations to their papers, because when later papers cite a scientist's original work, it provides a rough estimation of that original paper's value. Similarly, new patents regularly refer to "prior art" in old patents, so they can build their ideas on top of the solid ground of previous ideas. These precursors to Web links served the same purpose—they created a kind of "information economy" in which the best ideas are discovered because the most experts refer to them.

This information economy, not the content itself, is the most striking feature of the Web. Content on any subject can be created easily by anyone. Higher-quality information tends to attract more links than mediocre or poor content. When thousands or millions of pages are voluntarily linked to an article, it is a strong recommendation for its quality. You can think of the authors of each of those pages recommending that article, much the same way you might recommend a good plumber or a capable auto mechanic. When you recommend a person, you are providing someone access into your network of trusted associates. When your page links to another page, you are providing access to your network of trusted information. It is that trust, built up by the recommendations of thousands or millions of people, that allows search engines to conclude that the article in question is valuable, trustworthy information. In this way, we could say that it is not *what* your page knows, but *who* it knows—links to your page cause it to be treated with respect regardless of its actual content.

However, it is not that simple, of course. Just as that plumber must have knowledge (what he knows) to continue to attract recommendations from whom he knows, so does your page require strong information to attract links. But the links themselves are what we are interested in here. In Chapter 12, we looked at how search engines assess your content, but now let's see how they value links to and from your page.

How Web Sites Link

Links between Web pages use an HTML tag, just like all other content, as shown in Figure 13-1. The figure shows an **internal** link—a link from one page to another within the same domain (Web site). Of more interest to search engines are **external** links, which connect one Web site to another, because those links indicate more impartial recommendations. Web sites use these endorsements to determine which sites have the most linked-to pages—the pages with the most **inbound** links. Inbound links act as a surrogate for the quality and trustworthiness of the content, which search engines cannot discern from merely looking at the words on the page.

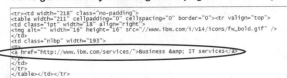

Figure 13-1   How links are coded in HTML. Web page links use the HTML anchor tag to show the (usually) underlined text on the screen for that link.

AltaVista, Compaq, and IBM have advanced the **bow-tie theory**—that the Web is actually composed of four kinds of pages, each with its own peculiar linking patterns:

- *Core pages.* Comprising 30 percent of the Web, these pages are the most linked-to and linked-from on the Web. The most popular Web sites tend to have many pages in this group.

- *Origination pages.* Approximately 24 percent of all pages have numerous links *into* the core but relatively few *from* the core. These pages might be new or not terribly high quality, so they have not attracted the links back to them that would mark them as part of the core.

- *Destination pages.* Another 24 percent of the Web consists of pages that are commonly linked *from* the core, but do not themselves link back *into* the core. These pages are typically high-quality pages, but they might be corporate Web sites that tend to link internally more then externally.

- *Disconnected pages.* The remaining pages (22 percent) are not directly connected to the core—they might have links to or from origination and destination sites, or they might be linked only to other disconnected pages.

As you look at Figure 13-2, understand that the pages are categorized comparatively. Origination pages tend to have far more links *into* the core than *from* the core, with destination pages just the opposite tendency. Getting one directory listing for an origination page does not change it to a core page, but getting a number of inbound links from core pages would.

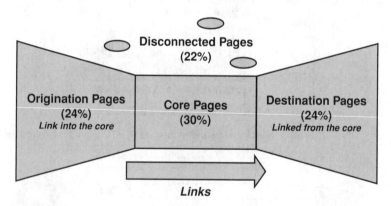

Figure 13-2   The bow-tie theory of the Web. Research shows a core of Web pages have the most links, with other pages feeding or being fed by the core.

For the search marketer, the importance of the bow-tie theory is that core and destination pages have the highest link popularity. Those are the best pages to get links *from*. As you can imagine, destination pages tend not to link to many other external pages, leaving just the core pages as the best targets to get links from. Garnering links from origination pages and disconnected pages will not bring you as many visitors and will not carry the same weight with search engines.

How Link Popularity Works

We introduced link popularity in Chapter 2, "How Search Engines Work," and in Chapter 12, "Optimize Your Content," where we explained that link popularity is a critical (for some search engines, *the* most critical) page ranking factor. Many search experts believe that as few as 25 *high-quality* links to your site can significantly increase your search rankings, but attracting 25 such links might not come easily for all sites. Remember, links from 25 mediocre sites (or worse, from 25 poor sites) will not help your page to rank any higher.

Figure 13-3 shows an exaggerated example of how important link popularity can be. If you search for the phrase "miserable failure" in Google, you will find President George W. Bush's official biography as the #1 result. Why? Because enough disgruntled Democrats have linked to that page with the words "miserable failure" as the anchor text in their links. (Not to be outdone, similarly vexed Republicans have made former Democratic president Jimmy Carter the #2 result for the same query.) As you can see from the figure, the words *miserable failure* do not appear anywhere on the page, but Google places such great weight on anchor text from links that it makes this page #1 anyway.

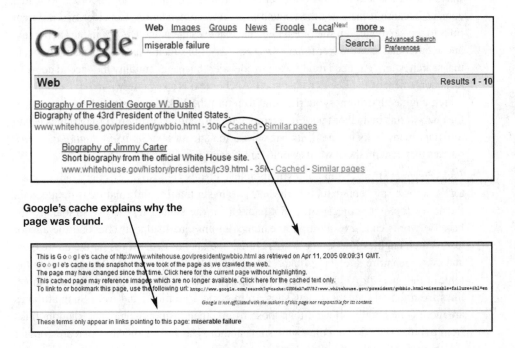

Figure 13-3 Link popularity run amuck. Google places such weight on link popularity that it overrides the page content, sometimes leading to comical results.

Not all search engines emphasize link popularity to the extent that Google does, but they all give it strong weight in their ranking algorithms. Search engines evaluate a page's link popularity in four basic ways:

- *Link quantity*. In general, pages receiving more links to them rank higher than pages with few links, but all links are not created equal, as discussed next.

- *Link quality*. Everyone has an opinion, but some are worth more than others. Opinions expressed by those creating links are no different. A link to a page is an endorsement of that page, but endorsements have more value from well-respected and authoritative sources than from others. Search engines determine authority by examining the link popularity of the site linked *from*. So, if a high-authority site (one that itself has many other high-authority sites linking to it) links to your page, it is conferring some of its authority on your page. Search engines attribute the highest page ranking factors to pages with many links from high-quality sites. But it is even more complicated than that. Search engines mathematically split the authority conveyed to each linked page based on the number of links—a high-authority page with 3 links conveys more authority to each linked page than an equally high-authority page containing 50 links conveys. The theory is that there is only so much authority to go around and the more links there are, the less of a recommendation each linked page is getting.

- *Anchor text*. The text that the visitor clicks to follow the link is very important to search engines because it provides the context of the recommendation. Consider two different links to the personal Web site of Pat Lee, one that uses the name *Pat Lee* in the anchor text and another that uses the words *tax expert Pat Lee* as the anchor text. Both clearly indicate that searches for "Pat Lee" might want to consider this page, but only the second conveys an endorsement of Pat Lee as a tax expert. Anchor text is a key query ranking factor in the search engine algorithms—queries tend to return the linked pages that have variants of the query terms in anchor text. For example, if our fictitious firm Snap Electronics began to attract many links to one of its pages with the anchor text *SnapShot digital cameras*, queries that contain those words would rank Snap's page higher than before.

- *Link relevancy*. Links from contextually relevant sites are also a key query ranking factor. When we say "contextually relevant," we mean that the information is on a certain theme (or topic or subject)—it is not enough for the anchor text to use similar words, because words can have multiple meanings on unrelated subjects. Beyond the anchor text, search engines look at the words around the anchor text, words on the entire page and even the entire site being linked from. Why? Because sites that are relevant to the topic of the query provide more relevant links than others. Continuing the Snap example, links from digital camera review sites, from camera retailers, and from Snap affiliates are more contextually relevant than those from a teen fashion magazine. Random links from popular sites do not convey the same authority as links from sites that are popular *and* thematically related.

If these factors seem hard to calculate, you are getting the idea. It is rather amazing that search engines can consider so many complicated factors in the second between the searcher's query and the results page, but they do. Search engines attribute high *page* ranking factors to pages with many high-quality links to those pages. Search engines attribute high *query* ranking factors to pages with inbound links that are both from contextually relevant sites and contain the query words in their anchor text. Those factors are mixed together, along with many other factors discussed in Chapter 12, to determine which pages rank first for a query.

So how do search engines calculate the value of links to a page (the biggest part of the page ranking factor)? As you might expect, each use different detailed techniques, but they have some basics in common, built around the theory of **hub** and **authority** pages:

- *Hub pages.* Web pages that link to several or many other pages on a similar subject. We have spoken of the hub page for Snap's digital cameras—it is the page with links to the rest of the pages on Snap's site on that subject. But other pages are hubs, too. If you create a page on your site that links to the best pages on the Web on a particular subject, that makes your page a hub for that subject. One reason that directory links are so powerful is that the subject (or topic or theme) of the directory is a powerful clue as to the subject of the pages linked to—these directory pages are also hubs.

- *Authority pages.* Web pages that are linked to by many other pages on a particular subject. Authority pages are the ones that search engines usually ascribe the highest page ranking factors to. And it makes sense. Pages that are most closely related to the searcher's keywords are probably authority pages.

We have expressed the concepts in terms of pages, but some search engines view hubs and authorities as clusters of pages within a site or even as sites themselves. Those engines would give more value to authorities that came from sites that had several pages that were also authorities on the same subject, for example.

Search engines try to rank authority pages higher, but the search engines use hub pages to do a better job of identifying authority pages. Because words can have multiple meanings (*windows*, for example), search engines that look only at anchor text might display pages about the wrong subject, even though those pages contain the words searched for. Hub pages can help search engines zero in on the particular meaning for a word—if an authority page is also linked by hub pages on a particular subject, search engines develop more confidence that the page is also on the right subject. Pella Windows will receive different hub links than Microsoft Windows, for example.

As discussed previously (in Chapters 2 and 12), the more pages that exist on the Web containing a keyword, the more important page factors become in the search result ranking. It makes sense, if you think about it. If your search marketing campaign is targeting a search term that very few sites use (such as a new brand name for your product line), optimizing your content and getting your pages indexed might be enough for high rankings. On the other hand, if you are trying to break through for *digital cameras*—a very popular keyword found on millions of pages—you must concentrate on factors in addition to content optimization. If it sounds confusing, it might be that you need a crash course in how to "think links"—that's next.

Your Linking Philosophy

What if all search engines got together and decided that links were no longer important? Suppose, in a blink, they all changed their ranking algorithms so that link popularity meant nothing to your page factors. Would that mean that you should not care about getting links to your site? Of course not!

Links are hugely important in and of themselves. The best links are always contextually relevant to the visitor. Those are the links you want—they drive *qualified* traffic to your site.

And that should be your linking philosophy. It sounds crazy, perhaps, but you should practically forget about search engines. If you chase what you think search engines want when it otherwise makes no sense, it will not make any sense to the search engine either. You want the links that drive the highest number of qualified visitors to your site, so that you can convert them. If you relentlessly pursue that strategy, you will find that the search engines reward you, too.

How *Not* to Get Links to Your Site

To prove the point that your best policy is to ignore what search engines think about your links, it is worth exploring the alternative. How have sites fared by chasing the algorithm to build up links? Well, it has been an interesting ride.

We begin our story back in the B.G. times—Before Google—because at that time no search engine ranked sites based on links. Sites linked to other sites purely because their visitors would benefit, so the number of links to a site was a good sign of how good its information was. From its inception, Google, in its wisdom, used the link information to determine which sites were of higher quality (that determination made up a huge part of its page ranking factors) and was able to rank the better sites at the top of its search results. This technique worked so well that many people began to use Google.

As Google began to attract more and more searchers, and as other search engines began to adopt similar page factor approaches that also relied on links, search marketers began to see how important links were. So they tried to get every site in creation to link to theirs. "Get more and more *links!*" they told themselves, no matter what the source. Search marketers with multiple unrelated sites heavily linked them all together, all in an effort to impress the search engines. For a short while it worked, but the search engines adjusted.

Search engines began to look at the quality of the site being linked from, weighing links from important sites more heavily than from unknown sites. They rated each site on the quality and quantity of links and used that rating to judge the strength of each link's endorsement. As a result, pages with links from only low-quality sites plummeted in the rankings, so the search marketers adjusted.

"Get links from the *biggest* sites!" the search marketers exclaimed. The directory frenzy was on. Find the sites that seem to be the most important and get your site listed. Yahoo! Directory and countless smaller directories were the places to be. However, the search engines noticed that many of these directories were not careful enough about what sites were linked and many popular sites seemed willing to link to almost anyone, regardless of how relevant the links were. So the search engines adjusted.

Search engines noticed that these links tended to go to the home page of each site, but the interior pages got very few links. The search engines began to place more and more emphasis on the anchor text of each link, looking for more than just the name of the company pointing to its home page. Sites with just home page links stopped getting high rankings for informational and transactional queries, so the search marketers adjusted.

"*Deep* links are what are important!" they told themselves. Soon, they started the *two-way* (reciprocal) linking frenzy. "I'll link to your pages if you link to mine," they told each other. Some sites set up dozens of links to each other to get those interior pages connected, causing the search engines to notice that two-way links do not call out quality sites as well as *one-way* links. So the search engines adjusted.

Suddenly sites loaded with reciprocal links began to fall in the search rankings, as sites with many incoming one-way links began to receive more weight. The search marketers noticed again, and they adjusted.

"We need as many *one*-way links as possible!" the marketers realized. They started littering the guest books and message boards of other sites with links to their URLs. Marketers discovered that posting to blogs was especially easy—you could even write a program to do it for you. Some of these links were legitimate services to visitors, but many were designed only for search engines to find—those links did not really identify the best sites, just the most aggressive marketers. So, the search engines adjusted.

Each search engine began to look more closely at the type of each link, placing more and more emphasis on how important the linking sites seem to be. Search engines also discounted links from pages with dozens or hundreds of links. The sites with thousands of random one-way links from guest books stopped ranking #1. Instead, the core sites (from the bow-tie theory) were thought to be more important than other sites, so *links* from those sites were also deemed more important. Again, search marketers noticed. And they adjusted.

"*Buy* one-way links!" was the new rallying cry. Because a search engine cannot tell the difference between a one-way link that was freely given from one that was purchased, search marketers went out to buy as many links as they could. They had to pay top dollar to get links from those very best core sites, on pages that did not have many other links on them, but it was worth it. For a while, at least. Until the search engines noticed that little-known sites would suddenly leap up in the rankings when nothing about the site had improved—but they had begun to get a lot of important links. So the search engines adjusted.

Search engines started downgrading links between sites that had wide disparity in popularity with no strong relevance between them. (Just why *did* that popular technology newsletter suddenly start linking to this new gambling site?) Search engines began to downgrade sites that were new or small that take sudden leaps in link popularity, assuming that they have bought their links.

"Relevant links are what are important!" they told themselves. And they were right. Relevant sites linked to other relevant sites. They linked to home pages and to deep interior pages. Is that the way the story ends? Only in fairy tales. This story never really ends. It will go on as long as there are search engines and search marketers to adjust to each other.

And our story was a fairy tale, too. The evolution of ranking algorithms and search marketer behavior is far more complex than our little story shows—it did not play out in the neat order we show here—but you get the point. You can decide to play this game of cat and mouse with the search engines, but we recommend that you play a different game instead. Our game takes a lot less energy, and you will not be subjected to bumpy ups and downs in your rankings every time the algorithm zigs when you zag.

So what should your linking philosophy *really* be?

STUPID LINKING TRICKS

Just like there are many excellent places to look for links, there are a number of techniques to avoid. Many people attempt to fool the search engines, but they are getting harder and harder to fool with tricks like these:

- *Blog spamming.* A *blog* (short for Web log) is an online personal journal—kind of a periodic column on the Web. Sometimes blogs are almost like reading someone's private diary, but others are more like magazine columns that tightly focus on a subject of interest. Many blogs are very popular and well written, and search engines treat them with the same importance as a well-crafted Web page, so links from these blogs are important to search marketers. Readers can subscribe to blogs to read the latest post and usually post comments themselves—which is where the trouble is. As Figure 13-4 shows, blog spammers post unrelated messages containing links to URLs that the spammer wants to boost in the search rankings. Many bloggers now block readers from posting comments.

- *Guest book spamming.* This trick is similar to the blog trick. A **guest book** allows visitors to post their contact information and comments about a Web site. Unfortunately, spammers began to post their site's URLs in guest book comments to impress search engines. Both blog and guest book spammers actually use programs to automatically post their URLs, allowing them to add thousands of links with no manual effort.

- *Link farms.* Tricky search marketers set up dozens or hundreds of sites that can be crawled by search engines, just so they can put in thousands of links to sites they want to boost in search rankings. "Free-for-all" sites allow anyone to post a link on any topic, and are similarly not recommended. Later in this chapter, we explain how to steer clear of links designed just to fool the search engines.

- *Hidden links.* Just as we discussed hidden text in Chapter 12, you can hide links using the same techniques. Hiding links allows your links to be seen by spiders but not by people, so you can load up lots of links on high-ranking pages to other pages that you are trying to boost.

As with content tricks, it is not very easy to fool the search engines, so tricks designed to fake out search engines usually do not work. You should also be aware of a couple of tricks designed to fool *you*:

- *Link e-mail spamming.* Rather then spamming the search indexes, this trick spams the inboxes of Webmasters, requesting links from their sites. Spammers even buy programs adept at unleashing this e-mail spam on unsuspecting Webmasters. Later in this chapter, we show you the right way to collect links from other sites. (If you are on the receiving end of a link request that does not look as though the person has ever seen your site, treat it like all spam and do not respond.)

- *Fake two-way links.* Many sites will link to yours if you link to theirs in return, but some try to trick you by employing links that search engines cannot see. That way, you think you got the link back but the search engines fail to give you credit for it, allowing your "partner" to get credit for the more valuable one-way link from your site. Chapter 10, "Get Your Site Indexed," explained which links spiders do not see, so you must check your two-way links to make sure you get what you bargained for. Go to the linking site with JavaScript turned off and see whether the link to your site works.

Our advice: Make sure you are not being fooled and do not be in the business of fooling search engines or anyone else.

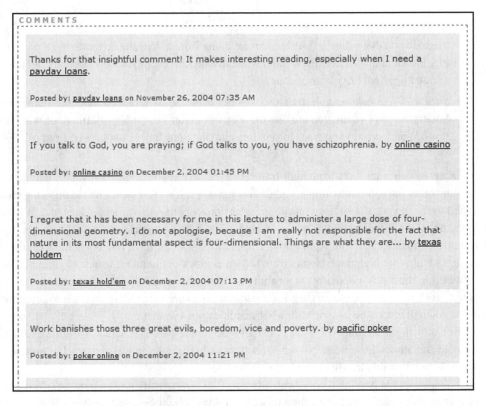

Figure 13-4 Blog spamming. Off-the-subject comments are posted to this blog merely to show search engines one-way links to two gambling sites.

Think About Visitors First

Sound familiar? Yeah, it's the same advice we gave you for content in Chapter 12. It works just as well for links. And it makes sense, if you stop to think about why links are valuable to you. First and foremost, links drive visitors to your site—visitors who come to your site because they followed the links. These extra visitors can complete your Web conversions the same way that searchers can.

So how do you drive the most conversions from visitors who follow links? You start by thinking about which sites can deliver the most qualified visitors to yours:

- *Sites with lots of traffic*. It's nice to get a link, but all links do not drive the same amount of traffic. The same links on a site with heavy traffic will drive a lot more visitors than one on an unpopular site.

- *Sites related to yours*. Heavy traffic to your site is nice, but you want *qualified* traffic. If you want to sell digital cameras, you want links from sites that prospective camera purchasers frequent. You want links from camera review sites, from digital photography magazines, from photo software sites—you get the idea. If you would buy an ad in a magazine on that subject, you should want a link from a Web site on that same topic. Getting lots of unqualified extra visitors who have no interest in your site does not help anyone and does not drive conversions.

- *Sites with less competition.* It can sometimes be better to attract an inbound link from a low-traffic page where you are one of three links than from a high-traffic page with 100 links. What odds do you want for visitors clicking your link (1 out of 3 or 1 out of 100)?

Okay, so you want links from high-traffic sites related to yours, especially sites that do not have many other links. Sounds simple, right? In some ways, it is. You want links to drive the most qualified traffic to your site so that you can increase conversions—this strategy does that. What is amazing about this simple strategy, however, is that it will give you the best search rankings, too. If you attract links to your site from popular relevant pages that have few other links on them, your pages will score high page factors from search engines. Remember, search engines are forever tweaking their link popularity algorithms to better reflect the quality that human visitors impute to each page. If you identify the links you want because they will draw the most qualified visitors, you will always be in sync with what search engines want, too.

But knowing what links you want is actually the simple part. It is harder, we admit, to actually go out and attract those links, but we cover how to do that later in this chapter. For now, let's look a little more closely at what kind of links you want.

Think about the bow-tie theory, with a twist. (Can you actually twist a bow-tie?) You want to be part of "the core"—and depending on your site, you might be able to achieve that (maybe even do it rapidly). However, it might be helpful to think about every subject or theme having its *own* bow-tie with its own core. Snap Electronics wants its site in the core, yes, but it should think about placing the digital camera area of its site in the *core for digital cameras*. Because a search engine looks at the thematic content of your pages and of your overall site, it asks, "What subject is this page about?" It checks which words are commonly used on your site and correlates those words to popular subjects. You can think about the search engines discerning the bow-tie relationships between all the sites on a certain subject—these are the sites that get the highest page ranking factors for queries on that subject. Any query relating to digital cameras will tend to find core and destination sites from the digital cameras bow-tie.

If you seek out relevant, popular sites, especially sites that do not have many competing links on them, you will be targeting the right sources for your inbound links.

The Harder a Link Is to Get, the More Valuable It Might Be

Attracting links to your site is, unfortunately, one of the tougher things to do in search marketing. If you start with the right philosophy—think about your visitors first—you will be off to a great start. However, you must realize that there is no quick fix in building quality links to your site.

It isn't hard to get links to your site—if you aren't picky about their quality. If you do not mind getting links that drive little traffic, you can get them quite easily. You send out some e-mails to a bunch of Webmasters and offer them a link if they give you one. You both dump links on rarely visited pages that have dozens of other links on them and off you go. You have links.

But how valuable are those links? If the pages containing the links are not heavily visited, how many visitors will come? If the sites are not related to yours, how qualified will they be? If the sites are not well respected, will their recommendation of your site engender deeper trust? Exactly what do you get from such links? Table 13-1 shows the value that you should place on links from different places—it is the same value that search engines place on the links, by the way. The table is a gross oversimplification—there are more than just two kinds of Web sites and five kinds of links—but is instructive anyway. Look closely at the table and see the pattern. The more-popular site's link is always better than the less-popular site's link of the same kind, but some links from average sites can be valuable (and are often easier to get).

Table 13-1 The Value of Links to Search Engines (Search engines increase your page ranking factor by different amounts based on where the links originate.)

Type of Link	From an Average Site	From a Popular Site
Internal links From one page on your site to another page on your site	None	Very low
Within the family From a page on one of your sites to another of your sites	Very low	Low
Two-way Trading links back and forth with another site	Low	Medium
One-way crowded A link from a page with many links from another site	Low	Medium
One-way sparse A link from a page with few links from another site	Medium	High

You might see a pattern here. The links that are most valuable are actually the toughest to get. Anyone can set up internal links from one page on a site to another, but it takes more effort to negotiate two-way links with another site. It is harder still to get a popular site to send a one-way link in your direction. For example, it typically takes three to six months (or more) to get added to the Open Directory (www.dmoz.org). This exclusivity is one of the reasons search engines give "extra credit" to pages included in DMOZ. Because there is a human review process, directory links are highly regarded by search engines.

In general, search engines are smart and getting smarter. The best links for your visitors might be difficult to get, but they are the ones that search engines reward, too. Later in this chapter, we show you how to go about getting those links so that you attract both visitors and search engines.

HOW SEARCH ENGINES DETECT LINKS THAT ARE "WITHIN THE FAMILY"

At this point, some of you might be looking for the shortcut. You probably did not pick up this book to drive traffic to your site based on links—you care about links only because they are a means to higher search rankings. And you already know that search engines value some kinds of links, such as one-way links, more than others, such as two-way or internal links. Maybe you do not believe that search engines can recognize each type of link, but they can.

Actually, you probably *do* believe that search engines can identify internal links, and you are right. Obviously, a link between two URLs with the same domain (www.your-company.com) is easy to spot. You might also be convinced that search engines can detect whether there are numerous links on a page, or whether two sites link back and forth to each other. But perhaps you are wondering whether there is a loophole for links "within the family."

Well, sometimes tricky operators *can* set up sites that evade the search engines' suspicions. But search engines continue to tweak their algorithms to detect the tricks. Search engines seek to downgrade these links because they are not between neutral parties—the endorsement that the link provides is biased. Here are three ways that they detect when sites are not exactly neutral parties:

- *Similar IP addresses*. Although the names of the domains might be very different, their IP addresses might be similar. IP addresses consist of a series of **blocks**, named the A block (the first one), the B block, and so on. If a Web site has the IP address 209.164.68.129, its A block is 209, its B block 164, its C block 68, and its D block 129. If a different Web site is located at 209.164.68.105, they would have the same IP address, right down to the C block, making it appear that they are hosted in the same place and possibly related to each other. Links between those pages would be discounted by search engines, even though their domains have different names. You can check the IP addresses of your domains at the Webmaster Toolkit site (www.webmaster-toolkit.com/class-c-checker.shtml) to see whether they are in the same C block.

- *Similar Whois information*. When you register your domain, you provide information about yourself or your company as the owner of the domain—this information is stored in the **Whois** database for anyone to see. If domains that link to each other have the same name, address, or telephone numbers in their Whois entries, the search engines might devalue the links, because they assume that the links are biased. There are lots of ways to check Whois entries, but Domain Dossier (www.domainwhitepages.com) is a good one.

- *Similar anchor text*. Search engines also downgrade the value of links that seem to have the same pattern to them over and over—such as a page that gets hundreds of links with the exact same anchor text. It is likely that these links are being orchestrated merely to manipulate search rankings because naturally occurring links usually have some variation.

Because search engines do not reveal their algorithms, it is reasonable to expect they have other ways of identifying links in the family. If we all know that Procter & Gamble owns www.tide.com and www.gain.com, maybe Yahoo! does, too. Don't be concerned if you have multiple domains that are honestly linking to each other. The search engines will downgrade those links, but will not penalize your sites. Just don't expect search engines to give your links the same weight they give to links between neutral sites.

Think About Links *from* Your Site

You need to have an *outbound* link philosophy, too. What sites should you link *to*? If your site links to mediocre (or worse) sites, you devalue your site's authority—to visitors *and* to search engines. Ask yourself whether the link to that site enhances the value of *your* site in your visitors' eyes. Some experts say that you should have very few outbound links, so that you take no chances of devaluing your site, but that makes no sense for many sites. Very successful sites can have few outbound links (those are the destination pages from our bow-tie diagram) or they might have *many* outbound links (they are the core pages)—it all depends on what fits your site. You do want to avoid having a site full of origination pages, where you have many links into the core but attract few back to your own site. If you think about it, pages that have lots of links to low-quality sites mixed in with links to core sites are probably origination pages, because they attract fewer links back from the core.

So what should you do? As usual, consider outbound links based on their effect on your *visitors* first, not the search engine. Here are the key questions to ask when considering an outbound link from your site:

- *Is the site well written and credible?* Note that the question was not, "Does the site have high PageRank?" A site already respected by the search engines is great, as long as it continues to deserve that respect. But don't be afraid to present unknown sites that have great content—that is a terrific service to your visitors (and to the search engines, too). If your site develops a reputation for finding great new content, you will attract a lot of links to your site.

- *Is the site's content strongly related to yours?* Don't link to your brother-in-law's Web site to do him a favor. Every link from your site is part of your credibility, both with visitors and with search engines. Make sure that every link is a service to your visitors—it is a link to a site that is highly relevant to them and that you strongly believe in.

- *Is the site a competitor to yours?* Consider this kind of arrangement very carefully. When considering a reciprocal (two-way) link arrangement, make sure that this is a very well-respected site that will help you more than it hurts you (because you draw less traffic than the competitor site, perhaps). Otherwise, it would be rare to have a reason to link to a competitor. Be wary of competitors that offer reciprocal links and do not deliver their side of the bargain.

If you create an outbound links page, it sounds better to call them "resources" than "links"—it is more oriented to your visitors' needs and helps to set the tone of what the value is to your visitor. Snap Electronics thought carefully about their outbound links and decided to avoid a "links" page entirely. Instead, they made sure that each product linked to camera review sites that posted favorable reviews, both because they wanted their visitors to see them and because they wanted those reviews to be found by search engines. (They made sure to use anchor text that would be useful for searching, such as *SnapShot digital camera review*.)

Some experts advise that all outbound links open a new browser window, because it makes it more likely that visitors will return to your site—they will eventually have to close that window, at least. Although this is true, it is also widely believed that opening new browser windows can confuse novice Web users and those that are visually impaired (because their screen readers do not always handle this technique well). In addition, new windows often annoy experienced users who want to control their own browser. We advise avoiding new browser windows because annoying your visitors is not the ideal way to get their attention.

By now, you should have made some decisions on your link philosophy—who you want links from and who you are willing to link to. Because search marketing revolves around inbound links far more than outbound ones, we spend the rest of the chapter showing you how to go about attracting those inbound links you need.

Step-by-Step Link Building for Your Site

Building links is a slow process. If you commit yourself to keep at it, however, you will eventually succeed when competitors with less stick-to-itiveness falter along the way. Attracting quality links to your site is not easy, but you can do it if you carefully follow the right steps:

- *Make your site a link magnet.* The best way to get links is to create a site so excellent that it draws links without them being requested. You can take specific actions to make your site attractive to linkers—we show them to you.

- *Perform a link audit.* As with anything, you have to measure your success. You need to know where you stand before you can track your improvement.

- *Identify sources of links.* Before requesting any site to link to yours, you have to explore all of your options and determine why each site will give you the link you want.

- *Negotiate your links.* How do you request a link? What can you offer in return? Are there alternatives to just promising a reciprocal link in return? Why would the other site agree? Learn how to bargain for the links you need.

The process of finding and requesting links from other Web sites is very important, but unless your site is high quality, it will not matter. Let's start with how to spruce up your site so that it attracts the most links possible.

Make Your Site a Link Magnet

Some might call it **linkability**, whereas others might dub your site **link-worthy**. Regardless of the name, you need to make your site a **link magnet**—your site must *attract* links from other sites.

So how do you attract those links? Page by page. You know which pages on your site might attract links—those are your **link landing pages**. Just as a search landing page can attract search engines, you can design your link landing pages to attract links. Each link landing page must provide a strong reason to be linked to:

- *A complementary product or service.* If your landing page shows an offering for sale, you must approach sites with related but noncompeting offerings. Ask yourself which companies would link to your product. How would it complement their product line?

- *Valuable information.* Many link landing pages provide important information. The information could be an article, a set of FAQs, a blog, a newsletter, a white paper, an e-book, or something else. What sites have visitors who need your information? What makes your information a "must-have" for them?

- *An authoritative source of information.* Your landing page need not have original information—it can be the right place to find links to the most trustworthy pages on the Web about a subject. In scientific research, "survey papers" examine all the other papers about a subject and critique them. Your landing page could list links to the important documents on a topic, along with your review of each document—you would be creating a small Web directory on a particular subject. Which sites could use your page as background for their visitors?

- *A desirable tool.* You can attract many links with a software tool that provides value to the visitor. If you can develop a simple (or not-so-simple) program that does something useful, you will attract links to it. In this book, we have shown you numerous free tools to help with your search marketing, but you can develop a tool on just about anything people need help with. A life insurer can provide a calculator to determine how much coverage is needed. A charity can show how much of a contribution is tax deductible. A travel site can suggest vacation ideas based on interests. If your tool helps people, you will get your links. To get the most links, your tool needs to be both helpful and unique—give people something useful that they cannot get anywhere else and see how many links you get.

- *A business relationship.* Don't overlook the built-in links you can request from your business partners. If you are a manufacturer, get links from your resellers. If you are a retailer, use your affiliates. Every organization has relationships with other organizations. Use yours! In addition, you can create a business relationship by purchasing links—a careful purchase can often provide good results. Be sure each link goes to the most relevant page on your site, not just the home page.

Use this list to come up with ideas for link landing pages for your Web site. But beyond pages that you can put on your own site, you can also get links by providing content to *other* sites, through **link backs**. For example, you can send an article you write to another site, allowing it to be placed on the site in return for a link back to *your* site as the article's author. You can take this approach with tools, too. Provide a tool that can be used on any site as long as that site displays the "Powered by" notice that links back to your site. Atomz (www.atomz.com) uses this approach with its free site search tool—it has become one of the most-linked pages on the Web.

No matter what type of landing page you set out to create, you need to think through the experience that the visitor will have when they get there, just as you did for search landing pages. The landing experience is important for visitors—without a good experience, your visitors will not follow through to your Web conversion—but it is also critical to attract the links in the first place. Who will link to your site if they see that the experience is not a good one for *their* visitors? You must design the right landing experience both to attract the link *and* to get conversions after it is in place. So, how do you design your link landing pages?

- *Reinforce the topic*. To attract links, you must know what the subject of your page is. Why should people link to you? Why should visitors follow the link? You should have a strong idea of what you want the anchor text to be on the link—use that same text as a prominent heading on the page and in the title tag. Remember that the visitor to that page could have been anywhere on the Web before reaching you, so smooth the visitor's transition to your site by showing that the link topic followed is exactly what your page is about. Avoid cutesy marketing names—be 100 percent sure that the heading of your page is exactly what you expect visitors to call your topic.

- *Never change the topic*. Once you have attracted some links, do not change the subject of the page. You may be tempted to put your new MP3 player on your withdrawn PDA page, because they share the same target customers, but the links to that new page will be all wrong. Those links will flee and you will attract fewer links to the rest of your site because linkers believe you will pull another switcheroo.

- *Deliver excellent content*. Your page must be well written and high quality in every way. If you have a well-known brand name, use it. The people whose links you must attract have many choices of pages to link to—yours must be the *best*, or you will draw far fewer links. The better your page is, and the more it completely fulfills the visitor's need, the more links you will attract. The single most important tip to attracting links is to make your landing page one that sites *must* link to—or else their visitors have missed out on a gem. Create that gem, and the links will follow.

- *Use link-friendly URLs*. Make your URLs short and easy to spell and remember. Use "URL rewrite" techniques (covered in Chapter 10) to transform dynamic URLs. Make your URLs look permanent; the shorter and more readable they are, the more fundamental they appear to your site. Check Figure 13-5 to decide which URLs *you* would link to. Unfortunately, some Web sites have the opposite problem, using the same URL for multiple documents (usually through frames or tricky programming). This shared URL technique is death for link campaigns because there is no way to link to the exact page unless every link landing page has a unique URL. In addition, use 301 server-side redirects (explained in Chapter 10) to ensure that the search engines count all of your links for the same page—your rankings will be lowered if the links to the same page are split between two URLs, such as www.domain.com and www.domain.com/index.html. Beyond 301 redirects, you can use the preferred domain feature of the Google Sitemap protocol (also covered in Chapter 10) to collect all your links into one name for your pages indexed in Google.

- *Take down the roadblocks*. If you think that people will link to pages that immediately pop up a registration page or a "choose your country" page, you are wrong. You will drive away many more links than you attract. We know that the marketing department wants to collect the e-mail address of everyone who downloads the white paper, but forcing entry before viewing just will not fly. You might coax some people to comply, but you will see many more visitors abandon. Worse, you will drastically reduce the number of sites willing to link to you in the first place. Take down the roadblocks for all link landing pages.

- *Keep good company.* If you have links to other sites on your link landing page (or pages surrounding the landing page), make sure they link to very high-quality sites. Potential linkers often examine a site carefully before they link to it—they look at far more than the landing page. Don't let questionable links on your site damage your linkability.

- *Draw visitors deeper.* Just as with search landing pages, you must be sure that visitors know where to go after they get to the link landing page. Be sure that they are invited into your site so that they can complete their task.

If, while reading the list of landing page tips, you asked yourself, "Why shouldn't I do these things for *every* page on my site?" then you are getting the idea. If you think of every page on your site as a potential link landing page, you will drive far more links to your site than if you reserve the star treatment for a small subset of pages. But many sites would find this a daunting task—they have too many pages that would require correction, just as performing organic search optimization on every page might be too expensive for many sites.

Snap Electronics believed that they could not afford to treat every page as a link landing page, but they decided to treat each of their *search* landing pages as link landing pages. As they upgraded their pages for organic search optimization, they tweaked their content to attract links, too. Snap also created new content to attract links, ranging from a white paper explaining their OneTouch auto-focus technology to employee blogs with new ways to use SnapShot cameras.

---

www.domain.com/2005studies/FebMarket.html

www.domain.com/studies/Feb2005market.html

www.domain.com/studies/0205market.html

www.domain.com/studies/current.html

www.domain.com/studies/2005/FebMarket.html

www.domain.com/studies/2005/February/market.html

www.domain.com/studies/marketreport/2005/February/market.html

www.domain.com/studies/reports.pl?docid=152454

www.domain.com/studies/reports.pl?month=02&year=2005&doc=mkt

Figure 13-5 Link-friendly URLs. If each URL was pointing to this month's market analysis report, which ones would make you more likely to link to them?

If your company cannot make every page a link landing page, start out by identifying the pages that are the most closely related to your targeted keywords for your search marketing campaigns. Don't limit your list to the main navigation pages of your site—frequently that white paper on a new technology will draw a lot more links than the page for the product that uses that technology. Make sure you dress up interior pages to your site as link landing pages for the same reason you want them found by search engines. The deeper into your site that you pull the visitor, the closer they are to a conversion.

After you have identified your landing pages, it's time to see how many links they are already attracting.

Perform a Link Audit

As with everything else in search marketing, we always measure whatever we do. To measure success at attracting links to your site, you perform a **link audit**. What sites are linking to you? Your link audit analyzes every link to your landing page, or even to your whole site.

The simplest metric for a link audit is the sheer number of other pages that link to your page—what we have called the inbound links. There is no shortage of ways to check inbound links, which are also known by search experts as **back links**. If you use the Google toolbar, just navigate to the page you want to check, and then click the blue circle with the white *i*. The resulting pull-down menu enables you to do a back links search, as shown in Figure 13-6. Google will count and display the highest-quality pages in its index that are linked to that page. Although simple to do, the toolbar unfortunately does not work very well. First, Google shows only a small subset of your links—those with lower PageRank are often omitted. Second, Google clutters up the list with *internal* links as well, which do not drive any traffic to your site (and which search engines discount in importance). As we write this, there is no way to get a complete list of external links to your page from Google. (Because search engines change frequently, keep up with the latest news using the resources in Chapter 16, "What's Next?")

This page has 1,030 links.

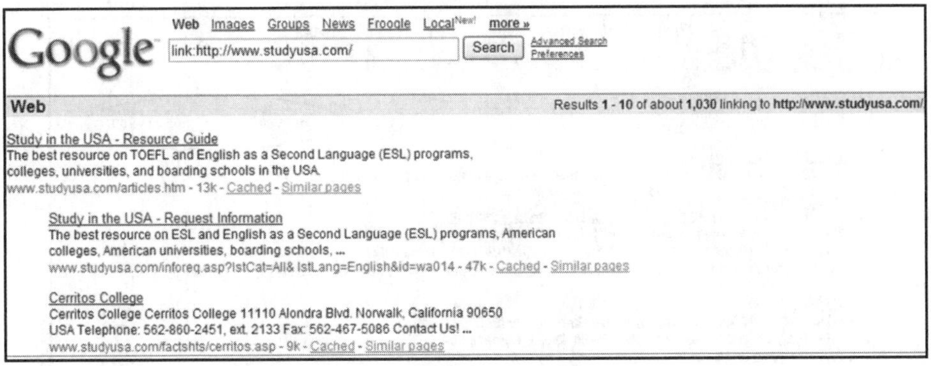

Figure 13-6 Displaying inbound links with the Google toolbar. If you use the Google toolbar, you can easily display a partial list of inbound links for any page.

Fortunately, there are ways to find almost all the inbound external links to your pages. Yahoo! Search provides several operators you can use, as shown in Table 13-2. Combining several operators provides excellent analysis, as the table shows, but be very careful with the syntax. Yahoo! expects the "http://" for the "link:" operator but not for the "linkdomain:" operator. Use of these operators is not an exact science, so experiment to see what works the best for you and keep up with changes the search engines make.

Table 13-2 Displaying Inbound Links with Yahoo! Search (Combining operators shows total or external links both to individual pages and to entire sites.)

	Search Query	Link Count
Links to a single page	link:http://www.studyusa.com/articles.htm	About 642
External links to a single page	link:http://www.studyusa.com/articles.htm site:www.studyusa.com -site:studyusa.com	About 50
Links to an entire site	linkdomain:www.studyusa.com	About 12,900
External links to an entire site	linkdomain:www.studyusa.com site:www.studyusa.com site:studyusa.com	About 10,700

In addition to checking the number of links, you can also check links to your site that contain specific anchor text, as shown in Figure 13-7. You can see that the query "inanchor:digital camera site:canon.com" lists every page on canon.com linked to using the words *digital camera* in the anchor text.

514 pages on canon.com are linked to with *digital camera* in the anchor text.

Figure 13-7   Finding pages with specific anchor text. Google allows you to see pages on your site with links containing your targeted keywords.

As you might expect, each search engine's spider crawls a somewhat different set of pages on the Web, so they find a different set of links to your landing page. Checking each search engine by hand can get old rather quickly, so you can use a link audit tool to eliminate most of the drudgery. All link audit tools will automatically count links to your pages, but Table 13-3 shows the other features that each tool possesses:

- *Finding links.* Most tools can help you identify pages that are good link candidates for your pages, through two main methods. The first, shown in the table as Keyword, identifies every link that contains a particular word or words in its anchor text. The second link-finding method, referred to as URL in the table, displays the sources of links to a particular URL (usually a competitor's page). When you see these lists of links, you can evaluate whether those site owners might be approached to link to your site.

- *Scoring links.* Some tools can evaluate each link to identify the ones that might have the most value. Different tools use different scoring methods, including the number of visits to the linking page by users of the Alexa toolbar (www.alexa.com), whether a link is "in-family" (from the same C block in its IP address), the relevance of that page to the theme of your page (whether it contains appropriate keywords in its title and its body text), or by its Google PageRank score.

- *Managing links.* A few of the tools help you to manage a full-blown link campaign, which we discuss later in this chapter.

Table 13-3 Link Audit Tools (All link audit tools count links to your page—here are some of the most popular, along with the other features that each offers.)

	Finds Links	Scores Links	Manages Links	Pricing
Arelis www.axandra-link-popularity-tool.com	Keyword and URL	Alexa	Yes	Trial version: Free Standard version: $100 Business version: $300
Link Popularity Check www.checkyourlinkpopularity.com	No	No	No	Free
MarketLeap Popularity Checker www.marketleap.com/publinkpop	No	No	No	Free
OptiLink www.optilinksoftware.com	Keyword and URL	In-family, theme, and PageRank	No	Up to 10 links: Free Unlimited: $149
PR Prowler www.prprowler.com	Keyword and URL	In-family, theme, and PageRank	No	$97
PR Weaver www.prweaver.com	Keyword	In-family and Page Rank	No	Free Beta
SEOElite www.seoelite.com	Keyword and URL	Alexa, in-family, theme, and PageRank	Yes	$167
Zeus www.cyber-robotics.com	Keyword and URL	In-family, theme, and PageRank	Yes	Up to 50 categories: Free Unlimited: $195

The table reveals a wide variation in pricing, ranging from free to several hundred dollars. There is an equal disparity in features—some of the simplest tools just count the number of links, whereas others perform several additional functions. Some of the "professional" versions are designed for search marketing consultants who regularly export link audit data into spreadsheets for even deeper analysis, or conduct analysis on multiple client sites. We do not look at every tool, but we examine a few more closely to give you insight into what kinds of features are available.

A free tool that eliminates a lot of manual work is MarketLeap's Link Popularity Check, as shown in Figure 13-8. You can see from the picture that every search engine has a different idea of how many links refer to this page. (As noted earlier, at the time we ran this report, Google was vastly underreporting the true number of links.) MarketLeap's tool shows the number of links reported by each of the major search engines, and even enables you to benchmark your page against pages from competitors or against your entire industry.

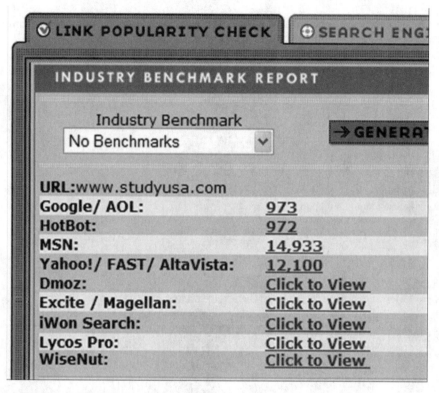

Figure 13-8   Counting links across search engines. MarketLeap's tool enables you to see the links to a page from each major search engine at a glance.

A serious link-building campaign needs to examine more than raw link counts, however. As search engines do, you will want to score your links according to the quality of the sites they come from. Several of the tools in the table perform these functions, but two that specialize in link quality analysis are OptiLink and SEOElite.

OptiLink can quickly fetch hundreds of links from the major search engines, analyzing them in several ways, including checking to see whether your targeted keywords appear in the link's anchor text. As interesting as it might be to check your own links, it can be even more illuminating to see how your competitors are faring. Snap Electronics ran the report shown in Figure 13-9, and found that 82 percent of links to nikon.com used the word "nikon" and not one of them used the word "digital"—that's not too many links for the keyword *digital camera*. This intelligence showed Snap how vulnerable Nikon was to a link campaign for *digital camera*.

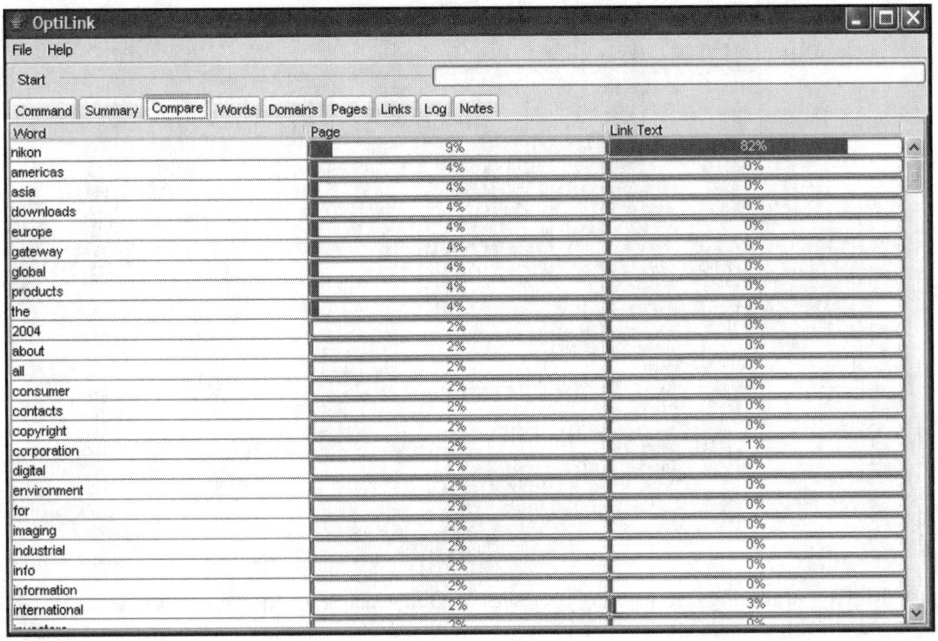

Figure 13-9   Analyzing the anchor text for your links. OptiLink analyzes each links and aggregates them according to their anchor text.

SEOElite, from Bryxen Software, can also help you research and analyze link candidates. It is absolutely the fastest performer with the most features of any link audit tool. SEOElite is unique in its capability to search and score potential link partners by finding keywords in anchor text, in the title, or in body text. SEOElite also has a nice screen layout that some search marketers find easier to use than some other tools. Figure 13-10 shows SEOElite's analysis of Nikon's links, which confirms OptiLink's analysis that no links exist with *digital camera* in the anchor text. Two other features distinguish SEOElite from OptiLink:

- *Filters by Google PageRank.* Whereas some tools will score links by PageRank, SEOElite enables you to limit your list of links to just those pages higher than a particular PageRank value. You can ask for a list of links that have a PageRank of four or higher, for example, eliminating links from the list that you would not consider as candidates. Remember, we do not advise that you cull your list exclusively by PageRank—unknown sites might be high quality but as yet undiscovered by linkers.

- *Uses the Google API.* Currently, only SEOElite and PR Weaver comply with Google's terms of service by using the application programming interface (API) provided for search tools. Google's link counts using the API are accurate, even when the Google toolbar itself is inaccurate. To make it even friendlier to the search engines, SEOElite uniquely offers a "courtesy pause" between each query, which keeps the search engines from being bombarded with queries.

Google PR	Alexa Rank	Page title	Anchor text	Outbound links
3	67749	Nikon MH-60E - (950 EN-EL2) - Ferra.ru	N/A	N/A
2	4684171	Fiorano.net	Nikon	92
4	1280614	Photo gallery	Nikon	4
3	720601	NPS Gallery	N/A	N/A
3	3139025	Welcome to Leadheads Bullets Firearm...	Nikon	214
5	440349	Digital Tallinn - city guide of the Capital...	Nikon Corporation	36
3	42173	Nikon 35-70mm f/2.8D AF Zoom-Nikkor ...	N/A	N/A
5	761548	American Photo - MentorSeries	http://www.nikon.com	42
4	26007	APIII 98 -- Exhibitors	Nikon, Inc.	72
0	4629041	Treiberlinkliste.de - Treiber- und Firmen...	http://www.nikon.com	184
0	5146945	migawka.com.pl - internetowy sklep fot...	<image>	20
0	467426	EdgeReview: Digital Imaging: At ...	www.nikon.com	10
4	5492427	Welcome to Algarve Images! - Associat...	www.Nikon.com	9
4	252038	C O E A J Z N W i p \ R A j	Nikon	246
4	1764416	Thailand Geographic	no anchor text	394
6	31408	Nikon	Global Gateway	50
2	3528072	Through The Eye Of The Beholder Phot...	<image>	346
2	58443	Nikon LS1000	Nikon	4
4	1196025	TSS Manufacturers - General	www.nikon.com	130
6	132772	Driver Links	Nikon	152
4	576496	The Mac Night Owl's Weekly Newsletter	Nikon	42
3	0	Pickashot.com - Pick-A-Shot of your fa...	Nikon	112
4	598967	Odyssey Expeditions Tropical Marine Bi...	Nikon	70
3	1081	Austin History Center Business Case fo...	no anchor text	96

Figure 13-10 Analyzing each link to your site. SEOElite displays each link along with its Google PageRank and its anchor text.

PR Weaver, another audit tool, is unusual in several respects. First, at this writing, it is available *free* as a beta release, but will eventually be a priced offering. PR Weaver, unlike all of the other tools, reports links using only Google—the rest of the tools report links from multiple search engines. Being Google-centric can be a drawback, because PR Weaver misses whatever links Google misses. However, this focus on Google causes PR Weaver to filter by Google PageRank and utilize the Google API, like SEOElite, *and* to display Google snippets for each links source. No other tool displays Google snippets—they just show the URLs. Snippets aid selection of potential link candidates for the same reasons they help searchers choose the search results they want to click.

Snap Electronics was quite interested in performing a link audit, but were more intrigued about auditing a competitor than their own site. You recall from Chapter 12 that Black Hat Cameras, a relatively unknown retailer, was solidly entrenched with the third result in Google for the keyword *digital camera*. Table 12-5 showed Black Hat's link popularity was a major factor in its ranking success, so Snap decided to audit Black Hat's home page.

Snap used a link audit tool that scored Black Hat's links by Google PageRank, confirming what we saw in Chapter 12—all of Black Hat's links come from pages with PageRank 4 or less. That is exceedingly rare for a highly ranked page for such a competitive keyword. Given normal random chance, a site ranked this highly would likely have a couple of higher PageRank pages linking to it. Perhaps Black Hat could be knocked from its #3 perch if Snap's digital camera hub page attracted a few high PageRank links.

Even though Black Hat did not have links from the most authoritative pages, it had a *huge* number of links—more than 9,000. The next step in the link audit is to see where those links are coming from. You remember that "in-family" links (links between two sites with the same C block in their IP addresses) a devalued by search engines because they are likely to be controlled by the same site owner. Snap decided to randomly check some of Black Hat's links to see whether multiple sites shared the same C block. To do this, Snap performed a **reverse IP lookup** on Whois Source (www.whois.sc); for $15 a month, Whois Source displays the names of the site owners along with their IP addresses. Figure 13-11 shows the results—hundreds and hundreds of domains from the same C block, many of which are linked to Black Hat's site. Moreover, they all have odd-looking hyphenated domain names, raising suspicion of a spam technique called a **link farm**.

Reverse IP Lookup

Member Area > Reverse IP Lookup

Advanced View of 68.167.234.66

Displaying results 1 - 500 of **1985**

Result page: 1 2 3 4 ≥ >>

Website
www.0-apr-card-credit-4u.info
www.0-apr-credit-card-4u.info
www.2004-tax-software-advisor.info
www.2nd-loan-mortgage-advisor.info
www.2nd-mortgage-e-bank.info
www.375-mg-phentermine-pharmacy-2003.info
www.375-phentermine-90-pills-pharmacy-2003.info
www.375-phentermine-pharmacy-2003.info
www.375-phentermine-top-deals.info
www.4-handed-texas-holdem-strategies-game.info

Figure 13-11   Suspicious links. Snap Electronics found that hundreds of links to Black Hat Camera's home page came from the same place.

Link farms attempt to artificially build link popularity by fabricating sites that have many links to other sites—the sites that the spammer wants to boost. Link farmers craftier than Black Hat spread their domains over many different servers with different C blocks, to avoid detection.

Snap decided to look more deeply into the Black Hat links by visiting some of the sites. A large number turned out to be blogs, but the blogs did not seem to talking about digital cameras. Blogs discussing completely unrelated subjects suddenly had a post linking to Black Hat's site, usually amid a list of many links to other unrelated sites, as shown in Figure 13-12. None of these links were terribly valuable, but apparently the sheer number of links (more than 9,000) was having a strong effect on Google.

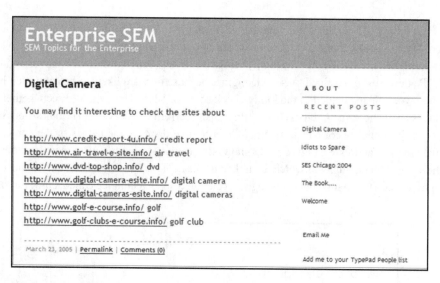

Figure 13-12   Blog spam. Many of Black Hat's links were from unrelated blogs that listed dozens of irrelevant links to fool the search engines.

Snap became convinced that Black Hat was using unethical spam techniques to fool Google and decided to report this activity to Google as a violation of their terms of service. Each search engine and directory provides a means to report violations, as shown in Table 13-4.

Table 13-4   Reporting Spam Violations (The major search engines all have mechanisms for reporting deceptive practices related to their search results.)

Search Engine	Contact
ask.com	reportviolations@askjeeves.com
Open Directory	staff@dmoz.org
Google	www.google.com/contact/spamreport.html
MSN	support.msn.com/feedbacksearch.aspx
Yahoo!	add.yahoo.com/fast/help/us/ysearch/cgi_reportsearchspam

Search engines receive many spam reports each day and they take each one seriously, acting quickly to penalize or ban true violators. If, like Snap Electronics, you ever need to report someone for spam techniques, include the following items in your report:

- Your search term and the URLs that were found that you believe are inappropriate.
- The spam technique you believe is being used and your evidence for that belief.

- Why you believe this technique is detrimental to searchers finding the best results. (It is not enough for you to want your competitor penalized unless you can explain why it hurts searchers.)

As you have seen, examining your competitors' sites can be very instructive. You can see which sites link to them and what anchor text they use. You might even catch one of them playing a few tricks. Next we show you how to identify dozens of sites that can provide high-quality links.

Identify Sources of Links

Now that you know where you stand, what are you going to do about it? Perhaps you find that you already have many high-quality links to your link landing pages—some large sites do—but you can always improve. If your audit uncovered a more disappointing situation, you have your work cut out for you.

If too many of your pages are "link-free" (or at least free of quality inbound links), what do you do now? Apparently what your Web site has been doing up to now has not been attracting the links you need. Your first step on the road to improvement is to review the advice we gave earlier: Make your site a link magnet. Sites with few quality links are typically violating some of this important advice.

It is not always that simple, however. Perhaps your site truly has high-quality content and it *should* be attracting more links than it does. Maybe your site just is not as well known as you would like it to be. Or it could be that people take your site for granted and do not bother to link to it. Or maybe you just do not have the patience to wait for folks to discover how great your site is—you want to jump-start the link-building process. What do you do?

We should warn you that link-building campaigns are not easy. You have to find sites that would be great sources of links. You need to give them a reason to link to you. And you need to keep track of what you are doing so you stay organized with your requests and measure your improvement. It's hard work, but we show you how it's done.

Let's start with motivation. To get a site to link to you, you need to give them a *reason*. Why should they link to you? How does that link help *their* visitors? Do you offer a complementary product or service? Information their visitors need? A useful tool? Do you have an existing business relationship? Are you going to offer their customers a discount? Will you pay them for the link? Link back to them?

Similarly, for each link, *you* need a reason. Why do you want this site to link to you? Does it draw high traffic? Is it qualified traffic for your Web conversions? Does it have high-quality content? Is that content relevant to your site's subject and its industry?

HOW IMPORTANT IS A SITE'S PAGERANK?

In Chapter 12, we introduced **page ranking factors**, a search engine's way of evaluating your page's quality. The most well-known compilation of page factors is Google's **PageRank**, which is often used as a shorthand way of referring to page factor scores for any search engine.

You can find any page's PageRank by navigating to the page in your browser and checking the Google toolbar. Rolling your mouse over the green PageRank bar will reveal a number between zero (not indexed) and ten (the meaning of life) that shows Google's perceived importance of that page. The toolbar shows the page's PageRank on the PageRank scale, so it will display "10/10" for a page with the highest possible PageRank score.

PageRank is not calculated on the normal linear scale, but rather an *exponential* scale. That's a fancy math term that means that PageRank 4 is not one better than PageRank 3—it is six or seven *times* better. So the difference between a PageRank 5 page and a PageRank 8 page is much larger than you might think.

We have discussed how search engines transfer some of a page's authority to your page when it links, so you want links from the pages with the highest PageRank scores, right? Yes you do, but it is more complicated than that. Remember that the authority conveyed is relative to the number of links on the page—the fewer the links, the more authority is passed on each link. So, it is frequently more valuable to be the only link on a PageRank 5 page than one of hundreds on a PageRank 7 page.

Don't fall into the PageRank seduction trap. It is most important for your pages to be linked from sites that will drive heavy, high-qualified traffic to your site, regardless of their PageRank. So, use PageRank as a tool to help validate your own judgment of the quality of a potential link source, but do not blindly follow PageRank or any other scoring system when you make your list and check it twice.

So what kinds of links can you get? They fall into a few major categories:

- *Internal links*. They might not be the most important to search engines, but you have the most control over them. See what you can do to make the links within your site the best possible.

- *Relational links*. Your company probably has many existing business relationships that can be parlayed into Web links. Suppliers, resellers, and even customers can be tapped.

- *Solicited links*. These are the links that everyone talks about, when you "cold call" someone and request a link to your site. What sites would want to link to yours? We help you make your target list.

- *Paid links*. Can you pay for links without wasting your money? We show you how.

We start with the easiest part of any link campaign: optimizing links between two pages on your own site.

Internal Links

We told you earlier that the easiest links to get are frequently the least valuable, so why spend any time talking about *internal links* between two pages on your site? Some search experts believe that search engines pay little attention to internal links, but we believe that some internal links can be helpful to search rankings.

Frequently, what *you* might consider your "site" might be considered multiple Web sites to a search engine. Although *you* know that www.yourcompany.com is from the same organization that brings you www.yourcompany.co.uk and www.yourcompany.de, the search engines sometimes give more credit to links between those domains than they would to links within the domains. So, the first way that internal links can help rankings is that sometimes they look like external links.

Some search experts believe that internal links can help in another way—through careful use of anchor text. The experts mainly agree that internal links do nothing to help your site's page ranking factors. Because internal links are biased, search engines do not weigh them heavily to decide which pages are the highest-quality ones. But some believe that the anchor text for those links is considered as a query ranking factor.

No matter who's right about what the search engines do, it's not hard to optimize your anchor text, so it's worth doing. Figure 13-13 demonstrates how you can change your writing to emphasize keywords in your anchor text, just in case the search engines are paying attention. To optimize for the phrase *digital camera*, the figure shows how little attention it takes to boost those keywords in the anchor text.

Before:	Click here for the latest Snap Electronics digital camera.
After:	Check out the latest Snap Electronics digital camera.
Before:	Snap Electronics is your best source for digital cameras.
After:	Snap Electronics is your best source for digital cameras.

Figure 13-13   Optimizing anchor text for internal links. Search engines might use anchor text on internal links, so write it as carefully as possible.

Internal links might not affect search rankings much, but because they are under your control, you might as well do whatever you can. (You know they are important to drive Web conversions.) Let's turn our attention to the kinds of links that make a big difference in search rankings.

Relational Links

The most overlooked source of links stems from your existing business relationships. Most companies, especially large companies, have an extensive set of partners that they do business with. Resellers, dealers, affiliates, retailers, suppliers—it does not matter what you call them. These partners often provide the easiest and most valuable links you can attract—what we call **relational links**.

Relational links are valuable because they are from neutral parties—any of these companies can freely decide to link to your site or not. If their relationship with your company ends, the link will, too. These companies are independent from yours—*that* is what makes a link from them such a valuable endorsement.

And, although we have said that the harder a link is to get, the more valuable it is, these links are not tough to get. It is far easier to attract links from your existing business partners than from a company you have no relationship with at all.

So start making your list. What companies will want to provide links to your site? Do you manufacture a product they sell? Are you a reference customer for a supplier? Do you have a deal to sell another company's product? Will your customers provide testimonials on their Web sites? Stop and think. What relationships exist between your company and others?

Depending on the nature of your company's relationships, you might be in a commanding position. If your suppliers want your reference, you can insist upon a link. You can require that all affiliates include links. Examine all of your relationships and see whether you are in position to request links (preferably one-way links) that they are very likely to agree to.

Even if your company already has plenty of links from your partners, you might still have work to do. Frequently large companies have an abundance of links to their home page, but not enough links to interior pages. Snap found its digital camera accessories suppliers already had links to the Snap site, but the links were all to Snap's home page, using *Snap Electronics* as the anchor text. Snap went back to each company and requested a link to the digital cameras product category hub page, with some variation of *SnapShot digital cameras* as the anchor text. Snap's experience is the norm for big companies—their big link totals are mostly links to their home page using the company name as the anchor text (as we saw earlier for Nikon). To nudge your search rankings for informational and transactional queries, you need links to your interior pages for your individual product lines, such as digital cameras. One way to find the best anchor text is to examine paid placement results. You will see what paid keywords are being entered by searchers that click through to your pages, so you can request those variations in your link partner's anchor text, too.

AFFILIATE LINKS: THE LOST OPPORTUNITY

If your company runs an affiliate program (where Web sites drive traffic through links to your site in return for a sales commission), you might believe that all of those affiliate links to your product pages are just what the doctor ordered—high-quality, one-way interior links. And they might be, if the search engines can see them. Unfortunately, most affiliate links are completely missed by search engines.

Because affiliate programs pay your affiliate every time a visitor follows a link to your site and buys your product, you have implemented an affiliate tracking tool to accurately count all visitors from affiliates that make a purchase. All affiliate tracking tools provide this essential function, but Rob Key, the CEO of Converseon (www.converseon.com), a leading affiliate program management company, says most tracking tools are not search-friendly.

Every affiliate tracking tool forces your affiliates to code the links to your site in a certain way, so that the tracking tool can perform its function. Unfortunately, many affiliate tracking tools require your affiliates to use links that employ the fancy redirection techniques that we advised against in Chapter 10. Others use strange-looking dynamic URLs that search spiders might choose not to follow or that accrue no value to your site. If your affiliate tracking system requires each affiliate link to add a tracking code to the end of a static URL (such as www.snapelectronics.com/digitalcameras/?afflink=affiliate327), the spider might treat each URL with a different affiliate code as a unique page, leaving the main page (www.snapelectronics.com/digitalcameras) with no credit for each link.

An opportunity often missed in large companies is **sponsorships**. Whenever corporate largesse funds a nonprofit or industry activity, it is customary for the funded Web site to thank your company and provide a link back to your site. If your company sponsors research at a local university, or endows a chair, get links to your site. Perhaps your company sponsors an external organization, or one of its programs or events. Because you probably do not need any more links to your home page with your company name, ask instead for a link to an interior page of your site that is focused on the event topic. IBM's Globalization team, for example, sponsors the Localization Industry Standards Association (LISA) conference, which dutifully placed a sponsor link on their site to IBM's home page. A quick e-mail from IBM got the sponsor link pointed to the IBM Globalization home page—a much more relevant link for that page. This link generated more qualified visitors following the link as well as improved search rankings. Your site might have similar opportunities.

Don't overlook **trade associations**. Your company might be a member of one or more of these industry organizations. Each trade association has its own Web site, and most have a member list page, as well as other pages on the site that might link to member Web sites. Make sure that your organization is listed in the member directory of each trade association you belong to—and the Web directory entry links to your site. Investigate whether there are other opportunities for your company to provide news or information for posting on the site (along with a handy link back to your site, too). These links are especially helpful in establishing your company's credentials in searches for the name of your industry and other industry terms.

For many companies, **press releases** are a surefire way to grab links to your site. If you have a Public Relations team, it probably already sends out press releases—you just need to get that team to "think link" when it does them. Snap Electronics changed its press release procedures to add the URL for the Snap Electronics home page (www.snapelectronics.com) in the "About Snap

So how can you tell whether your affiliate links are adding to your link popularity score? Go to one of your affiliates and check out the link for yourself. While viewing the page, mouse over the link and check the URL in the status bar of the browser. If you see anything on that link other than the unvarnished URL for your page, you might have a problem. If the URL looks okay in the status bar, you should perform one more check by viewing the source HTML of the page—you should find a tag that contains your page's URL (in the "href" attribute). Make sure that it has your exact URL coded with nothing added.

The bottom line is that your affiliate tracking tool might force your affiliates to create links that are invisible to search spiders. So all of those fantastic one-way interior links will not help your search rankings one bit. A couple of affiliate tracking systems that do seem to work are My Affiliate Program (www.myaffiliateprogram.com) and AffiliateShop (www.affiliateshop.com). Carefully inspect your affiliate tracking tools to see whether the links your affiliates use can be tracked by search engines. If they cannot, changing to a tracking tool that supports links that spiders can see will provide a vital boost to your organic search marketing efforts.

The basic purpose of affiliate tracking tools is to ensure that your affiliates are paid for the traffic they send to your site, so if you are stuck with a tracking system that trips up the spider, just remember that your affiliate program is extremely valuable to your business apart from its impact on search. If you can adjust your tracking system, however, your affiliate links might help you in search, too.

Electronics" title (in the company biography section at the bottom of each press release). Snap also added the URLs for interior pages for products and other related information in every press release—they made sure that the reader of the release could always go to the Web site for more. These techniques prove quite useful in printed press releases to drive traffic to your site, but they have more value, too. Press releases are increasingly read on the Web, so visitors can click through and come to your site. If you distribute your press releases through PRWeb (www.prweb.com), PR Newswire (www.prnewswire.com), or another press release distribution service, they can feed the search engines and relevant blogs with your release as soon as it is issued, providing many ways for people to reach your site. For the search marketer, these press releases will contain highly relevant links from important sites that help the search rankings of the pages on your site that they link to.

Look for opportunities to create new business relationships, too. If you can create a software tool that people need and make it available on your Web site, you will draw links. Just make sure that you are drawing qualified visitors. Snap will not raise conversions by adding a tool for planning your retirement, but offering a scrapbook for digital photos might be very enticing to their target market. Sometimes, like Atomz, you can offer software for use on other Web sites, as long as they agree to show "Powered by" links back to your site.

Relational links can often be the easiest ones to get, and they are frequently those precious one-way links. Don't miss this big opportunity for your site.

Solicited Links

When most people think about link campaigns, they have **solicited links** in mind. They have heard about the process of contacting strangers and wheedling and cajoling a link out of them. If it sounds like hard work, you have analyzed it correctly, but it can pay big dividends, both in terms of visitors following the links to your site and raising your search rankings. Those benefits are yours, however, only through careful selection of the sites to link to yours. Here are the kinds of questions you must ask yourself before soliciting a link from another site:

- *Does the site contain credible, well-written information?* Most experts would have phrased this question, "Does this site have a Google PageRank of at least 5?" But that's not the way to think about it. Having a high PageRank can be very good if the content is being maintained and continues to be well written and credible. But sites change. A site allowed to atrophy might lose its high standing. Similarly, if you have found a site that you think is very good that search engines have not yet discovered, now might be the best time to request a link—it might never be easier to get. (Perhaps you can pass along some tips for search marketing that will help the site gain the search engines' attention—after they link to you!) You know the subject matter of your site's content—trust your own judgment on whether a site is high quality.

- *Does the site's content relate to yours in a strong way?* There is no use getting links from a local accountant to your digital camera page, even if he loves your cameras. Your visitors would not place any stock in an accountant's recommendation, so why should a search engine?

- *Are the visitors to the site the kinds of visitors you want at your site?* If not, why do you want them to visit your site? Remember, you are not looking for higher rankings or more referrals—you want more conversions. Make sure the links you solicit drive qualified traffic to your site. Plenty of such sites are out there, so spend your time soliciting *them*.
- *Is the site a competitor of yours?* You need to think broadly about this question. A consulting firm probably would not want to link to a software company whose product performs one of their services. Don't waste time requesting links that you will never get.

These questions should seem familiar; we asked some of the same questions when we thought about your outbound link philosophy. In the rest of this section, we provide ideas on where to find potential link partners—for each partner, you need to ask yourself these questions before adding them to your list.

The most important links to your site come from Web **directories**, as we first explained in Chapter 3, "How Search Marketing Works." The Yahoo! Directory (www.yahoo.com) and Open Directory (www.dmoz.org) are the two most important directories that every Web site ought to pursue. However, many other directories can boost your site's traffic and search rankings:

- *Yellow Pages.* Many sites provide the Web equivalent of the telephone book's White Pages and Yellow Pages. Many of these directories receive top billing in search results, especially when the search engine believes the searcher is in the same area as your company's location. We cover the leading Internet Yellow Pages providers in Chapter 14, "Optimize Your Paid Search Program."
- *Specialty directories.* Sometimes known as *niche* or *vertical* directories, they cover only a single subject area. No matter what your organization does, there are sure to be several specialty directories for your industry, location, and other purposes, such as a directory of blogs or podcasts. Links from these directories can be very powerful evidence to the search engines as to what your site is about, which can translate into boosts for certain queries. The California Energy Commission developed a specialty directory to promote solar energy (www.energy.ca.gov/links/solar.html), as shown in Figure 13-14.

Figure 13-14 A specialty directory. The California Energy Commission's Solar Energy resource page promotes renewable sources of energy.

Locating specialty directories can be a bit time-consuming, but you can use the search engines to help. Michael Wong suggests combining keywords related to your company (product category, industry, and locale, for example) with the words listed in Figure 13-15. For example, you could enter a search query for financial services directories—"add url" + "financial services"—that would show all the pages with those words. (Although some of the terms in the list are parts of URLs, the queries will work just the same as for words on the pages, such as "submitasite.html +insurance.") You will find thousands of results for some of these queries, but you need not look at them all. See whether the ones at the top of the list make any sense by asking yourself the previously listed questions. Many of these sites are not worth the electrons they are printed on, but some might be valuable link partners.

add site	add url	submit_a_link.html
add a site	add a url	add link
submit site	submit url	add a link
submit a site	submit a url	submit link
addsite.html	addurl.html	submit a link
addasite.html	addaurl.html	addlink.html
submitsite.html	submiturl.html	addalink.html
submitasite.html	submitaurl.html	submitlink.html
add-site.html	submitalink.html	add-url.html
add-a-site.html	add-a-url.html	add-link.html
submit-site.html	submit-url.html	add-a-link.html
submit-a-url.html	submit-link.html	add_url.html
submit-a-site.html	submit-a-link.html	add_link.html
add_site.html	add_a_url.html	submit_site.html
add_a_site.html	add_a_link.html	submit_a_site.html
submit_url.html	submit_link.html	submit_a_url.html

Figure 13-15 Finding directories. Clever use of search queries can locate specialty directories relevant to your site.

Source: Search Engine Optimization eBook (5th edition) by Michael Wong

  So how can you tell which of these sites are legitimate sources of links, and which ones are link farms—mere shams to try to fool search engines? Unfortunately, it is not always easy, even for experts, but you can use a few clues to spot a spammer:

- *More form than function.* The site appears to have many links to sites that do not seem very valuable, especially if those links look like advertisements. Large collections of links labeled "sponsored links" that are paid placement or contextual advertising spots are a red flag.

- *Trade secrets.* Although many companies are listed in your industry's category, you do not recognize any of the company names.

- *Link "unpopularity."* The site has a low Google PageRank, or is an accident waiting to happen. Some spammers artificially inflate a site's PageRank for a while, but if Google catches on, it is penalized and gets a low PageRank. If you are unsure about a potential linking partner, try waiting a few weeks to see whether its PageRank suddenly drops.

- *Non sequiturs.* Your directory has links that seem irrelevant to its topic, or it seems to have no central theme at all. Links to pharmaceutical, banking, or e-business services all sit side by side with no rhyme or reason.

- *A family affair.* A large number of the links in a category come from the same Class C block—use an IP checker to detect this.

- *The more the merrier.* Each directory category has far more links (more than 100) than any visitor could ever use. When you click the links and look at the sites, many seem to have long hyphenated URLs and the sites resemble each other.

If you look over a directory carefully, and do not see these telltale signs of a link farm, go ahead and request the link. In the unfortunate case that you do get tied up with a link farm, tell the search engines what happened and turn in the link farm yourself. The search engines are not out to penalize anyone for an honest mistake, and they will be much more likely to believe you made an honest mistake if you are the one reporting it to them. You are unlikely to be banned for this kind of infraction, but you should expect that the links to your site from link farms will be devalued. If links from link farms are the majority of links to your site, you should expect your site to be penalized in the rankings.

Even if you find a legitimate directory, remember to verify that the directory page your link comes from is itself indexed by the major search engines. Then, check out the nature of the link itself, the way we did in Chapter 10. Many directories use fancy redirect techniques to let them count the number of visitors they send your way, but search spiders will not follow the link. So maybe you get visitors from the link, but it will not add to your link popularity with search engines. Check the links from directories the same way we showed you how to check affiliate links. If a link will get you qualified traffic, that is the most important thing, but know going in that these redirection tactics will not help your PageRank at all.

Before leaving the subject of directories, here is one more tip. A directory is more than just a great way to get a link; it is also a great place to find sites that will link to yours. As valuable as directories are for listing your business, they might even be more valuable for the lists they provide of thousands of other businesses neatly categorized for you to explore. Google proves especially helpful in this regard, because it lists the Open Directory in PageRank order (at www.google.com/dirhp). But you can mine specialty directories for link partners, too. Every time you find a quality directory that you want to be listed in, go the extra mile and examine all of their current listings in your category. You might find a company in the list that is a perfect link partner for you.

Directories are only part of the story for solicited links, however. Many other sites on the Web make great link partners if you know where to look:

- *Trade magazines*. Their journalistic integrity makes them highly respected links. Make sure that when your executives are interviewed or your product is reviewed that you work with the reporter to sneak your URLs into the story. The reporter will be interested if the pages you suggest have short URLs and provide a legitimate service for readers seeking more information. You will get more visitors to your site and higher search rankings from the online versions of the articles. Remember that your company can write articles for many of these publications, too.

- *Blogs*. Most blogs have blocked the spamming techniques that plagued them not too long ago, so blog links are once again very valuable. If you can interest well-respected and popular bloggers to write about your company and link to your site, you will benefit from strong endorsements to your page.

- *Research sites*. If your product is innovative in some way, you might be able to attract links from educational or commercial research sites that show the relationship between your product and the innovation. Many researchers are proud to link to commercial uses of their inventions or other inventions in their field. If you can find research papers that touch on some aspect of your product, you might persuade researchers to link to your site.

- *Related sites*. Be creative. Snap created pages filled with tips on taking digital pictures, and then solicited links from travel sites. Use the search engines to search for your targeted keywords and see which sites come up—the noncompeting sites would be excellent link partners. What can you provide that will cause them to link?

- *Your personal network*. Do you know anyone whose site might be helpful? Don't be afraid to ask for help from friends, or even friends of friends. One of the hardest parts of soliciting links is the "cold call" nature of the initial contact, so anything you can do to warm it up can go a long way to success.

It will not take long for you to develop a wish list of potential partners to approach. Before we discuss how to go about requesting each link, however, some of you might have the budget to *pay* for links.

Paid Links

You might never need to pay anyone to link to your site (except maybe the Yahoo! Directory). But *paid links* can be helpful if you must raise your search rankings in a hurry and you just cannot wait for all those solicited links to be agreed to. Just as paid placement can be used temporarily while you are building organic search rankings, you can also pay other Web sites to link to yours while waiting for the rest of your link campaign to bear fruit.

Because search engines put such a big premium on links, they have soared in value. It stands to reason that some links that were given freely a few years ago might require payment today. Some people believe it is unethical to buy links, and the search engines certainly devalue paid links when they can identify them. But those same search engines are quite happy to sell you links themselves—their paid placement programs are nothing more than links bought by the highest bidder. A cynic might say that search engines are against paid links when anyone besides a search engine gets paid. (*We* would never say such a nasty thing.)

Paid links are valuable because they drive qualified traffic to your site—whether you pay search engines for paid placement links or you pay a popular Web site to provide a link to yours. But you know that already. What you want to know is whether paid links can help your search rankings, and the clear-cut, definitive answer is . . . *sometimes*.

Let's start with the simplest part of the answer: Paid placement links you buy from the search engines *never* help your organic search rankings. Search engines can easily identify paid placement links as being paid links rather than unbiased ones, so they assign them no credit. Now for the tougher part of the answer: *Sometimes* your other paid links—the ones you buy from popular Web sites—will boost your search rankings. But *sometimes* they do not. Let's examine why.

You certainly cannot buy your way to the top of organic search listings by opening the money spigot to pay for lots of valuable links from other Web sites. The secret to link popularity is more complex than that. If it wasn't, every company with deep pockets could buy lots of links and boost their organic rankings. Search engines wouldn't like that, because it would make their organic results less valuable to searchers—the richest companies would show up at the top rather than the most relevant ones.

Search engines also have another reason to dislike paid links—they reduce the incentive to buy paid placement keywords from the search engines. (Gee, there is that cynic coming out again.) There is only so much search marketing budget available, so the more search marketers spend on paid links to popular Web sites, the less they have to spend with paid placement programs from search engines.

Whether from altruism (protecting the integrity of their organic results) or from greed (wanting search marketers to spend every nickel with them), search engines have strong incentives to devalue paid links in their link popularity calculations for organic search rankings. To devalue paid links, however, search engines must first *identify* them. Google recommends that paid links use a nofollow attribute, so that no search benefits accrue to such links. But, as you may suspect, few link sellers comply with that requirement, so the HTML for a paid link and an unbiased one usually looks the same. The money changes hands out of the sight of even the most inquisitive search spider. Spiders are smart, but they cannot check your accounts payable ledger.

So, what do search engines do? They play the odds. They look for patterns that are associated with paid links, and they devalue links that fit those patterns. Sites tend to get links from smaller sites before slowly attracting the bigger fish. Links from several high PageRank sites typically do not come out of nowhere unless they were purchased, which means that the endorsement is suspect. Those links do not indicate that the page is high quality, but rather that the site owner is flush with cash.

So search engines look for link patterns that resemble paid link activities and devalue those links. For example, search engines pay close attention to a sudden jump in a page's link popularity. If Google saw your page had links from a dozen PageRank 3 and 4 sites last month, but sees five PageRank 7 links added today, those new links will be viewed with suspicion. Odds are that those new links were purchased. Those links fit a particular pattern of being from sites much higher in PageRank than your other links, and cropping up suddenly rather than gradually over time. The new links will likely be discounted when calculating your page's PageRank.

Search experts refer to the "Google sandbox effect"—what Google and other search engines do to discount the effect of a quick change in link popularity. They say that your page can play around all it wants, but it will stay in its sandbox, without breaking into the top rankings for any queries. If its new-found popularity, over time, remains constant or even gradually grows larger, the search engines begin to remove the discounts and give full weight to the link popularity, allowing search rankings to rise. You can think of this technique as a probation period for the links. As with any insight to relevance ranking, search engines change all the time, so keep up with the ebb and flow with the materials we list in Chapter 16.

Occasionally, sites *do* come out of nowhere and become instantly popular. Perhaps your company was plastered all over the news for discovering a new wonder drug, or you executed a TV ad campaign that grabbed people's attention. When these kinds of events occur, your site's new-found notoriety can suddenly attract unbiased links. In this way, it *is* possible to shoot up in the number of links to your site without having bought any of them, but search engines will be suspicious, regardless, because that popularity jump fits the purchased links pattern. Your site will be placed in the "sandbox" anyway, at least until the search engines determine your sudden popularity is no flash in the pan.

So if search engines will not count your most expensive paid links, how can you purchase links for maximum effect? That depends on what effect you are looking for. If you want to drive the most qualified traffic to your site, buy, buy, buy! Find the sites that drive the traffic and forget about the search engines. You will get visitors to follow the links and you will get the conversions you want. Eventually that increase in traffic will result in more unbiased links to your site—so the search engines will have to sit up and take notice.

But if, against our advice, you are buying the links primarily to boost your search rankings, buy links from relevant sites that have a PageRank similar to or lower than yours. It can be higher, but just a little higher. Over time, you can buy links from pages with increasing PageRank without raising search engine suspicions.

Let's repeat that advice so you notice we said to buy links from *relevant* Web sites—buying links from higher PageRank sites that are not thematically related to yours is at best pointless, and at worst a sign that you are trying to spam the search engines. Relevant links are what make search engines take notice, so unless you are willing to work as hard as spammers do, you are better off playing it straight. Buying a link from a relevant site is just good advertising.

So where do you find the sites to buy links from? One way is to look for them using the same techniques we showed you for solicited links. Whenever someone turns you down for a free link, you might be able to sweeten the pot with a little cash. Sometimes offering some money to someone agreeable to a free link might get you a more prominent link that drives more traffic, or might garner a link from a more highly visited page.

Link brokers and link auctions are two more sources of paid links. Text Link Ads (www.text-link-ads.com) offers links for sale at fixed prices and even provides a service suggestion for new link opportunities on your specified topic. Another link vendor, LinkAdage (www.linkadage.com), sells links at auction, so that the highest bidder walks away with each link available. Thousands of links are available for sale, and the use of a middleman gives you some protection against fraudulent operators that try to cash your check but renege on providing the link.

Another way of buying links is to buy an entire Web site. Many Web sites are started by people with a passion for a certain subject, such as digital cameras. They create Web sites with excellent content and build a following, but they cannot figure out how to make enough money to quit their day jobs. Because they cannot quit their day jobs, they cannot find the time to maintain the sites at the expected level of quality. This situation offers a huge opportunity for your company to buy a Web site. You might buy the domain name and content and have your own employees update it, or you could hire the original owner to do what he loves to do—now for money. You can add subtle promotions for your products and links to your site in return for your investment. Keep in mind that some unethical search marketers purchase popular Web sites and then use them to link to all sorts of unrelated content, just trying to capitalize in the short term by inflating their page factors. We are not advocating any such tricky tactics. If you buy a Web site and use it to increase its popularity and improve its content, while driving more traffic to your site, everyone wins.

Deciding how much to pay for a link is not easy. As we have advised throughout this chapter, value the link for the qualified traffic that it drives to your site, treating its effect on your link popularity as a welcome bonus. Some search marketers pay thousands of dollars each month for a relevant text link from a popular page (which Google might score as a PageRank 9). At other times, you can buy a less-popular link that nonetheless feeds qualified visitors to your site for $10 a month.

As with any enterprise where money changes hands, you must beware of scams. Never respond to unsolicited paid link opportunities. Cold calls and spam e-mails are frequently coming from someone out to separate you from your cash without delivering anything of value. Also be aware that link farms are often paid link scams—use the link farm checklist we offered earlier in the chapter to evaluate any paid link opportunities.

Paid links are not for everyone, but, handled wisely, they can jump-start your popularity with search engines while driving highly qualified visitors to your site.

Negotiate Your Links

In the rest of this section, we offer some specific advice on how to negotiate links to your site. But first, you need to consider a basic question. Why should this site link to you? What's in it for them? You have asked yourself this just about every step of the way in this process, but now you need to provide a personal answer—one just for the site you are requesting from. That answer usually depends upon the kind of link you are pursuing:

- *Paid links*. The answer is simple: You give them the cash, and they give you the link. If you are dealing with a link broker or link auction site, you just follow their procedures; but what if you are negotiating directly with your potential link partner? First, ask for references from their satisfied link customers. Make sure you have a deal in writing—maybe a formal contract is overkill, but at least insist on a signed memo or a traditional **media insertion order** (sometimes called a "terms sheet"). Get the details in writing somehow. When does the link start and end? Where it is from and to? Just make sure that you both agree on what you are getting for the money—in writing. And always pay using a credit card or an escrow service such as PayPal (www.paypal.com) so that you have some recourse if your partner fails to live up to your agreement.

- *Solicited links*. The obvious deal would be to offer a link back from your site, but, because one-way links are so valuable, you should look at alternatives. Are you providing background information on a concept their visitors need to understand? Do you have a product that enhances their product? Will you offer a discount to customers from their site? Will you pay them a commission on sales? It might be advantageous for you to have other value than merely providing a link back. If you do offer a reciprocal link, remember that any link from your site should conform with your outbound link philosophy, so that you are linking only to high-quality sites that are beneficial to your visitors.

- *Relational links*. An existing relationship can provide immense power in getting the links you want. If your relationship is more important to your link partner than it is to you, you can demand (nicely) almost anything. When you sponsor an event, you can get whatever links you want. If your supplier wants a customer reference for their Web site, you can get a wonderful link in return. For relational links, the value of the relationship can help you get one-way links.

- *Internal links*. Although seemingly the easiest of all, sometimes you need to negotiate these too, especially in large companies. As discussed in Chapter 9, "Sell Your Search Marketing Proposal," you need to be very persuasive with your extended team as to why you need their help. If you are, you will get whatever links you want.

To get any of these links (with the possible exception of paid links), you frequently initiate the request with an e-mail. Here are some tips for crafting an e-mail that will get you the link you desire:

- *Address it to a person*. If you are stuck sending your request to an impersonal address, such as webmaster@pleaselinktome.com, your odds of getting the link drop sharply. Identifying a personal e-mail address along with the person's name will improve your chances enormously.

- *Use a compelling subject line.* Your first job is get your e-mail opened, so a subject of "Link request" is not going to get it done. You thought through why your prospective partner would be motivated to say "yes," so put that thought in subject line: "Free Digital Photo Album from Snap Electronics" or "SnapShot Digital Camera Sale Just in Time for Summer Getaways." Make sure your subject also includes the name of the target company so that it does not look like another spam offer.

- *Use a simple body format.* Don't use HTML e-mail. No pictures. No colors. Make it simple with a universal, nonproportional font (such as 10-point Courier), so you will know how the e-mail will be formatted in any e-mail program. There is no e-mail easier to ignore than one that makes your brain hurt because its lines are wrapping in all the wrong places.

- *Prove you visited the recipient's site.* In the first paragraph, compliment something about the site to distinguish your request from all the other generic e-mails received every day. Show that you took the time to send a personal request so that you look like someone to pay attention to.

- *Sell.* Explain why this link is good for visitors to your partner's site. This is the most critical part of the e-mail. You need a very simple but compelling reason for an endorsement to your site. Your e-mail will only be read once, probably hurriedly, so make the sale in these few sentences. For two-way link requests, make sure that you have already placed your link to your partner's site and that you identify what page on your site has that link.

- *Identify the page to be linked from.* Obviously, choosing pages with high PageRank and few links is nice, but you need to get the link from the page on your partner's site that makes the most sense for visitors, not for search engines. Don't be afraid to include the sentence with the anchor text, or a description of where the link is headed on your site, if that fits with the page you have identified. You can even send the actual HTML for the linking site to use. Anything you can do to make it easier for the Webmaster to add the link is to your benefit, but just be careful not to use the same tired anchor text and description on every request. You want variation so that the links appear natural to search engines and so each searcher will find a link pointing to your site no matter what keyword variation was used.

- *Identify the page to link to.* Be specific about the exact, existing URL on your site you want the link to. Make sure that your URL looks permanent so that the Webmaster does not think it will disappear soon. Make sure that it starts with "http://" and that it is short—an incomplete URL or a URL that wraps to the next line in the e-mail makes it much harder for the recipient to click it to go to the page. As discussed in Chapter 10, use "URL rewrite" techniques to shorten your URLs if necessary. It sounds silly, but the ability for a busy Webmaster to click your URL from the e-mail can mean the difference between getting a link and having your message deleted.

- *Ask for a response.* As with any sales pitch, close with a call to action. If you can inject some urgency into the request, that's even better: "I will keep this link to your site on my page for the next two weeks while you consider my request." Or "My summer blowout sale on digital cameras starts on June 6, just in time for vacation travelers, so you will want to have your link in place by then."

It will be hard for you to hear, but everything that we have discussed so far is actually the easy part. What's harder is keeping track of all of your link requests. Which ones were sent? Which ones did you get responses to? When should you follow up? Did you say thank you to the people who responded? Did you take down the links from sites that turned down your two-way link offer? Are the sites that agreed to two-way links last year still linking to you?

Welcome to the world of link management. We cover some of these issues when we get to Chapter 15, "Make Search Marketing Operational," but you need to learn a little bit now. Fortunately, software tools can help you manage large link campaigns and can do much of the tracking for you. We identified three tools back in Table 13-3 that perform link management functions, so let's look at their link management functions now.

Zeus (www.cyber-robotics.com) is a full-featured tool that manages your entire link-building process. A spider crawls the Web looking for sites that match the criteria you specify, using adaptive filtering to "learn" to identify the most relevant sites as potential link partners for you. Zeus captures the title tag, metatags, page content, and inbound and outbound links, giving the page a score. Zeus stores this information in a database for you to analyze and organize. You can create an outbound links page for your site and generate custom e-mails to each site owner requesting a link to your site. Zeus enables you to track the status of each request to help you follow up when site owners are unresponsive.

Arelis is an easy-to-use tool that finds potential link partners in two ways. Arelis can show you all the links to a URL that you specify (a competitor's site, perhaps) or find all the pages linked with a particular keyword in the anchor text. Like Zeus, Arelis enables you to choose any of these links to be added to a database. From there, you can classify, analyze, and select your link candidates, and generate a links page for your site. Arelis can send out e-mails soliciting links from templates or can help you compose personal requests for each site—you have complete control over the message and can craft it for maximum effect. Arelis provides status reporting and reminders of open requests.

SEOElite, in addition to being a whiz at identifying and scoring links, has added management features, too. Neither Arelis nor Zeus are exceptionally strong at scoring links, so some search marketers use one of the other tools shown in Table 13-3 to collect and score the links and then move the best candidates to the Arelis or Zeus database to manage the rest of the campaign. Using SEOElite can save you this extra step because it offers strong scoring features and helps you manage your links within the same tool.

All three of these tools help you send e-mails to site owners and keep track of the status of each request. You might find that the number of requests that you have going at any point in time makes one of these tools a real time-saver. You should know that any of these tools can be abused by a spammer who sends scattershot e-mails to every Web site with a "dot" in its name, but that is not the fault of the tools. Used properly, these tools can help take some of the disorganization and drudgery out of link campaigns.

Summary

Links are important to organic search marketing, and they rise in importance as competition for your keywords get stronger. The most searched-for keywords have the most pages vying to be shown at the top of the results, so your page's link popularity is often the key component in its search ranking.

But links are valuable far beyond search marketing. High-quality links to your site from all the "right" places (in the popular core of the Web) can drive many qualified visitors to your site through those links. In fact, we believe that attracting links to your site should be based on the qualified traffic those links will bring, not based on any calculated effect you are expecting in your search rankings. If you attract the links that bring the right visitors, the search engines will follow.

You learned that solicited links are important, but that cold-calling another site is hard work that requires perseverance. We discussed alternatives, ranging from internal links to relational links to paid links that might bring the link popularity you need with less effort.

Paid links are just one way to spend your search marketing budget, however. In Chapter 14, we explore every kind of paid search and show how your search marketing program can maximize the impact of your marketing spending.

Optimize Your Paid Search Program

"Money is better than poverty, if only for financial reasons," Woody Allen reminds us. So too, search marketers who are flush with cash have the advantage, but only if their money is spent wisely. We all know that a fool and his money are soon parted, but with paid search you might be shocked as to how *quickly* they are parted.

Paid search is deceptively simple in concept, yet never mastered. The paid search programs are constantly changing and your competition is always on the move. However, you *can* succeed in paid search if you learn some basic principles and stick to them. We do not examine every tiny angle in each search engine—you can use the resources in Chapter 16, "What's Next?" to learn more. Instead, this chapter will equip you to judge the soundness of more detailed advice by providing a solid grounding in the basics:

- *Paid search opportunities*. Paid placement and shopping search engines are the two top ways to drive return on your search marketing investment. We explain each, and help you decide whether they are for you.

- *Your paid search philosophy*. As with everything in search marketing, a successful paid search program requires some upfront thinking. You need to think clearly about what paid search means to your business and what approach you will take, both at the start and as your paid search program unfolds.

- *Step-by-step paid search optimization*. Paid search requires careful attention to details. We walk you through the typical process of implementing a paid search campaign.

When you have completed this chapter, you will be ready to plan and execute a comprehensive paid search campaign. We begin with a close look at the paid search opportunities available to you.

Paid Search Opportunities

Every search marketer ought to at least consider paid search opportunities. For some, paid search will not be cost-effective, but many search marketers find paid search to be more valuable than organic search. It all depends on your site and your situation. We help you decide whether paid search is right for you, and, if it is, how to make the most of it.

But first, let's review some of the main benefits of a paid search program that we introduced in Chapter 3, "How Search Marketing Works":

- *Highly qualified visitors will come to your site*. Just as with organic search, paid search referrals produce highly qualified visitors. If your Web site sells products carried by shopping search engines, you might find a way to attract those transactional searchers at the moment they are ready to buy. Even if shopping search does not fit your site, however, paid placement can generate sales, leads, and any other Web conversions that drive your site's success.

- *You see immediate results*. As you have seen, organic search success requires painstaking attention to detail to get your site indexed and to optimize its content for both search engines and for visitors—all of which can take months. Paid search, conversely, can require upfront work on landing pages and with trusted feeds for shopping engines, but often it can be initiated in a few days with an instant impact on your site.

- *It's inexpensive to get started*. As you learned in Chapter 1, "Why Search Marketing Is Important . . . and Difficult," paid search offers one of the lowest costs per action (conversion) of any form of advertising. And, unlike organic search, there are no expensive upfront costs. Anyone with $100 can experiment with a paid placement campaign in Yahoo!.

- *You pay only for visits to your site*. No matter how many times your paid search results are shown, you pay only when searchers click through to your site. If you design your site to efficiently convert searchers who click through, your return on your paid search investment can be very profitable.

- *You can target your audience*. Whereas keyword planning enables you to target searchers by their interests (for both organic and paid search), paid search provides more pinpoint precision. Shopping search isolates transactional searchers ready to buy, and paid placement can identify searchers by geographical location—both of which might be important to your business and well worth paying for.

As you have journeyed past Chapter 3 in this book, you have discovered that paid search offers other benefits, too:

- *Unlimited keyword targeting*. As discussed in Chapter 11, "Choose Your Target Keywords," organic search has a natural limit in the number of keywords that can be targeted. Although it is best to use existing pages on your site as search landing pages for both organic and paid search, inevitably you will find the need to add new landing pages as your keywords become more obscure. For example, you might find that your conversions increase when you write a product description page for your digital camera specific to an audience—serious photographers as opposed to gadget freaks. As you add landing pages for more and more keywords, each new page becomes very similar to other landing pages. You can imagine that the landing page for the serious photographers and gadget freaks must contain a lot of duplicate material, because you are expecting each visitor to read just one of them. Because organic search landing pages *must* be deeply linked into the navigation of your site, the constant repetition of similar landing pages damages the user experience and ruins your conversion rate, because your visitors will see links to the photographer and gadget pages (and might look at them both). With paid placement, however, you can create many more of these landing pages that link one way—*into* your site—so that searchers are guided from the search engine to your landing page to the core navigation of your site. That way, queries you think are coming from gadget freaks ("8 megapixel autotouch camera") are directed to a different page than those from serious photographers ("slr digital camera optics"). Your core site need not link *to* the repetitious paid search pages, so your visitors are not distracted by them—they see only one landing page and never link to another one after they reach your site. This enables you to target as many paid search keywords as you can justify the investment for.

- *Unequalled adjustability.* You have learned how difficult it can be to make changes to your Web site to support organic search, especially if you have a medium-to-large site. If your inventory runs low on your best-selling product, your organic search results will keep pouring visitors into your site. If you put a product on sale, it could take weeks for the organic search results to reflect the new price and weeks more to go back to normal after the sale ends. Paid search, on the other hand, can adapt to these changes as they occur. You can stop buying the keyword for an out-of-stock item in paid placement, and you can remove the item from your trusted feed to the shopping search engine. You can change your paid search ad and your shopping search trusted feed to reflect price changes as they happen. You can ratchet up your investment during your busy season and taper it off at other times. What's more, you can constantly monitor the return on your investments and make changes each day to increase conversions. Paid search is probably the most flexible form of advertising available today.

- *Near-total message control.* As you learned in Chapter 12, "Optimize Your Content," organic search requires your pages to be designed to please both search engines and visitors. Organic search engines will present only the pages that are considered the best matches, and searchers will not convert unless the pages appeal to them. With paid search, you must of course entice your search visitors to convert, but there are very few restrictions on the content of your message. Paid search offers far more message control, because the message can be directly targeted at searchers, with little concern about what the search engines want—you need only abide by their simple editorial guidelines, which we review later in this chapter. In fact, you can continually tinker with your message to test which ones get the highest conversion—modifying your copy, your offer, your price, or anything else. You can change the content in your trusted feed every day, and modify your paid placement ads even more frequently. You can also change the content on your landing pages at will. Your ability to control your message is unmatched by any other advertising medium.

Despite all these advantages, paid search is not for everyone. If you sell low-priced, low-margin products, you might find that the cost of advertising is more than you can justify in return. If you are unable to place any monetary value on your Web conversions, it will be hard to justify paid search spending. Many noncommercial and nonprofit sites find that paid search does not help them sustain their operations. For businesses, however, especially businesses that are trying to attract prospective customers to their site, paid search increasingly has a place in even the smallest marketing budgets.

Throughout this book, we have discussed many ways to spend money to improve your search marketing, including paid directory listings (in Chapter 3, "How Search Marketing Works"), paid inclusion (in Chapter 10, "Get Your Site Indexed"), and paid links (in Chapter 13, "Attract Links to Your Site"). Each of those techniques is important, but the two biggest paid search opportunities are in **paid placement** and **shopping search**, which we concentrate on in this chapter.

Paid Placement

We covered the basics of paid placement in the first three chapters of this book, but there is more that you should know to run a successful program. You recall that paid placement allows search marketers to "buy" a keyword by bidding an amount they pay each time their advertisement is clicked. As a result, paid placement is sometimes called cost-per-click (CPC) or pay-per-click (PPC) search.

In Chapter 3 (in Table 3-2), we listed the leading paid placement vendors. Keep in mind that you work with the paid placement vendors directly, but that your ads might appear on many different Web sites—Google's ads appear on AOL Search, for example. Although the top three paid placement engines (Google, Yahoo!, and MSN Search) combine to deliver 97 percent of all paid placement clicks worldwide, some of the second-tier vendors have strengths, too. MIVA (www.miva.com) has a large European network, and is an excellent vehicle for reaching highly targeted niche audiences, as its ads are presently shown on CNET and some other popular sites. Two growing vendors are Enhance Interactive (www.enhance.com) and ePilot (www.epilot.com). Each of these minor vendors drives far fewer clicks than Yahoo! and Google, but their per-click rates tend to be significantly cheaper, so they might be worthwhile for inclusion in your paid search mix.

Beyond these vendors, some very small programs might also make sense for you. These micro-vendors collect very few clicks, and lack the reporting of the big guys, but their high degree of specialization might deliver extremely qualified traffic. The best resource for locating these engines can be found at www.payperclicksearchengines.com—it has a list of more than 600 sites that accept paid placement advertising. It has reviewed a number of these programs to help you select the ones most appropriate for your business.

IF IT AIN'T BROKE, DON'T FIX IT: IS FIXED PLACEMENT FOR YOU?

Paid placement is actually a blanket name for just about any technique that gets your message in front of searchers for a fee. We concentrate in this chapter on auction-style paid placement, by far the most predominant form, but an older form, called **fixed placement** is still around.

Fixed placement is not emphasized by the major search engines the way it once was, and some no longer offer it at all. But specialty search engines and lesser-known search engines continue to make fixed placements available for many of their keywords.

The "fixed" part of fixed placement refers to the fact that the place your ad appears on the page does not change, regardless of what other advertisers do—this is in strong contrast to auction-style placement, where your competitors' bids give them as much influence over where your ad appears as you have. Fixed placement is also fixed in another way—the price is typically fixed for the duration of your agreement—you can negotiate the same price for months on end. This fixed pricing also differs from the minute-by-minute bidding changes that auction-style placements allow.

Fixed placement is usually priced per **impression** rather than per click, so you must pay the negotiated price each time your ad is shown, not each time it is clicked. And it is typical to buy 100 percent of the impressions, rather than having your ad rotated, although this is negotiable. Buying all of the impressions blocks your competitors from being shown in your spot. Although this sounds more expensive, it can often be cheaper if your per-impression cost is low and your click rate is high. But not all fixed-placement contracts are charged that way—you can negotiate per-click or even per-action (conversion) pricing sometimes. In fact, negotiability is another major difference between fixed placement and auctions. Savvy marketers can negotiate price, of course, but they also frequently receive throw-ins as part of the deal, such as extra impressions for the same price (perhaps in return for a longer monthly commitment).

But fixed placement is *not* for beginners. First off, you need to have a very good understanding of your impressions, your clickthrough rate, your conversions, and your profitability before you are ready to negotiate a fixed-placement deal. With auction placements, you can stop at any point if you have overpaid, but fixed-placement contracts are long-term commitments (think months) with limited ability to cancel.

Fixed placement is also inflexible in other ways. Search marketers accustomed to changing auction listings every day (to tweak their click rate and better qualify their customers) are in for a surprise. Fixed-placement listings are often manually updated, so your contract limits the number of changes you can make. Moreover, your changes can take days to be reflected on the live site, rather than minutes. And it can be almost impossible to change the keywords you bought—whatever you picked you are likely stuck with for the duration.

So, you need to be very sure of what you are agreeing to before you sign a fixed-placement contract. You might be able to get the same highly qualified traffic from fixed placement at lower rates than you pay in auctions, but a couple of mistakes can wipe out all of your savings and then some. Experienced marketers can lock their competitors out of fixed-placement positions with the right long-term deal and can drive extra visitors at lower costs. Just don't jump in before you know what you are doing.

Although the smaller paid placement programs might be valuable to some search marketers, all of you need to understand how to work with Google, Yahoo!, and MSN Search, who manage the lion's share of the paid placement listings, so we focus on them throughout the chapter whenever discussing paid placement.

As explained in Chapter 2, "How Search Engines Work," the biggest difference between paid placement engines is how they rank the paid search results. Overturn (now owned by Yahoo!) introduced the straight auction—the high bidder for a keyword gets the #1 position. Google's AdWords program, in contrast, pioneered the hybrid auction ranking algorithm that weighs both the auction bid and that ad's clickthrough rate to decide which one will provide the most money to Google. In doing so, not only is Google richer, but listings with higher click-through rates rank higher, raising the value to the searcher. MSN Search also uses a hybrid auction, and Yahoo! has announced plans for it, but less-popular paid placement engines generally stick with high bidder auctions. Search marketers need to understand the differences between the two approaches:

- *Predicting high bidder cost is simpler.* With a high bidder auction, you can look at what others are bidding and assume that if you bid high enough, you can take a high spot. You can then examine keyword demand and estimate your clickthrough rate and *voilà*, you "know" your costs (as shown in Chapter 8, "Define Your Search Marketing Strategy"). With hybrid auctions, however, you have no idea how much to bid to take any particular spot, because you do not know your click rate or your competitors'. So you can neither estimate how many times your ad will appear nor how many visitors will come to your site—until you try it. Neither Google nor MSN divulge keyword demand, but Yahoo! has announced that it will continue to do so when it adopts a hybrid auction.

- *High bidder auctions are more volatile.* Because bidders can raise or lower their bids at will, rankings can move up and down with alarming speed. Because clickthrough rates tend to be more stable, hybrid auctions tend not to be as erratic even if bidders make many changes. Further, because bid changes have less of an effect on rankings, bidders have less incentive for frequent changes.

- *High bidder auction bid management is more complex.* Because bidding is open and because bids directly correlate to high bidder rankings, gamesmanship ensues. Powerful software tools monitor competitive keywords to perform bid jamming, and several other interesting tricks that we explain. Hybrid auctions render these techniques unnecessary.

Generally, it's harder to plan a paid search campaign for a hybrid auction, while a high bid-der auction requires more management after setup. Later in this chapter, we show you how to succeed at paid placement programs, but before we do, you need to understand two relatively new twists in paid placement called contextual advertising and local search.

Contextual Advertising

Contextual advertising is an increasingly popular offshoot of traditional paid placement (if you can call anything in our young search marketing industry "traditional"). In its most basic form, contextual advertising depends on the paid placement vendor striking a deal with an information site to show ads on the information site's pages. Any site that draws heavy traffic is a strong can-didate to display contextual ads—think CNN or ESPN or weather.com or CNET. Every article on these sites offers possibilities for contextual ads. As Figure 14-1 shows, an ESPN story about the Yankees might attract Yankee fans who want to buy Yankee tickets, so why not advertise Yankee tickets from *your* store on that page?

Figure 14-1   Contextual advertising. ESPN targets its advertising to the content of each individual news story so that highly qualified visitors click through.

MapQuest (www.mapquest.com) further illustrates the use of contextual ads. When people search on a specific location at MapQuest, they not only get maps and directions but also ads for hotels, shops, and restaurants along the route. MapQuest and other information sites could easily sell advertising directly, without any help from the paid placement vendors, and some do. But because their content changes so rapidly, some of them are unlikely to be able to charge high prices to show the ads—they could sell only banner ads that do not promise what content will be on the same page as the ad. You would undoubtedly pay less for an ad for your Yankee tickets that might appear on the same page as a tennis story, because the readers of the tennis story are less-qualified buyers for your baseball tickets.

However, paid placement vendors already know how to display different ads depending on what the searcher enters, so why not apply that same technology to rapidly changing information sites? In the example in Figure 14-2, Google has already indexed the page on PetPlace.com (www.petplace.com), so it knows what the page is about—in this case, dogs. Google can easily select ads related to dogs to be displayed on that page alongside the story. Readers can click the ad to go to the advertiser's URL, just as with paid placement. The advertiser pays for the click and PetPlace.com and Google both take a cut. You can also see how ScubaBoard (www.scubaboard.com) uses Google contextual ads, too, but those ads are on a very different subject—scuba diving. Each information site might place the ads in different spots on their pages, but they all attempt to drive qualified visitors to the advertiser's site.

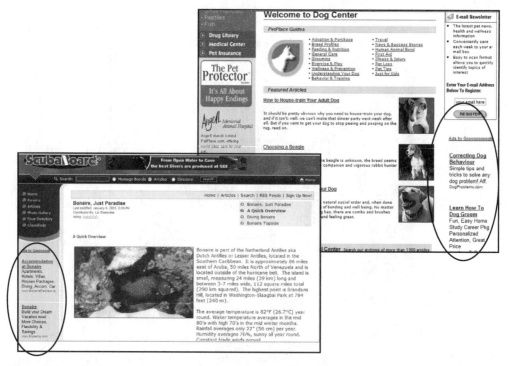

Figure 14-2   Top Shopping Search Engines. Yahoo! Shopping offers more products from more merchants than the other engines combined.

Contextual advertising programs work like any other paid placement program in which you pay for each click on your ad—both Google and Yahoo! offer such programs and Microsoft is readying one, too. Yahoo! and Google compete strenuously for the best information sites to display their ads. Google's AdSense program signs up information sites willing to display contextual advertising; Yahoo! fights to add similar sites to its Content Match network. Google is even exploring whole new services to serve as attractions for its contextual ads, such as the free Gmail service (gmail.google.com). Each side touts the quality of its advertising network to persuade you that highly qualified visitors will come to your site after clicking your contextual ad.

In these image-conscious times, *where* your ad is placed reflects upon your company. So you are probably concerned about exactly which Web sites and exactly which pages your contextual ads will appear on. Snap Electronics would not want its digital camera ad shown next to a somewhat risqué article that advised using photography to spice up your sex life, even if it was a mainstream men's magazine. The search engines are quite aware of the sensibilities of their advertisers, and they take great pains to avoid embarrassing situations, but most search engines offer no ability for advertisers to *choose* ad venues, the way you can with other media buys.

Not only that, but most do not even report where your ad ran after the fact. Why? If the vendors disclosed where your ads were appearing, they fear that you would make fixed-placement or banner deals directly with those sites and cut the paid placement vendors out of the action. Although this is frustrating for your public relations team, to address the problem you need to opt out of contextual advertising.

Except with Google. Google offers its advertisers *site exclusion*, so that a list of Web sites can be prevented from displaying their ads. (This is exactly the kind of function Snap Electronics was seeking in our earlier example.) Google does ask that site exclusion be used as intended, and that very long lists of sites not be provided in order to target ads to the few sites that are left in Google's content network. Advertisers that wish to target sites have another technique available to them.

Google offers that technique, understandably named *site targeting*, which allows advertisers to provide a list of sites that alone may show that advertiser's ads. But there is one twist. Unlike all other Google contextual advertising, site targeting ads are not charged by the click, but rather by the impression. So, each time a site targeting ad is displayed, the advertiser is charged.

Google also offers demographic site targeting, choosing sites by gender or household income, but only for contextual advertising (not search advertising as MSN does.) Ads are not filtered visitor by visitor—instead, a golf site attracting men can be targeted for ads for males. All readers see the ads, but the advertiser reaches more of the target male market this way.

In the past, Yahoo! offered advertisers separate bidding for their paid placement and contextual advertising programs, while Google did not. All that changed in 2005 when Google decided to separate its bidding also. Separate bidding is important to advertisers who believe that people who navigate pages and click contextual ads are not as highly qualified as those entering a search query. As a consequence, those advertisers believe that contextual ads should not cost the same per-click fee as search ads. Everyone agrees that far less traffic is driven from contextual ads than from paid placement, justifying separate bidding. Google, in addition, has responded by automatically adjusting pricing.

Google's "Smart Pricing" might reduce the cost of clicks from contextual advertising when Google believes that the conversion rate for those clicks is lower than expected. Google offers an example that caught Snap Electronics' attention: "A click on an ad for digital cameras on a Web page about photography tips might be worth less than a click on the same ad appearing next to a review of digital cameras."

Contextual advertising is perfect for products predictably related to certain kinds of information. For example, if you make camera lenses, you want to advertise on the most popular photography sites, especially camera review sites. The lens maker can show contextual ads only on relevant sites that cost nothing until the reader clicks.

Despite the promise, most advertisers are convinced that those who click contextual ads are not as highly qualified as searchers. Moreover, contextual advertising's biggest challenge is the quality of the pages where the ads appear. Many contextual ad sites are highly relevant sites for your ad, but not always the most popular destinations. Those popular destinations often find they can sell ads directly to advertisers, without giving the paid placement vendors a cut. Contextual advertising, in the minds of some marketers, is associated with sites that, although relevant, are not of the highest popularity or quality.

But better technology might already be changing the quality of contextual traffic. As search engines do a better job of targeting contextual ads to the content it appears with, click rates and conversion rates might increase. Kevin Lee, co-founder of paid search management company Did-it.com, has found that improved targeting and lower prices for Google's contextual advertising are yielding contextual returns that rival search paid placement for some clients.

To see whether contextual ads are cost-effective for your keywords, you can run a test with one campaign that uses your keywords in the traditional search paid placement and a second campaign with the same keywords enabled for contextual placement only. The search engine will report each campaign separately, and you can compare to see whether the contextual campaign delivers enough value to be worth your while. Some search marketers report that contextual advertising has been a gold mine, whereas others have been disappointed; so test it for yourself. In spite of some challenges, contextual advertising continues to grow each year and might be appropriate for your search marketing mix.

Local Search

If your Web site attracts visitors from an entire country, or from multiple countries, paid placement works just fine. You can choose the countries for your keyword purchases and target your searchers effectively. But what if your business is local? You do not want to waste your budget paying for clicks from searchers outside your area. What do you do if your Web site is for a retailer that operates in a single region within a country, or for a business with just one location?

Step up to **local search**. As discussed in Chapter 3, several of the major search engines, as well as traditional Yellow Pages publishers, offer local search engines that help searchers find companies within a particular geographic area.

Your business can benefit from the huge increase in searchers' propensity to think local. Research conducted in 2004 shows that more than one fourth of all searches are for merchants "near home or work"—more than twice the rate previously reported. Seventy-four percent of all searchers say they have conducted local searches, with 45 percent of local searchers intending to buy. Some large businesses can benefit from local search, too, such as a retailer that wants to make it easy for customers to find the nearest location. Table 14-1 lists the top local search programs. Verizon and SBC have made a transition from printed Yellow Pages to the Internet; the rest of the leaders have their roots in Internet search.

Table 14-1 Local Search Programs (Local advertisers can advertise on the Internet the same way they do in the Yellow Pages in the printed phone book.)

Company	Program	URL	Monthly Traffic	Inclusion Fees	Local Filters
Yahoo!	Yahoo! Local	local.yahoo.com	Undisclosed	Monthly and per click	Zip code city
	Yahoo! Yellow Pages	yp.yahoo.com	30 million	Monthly and per click	Zip code city
Verizon	Super Pages	www.superpages.com	16 million	Fixed fee and monthly per click	Zip code city phone number
InfoSpace	InfoSpace	www.infospace.com	6 million	CPM (per-impression) and per click	Zip code phone number
	Switchboard	www.switchboard.com	8 million	(per-impression) and per click	City phone number
SBC	SMARTpages.com	www.smartpages.com	12 million	Fixed fee and per click	Zip code city phone number
IAC/Inter-activeCorp	CitySearch	www.citysearch.com	8 million	Fixed fee and per click	Zip code city
Google	Local Search	local.google.com	Undisclosed	None	Zip code city

Yahoo! is the biggest player at the moment, with more than 15 million Yellow Page-style listings for U.S.-based businesses, in addition to a local search engine. These two services are very similar and might be merged at some point. Yahoo! compiles its business listings from its Yahoo! Shopping member list as well as various data sources, including InfoUSA (www.infousa.com). You can add your business to the lists for free by visiting listings.local.yahoo.com, but to get a prominent advertisement, you need to pay. For $10 a month, your business can add your company's slogan, a detailed description, links to your Web site, and up to 10 photos. Most of its competitors offer similar features, with traditional printed Yellow Pages vendors offering online tie-ins with its print advertising plans.

Local search depends on searchers telling the search engine the location as part of their search query. Beyond local search, **geographic targeting** is a way for paid placement advertisers to purchase general-purpose keywords (for which searchers have specified no place names), but show their ads only to searchers at a particular location. We talk about this opportunity later in this chapter.

Whether your business takes advantage of local search, contextual advertising, or any other form of paid placement, you are employing only some of the paid search programs available to you. Next we explore the other significant paid search prospect.

Shopping Search

Paid placement is not the only paid search opportunity. For some companies, **shopping search** is a much more important part of their paid search budget. If your business sells the kind of product online that is offered by shopping search engines, you might find it very profitable to be listed. In fact, many advertisers say that shopping search is their most consistently profitable marketing program.

We discussed shopping search engines briefly in Chapter 1 and showed the market share of each one in Figure 1-14. Now let's look more deeply at shopping search in general and at the leading shopping search engines in particular.

Shopping search engines are primarily designed to offer "one-stop shopping" for a particular product. A shopping searcher has already moved past informational searches and is ready to conduct a transaction. The searcher has decided, for example, to purchase a digital camera, and knows the desired features, but might not know exactly which camera to buy. Or the searcher has chosen a model, but is shopping for the most favorable price or the quickest delivery. The numbers back up these assumptions. One study showed that searchers at shopping.com are twice as likely to buy *and* they buy twice as much as searchers at traditional search engines.

Shopping search engines support these transactional searchers by consolidating the offerings of numerous manufacturers and retailers into one searchable "mall." If shoppers are choosing between multiple cameras, for example, each camera might be listed in the search results (along with a picture, a short description or feature list, customer reviews, and the price range). As shoppers hone in on particular models of digital cameras, the Web sites (often called "stores") that offer the camera are displayed in the search results. Each store might show its logo, its merchant rating (voted on by its previous customers), its price for the camera, and other distinguishing information to coax shoppers to click through to the store's site. When shoppers click results, they are taken to Web sites ("stores") to complete their purchases. Shoppers are beginning to appreciate this approach, with 54 percent of them citing the time savings and 52 percent valuing how much money they save when they use shopping search.

Shopping search engines offer varying user interfaces to shoppers. Some shopping search engines allow searchers to narrow down their selections by product features and price, whereas others support sorting the list based on price or merchant rating. Many calculate prices including tax and shipping charges if shoppers disclose their location.

Shoppers are responding. In 2004, BizRate and the Kelsey Group found that 37% of online consumers were very familiar with shopping search sites. Shopping search increased 22% from 2003 to 2004, comprising nearly one half of one percent of Internet traffic!

To garner shopping search traffic, get to know the leaders shown in Table 14-2.

Table 14-2 Top Shopping Search Engines (Yahoo! Shopping offers more products from more merchants than the other engines combined.)

Search Engine	Monthly Traffic	Merchants	Products	Product Submission	Product Minimum
Yahoo! Shopping shopping.yahoo.com	18 million	200,000	50 million	Trusted feed	15¢
Shopping.com www.shopping.com	15 million	5,000	Undis-closed	Crawl or trusted feed	5¢
PriceGrabber www.pricegrabber.com	15 million	6,000	10 million	Trusted feed	15¢
Shopzilla www.shopzilla.com	13 million	50,000	28 million	Crawl or trusted feed	10¢
NexTag www.nextag.com	10 million	3,000	3 million	Trusted feed	15¢
Become www.become.com	Undisclosed	250,000	20 million	Crawl or trusted feed	10¢
Froogle froogle.google.com	Undisclosed	Undisclosed	Undisclosed	Crawl or trusted feed	Free

Yahoo! Shopping is the leader, in products offered as well as traffic, but Shopzilla is nipping at its heels, with plans to reach 45 million products in 2005. Froogle, Google's shopping search entry, is the most interesting play, because you can provide a trusted feed containing all of your product data without incurring any per-click fees—at least as long as Froogle remains in beta test. Perhaps Froogle will emerge from beta test soon, after posting 270 percent growth in 2004 over the prior year.

 Although most shopping search visitors buy from U.S. merchants, shopping search engines are springing up around the world, and increasing in popularity. In Japan, Rakuten (www.rakuten.co.jp) is the second most popular site in Japan, ahead of Google. Rakuten is a combined shopping search and shopping mall site that caters to Japanese online shopping habits, including the tremendously popular "shoppers clubs." Merchants pay monthly fees for their shops and also fork over a percentage of all sales.

Table 14-3 shows the top shopping search engines in Australia, Hong Kong, and the U.K., as Yahoo! and MSN jockey for the top spots. Kelkoo, the leader in the U.K., is owned by Yahoo! and is the third most-visited site there—it also operates in nine other European countries.

Table 14-3   Top Shopping Search Engines Around the World (Most sales are in the United States, but shopping search is catching on in other countries, too.)

Rank	Australia	Hong Kong	United Kingdom
1	MSN eShop eshop.msn.com	Yahoo! Hong Kong Shopping hk.shopping.yahoo.com	Kelkoo UK uk.kelkoo.com
2	PriceGrabber www.pricegrabber.com	MSN eShop eshop.msn.com	Shopping.com UK uk.shopping.com
3	BizRate www.bizrate.com	PriceGrabber www.pricegrabber.com	Pricerunner www.pricerunner.co.uk
4	All the Brands www.allthebrands.com	Yahoo! Shopping shopping.yahoo.com	DealTime UK www.dealtime.co.uk
5	Epinions www.epinions.com	DealSaving www.dealsaving.com	Froogle UK www.froogle.co.uk

Source: Hitwise from survey on November 24, 2004

As you can see, the leaders in shopping search vary among countries, owing to different languages, currencies, and shipping feasibility. If you list your product with a shopping search engine that serves the entire United States, for example, you must be willing to ship anywhere in the country. You are wasting your click fees if you cannot fulfill an order, and searchers will be frustrated with your company, which harms your reputation.

Before plunging into shopping search, realize that it is a very competitive marketplace. You must be prepared to compete against other merchants on price, shipping speed, and reliability. Having a more informative or easy-to-use Web site is important for conversion, but shoppers will compare you to other merchants before they click through to your site. If you can compete on these factors, you can succeed in shopping search.

Shopping search and paid placement are the biggest opportunities in paid search, so let's examine how to think about them.

Your Paid Search Philosophy

You're probably getting used to it, but we're going to get philosophical again. Just because it is so easy to start a paid search program doesn't mean that you should not do some thinking first. In fact, because it *is* so easy to shoot from the hip, it is probable that some of your competitors run their programs that way. So, just a little thinking on your part can pay big dividends.

We spend the rest of this chapter explaining how to optimize your paid search campaign, but before we do, do you know what it is worth to you? As we have throughout this book, we harp on measurements. So, let's look first at what we know about the value of paid search.

Look for Value

Gunning for #1. *That* is the philosophy of the rookie search marketer. But let's take a step back and see whether we can adopt the philosophy of a cagey veteran marketer instead. The savvy marketer is looking for value, so let's examine how you find value in paid search.

We know that paid search drives traffic. You learned earlier that shopping search, in particular, drives visitors that are much more likely to buy than garden-variety searchers. But what about paid placement? Atlas DMT, a paid search software vendor, has demonstrated that paid placement can be highly effective in driving traffic, and that garnering the top positions drives the most. (Not exactly rocket science, huh?)

What might surprise you is the disparity in traffic from each paid placement rank—the #1 position drives about ten times more traffic than #10. With Google, even the drop-off from #1 to #2 is dramatic—about 40 percent. Although Atlas studied only paid placement, you can assume that having the top ranking in a shopping search category is valuable, too.

So what's wrong with gunning for #1? It seems to make a lot of sense. You are in paid search to drive traffic and ranking #1 drives the most traffic. Well, if you have an information site, you might be happy with merely generating traffic—perhaps your goal is to sell advertising on your site. For most of you, however, Web *conversions* are your focus. So, does getting a top paid search ranking give you the greatest number of conversions? Not always. Another study from those busy Atlas folks showed that the highest conversion rate is generally found for the top ranking results, but conversion rates vary by keyword demand. The 20 percent of keywords in the greatest demand had high conversion rates for the highest-ranked results, but the remaining 80 percent were all over the map—those 80 percent lower-demand keywords frequently produced higher conversion rates for their lower results than for top slots. Some Google results that landed at positions 8–10 had higher conversions than the #1 for the same keyword, for example. Less markedly, less-popular Yahoo! queries often showed similar conversion rates for the #1 and #10 results.

So what do we make of this research? Well, the good news is that you can pay considerably less than what it costs to rank #1 for many keywords and still convert at a high rate. However, the bad news is that you will have to redouble your keyword research efforts to find those low-volume keywords. You will also have to work harder at measurements, so that you can see when you are converting and when you are not. We also might conclude that Google's ranking algorithm might give the savvy search marketer an edge, because it places so much value on click-through. Perhaps those #8 ranking keywords are converting well in part because they get high clickthrough, and their per-click costs are modest.

Search marketers seem to be warming to this approach of purchasing deeper keywords. In 2004, the average advertiser's number of keywords rose 50 percent, reported *BusinessWeek* magazine.

No studies yet tell us whether shopping search conversion rates are high for lower-ranked results, but because most shopping engines charge every competitor in the product category the same per-click fee, there is no reason to be anyplace except at the top. Ranking lower usually does not save you money the way it can for paid placement.

You also need to develop your philosophy on local search and geographic targeting. If your business is listed in the printed phone book, you might as well take advantage of the free listings by Internet Yellow Pages providers. But should you employ enhanced listings for a $10 monthly fee? Should your paid placement campaigns use geographic targeting? You should think through the advantages of such programs and decide whether you want to test their effectiveness for your site or skip them completely.

So the first part of our philosophy is that you are looking for *value*, regardless of the rankings. Although top rankings generally drive more traffic to your site, you saw that rankings do not always correlate with traffic. And besides, your goal is to drive the most conversions at the lowest price—*that* is what "value" means. We know that we might need to do a little extra work to find value, but the studies say that the value is there.

Play the Market

Paid search is a marketplace, so you might as well apply what you know about markets as part of your paid search philosophy. All markets are made up of buyers and sellers, and prices fluctuate based on supply and demand. When supply is high relative to demand, prices are cheap. As more and more buyers chase after fewer and fewer goods, however, prices rise, the economists will tell you. So how does that apply to paid search? There aren't any "goods," after all—it's just a spot on a Web page, isn't it?

Let's take a tour of the important market principles that underlie paid search markets, starting with the basics.

Paid Search Market Basics

Although economists like to talk about "goods," market forces apply to services, too. Think about how passenger seat prices are set for an airline. Tickets bought far in advance are usually discounted because the airline collects the passenger's money long before the flight. Nonrefundable tickets are cheaper than refundable tickets because the airline locks in a sale. Because early payments and guaranteed sales have value to the airline, the airline lowers the price of the ticket in those circumstances. But what happens as the day of the flight approaches? If there are few remaining seats, the airline raises prices, so that last-minute business fliers pay top dollar because they have no alternative. If many seats remain, however, the airline might deeply discount each ticket hoping to attract impulse vacationers, because every ticket sold, even at a deep discount, is worth more than an empty seat.

Paid search markets have some of the elements of airline pricing. Shopping search engines do not charge the same per-click fee for every category because some categories are worth more than others to search marketers. Categories for products with higher prices (and presumably higher profits) tend to cost more than those for inexpensive items, just the way airlines try to offer vacationers bigger discounts than business travelers.

Other forms of advertising follow market principles, too. Commercials on highly rated prime-time TV shows cost more than those during the *Late Late Show*. When more people watch the show, advertisers pay more to reach them. For the same reason, high-demand keywords tend to cost more than less-popular ones because search marketers are paying for traffic (and they hope conversions).

But shopping search and paid placement are two different kinds of markets. You do not typically bid on your per-click fees with shopping search engines, where the seller sets the price and the buyer decides whether to pay the price or not. Paid placement is an auction market, in which only minimum bids are set and the price is set by whatever buyers are willing to pay.

For shopping search, your philosophy, as you saw earlier, is to find value. You need to determine which products you should sell through shopping search and which ones do not pay. You must know when the per-click fee charged for your product category by a shopping search engine does not allow you to turn a profit, so that you can walk away from that "opportunity." Later in the chapter, we show you how to calculate that. If the price is too high for you, you might check other shopping search engines to see whether they are cheaper or avoid them altogether.

Auction Pricing

Auction markets have a different ethos than fixed-price markets. When the number of buyers is high, the prices at auction markets tend to be high, too, because more buyers are chasing fewer goods (and perhaps because the prices more accurately reflect the value of what is being sold). Auction markets also result in more sales, because items that would go wanting if priced too high are sold at a price that might disappoint the seller, but they are still sold.

Think about how eBay works. Many unique items sold on eBay would have brought a fraction of their price at a garage sale, simply because a higher number of serious collectors are exposed to the item on eBay. On the other hand, commonplace items sell for cheap prices because of the high number of sellers who make them available compared to the size of the buyer market for those items.

Economists call this phenomenon **scarcity**—scarce items cost more when many people desire them. And scarce items fetch far higher prices at auction, which is why auction houses are always selling memorabilia or a celebrity's estate. If there is only one of something, and two rich people both want it, the price can go sky-high.

Paid placement follows the scarcity principle—only one result ranks #1 for every keyword within a search engine. If two bidders are determined to be #1 for a keyword, prices can skyrocket in a matter of hours.

Efficiency Is Everything

When you are faced with markets such as shopping search and paid placement, you can watch prices gradually rise to the highest sustainable point. As more and more search marketers begin to play the paid placement game, prices tend to rise. They aren't making any more #1 positions for the *digital cameras* keyword. There's only one. The more bidders that want it, the higher per-click fees will go. (Similarly, the more players enter the digital camera product category, the higher the per-click fees that the shopping search engines can charge.)

Economists call this tendency market **efficiency**—sellers will, over time, maximize the price based on the value to the buyers. And economic **price theory** holds that, over time, all benefits of an item will be incorporated into its price as buyers' knowledge becomes "perfect." Well, nothing is perfect in real life, only in economic theory, so inefficiencies exist everywhere in markets, just waiting to be exploited.

Your job: Find them. Think about how the stock market works. If everyone knew exactly what every stock was worth at any given moment in time, there would not be much point to buying and selling. However, one of the reasons that shares of stock are bought and sold is that two people have very different opinions about what the stock is worth. One reason this is so is that, economic theory notwithstanding, some of the "knowledge" that people have is irrational. It makes no sense at all. Search marketing is no different. If you are rational, you will usually outdo emotional types and guessers. It is like the stock market in that you need information to get an edge, but not hot tips. The information you need is right under your nose and you can gather it.

Unlike the stock market, paid search is not worth the same amount to every company. Even if every site paid the same 25¢ per click, some companies would make more money on that click than others. If you gather the information available to you, you will know what each keyword's position is worth to you, so you will never overpay.

So how do you know what to pay? How do you know whether that shopping search click is worth 25¢? Or whether the #1 placement for that keyword is worth 93¢? *That* is where the Web Conversion Cycle comes in. If you know the value of every conversion, and you know your conversion rate from your search referral, you know what that referral is worth. Then you can decide what to pay.

But it is usually more complicated than that, because the shopping search engines might be charging more than you can afford for some products, or the high rankings in paid placement are bid through the roof. How can others afford to pay when you cannot?

Two answers are possible. One is that they are nuts. They are bidding to keep that #1 position, and they lose money on every sale. If that's the case, you probably have a short-term problem; economics has this funny way of correcting problems such as money-losing bidding. Although annoying, you can withstand that situation for as long as it lasts.

But you might, in fact, have a more serious problem. Perhaps they can pay higher prices because they are more *efficient* than you are. Maybe they *can* make money at that high rate, but you cannot. Several reasons could account for this:

- *Their costs are lower*. If they can turn a much higher profit per item than your business can, they can afford to bid higher per-click costs and drive their sales up from improved traffic. Or they can pay the shopping search per-click costs for more of their products than you can.

- *They turn their inventory faster*. If they can sell twice as many items per month as you do, they tie up their cash in inventory for far shorter periods of time for the same amount of merchandise. (In brick-and-mortar-retail, grocery stores can operate profitably with a much lower profit margin than furniture stores because grocers "turn" their inventory so many times more each year.) Their higher turn rate will lower their costs and allow them to bid higher in paid placement and cover more items in shopping search.

- *Their clickthrough rate is higher.* If their ad copy (or their brand name) causes higher clickthrough rates, they might drive more traffic for the same ad budget than you do. That means each click costs them less than it costs you.

- *Their conversion rate is higher.* If their Web site visitors convert at higher rates, they sell more items than you do for the same ad budget. Each click is worth more to them than to you.

- *They know something you don't know.* Maybe you are trying to get the lowest cost per order, and they are going for the highest revenue. Perhaps you are budgeting based on profit margin, and they are budgeting based on lifetime value. Later in this chapter, we highlight your metrics choices and you can decide which one truly captures the value of every search click. The higher that you are able to justify the value, the higher you can profitably bid, so having the most complete model of value puts you in the strongest competitive position.

So, to take advantage of inefficiencies in the market, you must make your business as efficient as possible, so that you will have all of those advantages over your competitors, rather than the other way around. As a search marketer, you will not have much impact on whether your company is the low-cost producer in your field, and you will not have a great deal to do with how fast your inventory turns, but there are a lot of things you can affect, which we discuss later in this chapter.

Keep in mind that the only way to affect anything is to have the necessary information. As you drive for efficiency, you want to know the conversion rate for every product you sell (for shopping search) and for every keyword you buy (for paid placement), but you want to know much more. Are conversions higher

- From certain search engines?
- In certain positions?
- With certain copy?
- With certain landing pages?
- At certain times?

If so, you can take advantage, as we explain later. By gathering the most detailed information possible, you will know the right situations to play the market and when to hang back. But ratcheting up your efficiency is only part of the game. You also need to learn about an old business maxim of using other people's money.

Other People's Money

Some of the richest people around got there by investing other people's money. If the investment fails, they lose nothing; if it succeeds, however, they will get something out of it. Frequently these smart people get a management fee or a cut of the proceeds for their contribution to the success.

Smart search marketers can use other people's money, too. Here are several ways to do that:

- *Raid sales budgets*. One of the best ways to get investment in your paid search campaign is to raid other budgets, and the sales budget is one place to start. If you can show that your paid search program is wildly profitable, but you do not have a high enough budget to fund any more of those oh-so-profitable clicks, maybe your sales team does. If you can show that your return on spending is higher than the payback on their latest incentive program, you might get some of their money.

- *Raid marketing budgets*. If your company spends money on brand marketing, maybe you can take some of it for paid search. You are already showing how paid search delivers conversions, but did you know it can raise brand awareness, too? Surveys show that searchers are 27 percent more likely to recall a well-known brand returned as the #1 paid placement result than searchers who did not see that ad. Contextual ads show a 23 percent lift. If the marketing team is willing to kick in extra money, you can afford higher bids for the most popular keywords. According to Piper Jaffray, 10% of search spending is already driven by branding impact.

- *Raid other product budgets*. Does your product "drag" other sales in its wake? A sale of a computer might include software, services, and financing. Selling a washing machine might include a maintenance agreement. A sale of a stapler might include staples. Think about your product. If there are other things that can be sold along with your product, other people in your business are just as interested in you selling your product as you are. Can you offer these tie-in products on the checkout page? If so, will other product lines help subsidize your paid search costs to help improve their sales?

- *Raid your supplier's budgets*. Do you sell a product that your supplier is as anxious to sell as you are? Steal a page from the offline marketing playbook and suggest **cooperative advertising**. Relatively new to search marketing, Intel, among others, is working with its key customers to defray the costs of search marketing. They pay part of your per-click fees for products that contain their components. You might want to approach your suppliers with a similar idea.

- *Raid your supply chain's budget*. Suppose you are a business-to-business marketer but your paid placement keywords are attracting consumer clicks that just go to waste? Perhaps you can team up with one of your resellers to share the clicks (and the costs). If you sell wholesale and they sell retail, put up a landing page for those keywords that siphons searchers to the right site (yours or your retailer's) and you can split the per-click charges for the traffic you get. By doing so, you can share much higher bids for those keywords because none of the clicks are wasted.

Any of these techniques can make your budget go much further than if your philosophy is to go it alone, but you will be forced to share more information with your new-found partners than ever before, so you need to have close relationships for it to work well.

So far, you have learned a lot about how to develop a paid search philosophy, but the most important lesson is humility—you will never get it completely right. Next we show you how to get it a little less wrong every day.

Iterate, Iterate, and Then Iterate Some More

Here's a secret: Paid placement won't work. At least, it won't work at first. When you start, you will find that your ads get so few clicks that they are disabled by the paid placement engine. Or you will find that your ads get loads of clicks, but almost no sales. Expect this. Expect it not to work. Your program *will* start badly.

But no matter how badly you start out, if you are willing to track your numbers and keep tuning your program, you will eventually succeed. The secret is to start small. You *know* you are not going to get it right, so why not lose as little as possible while you learn? You learn just as much about horse racing betting at the $2 window as you do at the $100 window—you just have a lot more money left over after the last race.

The secret is not how well your paid search campaign starts—it is how you improve it every day. If you have chosen the right metrics to track, and you religiously measure your success, you can keep adjusting until you are as efficient as you can be.

If you can afford to start out with a large budget, the best way to spend it is on as broad a set of targets as possible. Don't shoot your wad of cash trying to be #1 for a popular query. Instead, buy as many keywords as you can, even if they are very low positions. Buy different keywords every day if you need to spread things around. If it doesn't cost any more to set up, put your entire catalog into a shopping search engine. Why? Because that way you will gather the most data. You will start getting click rate data and conversion data for as many targets as possible—as many paid placement keywords and as many shopping search products as you can afford. Do *not* overspend. Spend as little as possible on the widest possible set of targets.

After you have collected this early data, see who the winners are. Do you have some keywords that are highly profitable? Spend more on them to see whether higher rankings bring more traffic (and more profits). Do you have catalog items that are not worth the per-click costs for shopping search? Watch them carefully and remove them if they do not improve. In the rest of this chapter, we show you how to improve your clickthrough rates and your conversions rates so that you make more and more of your targets profitable. But *that* is not the most important lesson.

The most important thing to learn is that you must iterate. You will not get it right the first time—don't try. Instead, commit yourself to a constant feedback loop. Then adjust to that feedback for continuous improvement.

Let's look at how Snap Electronics handled the situation. They budgeted $150,000 for paid search in the first year (as discussed in Chapter 8), which comes to about $12,500 a month. They knew that they needed to test, so they decided that they would spend much less—about $1,000—to start, believing that they could experiment to see what works before putting a lot of money behind their campaign later. Snap bought dozens of keywords for digital cameras and ran their keywords for just a few hours each—the same hours each day—for a week. By analyzing their results, they had a much better idea of the keywords that would be the most profitable in a full-blown campaign.

Start out by going broad to gather the most information possible, but do it at the lowest possible cost. Then study your results to optimize your success. Like the stock market, past performance is no guarantee of the future, so be alert to ongoing results so that you can adjust your valuations.

Clearly, you have a lot to think about before plunging into your first campaign, but don't feel like you have to figure out everything before you start. One of the biggest advantages of paid search is its incredible adjustability. No matter what you start out doing, you can see what works and what does not in a few days and then do something else. The most important philosophy for paid search is no different than for search marketing as a whole—try something, measure its success, and then try something better. That way, you optimize your campaigns for the biggest return. Let's go step-by-step through a paid search campaign to see how it's done.

Step-by-Step Paid Search Optimization

Just like everything else in search marketing, paid search can be broken down into a series of steps that you can take, one by one. Paid search might look complicated, and sometimes it is. Every search engine has different program rules—and they change. You will never be able to predict what your competitors will do next, which has a huge impact on your results. By focusing on each step in the process, however, you *can* make paid search as simple as possible. Here are the high-level steps that every paid search program must take:

- *Set up your paid search program.* Every program has certain startup tasks, such as setting up accounts for each paid search program and choosing your bid management software. Although you can revisit these decisions at any time, you do need to make some choices up front because you will not change your mind for every campaign.

- *Choose your targets.* For each campaign, you must identify the keywords you are targeting for paid placement, and the products that you are focusing on for shopping search.

- *Attract searcher's clicks.* Paid placement campaigns rely heavily on strong copywriting to get searchers to click your ad. Shopping searchers have specific ideas of who they will buy from. We show you how to draw the most clicks from searchers for any paid search campaign.

- *Optimize paid search landing pages.* Just as with organic search, you must carefully consider the way your paid search landing pages are designed so that you drive the maximum number of conversions for your search referrals.

- *Measure and adjust your campaign.* Remember, search marketing, especially paid search marketing, depends on constant refinement. Learn how to track your success and how to improve your campaigns every day.

Those are a lot of steps, so let's get started with the first one, setting up your paid search marketing program.

Set Up Your Paid Search Program

Setting up your program has three major tasks: deciding your budget, setting up your accounts, and choosing your bid management software. We start with the budget.

Decide Your Budget

We spent some time in Chapter 8 developing a budget, but you might need a more precise method than we showed you there. Unfortunately, it is not all that easy to do. The tools you have at your disposal limit the amount of information you can gather, and what you ultimately spend depends in part upon what your competitors do, which is unpredictable. However, you can make better guesses about your budget.

The first thing to do when setting your budget is to decide how you want to do it. Do you want to build to budget? Or budget to build? In other words, will you add up all your possible costs and ask for that budget (budget to build)? Or are you being handed a budget to do whatever you can afford under the budget (build to budget)? Either way, your biggest challenge will be to properly estimate the costs. As you recall from Chapter 3, there are three major costs in paid search:

- *Creative costs.* It costs money to get your information into the search engine. For paid placement, you will develop titles and descriptions for your advertisements for each keyword you buy—that can run anywhere from around $15 to more than $50 per ad if you contract with an agency, but might be cheaper if you have the skills to do it in-house. For shopping search, some engines will crawl large sites for free, but most require a trusted feed (as discussed in Chapter 10), whose cost can vary widely depending on the flexibility of your product database and its associated software program.

- *Management costs.* You can contract an external vendor to manage your paid placement bidding (and shopping search submissions), and they can provide a free estimate for your costs. If you plan to do it yourself, you need to project the amount of time your central search team will expend. Later in this chapter, we review the free and licensed management tools—you will want to add those costs into your budget if you decide to buy a tool.

- *Media costs.* Most of your budget will go to the search engines in the form of per-click fees—the results of your paid placement bids or the fixed fees for shopping search. We spend the rest of this section estimating those costs.

In Chapter 8, we walked through a relatively simple process for projecting a paid placement budget for Yahoo! By examining your keyword demand in each paid placement engine for each campaign, and by religiously following the technique from Chapter 8, you can take a stab at your media costs is any high bidder auction, but not hybrid ones.

Any hybrid auction is tricky to project costs for, because of their clever ranking algorithm—the one that shows your ads based on a combination of your bid rate and your clickthrough rate. As discussed, hybrid auctions ensure that search marketers with relevant ads are rewarded. If you design your ad to get a higher clickthrough rate than your competitor's, you will get a higher ranking for the same bid. However, the same cleverness that can give you that edge wreaks havoc with your attempts to budget for Google (or any hybrid auction engine).

Here's why. With high bidder auctions, you can take a guess at what your bid must be to get a particular ranking. You can look at the bids from the current bidders for a keyword and estimate that your bid must be in that top range to get a top ranking—to be conservative, you might estimate that your bid must be significantly higher than the current #2 bid if you want to rank #2, for example. You are taking a guess because you cannot predict how bidders will change their bids in the future; they might even change their bids based on your bid, because the former #2 bidder wants to regain that spot.

But with high bidder auctions, you can at least get a feeling for what your bid must be to get that #2 ranking, for example. With Google (and other hybrid auctions), you cannot. Google will show you an "average bid," but it cannot offer any way for you to target your bid to achieve any particular ranking. It cannot because the clickthrough rate is just as important as the bid in determining the ranking. If your ad gets heavy clicking from searchers, it will take a lower bid to rank #2 than if it has a below-average clickthrough rate.

Because you cannot easily project your ranking in Google, you also cannot easily project your clickthrough rate, because you know that your rate in part depends on where you are ranked. (Does your brain hurt yet?) In high bidder systems, you take your guess at your click rate and multiply it by the keyword demand (the number of searches for that keyword) and you can estimate the number of clicks you will get. Multiply the clicks by your bid, and you have a projected cost. In Google, you can only get an average number of clicks based on your average bid, so your projections could be wildly off if you bid higher or lower than average and if your clickthrough rate diverges from the average (higher or lower). (Now do you have a headache?) But there is even more complexity, unfortunately. If Google's ranking formula were as simple-minded as multiplying the click rate by the bid, no new ads would ever be shown, because their initial click rate is zero. So, Google actually has a default clickthrough rate it uses to put new ads into rotation, and waits for a certain number of impressions before applying the ad's actual clickthrough rate to determine its ranking. (Head pounding by now?) It gets even more complicated. Google even assesses the quality of your landing page as part of the formula—well-designed landing pages that are closely related to your ad copy are favored, according to Google. MSN Search factors demographics such as searcher gender into its results. Yahoo! has announced its own unique hybrid auction system is on the way. You should expect hybrid auctions to become even more complex as time goes on. (There, now you are finally reaching for the Excedrin.)

So what do you do? You have a few options:

- *Give up.* You can give up the whole idea of "building to budget." This is not as dumb as it might sound to some of you. It is perfectly valid to "budget to build" instead, by deciding on the investment you would like to make, starting with a small test budget, and testing and testing until you gain experience with the bids and clickthrough rates that you see from Google and other hybrid auctions.

- *Use the averages to estimate.* Google will show you your cost per day, if you make the bid shown. If you want to bid more or less than the cost shown, you can guesstimate how that will affect your clicks.

- *Test with Yahoo! first.* You might get a better idea of your ad's clickthrough rate if you have already tested it on Yahoo! You will still be guessing at where you will rank and what the keyword demand is, but you might have a better idea of the relevance of your ad. If your ad gets high clickthrough (more than 5 percent), you might guess that an average bid might actually draw more clicks than the average number shown by Google or by MSN Search. At this writing, Yahoo! is still a high bidder auction, but Yahoo! has announced that its impending hybrid system will differ from Google and MSN Search—Yahoo! will provide estimates based on your *actual* bid amount, not the average bid, so Yahoo! may remain the place to test all new paid search campaigns.

Snap Electronics initially chose to use only Yahoo!, and they set a budget for their Yahoo! campaign back in Chapter 8. But Snap eventually wants to use Google, too, so they investigated what a Google budget might be. In Figure 14-3, you can see that the average *digital cameras* bid costs 85¢, the same price as Yahoo!'s top bid, but the way Google displays paid results makes it tougher to estimate your true costs. Sometimes the rates vary widely—the bid for *digital camera* (without the *s*) averages $1.23. Snap can use the cost per day to decide whether its estimated budget should be higher or lower than the averages. Snap can use similar guesswork to estimate their costs for an MSN paid search campaign.

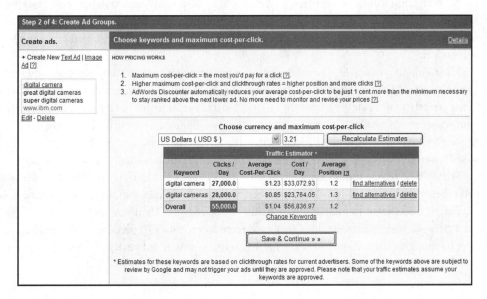

Figure 14-3 Snap's Google bid limits. Google shows both the maximum and average bids your competitors will pay per click for your targeted keywords.

Even if you do all the work to estimate your paid placement costs, you will never be accurate, for several reasons:

- *Bid gaps reduce your actual fees.* Every high bidder paid placement vendor has a way of discounting your fees based on **bid gaps**—situations where the bids are separated from each other by more than a penny. For example, if the #1 bidder has a maximum bid of $1, and you, as the #2 bidder, bid 85¢, every click on the #1 ad is charged at 86¢, one penny more than your bid. Similarly, if the #3 bidder has a max bid of 79¢, your per-click charge is 80¢. So, when you estimate your budget based on your max bid, you might be estimating higher amounts than what you will actually pay.

- *Lower conversion reduces your fees.* If fewer searchers click your ad than you expected, your fees will be lower (and higher clickthrough has the reverse effect). But Google goes further, as discussed earlier, where its Smart Pricing algorithm reduces per-click fees for keywords that its research shows get lower conversion. So, you might budget more than what Google actually charges you.

- *You cannot predict what other bidders will do.* The biggest reason you cannot predict fees with accuracy is that people are unpredictable. You do not know whether raising your bid will cause a competitor to "chase" you with a higher bid or just stand pat with the same bid. You might have budgeted for a maximum bid to get you a #2 ranking, but your competitors must cooperate for that to happen.

No budgeting techniques for paid placement bids are terribly accurate, but most marketers would prefer to have at least a guess at their costs rather than shooting completely in the dark. And if you think estimating your paid placement budget is hard, just try to predict a shopping search budget.

Most shopping search engines are targeted at small retailers who start by plopping down $50 on a credit card to "see how this works." Or large manufacturers that can get some cost guesses by working directly with a sales rep from the engine. No tools exist to predict the number of searches for any category of product—there is no analogue to the Yahoo! Keyword Selector tool, for example. So, although you have much better per-click cost certainty in shopping search as opposed to the bidding style of paid placement, you have no clue how many clicks you will get.

So, the best advice might be to conduct a controlled experiment. As we write this, Froogle is still a beta offering (read: free). You can load your product catalog into Froogle and see how well your products seem to rank and how many clicks you get. Then you might want to branch out to a paid shopping search engine—maybe devote 5 percent to 10 percent of your paid search budget to shopping search, just to see what happens. You will not really be able to plan your budget before you start, but you *can* take some baby steps before committing yourself with a large investment.

Set Up Your Accounts

Setting up your program can often be one of the simpler steps, but it is very important. As with the other steps, you can always go back and change your setup later, but getting it right upfront can save you some time.

As you have read through this chapter, you have probably made some decisions on which paid search programs make the most sense for your business. If you sell the kinds of products offered in shopping search engines, you might want to sign up and give it a try. If you know from your organic search experience what keywords your visitors are likely to search for, you have all the information you need to test paid placement for your business. You can use the tables presented earlier in this chapter to analyze each vendor that offers paid search and decide which ones seem to be the best candidates to start with, based on cost, market share, or other factors.

It might be tempting to sign up with every vendor out there. Don't. The work that goes into managing a paid search campaign is larger than you think. To be successful, you must focus on your content, your per-click charges, your clickthrough rates, your conversions, and your profitability. You need to do that for every campaign with every vendor, because each one is different. Don't become overwhelmed with work before you even know how it's done. Start small.

If you decide to start with just one vendor, you will probably want to use a paid placement vendor rather than a shopping search engine, because setup is usually simpler. Google, Yahoo!, and MSN Search are the big three in paid placement engines, so pick one of them. Choosing a single vendor also simplifies your decision on bid management and reporting tools—you can avoid investigating and paying for a third-party tool until your program gets bigger later. (We walk you through all of your bid management choices shortly.)

But how do you choose between the big three? Yahoo!'s high bidder auction is far simpler to budget for, as you saw earlier, but it is moving to a hybrid auction like Google and MSN. Yahoo! says that its coming hybrid auction will continue to help search marketers estimate their number of referrals based on their actual bids. Google's and MSN's keyword tools don't reveal keyword demand, so it is hard to know how often your ad will be shown.

Although it is harder to budget for a hybrid auction, its ranking algorithm gives you less to manage after the campaign is up and running. Hybrid algorithms, which rank listings by bid and clickthrough rate, produce less volatility than algorithms that employ bid alone, so your hybrid rankings will not jump up and down as erratically as with high bidder auctions (meaning you can watch them less). In addition, several bidding tactics you must pay attention to when using high bidder auctions—**gap surfing**, **bid jamming**, and **friendly URL**—are not used with hybrids, making your bid management efforts far simpler.

PAID PLACEMENT BIDDING TACTICS FOR HIGH BIDDER AUCTIONS

We spent time discussing your paid search philosophy earlier in this chapter, but much of paid search marketing is fought in the trenches, using tactics that can drain your budget if ignored. Because the hybrid auction ranking algorithms of Google and MSN include clickthrough rate, it is not possible to use these techniques, because you cannot juggle your positions by tuning your bids alone—they depend on your click rates, too. But all the other paid placement engines are ripe for use of these approaches.

Gap surfing is a technique in which you scan the list of paid placement results, looking for significant differences between bids. You then adjust your bid to be just higher than the lower bid in the gap. For example, suppose that you have determined through experience that you receive about the same number of clicks whether your listing is anywhere in the top three Yahoo! paid results. If the #1 result is bidding $1, the #2 result is bidding 50¢, and the #3 result is bidding 32¢, the largest gap is between the first two results, so a gap surfer would bid 51¢ to claim the #2 ranking.

True gap surfing means that you will never be #1 for a query, but most tools have a setting that will bid for the #1 setting if the gaps found are less than an amount you specify. For example, if the #1 result is bidding $1, the #2 result is bidding 99¢, and the #3 results is bidding 96¢, your tool could place you at #3 with a 97¢ bid. If you require a minimum of a nickel gap, however, your tool would place you at #1 with a bid of $1.01.

Gap surfing can be valuable because it can sneak you into the most cost-effective position, but it can also lower your revenue. As you will see later, having the most cost-effective bids is not usually as good as having the most profitable bids. The conversions you would get from the #1 ranking might be far more valuable than saving a few cents on the clicks.

Bid jamming is an offensive technique that does not lower your costs or raise your conversions. What it does is to raise your competitor's costs, which might drain his budget a bit faster. Sometimes you can knock a competitor's ads "off the air" if his budget runs out.

Bid jamming uses some of the same concepts that gap surfing does. A bid jammer specifies a range of ranks (say, #1 to #3, as you saw earlier) that are equally valuable. Once again, the bid management tool looks for the largest gap, but this time it bids just below a competitor's maximum bid, forcing the competitor to pay its highest per-click charges. If the #1 bidder is bidding $1, and the #2 is at 50¢, and the #3 result is bidding 32¢, the largest gap is between the first two results, so a gap surfer would bid 51¢ to claim the #2 ranking, but a bid jammer would bid 99¢ for that same #2 result. That forces the #1 bidder to pay $1 per click instead of 51¢, as before, whereas your 99¢ bid costs you just 51¢ per click until the #2 bidder goes higher.

Friendly URL is a tactic that many marketers employ to stay out of costly bidding wars. If two divisions in your company are bidding on the same keyword, it does not do your company much good to bid against itself. You can ask some bid management tools to bid your keyword just below your sister division and they can set their tool to bid just above. You can use this feature with unfriendly companies as well—if you know from experience that a competitor will bid both of you up to very high levels, you might want to target your bid just below theirs to keep your costs down. (This technique keeps your competitor's costs down, too, where bid jamming has the opposite effect.)

Some people find all these bid games fun; their competitive juices start to flow as they try to outsmart the other players. It might feel like a waste of time to you that is better spent on other, more profitable tasks. Regardless of how you feel, don't let the games take over your strategy. These techniques are tactics—important at times—but not your top priority.

Snap Electronics wanted to start with one paid placement vendor and one shopping search vendor for its digital cameras campaign. They had done all the work to estimate their budget for Yahoo!, so they chose Yahoo! as their paid placement vendor, knowing they could add others later. Even though it was free, they decided not to make the effort to sign up with the Internet Yellow Pages services, because each one would drain some of their time and they thought that relatively few people would find their company that way. They ran into their first surprise when they went to sign up for shopping search, as shown in Figure 14-4. MySimon was no longer accepting new merchants selling digital cameras.

Figure 14-4 Shopping search overload. At times, so many merchants want to sell a product that shopping search engines stop accepting newcomers.

Having struck out with a smaller player, Snap decided to go with one of the top-tier players, choosing Shopzilla. If you are working with an external search marketing vendor, perhaps they can set up your shopping search account for you, but Snap wanted to do it themselves without paying the vendor's hourly rate.

When Snap went through the sign-up process at Shopzilla, they were pleasantly surprised to see that they could merely enter their product list into a Web form, as shown in Figure 14-5, because Snap had fewer than 30 models of digital cameras. Although they would have to figure out trusted feeds or other update mechanisms later, this certainly made it easy to get started.

Product Title	Snap Shot X6 digital camera
Price	348.99
Shipping Cost	
Shipping Weight	
SKU	127558
Manufacturer	Snap Electronics
# of Products on Hand	1000
Product Condition	New
Product Description	The Snap Shot X6 digital camera is the most advanced 6.0 mega pixel camera on the market today. Featuring the patented Auto Touch focus and Snap's renowned ease of use, the Snap Shot X6 is the perfect camera for the serious photographer
Product URL	http://www.snapelectronics.com/stores/prd=33&lang=1&cntry=8
Image URL	http://www.snapelectronics.com/images/cameras/snapshotxz6.jpg
CPC Bid	0.5

Figure 14-5 Signing up for shopping search. Some shopping engines, such as Shopzilla, allow product data to be entered as paid placement ads are.

Setting up paid placement accounts can sometimes be a bit more complex than shopping search account setup. For example, the way you set up a Yahoo! account varies based on your situation:

- *You are working with an external search marketing vendor.* As discussed in Chapter 8, you can hire a vendor to perform all sorts of search marketing tasks. If you did so, as Snap Electronics did, you can leave the setup work to them. They help you develop and manage the program from start to finish. Their experienced staff has the tracking tools and the relationships with the paid placement vendors to drive the maximum return from your paid search investment.

- *Your click fee budget is more than $10,000 per month.* If you plan to spend a substantial amount with Yahoo! each month, a sales representative will be assigned to work with you. Remember, the $10,000 figure is what you spend with Yahoo!, not your overall paid search budget.

- *You have a smaller budget, but are willing to pay for assistance.* If you are spending less than $10,000 a month with Yahoo!, but you want help setting up your account, Yahoo! charges $200 to do so. Yahoo!'s Fast Track program not only helps you with account setup, but also in designing the ads for your first campaign, so it can be very worthwhile.

- *You want to do it yourself for free.* If you are willing to do the heavy lifting, there is no setup fee. If you know what you are doing, and you can get by with just online support from Yahoo!, this is the way to keep your costs down. $200 can buy a lot of clicks.

If you are setting up your Yahoo! account yourself, rather then having a search marketing vendor do it for you, you will be presented with the page shown in Figure 14-6.

	⬔ Fast Track®	⬔ Self Serve
Sign-Up Options	Online or call 866-747-7327	Online
Turnaround	3 business days	5 business days
Expert Assistance with Search Term Selection	Yes	No
Expert Assistance with Titles & Descriptions	Yes	No
Expert Assistance with Budget Management	Yes	No
Customized Proposal	Yes View sample	No
Control of Your Campaign	Yes	Yes
Free Account Optimization	Yes¹	No
Expert Assistance with Tracking URLs	Yes	No
Editorial Approval	Automatic	Subject to review
One-Time Service Fee	$199²	No Service Fee²

Figure 14-6   Selecting a Yahoo! program. Yahoo! has various options for you to get started with its paid placement advertising.

Reproduced with permission of Yahoo! Inc. © 2005 by Yahoo! Inc. YAHOO! and the YAHOO! logo are trademarks of Yahoo! Inc.

Signing up for a Google account is not much different from Yahoo!'s process. Google accounts are self-service (similar to Yahoo!'s free program), but they cost $5 to sign up.

For any paid placement account, you provide a credit card number and decide how much money to place into your account (as little as $50) and you are on your way. When a searcher clicks your ad for a keyword, the amount you bid for that click is deducted from your account. You can have the account automatically replenish from your credit card, you can have a set amount taken from your credit card each month, or you can be notified when your account dips below a certain point (so that you can manually add more funds).

As you set up your account, you are asked to specify the geographic locations for where your ads should run, as Figure 14-7 shows. The default country for MSN, Yahoo!, and Google is the United States, but you can specify any other country where they currently show their ads (from their own sites or from the sites of the syndication partners). Think carefully before you decide what to do—if you do not do business in all of these countries, you do not want your ads running there. Similarly, if you do not intend to translate your ads and landing pages to local languages (to tie into your country Web site), you will not drive any conversions.

You can further select location down to city and zip code if you want to refine your targeting using the geographic targeting capabilities discussed earlier in the chapter. We discuss this technique more later.

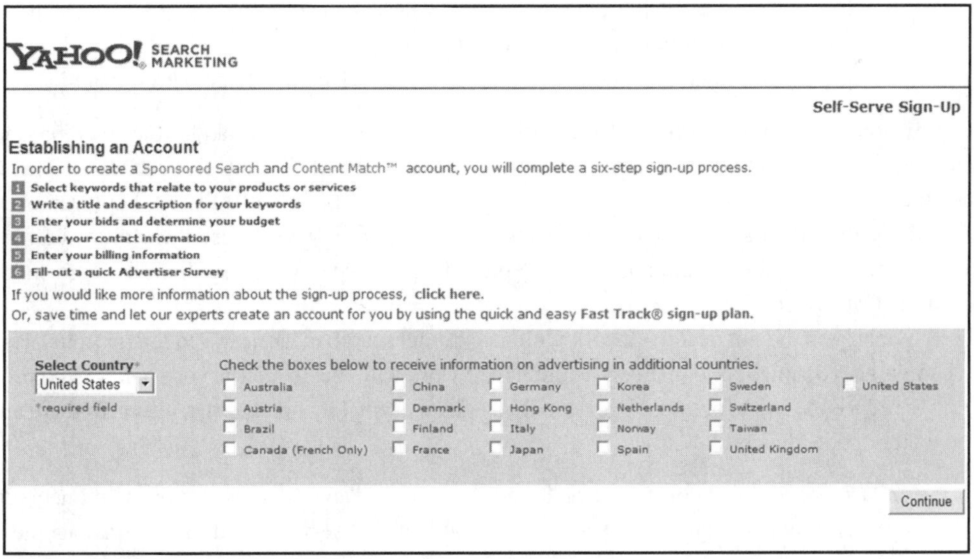

Figure 14-7   Selecting Yahoo! countries. Yahoo! offers U.S. targeting by default, but allows selection of other countries during the account setup process.

Reproduced with permission of Yahoo! Inc. (c) 2005 by Yahoo! Inc. YAHOO! and the YAHOO! logo are trademarks of Yahoo! Inc.

Select Your Bid Management Tool

Now that you have set up your paid placement and shopping search accounts, it is time to choose the software you will use to manage your campaigns, which is called a **bid management tool**. Bid management tools automatically adjust your paid placement bids and aggregate click and conversion data. A good bid management tool can spell the difference between a successful campaign and a failure.

A few bid management tools are distributed as software you install on your own computer, but most are offered as services from Web sites. Which specific tool you choose depends on what search engines you have selected:

- *Shopping search engines only.* This situation's easy. If you are only using shopping search engines, you do no bidding and need no tool to manage bidding. Most bid management tools also monitor your trusted feeds and your shopping search reporting.

- *Just one paid placement engine or a small paid search budget.* If you use just Google, or just Yahoo!, for example, you can use the tool they each provide for free with your paid placement fees. (If you use the paid placement vendor's free tool, it will monitor only the bids placed with that vendor.) Also, if your budget is less than $10,000 per month, it might not make sense to pay the fees for a high-end bid management tool.

- *Any other combination.* If you use more than one search engine or you have a large paid search budget, you will probably want to use a third-party bid management tool that can monitor bids across search engines and provide enhanced tracking and adjustment of bids. If you choose a third-party vendor, you must be sure to pick one that is authorized by the paid placement vendors you are working with. Double-check before you buy.

If you are working with a search marketing vendor, they might handle the tracking and reporting for you, so you might not need to choose a tool yourself. Twenty-five percent of search marketers choose that route. Some search marketers prefer to be more hands-on, however, even when delegating the paid search campaigns to a vendor. If you want to use the tool to see how your campaigns are doing, you might want to provide guidance to your search marketing vendor about the features you want.

Even if you did not decide to work with an external search marketing vendor for your overall campaign, you might find that you would like to work with one to handle your paid search program to reduce the work for you. Here are a few that are especially noteworthy, although there are many other good choices:

- *Did-it* (www.did-it.com). The co-founder of Did-it, Kevin Lee, is one of the pioneers in paid placement search marketing. He's built a full-service paid search management offering based on customizable technology that uses proven strategies and metrics to optimize your campaigns.

- *MarketLeap* (www.marketleap.com). MarketLeap, with its parent company Digital Impact, is one of the leaders in organic search marketing and have the resources to handle any size campaign in paid search.

- *Performics* (www.performics.com). Acquired by DoubleClick in 2004, the main advantage of Performics is its capability to integrate reporting with tags used by DoubleClick for banner advertising. Performics is one of a few Yahoo! Strategic Partners, signifying skill in successfully managing Yahoo! campaigns.
- *The Search Works* (www.thesearchworks.com). BidBuddy offers full-service paid search management and is currently the only tool approved to work with all leading European paid placement vendors.

For those on smaller budgets, or those who would prefer to manage their campaigns themselves, bid management tools that do not require a full-service relationship with a search marketing vendor are available. However, bid management tools are no one-size-fits-all proposition. What you need depends on your circumstances. Here is a checklist of questions you should answer before researching the right bid management tool for your program:

- *How much time are we willing to invest in this project*? Full-service vendors do all the work for you, high-end tools automate most of the work, and inexpensive tools leave a lot of manual work for you.
- *How many keywords will I need to manage*? Most bid management tools are priced based on the number of keywords that must be monitored. The more keywords, the higher the price.
- *How many times per day will I need to monitor and update my bids*? Some tools can update only a few times per day, or they require higher-priced versions for more frequent updates.
- *How high is my paid search budget*? As you might expect, the lower-end tools often lack the functions needed for large paid search budgets—$100,000 a month or more. Better tools can handle high volumes of click and conversion data while providing strong analysis functions. Don't skimp on your tool when it can mean so much more in revenue and savings.
- *How detailed must my reporting be*? If you want to calculate your statistics by keyword, by engine, by time of day, and by other very detailed breakdowns, choose a tool with the strongest reporting capabilities. If you are serious about search marketing, and have a large budget, you will need the detailed reporting to give yourself the information that keeps your efficiency high. We discuss reporting on paid search in Chapter 15, "Make Search Marketing Operational."

To make decisions on the precise features you are looking for in your bid management tool, you need to understand some of the most-used tactics in paid search marketing, such as gap surfing, bid jamming, friendly URL, and **dayparting**. If you plan to use any of these tactics, select a tool that supports that tactic.

TIMING IS EVERYTHING: ARE YOUR CONVERSIONS ON A SCHEDULE?

In your relentless drive to become more efficient in the paid placement marketplace, your business might benefit from analyzing the timing of your conversions. Some businesses have obvious timing characteristics—the toy industry sells a huge portion of its inventory before Christmas, for example. But such seasonal shifts do not always matter in search marketing unless conversion rates change, too.

Here's why. If all that happens during the Christmas shopping season is that more searchers are looking for toys, but they click through and buy at the same rate, your per-click bids should be the same all year round. If conversion rates are higher at Christmas, however, those clicks are worth *more* than the rest of the year. If you have analyzed your business and found that Christmas shoppers convert at a higher rate, you can raise your bids (and lower them the rest of the year) to increase your sales with the same search marketing budget. If your competitors bid the same year-round, they might be bidding a bit too low at Christmas and a bit too high at other times.

Your analysis might uncover patterns much more granular than seasonal swings. Suppose that Snap Electronics found that their digital camera conversion rate is much higher on weekends than on weekdays. Perhaps their customers are more likely to spend the time to research the model they want and make a purchase decision in the comfort of their home when they have some free time, rather than while they are busy at work. If true, the clicks Snap gets on the weekends are more valuable than those on weekdays, and thus worth higher bids. Snap could drive more revenue by raising their bids on weekends to reflect the true value of those clicks, and lowering them on weekdays. That way, they will land higher in the rankings at the times their customers are most likely to convert.

But why stop there? **Dayparting** (called "Ad Scheduling" by Google) is a technique that enables you to set your bids based on time of day. What if Snap analyzed its conversions and found that, during weekdays, conversions dipped under 1 percent during working hours (except for a three-hour window for U.S. lunchtimes) and peaked at 3.5 percent just after 8 p.m. U.S. Eastern time? Wouldn't it make sense to tune the bids by time of day to reflect the value of the clicks? Bid management tools that support dayparting do just that, automatically adjusting your bids through the day based on rules you provide. You might even find times you should "go dark" by shutting off your bids completely.

You should notice that even during periods of low conversion, if your conversion *rate* is high, it might still be very profitable. Snap might find that early morning hours, although delivering low sales compared to other times of day, has a high conversion *rate*. Although conversions are not very high, clicks are also low, so the low fees with high conversions make it a very profitable time period.

It is typical for conversion rates to fluctuate for every business, but you want to know, "Is there a *pattern*?" Without a repeating pattern, timing techniques do not work. After all, you need to know what *will* happen, not what *has* happened.

All this analysis can be a lot of work, but it pays off. Many times, the pattern crosses your whole product line; as the market gets more efficient, however, you might need to analyze product by product or even keyword by keyword to keep finding the edge you need. If you keep looking, however, you *will* find it.

Table 14-4 shows some standalone tools that do not require a full-service commitment from a consulting vendor. (Some of these tools are offered by vendors that will operate them in full-service mode if desired.) We have included the Google, Yahoo!, and MSN tools in the table to help you compare.

Table 14-4　Bid Management Tools (Many vendors provide software and services that help automate paid placement bidding and reporting for you.)

| Tool | Type | Engines | Features | | | | Price |
			Gap Surf	Bid Jam	Day-part	Bid Rules	
Atlas One Point www.atlasonepoint.com	Service	28	✓	✓	✓	CPA ROAS	$80 per month
BidRank www.bidrank.com	Software	14[1]	✓		✓	Basic only	$15 per month
Dynamic Bid Maximizer www.keywordbidmaximizer.com	Software	35[1]	✓		✓	CPA ROAS	$20 per month
Google www.google.com	Service	1	N/A	N/A	✓	Basic only	Free
KeywordMax www.keywordmax.com	Service	13	✓	✓	✓	CPA PM ROI	$99 per month
Yahoo! (formerly Overture) www.overture.com	Service	1			✓	Basic only	Free
MSN Search advertising.msn.com/ microsoft-adcenter	Service	1	N/A	N/A	✓	Basic only	Free
PPCBidtracker www.ppcbidtracker.com	Service	7[2]			✓	Basic only	$50 per month
Performics www.performics.com	Service	4			✓	CPA ROAS	Custom Bid

[1] Yahoo! version is priced and packaged separately from version supporting all other search engines.

[2] Version supporting U.S. search engines is priced and packaged separately from version supporting European search engines.

Each tool listed in the table supports a different number of paid placement search engines and provides varying features for its automated bidding functions. Gap surfing, bid jamming, dayparting, and automated bid rules are some of the most-requested functions for these tools, so we highlighted which tools offer them, even though gap surfing and bid jamming are used only with high bidder auctions. You can see that some tools offer more automation than others, with objective bidding optimization based on some metrics we explain later in the chapter, such as cost per action (CPA), profit margin (PM), return on advertising spending (ROAS), and return on investment (ROI). The other tools offer only basic rules that do not use objective analysis.

Due to agreements with Yahoo!, several tools are offered as Yahoo! versions and separately priced versions for managing all of the other PPC programs. This adds to the tool's cost, obviously, but worse yet is its impact on ease of use. You cannot integrate all of your bid adjustments and tracking in one place, causing extra work for your team.

The pricing shown in the table is the lowest offered for any version of the tool, but might run considerably higher for large paid search programs. Some packages limit the number of users, some the number of keywords, others the number of bid adjustments per day. Regardless, the lowest-priced version of each tool usually has some limitations.

Each of these tools can raise your efficiency while reducing your workload, but they cannot eliminate human monitoring. For example, they might lower your bid to the minimum amount if it gets few conversions, but it will not drop the keyword completely, which might be the best thing to do with a real loser. Regardless, the higher your paid placement budget, and the more competitive your keywords, the more you will need a strong bid management tool.

Well, there you have it. You have learned all the tasks necessary to set up your paid search program. Now it's on to step two, where we crank up our first paid search campaign by deciding our target paid placement keywords and shopping search products.

Choose Your Targets

After setting up your paid search program, your next step is to choose the targets for your first campaign. For paid placement, this means selecting your keywords, whereas for shopping search it entails choosing the products you want to offer.

The shopping search decision is simpler, so we discuss that before moving on to the complexity of paid placement. To start with, shopping search engines are limited to a fairly small set of products, so you can only offer the subset of your product line that corresponds to the product categories handled by each shopping search engine.

If your site does sell some of the products offered by shopping search engines, you need to determine whether the per-click fee charged will allow your sales to be profitable. In general, shopping search engines have focused on products whose price tags are high enough that the per-click fees are worth the cost, even with a rather low conversion rate. However, you should have some confidence that your site can convert the referrals sent from shopping search engines before you sign up. If you are struggling to convert visitors now, getting more visitors who you have to pay for will not help—you need to correct your conversion travails first.

The last step is one we covered in Chapter 10—getting the data to the shopping search engine. Some shopping search engines crawl your site for free, but you must develop a trusted feed for most of them. That can cost some money that eats into your profitability, but it is typically a one-time hit. Sending the data each day has a rather low operational cost after you have automated the process.

Most merchants should start by sending some of their best-selling products to shopping search engines to see whether they can compete on price, shipping speed, and reliability. Will customers click through to your site above the rest? Will customers convert after they click through? Start testing some of your strongest products to see how you do, and then go from there. Later in this chapter, we provide tips on attracting the shopping searcher's click.

Paid placement is a much more complicated game. Because it is based on search queries, it is not restricted to any subset of your products or services—you can sell anything that searchers can type. Paid placement keyword planning requires four steps:

- *Select good paid placement keywords.* In Chapter 11, we helped you identify the best keywords for your target market, and we don't rehash all of that advice here, but we do want to emphasize a few points important to paid search.
- *Organize your keywords.* Paid placement engines enable you to group your keywords to make them easier to manage and to measure. We show you how to think about organizing yours.
- *Decide your match type for each keyword.* You need to decide how the paid placement engine should match every keyword you bid on against the searchers' queries. You will see what your choices are and how to decide in every case.
- *Decide geographic targeting for each keyword.* You might want to pinpoint which searchers should see your ad based on their physical location. Learn how.
- *Select your bidding strategy.* Search marketers use many strategies for choosing the bids for their keywords. Some of them make sense, and some of them don't. Read on to avoid the rookie mistakes.
- *Make your bids.* After you know your strategy, it is relatively simple to make your actual bids, but there are still a few pitfalls to avoid.

Let's start by discussing a few tips specific to choosing paid placement keywords.

Select Good Paid Placement Keywords

You might recall from Chapter 11 that natural limits exist when planning for organic keywords—you cannot put landing pages in place for an unlimited number of organic keywords without ruining your site. With paid placement, you can target as many words as you want. But *should* you? Probably not.

Just as organic search has a natural limit, paid placement does, too. You will eventually get to the point that more keywords do not bring you more conversions—they are not worth their costs. They might not be worth the per-click costs, or perhaps it just costs too many people to manage them. So although most businesses find that they can target more paid placement keywords than they target for organic search, they need to prioritize even those paid ones.

If you are just starting out, it makes sense to concentrate on the keywords that might bring the highest returns. Definitely start out with transactional queries, especially those with your own brand names in them. Add informational queries that you believe will convert. (If you have done a good job tracking your conversions for organic keywords, you have an excellent head start.)

One of the biggest mistakes for paid search rookies is to chase keyword demand. Just because a keyword gets high demand does not mean it will convert for you. Remember the lesson of "too hot" keywords. As challenging as those overheated words are for organic, with paid search you are *paying* for every one of those nonconverting clicks.

Paid placement also has some advantages for search marketers who want to increase brand awareness. You can buy keywords that hit your target market for brand awareness and design relevant landing pages. For example, if you have a famous spokesperson, buy her name. Now, we know that searchers are not actually looking for your company, but if you put up a "fan-zine" site about her that happens to have a bunch of ads about your product, you might be pleased with the brand awareness you can raise at a very low cost. For example, Adidas could buy the names of the tennis players who wear their shoes. If you sponsor a golf tournament, buy golf words before the start of the tournament—you not only get brand awareness, you also get viewers for the event. The Web site for Castrol motor oil (www.castrol.com) has a page about its spokesman, soccer star David Beckham, as shown in Figure 14-8, so Castrol might consider adding additional content and purchasing his name as a keyword.

Figure 14-8   Buying brand awareness. Castrol's Web site contains information on a celebrity spokesperson whose name draws many search clicks.

Remember that your search for keywords will pay off handsomely. Your friendly search engine rep will happily give you a starter list of words to buy for your industry, but don't you think your competitors get the same list? Those words are bound to be somewhat overpriced because they are the only ones being bought by any of your competitors that are too lazy to do the hard research work. This is where your iteration philosophy comes in. Continually expand your keywords to find new ones that convert at an acceptable rate. Find that keyword your competitors have not discovered yet.

"HEY! THAT'S MY TRADEMARK!"—WHAT TO DO WHEN SOMEONE BIDS ON YOURS

When people think about trademarks and search, they always think about their competitors first. What would you do if your competitor bid on your trademark? Fortunately, it does not happen all that often. If it does, you can probably get it stopped easily (as we explain below). The more interesting cases, however, are not your competitors—they are your partners.

The most common instance of other companies bidding on your trademark stems from your own distribution channels. Your affiliates bid for the names of your products that they sell. So do your retailers and resellers. And you are probably okay with that. Sure it's a little annoying that your distributors might outbid you and have a higher rank for your product. Yes, it's not the greatest when a searcher buys from the more expensive affiliate channel than direct from you. (It is more expensive because you have to pay the affiliate for the sale.) But after all, that is just good marketing, and that is why you have distributors—so they can sell your product.

Unfortunately, it is not always such a positive story. Sometimes your partners can be your worst enemy in paid placement. Suppose we told you that your affiliates were sending searchers for your trademark to a landing page that showed not just your product, but also several cut-price knockoffs from your competition? Or used versions of your product? Now how do you feel? Your affiliates might be taking searchers predisposed to buying your product and parading them in front of other companies' products, too. To them, it is just a way to pump up their sales—they do not particularly care whose product they sell. But to you, it is a variation on the old bait-and-switch scam.

As long as your partners feature your products on the page, it is unlikely that you can win a suit against them for trademark infringement. However, you have a few other remedies available to you. First, they are your partners. You can set ground rules for how they sell your product. You can insist in the affiliate agreement that affiliates put no other products on their landing pages except your (new) offerings. Some marketers are banning affiliates from bidding on trademarked names at all, ensuring that you get the traffic for your trademark keywords.

In many situations, you can also take your case to the search engines. Both MSN and Yahoo! have trademark policies that put you in the driver's seat for your own trademarks. Both have stringent rules allowing the use of trademarked names in paid placement keywords only for sales of that trademarked product or informational commentary about that trademark. Google's policy is looser, requiring the trademark owner to provide Google with either a blacklist of companies who are banned from buying that trademarked term, or a "whitelist" of the only companies that may. Trademark owners must initiate any actions to protect their trademarks, which they may do regardless of whether they have any advertising relationship with the search engines. Despite these policies, trademark handling is controversial and is increasingly being played out in court. As with so many things in search marketing, use the resources in Chapter 16 to stay abreast of this fast-changing topic.

Despite these protections, you must remember that some conflicts over trademarks are inherent in the trademark law itself. Trademarks are issued within particular industries, so do not be surprised if several companies have trademarked the exact same product name, albeit in different contexts. So if you work for Sun Microsystems and you are annoyed about sharing your trademark with dozens of newspapers named "Sun," you will just have to get over it. It's their trademark, too.

Organize Your Keywords

Even if you are a habitually sloppy type, you need to think about how to organize your paid placement keywords. How you group your keywords will simplify the management of your paid search program and enable you to measure performance you could never track any other way.

MSN Search, Google, and Yahoo! all provide ways of organizing your keywords. It would be no fun at all if they did it the same way, so we explain their approaches—they are similar. All three have the concept of an **account**, as we explained when you set up your account earlier in this chapter. Even small accounts are too large to be manageable without logical subdivision, however, so each engine gives you ways to slice and dice your keyword lists.

Yahoo! enables you to divide your keywords into **categories**, which you can use to store keywords that are somehow related to each other. It is completely up to you which keywords you put together in categories, but several ideas predominate:

- *Division of labor*. If you have several people or several organizations managing your keywords, it can make sense to ensure that they store their keywords in separate categories. (Very large organizations sometimes have several Yahoo! accounts.)

- *Division of market*. You might have some keywords directed at business customers and others at consumers. You might want to separate keyword by the country they are directed at.

- *Division of bidding*. If you are employing different bidding strategies or tactics with different groups of keywords, you might decide to organize them into separate categories. For example, if one of your competitor employs bid jamming on several prominent keywords, you might want to put them in a separate category so that you can use a friendly URL or other technique that avoids a bidding war for those keywords.

- *Division of product line*. Snap will probably place the *digital camera* keywords into a different category than the *home theater* keywords.

- *Division of reporting*. Because you can roll up your measurements by category, you might want to isolate keywords from each other if you are testing something. For example, you might separate traditional paid search keywords from contextual keywords in Yahoo! so that you can test the contextual advertising effectiveness.

- *Division of message*. Frequently, it can make sense for all of the keywords in a category to share the same advertising message. So all of the Snap keywords for a certain product might have the same (or very similar) ad and the same landing page, whereas those for other products would not.

You can see that there are many reasons to separate keywords into categories, but luckily many of them overlap. You can decide to have categories for each individual product within a country that share the same message, for example, and you are happy to have the reporting divided on that basis, too.

Google gives you the equivalent of categories, too, but refers to them as **ad groups**. Ad groups contain the individual keywords and the ads associated with them, just as Yahoo!'s categories do. But Google goes Yahoo! one better, by enabling you to collect multiple ad groups into **campaigns**. Google campaigns give you a higher-level organization that can make reporting much simpler. If you placed each related product within a country into an ad group, you could decide to do your reporting by *country* (by creating a Google campaign with all of the ad groups for that country) or by *product* (using a campaign that collected all of that product's ad groups). Google campaigns enable you to have very specific ad groups to manage your keywords within broader campaigns used for reporting.

MSN Search organizes keywords similarly to Google (even using the word comapign), except that what Google calls an ad group MSN calls an **order**.

Google recommends placing keywords into ad groups that share the same messages, or two to four variations of the same message. You will want to place synonyms, for example, in the same ad group because they might share the same ads and landing pages.

However you decide to divide your keywords, take advantage of what Google and Yahoo! offer you; it will simplify your reporting and your management. Next we look at another choice you make for your keywords: Which of the searchers' queries should they match?

Decide a Match Type for Each Keyword

As we continue to look at how to tell the paid placement engines which keywords you want in your program, you need to specify how the keywords you choose ought to match the words that the searchers use. At first this might seem odd to you. After all, search engines decide which organic pages match searcher queries all by themselves, so why do they need your help for paid search?

Paid placement differs markedly from organic search in that the search engines do not look at the landing pages to decide which ones are the best matches. They look at the bids for the keywords (and in Google's case, the searcher click rate). That's why they need your help. Besides, you *want* to help them, because you will increase your conversions and lower your costs.

The way search engines get your help is through **match types**. The most inclusive match type—the one that matches the most searcher queries—is called **broad match** (by Google and MSN) or **advanced match** (by Yahoo!), but works almost the same way. If Snap Electronics bids on the keyword *digital camera* using broad/advanced match, any searcher query that contains all of those words can trigger Snap's ad. Word variants also match, such as any phrase that includes the words *digital cameras*. So, the queries "reviews for digital cameras" and "camera for digital photography" would both match Snap's keyword purchase for *digital camera*. The broad and advanced match types provide the most matches for your keyword, increasing your impressions and your referrals (as well as your fees).

The vendors differ on a couple of points. Broad match is the default for Google and MSN—the one you get if you do not select anything when you enter a keyword—but advanced match is not Yahoo!'s default. In addition, Google's broad match also matches synonyms.

More restrictive than broad match is **phrase match**, which matches any query that contains the keyword in order with no word variants. With phrase match, the queries "digital camera accessories" and "digital camera sale" both match *digital camera*, but "new digital cameras" and "digital slr camera" do not. Both Google and MSN offer phrase match.

One more restrictive match type remains, again with different names from Yahoo! (**standard match**) and Google and MSN (**exact match**). The most restrictive match type, exact match finds only the exact words as typed, so if Snap purchases "digital camera" with exact match, no other queries will match. Yahoo!'s standard match is slightly less restrictive, also matching word variants and misspellings. Standard match is Yahoo!'s default, and it always shows standard matches before advanced matches in its ranking. Using this match type drives fewer referrals, but might give you higher clickthrough rates (and thus better rankings) and higher conversion rates.

The final match type is called **negative match** (by both Google and Yahoo!) or **excluded keyword** (by MSN), and it is very important. Negative match enables you to specify words that, if found in a searcher's query, would prevent your ad from being shown. If Snap Electronics wanted to use a broad/advanced match type for *digital camera* but found they were getting too many clicks that do not convert for *digital video camera*, they could add a negative match for the keyword *video* to eliminate those queries while retaining more inclusive matching for all other queries. Similarly, many occurrences of *digital camera* might be the phrase *digital camera accessories*. Do you want to negate accessories because you want a lower bid for that phrase and a higher bid for *digital camera*? Or because your clickthrough rate will go up (raising your ranking)? Do your homework on what searchers enter and use negative keywords to target your keywords as tightly as possible.

Rather than getting bogged down in all the names, we refer to **expanded match** (advanced and broad) and **restrictive match** (exact and standard). More importantly, when do you use them?

Expanded match works best for very specific keywords, such as product numbers or unique product names ("snapshot slr" or "onetouch autofocus"), where virtually any query containing those words has a reasonable chance of converting. More common words can be good candidates for expanded match if their meanings always match your scope ("snap electronics") or if their meanings are unambiguous ("honda" or "ipod" or "cancun vacation"). Longer phrases can also be good candidates if you want to capture all variations—*snapshot digital camera* matches "buy a snapshot digital camera" and "snapshot accessories for digital cameras."

But expanded match does not work in all situations. Restrictive match is far better when your keywords have ambiguous meanings—they can mean more than one thing. Single words and acronyms are especially susceptible:

- Dallas (the city or the TV show?)
- Ivory (soap or some jewelry?)
- MP3 (a download or a player?)
- China (the country or a dinner setting?)
- Ford (a car or a person's name?)

For these ambiguous terms, you must use longer keywords (*Ford Taurus* or *MP3 player*) or add negative keywords to reduce ambiguity (Ford Motor can use *Ford –Gerald*).

One of the best strategies for match types is to start most keywords with expanded match, using your metrics to gradually identify which keyword variations have the highest conversions. When you do, you can buy those keywords using restrictive match (possibly with higher bids because they are worth more) and eliminate the original expanded keywords. An alternative is to add negative match keywords to your expanded match keywords to eliminate the low-conversion variations.

Regardless of what strategy you employ for match types, keep an eye on the search engines for changes to their match types—Yahoo! (then called Overture) completely revamped theirs as recently as 2004. The resources listed in Chapter 16 will help you stay informed.

Decide Targeting for Each Keyword

The newest type of targeting has been introduced by MSN, and allows targeting of searchers by demographics, such as gender and age. MSN allows you to incrementally increase your bids for keywords entered by searchers known to be in your targeted searcher group. So, Snap could increase their bid on "digital camera reviews" by 3 percent for consumers between 32 and 45 if they know that group to convert at higher rates.

Google, Yahoo!, and MSN all enable you to target the geographic locations of the searchers who should see your ad. If you do not take advantage of **geographic targeting**, your ad will be shown to searchers in the country or countries that you selected when you set up your account.

Geographic targeting might sound a lot like the local search concept we discussed earlier, but it is actually a completely separate way of using standard paid placement advertising to restrict your ads geographically—showing them only to searchers within the your area. With geographic targeting, a furniture store, for example, that delivers within 25 miles of its location can purchase the keyword *furniture* but ask the search engine to show that ad only on computers within the delivery zone. Local search, on the other hand, expects the searcher to enter the location as part of the query.

Search engines can restrict their results to the searcher's geography through a technique called a **reverse IP lookup**—they compare the IP address of the searcher's computer against a table that notes that address's geographic location. The location is usually accurate, but not always. When accurate, searchers located within 25 miles of that furniture store will see the ad when they look for "furniture" but others would not.

The three major search engines all support geographic targeting by city, but Google and Yahoo! also enable advertisers to specify the state or even the zip code of searchers who should see an ad. With Google, you can go further, even targeting by longitude and latitude coordinates, as Figure 14-9 shows. Because geographic targeting is a relatively new idea in paid search, the various paid placement engines provide different capabilities, and they are still evolving. Use the resources in Chapter 16 to keep up with the latest changes.

Figure 14-9   Geographic targeting for paid placement. Search marketers can target by searcher location, even by longitude and latitude with Google.

Select Your Bidding Strategy

As with so many other parts of search marketing, you need a strategy for something as complex as paid placement bidding. Some of the concepts covered here can also be useful for deciding whether shopping search per-click fees are affordable for your product. (Shopping search engines are also beginning to offer premium services that show more information in your ad in exchange for higher per-click charges, so you need to decide whether those premium fees are worth it.) But most of what we present here is exclusive to paid placement.

And paid placement is all about bidding, which at first blush seems simple enough. You don't need much smarts to able to submit a bid, or even to "win" by being placed at the #1 position. However, that is not really winning—winning is driving conversions that cost less than they are worth. That kind of winning demands a bidding strategy.

Rookie paid search marketers typically have no bidding strategy, or at least they do not know they have one. But the old saying "even no decision is a decision" applies here. If you do not make an explicit choice about your bidding strategy, you are basing your decisions on something, but you are just not articulating what it is.

Most "strategy-free" search marketers run through a series of strategies, moving on to the next one each time they get burned by their current one. Table 14-5 shows a range of philosophies—the ones at the top of the table tend to fixate on high rankings, traffic, and other measures of success, regardless of budget. In fact, two-thirds of all sites measure themselves based on nothing but pure traffic. The strategies at the bottom of the table tend to focus on budget constraints and efficiency rather than effectiveness. Most paid search marketers will benefit from one of the middle paths.

Table 14-5   Paid Placement Bidding Strategies (Some go all out to win the wrong game, whereas others pinch pennies—you should aim for the "sweet spot" in the middle.)

Nickname	Goal for Paid Search	Pros and Cons	Focus
Top dogs	#1 ranking	#1 rankings do not guarantee conversions, or even clicks.	Rank
Traffic reporters	Highest traffic	Better than focusing on rankings, but if the conversion rate is too low, the traffic might be unprofitable.	Maximize returns
Peddlers	Most conversions	An obvious goal, but if the conversions are not profitable, they are not terribly valuable.	
Marketers	Highest return on advertising spending	A useful goal, but it does not tell you if the return (revenue) is profitable.	
Financiers	Highest profit margin	A good goal, but your total profit could be higher at a lower profit margin.	
Go-getters	Highest profit or highest lifetime value	The best goal if you are not constrained by a budget.	The sweet spot
Executives	Highest profit within budget	For most search marketers, the optimal goal, but optimizing total profit might be more valuable.	
Accountants	Lowest cost per action	Useful for building support for raiding budgets from other groups, but does not maximize profit.	Minimize costs
Efficiency experts	Highest clickthrough rate or the highest conversion rate	Useful for building support for a higher budget, but does not maximize profit.	
Bottom feeders	Bargain keywords that have very low costs per click	You can uncover good value, but you will overlook high-performing keywords that cost more.	
Skinflints	Stay within budget	No focus on any measures of success means you cannot tell whether it is working.	

Newbie search marketers often choose a goal at the top or bottom of the table, without a great deal of thought. Sometimes these choices can be disastrous—two marketers both pursuing the "top dog" approach can burn through their budgets in a few days. Most of the time, poor choices are not so awful—marketers who look for bargain keywords at low prices hurt their company's return on their marketing program, but it is not a tragedy.

To be fair, those pursuing top rankings do have a reason—**syndication**. Paid placement ads are syndicated to partner sites, as you saw in Chapter 2. AOL, for example, shows Google's paid placement ads on the AOL search results page. However, AOL does not show *all* of the ads—they show just the top three or four. So, those that are constantly jockeying for the top positions do have their reasons; but if the top spot costs more than it is worth, it is not helping them.

A little thinking will lead you away from approaches at the extremes—the top or the bottom of Table 14-5. It is rarely as critical as top dogs think to be #1 in the paid placement rankings as opposed to #3. Likewise, skinflints that stay within their budgets without tracking any return on that investment cannot succeed at anything. Over time, successful marketers move to the middle, which some experts call **objective bidding**—using metrics to drive your bids. So what metrics are there?

Lifetime value is one way of quantifying what each new customer is worth. Direct mailers have used this metric for years to decide how much marketing investment to make in a customer—they do that by deciding what a new customer is worth, not just for the first purchase but for the lifetime of purchases from that customer. If your company can calculate the lifetime value for your customers, you can take the most long-term view for your search marketing.

Most companies are not so forward-looking, however. The next-best way of calculating the value of each conversion is its profit. If your company can calculate the profit on each conversion, a strategy of maximizing profit within your budget will probably be best. The problem with maximizing profit, however, is that it ignores the reality of a budget. For some companies, as long as you maximize profit, they will promise you the required cash flow to keep spending. This is good business, but it is a relatively rare approach.

More typically, your paid placement program will have some kind of budget constraint, and your job will be to maximize your returns within that budget. As you might expect, the best place to start is probably to maximize your profit within your budget. Some companies track profit margin—the percentage of profit per dollar of revenue. But not every company can track profit, either.

Most companies track success based on metrics built around sales revenue or advertising budgets (or both), rather than profit. Because your company's goal is to maximize profit, operating based on revenue and budgets is not necessarily wise. If your company already has a standard way by which it measures all marketing spending, however, you are best advised to use that same method for paid placement. By doing so, you allow paid search to be compared to other forms of marketing, which typically shows why search is such a good investment.

Because none of these other techniques maximize profit, you always need to be careful in placing too much faith in them. Still, they are frequently much easier to calculate—many of the bid management tools we showed earlier can calculate them automatically and even adjust your bids accordingly. So before we show you these magical formulas that enable you to place your paid placement campaign on autopilot, we once again warn you not to be seduced by them. If you can figure lifetime value or the profit on each conversion, that is great. Unfortunately, many search marketers cannot calculate these measures, so they need other approaches:

- *Cost per action (CPA).* If you cannot maximize profit, you might settle for minimizing costs. For companies selling a single product, minimizing the costs per action (Web conversion) might work out just as well as maximizing profit, but there are dangers. Remember that your ultimate goal is to have the highest amount of profit—not the lowest cost for each item sold. You might minimize cost per action with low paid placement bidding that generates far fewer sales than you could profitably make. A related concept is **cost per order** (CPO), which is just a more specific case of cost per action that refers only to the action of purchase. Cost per action can be applied to any Web conversion, not just purchases. CPA is calculated as the number of actions divided by the advertising costs (the paid placement fees), so 20 conversions that cost $20 in click fees yield a CPA of $1.

- *Profit margin.* Again, maximizing total profit is usually the best, but maximizing profit margin can be useful if you do not inordinately cut into your sales volume. As with cost per action, however, high profit margins on each sale might not be as good as slightly lower margins on much higher sales. Profit margin describes your profit per unit sold, but says nothing about your sales volume—low sales with high profit margins are not typically the optimal case. Profit margin is calculated as profit per unit sold divided by the sales price, so a $10 profit on a $100 item yields a profit margin of 10 percent.

- *Return on advertising spending (ROAS).* You can identify underperforming or expensive words by calculating each keyword's ROAS, which examines the revenue you get for those click fees. ROAS is not oriented toward profit, but it does help you optimize the revenue within your budget. ROAS is calculated as the dollars of revenue captured for every dollar of advertising, so $2,000 in revenue from $20 in advertising yields an ROAS of $100.

- *Return on investment (ROI).* Often batted around in common usage, ROI is calculated as the percentage of profit returned from your spending, so $200 in profit divided by $20 in advertising spending (paid placement fees) yields an ROI of 1,000 percent. Like ROAS, ROI can identify your worst-performing keywords, so that you can eliminate them or reduce your bids on them. Conversely, if your budget increases, the highest ROI keywords might be the ones you should test to see whether higher bids result in higher profits (even if ROI decreases), because the highest ROI does not always lead to the highest profit.

Table 14-6 shows how different strategies for objective bidding can result in very different outcomes. In each case, a bidder optimizing for one of these metrics can succeed in returning a profit, but a different strategy that optimized none of these metrics returned a higher profit.

Table 14-6   Objective Bidding Strategies (Different bidding strategies for selling the same $100 product can produce different overall profits.)

Metric Optimized	Sales ROAS	Profit per Sale	Paid Search Fees	CPA	Profit Margin	ROAS	ROI	Overall Profit
CPA	20	$10	$20	**$1**	10%	$100	1,000%	$200
Profit margin	20	$10	$20	$1	**10%**	$100	1,000%	$200
ROAS	20	$10	$20	$1	10%	**$100**	1,000%	$200
ROI	20	$10	$20	$1	10%	$100	**1,000%**	$200
Overall profit	50	$6	$250	$5	6%	$20	120%	**$300**

Understandably, if your company uses one of these metrics to judge the value of all marketing spending, it behooves you to do so, too. A variation on optimizing for a single metric is to use a *self-funding* strategy, which always ensures that your sales are profitable while possibly allowing you to reach higher sales volumes (and thus higher overall profits). To pursue a self-funding strategy, you start by calculating your *allowable*—the highest CPA that you will pay for a particular product. After you know your allowable, you can use the conversion rate to determine what your highest per-click bid should be, as shown in Table 14-7.

Table 14-7   Calculating Bids from Allowables (If you know how much each conversion is worth, and you also know your conversion rate, you will know your maximum bid.)

| Allowable | Maximum Profitable Per-Click Fees at Different Conversion Rates | | | |
	0.75%	1%	2%	5%
$5	4	5¢	10¢	25¢
$10	8¢	10¢	20¢	50¢
$25	19¢	25¢	50¢	$1.25
$50	38¢	50¢	$1.00	$2.50
$75	56¢	75¢	$1.50	$3.75

Using Table 14-7, Snap Electronics was able to pinpoint its optimal bid for its *digital camera* keywords. For example, Snap decided that it was willing to pay $50 for every sale of a Snap-Shot digital camera—$50 was Snap's allowable. (In real life, you would have a different allowable for every model of camera, so that you would allow more spending for models that returned higher profits.) Expecting to convert 2 percent of all keyword referrals into sales, Snap's opening maximum bid for *digital camera* keywords was set to $1.

We keep harping on the point that optimizing your bids for any of these metrics does not maximize your profit, but you can at least experiment with your allowable for each product to increase your profit (if you are able to calculate your profit in the first place, of course). You can increase or decrease your allowable, letting your bid management software adjust your bidding, and you can keep measuring your overall profit until you seem to have an allowable that maximizes profit—or gets it as high as you have been able to, at any rate. Economists refer to this as testing the **elasticity** of your market—stretching your allowable to see when profitability declines. Although not perfect, this strategy improves your overall profits without requiring expensive manual bid management.

You must also consider your philosophy for your incremental bids to target specific demographics, such as age or gender. Currently, MSN alone offers this capability, but you should expect others to provide demographic targeting over time. The bid premium that you pay for this targeting should be driven by the increased value of the conversions from this traffic.

Make Your Bids

Finally, let's get to what you have been waiting for—making your bids for your paid placement keywords. If you have adopted an objective bidding strategy and analyzed your numbers, you can either use your bid management software to control your bidding, or you can do it manually. For large campaigns or for competitive keywords, you need to rely on automated bid management to succeed.

The minimum bid that you can place on a keyword ranges from 1¢ to 10¢, depending on the search engine, and every bid must be at least 1¢ higher than the bid below it. The preceding section showed how you can use your allowable and your conversion rate to calculate your maximum bid. Except it is not so simple.

The maximum bid we calculated is just a starting point. Until you start buying keywords and you track your conversions, you do not know whether your conversion rate really *is* 2 percent. And even if you *do* average a 2 percent conversion rate across all of your keywords, some will undoubtedly convert at higher rates than others.

Snap Electronics struggled with this problem at the start of its paid search campaign for digital cameras. They wanted to start with the most popular keyword, *digital camera*, so they could drive the most conversions to the site from the start. They knew that they could bid $1 for that keyword, and they remembered when they did the budget exercise back in Chapter 8 that the top spot went for just 85¢ per click. Unfortunately, a few months had passed while getting their program approved—now it was Christmas season. Dozens of new competitors were bidding up this overheated keyword. Figure 14-10 shows the top Yahoo! bid has escalated to $2.50 per click! Snap would have to get an impossible 5 percent conversion rate to make a profit, according to its calculations from Table 14-7. Snap reluctantly decided to move on to less-popular keywords.

| | | | | | DELETE | | | | | | |

Keywords	Category	Monthly Search Volume	Your Max Bid ($)	Pos.	Top 5 Max Bids ($)				
			Update Bids						
digital camera	dc	1,182,747	2.51	1	2.50	2.30	1.88	1.88	1.87
snapshot digital camera	dc	4	0.10	1	-	-	-	-	-
snap digital camera	dc	24	0.40	1	0.39	0.39	0.38	0.20	0.18
digital camera reviews	dc	66,078	0.35	1	0.34	0.33	0.32	0.27	0.27
compare digital cameras	dc	8,374	0.57	1	0.56	0.56	0.55	0.54	0.53
best digital cameras	dc	17,014	0.95	1	0.94	0.79	0.75	0.75	0.75
digital camera comparison	dc	10,400	0.56	1	0.55	0.39	0.38	0.37	0.32
			Update Bids						

Figure 14-10   Making your bid. Yahoo!, like all paid placement engines, provides a simple way for you to make your maximum bid for any keyword.

Reproduced with permission of Yahoo! Inc. © 2005 by Yahoo! Inc. YAHOO! and the YAHOO! logo are trademarks of Yahoo! Inc.

Because Snap cameras get great reviews, Snap decided on the keyword *digital camera reviews*. Snap was excited to see the keyword had just a 35¢ bid for the #1 spot, although they knew it would drive far less traffic than *digital camera*. Snap quickly entered a maximum bid of $1 and took the top spot, knowing that they would never pay more than a penny higher than the #2 bidder. Unfortunately, a few days' worth of data revealed that the conversion rate for that informational keyword was distressingly low, less than 0.5 percent—it was not worth what they were paying. Snap was forced to temporarily withdraw the bid and to focus on other keywords that would convert at higher rates. Fortunately, they found that their branded keywords, such as *snap digital camera* and *snapshot camera* converted at more than 2 percent and their competition for those keywords was decidedly less—Snap took the top spots for less than 40¢ each, providing very strong returns.

Snap was smart to start their paid placement campaign by testing with a very small part of their budget. As soon as they got some results, they iterated their bids to go after new keywords that paid off. They will continue to do so as they gain experience.

Besides setting your maximum bids, you can also set **budget** maximums (either on a weekly or a monthly basis), so that you do not spend more than you should. If Snap Electronics had followed through on buying a popular keyword, such as *digital camera*, it would have drained its monthly budget in just a few days. Instead, Snap could set a daily maximum spending rate to spread out its budget throughout the month. The search engines accomplish this magic by rotating Snap's ad among other ads, so that even if Snap had the #1 bid, their ad would not be shown to each searcher with a matching query. The ad would be shown just enough to keep spending under the "cap" for the day.

Sounds great, right? It can be, when used properly, but spreading out your budget by letting the search engine randomly show your ad is no way to maximize your conversions. You would be better off taking other actions to stay within your budget:

- Target keywords with less demand but a higher conversion rate instead of the popular keyword.
- Use dayparting so that the clicks you receive for the popular keyword come at the times you get the highest conversion rate.
- Lower your bid for the keyword so that although you get fewer clicks, you pay less for each one.

Daily and monthly caps *do* have one good use—they protect you from sudden shifts that could be disastrous to your budget. Suppose that you were running the search marketing for Hilton Hotels in France. What do you think happened to your paid search budget the day that celebrity Paris Hilton burst upon the scene with a naughty video? If you had the top bid for the keyword *paris hilton*, you might have gotten a lot of erroneous clicks to drain your budget before you figured out what was going on. A daily cap could stop the bleeding.

Caps can also save you from yourself. Paid placement requires precision in keyword selection, bidding, and ad copy. Do it long enough and you are bound to make a mistake that drains your budget without any conversions. Caps can stop a run on the bank.

With MSN and Google, you set caps by campaign—Yahoo! has caps only for your whole account—so you can put lower performers in their own campaign and turn them on and off depending on how the rest of your campaigns are spending your budget.

But don't use caps to stay within budget when you could be making your spending more efficient. It's the lazy way to keep from blowing the budget, but it hurts your return. No random ad placement by search engines can drive as many conversions as your active management based on metrics will. Use caps as a firewall against disasters, not as an operational strategy.

Attract Searchers' Clicks

Take a deep breath! You're getting there, but you still have a little more to learn. It is not enough to set up your program and bid on the right keywords. Just as a direct-mail piece needs the right words to get you to open the envelope, you need to get searchers to click your listings. Effective copywriting is crucial for driving clickthrough rates for your paid placement listing, but for shopping search it is a different game. We look at both, starting with paid placement copywriting.

Optimize Your Paid Placement Copy

Nineteenth-century American humorist Henry Wheeler Shaw once said, "Money will buy you a pretty good dog, but it won't buy the wag of his tail." And so it is with paid placement, where your per-click fees can buy impressions for your ad, but only your copy will get the clicks you need from searchers.

You recall from Chapter 11 how difficult it can sometimes be to craft pages that contain the search terms (so that both the search engines and the searchers find what they are looking for). With paid placement, you will have no such difficulty—you can lead searchers to whatever pages you want with your paid ads. Well, *almost*.

Paid placement engines *do* have editorial guidelines designed to protect their business. Each search engine has somewhat different rules, but they are very similar:

- *Don't circumvent the click.* Search engines get paid only when searchers click, so they are understandably displeased with ads that show phone numbers or e-mail addresses that allow the searcher to buy from you without clicking.

- *Don't hype it up.* Excessive capitalization and showy punctuation (especially exclamation marks and question marks) are frequently rejected. Use of impossible-to-prove superlatives (best, most, greatest, cheapest, and so on) are also a quick ticket to a blocked ad.

- *Don't hide your identity.* Be clear about who you are. If you are an affiliate, for example, don't try to pass yourself off as the manufacturer.

Google, MSN, and Yahoo! publish extensive tips about how to follow their guidelines and how to make your ads as successful as possible. There are three critical parts to paid placement ads, as illustrated in Figure 14-11:

- *Title.* The first line of the ad must catch the searcher's eye or you will get very low click-through.

- *Description.* Your benefits and call to action go here. If you hooked them with the title, this is where you get them to click.

- *Display URL.* Not the URL that searchers will click through to, it is a shortened version that usually is just the domain of the company (www.yourcompany.com) so that searchers know where they are going when they click.

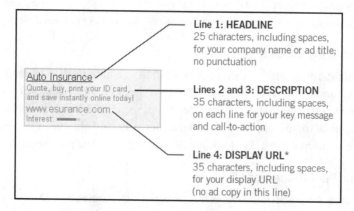

Figure 14-11   Anatomy of a paid placement ad. All paid placement ads have the same three components, as this diagram from Google demonstrates.

Source: The Maximum Effect p. 26

When you sit down to write your copy, you'll notice how little room you have—Google, MSN, and Yahoo! ads are all limited to just 70 characters. Make it punchy and edit your ad until all extraneous words are removed. Here's some more advice to guide you in creating good titles and descriptions for your paid placement ads:

- *Use the keywords.* Searchers are fixated on finding the words they just typed. They scan the search results page looking for them—ads with keywords attract nearly 50 percent more clicks. Sometimes, the keyword itself is so long that it does not fit in the title (and it would badly clutter up the description), such as *snapshot SLR x900 digital camera reviews*. In that case, strategically shorten the keyword, perhaps to *snapshot x900 reviews*. If you use the most important words in the searcher's query, your click rate should be strong.

- *Sell factual benefits.* Why should searchers click your ad? What do your customers want? Do you have a lower price? Free shipping? Quick delivery? Are you a reliable supplier? Do you have a key benefit for the product itself? Can you quantify that benefit? Try to say something factual that your competitors cannot. If you are the manufacturer, make sure you explain you are *not* an affiliate—that might improve your click rate. Small businesses using local search need to emphasize their location—use the name of the locality (*Central New Jersey*) and also use imagery words, such as *good neighbor*, that a national brand cannot always get away with. Fact-based ads get 50 percent more clicks than "sales-y" ones. Use full sentences to increase the fact-based effect, rather than breathless phrases that reek of hype. Unless you offer a compelling factual benefit to searchers, they will not click through to become customers.

- *Attract attention.* Although the editorial guidelines restrict your use of capitalization, exclamation points, and hyped-up copy, you should try to use the strongest words you can within those limits. You cannot use *greatest* but you can use *great*. Test your copy with different words that attract attention—*save* and *discount* are always attention-getters, but if you can find exciting words to describe your benefits while remaining factual (and not breathless), that approach is very successful. And do not hide your well-known brand names—recognizable brands cause searcher clicks, so highlight yours.

- *Call the searcher to action.* Make it abundantly clear what you want them to do. Not "click here," but rather, use words that speak to the searcher's task. If you are selling something, use "buy." "Download this case study." "Get a free quote instantly." If you appeal to the searcher's intent (remember Chapter 4, "How Searchers Work"), you will attract the searcher's click.

- *Create urgency.* Your call to action must be clear and must impel the searcher to click *now*. "Order today to receive before Christmas." "Only 50 remaining." "All orders placed in May receive this free gift." "Discounted 30 percent through Saturday." You get the idea.

After you have decided on your wording, it's time to actually place your ad. It can save time to use the same copy for an entire category (Yahoo!) or ad group (Google and MSN)—that is why you collected them together in the first place. You can then edit each keyword individually to fine-tune the copy, as shown in Figure 14-12.

Enter your copy into the bid management tool.

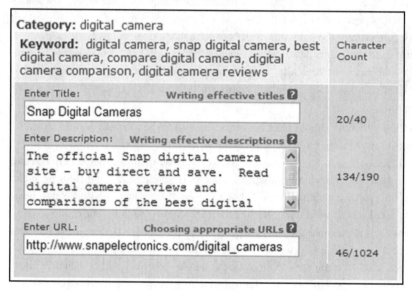

Preview the ad before approving it to be published.

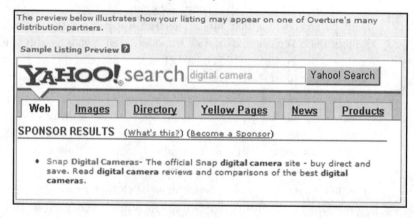

Figure 14-12   Editing titles and descriptions. Yahoo! shows exactly how your ad will look when presented in Yahoo! and the other syndication sites.

TOO MUCH OF A GOOD THING? HOW TO QUALIFY SEARCHERS BEFORE THEY CLICK

We have emphasized all the ways you can increase the clickthrough rate on your ad, but sometimes you have a different problem—you get the clicks but not the conversions you expected. Sometimes that is a problem with your landing page, or other pages on your site, but it can also be a sign that your ad is not properly **qualifying** your searchers.

Just as important as getting the right people to click is dissuading the wrong people from clicking. Write your ads so they attract the searchers who will actually convert. If you attract unqualified visitors, you will drain your budget with low conversion rates. Snap Electronics found that their ad for *digital cameras* keywords needed to emphasize Snap's exclusiveness and its quality. These words sufficiently positioned the camera away from bargain hunters who clicked and then blanched at the price. By dissuading those unqualified searchers, Snap lowered its per-click fees and raised its conversion rate.

Qualifying customers is important, but it has its risks, too. If the clickthrough rate for your ad drops too low, hybrid auction systems will rarely show it (because their ranking algorithms consider both click rate and bid). The other paid placement engines will also stop showing it because they flag any ad that drops below a certain clickthrough rate.

Sometimes the best way to qualify your customers is to change the way you buy keywords. If the click rates for Snap Electronics dropped too low, they could change their keyword strategy so that they purchased keywords that fit their product image. Instead of trying to target *digital camera*, Snap could add negative keywords (such as *cheap*, *discount*, or *bargain*, to eliminate the wrong searchers). Or Snap could go after more specific keywords, such as *best digital camera* or *8 megapixel camera*. Making your keywords more specific lowers your per-click fees and raises your conversion rates without lowering your clickthrough rates.

We have focused on titles and descriptions, but the last part of a paid placement ad, the display URL, is also important. Display URLs tell the searcher where their click leads them. If you have a well-known brand or Web site, make sure that the display URL plays it up.

Manage Your Paid Placement Ads

We have continually counseled you to go after as many keywords as you can profitably afford, and we have told you to place keywords in every ad, and to test variations against each other. How can you reduce the labor for all this work?

Let's start with inserting keywords into hundreds or thousands of ads. You have probably set up ad groups (or Yahoo! categories) for keywords that are similar in meaning. That's great, because those keywords can share the same ads, reducing your copywriting work. But it causes a new problem, because you want the keyword the searcher entered to appear in each ad. If you have used the same copy for each ad, how do the keywords get inserted?

With Google, you can use a clever tool called **Dynamic Keyword Insertion** (DKI). When you define your titles or descriptions, you can use curly braces to indicate the place where you want the keyword inserted into your copy. Snap Electronics has two dozen models that they placed in a single ad group so they could share the same copy for their ad across all models. But they wanted the model name in the title, so they coded their title as "Buy {Keyword: SnapShot Cameras} direct"—which inserts the searcher's keyword dynamically. For example, if the searcher entered "snapshot slr," the title of the ad would read "Buy snapshot slr direct." By controlling the match type of the ad group, Snap ensured that only phrases with *SnapShot* were part of this ad group. Sometimes, however, the keyword entered by the searchers are too long to fit in the title, such as "snap snapshot slr x900." In that case, the default text after the "Keyword:" in the braces would be inserted instead, creating a title of "Buy SnapShot Cameras direct." MSN has a similar capability it calls "dynamic text" that is similar to Google's DKI.

The dynamic capabilities of Google and MSN to insert keywords in your title or your description enable you to raise your click rate without much extra work. Yahoo! and most other paid placement engines do not offer any comparable tool, but they usually accept ad content submitted using spreadsheets, so you can use macros in your favorite spreadsheet to insert your own keywords into standard ad copy. You will have to code your macro to count the number of characters to ensure you do not exceed the length restrictions for the engine you are feeding (substituting default text in that case). It is not as elegant as dynamic text insertion capabilities, but can be equally effective. Whatever it takes, make sure that you get the searcher's keywords into every ad possible. It dramatically raises your clickthrough rate.

However, it is not the only way to raise your click rate. You can also test multiple versions of ad copy for the same keyword to see which one draws more conversions. As you might expect, this can be labor-intensive, too. So-called "A/B testing" (because you test version A against version B) can be automated by many bid management tools. Google offers a feature called **auto-optimization** that enables you to rotate up to six different versions of ad copy, with Google eventually settling on the one with the highest click rate automatically. Some advertisers prefer to test their ad copy themselves, because they want to conduct more extensive sampling than Google does or because they want to select the winning version based on conversion rate rather than clickthrough rate.

Regardless of how you manage your ad copy, finding ways to raise your clickthrough rates with the least possible effort is a winning strategy. You can also work on your shopping search listings to attract more clicks, as you will see next.

Fine-Tune Your Shopping Search Data

Optimizing your data in a shopping search engine is the key to attracting clicks from searchers. Figure 14-13 shows why shoppers use shopping search engines—you need to satisfy those needs to persuade them to click your listing.

To attract clicks on shopping search engines, you must concentrate on three major factors:

- *Metadata.* As discussed in Chapter 10, preparing your trusted feed properly ensures that your product listings will be found. (Some shopping search engines will also crawl your site or allow you to enter your listings.) If your product list does not contain complete and correct metadata, your products will not be listed for all of the searches that they should be.

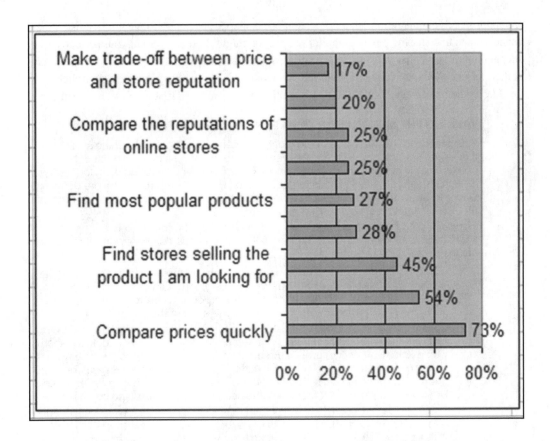

Figure 14-13 Shopping search uses. Shoppers like shopping search engines for many different reasons.

Source: ForeSee Results (December 2002)

- *Price.* Some shopping search engines rank results on price, so having the lowest price gets you to the top of the list. (PriceGrabber, Shopping.com, and Shopzilla rank by price.) As you might expect, having a low price attracts clicks regardless of whether the search engine ranks by price or not.

- *Merchant rating.* Yahoo! Shopping and Shopping.com can show listings with the highest merchant ratings at the top. As with price, your merchant rating is shown in all search engines, and high ones persuade more clicks than lower ones.

So, pay attention to your data to ensure that your listing is found, and pay attention to the ranking factors to be placed at the top of the list. Ranking at the top is important—one leading shopping search engine reports that 50 percent of all shopper clicks go to the top five listed merchants. When first starting out in shopping search, you might need to discount your price to attract shoppers until you boost your merchant rating. Some shopping search engines allow you to pay higher per-click fees to become a "featured" merchant—NexTag always ranks by per-click bids, just like a paid placement engine—so that is another way to be listed first in the search results.

WINNING THE MERCHANT-RATING POPULARITY CONTEST

Your **merchant rating** is one of the most important parts of your shopping search listing. Some shopping search engines rank the merchant results for a product by merchant rating (whereas other rank by price), but all display your rating with your listing. Searchers use merchant ratings as a quick check on your reputation before deciding whom to buy from. Shopping.com reports that highly rated merchants are 30 percent more likely to receive clicks than others.

Merchant ratings are calculated from your reviews by shoppers, so it *is* a popularity contest. How can you run with the popular crowd? Focus on the important things to get the reviews you need:

- *Correct content*. When an item is out of stock, remove it from your listing as quickly as possible to avoid frustrating customers with back orders. Fix any errors in metadata that would cause your product to be found for the wrong searches or would otherwise mislead searchers about the product.

- *Quality goods*. Make absolutely sure that your products do everything you claim, and that they are not damaged. If customers believe you have snookered them with a knock-off or a refurbished model when they thought they were buying a *bona fide* new item, your rating will suffer. So if you do sell knock-offs or used goods, be *very* clear about that in your description to avoid bad reviews later. Don't just mention it—hit them over the head with it so there is no confusion.

- *Quick shipping*. Customers want it, and they want it now. If it takes you a couple of days to get it off your loading dock, expect some impatient folks to nail you with a bad review. Be explicit about how long it will take so that expectations are not higher than what you can (literally) deliver. Use e-mail throughout the process to show the progress of the shipment.

- *Excellent service*. Things will sometimes go wrong. When they do, correct them immediately to make an unhappy customer happy again. It is strange but true that customers who were upset and had their problem fixed often rate you higher than those that had no problem at all. If customers post a bad review that contains specific complaints, answer those complaints online with a specific offer to fix the problem. (Sometimes those complaints are fakes from your competitors trying to drive down your rating, so answering them gives them less impact.)

Speaking of fake complaints, that is one of the things that merchants may not do to their competition. Similarly, merchants may not "encourage" anyone to offer a positive review of their service by crafting the words, providing financial incentives, or contacting them by e-mail or phone. Or by having employees and other biased parties post reviews. If the shopping search engines believe manipulation is occurring with merchant ratings, they change the ratings to compensate.

You don't need to resort to trickery to maintain high merchant ratings. Stick to the basics and your merchant rating will soar. That will do more to drive your conversions than anything else you can do.

Optimize Paid Search Landing Pages

Design your paid landing pages first and foremost for conversions. Most paid search engines pay no attention to landing page quality, except Google, whose Quality Score factors landing page relevance into paid search rankings. Review the tips we gave you in Chapter 12 for organic landing pages—you won't go wrong to follow them for paid landing pages, too.

For paid placement, a few editorial guidelines are insisted upon by paid placement engines:

- *Include the keywords*. Although you need not optimize your page the way organic landing pages require, the editorial department of every paid placement engine will inspect your landing page to make sure it is relevant to the keyword purchased. Do make it obvious that your searcher has landed in the right place for the query entered.
- *Stay on topic*. If you buy the keyword *racing cars* and try to sell automobile batteries, the paid placement engines will not approve your ad. Only pages relevant to the keyword topic will be accepted.
- *Reinforce your offer*. In addition to mentioning the keyword, you must ensure that anything you have called out in the copy be prominently shown on the landing page.
- *Drop pop-ups*. Visitors hate pop-up or pop-under advertising, so paid placement engines do not allow them. We recommend you dump them from your whole site, but you must at least eliminate them from your landing pages.
- *Enable the "back" button*. Some pages disable the browser's "back" button, so that the visitor cannot easily return to the search page. If you want to annoy your visitors, it is hard to top this practice, and paid placement engines will not let you get away with it.

These guidelines (and the rules we discussed earlier for the ads themselves) are not very hard to follow, but the search engines are quite serious about them. Catherine Seda, in her book *Search Engine Advertising*, reports that Yahoo! editors reject as many as 30 percent of all ads submitted to them, many for relevancy. Because hybrid auctions reward higher clickthrough rates, they do less policing of ads and landing pages for relevancy, although they reject many ads, too.

As with organic search landing pages, you must make it simple for visitors to convert. If you reinforce what searchers are looking for (their search keywords) and why they clicked your pages (your ad copy), you will likely get a good conversion rate. Remember that you might have several pages between your landing page and your conversion page, so make sure that the entire path is designed with conversion in mind. For shopping search, the path is usually much shorter—your shopping search landing page is typically the "buy" page for that product on your site.

Whether using paid placement or shopping search, your landing pages (and your entire conversion path) requires careful design and, above all, testing. Just as you test everything else about paid search, test your landing pages, too. Test the amount of copy on the page, the size of the product images, the kind of language used, the links to background information, and more. To test, you need to measure your conversions, which we discuss in Chapter 15.

IS FRAUD EATING AWAY AT YOUR PAID SEARCH BUDGET?

Fraud is the elephant in the living room that the paid search industry does not like to talk about. But fraud is very real, and you need to understand the issues and keep abreast of the latest news to protect your search marketing budget. Fraud comes in two flavors: click fraud and impression fraud.

Click fraud, in essence, drains your search marketing budget with clicks that are not intended to ever convert—clicks designed just to collect your per-click fee. It might be hard to stomach, but some experts claim that as many as 20 percent of all paid search clicks are fraudulent. Let's examine how click fraud occurs.

Whenever your paid placement or shopping search listing is clicked, you must pay your click fee, but you get nothing for that fee unless the visitor buys something from *you*. So, someone who wants to drain your budget could repeatedly click your listing without buying anything. But who would take the trouble to do that?

Competitors and hucksters, that's who. Your competitors might want to exhaust your paid search budget while their listings remain (to scoop up the customers you are missing out on). Hucksters are even more motivated—they can pocket a cut of your fees by accepting the paid placement ads on their site and then fabricating the clicks. No one believes that Google or Yahoo! or any of the other paid search vendors are instigating fraudulent clicks on their ads, but many suspect that their syndicators are. Any site that accepts paid placement (especially contextual ads) on their site could just start randomly clicking those ads to ring the cash register.

Your competitors might be engaging in "drive-by" click fraud—rogue employees clicking away at your listings from an overstimulated sense of competition (and a lack of ethics). The real problem stems from professional hucksters using this deviant technique to siphon your cash for themselves. Some use automated programs that click listings in random ways while disguising their locations, whereas others go so far as to hire networks of workers, sometimes in Third World countries, who click away all day.

It is unclear whether click fraud is illegal or merely unethical, but the paid search vendors are scrambling to control it, lest they lose the confidence of search marketers and imperil the whole industry. The major vendors have massive fraud squads to crack down on problem affiliates, but their efforts to date have proven no match for their fraudulent foes.

How *can* you protect yourself? Experts will tell you to monitor your reports for strange activity patterns, which you should; but if 20 percent of all clicks are fraudulent, that advice does not help much. Sure, you can spot a listing that suddenly gets a three-fold increase in clicks in a day, but the folks perpetrating this fraud are craftier than that. To combat the problem, some new companies claim to help you detect click fraud, such as Click Defense (www.clickdefense.com), ClickDetective (www.clickdetective.com), and PPC Audit (www.whosclickingwho.com). Additionally, Web metrics vendors, such as Coremetrics (www.coremetrics.com), have added click fraud detection features to their existing tracking tools. Also keep in mind that larger paid search vendors tend to have the strongest fraud detection programs, so the small vendors you located on www.payperclicksearchengines.com probably carry higher risk.

Impression fraud, the younger cousin of click fraud, stems from the switch to hybrid auctions that count clickthrough rates as part of the ranking process. Impression fraud is practiced by your competitors, who repeatedly execute searches to view your ads without clicking through, thus lowering your clickthrough rate and forcing you to bid higher to maintain the same position.

As long as fraud remains at its current level, it is merely an unpleasant cost of doing business, not unlike insurance fraud or shoplifting. It drives up everyone's prices, but if paid search is making money for your business, fraud is no reason to shy away.

Measure and Adjust Your Campaigns

Hey, you have a campaign up and running and your bid management tool is set up, so now you can just wait for the money to roll in, right? Well, not exactly. If you recall, your strategy is to iterate, so it's time to check out how you are doing and then make changes to improve. Bid management tools are *very* helpful, but they cannot substitute for your good judgment.

You must monitor new campaigns quite closely, because you are learning a lot. Over time, each campaign requires less monitoring, although nothing stays static forever. In Chapter 15, we talk about how to keep campaigns on track after the initial adjustment period, but now let's focus on how to track your campaigns as they come out of the gate.

Start out by tracking your campaign according to your objectives. If you are tracking profit, see whether it is meeting your projections. If all you can measure is your clickthrough rate, well, at least check that. And watch your bid rates for paid placement. If competitive bids are rising and your position is falling, it's time for deeper analysis. Measure as granularly as you can. Track your paid placement results by keyword within search engine within time of day, if possible. Examine your shopping search conversions by product within search engine. Notice which targets are performing and which are not, according to the metrics you have chosen.

When your paid placement keyword ads or your shopping search listings are not being clicked, take action:

- *Test new copy.* Your best way to attract clicks is with copy that demands searchers pay attention. If your paid placement ad or your shopping search listing seems to solve their problem, they will be compelled to click.

- *Test higher bids.* It is possible that accepting a higher cost per action might result in higher paid placement rankings. That increased exposure can sometimes dramatically raise click rates, providing stronger overall profits even though the profit per unit is lower.

- *Improve your merchant rating.* Shoppers *are* swayed by merchants they think they should trust. Make sure that you seem more trustworthy than your competition.

- *Look for ways they do perform.* Do they get an acceptable click rate at a certain time of day? Day of the week? Time of year? On a particular search engine? With a particular match type? With free shipping? For a discounted price? For searchers from a certain location? If you can find conditions of good performance, you can limit your purchases to those conditions.

- *Try new keywords.* Can you add negative keywords to restrict when your paid placement ads are shown? Can you add new terms to your keyword to achieve the same effect? Your keyword might be too broad or just plain wrong for your target market. Expand your horizons to get lower per-click fees and possibly higher conversion rates.

Some search engines have been known to disable ads whose clickthrough rates fall below a certain threshold. Google claims to have no threshold, so that if you bid a high enough per-click fee, Google will show your ad even with a very low clickthrough rate, but other search engines may have more stringent rules—they aren't saying. Scrutinize your clickthrough rates to avoid having ads disabled.

What if you are getting clicks, but not enough conversions? Again, look at when those paid placement keywords or shopping search products *do* perform well. If you catch them performing under certain conditions, dayparting and other restrictions on your keywords might be appropriate. Limiting your product catalog or restricting it to certain shopping search engines might make sense. As above, you might also want to experiment with new keywords—especially more specific keywords that might better target your audience. If those measures do not work, try some other ideas:

- *Reduce your bids.* Perhaps your conversion rate would be acceptable if the bid costs were lower. You can try reducing your bids to find out if the loss of sales results in a better return on (a smaller) investment.

- *Check your landing pages.* Did the URL change? Or did the ad copy change and the landing page does not reflect the ad copy as well as it used to? Is your offer competitive with your competitors? You might be able to use your Web metrics system to see whether visitors are abandoning your site on the landing page or abandoning deeper within your site.

- *Check the rest of your conversion path.* Are other related keywords slipping as well? Have any changes been made to the site in the conversion path? Again, your metrics facility might reveal where visitors stop their conversion process.

Oh, and one more thing. You should do everything listed above when your targets *are* performing, too. That is how you follow your strategy of being more efficient. It is far more likely that you will double your conversions by improving your already strong targets than by buttressing your weak ones. And getting more impact out of your winners is not any harder than fixing your losers—in fact, it is often easier. If you make your winners truly efficient, you will do well to spend more money on them and drop the targets that are borderline performers.

Snap Electronics had a lot to learn when they began purchasing paid placement keywords. You recall that back in Chapter 7, "Measure Your Search Marketing Success," Snap wanted to purchase the keyword *digital camera*, but earlier in this chapter they found themselves priced out of the market. Reluctantly, they decided to experiment with the keyword *digital camera reviews* instead.

Based on their allowable of $50, Snap needed to average a conversion rate of about 2 percent to justify a bid of around $1, but we saw that the top bid was only 35¢. Snap started by trying to top the current #1 bidder, knowing they would need to approach a 1 percent conversion rate if the price went up.

Well, the price did go up, because the previous high bidder topped 70¢, jockeying back and forth with Snap as the average per-click fees for Snap's campaign hovered in the low 70s. But within a few days, Snap saw that its clickthrough rate was way too low—less than 1 percent—so the conversion rate was minuscule, far less than the required 1.5 percent. Snap was forced to temporarily abandon this keyword to diagnose the problem.

Clearly the first problem was the low click rate. Snap took a close look at its ad copy (shown as "Ad A" in Table 14-8) and decided changes were needed. Snap quickly revised the ad copy to "Ad B" to try to boost its click rate. The results were dramatic, as clickthrough jumped to 5 percent, but the conversion rate was still less than 1 percent, much less 1.5 percent. Clearly, unqualified searchers were now clicking and then abandoning, so Snap set out to change the copy again, to what is shown as "Ad C," in an attempt to attract only those with a propensity to buy. It worked. Although click rate went down, conversion rate went up, but not quite to the magical 1.5 percent they needed.

Table 14-8   Snap's Shifting Ad Copy (Paid placement campaigns require great tinkering at first, especially with the words in your paid placement ad.)

Ad	Copy	Clickthrough Rate	Conversion Rate
A	Digital Camera Reviews Confused about what to buy? Find the best camera for you.	0.93%	0.21%
B	Digital Camera Reviews Don't know what to buy? Find your next camera and save 30%.	5.11%	0.87%
C	SnapShot Digital Camera Reviews Research Snapshot cameras and save 30% on yours.	3.41%	1.22%

What now? At this point, they examined their metrics, and found that many of their clicks were for queries such as "cheap digital camera reviews," "bargain digital camera reviews," and "discount digital camera reviews." They also found that some of the keywords contained the names of competitors ("nikon digital camera reviews) that drew few clicks and next-to-no conversions. *Digital video cameras* was a keyword that brought many clicks from hurried searchers, but near-zero conversions. By ferreting out a list of additional words that correlated with a lower conversion rate, Snap was able to add negative terms and increased their conversion rate to more than 1.7 percent. Not satisfied yet, they began to look at dayparting to see whether their conversion rates have any pattern to them. And the beat goes on.

Summary

Paid search is a myriad of details, but we have given you the basics to help you master them. Your most important decisions surround your paid search philosophy—if you can develop a feedback loop that responds to the right performance metrics, you can tweak your paid search campaign until it succeeds.

Search marketers can take advantage of both paid placement and shopping search opportunities, using the steps depicted in Table 14-9.

Table 14-9   The Steps to Paid Search Success (Some steps apply to both paid placement and shopping search, but others are specific to one or the other.)

Step	Paid Placement	Shopping Search
Set up your paid search program:		
Decide your budget.	✓	✓
Set up your accounts.	✓	✓
Select your bid management tool.	✓	
Choose your targets:		
Choose the products to list.		✓
Select good paid placement keywords.	✓	
Organize your keywords.	✓	
Decide your match type for each keyword.	✓	
Decide geographic targeting for each keyword.	✓	
Select your bidding strategy.	✓	
Make your bids.	✓	
Attract searchers' clicks:		
Optimize your paid placement copy.	✓	
Manage your paid placement ads.	✓	
Fine tune your shopping search data.		✓
Optimize paid search landing pages.	✓	✓
Measure and adjust your campaigns	✓	✓

You have learned everything you need to start your paid search campaign. At this point, you just have to begin your real education with your own program. "Learn by doing" is truly the only way to succeed at paid search.

In the next chapter, you will learn how to operate your entire search marketing program. You will staff your central search team, learn the best practices in search marketing, and measure, measure, measure. (Surprise!) You have got all the steps down by now, except one—how to run your program every day. *That* is what Chapter 15 is all about.

CHAPTER 15

Make Search Marketing Operational

If you're the kind of person who cleans your house once a year whether it needs it or not, this chapter might be a challenge for you. Some people are very good at starting something new—including starting a search marketing program—but tire quickly of the day-to-day work that turns a good start into a long-term success. Unfortunately, search marketing is not a one-time event; it is a new way to work. Making your search marketing program a smooth, ongoing operation is the only way you will succeed.

So, if process diagrams make you glaze over, and you do not have the patience to go over the numbers one more time to figure out what is going wrong, make sure you add people to your central search team who have the stick-to-itiveness you lack. And, come to think of it, setting up your central search team is the first of three actions you will take to make search operational:

- *Set up your central search team.* You need to know who to hire and how to train them, because the quality of your central search team can make or break your search marketing program.

- *Establish search marketing best practices.* In Chapter 9, "Sell Your Search Marketing Proposal," we talked about all the folks on your extended search team who you need to influence. Here we show you how to change the organizational rules to get the behavior you want.

- *Track search marketing success.* Anything of importance to an organization gets measured, and search marketing is no exception. Find out what statistics to track and how to use metrics to drive organizational change.

Are you ready to make it real? The startup tasks are almost behind you. It's time to see what makes a search marketing program succeed over the long haul—its operational excellence.

Set Up Your Central Search Team

Your central search team drives your success in search marketing. The central search team will prevent the search crises you live with today by collaborating with the extended search team to maintain proper page tagging, avoid technology "downgrades," head off ill-fated navigational designs, as well as dozens more.

Perhaps your organization already has a central search team, but most do not. In Chapter 8, "Define Your Search Marketing Strategy," we discussed the mission it ought to have. Now let's see how to staff and develop your central team.

Staff the Central Team

How large should the central search team be? As small as possible. Even if you convinced everyone that the search opportunity is huge, it is always better to start small and prove the concept. It is far easier to expand a success than to get cash infusions for something that started too big and did not show value right away. So, be conservative and grow slowly. Even a huge Web site can start with two or three dedicated people, and small sites can start with you doing it part-time. In fact, JupiterResearch found that most search marketers handle five other jobs in addition to their search role.

Remember, too, that the main purpose of your central search team is to help your extended search team. Your extended team must do the heavy lifting, with the central team setting strategy, performing training, answering questions, tracking metrics, and coordinating the overall program. So, staff your central team with the few subject matter experts needed to assist the larger extended search team.

When staffing your team, you need to think carefully about the skills you are looking for. Because a generic list of search marketing skills can be quite long, consider only those skills actually needed in your situation. You must also recognize that you will never find all those skills in one person, so prioritize a few of the most important skills and find the best person you can. Here are some skills you might need on your central search team:

- *Web content skills*. This array of skills ranges from copywriting to landing page optimization techniques to HTML coding. Because the central team will be working with the extended team on all of these tasks, the more familiarity the team has with those skills, the better.

- *Paid search*. If you are planning a paid search program, the central search team needs expertise in each search engine's paid services, either because the central team runs the paid program or because they provide advice to the extended team.

- *Keyword research*. The central team can aid the extended team by teaching them the basics of keyword planning, so the extended team can help choose the right search queries to target.

- *Search marketing tools*. Because the central team chooses the tools and trains the extended team in their use, it is very helpful for team members to know those tools well.

- *Global skills.* If your organization operates in multiple countries, having central team members that speak several languages and know the right local search engines to target in each country can be invaluable.

- *Web metrics.* The central team must teach the extended team how to analyze metrics to prove return on investment. The central team often must define and track metrics for page rankings and other search-specific reports.

As important as these technical skills are, other skills are also needed for the central team to lead the extended team:

- *Familiarity with your Web site's purpose, content, and technology.* Although easy to overlook, don't take for granted how much knowledge of your Web site is required to step in and be productive.

- *Knowledge of the company's products and customers.* Similarly, it is much easier to perform keyword research and to optimize pages when someone on the central search team knows the subject areas and audiences of the content.

- *Working relationships with the extended team.* As with any human endeavor, it takes time to build relationships, so bringing in someone who already has those personal connections will cut startup time.

- *Consulting experience.* All the technical expertise in the world is wasted if the central team does not communicate it to the extended team. A team member trained to listen to problems and solve them might have more impact than an uncommunicative expert. If you cannot hire experienced consultants, teachers are almost as good. Folks with teaching experience excel at explaining complex subject matter, but consultants might be better listeners when specific problems arise for your extended team.

Although it is tempting to hire only folks who have deep technical expertise, it might be useful to hire one central team member from the extended team, because that person might already have the requisite familiarity with the Web site and the company, and might also possess some important relationships.

Keep in mind that it is the rare central search team that grows large enough to hire people with all of these varied skills. Aim to create the mix of skills that are most valuable for your organization's team.

Develop the Central Team's Skills

Because you cannot hire enough people to have expertise in every area of search marketing, it is critical to develop the skills of the people you do hire. There is no shortage of ways to grow your team's skills:

- *Just do it.* There really is no substitute for trying to do something new. Even if you hire world-class experts, search marketing is changing all the time, so a good team will always have to experiment. Find people who learn by doing.

- *Read about it.* We highly recommend that you stay informed about the constant changes in search marketing, and you should buy a copy of this book for every member of your team and for your 100 closest friends. (Okay, the publisher made us put that in.) The rise of search marketing has spawned excellent free and low-cost sources of information, including numerous high-quality Web sites and e-mail newsletters.

- *Take a class.* Although not every search marketing technique is covered in formal classes, your team can learn HTML and technology skills this way. The Web has transformed training classes from time-consuming in-person experiences to quick online training that is ready when you are.

- *Attend a conference.* Some of the best search marketing information comes your way at conferences such as Search Engine Strategies and Webmaster World. Send your central search team and get them the quickest education possible.

- *Cross-train.* If you are able to staff a two- or three-person team, make sure they teach each other what they know. Not only does this help you over rough spots when team members move on to other positions, it also makes your team more well-rounded and better able to handle issues raised by the extended team.

- *Rotate extended team members.* A real win-win that can stretch your resources is a rotation program. Identify promising extended team members and offer them free training for a few months serving as a temporary member of the central team. Not only do you get someone else to help do the work, you also expand your relationships with the extended team and your team benefits from *their* expertise.

In Chapter 16, "What's Next?" we show you a list of Web sites, conferences, and other stuff that will keep your team busy for a long time. There is no shortage of information about search marketing, so you need to use your judgment about the best use of your time.

As with any team, constantly developing skills has many other benefits. Team members who learn new skills are more likely to remain in their jobs, and you benefit from employees who are better trained for those jobs. In addition, extended team members rotating back from central team assignments become your best allies among the troops. As important as it is to hire well, it is also important to develop the team you hire.

Establish Search Marketing Best Practices

After you staff and train your central search team, you need to put them to work assisting your extended search team. The central team must constantly evangelize, educate, and consult with the extended team, helping them implement each search technique. But that's not enough. The central team must work with the extended team to embed search best practices into the existing standards and processes of your organization.

Why is this important? Because search engine marketing is not a one-time thing. This is not the Year 2000 project, in which everyone gears up to do something once and then goes back to normal when it is over. Search marketing must be worked at every day. You must convince dozens, hundreds, perhaps thousands of people to undertake new tasks, sometimes changing the way they have done their job for years. Those kinds of behavior changes do not come about because you gave them a presentation once. They come about because every process in the organization is gently (and sometimes not so gently) nudging them to do what is needed.

The most important guideline is to go with the flow. Look at how work already flows in your organization and try to add tasks where they belong. Here are some examples:

- Every Web page being changed goes through a quality-assurance (QA) checkpoint before being promoted to production. Maybe you can get the QA team to enforce your new search standard at this checkpoint for each page?

- All technology projects have their designs reviewed by an architecture board before beginning development. Could you assign one of your team members to the board to ensure that designs are search-friendly?

- A content standard already exists that requires a title tag be present on every Web page. Can you get the standard updated so that all titles must be a certain length? And that they are unique, rather than the same title appearing on multiple pages? And that description tags must be present too?

- All new Web projects are starting to use a content management system. Can you update the publishing workflow so that all pages undergo both HTML validation and keyword analysis (for prominence and density) before they are promoted to production?

- Your site regularly executes a program that checks every page for broken links and reports the pages with errors to their owners to be corrected. Could you get the program expanded to check for proper title tags as well?

You get the idea. Take whatever processes already exist in your organization and tweak them to include what you need. It is much easier to change an existing process than to get agreement to start a new one—a new one can often arouse the corporate immune system (the one that rejects foreign ideas). Although your organization will undoubtedly have unique processes that you must think through, you should consider two key best practices: changing your standards and centralizing keyword management. Let's look at standards first.

Change the Standards and Enforce Them

Embedding search marketing best practices into existing standards and processes helps the extended team in several ways. First, it ensures that search marketing techniques get their attention, if only because their project is stopped to correct a problem. Second, it also helps extended team members justify the extra work to their managers. If there are no teeth in the standards, managers under the gun to cut budgets or meet impossible deadlines will cut the search work, even if the extended team members want to do it. By making search work part of what is required, it cannot be eliminated even when the pressure is on (which it always seems to be).

Now understand, merely enhancing existing standards and processes might not be enough—you might need to create new standards and develop new procedures to enforce compliance—but existing standards are the place to start. It is always easier to change an existing standard than to create a new one, and existing standards already have a compliance process in place. When you create a new law, you might be stuck hiring a new police force, too. It is difficult and expensive and should be a last resort.

We have covered all of these issues in other parts of the book, but here is a consolidated list of items that make sense for almost every organization to cover in their standards:

- *Content standards.* Ban frames, pop-up windows, "meta refresh" tags, JavaScript navigation, and the various other evils we preached against in Chapter 10, "Get Your Site Indexed." Demand correct robots metatags as well as validation of all HTML. Consign style sheets and JavaScript coding to external files, and do not allow pages to exceed 100K. Relegate Flash and other non-HTML formats to content that you do not need included in search indexes. Don't require typed entry of information in order to display any page that you want indexed. Also remember the lessons of Chapter 12, "Optimize Your Content," by insisting on unique and well-written title and description tags and keyword-rich content.

- *Technical standards.* Require robots.txt files to be coded correctly and checked frequently. Insist on 301 redirects when pages are moved to new URLs. Minimize the number of parameters in dynamic URLs. Don't require cookies, JavaScript, or any other technical requirement that spiders cannot fulfill to display a page. Order all servers to be available 99.5 percent of the time or more, and demand that all Web pages load within 10 seconds.

Use existing standards where possible to capitalize on existing compliance processes, but invent your own if needed. One place where you will undoubtedly need to invent your own process is our next topic: keyword management.

Centralize Keyword Management

After you have some experience with search marketing, you will find that some keywords that are very important to you are also very important to others. You will probably find there are a few keywords that are *highly* competitive—maybe you have someone constantly bidding you up in paid placement, for example. That's not an easy situation, but it's intolerable when that other person is inside your own company.

Yes, large companies often find the right hand bidding against the left hand. Maybe Buick is bidding against Cadillac within General Motors for the keyword *luxury sedan*. Or Tide is fighting with Cheer and Gain at Proctor & Gamble over *laundry detergent*. At other times, your company is struggling over customer sets—would a large consulting company have multiple groups battling over *small business marketing*? Sometimes the contested keywords are more subtle. How many departments fight over *Linux* or *Windows*? Different groups have servers that run Linux or software the runs on Linux or services to help you migrate to Linux—you get the picture. But it is not a pretty picture. It is upsetting enough when your competitors drain your paid search budgets with "crazy" bidding, but how galling is it when it is your own company?

That is why you need to consider centralizing all keyword planning. You recall from our discussion in Chapter 8 that *centralize* is a relative term, depending on your organization. When you decided the scope for your central search team, you wrestled with this question—the decision you made then will work now, too. Within that scope, centralizing all keyword planning is usually a good idea.

When you centralize keyword planning, you immediately get rid of runaway paid placement bidding against yourself. You also give yourself a chance to optimize organic search—if you have separate domains within your company (www.buick.com and www.cadillac.com), you might be able to get two listings for *each* of them in the top ten organic listings. (That's 40 percent of the organic results on the first page.) Although you might find some benefits in centralization for organic search keywords, you will accrue the bulk of your benefits by eliminating intramural bidding wars in paid search.

So how do you go about centralizing keyword planning? If you do not yet have any battles over keywords in your company, establish the practice before any damage is done. If the battles have already started, however, how do you wrest control? You start with evangelism—tell everyone about the problem. Long and loud. Calculate what it is costing the company in wasted paid placement fees. Use your metrics to show how much those wasted fees could have returned had they been invested well. Then offer to save that money by handling the coordination across the business units within your central search team. If the coordination work is extensive, you might need to take a cut of the savings to pay for additional resources for your team.

When you wrest control of the mission, you need to organize your approach to coordinate the job. Depending on how much coordination is required, one of these ways will make the most sense in your situation:

- *Manual*. This is the simplest method and the easiest way to start. Simply appoint someone on the central search team as the focal point for all business units to work with on all keyword planning. Some organizations require that this person get the passwords for all exiting paid search accounts so that all paid search activity goes through one place.

- *Automated*. If you have a large paid search budget, the manual labor of coordinating all that activity might cost too much. In that case, create a central database for all paid search requests. Anyone who has the budget to run a paid search campaign can submit a list of keywords to your central keyword tool. It does not matter whether your tool is a Web program, a database application, or any other shared resource—whatever is easiest for you to implement. What *does* matter is how the tool works. It should check the list of keywords submitted against all existing keywords to find any conflicts. If no on else in your company is using your keywords, you proceed with your campaign. If there is a conflict, the tool can resolve the conflict, as we describe later in this chapter.

- *Hybrid.* Perhaps you do not have enough money to fully automate the process. Then just automate the most painful part of the process. Maybe you can post the keyword list that is currently in use so that anyone proposing a new campaign can check the list before the campaign starts. Frequently, you can develop an automated process one piece at a time.

Now that you know how to identify a conflict, what exactly do you do when you find one? Your organization probably already has a style it uses for conflict resolution, so take advantage of the existing culture. If disputes between organizations are typically resolved by a high-level executive, you can bring the list of disputed keywords there each week for a decision. If your culture calls for the two parties to work out the dispute themselves, provide the contact information so they can talk to each other. If your company likes to have impartial boards of experts, go that route. Sometimes you can make the criteria for resolution objective:

- The group that had it first gets it.
- Each group rotates week to week.
- Both groups should use the "friendly URL" technique (discussed in Chapter 14, "Optimize Your Paid Search Program") to avoid bidding each other up. (This solution works only for high bidder auctions, unfortunately.)
- The group with the most profitable product gets it.

You can probably think of other ideas, too. But most organizations find that the best way to solve this problem is to develop a new landing page that features the offerings of both warring groups. If you think about it, the reason that each group wants the same keyword is that their customers would likely use it to find either group's product. If that is true, why not let the customer decide?

Think back to the Linux example. If five different groups within your company all have something to say to customers searching for "linux," why not put the messages of all five on a single landing page? Each group can have to a link to their old search landing page from the new landing page. So if your company sells five kinds of software that all run on Linux, show them all on a single landing page.

This approach helps in several ways. Obviously, it ends the bidding war and provides a seemingly fair solution to the five parties involved. (Yes, they will each argue about which group gets more prominent placement on the new landing page, but you can develop several versions of the page that rotate, if necessary.) But it also makes your company's message far stronger than before. Many more searchers will find your ad copy and your page to be compelling and some might actually be interested in *more* than one of your offerings, whereas in the past they would only have seen one.

No matter how you resolve the conflicts, make sure that your advertising agency or search marketing consultant (if you have one) is aware that your central search team arbitrates all conflicts. You can also work directly with the paid placement engines themselves, so that they know what your policy is. If you are a large enough customer account, the engines will be happy to let you know when they see internal bidding wars and will counsel the combatants to contact you for resolution. If necessary, you can go so far as to require that any new campaign must have your approval before the engines can place any ads.

Intel provides an excellent case study for how well central keyword planning can work. In 2002, 19 percent of all keywords were being bid by more than one Intel search marketer, sometimes by as many as nine at once! You can imagine that this was costing Intel a lot of money as well as making it harder for searchers to find the breadth of Intel's offerings. Intel's Martin Laetsch spent the next year centralizing all keyword planning, resulting in a doubling of click-through rates with a 50 percent reduction in per-click fees. Your company might be able to produce a similar success story with centralized keyword planning.

Track Search Marketing Success

Nothing is more important to search marketing success than tracking your progress. If you regularly track your key measurements, they will prompt you to do everything else required to succeed at search marketing. Your measurements help you identify problems when they occur, causing you to take corrective action. But metrics have other value, too.

Strategic use of disappointing metrics can motivate your extended search team to do what you want them to, and motivate your executives to approve more campaigns to correct the problems. Sharing successful metrics can prove the value of search marketing to accomplish the same purposes. So, whether the measurements are good news or bad news, you can use them to make your overall point—that we need to improve our search marketing.

Whether your new central search team tracks all your metrics for you or you can talk your existing Web metrics team into doing them, the tasks to perform are the same:

- *Assess your site's content.* Every page within the scope of your search marketing program must be checked regularly for compliance with your content standards and for inclusion in search indexes. Organic search landing pages for each keyword in your campaigns must be checked even more closely.

- *Check your search rankings.* Each keyword in your search marketing campaigns must have its ranking within your targeted search engines verified on a regular basis to see whether it is improving or degrading.

- *Monitor search referrals.* The number of visitors coming to your site from search engines must be routinely checked. All campaigns require even greater focus on search traffic referrals for their targeted keywords.

- *Calculate Web conversions.* Ongoing reporting of successful Web conversions from search referrals proves the value of search marketing and sometimes identifies problems on your Web site outside of search marketing.

- *Review your measurements with others.* None of these metrics are useful in and of themselves. Before we close this chapter, we explain how to use these statistics and how to drive the organizational behavior you want.

Search metrics help you to identify and diagnose problems as well as to prove success. We begin by putting your content under the microscope.

Assess Your Site's Content

For organic search, your site's content spells the difference between success and failure, as you learned in Chapter 12. Even though you have done the hard work of optimizing your Web pages, you must check your content frequently to ensure it does not deteriorate.

For paid search, you have a lot less to do. You are advised to check your paid search landing pages to make sure that their URLs have not changed. For both paid and organic search, your landing page copy affect conversion rates, but no easy way exists to check *that*.

Measuring the search friendliness of your content helps you identify problems and correct them—problems in content tagging, keyword prominence and density, links to or from your pages, and inclusion in the search indexes. You can decide that it is too much work, and that you would like to just react to problems as they occur. We advise against that approach—you will never maximize your conversions by just fixing what is wrong. Regular content monitoring will avoid problems and will improve content that is already successful. If you are ready to take a proactive approach, let's tackle the metrics for content tagging.

Content Tagging Measurements

Content tagging metrics report a wide variety of problems in the coding of your HTML pages. Here are some content standards that a content reporting tool can police, when run on a regular basis:

- *Malformed HTML.* Your pages might contain errors in HTML coding that affect the spiders' capability to interpret the page properly.

- *Poor titles and descriptions.* Some of your pages might be missing <title> and <meta name="description"> tags, or they might contain problematic content. Each page should have a unique title and a unique description—one that does not appear on any other page.

- *Incorrect redirects.* Your pages might use "meta refresh" redirects that are not followed by search spiders. Your URLs might also be redirected through multiple "hops" to get to the final page destination, which spiders will not always follow.

- *Bloated pages.* Your pages might be excessively lengthy (possibly because they contain JavaScript or style sheets embedded on the page).

A **content reporter** can detect all of these problems and more. At least monthly, you should evaluate each page on your site that falls within your search marketing program's scope, checking each page for compliance with your content standards. Your content reporter should analyze each page automatically and generate two reports:

- An **error log** that lists each page individually by URL, showing what problems were found

- A **content scorecard** that aggregates the statistics by business area

In Snap's case, each business area sells a separate product line, but in your case business areas could be divisions, countries, or something else—your business areas should correspond to your organization's structure. Snap kept its scorecard simple, as shown in Table 15-1, with just five items to check. Later in this chapter, we explain what you do with these statistics.

Table 15-1   Snap Electronics Content Scorecard (For each content standard, Snap's score-card shows the percentage of all pages that comply.)

Business Area	Have Titles	Have Unique Titles	Have Unique Descriptions	Avoid Illegal Redirects	Avoid Exceeding 100K
Digital cameras	81%	73%	26%	100%	97%
Home theater	100%	97%	74%	85%	100%
Televisions	56%	31%	11%	100%	100%

Depending on your budget and your team's ability to do some programming, you can either purchase a content reporter or build one yourself. If you can afford the cost, Watchfire (www.watchfire.com) offers a specialized spider that crawls even the largest site and can find all sorts of searchability problems, even enabling you to customize the rules it uses for checking. It can roll everything up into a set of scorecards that you can use throughout your organization. For those on a budget, WebCEO (www.webceo.com) crawls your site and reports on your content for less than $300.

BUILD YOUR OWN CONTENT REPORTER

If you want a content reporter that is totally customized to your own standards and environment, and you have access to programmers, you can build your own. You need three main components: a collector, an analyzer, and a reporter.

The **collector** is the component that assembles all of your HTML pages to be analyzed. If all of your content is stored in content management systems, the collector could be a small addition to your content management system that "pushes" its content into your analyzer every time a page is changed. If you cannot use that simple approach, the best way to collect your content is the same way search engines do, using your own spider. If you have a site search engine, you might already have a spider roaming your site. If not, you might look into a specialized spider, such as Xenu (http://home.snafu.de/tilman/xenulink.html). You will need to work with the spider's developer to feed the content to your analyzer—some have interfaces to do that, and some do not. If you need a spider, don't build it yourself—it is the most complicated technology in this system, and it will be smarter to acquire than to build.

The **analyzer** is the brains of the system. It parses HTML and checks it for compliance to your standards. If you just want to check simple things, such as the existence of title tags, or whether links are broken, you can easily develop a program to do that. If you want to thoroughly analyze your HTML for coding errors and compliance with a long list of standards, you might want to use a code analyzer, such as WebKing (www.parasoft.com/jsp/products/home.jsp?product=WebKing), which enables you to customize your rules.

Your **reporter** can take the output of your code analyzer and aggregate the findings into reports for all of the pages, for a product, a product line, a division, a country, or your whole organization. Database software or a report generator, such as Crystal Reports, can be used for this purpose.

Building a content reporter is not the right solution for everyone, but it can be done if you cannot afford the pricey turnkey solutions.

Keyword Prominence and Density Measurements

In Chapter 11, "Choose Your Target Keywords," you decided which pages would serve as organic search landing pages for each keyword in your campaign. You need to regularly inspect those pages even more carefully than the rest of the pages in the scope of your search marketing program. You worked hard on those pages when you started each campaign. Don't let them fall into disrepair.

You recall that a critical part of optimizing each landing page is improving keyword prominence and density—making sure that the keywords that page is designed to attract are present in titles and other prominent places, and sprinkled throughout the page. Your keywords should be found early and often.

It is worthwhile to regularly spot-check your search landing pages, using an auditing program as we did in Chapter 11. If you have only a few campaigns totaling several dozen landing pages, you should scrutinize every page once a month. If you have hundreds or thousands of landing pages—too many to check each one monthly—you might need to sample some of them each month. Regardless, regular checks of your landing pages will provide early warning for problems—you will be alerted before you see marked drop-offs in rankings or search referrals. Obviously, if you *do* see a drop-off in organic search rankings or referrals for a particular landing page, you need to look at that page immediately. And you *will* see fluctuations in rankings, possibly because your competitors have improved their pages or their offerings. You might see changes because the search engines change their ranking algorithms. Following an ongoing process of checking your organic search landing pages will allow you to maintain and improve your content.

Some auditing programs, such as WebCEO (www.webceo.com, less than $300) and Site Content Analyzer (www.sitecontentanalyzer.com, less than $100) can automatically crawl a set of pages on your site and generate reports, taking some of the drudgery away, but you will still need to stare down each report to see how you are doing.

Link Measurements

Links to and from your pages are critical to your search marketing efforts. The earlier you can detect problems with your links, the less impact they will have on your search marketing success.

Let's look briefly at links *within* your site. Each page on your site should be checked at least monthly for broken links. As you learned in Chapter 10, broken links stop the spider cold, just as they stop your visitors. Most content reporter tools, such as Watchfire, can detect broken links, but specialized broken link detectors such as Xenu can handle this, too. Broken links break the chain of pages that lead to conversion, for both organic and paid search, and must be diagnosed and repaired.

But for organic search marketing, you must also be concerned about broken links *to* your site. In Chapter 12, "Optimize Your Content," you learned about how important links to your pages are for organic search marketing. Whenever you change URLs on your site, you run the risk of breaking those all-important inbound links.

In Chapter 10, you learned how to redirect your old URL names to your new ones. You learned that the search engines transfer the value of inbound links to your new name when you do that correctly. But no one knows for how long search engines do that. Just as the post office eventually stops forwarding snail mail to a new address, eventually search engines must tire of treating links to your old URL as if they were to your new one.

For all of these reasons, you should regularly check your inbound links. When your URLs change, ensure that the proper redirects are in place, but also contact the important sources of inbound links and let them know they should change the URL in their link. (That contact is also a great opportunity to suggest better anchor text or an updated description in the link, if you want that.) Because you want to focus on the most important links first, you can prioritize them based on Google PageRank, using some of the tools profiled in Chapter 13. As an alternative, you can prioritize based on the referrals you get from each one, which your Web metrics facility can tell you. Whatever way you do it, you want each of those old links changed.

Even if you do not change your URLs, you still want to check inbound links to your organic search landing pages once per month—search experts often refer to these links as **back links**. If you are actively working on link-building campaigns, you should see progress every month. You also want to note any pages for which links are decreasing—they might be candidates for link-building campaigns. But you can track more than the sheer number of links to your site. You can analyze the links to your search landing pages compared to those to direct competitors for that same keyword.

You can decide to measure the efficiency of your link-building campaigns, too. For solicited links, how many requests actually result in links to your site? How can you improve the percentage? You might look at better targeting, improving your e-mail copy, or improving your site to see whether you can attract more links in your link-building campaigns.

Links are important for conversions and for organic search rankings, so check your link measurements each month to ward off problems.

Page Inclusion Measurements

No matter how well crafted your content is, it is useless to a search engine if your pages are not included in the organic search indexes. As you learned in Chapter 10, your pages can be missing from search indexes at any time and for any number of reasons. When you first began your search marketing program, you undoubtedly found a host of problems on your site, and you set to work correcting them. Regularly measuring your progress on getting your pages indexed is what we discuss here.

You probably recall the **inclusion ratio** metric that we introduced in Chapter 10, which shows the percentage of your Web site's pages that are included in search indexes. Two reasons stand out for why you should be checking your inclusion ratio at least weekly. The first is to track your progress at eliminating spider traps and enabling spider paths. A weekly check of your inclusion ratio can also reveal problems that have cropped up, however, before you have suffered long periods of harm to your search marketing program.

Springing the spider free from the traps that bedevil your Web site can sometimes take months. At times, you eliminate one spider trap just to find that there is another one in the same spot. By checking your inclusion ratio, you can track how correcting each trap (and opening each new path) allows the spider to include more and more pages in its index.

There is no need to exhaustively track inclusion in every search index. Many search marketers check just Yahoo! and Google, but you can check as many as you believe is necessary to monitor your search marketing program. (If you do not recall how to check the number of pages included in search indexes, Chapter 10 can jog your memory.)

In Chapter 10, we discussed how tough it is for some search marketers to estimate the number of pages on their sites. If this is an issue for your site, you can still easily monitor your inclusion ratio. All you need to do is choose a single, easy-to-calculate number that you can derive each week—the total number of documents in your three content management systems, for example. Although this total probably does not accurately estimate the number of Web pages on your site, it will correctly reveal trends and problems if you calculate it the same way each time.

Here's how it works. Each week, as you add up the documents across your three content management systems, the number of documents will fluctuate, as content is added or deleted. If a new product line is announced, for example, you might find 209 new documents across your 3 content management systems, although just 193 new pages were published to your site. If your site is crawled weekly, you should expect to see a couple of hundred new pages reflected in the search indexes the following week. If they are not, it makes sense to inspect that new site for spider traps or missing spider paths. Note that it is not important whether the number of documents truly correlates to the number of pages on the site for this method to work. As long as you measure consistently, you will spot problems and trends from week to week.

CASE STUDY: DETECTING AN INCLUSION CRISIS

Typically, IBM's Web site (www.ibm.com) has more than 4 million pages in Google's search index—until the day the weekly indexing check revealed just 5,000 pages. No one needed to run any fancy inclusion ratio calculation to know something had gone horribly wrong.

Because no major architectural or navigational changes had been made to the site, it was unlikely that all of the spider paths had been removed. Such a precipitous drop in indexed pages points to a new spider trap, so a specialized spider was unleashed to see what was wrong.

It did not take long to determine the problem. When the spider crawled ibm.com's home page, it stopped dead in its tracks, returning an error. A review of the page revealed that a new JavaScript had been added to the home page requiring anyone who wanted to enter the site to have JavaScript enabled. If you did not have it enabled, you were blocked from entering the site—you were shown an error message explaining that JavaScript was required.

The misguided Web developer who put this in place was trying to help visitors to ibm.com, because some pages on the site *did* require JavaScript (mostly pages in the ordering process of the e-Commerce site). But search spiders now could not index any page on the site past the home page, so only a few thousand pages were left in the index (only because they were linked directly from other sites).

Evidently the script had been live for about a month, and after numerous failed crawls, Google dropped most of the ibm.com pages from its index. (Yahoo! followed suit a few days later before the script was corrected.) After this script was removed from the pages, the spiders were again able to freely crawl the site, resulting in the return of the pages to the indexes.

Had IBM failed to conduct weekly inclusion checks, search referrals might have dried up for a week or more before anyone noticed the problem.

Check Your Search Rankings

After verifying your content is search-friendly and that it is stored in the major search indexes, now you are ready to check your search rankings. Just because your pages ranked well when you did the initial campaign work does not mean that those high rankings will last forever. Regular measurement of search rankings is a key operational function.

Every campaign in your search marketing program has a list of targeted keywords—the list you learned to choose in Chapter 11. To measure the success of each campaign, you need to check the search rankings for each keyword in that campaign at least once a month. (Most search marketers check their highest-priority terms weekly.)

As with inclusion, you do not need to check your rankings in every search engine around— just the ones that drive the bulk of your traffic. Most search marketers check Yahoo! and Google, while some check others, too. (Global marketers might need to check many local search engines in the countries they do business in.)

You know by now that high search rankings are important, because the higher your ranking for a keyword, the more clickthroughs you are likely to get. A #1 result sometimes has a 70 percent clickthrough rate, whereas results that fall below #10 can draw clicks less than 1 percent of the time.

Measuring search rankings on a regular basis is also important, both to show success and to identify problems when they occur. Publicizing high rankings within your organization helps convince people that search marketing can work, and motivates marketers whose campaigns have not yet succeeded. People like hearing about search rankings, possibly because everyone can understand what it means to go from #19 to #8, and maybe because it is thrilling to pass your competitors. As your search campaigns are executed, you should see steady improvements in the keywords targeted for those campaigns.

Conversely, regular monitoring can uncover a sudden drop in rankings, enabling your team to take quick action to correct what is wrong before losing any more search referrals. Although you would eventually spot a ranking problem in your other metrics (as referrals and conversions drop), you can see the rankings drop sooner. That speed allows you to fix the problem more quickly so that your campaign gets back on track before costing you any more precious conversions than necessary.

The problem with checking your search rankings, however, is that it is time-consuming for you (and time-consuming for the search engines themselves, which we discuss in a minute). Search marketing campaigns, once started, do not stop. As long as you still have a need to attract visitors, the campaign continues. By the time you have cranked up several campaigns, you have developed a long list of keywords for which to track rankings.

Consider our fictitious company, Snap Electronics, which built on early success to have four search marketing campaigns running after just a few months. Each campaign averaged 25 keywords, totaling 100 keywords in all. Because Snap targeted Google, Yahoo!, MSN, AOL, and Ask.com, it required 500 manual queries (5 search engines multiplied by 100 queries) to check their search rankings. And, for each of these queries, someone had to manually check the results, sometimes paging forward to multiple search results screens, to find what the highest ranking was for a page from Snap's Web site. This took days to do each time.

Fortunately, Table 15-2 shows some of the leading tools available to automatically check search rankings. As you look over the table, do not be overly swayed by the difference between 200 and 400 search engines supported—all that is important to you is that the tool supports the search engines that you have targeted for your campaigns. Every tool supports English, but if you are a global marketer you should check that the tool you choose supports all the languages of your campaigns. As explained in detail later, Google expects rank checkers to use a special API to do so, which two of the tools support. One tool is free, whereas the others are low-priced, fitting into most search marketing budgets.

Table 15-2   Rank-Checking Tools (Many good tools are available to check your search rankings—here are some of the most popular.)

	Supported Search Engines	Supported Languages	Google API	Pricing
AgentWebRanking www.agentwebranking.com	346	European and Asiatic	Yes	Business edition $150 Professional edition $500
Digital Point Rank Checking Tool www.digitalpoint.com/tools/keywords	Google, MSN Search, and Yahoo!	European, Asiatic, and Arabic	Yes	Free
Ranking Manager www.websitemanagementtools.com	476	European and Asiatic	Yes	Standard version $180 Professional version $250
Trellian SEO Toolkit www.trellian.com/seotoolkit	250	European, plus Arabic and Japanese	Yes	$300
WebPosition 4 www.webposition.com	216	European and Asiatic	Yes	Standard edition $149 Professional edition $389

You should know that automatic rank checking is considered a necessary evil by search engines, because it consumes precious server resources for queries run by software programs—not by people who might click through on an ad to make the search engines some money. So, not only don't the search engines make money from rank checking, it *costs* them money to host the extra servers to run all of those extra queries. Google has been the most outspoken about this issue and has actually banned Web sites that check many of their keyword rankings frequently—daily or even multiple times a day.

Google does understand that you and other search marketers need to check your rankings, but you are expected to use a rank-checking program that supports the Google application program interface, or Google API. (Table 15-2 above shows which programs do so, but you can also write your own program.) The API limits your rank-checking activity to 1,000 queries each day, which is sufficient for most search marketers.

One twist on search rank checking is competitor rankings. Sometimes you can motivate the extended search team to take the actions you need by showing where competitors rank, so it can be a useful metric to track regularly. There is no need to check competitor rankings on all of your keywords—most of your high-priority keywords do not apply to your competitors because they contain your brand name. When Snap Electronics decided to look at competitor rankings, only *digital cameras* and *easy digital camera* were selected, because those keywords were critical to Snap's branding goals. Snap decided that tracking competitor metrics for the other keywords was not worth the effort. If you decide to track competitor rankings, restrict the keywords you select to your critical branding or conversion battles.

Whether or not you track competitors' rankings, you should create a rankings scorecard for every keyword (or at least the high-priority ones). Your search rankings scorecard might average the rankings for each keyword across all of your targeted search engines. So Snap Electronics would average its rankings for *digital cameras* across all five targeted search engines, as shown in Table 15-3. Whenever a Snap page was not found in the top 100 results for a particular keyword, it was assigned a rank of 100.

Table 15-3 Snap Search Keyword Ranking Scorecard (Some queries return your pages at the same rank in different search engines, but others do not.)

Keyword Phrase	AOL Search	Ask	Google	MSN Search	Yahoo!	Score
digital camera	19	56	19	62	62	44
snap digital camera	2	1	2	2	2	2
snapshot digital camera	2	1	2	1	1	1
digital camera review	100	39	100	26	26	58
best digital camera	43	17	43	13	13	26
digital camera comparison	100	100	100	100	100	100
compare digital camera	100	84	100	71	71	85
Campaign average	52	60	52	39	39	48

If you would like to be more scientific about it, you could use a weighted average that gives Yahoo! and Google more emphasis based on their share of searches, but you might prefer to use a simple formula that is easier to calculate. You can check out the rankings for each keyword, for each campaign, even for your overall search marketing program, tracking your progress over time. Later in this chapter, we show you another use for this scorecard.

Another example of a search ranking scorecard is shown in Table 15-4, where we can track the positions of specific search landing pages. (For space reasons, we have eliminated the leading www.snapelectronics.com from the URLs in the table.) As you have already learned, driving visitors to key pages with specific messaging and navigation helps increase conversions. The landing page scorecard is a good way to motivate content owners and business unit managers to make the necessary changes to the site for increased organic search success.

Table 15-4   Snap Search Landing Page Ranking Scorecard (Content owners seem especially motivated by a scorecard that calls out their own pages.)

Landing Page URL	AOL	ASK	GG	MSN	YH	Score
/stores/Cat?cat=6&lang=1&cntry=840	19	56	19	62	62	44
/stores/Cat?cat=6&Prd=559&lang=1&cntry=840	2	1	2	2	2	2
/stores/Cat?cat=2&&lang=1&cntry=840	2	1	2	1	1	1
/cameras/digital_camera_reviews.html	100	39	100	26	26	58
/stores/Prd?prd=9&lang=1&cntry=840	43	17	43	13	13	26
/cameras/digital_camera_comparisons.html	100	100	100	100	100	100
/cameras/news/index.html	100	84	100	71	71	85

Search rankings are an important measurement because high rankings lead to more traffic to your site, in the form of search referrals. Next we measure those referrals directly.

Monitor Search Referrals

Search rankings are important, but high rankings are useless unless they lead to higher **search referrals**, a metric introduced in Chapter 7, "Measure Your Search Marketing Success." As you recall, search referrals are the visitors who come to your site from a search engine. We count overall search referrals—the number of visitors who come from search to any page within your search marketing program's scope—but we also slice and dice referrals to learn more. We examine the significance of referrals from each search engine, and you will learn to zoom in on your individual search campaigns to check referrals by keyword. And (say it with me now), we do it *regularly*. Checking referrals as a campaign first unfolds is exciting, but you need to continue to check them long after your enthusiasm has waned.

Overall Search Referral Measurements

The first way we track search referrals is across the scope of your entire search marketing program, from both organic and paid search.

Almost any Web metrics facility can report on search referrals, but you might need to customize your reports so that they fit your search marketing program. For example, Snap Electronics chose just its U.S. Web site as the scope for its search marketing program, so it wanted to look at just the search referrals to its U.S. site, ignoring those to the other country Web sites at snapelectronics.com—those referrals will become important when Snap increases the scope of its program. Snap customized the referral reporting by its Web metrics facility to examine its U.S. site only. Table 15-5 shows Snap's results for the first three months of its search marketing program.

Table 15-5   Snap's Search Marketing Program Search Referrals (Snap tracks all search refer-rals across the scope of its search marketing program, its U.S. site.)

	Baseline	May	June	July	Total
U.S. search referrals	12,112	19,457	71,890	90,030	248,650
Divided by U.S. referrals	326,543	317,986	289,786	327,045	1,261,360
Search share of referrals	3.71%	6.12%	24.81%	27.53%	19.71%
Search referral increase		61%	494%	643%	

As the table shows, search referrals increased markedly over the period, as the digital cameras campaign (and later others) made a dramatic difference. You will notice that search referrals did increase each month, but that a decrease in referrals for the entire site hid the extent of the improvement. That is why we also calculate the search share, the percentage of search referrals compared to the total referrals. This measure reveals that search marketing was still improving even during a downturn in overall traffic to the site.

If your site has seasonal ups and downs, you probably already have ways of interpreting your statistics to compensate. Some organizations use rolling averages, others use "year-over-year" comparisons, whereas your company might do something else entirely. Whatever method you use to smooth out seasonality should work just as well for search referrals as it does for everything else.

Search Referral Measurements by Search Engine

Although most organic search marketing work is not directed at any particular search engine, sometimes your efforts work better in one engine than in another. Segmenting search referrals by search engine can show you how your success differs in each engine. Moreover, for paid placement, your efforts are highly targeted to specific paid search vendors working with specific engines, so analyzing each engine separately is required.

Examining referrals by search engine will help you track progress as your campaigns take shape, but it will also aid in identifying problem areas that might affect one search engine more than the others, or one search engine *before* the others. A sudden drop in traffic from a single search engine might by caused by a decrease in rankings or fewer pages included in the index.

As before, most Web metrics facilities can separate referrals by search engine, but they might need some tweaking on your part to accurately categorize certain referrals as being from the correct search engine. For example, Google contextual search referrals are usually shown as coming from googlesyndication.com no matter what site they were actually from. Know that sometimes you will get clicks with no referrer at all—just remember that counting most of the traffic is better than nothing. Table 15-6 shows how Snap Electronics measured search referrals by each of the five search engines targeted by its search marketing program.

Table 15-6   Snap's Referrals by Search Engine (Snap tracks all search referrals across the scope of its search marketing program, its U.S. site.)

	Baseline	May	June	July	Total
Organic Referrals					
AOL	1,170	1,564	1,602	1,734	8,129
Ask.com	146	124	187	167	1,008
Google	5,623	7,647	10,556	15,840	59,369
MSN Search	2,365	2,126	3,542	3,970	16,097
Yahoo!	1,972	6,853	6,986	11,786	44,529
Other organic traffic	836	689	1,508	1,041	4,181
U.S. Organic Search Referrals	**12,112**	**19,003**	**24,381**	**34,538**	**133,313**
Paid Referrals Google AdWords	—	—	18,668	33,967	52,635
Yahoo! Overture	—	2,617	28,587	20,227	51,431
Shopzilla Shopping Search	—	65	254	1,298	1,617
U.S. Paid Search Referrals	**—**	**2,682**	**47,509**	**55,492**	**105,683**
Total U.S. search referrals	12,112	19,457	71,890	90,030	238,996
Total site visits	326,543	317,986	289,786	327,045	1,261,360
Search share of referrals	3.71%	6.12%	24.81%	27.53%	18.95%
Search Referral Increase		**61%**	**494%**	**643%**	

Beyond your need to track referrals to make decisions about your campaigns, you also need to track paid referrals to audit your per-click fees. But don't expect your referral reports to match the bills from paid search vendors, for several reasons:

- *Counting methods vary.* It is amazing how many different methods exist for counting referrals. The chances that your counts will match your vendor's counts are minuscule.

- *Time zones might differ.* If your Web servers are in different time zones from the vendors' servers, you will see different counts each day because the hours will put some clicks into different days on your report compared to the vendors' ledger.

- *Vendors remove fraudulent clicks.* When a search engine suspects a click is fraudulent, it will be removed from your bill, but that click will still be counted by your metrics system as a referral.

- *Vendors eliminate repeat clicks.* Sometime visitors inadvertently click your ad multiple times, especially when network speeds or other factors slow performance, but vendors delete fees for those clicks from your report.

Given all of these discrepancies, you might wonder why you should bother auditing your bills at all, but it is important. You should expect your referral reports to show as much as 10 percent variance from vendor ledgers. However, you should look for trends. If counts have varied by 3 percent to 4 percent for months, but this week they are 7 percent off, you should investigate.

Search Referral Measurements by Keyword

High search rankings typically create high search referrals, but occasionally a top search result does *not* garner heavy clickthrough by searchers. You will detect those situations by carefully tracking your search referrals by keyword for every search marketing campaign. Each month, you can calculate your referrals for each keyword, both for organic and paid search. Table 15-7 shows a sample report from Snap Electronics for July.

Table 15-7 Snap's Referrals by Keyword for July (For its digital camera campaign, Snap tracked the detailed data for each keyword for both organic and paid search.)

| Keyword Phrase | Baseline | Organic Search | | | | | Paid Search | | | |
		Referrals	GG	Rank YH	MS	Impressions	Clicks	Click Rate	Added Visits
digital camera	1,412	7,356	15	22	28	2,886,532	48,336	1.67%	50,636
snapshot digital camera	4,044	6,027	1	2	2	11,821	421	3.56%	1,404
snap digital camera	5,278	7,290	1	1	2	12,936	362	2.8%	2,374
digital camera reviews	—	394	20	31	31	160,227	5,464	3.41%	5,858
compare digital cameras	—	88	22	45	68	22,888	92	0.4%	180
best digital cameras	—	590	4	22	22	40,136	96	0.2%	686
digital camera comparison	—	152	16	18	6	26,539	451	1.7%	603
Totals	10,734	21,796	11	20	23	3,161,079	55,222	1.7%	61,740

As the months go by, you can examine the referral trends to see how your keyword referrals are trending. Snap Electronics used the simple form shown in Table 15-8 to track its monthly search referrals.

Table 15-8   Snap's Search Referrals by Keyword (For its digital camera campaign, Snap tracked the referrals for each keyword targeted in that campaign.)

Keyword Phrase	Baseline	May	June	July	Total
digital camera	1,412	5,231	32,687	55,692	95,022
snapshot digital camera	4,044	5,799	4,931	6,448	21,222
snap digital camera	5,278	6,325	6,874	7,652	26,129
digital camera reviews	—	163	3,652	5,858	9,673
compare digital cameras	—	66	210	180	456
best digital cameras	—	219	690	686	1,595
digital camera comparison	—	145	466	603	1,214
Totals	10,734	17,948	49,510	77,118	155,310

Tracking referrals is important, but you must keep your focus on the real prize: conversions.

Calculate Web Conversions from Search

None of the measurements we have discussed will make more of a splash than counting conversions. We have emphasized all along that search marketing is only useful insofar as it furthers your Web site's basic goals—coaxing more searchers to visit and more visitors to **convert**. You have chosen what events on your Web site constitute conversions. Regardless of what they are, the value of search engine marketing is to produce more visitor conversions. Now you need to count them, and count them regularly. Strong early results count for a lot less if they are allowed to atrophy from inattention.

Why would your conversions change over time? Because everything that causes conversions changes over time:

- *The competitive mix.* The other players jockeying for position for each keyword change over time. Perhaps a new company introduces a hot product, and its product page is crawled by the organic search engine. Or maybe an existing competitor cuts back its paid search budget and disappears from view. (In paid placement, especially, competitors can appear and vanish quite rapidly.) Whenever a player enters or exits the organic or paid competition for a keyword, it affects the rankings of every other player. Each time your rankings change, it affects your clickthrough rate (and can thereby raise or lower your conversions).

- *Paid placement bids.* Your bids and your competitors' bids can change multiple times each day, which changes your rankings, which (ankle bone connected to the shin bone) changes your conversions.

- *Ad and page copy.* Page copy directly affects rankings in organic search, and both page copy and paid placement ad copy affect conversion rates. Whenever you or your competitors change your ad or page copy, everyone's conversions can be affected. For example, if your competitor provides a more compelling offer, your click rate (and therefore your conversions) might go down. If you improve the wording on your landing page copy, your conversions might go up.

You might be wondering exactly what an acceptable conversion rate would be. You might be tempted to research averages for your industry, but that is the right answer for you only if you are an *average* business in your industry—average in every way. You know that across your product line, you have wide swings in conversion rates that are all rolled up into one homogenous average across your business. Some products convert at 4 percent and others are under 1 percent, perhaps. So what does it tell you that your average conversion rate is 2 percent? Not much.

Similarly, getting an average conversion rate across your whole industry is even less helpful. The only way to assess your success is to compare your present against your past. You should see that you are improving over time—not across the board perhaps, but overall. You should see that the conversions for each product tend to go up over time.

Now that you are convinced that you need to track conversions, we have bad news. Your Web metrics facilities might or might not enable you to accurately track the behavior of visitors who began their visits through a search referral. You should consult your local metrics expert to see how your system works, because there might be ways to get your existing measurement system to track conversions for you. Here are the kinds of devices that are most frequently used to track search conversions:

- *URL tracking parameters*. Metrics systems can usually record parameters passed in your landing page URL identifying a visitor who is on a certain path through your site—a search referral path, in this case. The URL itself can be changed, such as adding refer=Yahoo&ad=67 to the end of your existing URL, to tell you which ad in Yahoo! generated the referral. The metrics system might be able to tell you how many visitors who complete your conversion event followed this path.

- *Programmed tracking parameters*. Some metrics systems can handle tracking parameters passed programmatically. One tracking method requires you to add JavaScript code to each page in your conversion path—each page passes the tracking codes along in a daisy chain—but if your visitor goes to an unmarked page, you lose the tracking for that sale. Alternatively, as discussed in Chapter 6, "Measure Your Web Site's Success," you can use a tiny picture (called a single-pixel image) to track your visitors. However, if the picture is displayed from your vendor's server, your security folks might not allow you to use it.

- *Affiliate codes*. If your company maintains an affiliate marketing program, it already has an elaborate system for tracking referrals so that the affiliates get paid the proper commission. You might be able to get affiliate codes assigned for each search engine (or even each keyword for each search engine) and let the affiliate tracking system do the rest.

- *Cookies*. You can use some JavaScript for a few strategically placed pages to measure your search conversions. Here's how it works. On each search landing page, call an external JavaScript that checks the referrer URL (the page the visitor was on before reaching the landing page). When that page is from a search engine, it means that your visitor clicked a search result to navigate to your landing page. Your script can drop a cookie containing the name of the search engine and the keyword used. You then call a similar script on your conversion page to read the cookie. Whatever system you use to log the conversion can also note that this visitor was referred from a search engine (and log the keyword used). Later, when you add up the conversions, you will be able to count search referrals that converted separately from all other conversions, and you will know the keywords used each time. Note that some paid search engines will happily offer to drop the cookie for you, but that can cause security problems that most IT groups will not allow.

- *Microsites.* If all else fails, you can set up a completely separate site just for your search referrals. It is a lot of work, but if it is the only way to track your search conversions, it might be worth it for you. It is very easy to set up a microsite for paid search, but some do it for organic search as well, especially when their main site is full of spider traps. Figure 15-1 shows the microsite for Garelick Farm's new brand of low-fat milk (www.overthemoonmilk.com), developed by Dan Weingrod's Cronin and Company. Dan says, "It's often easier and cheaper to create a new domain than to correct all the infrastructure problems to get the metrics you need."

Figure 15-1   A microsite. If you cannot fix the reporting capabilities of your current Web site, a drastic approach starts a new Web site just for your campaign.

If you can use one of these methods to calculate your Web conversions of searchers, you can show how many referrals you are getting, the number of conversions (and the conversion rate), and the value in business terms of those conversions, just the way we did in Chapter 7. And you can track search conversions at any level of detail: a keyword, a group of keywords, an entire search marketing campaign, or even your overall search marketing program. (With paid placement, you can set up your categories or ad groups to simplify reporting.) So, if you can track that last month your site received 1,000 extra visitors from search for a particular campaign's keywords, and 2 percent (20) of them bought your $500 product, you generated $10,000 in extra revenue from that search marketing campaign. Table 15-9 shows the revenue scorecard for Snap Electronics.

Table 15-9 Calculating Snap's Incremental Revenue from Search (Incremental revenue can be tracked from your baseline to show the value of search marketing.)

	Baseline	May	June	July	Total
Search engine referrals	12,112	26,984	76,245	90,030	248,650
Conversions	101	413	1,510	2,044	4,067
Conversion rate	0.83%	1.53%	1.98%	2.27%	1.34%
Incremental revenue	$49,561	$203,538	$744,258	$1,00,753	$2,004,892
Cost of SEM	$0	$20,000	$37,500	$37,500	$95,000
Cost per search referral	$0	$.74	$.49	$.42	$.71
Cost per action	$0	$48.44	$24.84	$18.35	$23.36

When you can pinpoint the value that precisely, you can learn a lot. Suppose you find that 1 percent of visitors who come to the site by other means convert, whereas searchers convert at a 2 percent rate? That might justify a shift in marketing resources to search. If you find the search conversion rate lower, perhaps you need to examine whether there are ways of raising conversion, or whether there might be other keywords that convert at a higher rate. Remember that it is crucial that you analyze your conversion metrics at this detailed level to make good decisions. Looking at averages across your whole program is fine for a snapshot of progress but does not help you decide which organic search landing page to tweak or which paid placement keyword should be dropped.

Some companies, especially large companies, have complex infrastructure issues that make tracking search conversions difficult or impossible. If you find yourself in this position, it's not the end of the world. You can still estimate your business impact using the same method used in Chapter 7 to forecast our campaign's impact. Merely take the number of incremental visitors being referred from search for your campaign's keywords and multiply by your site's conversion rate. Using the example above, if we assume those same 1,000 extra visitors converted at a rate of 1 percent (the site-wide rate), we would estimate that 10 of them purchased the $500 product for $5,000 in incremental revenue from our campaign. It is not exact, but it is far better to estimate the value than to be silent about it.

If you can accurately tie Web conversions to the search referrals, you can track your conversions as granularly as your referrals. You can examine the revenue driven by each keyword in a campaign, as well as check conversion rates across your program for search referrals from individual search engines. This kind of analysis can help you gradually improve your campaigns, as you learn what works and what does not.

Review Your Measurements with Others

Well, we sure calculated a big pile of statistics in this chapter. Let's see what you can do with them.

As noted throughout, there are two main reasons to compile these statistics: to prove the value of search marketing and to identify problems that require action. When these metrics show your success, we suspect you will know what to do. Have a party, review the numbers with executives, and bring them up every time you want to do more. You will get the attention you need when things go well—congratulations.

But most people do not know what else they can do with these measurements—compel changes in behavior. That is what we talk about here. You can follow a simple a step-by-step process to change organizational behavior:

- *Change the rules.* Earlier in this chapter, we went over the standards you need to change in your organization. Your first step in changing behavior is to set up the rules in your favor and develop a policing system to enforce compliance as much as possible.

- *Set benchmarks.* Develop a set of statistical thresholds for acceptability that are attainable within a defined period of time. For example, if you start out knowing that only 70 percent of your pages even have titles on them, set a benchmark that 85 percent contain titles within one year. (For a small Web site, that would be very easy, but for a large Web site, that goal might be just right.) State that all business areas with 85 percent of their pages with titles are "green," whereas those with over 75 percent are "yellow," but all others are "red." Do this for every important statistic.

- *Review business area scorecards.* Every month, you calculate your scorecards for each business area—a content scorecard, a rankings scorecard, a referrals scorecard, and a conversion scorecard. Use just the scorecards you need to compel the behavior you want. If your site is loaded with content problems, start there. If you cannot get product managers to focus on search, start with rankings or referrals, perhaps. Show your scorecards to the executives responsible for the state of the metrics on the scorecards. (Table 15-10 gives a complete list of metrics and whom they should be reviewed with.) And post all scorecards throughout your organization. Avoid the temptation to save yourself some work by only reviewing scorecards when they are bad—it will be much harder to get the appointment to do that. Instead, review the scorecards *regularly*, good or bad.

- *Demand action plans to deliver improvement.* This will not be as hard as it sounds if you post your scorecards within your company. It is the rare executive who will sit still watching his area show up "red" month after month while other areas are "green" or at least "yellow." If you arrive each month to display the latest scorecard with helpful suggestions as to how to turn it around, eventually most executives will tire of the embarrassment and order their folks to "go along with the program"—your search marketing program, that is.

Table 15-10   Search Marketing Metrics (Tracking metrics on a regular basis proves your successes and pinpoints problems so they can be corrected.)

	Scope	Frequency	Audience	When Things Go Wrong
Content Metrics				
Content tagging	All pages	Monthly	Writers	Gain commitments to bring pages into compliance with standards.
Keyword prominence and density	Search landing pages	Monthly	Writers	Persuade to add keywords to the right places on each landing page.
Broken links	All pages	Monthly	Writers	Gain commitment to fix broken links.
Back links	Search landing pages	Monthly managers	Product	Persuade to solicit strong links to pages.
Inclusion in search indexes	All pages	Weekly	Writers and technologists	Diagnose root causes and gain commitment for corrective action.
Ranking Metrics				
Keyword rankings	All keywords targeted in any campaign	Monthly	Product managers	Diagnose root causes and gain commitment for corrective action.
Competitor rankings	Selected keywords	Monthly	Product managers	Diagnose root causes and gain commitment for corrective action.
Search Referrals				
Total search referrals	Site	Weekly	Product managers	Isolate the areas of the site that have dropped.
Search referrals by search engine	Top search engines	Weekly	Product managers	Isolate problems in specific search engines.
Search referrals by keyword phrase	Selected keywords	Monthly	Product managers	Determine why individual keywords are not performing.
Web Conversions				
Search conversions	All keywords and all campaigns	Monthly managers	Product	Diagnose root causes (usually changes to the site) and gain commitment for corrective action.
Conversion rate	All keywords and all campaigns	Monthly managers	Product	Diagnose root causes (usually changes to the site) and gain commitment for corrective action.

For some of these metrics, you need to see where you stand to decide what a good benchmark should be. If your site is riddled with "meta refresh" redirects on 15 percent of your pages, for example, you might choose a goal for 90 percent refresh-free pages earning a "yellow" score with 95 percent earning "green." On the other hand, if 95 percent of your pages are already clean, you might want to shoot for 97 percent and 99 percent.

For search rankings, you might decide that any keyword that averages a ranking below #30 should be scored "red," and that anything that drops out of the top ten is "yellow," because that is simple and everyone understands it. If you want to be more precise, you could have higher benchmarks for queries with your brand name in it (such as "snap digital camera") because it is so much easier to attain high rankings for those keywords.

For organizations that focus on organic search, benchmarking content and rankings might be enough. You can use those metrics to drive the actions you want to improve content tagging, keyword density, page inclusion, and any other behavior needed. If you have problems driving Web conversions on your site, or you have significant paid placement activity, you will want to focus on referrals and conversions, too. You can develop your own benchmarks for those metrics and assess each business area against them.

One study showed the average Web site gets about 13 percent of all referrals from search engines. So, for every 100 visits to your site, 13 percent of them are searchers clicking a search result; the rest are following links, using bookmarks, and directly entering the URL. Remember, 13 percent is the *average*. Well-known Web sites might have far more visitors that remember the URL or have bookmarked the site from a previous visit. Don't fall into the Lake Wobegon trap of needing all sites to be "above average"—take the baseline for your site and try to keep improving.

If you can track conversions, you have the best information of all. You can use conversion data to address pages that attract high search referrals but do not lead to high conversions. Perhaps those pages are at fault, or perhaps other pages between the search landing pages and the conversion page are the problem. Regardless, you know there is something wrong, and you can work on all of those pages and track improvement. Moreover, tracking conversions allows you to test which keywords convert at the highest rates. It is those keywords that should consume your organic optimization resources and command your highest paid placement bids. Management by conversions focuses your resources at the points of greatest returns.

This step-by-step approach using scorecards can prove quite successful when you stick to it, gaining attention for your search marketing program and forcing organizations to pay attention to the actions required. And year after year, it is the gift that keeps on giving, because every time your business areas reach the "green" benchmarks, you can raise them higher. Each year, your content gets a little cleaner and your rankings a little higher, because these metrics become part of everyone's job.

You can do even more with these metrics, however. In Chapter 9, we made a number of predictions to convince senior management and the bean counters that we would spend the money well. The metrics we have demonstrated should reveal whether your projections are coming true. Creating a simple matrix to share with key executives will keep them happy that they have invested wisely.

Summary

We have spent most of this book describing why search marketing is valuable to any Web site and helping you create a program to deliver that value. However, we don't want you to create a "where the rubber meets the sky" plan that looks good when projected on the conference room wall but has no basis in reality.

Your plan is worthless if it is not properly executed. In this chapter, you rounded out your search marketing education with the day-to-day best practices led by your central search team. You learned how to hire your central team, how to foster best practices in your organization, and how to track metrics on an ongoing basis to measure progress and identify trouble.

Above all, you discovered that search marketing is not a one-time event, but an iterative activity that must be improved every day. Armed with that knowledge, you are ready to bring search marketing success to your organization.

Perhaps by now you are asking yourself, "What's next?"—both for search marketing and for you personally. That's what Chapter 16 is all about.

What's Next?

It's been quite a ride. No matter where you started, you now have the knowledge you need to be a successful search marketer. But what's next?

That question has two answers—a personal one and an industry one. Let's start by looking at what's next for search marketing.

What's Next for Search Marketing?

Our crystal ball is as foggy as anyone else's, but we do see a number of trends that will play out over the next few years to change search marketing:

- *More content.* Every year, more and more information is made available on the Web, yet much information remains trapped offline or otherwise inaccessible to search engines. How will this change?

- *More technology.* Like any technology, search technology never stops improving. As software technology marches on, what are the implications for search marketers?

- *More personalized.* Every searcher who enters the same query gets the same results, right? That is something that will probably change in the future, as search results are tailored based on the person and current situation. What will that mean to you, the search marketer?

- *More competition.* The good news is that you are discovering search marketing, but the bad news is that everyone else is, too. How can you stay ahead of the increasing competition in search marketing?

Put on your long-distance glasses—let's examine the latest trends in search marketing, starting with what new content is expected to become available to search engines.

More Content

You know better than most people how much information is indexed by search engines today, but you also know that there is more information indexed every year. What are the burgeoning sources of content for search engines?

- *Multimedia content.* Although most search engines provide an image search capability today, many more content types will be added to search engines' indexes. As Web surfers upgrade to high-speed broadband connections to the Internet, many sites are providing audio and video information. As the Internet matures, there is no reason to believe that it will remain a bastion of textual information—sound and pictures make for a richer experience. Search engines will increase multimedia support. Today, specialty search engines, such as PODZINGER (www.podzinger.com), convert the words in the audio to text that can be indexed and searched. You'll see mainstream search engines do so also—they'll integrate the features of specialty search engines. When looking for the lyrics to a song, why shouldn't the searcher find the MP3 download of the actual song? When searching for breaking news, why can't the video news report be found? Search engines want to provide information in every form, and they will. You might even see new ways to search—finding clip art based on its color or locating a video clip based on an object in the picture.

- *Paid content.* Despite how much content is indexed today, vast amounts remain unavailable to search engines because content owners would rather be paid for their wares than have them dumped out on the Web for free. Both Google and Amazon already provide ways to search inside a book for sale, but searchers cannot see the whole book online—they must purchase it. There are many competing "digital rights management" systems that purport to protect content from theft, none of which have yet gained traction. Pundits have long talked about how surfers might someday purchase subscriptions to vast stores of content, not unlike the way cable television channels are bundled—a modest monthly payment split among all publishers participating. Others say no, that **micropayments** are the answer: Searchers pay the publisher a few cents or even a fraction of a cent to read a page found by the search engine. At some point, one or more of these methods (or one we have completely missed) will fire up the content money machine, and search engines will be in the middle of helping searchers find all that new content. Expect mountains of paid content to be indexed by search engines the minute their publishers know they can make money from allowing it.

- *Specialty content.* Some free content is also hard to find today because searchers want to find only specific kinds of documents, not any Web page that matches. Scientific researchers, for example, want to find only peer-reviewed journals for many of their searches. Patent attorneys want to search only for patents. These kinds of specialized searches are typically handled today with specialty search engines, but in the future this content might find its way into the major search engines, too. Expect that as search engines improve at finding specialized content, more of it will be made available for indexing.

- *Consumer-generated content.* More and more, new content does not come from publishers or other official media sources. Blogs and RSS feeds enable almost anyone to have a voice and be heard. These out-of-the-mainstream content providers are already changing the way we look at media—search marketers and PR people need to be aware of the ease with which messages can spread and gain an audience. Search engines can already find much of this content, but the larger trend to watch is where this goes next. Blogs lead to podcasting that leads to even more forms of self-publishing that get attention.

- *Desktop content.* Rumor has it that a future version of Windows will enable you to search your desktop and the Web at the same time. Google offers such a capability, as shown in Figure 16-1, as does MSN Search and Yahoo! Search and others. Wide adoption of search technology for finding information on the searcher's own computer could have broad implications for search marketing.

Figure 16-1 Google Desktop. If the same search that scours the Web can be employed on the searcher's own data, how will that change behavior?

How will these events change searcher behavior? That is what the search marketer wants to know. And the answer is (drum roll, please) . . . no one knows!

But you can start thinking about it now. You can start reading about it now—we show you how later in this chapter. And it is always fun to speculate, so let's think about what some of the questions are.

Will the advent of multimedia search force search marketers to provide their information in sexier formats? For example, do you need to adapt your radio and television commercials to the Web? Should your offline advertising agency craft more compelling content for your Web site?

If you are sitting on some of the paid content that would be liberated by either subscriptions or micropayments, which technique would work better for your business? If you work for a technical book publisher, could you offer subscriptions to the IT departments of large companies? If you are a newspaper, can you use micropayments to serve up stories from back issues? How are others in your industry addressing this opportunity? Are traditional media outlets under threat from bloggers and emerging nontraditional media?

Would searchers looking for information on their own computer find something on the Web that strikes their fancy? Would the search queries themselves look different? If Microsoft builds search into Windows, would searchers start using Microsoft's search capability over Google and Yahoo! Search? Many applications search the Web as part of their Help function—is more integrated searching within applications around the corner? Would all computer activity become more focused on search, driving up searches of all kinds?

After all, speculating is not just fun—it is instructive. Identifying the right questions gets you halfway to the right answers. So find the people in your company and your industry who are talking about these developments and discuss the effect on your search marketing efforts. If you are better prepared than your competitors, you will have a jump on them as these trends play out.

More Technology

Like all the software around us, search technology never stops improving. Even if you have the search marketing game wired today, you cannot be caught unawares as the rules change tomorrow. Let's look at some of the technology changes you should expect to see in the next few years. Although some of you might find the technology to be intrinsically interesting, *every* search marketer needs to ponder how technology changes might impact search marketing.

Direct Answers

You're probably familiar with what Google calls its "OneBox," where it offers quick answers to searcher queries, such as showing the weather forecast for "weather" (plus a zip code)—or showing the search engine's own content, such as the stock price and a link to the engine's finance site in response to a ticker symbol. Each search engine provides this kind of direct answer capability, where searchers don't need to click through to a search marketer's page—the search engine gives the answer itself.

Searchers like these direct answers, so expect to see more of them. But as search engines begin to provide product listings and other responses as direct answers, it may threaten some search marketers that don't have a deal with the search engines. If searchers begin to expect to see direct answers to their queries, search marketers need to take steps to be seen *there*, not just in the organic or paid results.

Keyword Assistance

Since the advent of text search in the 1960s, one problem has bedeviled searchers and continues to haunt them to this day—searchers often do not know the best words to use in their queries. In time, search engines will use some new techniques to help searchers pick the right words.

As we write this, Google is testing a new feature called Google Suggest (shown in Figure 16-2) that offers suggestions as you type in your queries. The figure shows what you would get if you typed in "dig"—several different queries are displayed that all start with those letters, ranging from "digital camera" to "digital camera reviews" and more.

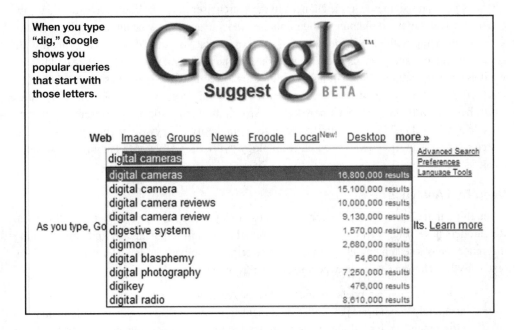

Figure 16-2 Google experiments with keyword assistance. Google Suggest tries to fill in the rest of the query as the searcher types the first few letters.

If Google Suggest remains a beta offering or is withdrawn, it will not have any effect on search marketing. If Google Suggest passes muster, and is made part of the mainstream Google search engine, however, it might cause changes in searcher behavior. Would searchers use fewer misspellings? Would searchers start using longer queries, such as "digital camera reviews," because they did not have to think up the words and type them in? Would the most popular queries get even more popular, with fewer variations in wording?

Other technologies could impact keyword planning, too. You are probably familiar with collaborative filtering technology, even if you do not know it by that name. Amazon and other Web sites use it to suggest items to shoppers (as in "Shoppers who bought books written by Max Readership also have bought books by Minnie Seller"). Suppose search engines started using it to suggest keywords to searchers (such as "Searchers who entered your query also tried these four related queries")? As search engines offer these alternative queries, they could emphasize the alternatives whose results have historically drawn many clicks (indicating the queries produced relevant results). If search engines did start using collaborative filtering to show popular queries, how would that change keyword demand? Would highly popular queries become even more popular?

What if search engines could look for synonyms of words that searchers enter? Search experts have toyed with this function for years, but the synonyms always seem to return more results that are off-topic than searchers are willing put up with. Still, you can bet that some researchers are still working on this.

As you can see, these simple changes in the search user interface could have drastic implications for your keyword planning. You might not know in advance what all the implications for keyword planning will be, but you would at least know that you should be looking for shifts in keyword demand, and perhaps even conversions, if one of the major search engines adds keyword assistance features. You will use your metrics to see how the game has changed and can react more quickly than your competition. Neeraj Agrawal of Battery Ventures (www.battery.com) believes that a new kind of search marketing specialist will emerge that he dubs "Keyword Man," to cope with the increased complexity of keyword planning. Regardless, search marketers must evolve as search technology evolves, in keyword planning and in other areas, as we see next.

Deep Text Analytics

If you think the technology that search engines use today is magical, you ain't seen nothing yet. Researchers have been working for years on breakthroughs in linguistics and pattern matching that make today's search engines seem positively primitive in comparison. Here are some of the text analytic techniques you can expect to emerge from the labs:

- *Summarization.* Snippets are nice, but some researchers are working on technology that accurately summarizes an entire document in a few sentences. Some implementations string together several sentences from the document, whereas others generate text from the central concepts.

- *Categorization.* Most documents have missing or inaccurate metadata, so computer scientists are developing programs that automatically generate correct metadata. Text analytics are already available to discover the subject (digital cameras) and type (white paper) of a document, as well as its grade level. In addition, some software can categorize the source of information (mass media, educational institution, corporation, and so on), its industry, geographic location, and publication date. All of this information can be used by search engines to limit the results of a search, such as "Find all case studies from the retail industry published after 2002 on the subject of credit card fraud."

- *Entity extraction.* Text analytic software already employs linguistics and pattern detection techniques to identify specific kinds of names within the text: person names, company names, and place names, for example. Some software can identify job titles, company mergers, product announcements, and other concepts. Other analyzers ferret out numeric information, such as company revenue, dates, and people's ages. Search engines could use this intelligence to allow more focused queries, such as "Find documents that mention product announcements from Snap Electronics and its competitors within the last two months."

The combination of these techniques might make true question answering possible, such as "When was George Washington born?" or "Where is Boeing's headquarters located?" or even "Which digital cameras have won awards?" Researchers can already demonstrate prototypes of search engines that answer questions, but this technology has not been generalized for use by the major search engines yet.

If these techniques come to fruition, search marketing might be profoundly changed. Although optimizing for keywords and drawing links would remain important, your content might need to emphasize facts as well, to continue to impress the search engines. Copy that mentions awards won or feature specifications that are meaningless for search today (although very valuable for driving people to convert) might suddenly become important answers for searchers' questions.

Even if this technology stops short of actually answering questions, it might allow searchers to use **natural language** queries; that is, they type in full sentences to find what they are looking for, such as "Show sales on digital cameras with at least 4.0 megapixel resolution." Searchers have historically been unwilling to do this much typing, because today's search results do not improve with extra words. Some search engine might come along to show better results with these longer queries, providing the incentive for searchers to change their behavior. Think about what effects that would have on your keyword planning.

Multifaceted Search

Our next technology is one of the most interesting of all. You might call multifaceted search the "anti-search" because it is often used without entering any keywords at all. In actuality, however, multifaceted search technology is just a more powerful addition to traditional text searching that enables searchers to restrict the search results by responding to choices offered by the search engine. Multifaceted search enables searchers to continually narrow down their results by choosing another constraint on their search.

Multifaceted search can already be spotted in some shopping search engines, such as shopping.com, as shown in Figure 16-3. Shopping search is a natural application for the multifaceted search approach, because some products, such as digital cameras, are bought based on the **facets** (features) of the product. Shoppers care about price, brand, resolution, and other facets of a camera. As they choose the facets they want (such as "more than 6.0 megapixel resolution" or "between $450 and $650 in price," and so on), invalid choices disappear, so shoppers never get a "not found."

When shoppers choose the "digital cameras" category, they
are shown the facets of the 1,800 cameras available.

A keyword can
be entered, but
is not required.

If neither price,
brand, nor
resolution is
the goal, other
facets are
available.

The matching
cameras are
sorted by
relevance, but
can be sorted
by price
instead.

Choosing "6.0+ megapixels"
narrows down the list to just 78.

"Interchangeable
Lens" is
expanded.

No "6.0+
megapixel"
cameras are
available for less
than $250, so the
choices for price
have changed.

The cameras
that match have
also changed.

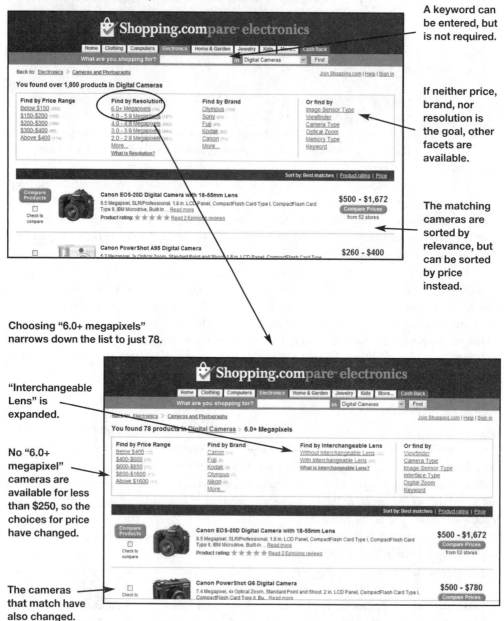

Figure 16-3   Search without searching. Multifaceted search allows multiple selections from
menus without ever serving up a "not found."

This multifaceted magic is made possible by the same XML trusted feeds discussed back in Chapter 10, "Get Your Site Indexed." Each digital camera retailer provides a data feed to shopping.com that includes the values ($649) for each facet (price) for every camera available. The multifaceted search engine does the rest, displaying the precise values available in the search index based on the current trusted feeds. If a particular model of camera sells out, it is immediately removed from the feed so that no shopper is disappointed.

 But shopping search is the tip of the multifaceted search iceberg. Multifaceted search could be used in the future for any kind of traditional text search application, if the search engine has enough information (values for facets) about the documents being searched. Remember the deep text analytics we discussed earlier? If search engines can automatically discern metadata, such as document type, subject, industry, and other information, each of these metadata fields can become facets in a multifaceted search. Imagine that specialty content being available through multifaceted search. Patent attorneys could perform their searches while limiting their scope to only patents. Transactional searchers in the Buy phase of the Web Conversion Cycle could eliminate all Use information from their results. As search engines apply categorization technology (the deep text analytics we discussed earlier) to every document on the Web, the metadata is created to enable multifaceted search technology to work on any search.

More Personalized

Beyond technology, a key search trend is toward a more personalized experience for searchers. Although many Web sites, led by Amazon, have personalized their user experience, search engines have been decidedly retro. Different searchers, by and large, get the exact same results when they type the same query into a search engine.

A quick review of the history of search technology reveals that the vast majority of improvements have been based on the content—analyzing it better, understanding it more deeply, and assessing its quality. But what about applying the same kind of thought to the searcher? After all, what makes a successful search is the best match between the content and searcher, so why have search engines focused on analyzing the content so much and ignored the searcher?

In part, the maniacal focus on content stems from the fact that understanding the content is easier than understanding people. However, despite the inherent difficulty, search engines are already beginning to understand searchers better, and you should expect to see more personalized search results based on several factors:

- *Geography*. Some search engines are already experimenting with local search and geographic targeting—they ask for place names in the query or they guess where searchers live and they try to show results from companies nearby. However, their only means of guessing is to analyze the searcher's IP address, which is not a flawless method. Someday search engines might entice searchers to register and disclose exactly where they live in a more permanent way, so that search engines can use that reliably to enhance results and provide more targeted paid placement opportunities.

- *Language.* AOL, MSN, and Yahoo! already have relationships with many of their searchers—they offer other services that cause people to identify themselves and provide information. If search engines knew what language each searcher prefers, they could restrict results to that language—even automatically translating results to the searcher's favorite language when necessary. Non-English Web pages and users are both growing faster than their English counterparts, so this capability is becoming more important.

- *Interests.* Could search results be improved if search engines knew searchers' interests? When searchers enter "jaguar," are they looking for the car, the animal, the football team, or the Apple operating system? If search engines understood the searchers' interests, they might be able to take a better guess. Eventually, one of the search engines will begin to collect information on searchers' interests to flavor the search results—we see whether searchers disclose this information willingly or if it needs to be collected as a byproduct of their Web usage, as Amazon does.

- *Demographics.* MSN's new adCenter offers search marketers the opportunity to increase their paid placement keyword bids based on searcher demographics, such as age and gender. Google is also beginning to experiment with demographics in its AdSense contextual advertising program. Expect to see all search engines charge premium prices for demographic targeting in paid search, and expect the engines to use demographic information to improve organic results as well. Expect *firmographic* features also, to target employees of certain companies or industries. Whether searchers will be concerned about the privacy implications of this targeting, only time will tell.

- *The wired home.* Web usage dramatically changed with the widespread adoption of "always-on" broadband connections. When surfers can use the Internet by walking up to their computer at any moment, they tend to use it more—and to search more. What will happen when there are Web browsers in the living room, the kitchen, and the bedroom—anywhere in the house? Will searching increase even more? Will the types of searches change? Will search engines explicitly support kitchen tasks, such as suggesting recipes based on ingredients on hand or locating the store that has stocked every item on a shopping list? Will voice recognition be required for a kitchen search engine to be truly useful? Regardless of the exact form searching takes within the wired home, it seems likely that devices built in to the searcher's home will have far more information about the searcher, which could then be used to personalize search results.

- *Handheld devices.* Will search results change as searchers use new devices to connect to the Web, such as personal digital assistants (PDAs), cell phones, or other small-screen devices? If you stop to think about it, these small screens with ubiquitous wireless access to the Web are tailor-made for a more search-centered user experience. There is no room to look at long Web pages with lots of links to navigate—you will want to search (maybe by pecking a small keyboard or using a stylus for handwriting recognition, or perhaps with voice recognition). Will Global Positioning Systems (GPS) that know where the searcher is located allow even *more* targeted geographic pinpointing of paid placement? ("Show me the hardware store nearest to where I am now.")

Handheld devices contain e-mail, calendars, to-do lists, and other information about their owner that might be used to personalize search results.

- *Information alerts.* Would the advent of more personalized search results fundamentally change information gathering behavior to a more passive activity? Once search engines know what searchers are interested in, will they begin sending it to them without waiting for them to search for it? If search engines know who wants to buy a particular car, would they send an alert message to the cell phones of each person when that car goes on sale at the local dealer? Would the dealer pay the search engine to do so? Time-saving information alerts might be just the incentive for searchers to disclose their interests and other personal information to the search engines—to get the alerts they want, they will need to reveal something about themselves, which allows the search engines to personalize more deeply in other ways.

We live in a world today where "one size fits all"—at least for search results. If one person finds a document using a search engine, another person can enter the same query and find the same document. Personalized search changes the game. Every person might get different search results from the same query, just as they each get different products listed on the Amazon home page. And the same person might get different results based on context—where he is, what device he is using now, and what he has been interested in lately.

Some searchers will be amenable to providing information about themselves to the search engines, just because they want to improve their search results. But others will not want to make any effort at all. Will search engines analyze each searcher's pattern of queries to determine interests? Will search engines provide other services to learn more about each searcher? When search engines perfect the technology to offer more personalized searching, many thorny questions might yet remain as to whether searchers will give up some privacy in return for the time savings of more relevant results.

It will take years to play out, but search marketers must be aware that personalization *is* coming, and the time to consider the implications is now. If the burden of translating your Web site into multiple languages were lifted, could you profitably operate in countries you avoid today? Perhaps you would benefit from learning more about how offline advertising works, so that you understand the demographics of your customers. It might be helpful to learn how impulse purchases can be influenced, because your retail store or restaurant might someday need to do more than hang out a big sign—you might want to digitally alert passers-by or nearby drivers thought to be interested in your establishment.

Regardless of your business, search marketing seems destined to become more fragmented over time, as today's purchase of a paid keyword might become the purchase of a keyword only for searchers fitting a certain demographic model. So, instead of buying the keyword *supply chain management*, you would buy that keyword only for searchers that work for companies over a certain size in specified industries. You would probably pay a higher price for this more segmented audience, but if your conversion rate were high enough, it would be worth the premium price.

In this brave new personalized world, how would you check your organic search rankings? Rank checking software cannot simulate personalized results, so the concept of ranking #1 becomes meaningless. Perhaps you really want to know for how many individual queries your page was ranked #1. Or maybe what your page's average ranking is across all queries, which only the search engines can reveal. Maybe search engines will start selling you organic search metrics, the way they offer paid placement reporting for search marketers today. We might move to an organic tracking system similar to paid search, where your organic search results are measured by the number of impressions (the number of times they are shown) and your page's clickthrough rate. By thinking about the effects of these changes, you will be more prepared when they arrive.

As you consider all of these changes afoot, you must remember that many others are being worked on, too. Moreover, many of these trends interrelate (keyword assistance could become personalized, perhaps, or maybe voice recognition makes searchers willing to use longer natural language queries), so their effects might be multiplied in ways that are hard to predict. That is all the more reason to stay alert for what is going on around you.

So far, we have discussed only those trends that will be seen by any searcher, but a hidden change is brewing that affects search marketers—increasing competition from *other* search marketers.

More Competition

You are not the only person joining the search marketing game. At the beginning of this book, we trotted out all the "gee-whiz" numbers to show you how search marketing is growing. So the good news is that you are catching the wave, but the bad news is there are a lot of other surfboards out there to contend with.

The biggest surfers are large corporations, many of which have been oblivious to search marketing, or have experimented and failed. You have seen in this book why search marketing can sometimes be difficult for big companies, but don't expect them to remain on the sidelines for long when there is this much money at stake. Large organizations are now becoming formidable search marketing competitors for three main reasons:

- *They are addressing their weaknesses.* If large companies harness their strengths while correcting the kinds of errors we describe in this book, they will become formidable competitors in search marketing. Enterprise-wide execution will allow large companies to counter the traditional search marketing advantage held by smaller, more nimble companies.

- *They are leveraging their brand names.* As you have learned in this book, large businesses have significant organic search advantages in attracting links and searcher clicks, due to well-known brand names. Larger marketing budgets can be applied to paid search, too. Conglomerates are beginning to see how portfolio management might apply to search marketing, the same way it applies in other marketing disciplines. General Motors, for example, has many different brands of sports utility vehicles ranging from the Chevy Aveo to the Hummer; each brand caters to market segments with different characteristics, sensibilities, and needs. A well-known brand such as Hummer draws many searches, whereas Aveo garners relatively few, but would Hummer searchers who cannot afford that pricey sports utility vehicle be interested in a less-expensive Aveo SUV? GM might be able to leverage its portfolio on the Web in ways that their Hummer and Chevy dealers never could. In addition, could GM have its divisions work together to dominate the listings for "sports utility vehicle"? You can bet they are going to try.

- *They are defending their brand names.* The ease of publishing to the Web has a downside for big brands—it makes it easy for "hate" sites to target a particular brand and get publicity for its complaints. Some search marketing vendors, such as Global Strategies (www.globalstrategies.com) and Converseon (www.converseon.com), are helping large companies with search engine reputation management. They monitor these negative sites and work to develop effective search marketing campaigns among friendly companies to give the negative sites less attention. If the top ten is dominated by your site and your partners, the hate site has less visibility.

But big businesses are not the only source of new competition. You might already be doing battle in global markets, and you see that competitors seem to be getting more sophisticated about search marketing, lessening your advantage. Or, worse, you do business in just a few local markets but you are starting to face competition from other regions or countries that could never do business in your territory before the Internet, but now they can. Not since the advent of the fax machine has such an important way of crossing geographic boundaries come along.

Before the Web, companies seeking to enter foreign markets used exporters, licensees, joint ventures, or wholly owned subsidiaries to create a local presence in each market. Although these techniques still have their place, the Web allows businesses to sell directly to a customer, no matter what country each one is in. The rise of global search engines help a business from across the world seem just as "local" as one a block away. It is likely that your business will be competing with new entrants around the world, if it is not doing so already.

But companies from around the world might not be the only new competitors you face. You might meet new combatants right in your own backyard—local businesses. If search engines can personalize results by location, as discussed earlier in this chapter, millions of local businesses whose ad budgets are spent on Yellow Pages advertising might now be able to profitably engage in search marketing. If you work for a large company, such as Home Depot, you might have had search marketing to yourself, but will someday face increased competition from local hardware stores.

What happens as more and more marketers realize how well search marketing works? As changes in search marketing make it profitable for more and more businesses? The simple answers are that it makes it tougher to rank at the top of organic search results and it also makes paid placement more expensive. So what do you do about that?

For organic marketing, your best approach is to redouble your efforts to make search marketing an ingrained part of your extended team's job. No more remedial programs to fix problems! Instead, prevent those problems from the start. Every new page must be designed with search marketing in mind, and no changes should be permitted without considering the search marketing impact. In that way, you will keep your costs as low as possible while reaping the highest possible gains. However, you must always focus on your message. If you truly create the content that is the best answer to a searcher's question, and you carefully optimize your site, you will continue to get high rankings. If you allow others to create better matches for your targeted searchers, however, increased competition will crowd you out of the top spots.

The growing competition in paid search is a much more difficult trend to cope with. Economics teaches that the marketplace in paid placement will force bids to the highest affordable levels for the players in your industry. This relentless efficiency will drive prices up as long as more competitors enter the market. To cope, your business must ruthlessly drive out costs so that your Web site is the most efficient conversion machine around and your product costs are as low as possible. That way, you have the maximum amount of budget available to raise your bids whenever necessary so you continue to drive conversions.

If the conversion rate of your Web site is lower than your competition's, or your product costs are higher, it leaves you with less money to put into search marketing. When the bidding gets too high, you will be forced to drop out. Consider the situation you will be in as bids mount. If you find yourself asking, "How can my competitor make any money bidding that rate?" then there are two possibilities. One is that your competitor is losing money, so you have only a short-term problem—eventually your competitor will lower the bid or go bankrupt. The other, more serious, possibility is that your competitor is actually *making* money with a bid that would *lose* money for you. In that case, you must address all inefficiencies in your Web site, in your manufacturing, and in every cost you have, so you can remain competitive in your bidding.

One way to cope with rising bid costs is to shift money from one budget to another. If search marketing is truly your most efficient marketing spending, you might want to reduce other marketing outlays (offline advertising, brochures, and so on) and move that money into search marketing. That way, you can keep up with rising bid prices without spending any more money overall.

Another way to improve your efficiency is with passionate attention to deep metrics. The kinds of metrics that you need to do by hand should become automated in the future. Adopt software tools that allow your campaigns to go on autopilot—the tool constantly monitors your bidding, your conversions, and your budget. The tool can make adjustments to take advantage of inefficiencies in bidding, not unlike stock market arbitrageurs looking for stock price anomalies. If you constantly automate your campaign management to be more adaptive without human intervention, you will drive your conversions to their maximums while keeping a lid on costs.

Before leaving the topic of competition, we should point out that the changes leading to more competition offer you business opportunities, too. Just as your business might face competitors from new places, your business can seek customers in new markets that were not cost-effective in the past. If you can become efficient enough, you can become a feared competitor in any market using search marketing and the Web.

Enough heady thoughts on where the search marketing industry is headed! What about you? As you get started in your search marketing career, what's next for you?

What's Next for You?

Get experience. Learn more. It's that simple. No one becomes a strong practitioner in any area with working at the craft. The craft of search marketing is no exception.

Get Experience

If you have begun executing your first campaign as you have read this book, you are already developing experience. As you have learned, it is critical that you measure everything you do so that you can see what's working and what's not. Using the techniques we have shown you, you can see how to do more of the "hits" and less of the "misses."

Undoubtedly, you learn a lot by doing things yourself, but don't overlook the benefit of *hiring* your experience. You can hire folks for your search marketing team that have more experience than you do. You can also hire a search marketing vendor to assist you along the way. Seek search marketing mentors wherever you go.

It is amazing how constant practice is often enough to develop the skills you need for any craft. Use the techniques we showed you in this book and repeat them over and over in your search marketing campaigns. You will gradually improve your results. Over time, you will develop excellent search marketing judgment—you will even learn when you should ignore the techniques we have taught!

If you have chosen the right goals for your site, and the right Web conversions to measure your success, you can track the results of every search marketing campaign. You can analyze those results and act on that knowledge to improve with each new campaign.

Keep Learning

No matter how much you have learned, you can always learn more. No matter how many tips we have crammed into this book, you should know that there is so much that we have left out. We have given you plenty to get started and maybe even explained concepts that some experts do not know, but search marketing is constructed from a whole range of details. There is always another way of designing your Web site that causes a crawling problem—and the workaround you need to know to fix it. Some smart person will always be figuring out a new bidding strategy for paid search—maybe one that is perfect for the situation you are in. Just about everything we have explained can be done some other way, and maybe that way would be better for you than the way we have shown.

If you still believe that you know everything about search marketing, just wait a minute—something will change. Even search marketing experts need to constantly learn what's new in this ever-changing field. If you need any convincing, just flip back to the beginning of this chapter and go over the trends that might change search marketing someday.

If you are keeping up with the changes happening in search marketing, you will know about what is coming before it hits and you will have time to think about what you will do differently. Do you want to be prepared, or caught flat-footed? There are new developments in search marketing every day—you need to keep up with what's going on to make sure that you will not be caught napping by your competitors. Two places to start are the Web sites of the authors:

- *Bill Hunt* (www.globalstrategies.com). Bill's well-respected Global Strategies International search consultancy is a good company to contact for any search marketing need.

- *Mike Moran* (www.mikemoran.com). Mike's Web site offers insights into the latest trends, and his free Biznology newsletter and blog provides tips that you can use long after you have closed this book. You can also head for www.mikemoran.com/updates to see corrections and significant industry changes since this book was published.

But if you are tired of listening to us, we don't blame you. Luckily, there is no shortage of other voices and helpful tools. You and your central search team can benefit from the vast amount of information available on search marketing, which we outline in the rest of this chapter.

Conferences

The quickest way to get up to speed in search marketing is to attend a conference. For a crash course, here are several excellent choices:

- *Search Engine Strategies* (www.jupiterevents.com). By far the largest and most comprehensive event, SES is held every few weeks throughout the year in cities around the world, moderated by Danny Sullivan and Chris Sherman of Search Engine Watch (www.searchenginewatch.com). Each conference lasts two to four days and features presentations and discussions for both novice and expert search marketers. In addition to the formal agenda, networking events each evening are designed for you to pick the brains of experts. *Around $600 per day*

- *PubCon* (www.webmasterworld.com). More technical than SES, catering more to Web Developers and Affiliate marketers, PubCon (now officially called "WebmasterWorld's World of Search") grew out of after-hours networking at the various search conferences into a three-day event that stands on its own, held a couple of times each year, with one always in the U.S. For Webmasters and other technical experts, this event is the valuable one for solving problems, learning new techniques, and keeping up with where the search marketing is headed. *As low as $500 to attend*

- *AD:TECH* (www.ad-tech.com). A very large event devoted to online advertising, AdTech has added search engine marketing segments in recent years. These introductory sessions are targeted at marketing managers and advertising agencies that want to start learning search marketing. AD:TECH is held for three days several times each year in cities around the globe. *As low as $1,000 to attend*

- *eMetrics Summit* (www.emetrics.org). Jim Sterne holds the definitive conference on Web metrics and analytics in several locations around the world throughout the year. This conference is broader than just search marketing, but all search marketers must understand metrics to be successful. *Around $2000 to attend*

Web Sites

Conferences are great, but if your budget is lower, you can use other information sources, including some free resources:

- *Search Engine Watch* (www.searchenginewatch.com). Danny Sullivan is probably the best known search expert in the world—this is the Web site he started, but he no longer contributes. Known for its industry statistics, Search Engine Watch offers free and paid newsletters as well as free and paid Web articles. The site's forum has become an excellent source of information for those with specific questions. *$99 for a one-year subscription*

- *High Rankings Advisor* (www.highrankings.com). Jill Whalen offers a free newsletter, Web site, and open forum for discussion. The site provides great advice on search-friendly copy writing, and the forum is well known for helping search marketers solve knotty problems. *Free*

- *Marketing Pilgrim* (www.marketingpilgrim.com). Andy Beal's excellent blog covers every news story in the search marketing industry. *Free*

- *Google Webmaster Central* (googlewebmastercentral.blogspot.com). Because of Google's large market share, no search marketer can ignore this treasure trove of information and tools. Google offers a suite of tools that help you determine how well Google's spider is crawling your site, and also provides a blog and discussion group for Webmasters.

- *Mike Grehan says...* (www.mikegrehan.com). Mike is a long-standing search consultant who specializes in the technology behind the search engines. His blog alerts you to his articles and interviews and provides a behind-the-scenes look at just about every search marketing conference. *Free*

- *Search Engine Journal* (www.searchenginejournal.com). Several writers update this blog on a daily basis. Known for interesting perspectives on the latest search marketing news. *Free*

- *Search Engine News* (www.searchengine-news.com). Planet Ocean Communications offer a monthly subscription-only newsletter. Subscribers also get access to a search marketing tactics manual with detailed search engine guidelines and other reference material. *$97 for a six-month subscription*

- *Search Engine Round Table* (www.seroundtable.com). The brainchild of Barry Schwartz, the site aggregates the best commentary from various forums into a central location. This is a daily "must read" for anyone in search marketing. Barry and his team also do an excellent job of recapping the highlights of the major search conferences. *Free*

- *Traffick* (www.traffick.com). A longstanding commentary site, home to several bloggers with regular insights into events in the search marketing industry. *Free*

- *WebmasterWorld* (www.webmasterworld.com). Brett Tabke and a series of moderators monitor excellent free discussion areas, and also host subscription discussions known for the presence of top search marketing pros. This is the top resource for Webmasters and other technical personnel. *$149 for a one-year subscription*

- *Occam's Razor* (www.kaushik.net/avinash). Avinash Kaushik's blog provides unequalled insight into every aspect of Web metrics, focusing on practical advice that questions conventional measurement wisdom to reveal true business value.

- *WebMetricsGuru* (www.webmetricsguru.com). Marshall Sponder follows all the news in Web metrics each day in his popular blog.

- *WebProNews* (www.webpronews.com). This site offers news stories on all Internet technology subjects, including search marketing. Updated daily, the extensive search marketing section features news and forums. *Free*

Summary

So, there you have it. You've learned a great deal about search marketing and, in this chapter, you've learned how to keep learning. You've developed an eye for some of the key trends that might shape our business over the next few years, and you have a list of resources that will help you keep up with every change that comes along.

Search marketing is a fast-changing industry—that's part of what makes it exciting, fun, and a good opportunity for your business. As you embark on your search marketing career, stay attuned to the constant changes, and always use your judgment on how you should respond. In the end, your judgment will serve you better than any methodologies extracted from this book. We hope that, beyond any specific methods, we've taught you how to *think* about search marketing and that you'll think your way to the top. Good luck!

Glossary

301 redirect   Also known as a *permanent redirect*, an instruction to Web browsers to display a different URL from the one the browser requested, used when a page has undergone a lasting change in its URL. A permanent redirect is a type of server-side redirect that is handled properly by search engine spiders.

302 redirect   Also known as a *temporary redirect*, an instruction to Web browsers to display a different URL from the one the browser requested, used when a page has undergone a short-term change in its URL. A temporary redirect is a type of server-side redirect that is handled properly by search engine spiders.

action   The searcher behavior that ultimately results in a Web conversion, usually the purchase of your product. Typically used in "call to action" to describe copy written to induce a conversion, and in "cost per action" to describe the fee for each successful conversion.

advertising agency   A company that helps clients to plan and purchase promotional announcements. *Interactive* agencies handle e-mail, banner ads, search, and other electronic promotions. *Traditional* ad agencies cover TV, radio, and print media, but might cover interactive media, too.

affiliate marketing   A technique of marketing and selling products in which a Web site (the affiliate marketer) directs Web visitors to another site (the affiliate program sponsor) and is compensated with a commission for visitor's purchases.

allowable   The highest cost per action that you will pay for a particular product. Your allowable is used with your conversion rate to calculate the maximum per-click fee that you should pay.

alt text   The descriptive text for an image coded in the HTML image tag. The alt attribute on the image tag helps visitors with visual impairments to determine what the images contain, by providing alternative (alt) text.

anchor text   The words that are shown on a page for a hypertext link, usually shown as underlined text in a different color from the surrounding text. Search engines use anchor text to infer the subject matter of the page being linked to.

antiphrase   A search term within a search query that is ignored by some search engines when it looks for matching pages. In the query "what is london's capital," search engines might ignore antiphrase "what is" and search only for "london's capital" (which will probably find better results because the searcher really does not care whether the words *what* and *is* are on the matching pages).

application server   The system software that executes the programs that run a Web site. Application servers, also known as Web application servers, are typically used to display dynamic pages.

audience   A Web term analogous to *market segment* in offline marketing that describes a particular group that a Web site's message is targeted to. Audiences are broader than market segments because they reach beyond customers. Typical Web site audiences include stock analysts, the media, and distribution channels, as well as each of their customer market segments.

authority   The perceived expertise level of a Web site, as measured by its network of inbound hypertext links. Search engines typically place great importance on sites that have many inbound links from other well-linked sites, and place those sites at the top of search results for queries on subjects that match the site's subjects.

authority page   A Web page that has many links to it on a certain subject.

back links   Also known as *inbound links*, the hypertext links from a page *to* your page. Inbound links to your page from outside your site are highly valued by search engines performing link analysis when they rank search results by relevance.

banner ad   A promotional message, typically presented as a large colorful rectangle in a prominent part of the page, analogous to an advertisement in a newspaper or a magazine. Clicking a banner ad takes the visitor to the Web site of the sponsor of the ad.

behavior model   An abstract embodiment of the activities of a group of people performing a task that is used to measure and analyze what they are doing. This analysis can suggest improvements to the process being followed for the task.

bid   The price paid to a paid search engine for each referral to secure a ranking in paid search results. In its simplest form, paid search results show a link to the highest bidder's page at the top of the list, and that bidder pays the bid price to the paid search engine each time a visitor clicks the bidder's link.

bid gap A significant difference between two bids in adjacent positions in a paid placement auction. For example, when the bidder currently ranked #3 has a maximum bid of 50¢, and the #4 bid is 40¢, the bid gap is 10¢.

bid jamming An aggressive paid placement auction bidding technique that raises your competitor's costs, which might drain his budget a bit faster. A bid jammer bids 1¢ less than the maximum bid of the next-highest position, forcing the other bidder to his maximum bid. For example, when the bidder currently ranked #3 has a maximum bid of 50¢, and the #4 bid is 40¢, the #3 bidder is paying just 41¢ per click. A bid jammer might bid 49¢ to ensure the #3 bidder pays his maximum cost (50¢) for each click.

bid limit The highest amount that a paid placement bidder is willing to pay for a keyword term.

bid management The technique used by Web sites to track and control the prices they pay to paid search engines to have their pages listed. Bid management is crucial for large paid search campaigns comprising multiple search keywords over several paid search engines, usually performed with software tools that automate bids based on constraints chosen by the Web site search marketers.

blog Short for "Web log," an online personal journal, a kind of a periodic column on the Web. Some blogs are reminiscent of a private diary, but others resemble magazine columns focused on a particular subject of interest.

body text Normal text written in paragraphs and lists on a Web page that have no special significance, as opposed to titles and headings, which connote more importance. Search engines look for query terms in body text, but accord them less relevance than emphasized occurrences, such as in titles.

bookmark Also known as a *favorite*, the browser function that enables surfers to store the URLs of a Web pages so they can return at a later time.

bow-tie theory A model of Web linking patterns that categorizes each page as core pages (strongly linked from and to), destination pages (strongly linked from the core), origination pages (strongly linked to the core), and disconnected pages (not linked from or to the core).

brand manager The marketing specialist responsible for promoting a particular set of products within your company. Brand managers are responsible for targeting the right people to buy your products and then reaching them with the message that causes them to take action.

brick-and-mortar retailer The Web-savvy name for a traditional physical store, to contrast it from a Web retailer.

browser The program that a Web site visitor uses to view and navigate the Web site. The two most famous browsers are Microsoft Internet Explorer and Netscape Navigator.

budget cap   The maximum amount you are willing to spend in a paid search campaign within a defined period of time, ranging from one day to one month. When you "cap" your spending, you are protected from sudden shifts that could be disastrous to your budget, because your ad or product is no longer shown by the search engine once you reach your cap—no more per-click fees will be charged.

call to action   The sales term for the message that causes the prospective customer to do something that closes a sale or gets them closer to a sale. Web pages that ask you to "add to cart" or "sign up for an e-mail newsletter" contain calls to action.

campaign   A marketing term for a marketing effort of relatively short duration with specific goals for success. A search marketing campaign might last a few months, during which specific keywords might be targeted for paid search, with success measured by the number of sales made from visitors referred by the paid search engines.

Cascading Style Sheet (CSS)   A set of formatting instructions for each tag in an HTML file that can be customized so that the same tagged file can be formatted in different ways with different style sheets.

case   The capitalization of letters in Western languages—UPPERcase as opposed to lowercase.

categorization   A technique in text analytics to discern document metadata that the author did not correctly provide, such as subject (life insurance), document type (prospectus), and other data.

central search team   The group responsible for coordinating search marketing work across the entire organization, directing the extended search team to execute the search marketing plan.

CGI   Common Gateway Interface, the original technique by which a Web server runs a program to dynamically create the page's HTML and to return it to the visitor's Web browser.

character encoding   The key by which a computer determines which patterns stand for which characters in a computer file. Different national languages contain different characters and require different character encoding schemes.

click   The action that Web users take with their mouse to navigate to a new page. Web metrics programs capture all visitor clicks for measurement and analysis.

click fraud   The unethical act of clicking a paid search listing with no intention of converting, but rather to simply cause the per-click fee to be charged.

clickthrough   The Web metrics term for visitors clicking a link and navigating to a new page. In search marketing, clickthrough rates of paid search results is a very important metric, because it can show search marketers the effectiveness of ad copy in attracting traffic.

clickthrough rate   The Web metrics term for the ratio of visitors seeing a link versus clicking that link and navigating to a new page. In search marketing, clickthrough rates of paid search results is a very important metric because it can show search marketers the effectiveness of ad copy in attracting traffic.

cloaking   An aggressive form of *IP delivery*, a technique by which a spammer, for the same URL, designs a program to return one page for human visitors and a different version of the page for a search engine's spider—one full of keywords designed to attain a high search ranking. The term *cloaking* originated from the way site owners blocked visitors from viewing their HTML code to reveal their search optimization secrets.

commerce server   The system software that displays products for sale, and securely takes orders from customers. Commerce servers often display dynamic pages, a fact that presents challenges for search marketing success.

Common Gateway Interface (CGI)   The original technique by which a Web server runs a program to dynamically create the page's HTML and to return it to the visitor's Web browser.

community   A naturally occurring subject theme among a group of interlinked Web sites used by the Ask Jeeves to return more relevant search results.

conglomerate   A highly decentralized form of corporate organization typically consisting of quasi-independent companies loosely organized into a single corporation.

consideration set   The sales term for the list of suppliers evaluated by a potential purchaser. Companies not "in the consideration set" cannot make the sale to that purchaser.

content   A Web term for the words and pictures shown on a Web page. Search marketing frequently depends on optimizing content so that search engines can more easily find a page for a relevant query.

content analyzer   A software tool that examines your Web page and offers advice to modify the page's tagging and text to improve search ranking.

content audit   A technique by which an organic search landing page is checked to diagnose problems to improve rankings, referrals, and conversions.

content management system   The system software that manages the process of creation, update, approval, and publishing of Web pages to a Web site. Search marketing success often depends on proper standards for the operation of the content management system.

content writer   The Web specialist of the extended search team responsible for crafting the words that appear on a Web page designed to convey information, as opposed to selling products.

contextual advertising   A paid merchandising spot displayed on the same page as an article about a related subject. Yahoo! Content Match and Google AdSense are the two leading programs.

conversion   The sales term for closing a sale—"*converting* a prospect to a customer." The traditional definition can be expanded to include *Web conversions*—any measurable, successful outcome of a Web visit—such as registering an account or donating to a cause.

conversion rate   The ratio of Web site visitors to Web orders—how many people came to the site versus how many actually purchased.

cookie   A method browsers use to store information that Web pages need to remember. For example, a page can store your visitors' names in cookies so that their names can be displayed on your home page each time they return.

cooperative advertising   A technique by which multiple companies pool their resources on a campaign that benefits them. In paid search, a company selling a product might split the per-click fees with the supplier of a critical component of that product.

copy   The words that appear on a Web page. Search marketing often depends on *optimizing* the copy so that search engines can more easily find the page in response to relevant search queries.

copywriter   The Web specialist of the extended search team responsible for crafting the words that appear on a Web page designed to sell products, as opposed to conveying information.

core page   According to the bow-tie theory of Web pages, one of the most linked-to and linked-from pages on the Web. The most popular Web sites tend to have many core pages.

cost per action (CPA)   A method of calculating fees whereby money is owed only when the searcher converts—typically by purchasing your product. In practice, CPA pricing is used only for fixed-placement or shopping searches, not bid-based advertising, and runs anywhere from $5 to $50.

cost per click (CPC)   A method of calculating fees whereby money is owed to the search engine only when the searcher clicks through on the paid placement advertisement. CPC prices range from about 10¢ (usually the lowest bid allowed) to $30 or sometimes more, with the average around $1.

cost per thousand (CPM)   A method of calculating fees whereby money is owed for each impression of an advertisement—each time it's displayed. Usually referred to as CPM (cost per thousand—M is the Roman numeral for one thousand), it is usually used for fixed-placement advertising, not bid-based advertising, and it varies from $10 to $30 per thousand impressions (or about 1¢ to 3¢ per single impression).

country map   A page consisting of spider-friendly links to the main page of every country site within your overall Web domain.

CPA   Cost per action, a method of calculating fees whereby money is owed only when the searcher converts—typically by purchasing your product. In practice, CPA pricing is used only for fixed-placement or shopping searches, not bid-based advertising, and runs anywhere from $5 to $50.

CPC   Cost per click, a method of calculating fees whereby money is owed to the search engine only when the searcher clicks through on the paid placement advertisement. CPC prices range from about 10¢ (usually the lowest bid allowed) to $30 or sometimes more, with the average around $1.

CPM Cost per thousand—M is the Roman numeral for one thousand—a method of calculating fees whereby money is owed for each impression of an advertisement—each time it's displayed. CPM is usually used for fixed-placement advertising, not bid-based advertising, and it varies from $10 to $30 per thousand impressions (or about 1¢ to 3¢ per single impression).

crawler Also known as a *spider*, the part of a search engine that locates and indexes every page on the Web that is a possible answer to a searcher's query. Successful search engine marketing depends on crawlers finding almost all of the pages on a web site.

creative The copy written for a paid placement advertisement.

CSS Cascading Style Sheet, a set of formatting instructions for each tag in an HTML file that can be customized so that the same tagged file can be formatted in different ways with different style sheets.

dayparting A paid placement bidding technique that allows you to set your bids based on time of day, so that your bids are higher at the times of highest conversion.

description tag The HTML element that contains a synopsis of the page. Search engines sometimes match search queries to page descriptions, so improving the description seems like a good way to begin to optimize your page.

destination page According to the bow-tie theory of Web pages, a page linked from the core but does not itself link back into the core. Destination pages are typically high-quality pages, but they might be part of corporate Web sites that tend to link internally more then externally.

developer A specialist who develops software. *Web* developers develop programs or HTML to display Web pages in your visitor's Web browser.

directory A list of hundreds or thousands of subjects (such as fly fishing or needlepoint) along with links to Web sites about those subjects. Yahoo! Directory is the most famous example, but most directories are lightly used in comparison to text search technology.

directory listing One of many hypertext links about a particular subject. Site owners submit a page to request that it be listed in the directory, and say that they have a "directory listing" when their submission is accepted. Yahoo! Directory and Open Directory are the most famous examples of Web directories.

disconnected page According to the bow-tie theory of Web pages, a page not directly connected to the core. Disconnected pages might have links to or from origination and destination pages, or they might be linked only to other disconnected pages.

disintermediation A Web-savvy term for "cutting out the middleman." Disintermediation was much discussed during the Internet boom, but has not been as sweeping as the hype would lead you to believe.

domain name   The spoken language label for an Internet Web site that can be used for Web surfing or e-mail. The domain name (dell.com) follows the "at" sign (@) in an e-mail address (michael@dell.com) and the www. in a Web URL (www.dell.com).

doorway page   Also known as a *gateway page* or an *entry page*, a spam technique by which a page is designed solely to achieve high search rankings, with no value to visitors to your site. Unlike search landing pages, a doorway page is usually kept as hidden as possible from visitors who navigate through the site.

dynamic page   Web page whose HTML is generated by a software program at the moment the page is displayed. Dynamic pages are necessary when a page contains content that must change based on the visitor, such as an order status screen. A software program must retrieve the order status for the visitor from a database and build the HTML that shows the correct information on the screen. Dynamic pages often pose difficulties for search marketing that *static pages* do not.

entity extraction   A technique in text analytics that identifies the type of noun in a sentence, such as person names, company names, and place names, for example.

entry page   Also known as a *gateway page* or a *doorway page*, a spam technique by which a page is designed solely to achieve high search rankings, with no value to visitors to your site. Unlike search landing pages, an entry page is usually kept as hidden as possible from visitors who navigate through the site.

extended search team   The collective group responsible for executing the search marketing plan coordinated by the central search team. The extended search team is a new name for the various Web teams that already maintain the Web site, connoting their critical role in search marketing success.

eXtensible Markup Language (XML)   A standard for a markup language, similar to HTML, that allows tags to be defined to describe any kind of data you have, making it very popular as a format for data feeds.

external link   A hypertext connection from one Web site to another, allowing visitors to move to the new site. Search engines treat these links as endorsements of the receiving site by the sending site.

filter   A constraint on a search that sets the scope of results, such as a country or language. Pages that are not included by the filters for a query do not appear in the results.

fixed placement   A technique by which a search marketer negotiates the appearance of an advertisement in a particular place on a page for a given search query, usually paying for impressions (the number of times the ad is shown), rather than for clicks.

Flash   A technology invented by Macromedia that brings a far richer user experience to the Web than drab old HTML, allowing animation and other interactive features that spice up visual tours and demonstrations.

frames An old technique of HTML coding that can display multiple sources of content in separate scrollable windows in the same HTML page. Frames have many usability problems for visitors, and have been replaced with better ways of integrating content on the same page—using content management systems and dynamic pages.

friendly URL A paid placement auction bidding technique that marketers employ to stay out of costly bidding wars by always bidding lower than the maximum bid of the identified bidder—the one with the "friendly URL" that a marketer does not want to compete with.

freshness The search name for how quickly pages that change have those changes reflected in the search. Search engines that reflect changes rapidly have a higher freshness than those that do not.

functional organization A highly centralized form of corporate organization typical of small-to-medium businesses with a small number of similar products that are sold to the same customers. The organization is divided by *function*, such as marketing or sales.

gap surfing A paid placement auction bidding technique in which you scan the list of paid placement results, looking for significant differences between bids. You then adjust your bid to be just higher than the lower bid in the gap. If the #1 result is bidding 70¢, the #2 result is bidding 50¢, and the #3 result is bidding 40¢, the largest gap is between the first two results, so a gap surfer would bid 51¢ to claim the #2 ranking.

gateway page Also known as a *doorway page* or an *entry page*, a spam technique by which a page is designed solely to achieve high search rankings, with no value to visitors to your site. Unlike search landing pages, a gateway page is usually kept as hidden as possible from visitors who navigate through the site.

geographic targeting A technique that search engines use to display paid search results from a particular geographic area. Search engines typically use the searcher's IP address to determine the correct location and then show the listings that their advertisers have requested be shown. Geographic targeting is different from *local search*, in which searchers enter the location as part of their query.

governance specialist The specialist of the extended search team responsible for enforcing your company's operational standards. A *Web* governance specialist enforces your Web site's operational standards.

guest book A part of a Web site that allows visitors to post their contact information and comments about that site.

hate site Also known as a *negative site*, a Web site whose primary purpose is to discredit another organization or Web site. These sites frequently use the name of another site with the word *sucks* appended to the domain name, such as yourdomainsucks.com.

heading tag   The HTML element that contains an emphasized section name that breaks up the body text. Search engines treat matches found in the heading tags as more important than those in body text, so improving headings seems like a good way to begin to optimize your page.

hidden links   A spam technique in which hypertext links are designed to be seen by spiders but not by human visitors. Spammers load up lots of links from high-ranking pages to other pages they are trying to boost.

hidden text   A spam technique in which text on a page is designed to be seen by spiders but not human visitors. Text can be hidden by displaying text in tiny sizes or in the same color as the background, or by placing keywords in areas overlaid by graphics and other page elements. Spammers load up the page with keywords to gain higher search rankings.

high bidder auction   The original technique for ranking paid placement bids in which the search marketer offering the top price for a keyword click gets the #1 ranking ad for that keyword.

home page   The page on a Web site that is displayed when the domain name (such as www.sony.com) is entered into the browser.

HTML   HyperText Markup Language, the markup tagging system used to denote the semantic element of all content. For example, all paragraphs are marked with a paragraph tag, and all headings are identified with heading tags. Web browsers interpret each tag to determine how to format the text on the screen when displaying that page.

hub page   A Web page that links to many other pages about a certain subject.

hybrid auction   The modern technique for ranking paid placement bids in which the #1 ranking ad is determined by a combination of factors, including the price offered for keyword clicks and the ad's clickthrough rate.

Hypertext Markup Language (HTML)   The markup tagging system used to denote the precise document element of every piece of text on a Web page. For example, all paragraphs are marked with a paragraph tag, and all headings are identified with heading tags. Web browsers interpret each tag to determine how to format the text on the screen when displaying that page.

impression   A term derived from banner advertising that denotes each time your ad is shown to someone. The number of clicks for your ad is divided by the number of impressions to derive the *clickthrough rate*.

inbound links   Also known as *back links*, the hypertext links from a page *to* your page. Inbound links to your page from outside your site are highly valued by search engines performing link analysis when they rank search results by relevance.

inclusion ratio   The percentage of your site's pages residing in a search index, calculated by dividing the number of pages found in a search index by the total number of pages you have estimated to be on your site.

index   The list used by the search engine of each word on the Web, along with which pages each word is on. When a searcher enters a query, the search engine looks for the words in that query in the search index and locates the pages that contain those words. The search index is the primary database of a search engine, and no search engine can work without a very well-designed index.

indexing   The process by which the spider stores each word on the Web, along with what pages each word is on. The search index is the primary database of a search engine, and no search engine can work if it does not have a very well-designed index.

informational searcher   A user who enters a search query looking for deep information about a specific subject. Informational searchers are looking for several top results that shed light on the subject, not one particular answer.

information architect   1. The Web specialist who decides the navigational structure of a Web site—how information is divided into separate pages, which pages link where, what nomenclature is used on a link to ensure people know what it is, and many other tasks. 2. The software specialist who determines the correct way to organize data fields in a database or a set of databases.

information retrieval   The name used by computer scientists to describe organic search technology.

interactive advertising agency   A company that helps clients plan and purchase online promotional announcements, such as e-mail ads, banner ads, search, and other electronic promotions.

interactive media   Electronic promotions such as e-mail, banner ads, and search, that drive visitors to your Web site. Advertising agencies often handle client purchases of interactive media.

interior link   A hypertext connection to a page deep within your site, rather than one to the home page, for example.

internal link   A hypertext connection from one page of a Web site to another page within the same site, allowing visitors to move to the new page. Search engines do not treat these links with much importance.

IP delivery   A technique by which a site owner can deliver customized content based upon the IP address of the visitor. When used within ethical standards, it allows a site to present local language or entitled content to specific visitors to reroute search engines around complex URL structures or give them exclusive access to databases that would normally require a query to retrieve the information. When used unethically, it is usually called "cloaking"—a spam technique, which, for the same URL, returns one page for human visitors and a different version of the page for a search engine's spider (one full of keywords designed to attain a high search ranking).

JavaScript   A programming language that can provide special effects inside a browser that cannot be performed in HTML. Search marketing success depends on certain standards about how and when JavaScript programming is used, because JavaScript, when misused, can prevent search spiders from indexing certain pages.

JavaScript redirect   A way of using a program to instruct Web browsers to display a different URL from the one requested (such as <script language="JavaScript" type="text/javascript">

window.location="http://www.yourdomain.com/newURL"</script>). JavaScript redirects, unfortunately, are usually ignored by search engine spiders, so this technique should be avoided.

KEI   Keyword effectiveness index, a mathematical representation of the popularity of a keyword (the number of searches containing it) compared to its popularity in usage (the number of Web pages it is found on).

keyword   A particular word or phrase that search marketers expect searchers to enter frequently as a query.

keyword demand   The number of searches for a particular query across all search engines within a defined period of time. Whereas search referrals tell you how many searchers click through to your site, keyword demand tells you how many total searches used that keyword at all search sites, whether the searchers clicked through or not.

keyword density   Also known as *term density*, the ratio of a particular search query's terms to all terms on a page. For example, if you want your 200-word page to be found for the query "insomnia" and your page contains 12 occurrences of that word, the keyword density of your page is 6 percent for the term *insomnia* (12 ÷ 200). Search engines typically consider pages with about 6 to 7 percent keyword density to be very high quality pages. (Higher keyword densities are sometimes suspected as spam.)

keyword effectiveness index (KEI)   A mathematical representation of the popularity of a keyword (the number of searches containing it) compared to its popularity in usage (the number of Web pages it is found on).

keyword loading   Also known as *keyword stuffing*, a spam technique by which keywords are overused in content merely to attract the search engines.

keyword placement   Also known as *term placement*, a measurement of the value of the location of a word on a Web page. All words do not have equal importance on a page. Words in a title or in a heading are more important than words in a body paragraph—these locations of keywords are their *placement*. Placement and position comprise *keyword prominence*.

keyword planning   The process of deciding which words and phrases a search marketer should target in a search marketing campaign.

keyword position   Also known as *term position*, a measurement of how close to the beginning of a Web page element that a word appears. For example, words at the beginning of the body element are usually more important than those that show up later in that same element. Position and placement comprise *keyword prominence*.

keyword prominence   A measurement that combines the *placement* and *position* of a term on a page to indicate its relative value to a search engine. The most *prominent* keyword location is the first word of the page's title, because the title is the best placement and the first word is the best position. Pages with a keyword in prominent locations tend to be good matches.

keyword proximity   Also known as *term proximity*, a measurement of the nearness of different search terms to each other within a matching page. Two words from the searcher's query that are adjacent to each other on a page have the highest proximity, and would tend to be ranked higher than pages where the terms were a paragraph apart, for example.

keyword research   The step in the keyword planning process during which search marketers discover all the possible words and phrases they should target.

keyword rarity   Also known as *term rarity*, a measurement of the frequency that a term is used on all pages across the Web. In a multiple-word search query, some words might be very common, whereas others relatively rare. The search engines gives higher weight to pages that contain rare terms than common terms when ranking the results.

keyword stuffing   Also known as *keyword loading*, a spam technique by which keywords are overused in content merely to attract the search engines.

keyword variant   A different form of a search query in which the individual terms in a keyword are presented in a different order, or use different forms of the words. For example, "hotels in london" and "london hotel" are variants of the same essential search keyword, even though the word order and the form of the word *hotel* (singular or plural) is different in each case.

landing page   The URL on your Web site where visitors will go when they click a particular link. A *search* landing page, for example, is the URL a searcher is led to after clicking an organic or paid search result.

language metatag   An HTML tag declaring the language of the page (such as <meta http-equiv="content-language" content="ja"> to indicate a page written in Japanese). Because in practice these tags are often syntactically incorrect or have the wrong language encoded, search engines never decide the language of the page based on this tag alone.

lead   A prospective customer passed from one business to another (or passed from one part of a company to another) who might eventually complete a transaction to become a customer. The number of leads passed is a critical measurement for businesses that cannot close a sale on the Web—they must attract interest in their products on the Web, but "pass the lead" to an offline channel to continue the sales process that might culminate in a sale.

lifetime value   A method quantifying what each new customer is worth, not just for the first purchase but for the lifetime of purchases from that customer.

link   A set of words, a picture, or other "hotspot" on a web page that, when clicked, takes the visitor to another Web page. Search engines pay special attention to outbound links when crawling pages and to inbound links when ranking pages by relevance to respond to a search query.

link analysis   Also known as *link popularity*, the technique used by search engines to determine the authority of Web pages by examining the network of connections between Web pages. Search engines use link analysis when ranking search results by relevance—pages that have many inbound links from high-authority pages are ranked higher than other pages in the search results.

link auction   A method of buying a high-value hypertext connection to your site by outbidding other sites. Some Web sites, known as link auction sites, specialize in running the bidding for parties that wish to buy and sell links.

link audit   A procedure by which you analyze every hypertext connection to your landing page, or even to your whole site. Link audits help you to identify which pages have few or low-quality links and would be good targets for link-building campaigns.

link-building campaigns   A method by which you attract more hypertext connections to your site, often by contacting other Web sites and making a request.

link farm   A spam technique by which search marketers set up dozens or hundreds of sites that can be crawled by search engines, just so they can put in thousands of links to sites they want to boost in search rankings.

link landing page   The URL a searcher is led to after clicking a hypertext link from another Web site.

link popularity   Also known as *link analysis*, the technique used by search engines to determine the authority of Web pages by examining the network of connections between Web pages. Search engines use link analysis when ranking search results by relevance—pages that have many inbound links from high-authority pages are ranked higher than other pages in the search results.

link within the family   A hypertext link between two sites that search engines consider to be biased, perhaps because they have similar IP addresses, Whois information, or anchor text. Search engines seek to downgrade these links because they are not between neutral parties—the endorsement that the link provides is not as valuable as others.

local search   A technique that search engines use to display results from a particular geographic area. Searchers might actually enter the location as part of the query (such as "philadelphia restaurant") or might have saved their location from a previous query. Local search is different from *geographic targeting*, in which paid placement results are selected based on the searcher's location, regardless of whether the query was intended to return results for a particular location.

local search engine   1. A search engine from a particular country or region, as contrasted with engines that attract searchers worldwide. 2. A search engine designed mainly to provide *local search*, such as Internet Yellow Page providers.

log file   A file on your Web server that serves as a record of every action the server has taken. Log files can be analyzed in complex ways to determine the number of visits to your site (by people and by search engine spiders) and the number of pages that they view.

markup A publishing technique where text is *tagged* according to its meaning within the document so that computers can format and find the text more easily. Markup languages such as HTML allow content authors to "mark up" parts of their documents with tags denoting each document element. For example, a title tag (<title>About Our Company</title>) identifies the title of a Web page.

marketing mix The combination of ways in which you spend your marketing budget (TV, radio, print, and so on). Making a commitment to search marketing usually implies that some other expenditure must be reduced in your marketing mix.

market segment A group of customers with similar needs that receive the same marketing messages for your products. For your Web site, market segments are usually defined as *audiences* that include groups beyond your customers (stock analysts, press, and others). Your Web site messages are usually targeted to several market segments (audiences).

match A Web page found by a search engine in response to a searcher's query. Search engines use various techniques to determine which pages match each query, and then rank the pages by relevance so the best matches are presented first.

match type The way that paid placement advertisers decide how their keywords correspond to searchers' queries. Paid placement vendors offer varying match types, providing control over how closely the keywords must match the queries before displaying the ad.

mega-keyword A search query that is entered frequently by searchers.

merchant rating A score assigned by shopping search engines to each company selling products, based on customer reviews of the company's service.

meta refresh redirect A metatag in the <head> section of your HTML that instructs a Web browser to show a different URL from the one entered (such as <meta http-equiv="Refresh" content="5; URL= http://www.yourdomain.com/newURL" />). This tag flashes a screen (in this case for five seconds) before displaying the new URL. Unfortunately, this technique is usually ignored by search engine spiders, so it should be avoided.

metasearch engine A search engine that sends the query entered by the searcher to several other search engines, collating the results from each into a single results list.

metatag A particular kind of document element that is "about" the document rather than an intrinsic part of the document. HTML tagging standards specify numerous metatags, including titles, descriptions, dates, and many others. Metatags are especially important to search engines because they contain key clues about a page's overall relevance to a search query.

metrics specialist The Web specialist of the extended search team responsible for compiling and reporting statistics—how many visitors come to the site, customer satisfaction survey results, the number of sales, and many more.

microsite   A small Web site, separate from your corporate site, designed to make Web metrics easier to collect for your search campaigns.

multifaceted search   A search technique that allows searchers to restrict the search results by responding to choices offered by the search engine. Multifaceted search allows searchers to continually narrow down their results by choosing another constraint on their search.

multinational organization   A form of corporate organization in which the company is divided by country.

natural language search engine   A search designed to accept natural language queries (such as "What is the capital of Florida?") and get an answer, not just a list of documents containing the words. The most famous search engine with this kind of capability is Ask.com.

natural search   Also known as *organic search*, the technique by which a search engine finds the most relevant matches for a searcher's query from all of the pages indexed from the Web. Natural search contrasts with *paid search*, in which bidders vie for the highest rankings by topping each others' bids.

navigational searcher   A user who enters a search query looking for a specific Web site as a result. A searcher using the query "cornell university" is looking specifically for www.cornell.edu, and no other result.

negative site   Also known as a *hate site*, a Web site whose primary purpose is to discredit another organization or Web site. These sites frequently use the name of another site with the word *sucks* appended to the domain name, such as yourdomainsucks.com.

noframes tag   An HTML tag designed to provide alternate content for (ancient) browsers that do not support frames. Search engine spiders use this alternate content to index your page, but you are better off eliminating frames altogether.

noscript tag   An HTML tag designed to provide alternate content for older browsers that do not support JavaScript. Search engine spiders also use this alternate content to index your page.

objective bidding   A style of paid placement auction bidding that relies on metrics to drive each bid.

offline sales   Revenue from product purchases in which customers began the sales process on the Web but transacted the purchase on the phone, in person, or through some other off-Web channel.

one-way link   A hypertext connection to a page with no corresponding reciprocal link back to the source.

online commerce site   A Web site that transacts sales of products, even though it might use offline distribution channels to ship the product to the customer. (Pure online sites, in contrast, need no physical shipment.) Examples include retailer amazon.com and competitor buy.com.

optimizing content   A search marketing term for modifying the words and pictures shown on a Web page so that search engines can more easily find that page for a relevant query.

organic search   Also known as *natural search*, the technique by which a search engine finds the most relevant matches for a searcher's query from all of the pages indexed from the Web. Organic search contrasts with *paid search*, in which bidders vie for the highest rankings by topping each others' bids.

origination page   According to the bow-tie theory of Web pages, a page with numerous links into the core but relatively few from the core. Origination pages might be new or not terribly high quality, so they have not attracted the links back to them that would mark them as part of the core.

outbound link   A hypertext link *from* your page to a different page on the Web, perhaps within your site, or maybe to another site.

page designer   The Web specialist of the extended search team responsible for the visual appearance of the page, frequently handling the HTML templates and style sheets used. Search marketing often depends on the page designer optimizing the templates so that search engines can more easily find the page in response to relevant search queries.

page ranking factor   Also known as a *query independent ranking factor*, any characteristic of an organic search match that is unrelated to the terms in the search query. Page ranking factors can take into account anything the search engine knows about the page itself—which pages that link to that page, the site that contains the page, and many other components. These factors are used in the organic search ranking algorithm to sort the best results to the top of the list. Because it does not vary by the query, any particular page's page factor score is exactly the same for every query—a page with strong page factors starts out with a high score for every word that is on that page.

page submission   A method of telling a search engine about the existence of a URL that you would like crawled. Search engines vastly prefer to find new sites by following links, but do offer ways to manually submit your home page's URL if your site is somehow not discovered.

page view   The Web metrics term used to count how many Web pages on a site have been viewed by individual visitors. If three people view a page once, and two people view that same page twice, that page is said to have seven page views.

paid inclusion   A service offered by some search engines (such as Yahoo!) that guarantee a Web site's pages are stored in the search index in return for a fee. Paid inclusion does *not* guarantee high search rankings for those pages—just that the pages will always be present in the index and that the spider will frequently revisit each included page to make sure the index is kept up to date with changes made on the Web site.

paid link   A hypertext connection to a target site that has been purchased from the source site.

paid listing   An entry in a Web directory. Directories contain hundreds or thousands of subjects (such as fly fishing or needlepoint) along with links to Web sites about those subjects. Yahoo! Directory is the most famous example.

paid placement   The technique by which a search engine devotes space on its search results page to displays links to a Web site's page based on the highest bid for that space. Most search engines distinguish paid placement results from *organic* results on its results page, but some do not.

paid search   Any service offered by a search engine in return for a fee, including paid inclusion, paid placement, and directory services.

parameter   The name of a variable in a software program that displays dynamic Web pages. The URL www.domain.com?product=45 contains a parameter named *product* and a value of 45. The software program uses the parameter and its associated value to decide which content to display on the page.

permanent redirect   Also known as a *301 redirect*, an instruction to Web browsers to display a different URL than the one the browser requested, used when a page has undergone a lasting change in its URL. A permanent redirect is a type of server-side redirect that is handled properly by search engine spiders.

phrase   A search term within a search query consisting of multiple words enclosed in double quotation marks, indicating to the search engine that those words be found as is on any matching page. If words are not enclosed in double quotes, they are treated as individual words to search for rather than as a phrase to be found together.

pop-under window   A browser window that opens in the background on your screen, frequently containing an advertisement.

pop-up window   A browser window that overlays the Web page on your screen, frequently containing an advertisement.

portal   The system software that manages the display of Web pages for a Web site, frequently including the use of personalization rules that dynamically choose what content to display based on what is known about the visitor. Search marketing success often depends on proper standards for the operation of the portal software.

precision   A search metric that measures the number of "correct" organic search matches returned by the search engine for a query compared to the number of total matches returned. If the search engine returns ten matches, of which nine are judged "correct," its precision for that query is 90 percent. (Precision is a subjective measurement, because it is based on someone's judgment of what is a "correct" match.)

primary demand   The name used by economists to describe the state of a prospective buyer in the very early stages of consideration of a purchase.

product-oriented organization   A form of corporate organization in which the company is divided by *product*, so that each product or product line sold by the company is run by a semi-autonomous group as if it were a standalone business.

profit margin   A financial term, the measurement of return on the sale per item. Profit margin is calculated as (Revenue – Cost) ÷ Price.

programmer   The Web specialist of the extended search team responsible for developing the software that runs the Web site. Search marketing often depends on the programmer following certain standards so that search engines can more easily find pages in response to relevant search queries.

pull-down navigation   A style of user interface in which a menu of links is hidden until the visitor clicks the exposed part of the menu—that action is referred to as "pulling down" the menu, because the links are then displayed underneath the area clicked.

pure online site   A Web site that not only transacts sales of products but also delivers products to customers without any physical shipment. Examples include stock purchases at schwab.com and music downloads at itunes.com.

qualified visitor   A person coming to your Web site that is within the targeted market segments for your product—a person who you are trying to attract because they are able to buy.

query   The words that a searcher types into a search engine to identify what information should be searched for. Some queries are a single word, but others can consist of multiple words and might contain search operators.

query-dependent ranking factor   Also known as a *query ranking factor*, any characteristic of an organic search match that is related to the terms in the search query. Query ranking factors—including prominence, density, frequency, and others—are used in the organic search ranking algorithm to sort the best results to the top of the list.

query-independent ranking factor   Also known as a *page ranking factor*, any characteristic of an organic search match that is unrelated to the terms in the search query. Page ranking factors can take into account anything the search engine knows about the page itself—which pages that link to that page, the site that contains the page, and many other components. These factors are used in the organic search ranking algorithm to sort the best results to the top of the list. Because it does not vary by the query, any particular page's page factor score is exactly the same for every query—a page with strong page factors starts out with a high score for every word that is on that page.

query ranking factor   Also known as a *query independent-ranking factor*, any characteristic of an organic search match that is related to the terms in the search query. Query ranking factors—including prominence, density, frequency, and others—are used in the organic search ranking algorithm to sort the best results to the top of the list.

ranking   The technique by which a search engine sorts the matches to produce a set of search results. Although some search engines can sort by the date of the Web page, the most common ranking method is by relevance. The software code that decides exactly how the ranking is performed is called the *ranking algorithm*, and is a trade secret for each search engine.

ranking algorithm   The software instructions that control precisely how search matches are sorted into the order in which they are displayed on the search results page. Search matches are sometimes ranked by the date of the pages, but are most frequently ranked by relevance. A search engine's relevance ranking algorithm is one of the most proprietary parts of its secret sauce.

ranking checker   An automated tool that analyzes where a particular URL or set of URLs appear in the search results for a query.

ranking factor   Any characteristic of an organic search match that can be used by a ranking algorithm to sort the matches for presentation on the search results page. Relevance ranking algorithms use myriad factors, including the location on the page that matches the query, the authority of the page (based on link analysis), the proximity of different words in the query to each other on the page, and many more.

recall   A search metric that measures the number of "correct" organic search matches returned by the search engine for a query compared to the number of "correct" matches that exist in the search index. If the search engine returns nine "correct" matches, but ten "correct" matches exist in the search index, its recall for that query is 90 percent. (Recall is a subjective measurement, because it is based on someone's judgment of what is a "correct" match.)

reciprocal link   Also known as a *two-way link*, a hypertext connection to a page that has a corresponding link back to the source.

redirect   An instruction to Web browsers to display a different URL from the one the browser requested. Redirects are used when the URL of a page has changed. They allow old URLs to be "redirected" to the current URL, so that your visitors do not get a "page not found" message (known as an HTTP 404 error) when they use the old URL.

referral   The Web metrics term for the event of a page being viewed after viewing a previous page. Web metrics systems capture the referrer URL for each page view so that referrals from particular places, such as search engines, can be counted and analyzed.

referrer   The URL of the page that a visitor came from before coming to the current page. Web metrics systems capture the referrer for each page view so that *referrals* from particular places, such as search engines, can be counted and analyzed.

relational link   An in-bound hypertext link to your site that you solicited based on an existing business relationship, such as the relationships your company has with suppliers, resellers, and customers.

relevance   The degree to which an organic search match is closely related to the query. A match with extremely high relevance is a candidate to be the #1 result for that query. Search engines typically sort the matches by relevance for presentation on the search results page using a relevance ranking algorithm. Relevance ranking algorithms use myriad factors, including the location on the page that matches the query, the authority of the page (based on link analysis), the proximity of different words in the query to each other on the page, and many more.

relevance ranking   The technique by which a search engine sorts the matches to produce a set of organic search results whose top matches most closely relate to the query. The software code that decides exactly how the relevance ranking is performed is called the *ranking algorithm*, and is a trade secret for each search engine. Relevance ranking algorithms use myriad factors, including the location on the page that matches the query, the authority of the page (based on link analysis), the proximity of different words in the query to each other on the page, and many more.

result   A link to a matching Web page returned by a search engine in response to a searcher's query. Search engines use various techniques to determine which pages match each query, and then rank the organic search matches by relevance so the best matches are presented first in the search results. Paid placement and directory results are typically governed by a mixture of relevance and the amount bid by the owner of the Web site listed.

results page   The Web page containing the search engine's response to the query. Each search engine has a unique layout for its results page, but it is typically a mixture of organic and paid placement results, with directory listings also possible.

return on advertising spend (ROAS)   A financial term measuring the revenue impact of media expense using a formula such as Revenue ÷ Expense. Calculating the ROAS of several advertisements can help increase spending on the best ones.

return on investment (ROI)   A financial term measuring the monetary impact of an investment using a formula such as Profit ÷ Cost. Projecting the ROI of several possible investments can help you choose the best one.

ROAS   Return on advertising spend, a financial term that measures the revenue impact of media expense using a formula such as Revenue ÷ Expense. Calculating the ROAS of several advertisements can help increase spending on the best ones.

robot   A little-known name for a *crawler* or *spider*, the part of a search engine that locates and indexes every page on the Web that is a possible answer to a searcher's query. Typically used only when discussing the robots HTML tag or the robots.txt file.

ROI   Return on investment, a financial term that measures the monetary impact of an investment using a formula such as Profit ÷ Cost. Projecting the ROI of several possible investments can help you choose the best one.

RSS   Really Simple Syndication, a method of sending information to subscribers automatically, often used for blogs and produt catalogs.

sandbox effect   The informal name used by search marketing experts to describe the treatment of new sites by Google and other search engines when they discount the effect of a quick change in link popularity. Your page can play around all it wants, but it will stay in its "sandbox," without breaking into the top rankings for any queries. If its new-found popularity, over time, remains constant or even gradually grows larger, and then the search engines begin to remove the discounts and give full weight to the link popularity, allowing search rankings to rise.

search engine marketing (SEM)   The activities that improve search referrals to a Web site using either organic or paid search. Search engine marketing is also known as *search marketing*.

search engine optimization (SEO)   The set of techniques and methodologies devoted to improving organic search rankings (not paid search) for a Web site.

searcher   The Web user who enters a query into the input box of a search engine and request that a search be performed.

searcher context   The conditions under which a searcher enters a search query, including permanent or semi-permanent characteristics (such as gender, job role, and marital status) and more ephemeral factors (such as current geographic location, the subjects of pages viewed recently, and recent search keywords).

searcher intent   The goals that a Web user has when entering search queries, examining results, or choosing the result to click.

search filter   A constraint on a search that sets the scope of results, such as a country or language. Pages that are not included by the filters for a query do not appear in the results.

search index   A special database that stores every word found on every Web page, along with the list of pages that each word was found on. When a searcher enters a search query, the organic search engine consults the search index to find the list of pages that match the query.

search landing page   The URL a searcher is led to after clicking an organic or paid search result.

search marketing   The activities that improve search referrals to a Web site using wither organic or paid search. Search marketing is also known as *search engine marketing* (SEM).

search operator   A character with a special meaning to a search engine that controls the way the engine matches the query for organic search. Common operators include double quotation marks (treat enclosed words as a phrase), the plus sign (the following term is required), and the minus sign (the following term must not appear in any results).

search query   The words that a searcher types into a search engine to identify what information should be searched for. Some queries are a single word, but others can consist of multiple words and might contain search operators.

search referral   The Web metrics term for the event of a page being viewed after viewing a search results page. Web metrics systems capture the referrer URL for each page view so that referrals from search engines can be counted and analyzed.

search result   A link to a matching Web page returned by a search engine in response to a searcher's query. Search engines use various techniques to determine which pages match each query, and then rank the organic search matches by relevance so the best matches are presented first in the search results. Paid placement and directory results are typically governed by a mixture of relevance and the amount bid by the owner of the Web site listed.

search term   One word or phrase from the search query. Words enclosed in double quotation marks (the phrase operator) are treated as a single search term, but other words are treated as individual single-word terms.

search toolbar   A program used to enter search queries on your browser screen without first going to a search engine's Web site.

seed list   The enumeration of starting URLs for a spider to begin crawling Web pages. Spiders examine each page to see what other linked pages it should go to next, but it requires a seed list of starting points when it begins crawling.

selective demand   The name used by economists to describe what a prospective buyer exhibits when weighing the purchase of a particular brand or model of a product.

SEM   Search engine marketing, the activities designed to improve search referrals to a Web site using either organic or paid search. Search engine marketing is also known as *search marketing*.

SEO   Search engine optimization, the set of techniques and methodologies devoted to improving organic search rankings (not paid search) for a Web site.

server   A computer (or a program running on a computer) that responds to a client program's request. For example, a Web server responds to its client, a Web browser.

server-side redirect   An instruction from the Web server to Web browsers to display a different URL from the one the browser requested. Two common forms of server-side redirects are 301 (permanent) and 302 (temporary) redirects, named after the HTTP status codes they return to the browser. Server-side redirects are handled properly by search engine spiders.

session   Synonymous with a *visit*, a Web metrics term for a single series of pages viewed from a single Web site. If a visitor comes to a Web site and views five pages before leaving to go to a new site, the metrics system logs five page views but just one session.

session identifier   Dynamic URL parameters (usually named "ID=" or "Session=" or some other similar name) used by a Web metrics system to keep track of each unique visitor looking at a single page or at a series of pages in a visit to a site. Search engine spiders typically do not index pages with a session identifier.

shopping search engine   A search engine specially designed to allow comparison of features and prices for a wide variety of products.

site map   A page consisting of spider-friendly links to the rest of your Web domain. For a small site, your site map can have direct links to every page on your site. Medium-to-large sites use site maps with links to major hubs within the domain (which in turn allow eventual navigation to every page on the site).

snippet   The short paragraph that a search engine generates under the title (on the results page) to display the relevant passages on the page for the query.

solicited link   A hypertext link to your site that you received by explicitly requesting the other site to link to yours.

spam   1. Unsolicited illegal e-mail, usually containing a sales pitch or a fraudulent scheme offered to the recipient without permission. 2. Also known as *spamdexing*, unethical (but legal) techniques undertaken by a Web site designed to fool organic search engines to display its pages, even though they are not truly the best matches for a searcher's query.

spamdexing   Also known simply as *spam*, unethical (but legal) techniques undertaken by a Web site designed to fool organic search engines to display its pages, even though they are not truly the best matches for a searcher's query.

specialty search engine   A search engine that focuses on just one or two product categories or subject areas.

spelling correction   A feature of most engines that suggest possible changes to the searcher's query when it appears to be finding relatively few matches and a different spelling yields many more matches. Google's "Did you mean . . .?" ability is a classic example of spelling correction as applied to search.

spider   Also known as a *crawler*, the part of a search engine that locates and indexes every page on the Web that is a possible answer to a searcher's query. Successful search engine marketing depends on crawlers finding almost all the pages on a Web site.

spider paths   Easy-to-follow navigation routes through your site, such as site maps, category maps, country maps, or even text links at the bottom of the key pages. Spider paths include any means that allow the spider to easily get to all the pages on your site.

spider trap   A barrier that prevents spiders from crawling a site, usually stemming from technical approaches to displaying Web pages that work fine for browsers, but do not work for spiders. Examples of spider traps include JavaScript pull-down menus and some kinds of redirects.

static page   A Web page whose HTML is stored in a file for display by a Web server. Static pages typically do not change based on the visitor—they look the same to each person who views them—in contrast to *dynamic* pages.

stop word   Words that occur with very high frequency (such as *an* or *the*) ignored by search engines when entered by a searcher.

style guide   The rules governing the look and feel of the Web site, including page layouts, color schemes, information architecture, and many other areas.

style guide developer   The Web specialist of your extended search team that maintains the style guide— rules governing the look and feel of the Web site.

style sheet   A set of formatting instructions for each tag in an HTML or XML file that can be customized so that the same tagged file can be formatted in different ways with different style sheets.

summarization   A text analytics technique whereby an entire document can be condensed into a short abstract of a few sentences.

syndication   A business arrangement by which results from one search engine are provided for display by another search engine. AOL, for example, shows Google's paid placement ads on the AOL search results page, and is thus a syndication partner of Google's.

tag   A method of marking text in a document with its meaning so that computers can format and find the text more easily. Markup languages such as HTML allow content authors to "mark up" parts of their documents with tags denoting each document element. For example, the title tag (<title>About Our Company</title>) identifies the title of a Web page.

temporary redirect   Also known as a *302 redirect*, an instruction to Web browsers to display a different URL from the one the browser requested, used when a page has undergone a short-term change in its URL. A temporary redirect is a type of server-side redirect that is handled properly by search engine spiders.

term   One word or phrase from the search query. Words enclosed in double quotation marks (the phrase operator) are treated as a single search term, but other words are treated as individual single-word terms.

term density   Also known as *keyword density*, the ratio of a particular search query's terms to all terms on a page. For example, if you want your 200-word page to be found for the query "insomnia" and your page contains 12 occurrences of that word, the term density of your page is 6 percent for the term insomnia (12 ÷ 200). Search engines typically consider pages with about 6 to 7 percent term density to be very high-quality pages. (Higher term densities are suspected as spam.)

term frequency   The search metric that describes the number of occurrences of a particular searcher's query term in a Web page. Search engines use the term *frequency* as a ranking factor in the relevance ranking algorithm for organic search.

term placement   Also known as *keyword placement*, a measurement of the value of the location of a word on a Web page. All words do not have equal importance on a page. Words in a title or in a heading are more important than words in a body paragraph—these locations of keywords are their *placement*. Placement and position comprise *keyword prominence*.

term position   Also known as *keyword position*, a measurement of how close to the beginning of a Web page element that a word appears. For example, words at the beginning of the body element are usually more important than those that show up later in that same element. Position and placement comprise *keyword prominence*.

term proximity   Also known as *keyword proximity*, a measurement of the nearness of different search terms to each other within a matching page. Two words from the searcher's query that are adjacent to each other on a page have the highest proximity, and would tend to be ranked higher than pages where the terms were a paragraph apart, for example.

term rarity   Also known as *keyword rarity*, a measurement of the frequency that a term is used on all pages across the Web. In a multiple-word search query, some words might be very common, whereas others relatively rare. The search engines give higher weight to pages that contain rare terms than common terms when ranking the results.

term variant   Also known as *word variant*, a linguistic form of another word. *Mouse* is a variant of *mice*, and *will* is a variant of *be*. Search engines often treat variants interchangeably for matching purposes unless the searcher requests otherwise.

text analytics   A technique whereby software employs linguistics and pattern detection techniques to impute some larger meaning to the words in a document. Entity extraction and document categorization are two emerging types of text analytics.

title tag   An element of an HTML document that stores the main heading of the entire page, which will be used on the title bar or bookmarks for its page. Search engines pay more attention to what is in the title tag (<title>About Our Company</title>) than any other tag on the page.

toolbar   A program that adds a function on your browser screen you can execute without having to first navigate to a Web site. A search toolbar, for example, allows Web users to enter search queries without first going to a search engine's Web site.

traditional advertising agency   A company that helps clients plan and purchase promotional announcements for TV, radio, and print media, but might cover interactive media, too.

traffic   The Web metrics term to describe the number of visits to a Web site. Web metrics reports will frequently analyze increases or decreases in traffic, and they typically evaluate search marketing success in attracting visits from search engines.

transactional searcher   A user who enters a search query intending to complete a specific task, such as purchasing a product or downloading a file.

trusted feed   A way of sending your data to a search engine, instead of having the spider crawl your site. Some specialty search and almost all shopping search engines require the use of trusted feeds to load your data into their search indexes.

two-way link   Also known as a *reciprocal link*, a hypertext connection to a page that has a corresponding link back to the source.

Uniform Resource Locator (URL)   The address of a Web page that a visitor can enter into a browser to display that page. For example, www.bn.com is the URL of the Barnes & Noble home page.

unique visitor   Synonymous with *visitor*, a Web metrics term for a person who visits a Web site at least once in a period of time. If the same person came to a Web site three times in one month, the metrics system would log three visits for that month, but just one unique visitor.

URL   Uniform Resource Locator, the address of a Web page that a visitor can enter into a browser to display that page. For example, www.bn.com is the URL of the Barnes & Noble home page.

URL parameter   The name of a variable in a software program that displays dynamic Web pages. The URL www.domain.com?product=45 contains a parameter named *product* and a value of 45. The software program uses the parameter and its associated value to decide which content to display on the page.

URL redirect   An instruction to Web browsers to display a different URL from the one the browser requested. Redirects are used when the URL of a page has changed. They allow old URLs to be "redirected" to the current URL, so that your visitors do not get a "page not found" message (known as an HTTP 404 error) when they use the old URL.

URL rewrite   A method of modifying the appearance of your URLs so that dynamic URLs look like static URLs. URL rewrite helps make your URLs more readable for your human visitors, but are also very important in getting spiders to crawl your site.

URL value   The number or character string assigned to a variable in a software program that displays dynamic Web pages. The URL www.domain.com?product=45 contains a parameter named *product* and a value of 45, which the software program uses to decide which content to display on the page.

usability engineer   The Web specialist of the extended search team responsible for the user experience. Search marketing often depends on the usability engineer's recognition that search is a critical user scenario that must be considered in all user experience strategy.

user agent   The name of the software program that made a request of your Web server, as shown in your log file. Most browsers generate a user agent name with *Mozilla* in it, but search engine spiders each have unique names that allow you to see when they have visited.

user experience   The total environment a Web visitor is exposed to that shapes satisfaction with each visit to a site, including content, visual design, navigation, and technology.

value   The number or character string assigned to a variable in a software program that displays dynamic Web pages. The URL www.domain.com?product=45 contains a parameter named *product* and a value of 45, which the software program uses to decide which content to display on the page.

visit   Synonymous with *session*, a Web metrics term for a single series of pages viewed from a single Web site. If a visitor comes to a Web site and views five pages before leaving to go to a new site, the metrics system logs five page views, but just one visit.

visitor   Synonymous with *unique visitor*, a Web metrics term for a person who visits a Web site at least once in a period of time. If the same person came to a Web site three times in one month, the metrics system would log three visits for that month, but just one visitor.

visitor behavior   The study of what Web visitors think and do when using the Web.

visual design   The appearance, often called the look and feel, of a Web page, including page layouts, colors, fonts, images, icons, and buttons.

Web   Known formally as the World Wide Web, an interlinked network of pages that display content or allow interaction between the Web *visitor* and the organization that owns the *Web site*.

Web application server   The system software that executes the programs that run a Web site. Web application servers, also know as application servers, are typically used to display dynamic pages.

Web conversion   Any measurable, successful outcome of a Web visit—such as registering an account or donating to a cause—based on the behavior model developed for the Web site's specific goals.

Web Conversion Cycle   A behavior model that describes what visitors do when they come to your Web site and that helps you count your successes as Web conversions.

Web conversion rate   The ratio of Web site visitors to Web conversions—how many people came to the site versus how many successfully achieved the goal (buy the product, sign up for a newsletter, fill out contact information, and so forth).

Web developer   A Web specialist who develops programs or HTML to display Web pages in your visitor's Web browser.

Web governance specialist   The Web specialist of the extended search team responsible for enforcing your Web site's operational standards.

Web log   1. A file on your Web server that serves as a record of every action the server has taken. Log files can be analyzed in complex ways to determine the number of visits to your site (by people and by search engine spiders) and the number of pages that they view. 2. Also knows a *blog*, an online personal journal, a kind of a periodic column on the Web. Some blogs are reminiscent of a private diary, but others resemble magazine columns focused on a particular subject of interest.

Webmaster   The Web specialist of the extended search team responsible for planning and operating the servers that display Web pages when visitors arrive. Search marketing often depends on the Webmaster understanding the importance of Web search so that proper priority will be given to needed search marketing tasks.

Web page   A combination of text and pictures, often augmented by software, that allows visitors to interact with the organizational owners of the *Web site*.

Web server   The system software that displays *static* Web pages from HTML files and can execute some programs to create *dynamic* pages.

Web site   A set of interlinked Web pages managed by a domain team that allows interaction between visitors and the site's owner. For example, visitors speak of "going to Amtrak's Web site," which is at www.amtrak.com. All pages whose URL starts with www.amtrak.com are considered part of the Amtrak Web site.

within the family link   A hypertext link between two sites that search engines consider to be biased, perhaps because they have similar IP addresses, Whois information, or anchor text. Search engines seek to downgrade these links because they are not between neutral parties—the endorsement that the link provides is not as valuable as others.

word variant   Also known as *term variant*, a linguistic form of another word. *Mouse* is a variant of *mice*, and *will* is a variant of *be*. Search engines often treat variants interchangeably for matching purposes unless the searcher requests otherwise.

World Wide Web   Usually abbreviated as WWW, or simply "the Web," an interlinked network of pages that display content or allow interaction between the Web visitor and the organization that owns the Web site.

XML   eXtensible Markup Language, a standard for a markup language, similar to HTML, that allows tags to be defined to describe any kind of data you have, making it very popular as a format for data feeds.

Index

V

W

X-Y-Z